International R

The Changing Contours of Power

Donald Snow
University of Alabama

Eugene Brown
Lebanon Valley College

 LONGMAN

An imprint of Addison Wesley Longman, Inc.

New York • Reading, Massachusetts • Menlo Park, California • Harlow, England
Don Mills, Ontario • Sydney • Mexico City • Madrid • Amsterdam

Editor-in-Chief: Priscilla McGeehon
Acquisitions Editor: Eric Stano
Marketing Manager: Megan Galvin-Fak
Supplements Editor: Mark Toews
Full Service Production Manager: Eric Jorgensen
Project Coordination, Text Design, and Electronic Page Makeup: Electronic Publishing Services Inc., N.Y.C.
Cover Designer/Manager: Nancy Danahy
Map Studio: MapQuest.com
Photo Researcher: PhotoSearch, Inc.
Senior Print Buyer: Hugh Crawford
Printer and Binder: The Maple-Vail Book Manufacturing Group
Cover Printer: Phoenix Color Corp.

Library of Congress Cataloging-in-Publication Data
Snow, Donald M., 1943-
        International Relations : the changing contours of power /
Donald M. Snow, Eugene Brown. - - 1st ed.
        p. cm.
    Includes bibliographical references and index.
    ISBN 0-321-07046-1
    1U   International Relations. I. Brown, Eugene, 1943- II. Title.
    JZ1242 .s663 2000
    327.1'01- -dc21
                                                99-37222
                                                CIP

Please visit our website at http://www.awlonline.com

ISBN 0-321-07046-1

12345678910—MA—02010099

CONTENTS

PREFACE

When we began thinking about writing this book, our primary concern was the major events since the end of the Cold War. Patterns of behavior associated with the Cold War system had unraveled and had rendered much of the textbook literature of questionable relevance to understanding the world we face in the new millenium. It seemed to us that a book grounded explicitly in a post-Cold War framework would be of some value. The result is *International Relations* and its emphasis on the "changing contours of power."

We have tried to emphasize phenomena and trends that capture the important attributes of our post-Cold War world and are either missing or not so prominent in the older texts: the globalizing economy, the role of high technology in political and economic activity worldwide, the newer roles being played by traditional entities like the United Nations and newer entities like the Asia-Pacific Economic Cooperation, and changing patterns of violence, like the Kosovo-style wars so common to the developing world. To deal with these changes, we propose a new and unique framework, a world of tiers, to help organize and think about how the new system works. The framework consists of two tiers: a First Tier composed of the most advanced market democracies, and a Second Tier of the developing world made up of a series of developmentally distinguished subtiers. We contend that the emerging system can only really be understood in terms of the dynamics of these two parallel tiers and the relationships within and between them. Our central theme, as reflected in the subtitle of the book, is that although power relationships remain the basis of the system, the way they operate is being altered, often at incredible speeds.

Ours is not the only post-Cold War text in the field, but the consciously student-oriented approach of this text sets it apart and better helps students to understand the complex field of international relations. A quick glance will reveal a number of features designed to enhance the comprehension and even enjoyment on the part of the student reader. Each chapter, for instance, begins with a preview of the chapter contents and a list of key concepts to be grasped, presented in the order in which they appear in the text. Each chapter ends with a brief review of what the student has read.

That is not all. Each chapter includes a number of "boxed" features presenting additional material within eight recurring categories. *Summary* boxes preview lists of materials covered in the text. *Amplification* boxes provide fuller explanations, rosters of members of organizations, and the like. *Coming to Terms* boxes elaborate on definition or conceptual matters. *Cases in Point* boxes are short case studies illustrating points made in the main text. *The Impact of Technology* boxes provide examples of how technological changes affect international relations. *Views from Abroad* boxes reflect non-American views of international matters as reflected in the foreign press. *Contours of the Future* boxes offer speculations on how events and trends may change in the future and, as such, parallel the "Changing Contours" sections that end most chapters. Finally, *Web Sitings* boxes direct students to Internet sources of additional material. At the end of each chapter, except the first, a longer case study explores a topic related to the main chapter subject.

We have also tried to make this a student-friendly text by making the text as readable and comprehensible as possible. Wherever possible, we have avoided technical language or have tried carefully to explain terminology and ideas. We have purposely avoided footnotes and quotations that might detract from the flow of the text. Rather, we have provided selected readings at the end of each chapter and a bibliography at the end of the book appropriate for an introductory student to use for research or future inquiry. A glossary provides a ready resource and reminder of the definitions of key concepts throughout the book. An extensive program of maps and photographs serves as a further guide to aid student understanding and interest.

Supplements

Instructor's Manual/ Test Bank

The Instructor's Manual includes chapter outlines, chapter glossaries, a list of key ideas and objectives for each chapter, and a variety of thought-provoking discussion questions and student projects. The Test Bank contains hundreds of challenging and throughly revised multiple choice, and essay questions.

Longman Atlas of War and Peace

Adapted from the work of Dan Smith, Director of the International Peace Institute, and introduced by James N. Rosenau of George Washington University, this series of pedagogical maps and explanations offers a nontraditional approach to cartography: how do nations compare to one another in such terms as military spending, ethnic strife, control of natural resources, and internal conflicts. FREE when packaged with the text.

A book of this length and complexity is a large task, and one that cannot be undertaken without the assistance of others who deserve acknowledgment. First, we want to thank our Addison Wesley Longman editor, Eric Stano, who inherited this work and has shepherded it to completion. Brooks Ellis at Electronic Publishing Services, Inc. and Gia Forakis at PhotoSearch, Inc. have done yeoman duty in bringing this to fruition. Very conscientious and helpful reviews have been provided by Gregory Hall of St. Mary's College of Maryland, Randy Kleff of Virginia Union University, Philip Meeks of Creighton University, Michael A. Preda of Midwestern State University, Renee Scherlin of Appalachian State University and Marc Simon of Bowling Green State University. We wish to thank our former editor and good friend, Don Reisman, who convinced us to undertake this work, and Paul Smith, who had faith in and directed it before the merger of Allyn & Bacon and AWL. Finally, thanks are due to our families for putting up with us while this was underway and to our home institutions, the University of Alabama and Lebanon Valley College, for the physical and moral support.

Donald M. Snow
Tuscaloosa, Alabama

Eugene Brown
Annville, Pennsylvania

INTRODUCTION
International Relations and You

Why should you care about international relations? The term, often abbreviated as IR, refers to the ways that the countries of the world and groups of people and even individuals within those countries interact with and affect one another. In a rapidly shrinking world, those interactions increasingly affect your life, often in ways of which you are unaware. An understanding of international relations thus has a personal and instrumental value in addition to its intrinsic value. In short, what happens in IR is important to you, and because of dynamics that will be explored in the pages that follow, that importance will almost certainly increase during your lifetime.

The personal relevance of IR to you needs to be demonstrated, not merely asserted, and hopefully the text will provide adequate evidence. To give you an initial exposure to how IR affects you, we will briefly present three examples of how international matters have ramifications for people around the globe, including the United States.

The NAFTA Agreement

The first example is the North American Free Trade Association (NAFTA) agreement among Canada, Mexico, and the United States. NAFTA was negotiated during the waning months of the Bush administration (1992) and then, over considerable opposition, shepherded by the Clinton administration through the two houses of Congress. It has two general goals.

First, it seeks to stimulate trade and economic growth among the three major North American countries by gradually removing tariffs (taxes or duties on imported goods) and other restrictions on trade among them. Thus, goods and services will flow freely across North American borders at prices not raised by imposed duties. Theoretically, U.S. goods will be cheaper in Canada and Mexico than they were before NAFTA, thus enticing Canadians and Mexicans to buy more of them. Similarly, Canadian and Mexican goods will cost less in the United States, allowing Americans to buy them more cheaply.

The second goal of NAFTA is to create a trading bloc to compete with other advanced economies such as Japan and economic groups such as the European Union. It does so by creating a common set of tariffs and restrictions on all goods and services entering the NAFTA area. The tariff on a German car, for instance, will be the same whether it enters a port in Canada, the United States, or Mexico. (Before the agreement, tariffs varied by country.) If Germany seeks to lower tariffs against its cars in one country, it will have to negotiate with all three, and those three presumably can drive a better bargain than any one of them could do on its own.

In theory, everyone—American, Canadian, or Mexican—will benefit from NAFTA because it will stimulate economies by creating more jobs and greater markets for goods, as well as lowering the prices to consumers of some imported items. Yet the agreement generated strong opposition that almost blocked congressional approval. Why?

The answer is that any economic change produces losers as well as winners. Most experts agree that in the broad sense all three countries (and others may join) will benefit from NAFTA. That does not mean, especially in the short run, that every individual American, Canadian, or Mexican will benefit.

Some U.S. industries, for example, are in direct competition with counterparts in Mexico and depend on trade restrictions for their survival. A man's shirt may cost $15 to produce in North Carolina, while lower labor costs allow the same shirt to be manufactured in Mexico for $10. The North Carolina product, then, can compete in the U.S. market only with the aid of protective measures such as a $5 tariff on Mexican shirts or a strict limit on the number of shirts imported from Mexico. NAFTA removes the ability to impose that restriction.

Is this a good deal for you? The answer is, of course, that it depends. If you are a consumer not associated with the North Carolina textile industry, it is a good effect because you can save $5 on a shirt. If, however, you are part of that industry, the result may be disastrous. Either your company must find a way to lower costs, such as drastically lowering wages or moving to a lower labor cost location overseas, or it will go out of business. In the latter case, someone—you, the government, or private sources—would have to bear the cost to retrain you to produce something at a competitive price: for the sake of symmetry, something that Mexican textile workers will buy.

This kind of impact on you will increase with time. At the December 9–11, 1994, Summit of the Americas meeting held in Miami, Florida, the 34 democratically elected heads of government of the Western Hemisphere (only communist Cuba was not represented) agreed in principle to form a Free Trade Area of the Americas that will, if implemented, result in the gradual elimination of trade barriers among the countries of the hemisphere, a commitment

An anti-NAFTA rally in New York City in 1993. Although economists virtually all agree that the association will benefit Americans as a group, many individual workers know it will probably cost them their job.

Contours of the Future?

The Free Trade Area of the Americas

When the heads of government met in Miami for the Summit of the Americas, it was the first time such a large number of freely chosen Western hemisphere leaders had ever assembled. Anxious to reinforce the emergence of political democracy that had allowed the convocation, they sought to devise ways that would enhance and strengthen hemispheric democracy in the future.

They agreed that economic prosperity was a key element in legitimizing regimes and thus reinforcing democracy, and this position formed the rationale for the Free Trade Area of the Americas initiative. As they put it in their joint declaration at the end of the conference, "A key to prosperity is trade without barriers, without subsidies, without unfair practices, and with an increasing stream of productive investments. Eliminating impediments to market access for goods and services among our countries will foster regional economic growth." Based on this assumption, they declared the "resolve to begin immediately to construct the Free Trade Area of the Americas (FTAA), in which barriers to trade will be progressively eliminated ... no later than 2005."

This is an ambitious agenda, and one which, if carried out, could have huge consequences for the economies of the countries involved and the hemisphere that would make the effects of NAFTA seem minor. At this stage, however, the declaration is not a binding treaty or other obligation that will lead inexorably to a hemisphere-wide trading bloc. Rather, it instructs the member states, acting individually and collectively, to devise ways to move toward the common goal.

The barriers are complicated and formidable, and it may well be that FTAA will never come into being. Much the same, however, has been said about a number of other proposals over the past few years. If our experience in the globalizing economy, which we explore at length in Chapter 9, is any indication, the possibility cannot be ignored, and the consequences for you could be considerable.

Source: Summit of the Americas, *Summit Documents.* Washington, DC: U.S. Department of State, 1994.

reiterated at the second summit in 1998 in Santiago, Chile. Such an arrangement could dwarf the effects of NAFTA. The "Contours of the Future?" box examines the prospect.

Cutbacks in Defense

The end of the Cold War has reduced military threats to the United States and most other countries. As the threat of large-scale, systemic war involving the United States leading one coalition and the former Soviet Union the other has faded into memory, so too has the apparent need to maintain a large and expensive standing military establishment. During the Cold War, the need to spend on defense was rarely questioned; today it can be, and is. The end of the Cold War thus allows a redirection of resources to other needs. The long list of deserving candidates may include some you favor: debt and deficit reduction, repair of a deteriorating infrastructure (e.g., roads and bridges), environmental cleanups, rehabilitation of the inner cities, housing for the homeless, tax credits for a college education, guaranteeing the future solvency of Social Security. Given these needs, the end of the Cold War provides a veritable bonanza. Or does it?

The problem is that scaling back on defense also has human and economic costs. People and places whose livelihoods were sustained by the Cold War competition are suddenly the victims of its end in ways not unlike those suffered by North Carolina textile workers. Three groups particularly bear the burden in ways that may be personal to you.

The first are military personnel. One consequence of a reduced military threat means the need for less military personnel. Cutbacks have thus been accompanied by a growing number of discharges from active and reserve forces, in some but not all cases voluntary. Many jobs have simply been eliminated, which carries a special irony: the efforts and diligence of those "downsized" contributed to the collapse of communism and "victory" in the Cold War, but their reward is to have their jobs eliminated and to have to pursue second careers they had not anticipated. For you personally, the opportunity for a military career may now be closed or sharply constricted.

The second group affected are those individuals and communities associated with defense industries. The need for newer and more weapons to confront the Soviet menace meant that military procurement and the contracts it produced became the backbone of those places where it occurred. The apex of that prosperity was the aerospace industry, feeding the apparently insatiable appetites of both military and civilian aviation and underwriting the prosperity of metropolitan areas as diverse as Seattle, Atlanta, and Long Beach, California.

The end of the military competition has put a damper on that prosperity, most dramatically, but not exclusively, within the aerospace industry. Why, some critics maintain, does the United States need any more B-2 bombers, designed as they were to penetrate Soviet antiaircraft defenses—then the most sophisticated in the world—that no longer exist. Similarly, does the United States need the highly sophisticated F-22 fighter when it already possesses the most capable fighter aircraft in the world in the F-15, F-16, and F-18A, especially to deal with likely contingencies in the developing world where the opponent probably has no air force at all? The same arguments can be made about army equipment (Abrams tanks) or naval vessels (a new generation of attack submarines). If the United States does not need new airplanes or other weapons, it also does not need the engineers who designed or the workers who built these weapons in those roles. If you plan an engineering career, you might think about the impact on the engineering field you are going to pursue.

The third group of Americans affected are civilians associated with military facilities. As the military becomes smaller, its physical needs for facilities, notably bases, becomes smaller as well (especially if one makes the argument, as many do, that there were excess bases even during the Cold War). A military that is two-thirds its former size—or even smaller—simply does not need as many bases and posts as it did previously.

This recognition has spawned a phenomenon that is the horror of many base towns: the base relocation and closing (BRAC) process. The series of BRAC rounds in 1991, 1993, and 1995 will be followed with yet another in the near future. Each time, the possibility of having a base closed horrifies communities and brings about monumental efforts to save "my" base from the cutter's axe. These communities know the consequences of being the victim of BRAC: civilian housing markets declining as military personnel living off-base are mustered out of service or moved to consolidated facilities; merchants losing the business of military customers; civilian employees being furloughed or fired; and local tax bases shrinking in response to all these developments. Many who cheered the fall of the Berlin Wall did not realize it would hit them directly in the pocketbook, but it has. While reductions in military spending may be beneficial to the economy as a whole, they can be very difficult for those directly affected.

Trading with China

Thanks to policies enacted in the latter 1970s (and discussed in more detail in Chapter 7), the Chinese economy has become one of the largest and fastest growing in the world, with some predictions that it will become the world's largest sometime in the early twenty-first century. As a result, how to interact economically with the People's Republic of China has become an important foreign policy consideration for all countries along the Pacific Rim, including the United States. The status of U.S.-China trade has become a particularly contentious issue between Congress and the Clinton White House over the renewal of something called *most-favored nation (MFN) status.*

This whole issue and how it is resolved has direct relevance to you because of the nature of trade between the countries. Between 1992 and 1995, imports of Chinese goods into the United States rose from $25.7 billion to slightly over $45.5 billion, an increase of about 80 percent, and the trend continues. This is important to you, because the vast bulk of American imports of Chinese goods is in consumer products, notably clothing, athletic shoes, toys, and the like. A quick inventory of the labels in your wardrobe will reveal the extent to which trade with China has a direct effect on you.

But trade with China has become politically volatile over the issue of MFN status. That arcane term refers to the trade conditions between trading partners: a country accorded MFN status (and almost all countries are) has its goods and services imported into a country at the lowest tariff rate charged against any country. A country that does not have MFN status with the United States (or anyone else) is thus at a tariff disadvantage selling its goods in the United States.

The renewal of MFN status for China has become politically controversial in the United States. Why? There are three basic reasons, only one of which is directly economic in content. The economic argument has to do with the trade balance between the two countries. By 1995, the United States had developed a trade deficit with China of over $33 billion, making it the second largest (after Japan) in the world. In 1996, the China-U.S. trade imbalance topped $50 billion.

The dynamics of this imbalance are simple enough. U.S. imports from China have grown rapidly, as Americans buy more and more cheaply produced Chinese consumer goods. Chinese imports of American-made goods, however, have grown much more slowly. In 1992, for instance, China imported $7.4 billion in U.S. goods; for 1995, that figure had only risen to $11.75 billion. This failure of the Chinese to import more American goods has become a source of contention between the governments of the two countries in

U.S. President Clinton addresses the
Chinese people, June 1998.

trade negotiations; it was a major item on the agenda when President Clinton visited China
in June 1998.

The second issue is China's human rights record, including its active and well-documented
resistance to democratic reforms. Some observers describe the Chinese system as one of
"market Leninism," with a fairly free market sector in an economy encased in a heavily authoritarian political regime. Political dissent is sometimes brutally suppressed, with the
most dramatic symbol being the squashing of the pro-democratic movement in Beijing's
Tiananmen Square in 1989. Critics of American China policy argue that trade restrictions
should be imposed to force the Chinese government to alter its human rights policies. Dissenters counter that such tactics will not work and that if the United States partially pulls
out of China, others, notably the Japanese, will fill any void without demanding political
changes by the Chinese. A major purpose of the Clinton mission to China was to publicize
this problem, which it was allowed to do when the President spoke live on Chinese state
television directly to the Chinese people.

The third issue has to do with Chinese arms sales throughout the developing world. Although China occasionally vigorously denies that it does so, there is a good bit of evidence
that the Chinese sell weapons systems to a number of countries. These include deadly and
highly sophisticated weapons that the most advanced countries are seeking to restrict, such
as the ballistic missiles sold to countries like Pakistan, which is locked in a regional conflict with neighboring India that intensified in 1998 when both countries publicly detonated nuclear weapons.

How should trade with China be handled? Should it be restricted until such a time as
China becomes a more "normal" country that honors human rights, democratizes, quits the
clandestine sale of weapons, and buys more American goods? The decision to impose restrictions would have a direct influence on the things you buy. As an experiment, go to a
shoe store specializing in athletic shoes, look at the displays, and calculate what those

racks would look like if all the shoes made in China were removed. Then calculate what prices might climb to if there were no Chinese shoes. The same kind of analysis can be applied to apparel and other consumer goods.

At the same time, the reason those goods are so cheap is because they are made by suppressed Chinese workers who are paid very little for their efforts. Is that right? What is more important to you, cheap consumer goods or a more responsible China in world politics? From a strictly individual standpoint, you may reach one conclusion. From a broader international perspective, you might reach another.

Conclusion

The purpose of this introduction has been to present a hint of the ways in which international relations has a direct impact on you. Two of the three examples were economic. This is not surprising in a post–Cold War world that is no longer inevitably obsessed with the military confrontation between the United States and the Soviet Union, as was the Cold War system. Economic concerns are more central now; it was not a coincidence that the one security-related example was about the impact of the shrinking importance of military affairs.

These examples represent no more than a hint at how IR can have a direct impact on you, whether the study of the subject matter becomes a matter of central concern for you or not. In the pages that follow, we hope you will recognize both the fascinating and important nature of the dynamics of the international system.

The Nature of
International Relations

PART 1

THE STUDY OF INTERNATIONAL RELATIONS

THE INTERNATIONAL SYSTEM

HISTORICAL EVOLUTION OF THE STATE SYSTEM

FOREIGN POLICY DECISION-MAKING

THE FUNCTIONS, ORIGINS, AND FORMS OF WAR

The Study of International Relations

PREVIEW

In this chapter, we will look at the discipline of international relations and how it is studied. To accomplish that goal, we will begin by looking at the substance of what constitutes international relations. With the basic framework of the discipline established, we will move on to a discussion of basic ways to think about international relations in a period of major change and how the international system works. We will conclude by looking at the "world of tiers," the organizational device that we will employ to describe the current international system.

KEY CONCEPTS

intermestic policy
international relations
nation-state
state actors
subnational actors
supranational actors
foreign policy
system

transnational issues
idealism
realism
realist paradigm
anarchy
First Tier
Second Tier

OUTLINE

As he surveyed a scourged battlefield during the bleakest hours of World War I, French Marshal Ferdinand Foch repeated to himself Alphonse Karr's famous phrase, "Plus ça change, plus c'est la même chose" ("the more things change, the more they remain the same"). Appalled by the suffering he saw around him, Foch was profoundly skeptical of the idealism of U.S. President Woodrow Wilson and others who saw the conflict as a crusade to bring about freedom and democracy worldwide, a war to end all wars, as Wilson had publicly hoped. To Foch, and many others since, the international system might witness much outward change—new powers rising while others fall, periods of horrific warfare giving way to seasons of tranquility—but beneath such tides, Foch suspected, the ancient cycles of international rivalry and the struggle for power would sooner or later lead to yet another collapse of order and another period of war and suffering.

Wilson had a different vision. As a young man growing up in the South, he had seen firsthand the Reconstruction period after the American Civil War, and he was determined not to repeat that bitter, divisive outcome, despite the enormous sense of vindictiveness toward the defeated Germans. Wilson believed profoundly that through democracy and the ability of national groups to determine their own governments, a better and more peaceful world was attainable. That the two concepts could be contradictory in practice (national self-determination sometimes being antidemocratic), as has occurred in the post–Cold War period, was a possibility he did not foresee.

Like the world of Wilson and Foch, the contemporary world is poised at a historic moment that many hope represents a profound break with the old cycle of international hatred and war. In 1918, the major powers had just concluded an extraordinarily gruesome four-year war that stimulated the desire for a better world, a desire that would be frustrated by a second global conflict between 1939 and 1945—World War II. In the 1990s, the international system is emerging from the grim shadow of the Cold War, a 45-year series of crises splitting the great states of Europe and North America into two hostile camps, each armed with enough nuclear weapons to end civilized life on earth. But what lies ahead? Will there indeed be a "new world order" of peace and decency? Or did Foch have it right: will nothing really change? Or will the result be somewhere between these extremes? What does the new millennium hold for us?

Our search for an answer to these momentous questions might begin by noting that the way World War I was resolved contributed to the fulfillment of Foch's pessimistic prophecy. The victorious Allies not only defeated the German Empire militarily, but they proceeded to impose a vindictive settlement humiliating the German people, who were forced to accept the entire official burden of guilt for the war and to pay huge reparations as well. Over the long run, neither the Germans nor the democratic government imposed upon them by the Allies could embrace such a bitter peace. Sooner or later, Germany would recover its strength, and once it did, Germans had little reason to uphold a peace they could only consider unjust.

No two historical periods are exactly alike, of course, but it is tempting to wonder if the kinds of miscalculations made by the victorious statesmen in 1918 might be repeated in the wake of the Western system's triumph over communism in the Soviet Union and Eastern Europe. The choice is again how to treat a former adversary. Can the peace be won now that the Cold War is over? The global system is very different from what it was

A 1918 view of Ypres, Belgium, the site of three major battles in World War I, offers graphic testimony to the devastation of war. The end of the Cold War raised widespread hopes for a more peaceful future in international relations, although history provides little encouragement for such a prospect.

even 10 or 15 years ago. But is the promise of change genuine or an illusion? Is the change deep-rooted or merely superficial?

The process of global change is one of this book's twin themes. Things are different today than during the Cold War. At the very least, the old Soviet-American ideological and geopolitical standoff that left the world apparently poised at the brink of nuclear Armageddon has dissolved. Much of this text's attention will be aimed at trying to understand how things have changed and what those changes mean. Moreover, the process of global change is beginning to form a two-tiered international system, the outlines of which will be introduced later in this chapter.

The book's second theme is how international matters now affect everyone, a point raised in the Introduction. At one level this observation may seem a cliché, but the world is becoming increasingly interdependent, knit together by an ever-growing flow of peoples, goods, images, and ideas. Once-distant international matters are now a routine part of people's lives, and they become more so daily. They command the pages of your newspaper and virtually leap off your television screen and into your homes. Your home computer has become a medium of global communications via the world wide web, international "chat boxes," and the like. Some of these images are large, spectacular, sometimes painful, and even grotesque. The most obvious are wars—in Bosnia and Herzegovina, Kosovo, Iraq, Somalia, and Rwanda.

Not all important international events are as vivid and dramatic as war, however. In fact, it is striking how many of your daily routines now contain an international element. In everyday shopping, for instance, you can seldom escape the reality of a world made small and interdependent by modern technologies of communication, transportation, and trade. Look at the labels in your clothing sometime—chances are your wardrobe is a veritable international potpourri.

Political scientists have devised a term, *intermestic policy,* to describe the phenomenon of issues and events that are simultaneously *inter*national and do*mestic.* For example, a rise in oil prices in the Persian Gulf sends gasoline prices soaring at your service station. A rise in interest rates in Germany affects the value of stock on Wall Street. The decision by the U.S. government to place restrictions on goods imported from foreign lands affects the availability of jobs in those areas of the United States where comparable goods are produced, as well as the retail prices we pay for goods.

The broad purpose of this chapter is to provide you with some context for the nature of international relations and how it is studied. The first matter it will address is what constitutes the field of international relations and how the international system is distinct from the domestic scene. International relations is fundamentally unlike domestic politics (see the discussion in Chapter 2 on the consequences of sovereignty), so that understanding how your own national political system operates does not automatically translate into a parallel understanding of how international relations works.

International relations has been studied in some form or another for as long as independent political groups have come upon and had to interact with one another. The many theoretical and pragmatic ways by which scholars have pursued such studies are a matter of concern primarily for professional students of the field. The basic divisions among political scientists are not, in our view, a necessary element in introducing the subject matter of international relations. Because we are undergoing a profound process of change in the international system, it is, however, worthwhile to see how practitioners and many scholars viewed the international system and how changes in that system affect the way we view it. This will provide the setting for our view of system organization, the world of tiers.

What Is International Relations?

At its most fundamental level, international relations deals with the interactions between the countries of the world, the most basic building blocks of the international system. This definition is admittedly oversimplified, and the chapters that follow will attempt to make it more complete, sophisticated, and realistic. Nonetheless, it contains three important terms: international, relations, and system. Examining each provides a first step to answering the question of what the field entails.

The word *international* reveals two important qualities of international relations. First, the prefix *inter* differentiates the field from the study of the politics, history, or economy of individual countries. Those who concentrate on that level of politics, for instance, are studying domestic politics, what goes on in government within countries and why. International relations, on the other hand, deals primarily with the relations between or among countries.

At the same time, it is impossible for students of international relations to ignore domestic events, because most of the decisions that affect international relations are made by policymakers within individual countries. What national decision makers decide and how and why they make their decisions are important in understanding and predicting international affairs, and for that reason Chapter 4 is devoted to that subject.

The other part of the word international is *national,* which defines the basic units of study in the field. The nation-state—more commonly and more correctly referred to as country or state—is the leading actor on the international stage; therefore, the most important object of study in international relations is how state actors, principally but not exclusively through their governments, interact with one another. This central aspect of international relations is best illustrated by a political map of the world (one that features boundaries between independent countries).

Although they play the most significant parts, state actors are not the only players on the international stage. Increasingly, subnational actors—individuals like former president Jimmy Carter and groups like the United Automobile Workers—take prominent roles in international relations. At the same time, supranational actors—governmental and nongovernmental organizations bridging several or many countries, such as the Red Cross or the United Nations—increasingly assert their autonomy and place in the system. The profusion of nonstate actors contributes to the increasing difficulty of distinguishing domestic from international politics.

The second important term in our working definition is *relations,* and it also reveals at least two characteristics of the field. First, it suggests that international affairs are composed of a series of interactions among states and other actors. The most important of these are between the states' governments, whose interactions with one another constitute the foreign policy of the individual states. These intergovernmental interactions are supplemented by interactions across national borders by the subnational and supranational actors.

The term relations is also significant because it encompasses a broad variety of forms of interaction, ranging from the political and military to economic, social, cultural, and even humanitarian concerns. In reference to the field, terms like "world politics" or "international politics" are often used as synonyms for international relations. Using the terms interchangeably is harmless as long as one realizes that political interchange is not the sole form of international activity—even if it is the most prominent and, for many purposes, the most consequential.

The third key term in our working definition is *system.* The idea of systems is found in a variety of areas, from biology (the circulatory system) to astronomy (the solar system) to the social sciences (social systems) to athletics (offensive and defensive systems in football or soccer). When we refer to the international system, we are adding several additional characteristics to the definition of international relations. First, a system comprises a number of distinct, interdependent units whose interactions affect one another. When the United States imposes environmental regulations on automobile emissions, this action has an impact on other member states in the international system—notably those who manufacture automobiles that are exported to the United States, such as Japan, Germany, or Sweden.

The second characteristic of a system is that there is an orderly regularity and predictability to the interactions between the units. Things do not happen randomly in the international system; rather, through experience and conventions devised by the members, there are rules and expectations about what happens when governments or other actors interact. For instance, there are rules governing how the representatives of one country can be treated in another country. Diplomats are given immunity from civil and criminal laws so that the host government cannot harass them or impede them from carrying out their duties, as might be the case otherwise.

There are good reasons for such rules. The most basic is reciprocity: if you do not inter-fere with my diplomatic personnel, I will not interfere with yours. Moreover, it would be difficult to recruit members for the diplomatic corps if they had no idea from day to day and from country to country whether they would be safe or not. These kinds of conventions and rules cover most interactions between member units, because they provide predictabil-ity and order. When the conventions are violated, as was the case when militant Iranian "students" seized the American embassy in Tehran in 1978—with the complicity of the Iranian government—and held American diplomats hostage for over 14 months, there was broad international condemnation of the Iranian government.

The third characteristic of a system is that it exists within the context of a broader envi-ronment that is dynamic and itself forces the units to adapt and change. Political events such as the collapse of communism in Eastern Europe and the Soviet Union, economic events such as the crises in a number of Asian economies in 1997 and 1998, and even nat-ural events such as population growth and droughts constitute the environment that helps to shape the system.

From the combination of these attributes we can begin to define international relations. First, it is about how people and governments in different countries deal with one another. The principal participants in these interactions are national governments, but they are by

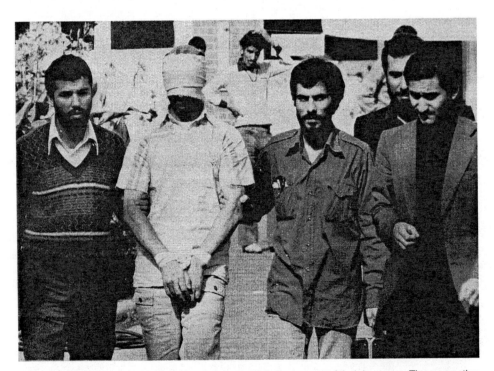

Iranians who seized the U.S. embassy in Tehran in 1979 display one of their hostages. The occupation of the embassy and the 14-month detention of its staff violated the principle of diplomatic immunity, a key rule providing order in the international system, and the Iranian government was internationally condemned for its complicity in the actions.

no means the only actors. Second, international relations deals with a broad range of inter-actions. The most dramatic and prominent are political, issues dealing with the allocation of scarce resources within and between countries. International relations is not limited to purely political matters, however, but encompasses other forms of interaction as well.

Moreover, the "menu" of international relations is growing rapidly. If international relations once dealt primarily with the diplomatic relations between states and matters of peace and war, in recent years a proliferation of international activity has come from two other sources.

One source is an expansion of the range of issues and problems that have become inter-national in scope, the rise of the so-called *transnational (or transstate) issues*. These are problems that transcend state boundaries in ways individual states have very little control over. Air pollution, for example, used to be thought of as a local (smog in Los Angeles) or at most regional (acid rain in the Northeast) problem. Now environmental degradation and renewal are viewed as global problems with solutions that must be arrived at cooperatively worldwide, as argued at the Earth Summit in 1992 and reinforced in forums such as the Summit of the Americas in 1994. Similarly, the question of whether to promote or to regu-late population growth used to be considered a domestic issue; however, migration from overcrowded, underdeveloped countries to the economically most advanced countries (from Central America to the United States, for example, or from Africa to Europe) has made it an international issue as well. The 1994 Cairo convention on population issues sponsored by the United Nations Conference on Trade and Development underscored the transstate nature of the problem by showing that population growth in one country in-evitably affects other states as well in terms of strains on the food supply, pollution, and migration, for example.

Another source of proliferation of international activity is the growth in the number and kinds of individuals and groups who are participating in and demanding rights under international regimes (conventions and agreements that regulate behavior). In the early days of the modern international system (as described in Chapter 3), only states and their governments had standing in the international arena. Today, they must share this privilege with a large number of subnational and supranational claimants, whose ranks have been growing especially fast in recent decades. The explosion in the number of truly international business corporations—sometimes called multinational corpora-tions (MNCs)—is an example of this phenomenon, as is the growing importance of the global electronic media.

This process of change is what gives contemporary international relations its dy-namism and interest. Over the past few years policymakers and scholars alike have gone through the initial euphoria of talk about a "new world order" to a more restrained view that the new order is not so very different, and possibly even a bit less orderly than the old one. Many of the contours of the new order are evident, even if not in precise de-tail. What can be discerned today in areas such as the changing international economic system, for instance, is like an artist's sketch. The sketch shows what the general shape and composition of the finished painting will be; the painting adds the details and tex-ture. In the case of the international system as a whole, the extreme dynamism may sug-gest that what we need is a series of sketches like those that are combined into an animated motion picture.

Thinking About International Relations

The international system has occasional convulsions that alter some of the basic ways in which countries interact and hence in the way that we think about our subject. As we will see in Chapter 3, such changes are typically associated with major systemic traumas such as general wars—for example, the Napoleonic Wars and the world wars of the twentieth century.

We have gone through a similarly traumatic change in the fabric and nature of international relations in the past decade. One of the signal events was, of course, the implosion of the Soviet Union into 15 successor states. This in and of itself was a virtually unprecedented event: the peaceful disintegration of a country that was in fact the world's last major empire. The other and closely related event was the end of the Cold War, which occurred gradually between 1989 and 1991. It began with the election of a noncommunist government in Poland in September 1989, reached its symbolic height with the destruction of the Berlin Wall later in that year, and became an accomplished reality when the Soviet flag came down from the Kremlin on the last day of 1991, replaced the next day with the flag of Russia (these events are discussed in more detail in Chapter 6).

The results were intellectually and physically stunning. Hardly anyone inside or outside government or in academia saw the collapse of the Cold War coming; the peaceful implosion of the Soviet opponent of the Cold War was envisaged as a possibility only by a few (New York Senator Patrick Daniel Moynihan, most prominently). The Cold War, which began to develop shortly after World War II and which seemed a permanent anchor for international politics by the time that North Korea invaded South Korea in 1950, was the central reality of world politics (although, by no means, its only concern). Most students and practitioners believed the Cold War could only end by becoming hot; since a "hot" war between the two superpowers could become a thermonuclear war that threatened mankind, keeping the Cold War cold was an obsession. We believed the Cold War could only end with a bang; we were unprepared for it ending with a whimper. We are still adjusting.

The "rules of the game" for international relations during the Cold War were captured in something called the *realist paradigm*. The tenets of that paradigm included the centrality of state sovereignty as the principal value of the members, state-centrism (meaning individual countries were the most important units in the system), power (sometimes but not always military) as the means to adjudicate international differences between states, and the realization of national interests as the primary motivator of states in their relations with one another. These distinctions are described in detail in Chapter 2.

This set of values and resulting principles for conducting international relations is not new. Many observers trace the roots of realism back to *The History of the Peloponnesian Wars*, an account of a long conflict between Athens and Sparta written by the Athenian historian Thucydides in the fifth century B.C. Certainly, *The Prince*, Italian statesman Niccolò Machiavelli's manual for rulers written in the sixteenth century, is based on realist principles. Realism, and its operationalization in the realist paradigm, have been around for a long time.

Realism and the paradigm have always been controversial and are particularly so today. Part of the controversy is philosophical and methodological; part arises from the operational implications of implementing world politics from the realist perspective. Put more simply, realism is an approach to organizing action in the international system and a

The ancient Greek historian Thucydides and the sixteenth-century Italian statesman Niccolò Machiavelli are often considered the "fathers" of the approach to international relations scholarship known as realism.

construct around which one can organize studying and understanding international relations. Because the two aspects are intertwined, the result is maximum confusion.

Because this is not a book about international relations theory, we will not present the methodological debate in great detail. The emphasis of realism on power has always been controversial. Part of the criticism arises philosophically from the fact that realism makes the use of military force to achieve national goals a "normal" activity; those who are opposed to war (or who at least want to see it viewed as more abnormal) thus object to the approach because of its implications for international life.

Others disagree with realism on methodological grounds. As an approach to the study of international relations (as opposed to an operational principle), realism places great emphasis on the concept of *power*, and in its most pure forms it uses the concept of power to explain essentially all international behavior. The numerous critics of realism argue that this emphasis is overdone and that it distorts a comprehensive understanding of the subject matter.

We take no particular position on the realist paradigm at either the philosophical or the methodological levels. We do, however, assert that the realist paradigm has been, at least through the end of the Cold War, the dominant way in which real decision-makers have viewed international relations. Because of this reality and our underlying concern that the reader come to understand international behavior in the ways that international decisions are actually made, much of the discussion will be couched in terms that realist-paradigm-driven policy makers (whether they knew it or not) would understand.

The Realist Paradigm and the Cold War

The realist paradigm was almost perfectly fitted to the Cold War environment, and it is no accident that it developed to its complete structure during the conflict between the communist and noncommunist worlds. The Cold War construct was the kind of international system for which realist ideas provided a "natural" way of thinking about and operating the system.

Without making redundant the extensive discussions in Chapters 3 and 6 of the Cold War and its end, we can look at the fit between the realist paradigm and international reality through two of the primary lenses that focused the Cold War. One of these foci was the overwhelmingly military, geopolitical nature of the East-West competition that was the central feature of the system. The other focus was the competition as a zero-sum game in which the successes of one side were seen to be the failures and setbacks of the other.

Above all other things, the Cold War was a geopolitical competition, the chief coin of the realm was the military competition between the two sides. Both the West and the East developed and maintained enormous and expensive military apparatuses aimed at the other for the purpose of deterring an attack or, should deterrence fail, of fighting a World War III that could have gone nuclear. The need to spend large amounts of dollars or rubles was virtually unquestioned: the failure to match the enemy gun for gun, missile for missile, was potentially disastrous.

The military fixation, with its emphasis on the so-called military instrument of power, fit into two corollaries about the use of military force during the Cold War. One corollary was Clausewitzian, reflecting the impact of Carl von Clausewitz, the nineteenth-century author of *On War*, his account of the Napoleonic Wars. The central tenet of Clausewitz's analysis was the subjugation of the use of military force to the political purposes that force sought to attain. "War," as he put it in what became known as the Prussian dictum, "is the continuation of politics by other means." The second corollary was Napoleonic, and it suggested that, like the use of force by Napoleon to spread the values of the French Revolution, military force should be reserved for the grand, and most important, interests of state.

This perception was clearly evident in the Soviet Union, and it came to dominate American thinking in official circles as well. The idea of military force reserved for the most important political purposes fit both the realist paradigm and the nature of the Cold War competition. The Cold War was, among other things, a clash between ideas held by two evangelical opponents. Sometimes military weapons were the *lingua franca* for the competition to turn parts of the world map red (communist) or blue (anticommunist).

The competition was so fierce because the stakes were high (the survival of one system or the other) and the outcomes were conceived as zero sum (victories came at the other's expense). In the 1950s, for instance, Americans seriously debated the prospects of "better red than dead" or "better dead than red" as the possible eventual outcomes of the competition. The notion of cooperation from which both sides could benefit (positive sum outcomes) were generally overwhelmed by notions about the protracted, encompassing nature of the conflict. The one major exception was the growth of arms control agreements after 1963 that had as their purpose and effect reducing the likelihood of nuclear war between the two sides (see Chapter 5).

This vision of the world never lacked critics. From academic circles, there was the criticism that the emphasis on power distorted reality and that things like the supremacy of sovereignty never were as all-encompassing as the realist paradigm would have it. For a growing number of analysts and citizens, the specter of nuclear war dictated breaking out of the paradigm and its normalization of war as a legitimate activity. Within academic circles, the growth in quantitative approaches to the study of politics moved scholarship away from the grander levels of theorizing to more narrow concerns about the relationships between different factors (variables) operating in the system. Moreover, the realist paradigm tends to emphasize the state as an international actor at the expense of other actors in the system. The feature box, "Coming to Terms: Levels of Analysis," introduces this notion.

Deciding whether the realist paradigm was the most appropriate way of thinking about international relations during the Cold War period goes beyond our purposes here. What is of greater importance is whether the approach remains as the central most helpful way to look at international relations in a very changed environment, the post–Cold War international system.

The Realist Paradigm and the Post–Cold War World

The realist paradigm was clearly the dominant set of operating values and principles by which the Cold War period was conducted. It is arguable that a large number of those values (the defense of the homeland as the supreme and overriding value, for instance) have been present well before the founding of the state system, generally dated to the peace of Westphalia that ended the Thirty Years War in Europe in 1648. Whether organizing the study of international relations in the attempt to discover scientific theory about the subject using realist principles is the most fruitful approach for inquiry is a debatable point that goes beyond our present purposes.

What is principally interesting to us is whether the realist paradigm holds as well today, in the post–Cold War world, as it did before. As already noted, realism has never wanted for critics who would like to invalidate its operational principles because of their consequences, notably war. Critics have quite rightly, for instance, faulted rigid realist interpretations of the sovereignty concept that is the central tenet of realism, arguing that sovereignty has never in fact been as overriding and powerful as it is often made out to be by proponents of the realist paradigm (see discussion in Chapter 2).

Does the realist paradigm still maintain its prescience as a way to understand how policy makers confront and deal with the world? Put another way, has the world changed sufficiently since the end of the Cold War to require modifying the paradigm as a descriptive device?

In some ways, it clearly has. As noted at the outset, change is a recurring theme of this text, and one of the objects of that change has been the validity of realism to provide an overarching explanation of international behavior. Many of the instances and trends will be discussed in detail in the following chapters and emphasized in the "Changing Contours of Power" sections found at the end of most chapters. Here, we introduce a few examples of that change.

Coming to Terms

Levels of Analysis

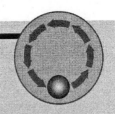

An ongoing area of methodological debate within international relations that cuts across the various distinctions we have made in this chapter is the question of the appropriate level of international actor on which to focus attention. This levels-of-analysis debate generally focuses on the advocacy of one of the three levels already identified: the level of the state actor, of the subnational actor, or of the supranational actor.

Traditional realists place their emphasis on the state and its actions as the appropriate level of analysis. States are the major actors in the system, they argue: the most important concerns of international affairs are the interactions between sovereign states, and so the state is the appropriate unit on which to concentrate. From a quantitative vantage point, most available statistical measures are accumulations of state-level data, and variations among states on particular measures may help explain variations in interstate behavior.

The traditional emphasis on the state level of analysis has been criticized in a number of ways, two of which will be highlighted here. To some, it is simply incorrect or inadequate. There are, after all, intrastate entities (including individuals) whose actions make a difference in what states do quite apart from their state affiliation.

Emphasizing individuals, for instance, opens new avenues of approach such as perception, cognitive dissonance, and the role of personality that are likely to be ignored in a state-centered level of inquiry. At the same time, supranational actors cannot be ignored, because they increasingly act either in concert with or independently of states to affect international relations.

A second objection argues that concentration on the state level of analysis perpetuates a traditional way of thinking about IR that is not only intellectually dysfunctional but also impedes desirable reform. Many feminists, for example, argue that state centrism is a male-derived construct whose emphasis on sovereignty, conflict, and the warrior ethic helps to perpetuate war. Emphasizing the individual or group subnational levels allows a reorientation of thinking toward less war-centered models of international reality (such as those focusing on gender differences in behavior) or more supranational ones.

Many critics of realism contend that its concentration on the state as the central focus of international relations helps to perpetuate war and other forms of conflict. They argue that more attention should be given to supranational structures such as those represented by the 1994 Cairo population conference.

One clear shortcoming of a slavish devotion to the realist paradigm is its state-centrism. Carried to the extreme, the paradigm suggests that states are the only legitimate actors in the system. This position used to be characterized by an analogy called the "billiard ball analogy," which argued that states were like billiard balls, hard, impervious entities that bumped against one another occasionally and that those collisions were international relations. Moreover, the analogy of imperviousness implied that what went on within states was the sole business of those states and could not legitimately be challenged by other states or other entities.

No realist would literally defend anything like the billiard ball theory today, since it is really a caricature of the extreme application of sovereignty. The consequences of sovereignty have long been decried because of the system it perpetuates—one based on power and war (this is a central criticism of feminist approaches to IR, among others). We would concur and restate some of these criticisms of the paradigm in two ways: it is descriptively deficient, and its application leads to actions that violate current values evident in the international environment.

The idea that states are the sole, or even overwhelmingly powerful, actors in international relations is challenged in two ways. One is through the emergence of numerous, influential *nonstate actors* (these are discussed more fully in Chapter 2). On the other hand, there are *supranational actors*, organizations that transcend international boundaries and who influence the international system. These include international organizations (IOs), either as entities in which governments are the members (intergovernmental organizations, or IGOs) or private entities in which individuals and groups in several countries are the members (nongovernmental organizations, or NGOs). More dramatically, aggregations of states in unions such as the European Union (EU) are influential supranational actors.

A more powerful form of obsolescence of realist principles is found in the evolution of the global economy (see Chapter 9). Thanks largely to the high-technology telecommunications revolution, economic activity leapfrogs national boundaries so regularly that international businesses regard those boundaries as essentially irrelevant to the operation of a progressively privatized, deregulated global business and financial system. To think about economic activity as something over which national governments exercise considerable leverage and control because that activity occurs within sovereign territory is to virtually guarantee missing the point.

The realist paradigm is, ironically, also inadequate to understand all the security challenges of the post–Cold War world. It is ironic because the realist paradigm is very much national-security driven and derived. Yet adherence to the dictates of realism inevitably distorts recognizing the security challenges in the world and deciding which ones to react to. The culprit is the Clausewitzian and Napoleonic influences on thinking about security within the paradigm. As already noted, realism drives one to calculate using force only when the vital interests of states are challenged (Napoleonic grand stakes) and when force serves the purposes of states (Clausewitz).

To preview material in the next section of this chapter, the most important interests of the most important states are hardly challenged at all in the contemporary environment in ways for which armed force would be an appropriate response. Instead, we live in a world where, for the most influential states (and those with the most powerful armed forces), there exists a condition of *interest-threat mismatch*: the most important interests are hardly threatened, and the threats that do exist are tangential, mostly well outside the realm of vitality. In fact, almost all the violence on the contemporary global stage is internal war (civil war) in areas of Africa and the like where there are few major power interests involved. Moreover, these conflicts are often chaotic in terms of conduct and political purpose. The result is that application of the realist paradigm will distort understanding of what is occurring in these situations and will almost always dictate avoiding involvement. The debate in 1999 over sending U.S. ground forces into Kosovo illustrates this point.

A final example has to do with the inviolability of sovereignty. As noted, the "billiard ball" analogy suggests that what goes on within states is the business of states and that

Iraqi President Saddam Hussein (*right*) meets with an official of the Japanese Socialist Party a few days before the beginning of the 1991 Persian Gulf War, in which his forces were driven out of Kuwait by a U.S.-led military coalition. Saddam had mistakenly calculated that the international system, and in particular the United States, lacked the resolve to use force against him.

outsiders have no legitimate basis for interfering with domestic concerns. Noninterference has never been absolute. The assertion that it is is one of the critiques of realism, but the criticism reaches particular intensity when states engage in particularly atrocious behavior against portions of their populations, as has been the case in Bosnia, Rwanda, and Kosovo, to cite the most obvious examples since the end of the Cold War. The idea that cold-blooded killers can hide behind sovereignty while they perform their grisly acts is challenged on the basis of what are called humanitarian interests—interests that override state sovereignty as the premier interest.

These examples of challenges to the structure are just that, examples, and they and others will be developed in the pages to follow. One area where we believe change has been especially evident is in the physical structure of the international system, and particularly the way groups of states are considered. As an alternative to the Cold War way of categorizing the system, we propose the world of tiers, to which the discussion now turns.

A World of Tiers

Although we do not have a strong set of methodological predilections through which to organize our inquiry, we do believe that a pattern of relationships is emerging in international affairs that incorporates both continuity from the past and the change in the post–Cold War world. That pattern forms a framework that allows us to organize and describe the new international reality. We call that framework a world of tiers.

Our central contention is that at present there is no single, unified system at work in international politics. Rather, there are two distinct subsystems, which we call the First Tier and the Second Tier, each with its own characteristics and patterns of interaction; and the set of relationships within each tier has different consequences for the system as a whole. Much of what is unsettled about contemporary international relations is how the two tiers will interact with one another.

Essentially, the idea of tiers resembles the way scholars described the Cold War system but restates it in a manner reflecting an adjustment to changed circumstances and in fundamental agreement with the categorization of Max Singer and the late Aaron Wildavsky in *The Real World Order.* In the past, it was commonplace to divide the international system into three or four "worlds": a First World made up of the wealthiest industrialized democracies, a Second World generally considered to be composed of the communist states, a Third World containing the "less developed" or "developing" noncommunist states, and sometimes a Fourth World including the most destitute countries. The clearest reason to change these designations is the virtual disappearance of the Second World. While there remain—at least for the time being—isolated communist regimes in China, Vietnam, North Korea, and Cuba, they hardly constitute a coherent descriptive division of the world in the way the Soviet bloc did. Of those communist regimes that endure, the Chinese is the only one to rule a country of real consequence, and it has openly abandoned communist ideology in its quest for economic modernization through capitalism. North Korea still poses a military threat to a South Korea poised on the edge of joining the First Tier, but German-style unification of the Koreas is more plausible than war.

The idea of the two tiers is straightforward. The First Tier is composed of the 25 or so countries of the world that U.S. President Bill Clinton refers to as the "ring of market democracies"—the United States and Canada, the European countries that never had communist governments, Japan, Australia, and New Zealand. The "membership requirements" for First Tier status are a stable democratic political system and a structurally advanced market-based economy. The Second Tier consists simply of all those states outside the First Tier. As such, it accounts for the vast majority of the world's states and people (Singer and Wildavsky, who employ a similar set of distinctions, set the population proportion at six-sevenths). It also incorporates a broad diversity of states under one umbrella, from near members of the First Tier—industrialized "fragile democracies" like Brazil and Taiwan—to extremely poor places like Mali and Bangladesh and extremely undemocratic ones like Iraq and North Korea. Obviously, designating a state as a member of the Second Tier does not tell one much about it other than that it is not in the First Tier. As a result, we have divided the Second Tier into four subtiers, which are listed with examples of each in the Summary box "Second Tier Subtiers." A complete list of Second Tier countries by region and subtier, along with an explanation of each country's classification, appears in the Appendix.

Summary ————————————————————————————

Second Tier Subtiers

Subtier	Examples
Developed	South Korea, Israel, Mexico, South Africa
Partially developed	India, Ukraine, Colombia, Nigeria
Developable	Haiti, Bangladesh, Serbia/Yugoslavia, Somalia
Resource-rich	Saudi Arabia, Algeria, Trinidad and Tobago

These distinctions reflect an application of the political and economic criteria for membership in the First Tier. Second Tier states lack one or both of the characteristics that would enable them to join the First Tier—stable democracies or structurally advanced, wealthy market-based economies (what Singer and Wildavsky call "quality economies"). With the possible exception of the resource-rich states—a category created mostly for the wealthy semifeudal monarchies in the Middle East—the subtiers are arranged in a sequence representing progress toward these characteristics, and especially the economic one. The two criteria are related in that they are expressions of political and economic freedom, respectively, which together provide the incentives on which quality economies are based. Because economic and political development does not always progress at the same rate, however, we have chosen to give the economic criterion greater weight in such cases.

Each subtier contains a range of states. The most developed countries, found principally in the Pacific Rim, are those that are nearest to entering the First Tier: generally they have thriving economies, but their devotion to democracy is not well established. (It is not hard to imagine a number of the Pacific Rim states joining the First Tier, possibly using some form of association like the Asia-Pacific Economic Cooperation [APEC] as a foothold.) What distinguishes them from other developed Second Tier states is that the latter generally have had a high foreign debt burden acting as a deterrent to further development and making them less stable economically and often politically as well. (Nevertheless, NAFTA will almost certainly lift Mexico up the scale, along with any other Western Hemisphere states that may join the association or the Free Trade Area of the Americas.) The partially developed countries lack either economic or democratic development or both but have shown some progress. They range from fairly poor and nonindustrial countries with firmly established democratic traditions to formerly communist states with the industrial infrastructure characteristic of developed states but little experience or skill with a market economy or political democracy. The developable states have the human or material basis for development but lag behind. They range from states about to enter the developmental process to states that have no reasonable short- to medium-term prospect of development.

The political and economic rather than military bases of these categories, which are discussed in more detail in Chapter 8, reflect what we believe to be the higher salience of nonmilitary factors in the new international system. Large armed forces and nuclear weapons will make Russia consequential in some circumstances, but it is improvements in the Russian economy and government that will define its status in the system (Russia falls in the partially developed category currently). Similarly, although China has a huge army and the second largest and fastest-growing economy in the world, it will not fully join the global economy until its repressive politics change.

Views from Abroad

Toward a Unified Korea

The fate of the Korean peninsula, divided into the independent states of North and South Korea since the end of World War II, represents one of the dynamic and troubling problems of the post–Cold War world. The volatile relations between the two Koreas have been made worse by the economic collapse of North Korea, including widespread food shortages that became evident in 1996. The question is what will happen to resolve the problem.

Two possibilities suggested in the world press in 1996 are equally valid today. One is for peaceful unification into one state. As *The Australian* of Sydney suggests: "Lasting peace for the two Koreas will come only with reunification....The sooner the four key parties—U.S., South Korea, China, and North Korea—can sit together at the conference table, the closer we may come to achieving lasting peace and security on the Korean Peninsula."

While agreeing on the desirability of peaceful reunification, the *South China Morning Post* of Hong Kong warns of the second, more ominous possibility: "While neither side seems to desire conflict, one miscalculation could still lead to all-out war." The situation is all the more volatile, it maintains, because "this may also be P'yongyang's last chance to negotiate peace rather than simply disintegrate and be absorbed by Seoul." The *Straits Times* of Singapore agrees with this assessment, stating "Time is not on P'yongyang's side, however. A domestic economic crisis, combined with international isolation, gives it very few cards to play but the military one, which, should it be used and fail, may precipitate the downfall of its political system."

The impact of a unified Korea would greatly affect East Asia. As *Handelsblatt* of Düsseldorf, Germany, put it, "A reunified Korea, with a population of 67 million, would be a significant regional actor, third to China and Japan." This prospect is generally welcome in China, which views Korea as an economic partner, but *Handelsblatt* argues, the same is not true of Japan, because "for Tokyo, a reunified Korea would mean direct competition," since the two countries make many of the same kinds of products for sale in international trade, notably electronics and automobiles.

Neither reunification or war has occurred. The horrible drought in North Korea in 1997 has been partially alleviated, with some of the needed grain to feed the North Koreans coming from South Korea. Which track the peninsula will take, however, remains open.

Source: World Press Review, June 1996, 4.

The idea of tiers is an extension of earlier classification schemes. In *The Real World Order,* for instance, Singer and Wildavsky present a similar set of categories they call the "zones of peace" (the First Tier) and "zones of turmoil and development" (the Second Tier). Similarly, the distinction between the "developed" and "less developed" worlds goes back to the 1950s, when African and Asian decolonization began to create a category of states clearly different from the traditional international actors found mainly in Europe and North America (most of Latin America, on the fringes of the traditional system, also fell into this category). A problem then and now was devising categories that did not sound pejorative toward these newer states, since "less developed" sounds inferior to "developed," for instance. Our notion of tiers does not resolve this sensitive issue, but we do believe that this framework and our assumption that Second Tier states aspire to First Tier status provide a fair and accurate characterization of current international reality.

In essence, then, our depiction portrays the Cold War system stripped of the Second World; in our revised framework, the First and Second Tiers replace the former First and Third Worlds. What distinguishes it is that it allows the reader to focus clearly on what the very real differences are between the two groups of states, how members of each tier interact among themselves (intratier relations), how intratier relations are different within each tier, how the tiers interact with one another, and what consequences each of these distinctions has for international relations generally.

The First Tier

As suggested earlier, President Clinton's phrase "ring of market democracies" neatly captures the essence of what it means to be a part of the First Tier. A list of "members" is provided in the Summary box "The First Tier" and accompanying Map 1–1. The list is presented in no particular order, and one might quibble about whether one state or another should be on it. It encompasses the United States and Canada in North America, the European Economic Area (the memberships of the European Union and the European Free Trade Area), and Japan, Australia, and New Zealand. It conspicuously excludes the formerly communist states, although some—the Czech Republic, Hungary, and Poland, for instance—may join the First Tier in the foreseeable future. There are also other non–Pacific Rim aspirants to the First Tier. The continued successful implementation of multiracial democracy could easily qualify South Africa; membership in the European Union (for which it has applied unsuccessfully) could raise Turkey; and the completion of the Arab-Israeli peace process could unleash an Israeli economy shackled historically by defense spending, to cite the most obvious examples.

Summary ────────────────────────────

The First Tier

North America
United States
Canada

Asia and Pacific
Japan
Australia
New Zealand

Europe
Great Britain
Ireland
Norway
Sweden

Denmark
Finland
Spain
Portugal
France
Germany
Belgium
Netherlands
Luxembourg
Italy
Austria
Switzerland
Iceland
Greece

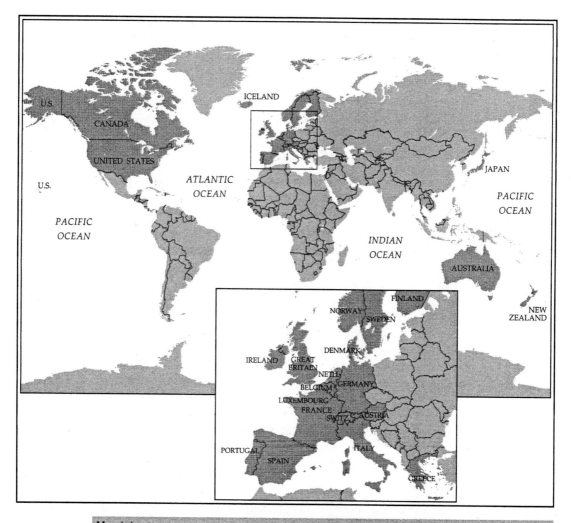

Map 1-1   **Members of the First Tier**

©1996 by St. Martin's Press, Inc. From: *Contours of Power,* by Snow/Brown. Reprinted with permission of Bedford/St. Martin's Press, Inc.

As previously noted, the exclusion of China and Russia, two of the major powers of the Cold War system, reflects what we believe is a fundamental difference between that system and the new order: political and economic freedom form more of the base of national power than they did before. The most important states in the world today happen to share the characteristics of market democracies, which in turn meet the criteria of quality economies: complex, information-based economies operated by highly motivated work-forces. As a result, these states are increasingly similar to one another, fully participative in the global economy, and are technologically advanced in ways that translate into economic and military superiority as well.

The Summary box "Characteristics of the First Tier" lists several common characteristics shared by countries of the First Tier. The first and most important, which we have already stressed, is the commitment to political democracy and a market economy. This common commitment to core values and ideologies means that the states of the First Tier are fundamentally similar and that their similarities outweigh any differences grounded in history, culture, religion, and so on. This does not mean they are all clones of one another; rather, it means they share common outlooks toward the world.

Summary

Characteristics of the First Tier

1. Commitment to political democracy and market economy
2. Inclusion of all the most important (core) powers of the world
3. Absence of conflict with war potential
4. Growing economic interdependence
5. Public opinion as the major constraint on use of force
6. General preference for peace and stability
7. Shared preference for collective security

Second, the First Tier is characterized by its inclusion of the most important, or core, powers of the world. One of the major criteria of effective power in the new international system is technologically driven economic supremacy, and the forefront of that process is one of the most important differences between the tiers. As the performance of the coalition in the Persian Gulf War—which was led by First Tier states—clearly demonstrated, this superiority translates into military prowess as well. Indeed, the First Tier's application of advanced technology to military purposes is increasingly described as a "revolution in military affairs," as discussed in Chapter 5. This does not mean that every First Tier country is a great power or that there are no consequential states outside the First Tier: as noted, Russian possession of nuclear weapons makes the major Soviet successor state impossible to ignore, as the populations of China and India so make those countries. It does mean that all the most important states—the core—are in the First Tier.

This commonality of worldview among all the core actors in the international system is unprecedented since the eighteenth century, when the major states of Europe were all monarchies and almost all (Great Britain being the exception) more or less absolutist monarchies. The result is a third characteristic of the First Tier—the absence of conflict between states that has any realistic prospect of leading to war. The reason is their shared commitment to political democracy: free peoples do not initiate war toward others who share their values, and their common values mean they have little to fight about.

This characteristic defines a tremendously important difference—or improvement—between the Cold War system and the present, the absence of a military confrontation that threatens the integrity of the system itself. During the Cold War, avoiding a nuclear war between the United States and the Soviet Union was the central problem with which the system dealt, the first and overriding international concern. That threat is missing today; it is difficult to imagine realistic circumstances in which any pair of First Tier states would go to war with one another and jeopardize the entire system. This statement applies as well to consequential nonmembers like Russia, which still has the wherewithal to incinerate the globe but clearly lacks the motivation to destroy a First Tier that is its only hope for economic uplifting. This does not mean there will not be much war and violence in international relations; there clearly will be. What it does mean is that the most important states will not fight one another unless conditions within the First Tier change substantially.

An additional source of peace within the First Tier is its fourth characteristic—a growing interdependence among First Tier economies. The idea of interdependence is not new, going back to the 1960s (see the discussion in Chapter 9). The First Tier is largely defined by the emergence of a truly global economy where national borders are of little economic consequence and where business operations and investments across those boundaries are routine, motivated by common economic philosophy. This shared sense of values does not always result in agreement on all things. Competition between firms and between countries on economic issues will continue and often be very lively. Economic differences will be subdued, however, by the increasing globalization of the economy, and it is fanciful to think of these issues deteriorating to the point that war is threatened.

A fifth characteristic of the First Tier has to do with the role of military power. Although lacking motivations to fight one another, the First Tier states will occasionally use force in Second Tier conflicts as they already have in places like Somalia and Haiti, with public opinion, not military capability, the principal limitation. Technological sophistication has already made the First Tier states militarily superior to their Second Tier counterparts, especially in the projection of military force outside their borders. Whether that force can be brought to bear or sustained will for the most part be a matter of whether democratic citizenries will support such applications. Public opinion in democracies generally opposes military action unless the public believes it has been forced to do so and the reasons for

U.S. troops patrol the seaport area of Port-au-Prince, the capital of Haiti, where the United States mounted a peaceful occupation in 1994 to restore an elected civilian government that had been overthrown by a military coup. Since the end of the Cold War, First Tier states have occasionally used military means to try to settle conflicts within the Second Tier. Public opinion, however, generally makes such interventions politically difficult for First Tier governments.

using force are very important. This reluctance has the positive effect of stabilizing military relations among First Tier states; for better or worse, it will almost certainly limit the ability of First Tier states to intervene in conflicts in the Second Tier.

A sixth and related characteristic of these states is a general preference for peace and stability in the world. The First Tier's prosperity is largely based on stability among its members, which creates a favorable economic climate. Expanding that tranquility to the Second Tier clearly is in the best general economic interest of the First Tier. Thus political democratization—expanding the ring of market democracies—is clearly a process that the First Tier wants to promote. What is less clear is exactly how much effort—and money—the First Tier is willing to expend toward this goal. The inclination toward peace is, moreover, not universal; the United States, for instance, would not be at all averse to instability in Cuba that resulted in the overthrow of Fidel Castro's regime.

Finally, a seventh characteristic of the First Tier is a shared preference for collective security as the means to promote and enforce international peace. For the foreseeable future, virtually all of the world's violence will be in the Second Tier. Where First Tier states determine the need to involve themselves in that violence, they will generally look toward burden sharing by the world community, acting through some legitimating agent like the United Nations' collective security provisions or North Atlantic Treaty Organization (NATO) auspices, rather than unilateral action. This preference is likely increasingly to be expressed by action in the UN Security Council, unless either Russia or China becomes obstructionist and exercises its veto power (a possibility discussed more fully in Chapter 13).

The Second Tier

In addition to violence, most of the world's other most difficult problems are also concentrated in the Second Tier. This is not a new condition—misery and despair have been the common lot of people in many Second Tier states for a long time. What is distinctive about the contemporary system is that the Cold War overlay has been removed, leaving Second Tier problems more central to ordering the system than before.

The same categories of characteristics we used to describe the First Tier can also be applied to the Second Tier. In each case, however, the characteristic is the opposite of its First Tier counterpart. These are listed in the Summary box "Characteristics of the Second Tier."

Summary ————————————————————————

Characteristics of the Second Tier

1. Absence of common political and economic values
2. Peripheral relationship to overall system
3. Considerable instability and violence between and within members
4. Diversity of economic development
5. Military capability as constraint on use of force
6. Lack of a uniform commitment to peace and stability
7. Preference for individual or collective defense rather than collective security

The first characteristic is the absence of common political and economic values across the entirety of the Second Tier. Politically, the Second Tier ranges from the last vestiges of communism to unreconstructed despotism to fragile democracy. The closest thing to an ideological rival to political democracy, fundamentalist Islam, is found in part of the Second Tier. Similarly, many Second Tier countries are strongly committed to market economies, while others cling to pre-market bases for economic activity. Chapter 8 elaborates the four subtiers already identified to capture this diversity.

A second characteristic is the peripheral relationship of all the Second Tier states to the overall system. Not all Second Tier countries are inconsequential or unimportant to the system. What the notion of peripheral status means is that none of them can engage in action that automatically or necessarily threatens the integrity or existence of the system as a Soviet-American clash would have during the Cold War. None of the wars between Second Tier states would necessarily draw in all or a sizable proportion of the First Tier states or other Second Tier states. Some—for instance, a renewed India-Pakistan conflict over Kashmir—could be quite bloody, especially if the nuclear weapons they publicly tested in 1998 were involved. It is, nonetheless, difficult to imagine any Second Tier conflict that would escalate to something we might think of as World War III.

When combined with the improbability of war between countries of the First Tier, this condition presents the remarkable emerging characteristic of the overall system that has already been mentioned: the virtual absence of any military threat that could threaten to destroy the international system as a whole. This condition may or may not prove to be transitory; for the moment, however, it represents a condition of stability not often seen in international affairs.

The third characteristic of the Second Tier is the presence of considerable instability and violence within and between states. Internal violence is likely to continue because the absence of legitimate governments makes power struggles an everyday fact of life. The current surge of ethnically based internal violence in much of the Second Tier, so vividly played out in places such as Somalia, Bosnia, Kosovo, Rwanda, and parts of the former Soviet Union, illustrates this phenomenon, which may well continue and spread to parts of the Second Tier that have not already experienced it. In addition, regional conflicts threaten to erupt in interstate violence as well.

A fourth characteristic is diversity of economic development. Whereas First Tier states share wealthy, structurally advanced economies, such uniformity is lacking among the states of the Second Tier. A number of the poorest states have yet to enter the first industrial revolution (basic industrialization), while a few countries are on the verge of the third industrial revolution, where information is the most valued commodity. Sandwiched in between is the anomaly of the oil-rich states of the Middle East, with their huge wealth but largely nonindustrial economic structures.

A fifth characteristic of Second Tier states is the limit placed on their use of force by military capability. By definition, most Second Tier states have fewer resources to invest in military power than do First Tier states (at least on a per capita basis), although they often spend proportionately more of their resources on weapons (the Middle East is the principal example). The arsenals and the ability to employ them are uniformly less sophisticated than their First Tier counterparts. This gap between the tiers is an important part of the reason that no system-threatening challenge exists within the international system.

A sixth characteristic is the lack of a uniform commitment to peace and stability. War and other violence as instruments of policy are still viewed as viable alternatives within many Second Tier countries and between some others. Where legitimate grievances exist and where ancient hatreds continue, the option of force will remain tempting. As noted earlier, one reason for the First Tier to push for enlarging its membership is to abate the amount of violence in the Second Tier.

The seventh characteristic of the Second Tier is its likely preference for individual or collective defense rather than collective security. Since force remains a viable option for some Second Tier countries, they may come to see the existence of an effective collective security mechanism—as favored within the First Tier—as a menace, since it would be a mechanism used to end Second Tier conflicts that not all parties will want stopped. In that case, assertion of the right of individual states or groups of states to defend themselves (individual or collective defense) may become an attractive option to ward off intrusion in internal affairs. This will not, of course, be a universal Second Tier position. A number of Second Tier members, such as Morocco, Pakistan, and Ghana, have consistently supported and contributed forces to United Nations peacekeeping enterprises.

Intersection of the Tiers

This discussion suggests three analytically distinct forms that the international relations of the future will take on. The first two forms involve the relations among states of each tier, and the contrasts we have laid out suggest that the patterns will be quite different.

The third form—the relations between the tiers—is the most problematical, and early experiences do not suggest concrete patterns. Will the First Tier attempt to impose peace and stability in the Second Tier, and if so, for what reasons? The experiences in Somalia and Bosnia suggest quite different answers. At the same time, the good offices of several First Tier states in engaging a peace process between Israel and the Palestinians that has expanded throughout the region hold out a different potential message.

The form that First Tier–Second Tier relations takes will be mostly a matter of the First Tier's determination. The First Tier may decide that sizable parts of the Second Tier are too marginal and hopeless for its concern and hence may further decrease its involvement. On the other hand, expanding the ring of market democracies more broadly could enhance the prosperity and well-being of the First Tier itself, a reason for involvement.

The Changing Contours of International Relations

As already noted, a major emphasis of this text is on change in the international system, including where change may be heading in the future. To facilitate thinking in terms of change, each chapter will end with a brief discussion emphasizing major sources of change that were raised in the chapter and questions about the direction of change.

Two major sources of change were raised in Chapter 1. The first, and potentially more profound, is the challenge to the realist paradigm and some of its most cherished underpinnings. No one is willing to admit (although some may dream) that power politics is going to disappear or that the state will, in Marxist terms, "wither" away into some grand utopian design. Nevertheless, sovereign control by states over the entirety of their affairs is indeed being eroded. Some of the erosion is voluntary, as in when countries agree by treaty to limit what they do internally or to one another. Some of the erosion may be the result of precedent: into how many countries like Somalia can the international system make a forced, uninvited entry without the sanctity of everyone's territory being compromised?

There will be resistance to the dilution of sovereignty, mostly emanating from national governments that realize what is happening to their authority. In 1998, for instance, the U.S. government came out in virtual singular opposition to a treaty proposing a permanent War Crimes Court with mandatory jurisdiction over all alleged instances of atrocities. To many, American opposition seems anomalous, because most Americans do not believe their soldiers would commit war crimes. The opposition, it turns out, came out on the basis of sovereignty; the U.S. government was unwilling to give up total control over the disposition of its citizens by being forced to turn them over to international jurisdiction. This suggests that although the assault on sovereignty and other vestiges of the realist paradigm will continue, its progress will be not be linear.

The other source of change is the emergence, largely thanks to the globalizing economy, of an international system describable in terms of tiers. The gist of the idea of tiers is its dynamism and the notion of change. Dividing the world into a First Tier and three economically sequential subtiers suggests progression upward toward, and ultimately inclusion into, the First Tier. But will that be easy? The lessons of the financial crises that began in eastern Asia in 1997 and spread more generally in 1998 suggest that the mechanisms of the globalizing economy are too new, fragile, and evolving to allow any linear predictions. Whether or how fast the globalizing system responds to the financial crises will help predict the direction and speed of change.

Review

This chapter has provided an examination of the nature of international relations and how it is studied. In the process, the following points were made:

1. International relations is, at heart, the study of how the sovereign states of the world interact with one another. In addition to states, both subnational and supranational actors play a role.

2. The largely unanticipated end of the Cold War has accelerated a process of change in the operation of the international system. The realist paradigm, by which the Cold War system was organized, is now being challenged in a number of ways by post–Cold War international relations.

3. The authors' major organizational device for looking at the current international system is that of "a world of tiers." The First Tier consists of the most technologically advanced states with market-based economies and political democracies. These include the most powerful and consequential members of the system; their economies are highly interdependent, they have no major conflicts among them that could lead to war, and they prefer a tranquil system regulated by collective security.

4. The Second Tier, which is composed of the rest of the world's states, differs from the First Tier in a number of ways. The states of the Second Tier lack a common political and economic philosophy and level of economic development, they are less consequential for the overall system, and conflicts within and between them account for most of the violence and instability in the system. Finally, they are coming to prefer a system of individual or collective defense rather than collective security.

Suggested Readings

Bueno de Mesquita, Bruce. *The War Trap*. New Haven, CT: Yale University Press, 1981.

Carr, E. H. *The Twenty-Years' Crisis, 1919–1939*. London: Macmillan, 1939.

Dougherty, James E., and Robert L. Pfaltzgraff Jr. *Contending Theories of International Relations: A Comprehensive Survey,* 3d ed. New York: Harper & Row, 1990.

Falk, Richard. *Legal Order in a Violent World*. Princeton, NJ: Princeton University Press, 1968.

Fromkin, David. *The Independence of Nations*. New York: Praeger Special Studies, 1981.

Gilpin, Robert. *The Political Economy of International Relations*. Princeton, NJ: Princeton University Press, 1987.

Grant, Rebecca, and Kathleen Newland, eds. *Gender and International Relations*. Bloomington: Indiana University Press, 1991.

Isaak, Robert A. *International Political Economy: Managing World Economic Change*. Englewood Cliffs, NJ: Prentice Hall, 1991.

Kaplan, Morton A. *System and Process in International Politics*. New York: John Wiley, 1957.

Keohane, Robert O., and Joseph S. Nye Jr. *Power and Interdependence*, 2d ed. Glenview, IL: Scott, Foresman/Little, Brown, 1989.

Morgenthau, Hans J. *Politics Among Nations,* 6th ed., rev. Kenneth W. Thompson. New York: Alfred A. Knopf, 1985.

Rosecrance, Richard. *Action and Reaction in World Politics*. Boston: Little, Brown, 1963.

Singer, Max, and the Estate of Aaron Wildavsky. *The Real World Order: Zones of Peace, Zones of Turmoil,* rev. ed. Chatham, NJ: Chatham House, 1996.

Spero, Joan Edelman. *The Politics of International Economic Relations,* 5th ed. New York: St. Martin's Press, 1996.

Thucydides. *The History of the Peloponnesian Wars*. New York: Penguin Books, 1954.

Viotti, Paul, and Mark Kauppi. *International Relations: Theory, Realism, Pluralism, Globalism*. New York: Macmillan, 1987.

Waltz, Kenneth. *Man, the State, and War*. New York: Columbia University Press, 1954.

The International System

PREVIEW

In this chapter, we will introduce the principal elements and aspects of the international system that will serve as the foundation for discussions in the rest of the book. We will begin by looking at the basic unit of the system, the state, and how it has evolved over time. This will lead to a consideration of the sovereign authority possessed by states and how sovereignty produces an international system marked by anarchy, or the absence of such authority. Because an anarchic world is necessarily one in which power and the balancing of power play a major role, we will next define and discuss these concepts. We will then look at nonstate actors in the international system. The chapter will conclude with a case study of the tragedy of Bosnia and Herzegovina, a consequence of the breakdown of a traditional state and an illustration of the changing nature of the system.

KEY CONCEPTS

nation-state	instruments of power
state	balance of power
failed state	unipolar system
nation	bipolar system
nationalism	multipolar system
multinationalism	nonstate actors
irredentism	intergovernmental organizations (IGOs)
sovereignty	nongovernmental organizations (NGOs)
anarchy	multinational corporations (MNCs)
vital national interests	stateless corporations
power	global television
politics	subnational actors
scarcity	

OUTLINE

W e begin our exploration of the international system by describing and discussing its basic nature and structure. As noted in Chapter 1, major elements of the international system, like those of other systems, include its parts or units, which we will often refer to simply as actors; a network of relations among the actors; and a systemic concern among the members about how to deal with change that reflects system dynamism. We shall proceed as follows. The most basic kind of actor in the international system is the state, also sometimes referred to as the nation-state, and it is with the nature of the state that we begin. Next we turn to the central organizing device for the relations among states, the principle of sovereignty (introduced in Chapter 1), around which the rules of the system are crafted. Because of sovereignty, we then turn to power, which is a major feature of those relations, including various ways power may be distributed among the members. Finally, we examine change in the system that can be seen in the proliferation of so-called nonstate actors and in the disintegration of some traditional states, notably Yugoslavia.

A World of States

The group of states represented by a political map of the world defines the central political reality of the globe. When you propose to travel abroad, your normal reference point about your destination is the country (a synonym for state) to which you are going—Germany, Japan, or Brazil, for example. The primary political entity with which most people identify, to which they have a sense of belonging, is their state.

The first thing to note about this most basic unit of the international system is its alternate name: nation-state. In fact, the term nation-state represents two different concepts; those of the nation and of the state, and its definition is an amalgam of the meanings of these two terms. It is thus necessary to look at them first separately and then in combination, because in situations where statehood and nationhood are incompatible, as they sometimes are, the result can be political instability and even violence.

The State

For the purpose of understanding international relations, the idea of the state is overwhelmingly important. The term is a legal and political one, and it refers to internationally recognized control and jurisdiction by a government over a piece of territory and a group of people.

As this definition suggests, states are normally thought of as possessing at least four characteristics. The first is a territory that is definable on a political map of the world and does not overlap the territory of other states (when claimed territories do overlap, there exists a territorial dispute). Second, a state has a population over which the state's government has jurisdiction. While this characteristic may seem self-evident, even trivial, it explains, for instance, why there are no states in Antarctica.

Third, a state has a political organization. The basic purpose of this organization is to create an authority or government capable of maintaining some form of order over the state's territory and population. When the authority is seen as unjust or illegitimate (lacking the willing allegiance of the population), instability and violence may result. When the political organization simply collapses, as it did in Somalia in 1991 after the fall of the authoritarian ruler Siad Barre, the state may continue to exist, but in a condition of anarchy wherein no government has authority. For instance, there was no governmental unit available to invite United Nations forces into the country to restore order. The term "failed state" is sometimes used to describe this condition.

The fourth and final characteristic of a state is its recognition by other states. This characteristic, which gives states their formal legal standing as equal units within the international system, is manifested in such ways as formal declarations of recognition, the exchange of diplomats, and membership in the United Nations. When a government claiming to represent a state is refused recognition by other states, the state's standing is ambiguous; this was the case, for instance, with the so-called Serbian Republic of Bosnia and Herzegovina during the war over that territory in the early 1990s (described in the case study at the end of the chapter).

A checkpoint along the U.S.-Mexican border in San Ysidro, California. Control of a definable territory is one of the basic characteristics of a state.

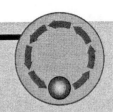

Coming to Terms

Nations, Nation-States, and States

Although the terms *nation, state,* and *nation-state* are often used interchangeably in general discussion about international relations, for our purposes, they need to be employed more precisely. When we talk about a political entity that governs territory and is the primary actor in international relations, we refer to a state, or less formally, to a country. We use nation, on the other hand, to refer to a group of people with common loyalties, which do not necessarily have any relationship to political authority. The hyphenated term nation-state will refer to an idealized state where all the inhabitants are members of the same nation. For various reasons, however, we will sometimes use the adjective *national* in referring to states. The term *national interest* is so conventional that it seemed the best choice, for example, as did *national governments* to avoid confusion with the governments of the U.S. states.

Despite its long history, a number of analysts suggest that the use of statehood to define the political and legal basis of the international system has become obsolete—or at least is in the process of becoming so. They base this assertion on several grounds, including the existence of international problems that a system organized on the basis of states is inadequate to deal with, such as environmental degradation, and the fact that state boundaries do not correspond to the structure of other significant international realities, such as the global economic system. These challenges will be discussed in detail later in this chapter and elsewhere.

The Nation

The concept nation is an anthropological and psychological term, and it refers to group identity and loyalty. Being part of a national group provides both a sense of belonging ("I am French") and a sense of exclusion and distinction from other national groups. As the post–Cold War world is evolving, these two contradictory sides of nationality are having some explosive, often deadly, consequences.

Nationality is normally thought of in terms of a group of characteristics common to the nation's members. A representative list of these characteristics includes:

1. *Race:* shared membership (or belief in such membership) in a group defined as different from others by virtue of its physical appearance, such as skin color or facial characteristics. In its purist form (hardly found in contemporary nationalities), the definition of race is based on a common, and distinct, gene pool.

2. *Language:* shared use of a language or dialect different from that normally spoken by others.

3. *Culture:* a shared set of beliefs about social organization, correct behavior, and the like that are different from those held by others.

4. *History:* a shared set of historical experiences, often including privation at the hands of other nations, and a shared interpretation of those experiences.
5. *Religion:* a shared system of religious beliefs or practices different from those of others.
6. *Feeling of belonging and identification:* a shared belief that one belongs to the nation or the acceptance of that status by others.

This list is not exhaustive, nor do all nations share all these characteristics. A common political heritage and set of political beliefs could be added, for instance. At the same time, the American citizenry as a whole displays none of the first five characteristics; yet despite the tendency toward the assertion of compound nationalism (describing oneself as Italian American or African American, for instance), almost all Americans view themselves as Americans and are, for the most part, accepted by others as such.

Nationality often differentiates even quite similar groups of people along so-called ethnic lines, based on differences in such characteristics as race, culture, or religion. As mentioned earlier, it thus creates feelings of distinction and exclusion as well as belonging. When members of different nationalities confront one another, therefore, the result is often misunderstanding, fear, and even loathing; in many cases, the actual differences between the groups are exaggerated completely out of proportion. Serbs and Croats, for instance, differ from one another in some respects—notably religion—but otherwise are virtually indistinguishable.

The Nation-State

Were all the world's states actually nation-states, each of them would be a place where all the inhabitants shared a common sense of nationhood that was closely related to loyalty to the state. In such a situation, ethnic and political loyalties would reinforce one another, adding legitimacy (willing consent to be governed) to the authority of the state and creating a unified feeling called *nationalism.*

Such a situation can, at least theoretically, come about in either or both of two ways: through an inclusionary method whereby a sense of identification with a state expands within the state until its boundaries approximate those of the state, or through an exclusionary method whereby state boundaries are changed or populations moved

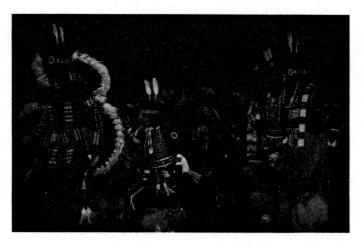

The people of the United States represent a variety of different racial, religious, and cultural groups, and many of these groups retain a sense of distinctive ethnic identity, as demonstrated by events like this American Indian ceremony.

so that a state contains only one nationality. The two methods have different appeals and consequences.

The inclusionary method, a product of democratic political theory, is based on the idea that through free and democratic interactions the political system acts as a kind of "melting pot" wherein different ethnic identities gradually blend together into a shared, inclusive national identity coterminous with the boundaries of the state. This idea, which may be more an expression of hope than a description of reality, is normally extrapolated from the pre–World War II experience of the United States and is a prominent part of theories of political development aimed at the African and Asian states that have become independent since World War II. Because this method weakens old nationalisms and the antagonisms they entail, it is preferred by those who seek to minimize violence in the international system.

The exclusionary method can be seen in operation in parts of post–Cold War Europe, peacefully in the separation of Czechs and Slovaks into two relatively homogenous states and violently in the form of "ethnic cleansing" in the former Yugoslavia. Although it has become a powerful force in recent years, hardly anyone except those seeking to use it to the advantage of their own national group favors the exclusionary method in principle, since it has at least three undesirable aspects.

First, it reinforces and even intensifies intolerance among groups, heightening the likelihood of instability and violence. Second, it tends to encourage the fragmentation of the state system into small, less economically viable units. Although the Czech Republic, for instance, will likely be a strong, viable entity, the prospects for Slovakia are not so bright. Finally, in many states national populations are already very intermixed, making the creation of ethnically homogenous states difficult. The only alternative means to this end is forced migrations, which is always a traumatic experience. As we shall see in Chapter 6, these problems are particularly vexing in parts of Eastern Europe and the former Soviet Union.

Imperfections in the State System

What the previous discussion suggests is the existence of imperfections in the nature of the basic units of the international system, with consequences for the system's operation. Indeed, there are two major kinds of problems in the alignment of nation and state in the contemporary international system, and each presents a different set of challenges in trying to fashion a more peaceful world order. These problems are multinationalism and irredentism.

Multinationalism.   The problem of multinationalism, in which more than one national group inhabits a single state, is a very common occurrence in the Second Tier, and especially in the former European colonies that gained their political independence after World War II. It is also found in much of the former Second World, and especially in the former Soviet Union.

In much of the Middle East, Africa, and (to a lesser degree) Asia, the underlying problem from which multinationalism arises is the existence of artificial states. This phenomenon had its origins in the colonial period, when borders were drawn with little knowledge, regard, or concern for the preexisting political realities of colonized areas. In the process, large pieces of territory inhabited by multiple national or tribal groups were often placed within a single state, a phenomenon that had occurred earlier in Western Europe itself.

Many of these groups were historical antagonists; but under colonial rule their relations appeared peaceful, because the authoritarian nature of colonialism was able to suppress open displays of antagonism in the same manner that communist authoritarianism hid similar national and ethnic hatreds in the Soviet Union and parts of Eastern and Central Europe.

When independence was gained, however, multinationalism became a problem. Suddenly, multiple nationalities within newly independent states were told that they were Nigerians or Iraqis or Pakistanis. The problem was that those Nigerians still thought of themselves as Ibos, Hausas, Yorubas, or one of the other tribes that had traditionally formed the basis of primary loyalty within "Nigerian" territory, just as many Iraqis thought of themselves as Arabs or Kurds, and Pakistanis thought of themselves as Punjabis, Baluchis, or Bengalis. Quebecois separatism in Canada demonstrates that this phenomenon also occurs in the First Tier.

The inclusive method of solving this problem called for the development of new national loyalties that would coincide with loyalty to the state, a process similar to that which had occurred earlier in the states of the First Tier. Just as most Americans have come to think of

Case in Point

Kosovo

The problems that can be caused by ethnically and religiously based multinationalism are no more clearly demonstrated anywhere in the world than in the Yugoslav province of Kosovo, until 1991 an autonomous region within the Yugoslav state of Serbia. The result has been an armed clash between the predominantly Albanian Muslim population of the province and the forces of the Yugoslav state, who are predominantly Serbian Orthodox Christians.

Fighting broke out in earnest in Kosovo in 1997, as the Yugoslav government initiated a series of raids using paramilitary forces against ethnic Albanian Kosovars suspected of fostering a secessionary movement to separate Kosovo from Yugoslavia and probably unite it with Albania. Documented reports of atrocities against ethnic Albanian Kosovars (such as leveling villages) caused international concern and eventual sanctions against Serbia/Yugoslavia in 1998, follwed by NATO attacks in 1999. In response, Kosovar separatists formed their own

military force, the Kosovo Liberation Army (KLA), which has received sizable military assistance from Albania and expatriate Kosovars internationally.

From an outsider viewpoint, the obvious solution would be to allow the separation of Kosovo from Serbia/Yugoslavia either to form an independent state or to federate with Albania, since the territory is overwhelmingly Albanian Muslim in composition. What frustrates this solution is that Kosovo has enormous significance as a symbol of Serbian nationalism. Kosovo was the site of the climactic battle of Serbia against the Ottoman Turks fought in 1389; the result was a crushing Serbian defeat and the loss of Serbian independence until the end of World War I. The Battle of Kosovo is of such symbolic importance to Serbs that they cannot rationally consider allowing Kosovo to escape from Serb control again. That most of the Kosovars converted to Islam only adds to the animosity between the two groups.

themselves as Americans first and Mississippians or African Americans second, citizens of Nigeria, for instance, were to undergo a transformation that would result in their thinking of themselves as Nigerians first and Ibos second. Unfortunately, the transfer of loyalties has not always occurred. Where it has not, the result has often been an exclusionary variety of nationalism in which various nationalities compete for political power within a state and where appeals to nationality and ethnicity are even used to encourage genocidal war, as in Rwanda.

As suggested earlier, under authoritarian rule much of this divisive national feeling was suppressed. In the Soviet Union, for instance, the Committee on State Security (KGB) routinely infiltrated and suppressed separatist national groups, thereby providing a veneer of unity facilitating the belief that communism was creating a "Soviet man." Ironically for those who favor liberal democracy and an inclusionary form of nationalism, the loosening of authoritarian rule that is one of the major results of the end of the Cold War is unleash-

Map 2-1   **Successor States of Yugoslavia**

©1996 by St. Martin's Press, Inc. From: *Contours of Power*, by Snow/Brown. Reprinted with permission of Bedford/St. Martin's Press, Inc.

ing the forces of exclusionary nationalism around the world. As political constraints are removed along with the psychological security of the old order, people are falling back on their old national identities for a feeling of belonging and a system of beliefs; old, simmering hatreds are being revived and manipulated. This is most dramatically the case in the former Yugoslavia, and manifested in the early 1990s in Bosnia and more recently in Kosovo. As political freedom spreads to Africa, Asia, and the Middle East, multinationalism almost certainly will become a manifest problem in many more countries.

Irredentism.   The other major kind of problem in aligning nation and state is irredentism, a situation in which a national group is divided between two or more states and a movement arises to unite it either by shifting territory between the existing states (the original meaning of the term) or by carving a new state out of the territory in which the members reside. Somalia and Ethiopia, for example, disagree about the status of the Ogadan region of Ethiopia, whose inhabitants are largely ethnic Somalis and would prefer to be part of Somalia; most Kosovars are ethnic Albanians and would rather be part of Albania or have their own state. The problem is most difficult to solve when the group is an oppressed minority in the states where its members reside and there is no state to which they can immigrate. A group that has no national home is called a stateless nation.

The most intractable case of the effects of states dividing a national group involves the Kurds, a group who meet all the criteria of a nation. They have a common history dating

Iraqi Kurdish refugees make their way down a steep hillside along the Iraq-Iran border. The Kurds are a prime example of a stateless nation: they meet all the criteria of a national group but have no state of their own and are an oppressed minority in all the countries where they live. The Iraqi Kurds came under fierce attack from the forces of Iraqi President Saddam Hussein after they rose in rebellion in the aftermath of the 1991 Persian Gulf War.

back to biblical times, a common religion (a form of Sunni Islam), and a common language (Kurdish) and culture; most important, they think of themselves as Kurds. In the twentieth century, however, they have represented a minority in the countries where they live: Turkey (where they make up about 20 percent of the population), Iraq (about 10 percent), and Iran (about 5 percent). In each case, they have been politically, culturally, and militarily oppressed more or less systematically by their "host" governments. The campaign by Saddam Hussein in Iraq, which included the use of chemical weapons against Kurdish villages in 1987, is the best publicized instance.

Almost all Kurds share a desire to forge a state called Kurdistan from Iranian, Iraqi, and Turkish territory, a goal nearly achieved in 1919 at the Versailles peace talks. The "host" states are, however, uniformly unwilling to cede parts of their territory, and as a result the Kurdish separatist movements that exist in each country are engaged in varying levels of civil war against the regimes at any given time.

Multinationalism and irredentism collectively constitute a threat to the stability of the international system that will continue to challenge the system's attempts to regulate war and peace in the future. Bloodletting in places as diverse as the republic of Georgia, Sri Lanka, and the Sudan can be traced to these causes. Given the very public nature of violence and other atrocities in a world of global television transmission, there will be mounting pressure for the international community somehow to interpose itself in and mediate conflicts where journalists choose to publicize them. Just as the international community agonized over what, if anything, it could do in Bosnia and Herzegovina, so it may in many other far-flung locations about the globe.

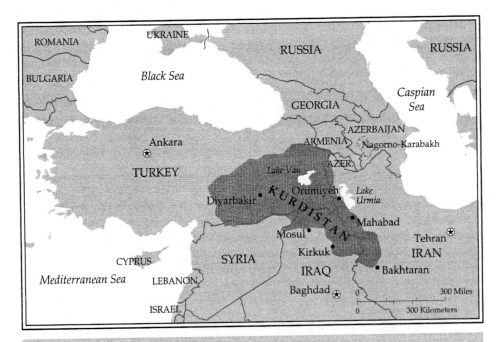

Map 2-2 **Kurdistan**

Sovereignty and Anarchy

One of the difficulties involved in deciding what to do about a conflict is structural: the basis of the international system is the principle of the sovereignty of the state to regulate its own affairs. Sovereignty is the fundamental principle that defines the interactions between the members of the international system. An idea first set forth in the sixteenth century and enshrined in the peace of Westphalia in 1648, sovereignty means complete and supreme authority. As the concept has evolved, sovereignty has come to be an attribute possessed by states, meaning that in their dealings with one another all states are (at least theoretically) equal and that there is no power above them.

To understand the role of sovereignty and how and why it is the central reality of international relations, we will look first at the origins and evolution of the concept, then at the consequences of sovereignty for the international system, and finally at contemporary critiques and attacks on the idea of absolute state sovereignty.

Origins and Evolution of Sovereignty

The author of the concept of sovereignty was a Frenchman, Jean Bodin, who lived in the sixteenth century, a time of considerable turmoil and disorder accompanying the breakup of feudalism in France and elsewhere in Europe. To Bodin, the central problem of the "international" system of his time was the absence of strong rulers, authorities who could order and control the relations between warring feudal lords within the territories that would eventually evolve into the modern European states. In 1576, he published a book, *De Republica* (Republic), expounding this observation. As a central part of the remedy he proposed, he coined the term sovereignty, which he defined as "supreme power over citizens and subjects, unrestrained by law." His idea was to create an overarching authority that could make and enforce a legal order. As Bodin formulated it, sovereignty was a principle intended not to govern the relations between political units but rather to empower those who maintained order within those units. It created the basis for domestic authority, and most observers believe Bodin would have opposed its extension to international relations.

The modern concept of sovereignty originated in the sixteenth and seventeenth centuries with Jean Bodin (left) and Thomas Hobbes (center left), who argued that an all-powerful central authority was necessary to preserve order within a state. The idea of popular sovereignty evolved in the eighteenth century out of the writings of John Locke (center right) and Jean-Jacques Rousseau (right); they asserted that sovereignty within a state resides in the people, not the monarch, and that governmental authority depends on popular consent.

The widespread adoption of sovereignty as an operating principle had to await the end of the Thirty Years War in 1648, one of the primary issues of which had been the secularization of political authority. Those who won the war and dictated the treaties that compose the peace of Westphalia wanted to wrest all political power from the Roman Catholic Church. The doctrine of sovereignty, wherein sovereign control was possessed by the monarch of each state (which is why kings and queens were sometimes also called sovereigns), served this purpose. In 1651, Thomas Hobbes published *Leviathan,* which also argued for the principle that supreme authority within the state should rest with the monarch and that secular legitimacy should replace the lost legitimacy of the Church.

Although Hobbes, like Bodin, did not discuss the international implications of sovereignty, others were already doing so. Hugo Grotius, often considered the father of modern international law, had asserted the sovereignty of the state as a fundamental principle of international politics in his book *On the Law of War and Peace,* published in 1625. In 1758, Emerich de Vattel published his *Law of Nations,* which also argued that states could not be restrained by superior authority or by law.

The other fundamental addition to the evolution of sovereignty was its popularization. Stimulated by the works of John Locke (*Two Treatises of Government,* 1690) and Jean-Jacques Rousseau (*The Social Contract,* 1762), the idea had emerged by the time of the American and French Revolutions that sovereignty within a state resides in the people, not in an individual (the monarch), but that the people agree to assign part of their sovereignty to the state to perform collective acts. This idea is known as popular sovereignty.

Through this process of evolution, the concept of sovereignty gained its contemporary meaning. From Bodin comes the notion of a location of supreme authority within the state that provides the basis for domestic order, a principle put into practical effect by the peace of Westphalia. From Locke and Rousseau comes the limitation that legitimate secular authority resides in the citizenry, which both confers this authority on the state's government and can rescind the grant. Therefore, the principle of sovereign authority is based on that of legitimacy. Both these principles remain in force within the international system today and form the conceptual basis of the realist paradigm.

Consequences of Sovereignty

As Grotius was the first to recognize, the sovereignty that provides the basis for domestic order also helps to create international disorder. By definition, there can be no power superior to that of a sovereign government. (As a practical matter, too, such a government is normally above any other form of law.) That being the case, there can be no international authority that is above or superior to the sovereign states that constitute the international system. As a result, international relations is a state of anarchy (the absence of government).

Moreover, because sovereignty gives states supreme control over what goes on within their territories, it has been considered improper, at least historically, for states to interfere with another state's internal exercise of power. This condition is traditionally described in terms of the "billiard ball analogy" raised in Chapter 1: the idea that states are like impermeable billiard balls, and that international relations consists of the balls coming into contact but not penetrating below the surface of one another. As we shall discuss next, this notion is under considerable assault from those who assert that there are state actions so heinous that they should not be tolerated by the international system merely on the grounds of sovereignty.

Anarchy does not mean chaos or disorder; it means more simply that there is no institution with the authority to regulate the relations among sovereign states. In fact, there is order in the vast majority of international interactions, because states have agreed to rules of behavior as a matter of convenience or self-interest. States normally honor the passports of the citizens of other states, for instance, even if they have no jurisdiction over the criteria by which those passports are issued. Why? The answer is simple: countries know that honoring one another's passports is a matter of mutual convenience. Even at that, some countries still assert sovereign control of access to national soil by requiring that people seeking to enter their territory obtain special permission in the form of a visa.

Why does the international system continue the anarchy that has always been present in the relations among states or their equivalents? The answer is straightforward: that is exactly the way states want the system to be. The reason lies in the notion of vital national interests, conditions deemed so important to states that they will not voluntarily compromise them. The most basic vital interest is the territorial integrity of the state itself; no state will willingly allow its territory to be invaded, occupied, or taken away by the forces of another state. Nor will a state generally accept without some form of resistance any threat it perceives to the safety of the citizens and their economic well-being or that of the state as a whole.

An international authority superior to the state could jeopardize the vital interests of states. For example, there are numerous disputed borders in the world where adjacent states claim the same territory and hold their claims to be vital. If there were a real international authority, it could adjudicate such claims; in the process, someone's claim would be at least partially denied. Since the issue is considered too important to be compromised, states prefer not to have an authority capable of making unacceptable judgments.

There is, of course, a World Court (technically, the International Court of Justice), but its jurisdiction illustrates the point. The Court has jurisdiction over international disputes only if both parties to a dispute give it jurisdiction for that specific case. Jurisdiction, in other words, extends only to those matters on which both states are willing to lose: matters not considered vital, where sovereignty can be waived.

This lack of a sovereign international authority results in a system where all states are legally coequal and where their interactions are "governed" only to the extent that they willingly agree to be regulated. Although this is technically the case, the reality of course is different. Just as in George Orwell's *Animal Farm*, where all pigs were equal, but some were more equal than others, so too are some states more equal than others in the sense that they are more capable of accomplishing their purposes. The reason is that the absence of governing authority makes international politics inherently power politics.

Critiques of Sovereignty

Before turning to the role of power in a system of sovereign states, it is only fair and balanced to point out that the view of sovereignty's role set forth to this point is not universally held by international relations scholars. Some argue that the case is factually flawed, that sovereignty in practice is not and never has been as pervasive as it is in theory. Others argue that sovereignty is undesirable, because it permits rulers to act in atrocious manners toward their own citizens, a critique that goes back to the gestation of the concept. The criticisms can be formulated in terms of at least five specific limits on the exercise of sovereignty that its critics see as actual, desirable, or both. While the criticisms do not necessarily lead to the conclusion that sovereign control should not remain the underlying principle of the system, the criticisms do point to practical limits that the contemporary world places on its absolute practice.

Summary ━━━━━━━━━━━━━━━━━━━━━━━━━━━━━━━━━━━

Limits on Sovereignty

1. Voluntary dilution of authority by states
2. Inability of states to control "national" economies
3. Inability of states to control telecommunications
4. Emergence of transnational issues requiring coordinated solutions
5. Assertion of the "rights of individuals and groups" over the "rights of states"

The first limitation is that states routinely dilute their sovereign control voluntarily. Signing the United Nations Charter, for instance, requires that a state denounce war as an instrument of policy; acceding to the Universal Declaration of Human Rights and the Convention on Genocide restricts the way it can treat its citizens. Further, membership in intergovernmental organizations such as the International Telecommunications Union or the International Civil Aviation Organization restricts states' options in various areas of policy, in this case on electronic communications and airport safety standards, respectively.

A second limitation also relates to the factual content of sovereignty, specifically in the area of economics: it is a pure fiction to assert that any state's economic activity can be totally controlled and regulated by that state's government. The international economic system is truly global, with individual corporations operating and owned by people in numerous countries. The so-called stateless corporation, about which more will be said in Chapter 9, is a case in point. As further example, the fact that a stock exchange is operating somewhere in the world all the time means that money to purchase stock flows routinely across national borders without governmental consent.

A third and related limit to sovereignty has arisen from the telecommunications revolution. Historically, a major lever of governmental control over a population was the ability to control access to information through censorship and interference with messages across national boundaries. With the rise of satellites and a number of other technologies, the global information system is making such control virtually impossible. In the process, it is becoming harder for rulers to lie to their populations. Global television news is a major source of change in the new international system.

A fourth limit on sovereignty comes from the emergence of those transstate issues discussed in Chapter 1. These issues involve problems that transcend national boundaries in ways that the governments of individual states have little control over; they cannot be solved by individual states alone but require coordinated international responses. The most prominent examples include environmental degradation, terrorism, worldwide food supply, and population growth. Although the designation of transstate issue or problem is of fairly recent vintage, the phenomenon itself is not. The rationale for forming

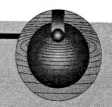

Amplification

The U.S. Sovereignty and the Permanent War Crimes Tribunal

The steadfast, and some would argue pernicious, extent to which states cling to sovereignty is well exemplified by the American position on the proposed permanent war crimes tribunal that was negotiated between 161 states in Rome in June and July 1998. The proposed tribunal would have automatic jurisdiction over military and other personnel if they are accused of war crimes. The United States argues that the automatic nature of the jurisdiction violates American sovereign control over its own citizens, and notably military personnel serving overseas who might be accused of crimes in carrying out their duties.

The American position derives from the unique U.S. position in the world and its historic opposition to international conventions intruding on U.S. sovereignty. The official U.S. position is that a tribunal with sweeping jurisdiction could bring politically motivated charges against American service members if, for instance, they were involved in incidents where civilians were killed in a peacekeeping operation. The United States wants protection for its citizens in these kinds of cases, either by limiting the extent of automatic jurisdiction or providing that jurisdiction only applies when it is specifically granted by the U.S. (or other country's) government. Jelena Pejic, a lawyer for the Lawyers' Committee for Human Rights, states the contrary position: "We understand the American concern, but the loopholes it is creating to protect American citizens are the same ones that would allow rogue countries to shield themselves."

The U.S. position is consistent with the position the United States has taken on other conventions. It was an American concern, voiced as the Connally Amendment, that limits the jurisdiction of the World Court, and the limits it proposes on the war crimes tribunal are similar. The United States was also one of the last countries to sign the Universal Declaration on Human Rights and the Convention on Genocide for the same reason.

Source: New York Times, national edition, July 10, 1998, A7.

the specialized agencies of the United Nations at the end of World War II was the existence of a set of problems not amenable to state-by-state solution, a perception captured in the motto of the World Health Organization: "Disease knows no frontiers." Attacking these problems requires international action in which some dilution of sovereignty does occur; the difficulty of reaching consensus on solutions was well demonstrated by the 1992 Rio de Janeiro Earth Summit, where declarations of sovereignty impeded, among other things, appeals to limit reductions in the destruction of rain forests by states like Malaysia (see the case study in Chapter 10).

Finally, sovereignty is under direct assault from those who deny the absolute right of states to do what they please within their borders. Such assertion of total control is known, in the shorthand of international law, as the "rights of states." In response to growing, publicized (via global television) evidence of obviously atrocious behavior by states against their citizens in places such as Cambodia, Tiananmen Square in Beijing, the Kurdish areas of Iraq and Turkey, Bosnia and Herzegovina, and Kosovo, a contrary assertion has arisen. Known as the "rights of individuals and groups," this argument suggests that when governments abuse their citizens in ways that offend international standards, the system has a right and an obligation to intervene in contravention of national sovereignty. In effect, this is an extension of the argument that the sovereign is not above the law.

This is a controversial position, one not widely accepted in theory and especially application. Some precedent for it has been set by the American "humanitarian interventions" to end Kurdish and Shiite suffering in Iraq (Operation Provide Comfort and Operation Southern Watch) and starvation in Somalia (Operation Restore Hope), but it has yet to be raised to an international standard.

All of these critiques of sovereignty, in fact, must be placed in proper context. The political sovereignty of states is not particularly under attack, except for the assertion of the rights of individuals and groups over those of states. It is in the nonpolitical aspects of international activity, such as the economic sphere, that the assault is most obvious and strongest.

The Concept and Role of Power

The continuing prevalence of political sovereignty affects the rules of international conduct. In the absence of a superior authority, states must resort to self-help to promote and protect their vital interests. The principal means by which they do so is through the application of power.

Like individuals and groups within a state, states and other actors in the international system occasionally come into conflict over issues in which both parties cannot have their own way. In domestic society, the order produced by sovereignty provides mechanisms for resolving these conflicts through, for instance, the legislative and judicial systems. International relations lacks such mechanisms because the perception or definition of certain interests as vital makes it impossible to create decision-making units that could compromise those interests. In that situation of anarchy, a state or other actor obtains a favorable outcome to a conflict to the extent it can convince its opponent or opponents to accept less than they wanted in the disputed area. It does so through the application of power, which is a more pervasive attribute of international relations than it is of domestic affairs.

A caveat is necessary here. What we will describe as the use of power in international relations does not describe all or even the majority of international interactions, most of which are governed by rules and procedures almost as routine and predictable as those occurring in domestic systems. For most purposes, international relations is not a Darwinian jungle where only the fittest survive; it is a condition of anarchy when those relations involving the most important interests of the state (the vital interests) come into play.

With that in mind, we can begin to look at power and its role in the system. First, we will define power and its characteristics. We will relate that definition to politics generally and the notion of scarcity underlying the relationship between power and politics. Second, we will introduce the mechanisms by which power is utilized, the instruments of power.

Power Defined

Within the realist paradigm, power is the most basic concept for understanding international relations, a perspective we basically accept. Although power is used to mean a number of things, the definition we will employ is as follows: power is the ability to get someone to do something he or she would not otherwise do.

This definition is somewhat vague, and the use of the power concept by classic realists is often criticized as either too vague or too all-encompassing to be helpful in explaining international phenomena. The key problem resides in the term ability within the definition: what makes someone do something he or she would not otherwise do?

This source of confusion can be clarified by making two distinctions about power. The first is that power is a relationship, not an attribute. Many scholars have attempted to clarify this distinction. Some have tried to conceptualize power as a quantifiable attribute (or group of such attributes) that states possess and can use to gain compliance from other states; from this basis these scholars have developed indices of power or power potential (see, for instance, Kegley and Wittkopf, 1993). The advantage of this approach is that it produces statistical measurements that can be compared to see which party to a conflict should prevail in power relationships. For instance, the United States is the remaining world superpower because it leads the world in both military and economic strength, as measured by such indices as striking force or industrial production. By contrast, Malawi has less power by any means of measurement; thus, the United States should "win" in a power relationship with Malawi.

The limitation of this quantitative approach, on the other hand, is that although measures of power are important in determining the capability of states to carry out the threats or provide the incentives that are inherent in power applications, knowing how much of a measure of power a state has is not enough. Thinking of power as a relationship clarifies this point: abstract amounts of power are relevant only to the extent that the state or other actor to whom power is applied is actually influenced, which is a psychological, political phenomenon. If measures of power were all there is to determining winners and losers, clearly the United States should have prevailed in the Vietnam War. But it did not. Why?

The answer leads to the second point of clarification in our definition: the extent to which power is effective is specific to particular actors and situations; it is not abstract and immutable. To understand this concept, consider that getting someone to do something he or she does not want to do is often accomplished through issuing a threat, a warning that something harmful will be done in the event of noncompliance. Effective threats will accomplish their purpose without being carried out; the object will comply based on the threat alone. The dynamic here is plain: once a threat is made, the focus of the outcome shifts from the party that made it to the one being threatened. First, he or she must decide if the threat is to be believed. This involves two calculations: whether the other party can carry out the threat (capability) and, if so, whether it actually would do so (intention). In combination, these calculations define the likelihood of hostile action: the credibility of the threat equals capability plus intention. The problem is that while capability may be known, intention quite often is unknown. After making this assessment, the threatened party must calculate the importance of the outcome and the acceptability of complying or resisting.

We will elaborate on this process later in the section, but at this point simply note how it illustrates the actor- and situation-specific nature of power. Since the burden of resolving the conflict lies with the party threatened, then whether power is available to the party issuing the threat or will be effective if it is used depends very much on the situation: the mindset of the party threatened and its assessment of the other party. The entire process takes place within an atmosphere of uncertainty and imperfect information.

If the strict comparison of power indices was the determinant of these situations, the outcome in Vietnam would have been quite different than it was. By any quantifiable comparison of power, the United States was clearly more powerful than North Vietnam and its South Vietnamese allies (the National Liberation Front and its military arm, the Viet Cong), and comparing measures would have resulted in a prediction of U.S. success. But it did not occur. One reason was that the absolute measures were not relevant to the specific situation; much of American firepower could not be employed effectively against guerrilla forces who would not stand and fight in the face of that firepower. At the same time, the Americans badly underestimated the importance of the war to the enemy. The war was simply more important to the Vietnamese than to the United States, a factor that quantitative comparison could not capture.

Power and Politics

Because the power relationships between states are primarily political in nature, it is necessary both to define politics and to show its linkage to power through the concept of scarcity. For our purposes, politics can be defined as the ways in which conflicts of interest over scarce resources are resolved. This definition is similar to the classic formulation of David Easton (politics as the authoritative allocation of resources); as such, it contains two major elements which allow one to differentiate a political from a nonpolitical situation.

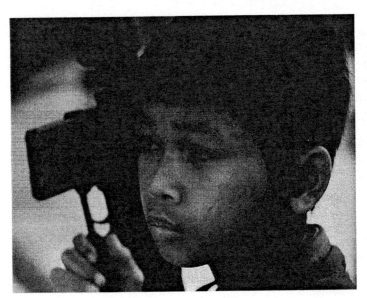

The intense determination and unconventional tactics of Viet Cong guerrillas, like the youngster receiving weapons instruction in this photograph, help to explain why the United States lost the Vietnam War. Despite having far greater military and industrial resources than the Viet Cong and their North Vietnamese allies, the Americans could not prevail against an enemy that attached much more importance to the outcome and used tactics against which American firepower was largely ineffective.

One element of the definition is substantive—conflicts of interest over scarce resources. The key idea here is scarcity, the condition in which all claimants to a particular valued thing cannot simultaneously have all of it they want or need, because not enough of it exists. The notion of scarcity often has an economic tone, since economics is the discipline that most utilizes it. Certainly economic resources—money, oil reserves, industrial goods—are among the more prominent valued things that are normally scarce. But anything that people want more of than they all can have can be a scarce resource; examples include social status (by definition everyone cannot be part of the elite), political power (there are more people who would like to be president of France than can be at any given time), and sovereign control of territory (as in Bosnia and Herzegovina).

When only one of the claimants to a scarce resource is actively pursuing its claim, the conflict between them is said to be latent, or inactive. Some Mexicans, for instance, undoubtedly hold irredentist desires to reclaim parts of the territory in the southwestern United States that were taken from Mexico during the Mexican War and by the Gadsden Purchase; as long as those claims are not pressed, the dispute between the two countries remains latent. Problems of scarcity become important and political when some or all of the claimants to a resource actively pursue more of it than can simultaneously be possessed. A simple diagram of such a situation is depicted in Figure 2-1. In this diagram, there are two parties, A and B, with claims on a resource, depicted as the circle. The extent of each party's claim is shown as a semicircle; the shaded area where the semicircles overlap represents the parties' mutual claim against a part of the resource that both cannot simultaneously possess. In many real cases, of course, there are more than two claimants, or claimants may pursue all of the resource or different amounts of it.

Presuming that both sides press their maximum claims, there are three possible outcomes, shown in Figure 2-2. In Outcome 1, party A gets all of the resource he or she desired; Outcome 2 has party B attaining his or her goal; and in Outcome 3, A and B compromise such that each receives less than the amount claimed. How is the outcome determined? The answer is through the second, or procedural, aspect of the definition of politics—the means by which conflicts are resolved. In domestic society, those means are defined by a series of procedures that are based in domestic sovereignty. In the international system, the lack of an overarching authority leads back to the notion of power. All

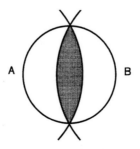

Figure 2-1   **Scarcity**

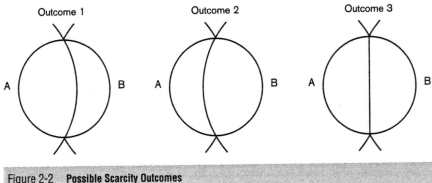

Figure 2-2 **Possible Scarcity Outcomes**

three of the outcomes require one or both of the claimants to do something they do not want to (or would not otherwise) do. Which outcome occurs will depend on which party is able to compel the outcome toward his or her preference and away from the other's preference—which, in other words, in the particular situation has the relevant power to compel the outcome.

It is because of this dynamic that international politics are inherently power politics. To see how power relationships operate, in turn, requires looking at the kinds of power available to states—the so-called instruments of power that were mentioned in Chapter 1.

Instruments of Power

The idea of instruments of power refers to the range of means that a state has available to it in attempting to gain compliance from other states. (Although this discussion will focus on states, nonstate actors possess and use many of the same means.) The list of these means is a varied and extensive one, and success requires finding the appropriate means for the specific problem at hand. Because of their situation-specific nature, understanding the instruments of power provides a more complete basis for comprehending the dynamics of power than does analyzing comparative aggregate measures of national power.

Traditionally, as suggested in Chapter 1, the instruments of power are divided into three general categories. The political/diplomatic instrument refers to a state's ability to use persuasive reasoning and diplomatic skill to get others to accept its position; the economic instrument, to its ability to use economic rewards or penalties to gain compliance; and the military instrument, to its capacity to threaten or use force. When the political/diplomatic instrument is employed, it is normally used in conjunction with one of the other instruments.

Each of these instruments includes a number of possible actions, and choosing any particular action involves an estimation of what will be effective at an acceptable cost. For instance, the actions available in the political/economic realm include a change in diplomatic relations, scientific and cultural exchanges, humanitarian assistance, technical assistance, dissemination of information and propaganda, economic and financial assistance, economic and trade policy changes, covert actions, United Nations Security Council debate, and trade embargoes and economic sanctions. Four general comments can be made about the items on this list.

First, all of these general categories of action offer multiple specific options. Economic and trade policy, for instance, includes such things as most favored nation (MFN) status (as discussed in the Introduction), preferential quotas on imports, and the like.

Second, most options offer positive, negative, and other suboptions. One can threaten to withhold diplomatic recognition to force acquiescence to a position, or one can extend recognition in response to compliance. Similarly, one can threaten to withhold the various forms of assistance for noncompliance and offer varying levels of assistance for varying amounts of compliance. Table 2.1 gives examples of some options and suboptions available within each category of action.

A third point to be made about the list as ordered is that it represents a sequence of actions of increasing cost or benefit to the state taking the action and the one toward which it is directed. It requires very little effort to offer or to withhold recognition of a regime or to send or not send a group of scientists or artists to another country, and being given or denied such privileges likewise has little practical effect. Enforcing or enduring an embargo requires much more effort on both sides.

A fourth and final comment about this list is that the availability of more or fewer of these actions more accurately reflects a state's power than does a static measure like the size of its economy. All the options and suboptions in Table 2.1 are available to a U.S. president seeking to use power in a situation in the interests of the United States. Other states do not have as many options available and thus are less likely to succeed in gaining compliance (they are less powerful). As noted, the United States has threatened to manipulate China's MFN status in order to improve the Chinese government's human rights record. Although China has not been dramatically impressed, similar threats from, say, Uruguay would carry even less weight.

A similar list of possible actions, to which the same general comments apply, can be made for the combined use of the political and military instruments. In ascending order of severity, this list includes military assistance, dissemination of propaganda, covert actions, UN Security Council debates, shows of strength, surveillance, a change in diplomatic relations, naval restrictions, mobilization of armed forces or evacuation of one's citizens from

Table 2.1 Examples of Political/Economic Instruments of Power	
Action	**Options and Suboptions**
Change in diplomatic relations	Extending or withholding recognition
Scientific and cultural exchanges	Sending or not sending ballet troupe
Humanitarian asssistance	Sending or ending disaster relief
Technical assistance	Sending business experts to formerly communist countries or withdrawing them
Dissemination of information and propaganda	Planting stories in press
Economic and financial assistance	Forgiving or not forgiving loans
Economic and trade policy changes	Granting or revoking most-favored-nation (MFN) status
Covert actions	Bribing officials
U.N. Security Council debates	Sponsoring friendly or hostile resolutions
Trade embargoes and economic sanctions	Blocking or unblocking critical goods

Table 2.2	Examples of Political/Military Instruments of Power
Action	**Options and Suboptions**
Military assistance	Extending or refusing credits for equipment
Dissemination of propaganda	Funding hostile radio broadcasts
Covert actions	Funding or not funding guerrillas
UN Security Council debates	Sponsoring friendly or hostile resolutions
Show of strength	Deploying fleet off coast
Surveillance	Engaging in overflights
Change in diplomatic relations	Withdrawing embassy personnel
Naval restrictions	Quarantining ships; blockading or mining ports
Mobilization/evacuation	Calling up reserves
Use of limited force	Bombing military targets
Threat of mass-destruction weapons	Putting nuclear force on alert

the target country, limited use of force, and threatened use of weapons of mass destruction (nuclear weapons).

Examples of options and suboptions for each action in the list are shown in Table 2.2. What differentiates this list from the list of political/economic actions is its more negative tone. Most of the actions involve threatening or actually causing physical harm to people. In a few instances, such as the provision or withholding of military assistance, there can be a carrot as well as a stick. With military actions, however, the stick is the more frequent option. Once again, more powerful states have the ability to threaten or carry out more of these actions than less powerful states.

Analyzing national strength in terms of the instruments of power lends support to the post–Cold War assertion that the United States is the world's only superpower. While other states rank high in possession of the economic or the military instrument, the United States is the only one that has available the full range of actions in both dimensions. Japan rivals the United States in terms of some elements of the economic instrument, but it has a self-limited, unassertive military instrument. Russia, on the other hand, still possesses some of the superpower-class military instrument of the former Soviet Union (principally its nuclear arsenal) but has little economic clout. Some American effectiveness also comes from what Joseph S. Nye, Jr. calls "soft power," the inherent international appeal of the American vision of the world.

The lists of economic and military instruments also speak to the limits of power. Even though the United States has by far the widest variety of actions available to it, that does not mean it will always prevail; there are always situations, just as in Vietnam during the Cold War, where none of the possible actions will move matters in the direction it wants them to go. The case study on Bosnia and Herzegovina particularly illustrates this problem. These limits on power arise because a given action must be measured against a set of at least three criteria:

1. *Controllability:* Does the state have enough control over the action to apply it effectively? This is especially a problem with economic actions that are not directly

governmental actions, such as boycotts; the theft of economic assistance by corrupt officials is another example.

2. *Relevance:* Does the action address the problem in a meaningful way? Sailing a naval fleet just off the coast of a country can inspire awe (especially if it includes a nuclear aircraft carrier), but it probably would not deter human rights violations.

3. *Credibility:* Will threats be believed? This concern applies most directly to the most severe actions—use of force or sanctions—where carrying out the threat could potentially harm the threatening as well as the threatened state.

Balances of Power

Analyzing the relative distribution of power among the members of the international system—the balance of power—is a basic use of the term "power" in international relations study. It requires examining which states are the most influential (or powerful) at any point in time, how these relate to one another, and how they relate to the lesser powers in the system. Moreover, international relations scholars have also attempted to assess the relative stability of various distributions of power.

The idea of a balance of power is as old as the study of relations among political communities. Thucydides, in his account of the Peloponnesian Wars, was the first to use the concept, describing its application among the Greek city-states and their neighbors; the analysis of power balances has been a part of international relations scholarship ever since. In general, such analysis tries to define the dominant characteristics of various forms of the international system and to assess the consequences of those variations. How many powerful states are there at a particular time? How do they relate to one another and to others? How much control is available to the various actors? Do the patterns of their interaction produce instability and violence or stability and tranquillity?

These questions take on particular relevance in the contemporary world because the system is in a period of transition, as the power balance of the Cold War and the systemic patterns it produced are being supplanted by a new balance and new patterns based in a world of tiers. Will the new system resemble one of the historical ones, or will it be something very different?

Forms of Balance of Power

Authors such as Rosecrance, Kaplan, and others have classified international systems along three basic lines: by the number of major actors in the system, by the amount of control the major players possess, and by the extent to which different configurations produce stability or instability. Actors are defined as major on the basis of their power, which has historically been equated mainly with military capability.

On the basis of the number of major actors, systems are normally divided into three categories. The first, if historically least common, is the unipolar system, a configuration where one state—or empire—so dominates the international system that no other political entity rivals it. The Roman Empire at its apex probably provides as close to a historical example as has existed; Rome did not control the whole world, but it did hold sway over the

Ruins of the Roman Forum. The Roman Empire at its apex is probably the best historical example of a unipolar international system, in which one political entity clearly dominates all others.

civilized Mediterranean world as well as many peripheral areas. With the end of the Cold War and the demise of the Soviet Union, some analysts suggest that because the United States is the only remaining superpower, the world is for some purposes unipolar, a notion we will discuss shortly.

The second category of this classification scheme is the bipolar system, where two states are so clearly more powerful than any others, that they become the organizational axes of the international system. The period between the end of World War II and the disintegration of one of the poles (the Soviet Union and its "empire") was an example of a bipolar world. In this instance, the clash of the ideological worldviews of communism and market-based democracy reinforced the polarity of the system.

The third possible configuration of actors is the multipolar system, where more than two states have significant power. The classic instance of a multipolar international system was the nineteenth-century Concert of Europe (sometimes referred to as Balance of Power) system, in which five states were significant independent sources of power and influence on the system: Great Britain, France, Russia, Austria (after 1867, Austria-Hungary), and Prussia (after 1870, Germany). The period between the world wars began as a multipolar system, but in the 1930s it effectively became bipolar with the formation of two military alliances that would contest one another in World War II.

When systems are classified according to the degree of control the major actors have over the system's operation, a form of analysis applied particularly to the Cold War bipolar system, the standard distinction is between tight and loose control. In a tightly controlled system, lesser powers fall under the effective domination of the major power or powers and can largely be directed by them. In a loose system, the most powerful state or states have less control over the actions of others, having to rely more on voluntary cooperation by lesser states.

The different forms of power configuration and control can be looked at in combination, as is done in Figure 2-3. Several points about this chart are worth noting. As suggested by our earlier reference to the Roman Empire, historical instances of tightly controlled unipolar systems are very few, whereas it is possible to think of the current system's evolution as unipolar, if in a more limited way (that it is also possible to think otherwise is indicated by the question mark). Certainly, even among those who regard the United States as the single pole, no one expects it to control the international system. The bipolar classification reflects the view, held by most analysts, that the Cold War system remained at least militarily bipolar throughout its existence, but that the superpowers' control of events gradually diminished. Finally, one can argue whether a tight multipolar system is impossible by definition, since by definition it contains multiple independent sources of power. This question is discussed in more detail in Chapter 3.

Determining which systems produce more or less stability, conventionally defined as the ability to regulate international relations short of war, is a difficult problem, and analysts disagree greatly. During the Cold War, the prevailing view was that bipolar distributions of power encouraged confrontation with potentially disastrous results (nuclear war), whereas multipolar systems were more flexible and preferable. The peaceful demise of the system may require some refinement of this notion.

Current Relevance

It is difficult to label the evolving system precisely in balance-of-power terms, and hence to judge its likely stability or instability in these terms. For one thing, the measurement of power is more complex than it used to be. As already noted, economic power is now a

		Amount of Control	
		Tight	Loose
Configuration	Unipolar	World Empire	Current?
	Bipolar	Early Cold War	Late Cold War
	Multipolar	Early Concert of Europe	Current?

much more important element in national, and thus systemic, power; adding to the confusion is that, with the exception of the United States, the most powerful countries economically are not the most powerful militarily, and vice versa. For another thing, the world is infinitely more variegated and complex than it used to be. The international system in 1945 was composed of about 60 states; the current system is about 180 and is growing as existing states split apart.

We can, however, make the observation that the evolving system will be one of loose control by the major actor or actors. No state or combination of states has shown a sustained interest in enforcing an order on the system. Were there a truly dominating power, for instance, the horror in Bosnia might not have been allowed to go on for as long as it did. If the United States is the pole, it will lead by example and persuasion (the political/diplomatic instrument of power), not by military force or economic predominance. If the world is thought of as multipolar, the major powers will exert leverage only when they can act in concert through mechanisms such as the Group of Seven (G–7, the most economically powerful states), the Group of Eight (G–8, when Russia joins with the G–7), or through organizations such as the United Nations.

Nonstate Actors

One other way in which the international system will be different in the post–Cold War world is the emergence and maturation of a group of actors claiming a role in international relations independent of states. As introduced in Chapter 1, these nonstate actors include two broad categories: supranational actors, organizations whose membership and activities transcend national borders, and subnational actors, individuals and groups representing portions of national populations.

The members of supranational organizations may be either states themselves or individuals and groups from two or more states. Moreover, the ends served by their activities may be either public (as in the case of organizations such as human rights groups) or private (as in the case of multinational corporations).

The most visible, prominent supranational actors are those international organizations of which states are members, known collectively as intergovernmental organizations (IGOs). The most obvious example is the United Nations system, the core of which is the United Nations (UN) itself and its specialized agencies, such as the World Health Organization and the International Monetary Fund. IGOs are created by agreements negotiated by the states who are the members, and they have authority to act only to the extent that the member states grant them such authority. Because of this restriction, whether the UN should be thought of as an independent actor is debatable. When the UN acts as a peacekeeper, for instance, it does so because member states have explicitly authorized a particular action, have volunteered forces for that action, and have agreed to pay national assessments for it. The UN does have a permanent Secretariat, or executive staff, with a permanent staff loyal to it, but even the activities of the Secretariat are subject to the approval of the member states. Just as the British Parliament has the power to legislate the monarchy out of existence, so the member states of the UN and other IGOs have the same theoretical capability with respect to those bodies.

The other group of public supranational organizations, those who have no governmental affiliation and whose membership consists of individuals or groups from more than one

Nongovernmental organizations, or NGOs—organizations dedicated to public goals and made up of individuals or groups from more than one state—are becoming increasingly prominent in international relations. Here, Hillary Rodham Clinton, wife of U.S. President Bill Clinton, delivers a ringing defense of women's rights at the 1995 NGO Forum on Women, held in conjunction with the Fourth World Conference on Women in Beijing, China. Delegates to the forum, representing well-known organizations like Amnesty International and Human Rights Watch as well as many smaller groups, gave her a warm response.

state, are called nongovernmental organizations (NGOs). These entities generally come into existence to deal with some problem or function that transcends national boundaries but for which states cannot or do not want to form IGOs. A prominent example is the International Red Cross, one of whose major functions is to assure that the Geneva Convention on treatment of prisoners of war is not violated during shooting conflicts. Because it has no governmental affiliation or political agenda, the Red Cross is trusted as a kind of "honest broker" in applying the rules of treatment. Another prominent NGO is Amnesty International, a group that attempts to monitor and publicize the conformance to human rights standards by various national governments. Most NGOs receive funding from individuals and private organizations (for instance, foundations) from different states.

The role of public supranational organizations is almost certain to expand in the future. Their continuation and proliferation suggests that they serve the useful function of providing otherwise unavailable services successfully.

The other major form of supranational actor is the private organization, a transnational association of individuals or groups whose purposes include private activity—promoting life insurance, for instance—and financial gain. The most prominent example of this growing phenomenon is multinational corporations (MNCs), the most advanced form of which are stateless corporations.

The importance of MNCs as a part of the rapidly evolving economic interdependence of the globe is discussed in detail in Chapter 9. When they first became a visible influence on

Case in Point

How NGOs and States Cooperate in Humanitarian Relief

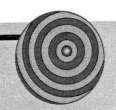

The spate of internal wars with their attendant atrocities in the Second Tier in the 1990s has produced millions of innocent victims who urgently need aid and comfort—the wounded and maimed, those fleeing out of fear, those huddled in squalid refugee camps rife with disease and starvation. There are no international structures adequate to deal with the current volume of suffering, both because such conflicts were fewer in number during the Cold War and because the system was less concerned with those that did occur. Nongovernmental organizations (NGOs) with specific humanitarian agendas have begun to fill this gap; a new concern is how humanitarian NGOs cooperate with major states like the United States to ensure the adequacy of these efforts.

A pattern is emerging in this interaction. When natural or other disasters occur, humanitarian NGOs like CARE are the first outsiders to arrive on the scene and provide assistance. In the case of internal wars, however, the conflict itself interrupts care-giving activities, or the extent of suffering swamps NGO resources. At this point, state (or international) military options become relevant: force to end the interruptions caused by war, military logistics to get adequate relief supplies where they are needed.

NGOs and military forces are only learning how to relate to one another, especially in preparing for the critical point at which forces are withdrawn and NGOs are left to fend for themselves. Their first major interface was in the Somalian civil war, where politically motivated actions by warlords interrupted—or even shut down—the provision of humanitarian aid by NGOs, making suffering greater and thereby necessitating military intervention. Neither party understood the other's needs and aims regarding the provision and security of future food distribution. Moreover, there was no real "hand-off" strategy to provide for the security of the NGO workers remaining in Somalia as the troops left. With their departure the aid distribution system quickly reverted to chaos.

The NGO-military relationship began to improve in the response to the carnage in Rwanda in 1994. When hundreds of thousands of panic-stricken refugees fled across the border to Zaire, now the Democratic Republic of the Congo (or Congo), the following NGOs responded rapidly; American-based groups included the Adventist Development and Relief Agency, American Red Cross, Americares, CARE, Catholic Relief Services, Church World Service, Concern Worldwide, Doctors Without Borders U.S.A., Oxfam America, Save the Children, and U.S. Committee for UNICEF. But their efforts, including global solicitation of resources, were quickly overwhelmed by the magnitude of the needs in areas such as medicine, food, potable water, and basic sanitation. The only organization with the logistical capability to service the refugees adequately was the U.S. armed forces, and the result was an informal alliance between the NGOs and the U.S. Department of Defense and the beginning of a dialogue about how they might cooperate in future humanitarian relief efforts.

Source: List of agencies from *Newsweek,*
August 8, 1994, p. 31.

the international system in the 1960s, they were generally thought of as nationally based corporations doing business in foreign lands. For instance, IBM (International Business Machines), a prototype of the MNC, was thought of as an American corporation that sold its wares abroad as well as at home and owned manufacturing facilities in multiple countries. Some observers raised concerns about the ability of governments to control the overseas operations of their corporations in cases where companies acted contrary to official national policies—for instance, doing certain kinds of business with the then-racist South African government. However, others saw MNCs as contributing to a growing "complex interdependence," whereby the increasing internationalization of economic activity would tie countries so closely together economically that they would become unable, or at least less likely, to come into violent conflict.

Among the countries of the First Tier, private-sector interdependence has progressed well beyond this level. Increasingly, MNCs have become true international corporations: their ownership, management, and workforce come from and their products are made in several or even many countries. As we shall see, this phenomenon is most advanced in the automobile industry, where the major (originally) American auto makers own parts of major (originally) Japanese and, in some cases, (originally) European automobile companies and vice versa. These are examples of stateless corporations, companies so internationalized that it is effectively impossible to tie them to a principal national base. The same is becoming true in the electronics industry.

A particularly intriguing supranational actor is global television, the first examples of which are the American-based Cable News Network (CNN) and the British-based Independent Television Network (ITN). Neither is technically a multinational; CNN, for instance, is essentially an American firm covering and broadcasting news worldwide (although increasingly in consort with foreign broadcasters and broadcasting systems).

Global television is the result of the high-technology, and more specifically telecommunications, revolution that began to become evident in the early 1980s and continues to expand its influence. Information-transmitting technologies such as fiber optics and satellites allow the sharing of information worldwide essentially instantaneously. Light, portable camcorders and satellite "dishes" linked to orbiting satellites allow news gatherers and disseminators instant access to events heretofore inaccessible. It is not too dramatic to say that the global eye of television is virtually everywhere. At one point in 1994, CNN claimed it broadcast into 143 countries; the list will certainly expand. Moreover, the network estimated that as many as 2 billion people worldwide viewed its coverage of the Persian Gulf War at one time or another. A similar number watched live coverage of the 1998 World Cup soccer finals.

The impact of global television is only beginning to be understood, and that impact keeps changing as it permeates more and more parts of international life. Some aspects of this impact will be highlighted at appropriate points in the text, but three of the major ones should be noted.

1. *High-level influence:* Among the many people who watch global television are numerous world leaders. Former President George Bush was an avid watcher, as was former British Prime Minister Margaret Thatcher. CNN or ITN coverage is often the first source of breaking news for world leaders.

2. *Agenda setting:* Although there is little evidence it does so purposely, global television affects public agendas by what it does and does not publicize. When coverage of Iraqi

Kurds huddled and dying on Turkish mountainsides filled the CNN screen, the United States felt impelled to intervene; in the absence of those images, it might not have.

3. *Difficulty of concealment:* Because it is increasingly more difficult to keep global television from covering and thus exposing events everywhere, it is becoming harder for governments and other parties to cover up unfavorable news or to lie about events. This difficulty is, of course, bad news for the world's tyrants and helps undermine their credibility and thus their authority. The Chinese government would certainly have attempted to cover up its actions against the Democracy Movement in 1989 in Tiananmen Square had CNN and others not been there to cover a state visit by Soviet leader Mikhail Gorbachev; since they were present, the Democracy Movement used their presence to publicize their cause, and the world watched the bloody suppression. The presence of tourists carrying camcorders makes it difficult to deny access to events in even the most oppressive countries; everyone is a potential CNN "stringer."

Although subnational actors, those individuals and groups within states who act internationally, have increasingly joined their supranational colleagues in taking major roles in world affairs, the question of what standing, if any, they have in the international system remains unsettled. When Jesse Jackson traveled to the Middle East to negotiate the release of Americans held hostage by various terrorist groups, was he acting simply as a private citizen of a single country, or did he have some greater status? Similarly, when Nelson Mandela, as representative of the African National Congress (ANC), traveled abroad before he became president of South Africa, what was his international status?

In the traditional, state-centered system based on the idea of sovereignty, individuals and groups have no international standing per se, unless they are official representatives (known as plenipotentiaries) of governments. Thus, Jackson was criticized for posing as a diplomat when he had no authority to act for anyone other than himself; if Mandela was accorded great respect, it was because of his personal, not his or the ANC's international, standing.

Case Study: *Bosnia and Herzegovina*

The war in Bosnia and Herzegovina (hereafter Bosnia for shorthand purposes) that engrossed world attention in the early 1990s illustrates a number of principles and arguments that we have highlighted in the previous sections. Yugoslavia and Bosnia are both classic instances where nation and state do not coincide and where the attendant problems of ethnicity and nationality reached their ugliest extremes. The problem of Bosnian sovereignty and the resulting official classification of the war as a civil conflict provided a cover for international inaction, despite the atrocities committed in sovereignty's name.

Moreover, the war has provided a vivid illustration of the continuing salience of power in international relations. Bosnian Serbs and Croatians employed military force ruthlessly in their campaign of dissection and annexation of Bosnian land, and their ferocity was matched by the Bosnian Muslims. The international community dithered well into 1995 over which instruments of power could be applied effectively and found great difficulty reaching consensus. Finally, supranational actors, principally the North Atlantic Treaty Organization (NATO) and the European Union, were asked to try to do what individual states could or would not, and the UN was caught in the middle, lacking the mandate and resources for successful intervention to end the killing. Finally, in December 1995, the

United States brokered a peace agreement (discussed in detail in the case study in Chapter 4) that included a 60,000 strong Implementation Force (IFOR) drawn from NATO countries and others to monitor its enforcement.

A Brief History

Before looking at how the Bosnian tragedy illustrates the operation of the international system, it is worthwhile to view, at least briefly, how the situation deteriorated to the awful bloodletting that ensued.

One must begin with the people of Yugoslavia, and especially Bosnia. The Yugoslav state (Yugoslavia means "Land of the Southern Slavs") was created in 1929 from the Kingdom of the Serbs, Croats, and Slovenes, which had itself been formed in 1918 from remnants of the Ottoman and Austro-Hungarian Empires that had dissolved after World War I. The population was and is very diverse. For instance, there are three major languages—Slovenian, Macedonian, and Serbo-Croatian—and Serbo-Croatian, the dominant language, is written in two different alphabets: the Roman alphabet in the republic of Croatia, the Cyrillic alphabet in Serbia, Bosnia, and Macedonia. Within Bosnia, the combatants are also divided by religion, reflecting a similar diversity among Yugoslavians as a whole. Those who identify themselves as Bosnian Serbs are primarily Orthodox Christians, the Croats are mostly Roman Catholic, and the largest Bosnian group adheres to Islam. The vast majority of Kosovars, as already noted, are ethnically Albanian Muslims.

The history of modern Yugoslavia, including that of its destruction, was born in World War II. When Nazi Germany invaded the country in 1941, several military and political movements emerged in Croatia and Serbia. One, the Ustashi, was primarily Croatian in composition, and it collaborated with the Germans (Croatia and Germany had a long history of friendship and cultural affinity). In opposition to the German occupation, two other groups emerged, the royalist-led Chetniks and the Communist Partisans; although they sometimes fought each other, both were mostly Serbian in membership and engaged in similar atrocities against the Croats. Accusations of atrocities during this period by both sides underlay much of the spirit of retribution during the fighting over Bosnia. Moreover, the wartime conflict between Serbs and Croats underlined Serbian domination and defense of the Yugoslav state, as opposed to the Croatian desire for an independent Croatia.

When World War II ended, Josip Broz Tito emerged as the leader of a communist Yugoslavia dominated by former Partisans. He sought to model the new Yugoslavia after the then-Stalinist state in the Soviet Union, a policy that had two major elements. First, he created an authoritarian government that could suppress any signs of conflict between Yugoslavia's rival regional, ethnic, religious, and linguistic groups. Second, he consciously drew arbitrary boundaries between the six "republics" he created (like those between the fifteen republics of the Soviet Union) and encouraged intergroup mixing through migration and the creation of mixed communities, hoping thereby to produce a new "Yugoslav" whose loyalties would be primarily to Yugoslavia, not Serbia, Croatia, and the like. This intermixing occurred especially in Bosnia.

The glue that held Yugoslavia together for as long as it lasted was the force of Tito's power and personality. In anticipation of his eventual retirement or death, a structure whereby power rotated among the six republics was created in the hopes of keeping the union together thereafter. In the event, the union survived Tito's 1980 death for a little over a decade, a period in which the Serbs became increasingly dominant. Beginning in 1991, following the spirit of a dissolving Soviet Union, Yugoslavia disintegrated. Declarations of independence by Croatia and the neighboring republic of Slovenia were quickly followed by the secessions of Macedonia and Bosnia, leaving only Serbia and the republic of Montenegro constituting what continued to call itself Yugoslavia.

Caught particularly in the middle of this tide of nationalist passion was Bosnia, and more specifically the Bosnian Muslims, a population segment distrusted by the others in that republic because it had earlier collaborated with the Ottoman occupation. With Bosnia sandwiched physically between Serbia and Croatia, which were themselves fighting over disputed territory along their border, the Muslims saw themselves in an impossible situation. They constituted a plurality (at about 40 percent) but not a majority of the Bosnian population, which also contained about 30 percent Serbs and slightly over 20 percent Croats. (This mixture, of course, was part of the volatile legacy of Tito's rule.) Many Serbs and Croats lived in parts of Bosnia where their group was in the majority; the general land grab that emerged suggested these areas would attempt to join Yugoslavia/Serbia or Croatia. The Muslims naturally anticipated that the land grab would extend to Muslim-dominated areas as well.

In their panic, they formed a government in early 1992 and declared the independence of Bosnia and Herzegovina. Fearing for their own futures in a Muslim-dominated state in which they were not represented in the government, the Bosnian Serbs and Croats then went into separate rebellions. The Muslims had, in a sense, created the situation they feared.

The result was a gruesome three-sided civil war wherein Muslims, Serbs, and Croats fought one another, although the Croats and Muslims were occasionally allied since both favored a maximum dismemberment of Serbia/Yugoslavia. The Muslims were depicted as the primary victims by global television because they were underarmed compared with the Serbs and Croats in Bosnia, who received aid from Serbia and Croatia, respectively, and because "ethnic cleansing" to force Muslims out of territory and move Serbs or Croats in was often accomplished through siege warfare, a particularly brutal method in which civilians are a target. Reports of widespread rape of Muslim women and the slaughter of the inhabitants of Muslim villages added to the image.

The search for villains within Bosnia and in the international community is futile. What the tragedy in Bosnia does illustrate, however, is some important principles, detailed throughout this chapter, about how the international system works. They are important not only as illustrations but also as potential lessons for the next Bosnia.

Bosnia and the International System

The most basic underlying cause of the sequence of events that tore Yugoslavia apart and that came to focus on Bosnia arises from the incompatibility of multinationality and the state. The ethnic, regional, linguistic, and religious groups that made up Yugoslavia never formed a nation. Although Yugoslavia did for a time act as an effective state, shared statehood did not overcome centuries of historical animosity; members of different national groups (except for some Serbs who dominated the country) never came to think of themselves as Yugoslavs first.

That this most virulent case of the failure of statehood should occur where it did is both predictable and surprising. The history of the Balkans, of which former Yugoslavia is a microcosm, is one of instability and violence, invasion and counterinvasion, colonialism and its disintegration. The result has been a tangle of cultures, languages, historical experiences, and loyalties from which forging common nationalisms is very difficult. The breakup of Yugoslavia, including the possibility of bloodshed, had been predicted for years; only the extent of the carnage was a surprise.

That something like Yugoslav nationalism did not emerge as a force was also surprising, however. Tito did everything in his power to create such an identification; his adoption of the Stalinist model was for that purpose. In fact, Soviets used to think of Yugoslavia as a kind of laboratory, a simulation, of their own society. The outcome of the "experiment" has been chilling for the republics of the former Soviet Union, many of whom share the same problems of disunity and multinationalism.

What is most troubling about Bosnia's travail is its precedent for the future, both in the center of Europe and elsewhere. There are many multinational states in the Second Tier for which the Bosnian tragedy is a potential harbinger. Clearly, this is a major system problem for the future.

A second impact of Bosnia has to do with the continuing role of sovereignty. When Bosnia declared itself independent and was recognized as such, it became a sovereign state, albeit with a government that lacked the loyalty of a large part of its population. In granting recognition so quickly, did the system help create the panic that inflamed the civil war? When peace was brokered and an international force was put in place to enforce it, was Bosnian sovereignty compromised?

The role of power is also well represented in the Bosnian case. Bosnia became a microcosm of the international system; there was no real sovereign, only a government representing a minority of the population and having neither the legitimacy nor the force to enforce an order. In the absence of a compelling sovereign, the factions—Serbs, Croats, Muslims—effectively acted as states in their own system; the military instrument of power was the weapon of choice.

All sides, notably the Serbs and Croats, could reasonably calculate the utility of force. The Bosnian Muslims' declaration of independence created for both an intolerable situation that required change. Their preferred outcome, annexation to Croatia or Serbia/ Yugoslavia, seemed attainable, given the balance of available means and the relative absence of effective opposition by the Muslims. They must have perceived the expected utility of grabbing land as quite high, as long as the international community remained inhibited from taking effective action.

The risk, probably imperfectly understood and calculated by the Bosnian Serbs, was the effect that televised siege warfare would have on public opinion worldwide. Siege warfare is and always has been atrocious, because it is committed against seemingly innocent civilians incapable of defending themselves. It is also an ancient form of warfare; what made the siege of Sarajevo different was that it was on the nightly news.

For several years, the only politically acceptable form of international action was economic sanctions and later the threat and then implementation of aerial bombardment, particularly against Serbian positions around Sarajevo. Such sanctions, however, even enforced by a naval blockade of sorts, work very slowly if they work at all. Higher energy costs and the unavailability of consumer goods in Belgrade did not translate for some time into noticeable pressure for the Bosnian Serbs or Croats to change their activities.

The alternative to sanctions, of course, was military action. Merely threatening it proved ineffective, because the Bosnian Serbs in particular never believed the threats

A woman and her son run for cover along "Sniper Alley" in Sarajevo, the capital of Bosnia, which beginning in 1992 came under intense shelling and sniper fire from Serbian forces in the surrounding hills. Live global television coverage of the siege of Sarajevo helped to turn world opinion against the Serbs in the Bosnian civil war.

would be carried out (except for the limited air strikes). This Serbian perception was reinforced by disagreement among the potential interveners about the possibility of actually using military forces to pry apart the combatants and prevent them from fighting, the kind of action the UN and the U.S. military call peace enforcement.

Ultimately, the inertia of inaction was broken by the Dayton Accords, which were ratified in Paris in January 1996. The key element in reaching a cease-fire and specifying the actions necessary for a stable peace to become possible was the NATO, and especially U.S., commitment of forces to enforce the peace process. Both the process by which the accords were reached and the nature of the military commitment to enforce them remain major variables in the ultimate outcome of the Bosnian nightmare.

The agreement to stop the fighting was worked out at Wright-Patterson Air Force Base in Dayton under the watchful eye of American mediators. Three of the principal parties were involved in the negotiations and signed off on the final accord: the governments of Croatia, Serbia/Yugoslavia, and the Bosnians (or as they now like to call themselves, Bosniacs). Significantly, Bosnian Serbs were unrepresented, largely because most of their leaders were under international indictment for war crimes and would have been arrested if they attempted to attend. Serbia purported to represent their interests; whether they did and whether the Bosnian Serbs accept the conditions so negotiated remain problematical.

The accords contain military and civilian requirements of differing levels of difficulty. The military requirements were to provide a shield against further violence to promote an atmosphere in which peace could be pursued. Actions included supervising the zone of separation between the parties, monitoring the inter-entity boundary line dividing the country into political units, disarming armed civilians, monitoring and confirming the withdrawal of foreign troops, monitoring heavy weapons, supervising troops and weapons movements to special areas and monitoring holdings in those areas, overseeing demobilization of excess personnel, monitoring mine removal, and ensuring freedom of movement.

The political requirements were more extensive, ambitious, and difficult, but absolutely necessary if a stable peace was to ensue. They included arbitrating control of Brcko and the Posavina Corridor (a transfer point of importance to Bosnians and Serbs), returning refugees and displaced persons to their former homes, building political institutions, restoring and developing Bosnia's economic system, negotiating and implementing arms control and confidence-building measures, and implementing the U.S. program to equip and train a Bosnian military.

To facilitate the agreement, a NATO force of 60,000, led by the United States, was commissioned. Originally called the Implementation Force (IFOR), it was renamed the Stabilization Force (SFOR) in 1997 after its mandate was extended. It consists of a number of members from NATO countries, NATO affiliates through the Partnership for Peace program (discussed in Chapter 6), and others such as Russia. It has managed to keep the peace, but its future remains cloudy as major members, including the United States, occasionally threaten to withdraw.

The ultimate disposition of the Bosnian tragedy, including its long-term impact on the new system, remains problematic. Large portions of the Dayton mandate remain unfulfilled; only in July 1997, for instance, did NATO forces begin actively pursuing indicted war criminals. Moreover, there is little doubt that portions of the population, notably many Bosnian Serbs, do not support the agreement and may, if SFOR is dissolved, begin the bloodshed anew. The Balkans have long been known for problems larger than they are capable of solving themselves; Bosnia is only the latest example of that phenomenon.

Review

This chapter has provided an overview of the structure and dynamics of the international system. In the process, the following points were made:

1. The principal units of the system are states. States are political and legal entities and are distinct from nations, which are anthropological and psychological entities. A major problem in the contemporary system is the conflict between national groups within states, a conflict manifested in exclusionary nationalism.

2. Traditionally the governments of states have possessed supreme authority, or sovereignty, within their territory. The concept of sovereignty goes back to the beginning of the modern state system.

Domestically, it creates the basis for order; internationally, its consequence is anarchy. A number of critiques suggest that the importance of sovereignty is exaggerated, undesirable, or both.

3. The importance of power in international relations is a major consequence of systemic anarchy. States thus strive to accumulate instruments of power—political/diplomatic, economic, or military—that provide them leverage in relation to other states.

4. The emphasis on power means that how power is distributed or balanced within the system is an important concern. Historically, the major forms that balances of power have taken are unipolar, bipolar, and multipolar. It is as yet unclear whether or how the current system fits within these categories.

5. Actors other than states are becoming increasingly numerous and important in international relations. They include intergovernmental organizations (IGOs) and nongovernmental organizations (NGOs). Other significant nonstate actors are multinational corporations (MNCs) and global television.

6. The disintegration of Yugoslavia and of Bosnia and Herzegovina illustrates the problem of maintaining statehood in a multinational state. The secession of most republics from Yugoslavia resulted in power struggles between national groups that were especially vicious in the most multinational successor state, Bosnia.

Suggested Readings

Bell-Fialkoff, Andrew. "A Brief History of Ethnic Cleansing." *Foreign Affairs* 72, 3 (summer 1993): 110–121.

Bodin, Jean. *Six Books on the Commonwealth.* Oxford, UK: Basil Blackwell, 1955.

Boutros-Ghali, Boutros. "Empowering the United Nations." *Foreign Affairs* 72, 5 (winter 1992/93): 89–102.

Brierly, James L. *The Law of Nations,* 6th ed. Oxford, UK: Oxford University Press, 1963.

Doder, Dasko. "Yugoslavia: New War, Old Hatreds." *Foreign Policy* 91 (summer 1993): 3–23.

Etzioni, Amatai. "The Evils of Self-Determination." *Foreign Policy* 89 (winter 1992/93): 21–35.

Gati, Charles. "From Sarajevo to Sarajevo." *Foreign Affairs* 71, 4 (fall 1992): 64–78.

Grotius, Hugo. *The Rights of War and Peace: Including the Law of Nature and Nations.* New York: M. W. Dunne, 1981.

Hobbes, Thomas. *Leviathan.* Oxford, UK: Clarendon, 1989.

Cvijeto Job. "Yugoslavia's Ethnic Furies." *Foreign Policy* 92 (fall 1993): 52–74.

Kaplan, Morton, and Nicholas Katzenbach. *The Political Foundations of International Law.* New York: John Wiley, 1961.

Kegley, Charles W. Jr., and Eugene R. Wittkopf. *World Politics: Trend and Transformation,* 4th ed. New York: St. Martin's Press, 1993.

Locke, John. *Two Treatises on Government.* New York: Cambridge University Press, 1988.

Machiavelli, Niccolo. *The Prince.* Irving, TX: University of Dallas Press, 1984.

Neuchterlein, Donald. America *Recommitted: United States National Interests in a Reconstructed World.* Lexington: University of Kentucky Press, 1991.

Nye, Joseph S. Jr. *Bound to Lead: The Changing Nature of American Power.* New York: Basic Books, 1990.

Palmer, R. R., and Joel Cotton. *A History of the Modern World: Since 1815,* 6th ed. New York: Alfred A. Knopf, 1984.

Rosecrance, Richard. *The Rise of the Trading State: Commerce and Conquest in the Modern World.* New York: Basic Books, 1986.

Rousseau, Jean-Jacques. *The Collected Works of Jean-Jacques Rousseau.* Hanover, NH: University Press of New England, 1990.

Historical Evolution of the State System

PREVIEW

In this chapter, we will examine how the international system has evolved over the roughly 350 years that a system based on state sovereignty has existed. The discussion will begin with the eighteenth-century balance-of-power system that emerged in 1648 from the peace of Westphalia and lasted until the French Revolution and Napoleonic Wars. We will then turn to the nineteenth-century system that emerged at the end of the Napoleonic era and organized international relations until World War I. This will be followed by an examination of the system between the world wars and of the Cold War system, which began after World War II and lasted until the revolutions of 1989 in Eastern Europe. The chapter will conclude with a case study looking at the emerging system of the post–Cold War world.

KEY CONCEPTS

system
context
distribution of power
war and peace system
collective security
collective defense
total purposes
limited purposes
total means
limited means
domestic change agents
international change agents
critical events

peace of Westphalia
apoliticism
ancien régime
Concert of Europe
flexibility of alliance
equality of power
colonialism
hue and cry
superpower
necessary peace
democratization
national self-determination

OUTLINE

As was noted in Chapter 1, the international system is not a static, unchanging entity. Rather, it is constantly evolving, adapting to new realities and challenges. Analysts of international relations are now in the midst of a fundamental process of adaptation as that system evolves from the Cold War format to the form it is taking in a post–Cold War world.

There is no precise, unimpeachable way to distinguish and characterize the different forms that the international system has taken through history. Similarly, there is no consensus about when things have changed to the point where it can be said without question that an old form or its patterns of rules have expired and been replaced by a new form or set of patterns. With these caveats in mind, in this chapter we will look at what we see as the five successive historical forms of the western-based international system and at the transitions between them—those occasions when relationships have changed so fundamentally that reference to the older set of rules is simply inadequate or irrelevant to understanding what is happening in the new setting.

Our purpose is not entirely academic and has considerable bearing on the present time. It is our conviction that the process of change beginning with the revolutions of 1989 in Eastern Europe created a historic process—a sea change—comparable in magnitude to other fundamental changes over the roughly 350 years that the modern international system has existed. To understand the change the world has undergone in the past decade requires an appreciation of the historical context in which it is occurring.

The classification scheme we will use to look at the system's evolution is shown in the accompanying Summary box "Evolution of the International System." A few initial observations about this scheme are in order.

Summary ——————————————————————————

Evolution of the International System

Eighteenth-century system, 1648–1789

Nineteenth-century system, 1815–1914

Interwar system, 1919–1939

Cold War system, 1945–1989

Post–Cold War system, 1991–present

First, dividing nearly three and a half centuries of largely European history into five periods is somewhat arbitrary. Others prefer to discriminate more finely: the nineteenth century, for instance, can easily be subdivided into three or more periods, and the Cold War can easily be divided into two. We have chosen the categories here because the break points that emerge are, in our view, monumental and fundamental. We have added a brief discussion of the situation in the two principal Asian countries, China and Japan, to provide some more global context.

It should be noted that all the break points occurred at times of system-wrenching and system-encompassing wars, except for the one between the Cold War and the post–Cold War systems. This pattern forms part of the rationale for the scheme; major wars involving all (or nearly all) of the major powers normally do result in a basic reordering of the relationships among them, with individual powers rising and falling in importance, depending on the outcome. The French Revolution and Napoleonic Wars clearly qualify as system-convulsing events; so do the two world wars. Many theorists note, however, that marking major system changes by wars may prejudice the way the system is viewed, leading to an overemphasis on anarchy and on war as a key "natural" agent of change when in fact other forces may be more important.

A third point to note is the gap in time between the end of one system and the beginning of its successor. This gap represents the major war or wars (or other convulsions) that ended in major change, times when the system did not operate within the

U.S. Vice President Richard Nixon (*right*) challenges Soviet leader Nikita Khrushchev during the "kitchen debate" at an American manufacturing exhibition in Moscow in 1959. Referring to the relative merits of the Soviet and American economic systems, Khrushchev boasted, "We will bury you"; Nixon responded with a defense of capitalism. When the major powers disagree about fundamental political or economic philosophies, as was the case during most of the Cold War, friction and instability within the international system will be at a maximum.

normalcy of some control. For example, the gap between 1789 and 1815 represents the period between the beginning of the French Revolution and the final defeat of Napoleonic France. The gap between 1989 and 1991 represents the period of crumbling of the communist system in the Soviet Union and Eastern Europe.

The Idea and Concerns of International Systems

The actors in the international system, principally the states who are the core members, will always be concerned with understanding the patterns by which their relations are ordered, as a matter of ordering affects future trends and of developing policies that further stabilize and facilitate the pursuit of national interests. For the largest part of the history of the system, the chief area of concern that states have needed to deal with is that of peace and war; as a result, that problem and its solutions will figure prominently in the following analysis.

Our framework for discussion of each historical form of the system will consist of five elements: (1) the context or setting in which the particular system came into being, (2) the distribution of power among the members, (3) the way the system organized itself to deal with the problem of peace and war, (4) major agents of change as the system evolved, and (5) critical events and dynamics leading to the transformation to a new system. Each of these elements requires a brief description before it is applied to the historical record.

Context

The transition from one system to another develops out of basic, probably traumatic, change that caused the old system to fail. This convulsion provides the principal context out of which a new set of relations among some or all members has to be fashioned. The context also includes an assessment of what went wrong; this assessment influences what will happen in the course of future restructuring.

Three important points need to be made about this notion of context. The first is that every event has a context—or put another way, nothing happens in a vacuum. When a major traumatic event precipitating system change occurs, such as the breakdown of the interwar system in 1939, those charged with the restructuring naturally ask, "What went wrong?" It is a question that cannot be answered without reference to what the pattern was previously. Thus, the peace treaty at the end of World War I contributed to the breakdown of the interwar system and is therefore part of the context for the agreements ending World War II and creating a new system.

A second point is that part of the context in which a new system is adopted involves understanding and accommodating previous changes. The international order after World War I, for instance, had to accommodate the fact that two of the major players of the previous order, the Austro-Hungarian and Ottoman Empires, had not survived the war and that another, Russia, had been drastically transformed. The post–Cold War system must adjust to the fact that there is no longer a Soviet Union. The way Russia and the other Soviet successor states are treated, for instance, will affect the stability of the currently evolving order.

Finally, in considering context it is important to recognize that the process of restructuring takes time. Major system change normally includes the appearance of novel phenomena and problems with which the new system must grapple, and deciding—or discovering—

what the role of these will be usually involves a period, often a prolonged period, of disagreement. After World War II, for instance, a major new reality was the atomic bomb and its awesome destructive capability. A similar controversial matter in the post–Cold War system is the significance of the dilution, even disappearance, of an active ideological opposition to western political and economic forms.

Distribution of Power

Four questions can be asked about the way power is distributed in the system. First, how many powers are there, and who are they? When the idea of a distribution of power in the system was introduced in the last chapter, under the rubric of balance of power, three basic possibilities were suggested: a unipolar system (one state dominates), a bipolar system (two powers are predominant), and a multipolar system (more than two states have significant power). A unipolar configuration has not existed during the 350-year history of the modern international system, unless a dilute form exists now. (Indeed, one can argue that a unipolar system cannot be described in balance-of-power terms, since by definition there is no countervailing power to do the balancing.) In any event, power has generally been distributed in bipolar and multipolar modes, the latter being the more common form.

A second question has to do with patterns of relations among the major powers. Are the powers like-minded, sharing a similar worldview or level of satisfaction with the system? If they do share a similar political and economic philosophy, as was the case in the eighteenth century, instability may be minimized because there is little to fight about. On the other hand, when the major powers are in fundamental disagreement, as was the case through most of the Cold War, friction will be at a maximum.

The third question is, how do the major powers interact with the lesser powers? The salient concern here is the extent to which the major powers can or attempt to influence the activities of the lesser ones. In the early days of the Cold War, for instance, both the United States and the Soviet Union were able to maintain a high level of control over the "clients" in their "blocs." In the system as currently evolving, on the other hand, the ability of the states of the First Tier to control events in the Second Tier, including the violent disintegration of states, is questionable.

The fourth question, arising from the rest, is, will the distribution of power result generally in a condition of stability or instability? Traditionally, this was a question of the level of warfare and other violence in the system: did the system promote or inhibit the recourse to violent change? An apparent characteristic of the emerging system today is the need to expand notions of stability to include new dimensions, such as stable economic relationships within the First Tier and between the First and Second Tiers.

War and Peace System

Since war is the most potentially traumatic and, in an age of weapons of mass destruction, system-threatening problem faced by the membership of the international system, devising a way for ordering and controlling organized violence—a war and peace system—is always a major priority for the members. The question is how security can reasonably be guaranteed. Three concerns must be addressed in formulating a security apparatus in the international system.

Organizational Base.   The first concern deals with the organizational base of the system to deter wars, or if deterrence fails, to fight them. Since the avoidance of war is normally a value held by the members of the system (except possibly by those who find the system does not provide them with security), the question of organizing the peace is paramount.

There are two basic organizational models available, *collective security* and *collective defense*. In a collective security system, all—or the overwhelming majority—of the major powers agree that peace is their principal value and that they will enforce that peace against those who would breach it. Theoretically, such a system will deter potential military aggressors (including any of the major powers themselves), who realize that their transgression will be met with the overwhelming power of the system, thereby ensuring their defeat. That conclusion requires a potential aggressor to assess the resolve of the members (or the other members), so their commitment to the maintenance of the system must be a clear and unambiguous one that does not allow misinterpretation. Critical to the operation of a collective-security system is agreement among the members that the status quo (or only peaceful change in the status quo) is desirable, their willingness to defend the status quo militarily, and the availability of overwhelming force to the defenders.

The alternative to collective security is collective defense. In a collective-defense system, a limited number of states with similar interests band together to defend one another in the event of an attack against one or all of them. Such a system deters aggression when a potential enemy—possibly in concert with a group of like-minded states—decides that such action is unlikely to succeed. The military alliance is the central element of a collective defense system.

Formality.   The second concern about an international security system is its formality or informality. In a formalized system, the arrangements for organizing and maintaining the peace are codified in written agreements among states (treaties). These may be bilateral or multilateral military alliances or international collective-security agreements. In an informal system, similar arrangements may exist, but not in written form.

As we shall explain, there has been a historical trend toward greater formalization, for at least two reasons. First, there is the general belief that written agreements make commitments more difficult to renege on, thereby making less ambiguous to a potential aggressor the likely consequences of action to upset the peace. Second, more formal agreements can spell out mechanisms for prewar planning and training, making force more effective should war occur.

Total Versus Limited War.   The third concern of an international system is the scope and function of war within the system. Wars may be characterized as either total or limited with respect to both purpose or means. The purpose for which a war is fought refers to the desired political outcome after the war, the so-called better state of the peace. Total purposes normally require the overthrow of the adversary's government as a preface to imposing a peace; limited purposes do not require overthrow of the government. Means refer to the extent that a society's resources are mobilized for a war effort. Total means thus refer to a situation of total mobilization of society; limited means refer to a lesser commitment.

This relationship can be placed in matrix form to show its dynamics, using a few twentieth-century wars as examples, as in Table 3.1. What this matrix suggests is that the two

Table 3.1	Ends and Means in War	
Means	**Ends**	
	Total	**Limited**
Total	World War I, World War II	
Limited		Vietnam, Korea

"pure" combinations (total-total and limited-limited) are the most frequent. In a war where the overthrow of the enemy government is the objective, the enemy is likely to be highly resistant, and hence putting forth the maximum possible effort makes sense if the objective is to be achieved; if the goal is less ambitious, then using all military force might well be excessive to the purpose. On the other hand, self-limitation of means when the objective is total usually makes little sense.

From the French Revolution through World War II, war tended to become steadily more total in both purposes and means. The watershed was probably the American Civil War, which began as a limited, eighteenth-century-style conflict but evolved into a total conflict (see Snow & Drew, *From Lexington to Desert Storm,* for a detailed discussion). The trend clearly culminated in the world wars of the twentieth century, in which ultimately the atomic bomb was used against Japan.

Since World War II, the trend has moved back toward limitation. As the major powers accumulated ever greater means of war, they were increasingly led to limit their purposes: nuclear weapons in particular are clearly excessive means for any political purpose for which their large-scale employment might be contemplated, and the fear that they might be used eventually led the major powers to conclude they had to avoid any war between them.

Change Agents

The process of change and adaptation is constant in international relations, and during the evolution of any form of the international system trends build that ultimately contribute to its replacement. For our purposes, these trends can be divided into two types: changes within the member states, or domestic change agents, and changes in the relations between the states, or international change agents. We recognize that this distinction is sometimes artificial: important changes within a state—such as the Bolshevik Revolution in Russia—can affect international relations, and the formation of an international alliance can similarly have an impact on domestic affairs.

Domestic Change Agents. The domestic change agents can be conventionally divided into three categories: political, economic, and social. Each can be given a commonsense definition. Political change agents are changes, or demands for change, in the relationship of the government and the governed within states. In the nineteenth century, for instance, the demand for greater citizen participation in government preoccupied the rulers of Europe. In the late twentieth century, political democratization in the old Second and Third Worlds (what Samuel Huntington calls the "third wave" of democracy) occupies a similarly prominent position.

Economic change agents are actual or proposed changes in the means or modes of production, the relationship between labor and management, economic philosophies, and the like. Over time, economic factors have become increasingly important in the operation of the international system. In the nineteenth century what has been called the first industrial revolution transformed economic production and stimulated great growth where it occurred. For much of the twentieth century, operational Marxism provided an active challenge to capitalism until it effectively collapsed to help end the Cold War system. In the contemporary system, parts of the Second Tier are undergoing a delayed experience of the first industrial revolution while much of the First Tier grapples to adjust to the great internationalization of economic activity inherent in the third industrial, or high-technology, revolution. (The second industrial revolution refers to the movement from a manufacturing-based to a service-based economy.)

Social change agents are changes in such areas as class divisions, ethnic relations, the role of religion in society (secularization versus fundamentalism), and the relationship of wealth to social status. Like their economic counterparts, social factors have been of growing importance. The nineteenth century saw the rise of the middle class as a social force in Europe, and in the twentieth century the atheistic "classlessness" of socialist/communist systems challenged existing standards of social organization. More recently, ethnicity has become a major social concern, especially where attempts at ethnic integration have failed and where migration, often precipitated by economic or political problems, has heightened tensions between ethnic groups.

International Change Agents. International change agents can be described more succinctly. These are changes in the relations among members of the system, particularly among the major powers, that create changes in how the system operates.

Traditionally, the major international change agents have been political and military. Changes in the military power of a state or group of states are examples: the emergence of Germany as the predominant military power toward the end of the nineteenth century, or the rise of a militarily significant communist bloc of states in the latter half of the twentieth century. The challenge of communist military might in opposition to the western political system certainly was a major factor in structuring the Cold War system.

Economic and social factors are at work as well. The communist-anticommunist confrontation was about economic as well as political orientations. Socially, the increasing reluctance of populations in the poorer parts of the world to accept their poverty in a docile manner is destabilizing many societies, besides being a major cause of large-scale migrations across state borders.

Critical Events

The cumulative effect of the change agents discussed above is normally a series of critical events leading to the large-scale turmoil that results in system transformation. As noted, the turmoil or "critical mass" that produces the fundamental transformation has normally been a general shooting war involving the major powers; the exception was the nonviolent collapse of the Soviet Union (an event without historical precedent).

The important point to be made about critical events is how they flow from and are the culmination of the influence of other factors (change agents or other critical events). Nazism, a movement that achieved popularity only in the harsh economic crucible of the

Great Depression, was partly the result of the punitive peace imposed on Germany at the end of World War I. Similarly, in retrospect it is clear (as discussed in Chapter 6) that the growing economic disparity between East and West, manifested especially in the widening gap in technological levels, helped propel the series of decisions by Mikhail S. Gorbachev and his associates that inadvertently resulted in the abandonment of communism, the implosion of the Soviet Union, and ultimately the demise of an international system predicated on East-West ideological and military competition.

The Eighteenth-Century System

As Rosecrance so clearly stated in *Action and Reaction in World Politics* over 30 years ago, it is almost nonsensical to talk about an "international system," in the modern sense, for the period between the end of the Thirty Years War and the outbreak of the French Revolution. The "states" of the international system were just being formed or, in places such as Germany, would not be formed until well after that period (the process of German and Italian consolidation occurred in the mid-nineteenth century). Modern forces such as nationalism did not exist until the American and French Revolutions effectively introduced the idea. Relations among political units were limited in scope and comparatively peaceful. The period is, nonetheless, the context from which the modern state system has evolved, and it is important for that reason alone.

The Summary box "The Eighteenth-Century System" provides an overview of the concerns that we raised in the preceding section. For clarity's sake, we will look at each category in turn.

Summary ───────────────────────────

The Eighteenth-Century System

Context
- Change: end of Thirty Years War
- Better state of the peace: secularized state system (Treaty of Westphalia)

Distribution of Power
- Major powers: Britain, France, Austria, Ottoman Empire, Spain, Russia
- Relationship: multipolar (powers like-minded)
- Stability: stable

War and Peace System
- Organizational base: collective security
- Formality: informal
- Purpose: moderation of conflict

Change Agents
- Most became significant only toward the end of the system.
- Domestic
  1. Political: ideas of Locke, Rousseau, and others
  2. Economic: beginnings of first industrial revolution
  3. Social: growing discrepancy between wealth and social status
- International: decline of Spain and Ottoman Empire, rise of Britain

Critical Events
- American and French Revolutions

Context

Clearly, the major source of change was the outcome of the Thirty Years War, which had wracked the international system between 1618 and 1648. That enormous religious conflict, largely pitting the Catholic states loosely aggregated as the Holy Roman Empire against the Protestant states of northern Europe, had been fought mostly in what is now Germany, and some estimates suggest that upwards of one-quarter of the German population perished from combat and combat-related diseases.

The peace of Westphalia ending the war also provided the final chapter in the struggle between secular and religious authority within states. An object of controversy throughout the Reformation, the secular state had gradually claimed increasing jurisdiction over the territory and population within its borders. This trend had been resisted by the Catholic Church on religious and moral grounds, including the notion of the unity of Christendom, but the victory of Protestant forces upholding secular authority brought an end to that debate in Europe. Extolling the doctrine of sovereignty introduced by Jean Bodin and popularized by Thomas Hobbes, the authors of the treaty declared the secular state supreme. The modern state system was born and began its evolution to its present form.

In Asia, China was beginning the long, slow decline of the Manchu dynasty, which in time paved the way for republican government. Before that could happen, though, this 5,000-year-old civilization would suffer through the death throes of a dying dynasty. Internationally, despite China's preference for isolation, the technologically superior European imperialists were gaining ever greater concessions from the Manchu court and were, unknowingly, sowing the seeds of an anti-western xenophobia that even today is seldom far from the surface.

Japan was enjoying a period of relative stability under the centralized feudalism instituted at the beginning of the sixteenth century by the *shogun* (military ruler) Tokugawa. Its foreign dealings were virtually nonexistent. After a century (1542–1639) of allowing Dutch traders and Portuguese missionaries within the country, the shogunate expelled the foreigners and entered a self-imposed isolation that would last until Japan was forcibly opened in 1853.

Distribution of Power

Because the distribution of power did change considerably over a period of time, it is difficult to talk about a group of major powers in the same way one can when discussing the contemporary system. A glance at a European map of the time shows a group of states that encompassed the effective international system of the western world. The most prominent members included Great Britain, France, the Austrian Empire, the Ottoman Empire, Spain, and Russia.

All the major governments shared the political feature of monarchism. This meant in practice that the rulers of Europe had very few political disagreements; certainly they shared adherence to the prevailing political ideology. Royalty from the various countries frequently traveled between capitals, married one another, and served in one another's courts. The result was a multipolar system with remarkable stability and tranquillity, which was only infrequently interrupted by major systemic violence.

Peace Mechanisms

There was no real, active war and peace mechanism during this period of time. Because the various states were more or less coequal in military power at a low level of capability (at least by today's standards), there was little military incentive for the major powers to confront one another, and their essential agreement politically also gave them scant reason to engage in war.

This essential moderation of conflict also reflected the particular internal conditions in these times. The consolidation of many scattered territories into larger states meant that central authority suppressed the marauding and lawlessness that had marked the Middle Ages: lower-level nobles could no longer attack one another with impunity. Sovereignty, that is, produced a reasonable internal order over time, as Bodin had hoped.

The military resources available to the ruling monarchies were also quite limited. Armies were made up mostly of mercenaries drawn from the dregs of society (although

Map 3-1   **Europe in 1740**

©1996 by St. Martin's Press, Inc. From: *Contours of Power*, by Snow/Brown. Reprinted with permission of Bedford/St. Martin's Press, Inc.

they were officered by the nobility), and they were expensive to recruit and to retain. The average subject had no particular attachment either to the monarch or to the state, and thus was unwilling—or at least reluctant—either to volunteer or to be conscripted into military service. Moreover, this lack of attachment meant a reluctance to pay taxes to support the monarch's adventures internationally. What is now thought of as international relations or foreign policy was "the king's [or queen's] business," not the concern of the subject.

These conditions made for a very limited set of purposes for which war could be fought. Since armies were small and expensive, they could not be employed for grand purposes such as the subjugation and occupation of other than very small states; they were large enough only for more limited tasks. Thus, restrictions on available military means restricted the political purposes for which force could be used.

Moreover, the style of warfare of the times was self-limiting. The normal form of military engagement was the face-to-face clash of lineal formations of armies with smoothbore muskets, and combat involved fierce hand-to-hand fighting in which casualty rates of 40 percent or more were not uncommon. The objective was to fight the decisive battle that would break the opposing force and allow victory to be claimed. This style and set of purposes were effective in the relatively small spaces of Europe: one did not require an enormous armed force or repeated military actions to attack and conquer a small province adjacent to national territory.

Understanding the prevailing pattern and underlying philosophy of eighteenth-century warfare is important in considering the critical events that ended the age. When the American Revolution broke out, Great Britain sent a mercenary army that never exceeded 35,000 to pacify a territory the size of the 13 rebellious colonies (over 1,400 miles from north to south); such a force could have occupied Belgium, but it was clearly inadequate to occupy the colonies. All that General George Washington had to do was to avoid losing a decisive battle in which the Continental Army was destroyed; the style of eighteenth-century warfare meant the British never really stood a chance.

The other critical event, the French Revolution, similarly revealed the military limitations of the eighteenth-century system. A major effect of the revolution was to instill nationalism into the French people. As a result, when the initial calls to arms in defense of France and the revolution were sounded, the French responded in numbers that produced armies much larger and more motivated than the mercenary forces they confronted, which were more typical of the times.

Change Agents

Europe from the last half of the seventeenth century through the eighteenth century was in a period of slow, gradual transition from the feudal conditions that preceded the Reformation to the modern era. Through much of the period, class distinctions remained very important within domestic societies, while on the international scene there was a condition of cosmopolitanism and commonality never achieved since.

Within domestic societies, the primary political reality was a combination of apoliticism and the absence of nationalism for all but a very small noble elite. Ordinary people had no ideas about politics and the efficacy of political participation, concerns they attributed to the monarch. Furthermore, they identified with a small local community, not with the state or its ruler; in other words, they had no sense of nationalism.

This situation had both positive and negative consequences for rulers. On the negative side, subjects were unwilling to sacrifice much for the monarch, thereby limiting the monarch's resource base. On the more positive side, the vast majority of the population was docile and hence did not challenge absolutist rule. Even in the American colonies, it would take the British monarch's bungling of the Americans' mild request to be treated as full British subjects, rather than as colonials, to produce political activism.

Economic and social realities reinforced this tranquillity. Although the impact of the first industrial revolution was beginning to be felt by the end of the period, the economic system was still centered on subsistence agriculture and cottage industry. In this type of economy, the average person did not acquire wealth that could be taxed; hence demands for political participation were not generated. The social system, which for the overwhelming majority of people was still based on the village structure, was also highly stratified and traditional. There was little social movement or social contact among classes.

Internationally, there was considerable cosmopolitanism. Members of the various national nobilities moved freely among the courts of Europe, serving in one another's military forces or governments. It was not unusual for Irishmen to serve the king of Spain; the Hanoverian kings of Britain were originally German. This free flow and interchange, nurtured by the commonality of political ideology, meant that members of the international ruling class of Europe had more in common with one another than they did with commoners in their own countries.

This condition made the rulers very conservative and moderated the relations among them. They were naturally conservative because they benefited greatly from the status quo and hence sought to preserve—or conserve—it. Because the consequences of change were unpredictable and potentially negative, the boat was not to be rocked.

By the second half of the eighteenth century, however, forces of change were stirring beneath this placid surface. Especially in Britain and France, in addition to the beginnings of industrialization, the discrepancy between the increasing wealth of many nonaristocrats and their continuing lack of social and political privileges was becoming apparent. At the same time, the spread of the political ideas of such thinkers as John Locke and Jean Jacques Rousseau was creating an intellectual climate of increasing hostility to the traditional order of things. Internationally, the continuing cosmopolitan harmony among monarchs and courtiers did not reflect long-term shifts in the relative strength of their states, such as the decline of Spain and the Ottoman Empire or the rise of Britain, evidenced by its triumph over France in the struggle for control of North America.

Critical Events

Two events coming within a decade and a half, although only tenuously related to one another, ended the tranquility of the eighteenth century and transformed the international system. The first, and in a systemic sense less important, was the American Revolution. The second, and far more influential for an international system centered in Europe, was the French Revolution.

The two revolutions in combination challenged the political basis of the old order. They represented (and were influenced by) the doctrine of popular sovereignty put forth by Locke and Rousseau; their success effectively placed sovereignty in the people rather than in the monarch, an idea that would become nearly universal during the following century within the western world. In the process, they shattered the absolutist monarchist consensus on governance; popularly based government became an ideological alternative that could not be extinguished even with the eventual defeat of the Napoleonic French armies.

In retrospect, the American Revolution was a rather mild protest. Even after the "shot heard round the world" was fired, it took the Americans 14 months to decide that independence was their purpose. In the interim, they sent King George III an entreaty that said if he would grant them the status of British subjects they would forget the whole rebellion. George, fearing a "domino effect" of cascading sedition in other colonies, rejected this Olive Branch Manifesto. The colonials had little alternative but independence; the rest is history.

The French Bourbon monarchy was, of course, no champion of political democracy, but in the Americans' rebellion it saw the opportunity to pay the British back for evicting France from North America in the French and Indian War between 1754 and 1763. The thread of connection between the American and French Revolutions was that in the process of aiding the Americans, the French king bankrupted the royal treasury. Faced with the need for revenue, Louis XVI summoned a body that had not met in over 150 years, the *parlements,* from which he asked taxes. The legislators demanded political concessions in return, which the king refused. The powder keg was lit.

The French Revolution represented the first continental assertion of popular sovereignty, initially through popular rule and participation and later through popular tyranny (the popularly backed yet authoritarian Napoleonic Empire). Furthermore, it became evangelical and spread its gospel of *liberté, égalité, fraternité* (liberty, equality, fraternity) across the continent on the back of the *levée en masse* (the French army). The military forces were eventually repelled; the ideas remained and were joined permanently to the political debate.

The Nineteenth-Century System

The period between the end of the Napoleonic Wars in 1815 and the outbreak of World War I in 1914 was one of the most turbulent, eventful periods in European and hence international history. It began with a doomed attempt to reimpose the old political system, the *ancien régime,* onto a population whose intellectual development had rejected it. As the century unfolded, great political, economic, and social change occurred within all the major countries. At the same time, the map of Europe was reconfigured as old empires crumbled and new states emerged. Internationally, a period of introspection managed by a collective security arrangement gave way to a collective-defense-dominated system, as power alignments changed. The basic features are outlined in the Summary box "The Nineteenth-Century System."

Summary ━━━━━━━━━━━━━━━━━━━━━━━━━━━━━━━━━━

The Nineteenth-Century System

Context

- Change: defeat of Napoleonic France
- Better state of the peace: restoration of ancien régime (Congress of Vienna)

- Formality: informal (Concert); formal (alliances)
- Purpose: deterrence of conflict (Concert); defense (alliances)

Distribution of Power

- Major powers: France, Britain, Russia, Prussia/Germany, Austria/Austria- Hungary
- Relationship: multipolar (powers like-minded to about 1870; divided thereafter)
- Stability: stable to about 1870; unstable thereafter

Change Agents

- Domestic
  1. Political: nationalism, ideologies (liberalism, conservatism, Marxism)
  2. Economic: first industrial revolution
  3. Social: urbanization, new wealth, class change and conflict
- International: unification and armament of Germany, colonization of Africa and Asia

War and Peace System

- Organizational base: collective security (Concert of Europe)/collective defense (military alliances) after 1870

Critical Events

- Crimean War, Franco-Prussian War, end of colonization, assassinations in Sarajevo

Context

The nineteenth-century balance of power arose out of an attempt to reconstruct the international system that had been convulsed by the ravages of the French Revolution and the Napoleonic Wars. These events had changed national boundaries, created new coalitions of forces, and broadened the nature and scope of warfare. Most important, however, the popular ideology of the Revolution and the nationalism of imperial France were now permanent characteristics of the system.

In the end, the monarchists had prevailed on the battlefield, and at the Congress of Vienna in 1815, they sought both to consolidate their victory and to turn back the clock politically to the pre-Napoleonic situation. In the act most symbolic of this attempt, they restored France as a full member of the system with its 1793 borders (the borders before the French began their expansionist campaigns). More important, they restored the Bourbon monarchy to power in France as the price of French readmission to the system.

The legacy of the French Revolution would not prove easy to kill, however. There were now supporters of its ideals in all the European countries, and their struggles against the reassertion of monarchism would be a major theme throughout the century.

The system evolved from these roots to the point that by the time of its collapse into World War I, it scarcely resembled what had been forged at Vienna. Different analysts break down this evolution differently. Because our concern resides largely with the issues of power distribution and the management of the war and peace system, we will subdivide it into two periods. In the first period, extending to 1870, the year of the Franco-Prussian War, the operative, if gradually deteriorating, peace mechanism was something called the Concert of Europe. After the Franco-Prussian War, the dynamics of the Concert no longer operated, and the system gradually drifted toward a basis in static alliances that ultimately contested what is euphemistically called the Great War (World War I).

The nineteenth century brought high drama to Asia. What is striking was the contrast between China and Japan when confronted by the powerful West: China collapsed and Japan set upon an extraordinary course of modernization to meet the West on its terms.

China's enfeebled Manchu dynasty was helpless in the face of the western powers, who often used their power for morally dubious ends. In the 1840s, for instance, Britain twice waged war on China to protect its right to sell Indian-grown opium to China's massive population (opium was illegal in Britain). The westerners grabbed chunks of Chinese territory, insisted their citizens be tried under their own rather than Chinese laws for crimes committed in China, demanded exemption from Chinese taxes, and more. The Manchus were powerless to stop the virtual partition of China.

Japan's story was quite different. Their isolationism was ended, once and for all, by an American, Commodore William Perry and his fleet of "Black Ships." Perry's non-belligerent display of the advanced technology of the West shocked Japan's elites. By 1868 the Tokugawa shogunate had been overthrown and replaced by a small group of young reformers, who would remake Japan along western lines. As they grew older, they set Japan on the path of representative government. Still, the slogan that would capture the dreams of both Asian powers was "rich country, strong military." By the end of the century, Japan was to flex its military muscle against its one-time cultural mentor, China. In 1895, Japan snatched Taiwan in a brief and decisive war that foretold things to come.

Distribution of Power

At the outset of the nineteenth-century system, there were five major powers anointed by the conferees at Vienna: Great Britain, France, the Austrian Empire, the Russian Empire, and Prussia (which led the unification of the German Empire during the middle of the century). As the accompanying Map 3-2 shows, the five dominated Europe except for the Iberian peninsula (Spain and Portugal).

These five states dominated a consciously multipolar system whose major purpose was to restore the international tranquility that had marked the previous century. Because it was recognized that contrary political and other forces had come into being thanks to the apostles of revolutionary France, the intent now was to regularize international relations so that individual states could concentrate on internal developments and problems. In fact, relative peace did prevail in Europe for three decades or more. The period also coincided with great social and political turmoil within a number of the major states, including major waves of revolutionary activity in 1830 and 1848, which to a great extent directed attention away from foreign endeavors.

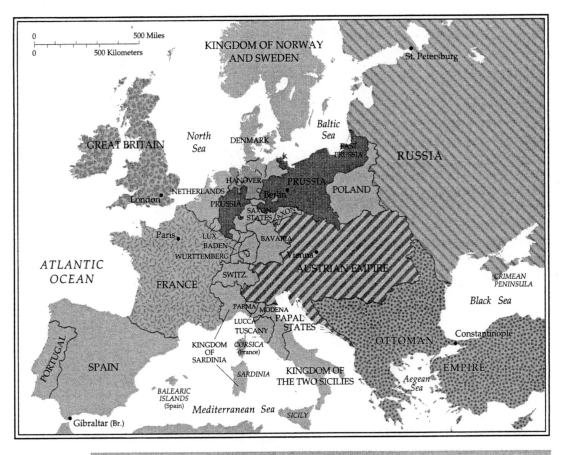

Map 3-2   **Europe in 1815**

©1996 by St. Martin's Press, Inc. From: *Contours of Powers,* by Snow/Brown. Reprinted with permission of Bedford/St. Martin's Press, Inc.

Peace Mechanisms

As suggested earlier, for a collective-security system to operate successfully, three conditions must be met: agreement on the desirability of the status quo, a willingness to defend it, and the availability of overwhelming force to do so. The availability of such force, known as *preponderance of power,* is normally ensured by two characteristics of the system. The first is flexibility of alliance: every member of the system must be willing and able to align with any other members in the event of a threat to or breach of the peace, whether caused by one of the members or by some outsider. The second characteristic is equality of power: the members all have relatively equal power and see that condition as desirable. Together these characteristics ensure that if one or even two members threaten to upset the status quo through military action, sufficient force will still be available to frustrate such attempts; the potential transgressor will thereby be deterred because it will conclude that military action is futile.

At one level, the collective-security system known as the Concert of Europe that emerged after 1815 satisfied the conditions just described. Thanks to the decision not to punish France, all the powers were relatively equal in military strength (Prussia was probably the weakest, which would create problems later). Their governments were like-minded enough ideologically that they could freely align with one another, and each was to some extent committed to defending the international status quo that kept all of them in power.

The agreement on ideology was not, however, complete. Two members in particular, Britain and France, had ambivalence about the absolute monarchy of the other three. In Britain, the principle of limitation on monarchical power was already established, and the century would witness the gradual democratization of the British polity. France had already tasted popular sovereignty, and although the Bourbons had been placed back on the throne, their power base was uncertain. In 1830, a weakened Bourbon monarchy would fall from power for the last time.

Thus, even within the Concert, there was some disagreement in world views, and hence a differential commitment to the status quo. This schism, which gradually widened, was manifested by the formation of a second, informal mechanism, the Holy Alliance, a kind of caucus of Austria, Prussia, and Russia to promote the interests of absolute monarchism. The split between these absolutists and the more democratic forces in Britain and France would grow as the century progressed.

The interplay of these forces resulted in an informal collective-security arrangement. No standing institution organized the peace; rather, the Concert involved an irregular, informal series of meetings that were convened as the need seemed to arise. Across time, the meetings became increasingly infrequent. The absence of a predictable mechanism that could be put into operation when war clouds loomed was cited after the outbreak of World War I as a major deficiency of the arrangement.

In fact, the Concert system was effectively dead after the settlement following the Franco-Prussian War (some would argue it had died some years earlier). Militarily the war was a walkover (the French Emperor Louis Napoléon surrendered at Sedan after a six-week campaign), and the political settlement shattered the operating conditions of the Concert system.

The most important outcome of the settlement was France's cessation of Alsace-Lorraine to Germany. As Map 3-3 shows, the area lies between the two countries, extending from Switzerland in the south to Luxembourg in the north. Traditionally it has been part German and part French in cultural, linguistic, and other terms, with political control alternating between the two countries through history. It was annexed to France in the sixteenth century as the French state consolidated, and its citizens became culturally French during the revolutionary period. Thus, the French had come to think of Alsace and Lorraine as an integral part of France; the Prussians disagreed.

The annexation of Alsace-Lorraine to the Second German Empire or Reich (the Holy Roman Empire is considered the First Reich) consolidated the modern German state and destroyed what was left of the Concert by undercutting all three operating assumptions. The iron ore of Lorraine and the coal of Alsace, in proximity to the industrial Ruhr and Saar basins, helped fuel the development of heavy, steel-based industry in the German Empire. Enough of this industrial development was channeled into military production to

Map 3-3   Alsace-Lorraine

©1996 by St. Martin's Press, Inc. From: *Contours of Powers,* by Snow/Brown. Reprinted with permission of Bedford/St. Martin's Press, Inc.Bedford/St. Martin's Press, Inc.

make Germany overwhelmingly the most powerful state in Europe; equality of power was shattered in the process.

The annexation also negated the other conditions. French public opinion was so outraged that no French government could align itself with Germany as long as the annexation stood. Alliance between the continent's two major powers was thus no longer possible. At the same time, agreement on a status quo worth defending could no longer be reached.

Germany's effective destruction of the Concert system is ironic. As the "weak link" of the original Concert, Prussia was protected under the system from the predators that had frequently threatened it in previous centuries (notably during the Thirty Years War). The Prussians worried, however, that the Concert might fail, thereby leaving it vulnerable once more. To guard against such a prospect, Germany had to become strong; the Franco-Prussian War was the culmination of this national "body building." Germany in effect therefore created a self-fulfilling prophecy; because it foresaw that the Congress might fail, it acted in a way that brought about its failure. German nationalism triumphed at the expense of systemic stability.

After 1870, the system gradually moved from a basis in collective security to a basis in collective defense. The Concert of Europe was replaced by the formation of static military alliances, of which Germany and France were the tethers. This system accelerated in the early twentieth century into the complex set of alliance commitments that greased the slide to war in 1914. On one side, Germany developed an alliance of Central Powers that included Austria-Hungary, the Ottoman Empire, and Bulgaria. The opposing Triple Entente, which expanded to include more than 20 states, was led by France, with Britain and Russia as its most prominent members in 1914.

Change Agents

The power map of Europe was not the only area where great change was taking place in the nineteenth century. It was a time of great turmoil within individual countries, as change was incorporated by some and resisted by others. Internationally, the major emphasis was

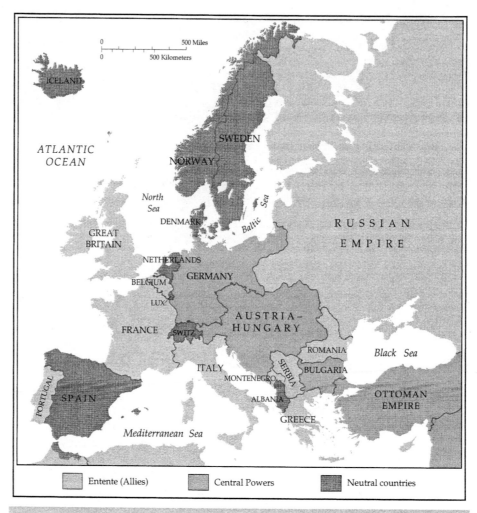

Map 3-4 **Europe in 1914**

©1996 by St. Martin's Press, Inc. From: *Contours of Power*, by Snow/Brown. Reprinted with permission of Bedford/St. Martin's Press, Inc.

on the avoidance of major conflicts among the important members and on the colonization of Africa and Asia.

Domestic Change Agents.   A number of domestic forces of change mingled in the countries of Europe, leading to new, interrelated political, economic, and social developments. Politically, a battle raged over ideology and hence the locus and basis of political control. Conservatives promoting a return to absolute monarchy clashed with Liberals supporting French revolutionary ideals based on popular sovereignty; in the second half of the century, the works of Karl Marx and Friedrich Engels added Marxism to the mix. The infusion of nationalism into politics only complicated this process of change. Economically, the first industrial revolution was widening the productive base and creating new social classes and demographic strains, as well as transforming military technology. Socially, the old nobility-based, highly stratified social system was challenged by a new, middle-class-based system resulting from economic and political change.

These forces preoccupied the members of the system and turned them inward. Revolutions arose periodically throughout the continent and had to be suppressed or accommodated. The membership of the Holy Alliance was, of course, most resistant. It was a time when the European agenda was consumed by domestic concerns.

The political debate was fundamental. On the one hand, the supporters of the ancien régime wanted desperately to regain the old political and social positions from which they had so benefited. The ideas of popular sovereignty and citizen participation in governance had been spread everywhere and would become the basis for universal demands for democratization across Europe. At the same time, French nationalism inspired others as well; the old cosmopolitanism of the eighteenth century, including its moderating influences, could never be reinstated. The liberals demanded change and a piece of the political action. The Marxists added their own version of that change, both economically and politically. Someone had to lose.

Economically, the effects of the first industrial revolution gradually spread from their roots in Great Britain to the Continent. A full discussion of the change that industrialization created goes beyond our purposes here, but we will cite three examples of the great impact it had on the political and social systems.

The first was a demographic shift. Before the first industrial revolution, most European countries were essentially rural, with most people making their livings by either farming or working in village-level cottage industries. Industrialization required large numbers of workers concentrated in cities to work in the factories. The result was a considerable migration to urban areas generally unprepared for the influx in terms of such resources as housing and public services.

The second aspect of change was the creation of new wealth by new groups. The new entrepreneurial, capitalist class, imbued with the economic theories of Adam Smith and others, built a much wealthier society than had preexisted. The old economically predominant class, the nobility, did not participate in this process and thus in this accumulation of wealth. Suddenly, there were economic rivals for the nobility.

The third aspect was the emergence of a number of new social classes. At a minimum, three new classes emerged or grew substantially. The entrepreneurial class of factory owners, as nouveau riche (newly rich), challenged the social dominance of the traditional upper class. The new middle class of managers, civil servants, professionals, and the like gradually expanded to become the dominant class of modern society. Finally, the proletariat of industrial workers were a new phenomenon altogether.

The emergence of these new classes as challengers to the old social order provided the major social dimension of change. For the old, conservative elite, the new classes were an unwanted intrusion on their positions, and they resisted the movement to a more egalitarian order. Where they were successful (in Holy Alliance countries such as Austria and Russia), the price was less economic modernization. Where they failed, economic modernization and redistribution of social status occurred.

These new phenomena, which were all interrelated, helped form the battle lines of domestic politics, as depicted in Figure 3-1. Politically, liberals favored a gradual enlargement of their political rights, which did come about largely as a result of their growing

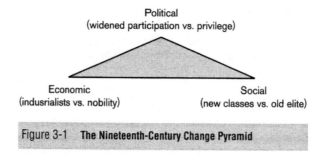

Political
(widened participation vs. privilege)

Economic
(indusrialists vs. nobility)

Social
(new classes vs. old elite)

Figure 3-1   **The Nineteenth-Century Change Pyramid**

contribution to national economies and, not unimportantly, tax revenues. Moreover, their wealth gave them a claim on greater social status, including political participation. The conservatives, and especially the absolutist monarchists, resisted liberal advances on all three fronts—political, economic, and social.

International Change Agents.   With all these domestic forces at play, the European powers wanted as tranquil an international situation as possible to allow energies to be concentrated on domestic issues. Most of the international activity focused on colonialism in Africa, Asia, and the Pacific. This meant the expansion of the British and French Empires as the Spanish and Portuguese were retreating, and later the expansion into the colonial business by countries such as Germany, Italy, and the United States.

For most of the nineteenth century, colonial expansion did not pose a major source of conflict within the system: territories for colonization were reasonably abundant, so that no one cared to fight over a given piece. By the end of the century, however, with the colonization of North Africa, most available territories had been taken. As colonial territory became scarce, competition among the powers intensified. It also came to focus on Europe itself.

Critical Events

As the nineteenth-century balance-of-power system evolved, a number of events defined and transformed it. As noted in the Summary box for the period, four stand out: the Crimean War, the Franco-Prussian War, the end of Afro-Asian colonization, and the events in the Balkans that triggered World War I.

The Crimean War (1853–1856) is often described as the first—and possibly last—time the Concert acted according to its principles. The conflict began as a dispute between Russia, Turkey (the Ottoman Empire), and France over access to holy shrines in Ottoman-controlled Jerusalem. Russia then invaded Turkey with the intent of seizing control of the strategic waterways out of the Black Sea into the Mediterranean, waterways that would provide Russia with a warm-water port. To have allowed Russian success would have increased Russian power and thrown the distribution of power out of balance. Hence, Great Britain, France, and Sardinia (a minor player) joined Turkey to repel the invasion and drive the Russians off Turkish soil, ultimately to the Crimean peninsula of Russia, where some of the most important battles occurred.

Two things stand out as examples of the Concert in action. First, Russia was not punished for its aggression but merely returned to its boundaries. Why? Russian power might be needed to defend the Concert later; equality of power had to be maintained. Second, the defense of the status quo was an action of the Concert's more liberal members; the other states of the Holy Alliance (Prussia and Austria) did not participate, an early signal of the fault line along which the Concert would eventually split.

The second critical event was the Franco-Prussian War of 1870, discussed previously. This watershed event completed the dismantling of the collective-security-based Concert of Europe and began the transformation toward a system of static alliances that ultimately would contest World War I.

The third event was the end of active colonization outside Europe due to the exhaustion of colonizable territory. With no place outside of Europe in which to seek influence or control, the major powers turned to those parts of Europe itself that seemed vulnerable. The focal point was the Balkans, where the Ottomans were gradually losing control and the scramble was on among ethnic groups (see the case study in Chapter 2) to see whether territories would become independent or be annexed to Austria-Hungary—whose deterioration was itself a major factor in the downward spiral to World War I.

The competition hardened as various powers scrambled to establish influence in particular areas. Great Britain became the patron of Greece, for instance, and newly independent Serbia became closely aligned with Russia, thereby creating the triggering mechanism that would later explode.

The fourth event, the assassinations in Sarajevo, provided the spark. For the first of two times in this century, the system came to focus on Bosnia and Herzegovina. The province was a part of the Austro-Hungarian Empire but was consumed with the kinds of ethnic nationalism with which the world has subsequently become all too familiar. On June 28, 1914, as Archduke Franz Ferdinand, the heir to the imperial throne, and his wife visited the Bosnian capital, they were assassinated by a Bosnian Serb, an adherent of the Black Hand movement to create separate Bosnian territories with Serbian majorities. When Austria-Hungary threatened retaliation against Serbia proper, the alliance commitments between Russia and Serbia were activated, thereby setting in motion a set of alliance commitments on both sides that no one acted decisively to deactivate. The result was war.

The Interwar System (1919–1939)

The convulsive event transforming the nineteenth-century system was World War I, the "war to end all wars." It was an event that hardly anyone tried very hard to avoid. Why? The reason is complex (see, for instance, Snow and Drew, Brodie, or Stoessinger for a more in-depth view) but can be summarized as an almost total misapprehension of what the war would be like and a belief that war was more desirable than the existing peace. Not anticipating the enormous changes that the industrial revolution had brought to warfare (see Chapter 5), all powers expected the conflict to be short and relatively bloodless, a reprise of the Franco-Prussian War. When the trench lines hardened, the generals did not know what to do. The result was warfare of unprecedented carnage that embittered the populations of all the states involved and contributed to a peace settlement virtually guaranteeing an unstable system and another horrendous world war.

Context

The context in which the international system had to be reconstructed was the ashes of a war that had killed millions (the casualties of the major participating states are recorded in Table 3.2) and greatly scarred the French countryside, on which the bloodiest European encounters occurred. The world was dazed and disillusioned; all the participants—especially the French, who lost a whole generation of young men—were bitter. The question was how to ensure that such a thing did not happen again.

The mechanism for reconstructing the peace was the Versailles Conference in Paris, where two visions of the postwar world competed. One, held by the U.S. President Woodrow Wilson, called for a reconciliatory peace based on his Fourteen Points plan and its centerpiece, the League of Nations. No one would be punished; victors and vanquished alike would be welcomed. This represented, as noted in Chapter 1, an idealist vision of the world.

The other vision, the one ultimately implemented, was held by French Premier Georges Clemenceau. Reflecting the enormous French hatred and frustration that had been building since the Franco-Prussian War, this vision called for the severe punishment of Germany, a vindictive peace. Its elements included forcing Germany to formally accept total responsibility for the war (in the War Guilt Clause, Article 231, of the peace treaty), exacting crushing reparations to pay for Allied reconstruction, and creating a disarmed, pastoral Germany that could no longer threaten the peace.

These conditions could be forced on a prostrate, defeated Germany, but the Germans could not be expected to embrace them. The War Guilt Clause was of questionable accuracy; the reparations stunted German economic recovery and guaranteed Germany would be hardest hit by the Great Depression; and a disarmed, pastoral Germany was as vulnerable to the whims of aggressors as Prussia had been to Napoléon's armies in 1806. The result, as it had been after 1870, was another self-fulfilling prophecy. Clemenceau's peace was motivated by fears of a resurgence of German might. He and his colleagues at Versailles accordingly created a set of conditions so obviously and overwhelmingly unacceptable to Germany as to guarantee the very resurgence they had tried to prevent.

Table 3.2	World War I Casualties (major participating states)	
	Killed	**Wounded**
Allies		
Britain	908,371	2,090,212
France	1,357,800	4,266,000
Italy	650,000	947,000
Romania	335,706	120,000
Russia	1,700,000	4,950,000
United States	126,000	234,300
Central Powers		
Austria-Hungary	1,200,000	3,620,000
Germany	1,773,700	4,216,058
Ottoman Empire	325,000	400,000

Summary

The Interwar System

Context
- Changes: end of World War I; collapse of Austrian, Ottoman, Russian empires
- Better state of the peace: punishment and restraint of Germany (Versailles Treaty)

Distribution of Power
- Major powers: Britain, France, Germany, Japan, Italy, (Soviet Union), (United States)
- Relationship: artificially multipolar (powers divided or isolated)
- Stability: unstable

War and Peace System
- Organizational base: collective security (hue and cry)
- Formality: formal (League of Nations)
- Purpose: deterrence of conflict

Change Agents
- Domestic
  1. Political: fascism and communism
  2. Economic: German hyperinflation, Great Depression
  3. Social: racist populism
- International: German repudiation of Versailles Treaty, spread of fascism

Critical Events
- Failures of League (Manchuria, Ethiopia, Rhineland)

For China, the interwar period is a misnomer. Following the abdication of the last emperor, China experimented with western-style political democracy under Sun Yat-sen. His regime, however, lacked the support to produce order, and the country slid into warlordism. The warlords stripped the country of whatever unity remained after the foreign-engineered humiliations of the nineteenth century. In addition, a civil war broke out between the Communists of Mao Ze-dong and the Nationalists of Chiang Kai-shek.

China was ripe for the picking, and the Japanese began their aggression by conquering Manchuria in 1931 (which some argue was the real beginning of World War II). In 1937, they attacked China proper, where their behavior toward soldiers and civilians alike was extremely cruel and barbaric. During the infamous "rape of Nanking," 300,000 Chinese were allegedly killed, often in the most gruesome manner.

For Japan, the interwar period marked a tragic turn. The country was hard hit by the Great Depression, triggering the dramatic rise of ultranationalism and militarism. Japan's budding democracy became a victim of the rising militarists. As their fascism grew in popularity, the military turned the country to war, especially in China. For Japan and China, the term "interwar" period was indeed a misnomer.

Distribution of Power

The end of the war also witnessed a change in the distribution of world power. Two of the old major powers who had been on the losing side, the Austro-Hungarian and Ottoman Empires, broke apart and simply ceased to exist, as the map of Europe in 1929 reveals (Map 3-5). Great Britain and France remained part of the mix but were badly weakened by the war's human and economic toll. New regional powers emerged in the Pacific (imperial Japan) and the Mediterranean (Italy). Of the two other potential major actors in the international system, the United States ultimately chose not to participate politically, while the Soviet Union was excluded because of opposition to its communist ideology.

The resulting system was multipolar but in an artificial manner: Britain and France were key players; Germany's role was confined by the terms of the peace; the roles of Italy and Japan were unclear and evolving; and the United States and the Soviet Union, the two sleeping giants, did not or were not allowed to play. This highly unstable and volatile mix produced a peace system with no meaningful chance of creating and regulating a peace.

Map 3-5   **Europe in 1929**

©1996 by St. Martin's Press, Inc. From: *Contours of Power*, by Snow/Brown. Reprinted with permission of Bedford/St. Martin's Press, Inc.

Peace Mechanisms

As is typically the case after a war, a major question facing those who framed the peace of Versailles was what had gone wrong to allow the war to occur in the first place. A major line of thought was that the system had lacked any formal mechanism or forum that could be mobilized to prevent war. The Concert had been too informal and had, after all, not been operative for a half-century. What should take its place?

The answer was a highly formal collective-security system under the auspices of the League of Nations. This intergovernmental organization was the brainchild of President Wilson, who believed unless the countries of the world banded together to prevent breaches of the peace, continuing war was inevitable. Moreover, he believed that only a formal commitment through a permanent, continuously active institution could overcome the deficiencies of the Concert of Europe.

Unfortunately, League-style collective security never stood a chance of success, because none of the conditions for collective security were met. Three of the major powers had reason to oppose, rather than to support, the status quo: German opposition was most obvious, but territorial claims of Japan (to Germany's Pacific colonies) and Italy (to parts of what is now Croatia) were also denied by the conferees at Versailles. Together with the early exclusion of the Soviet Union from any involvement and the ultimate refusal of the United States to join the League (the U.S. Senate declined to ratify the Versailles Treaty, including provisions for the League), the resignation of Germany, Japan, and Italy in the 1930s meant that the organization did not even include most of the major powers.

Even had the three powers not resigned, changes in their governments meant that by the mid–1930s the League would have failed to meet the preponderance-of-power standard. When fascists seized power in Italy and Germany and the military did likewise in Japan, the ability of any power to align with any other (flexibility of alliance) was undercut. In its place, two ideologically opposed static alliances emerged during the 1930s. Moreover, the rearmament of Germany and major military buildups in Italy and Japan gave these countries clear superiority to their rivals, at least in the short run, so that equality of power disappeared as well.

In addition, the League Covenant's provisions for collective security were deficient. The League Council could, and occasionally did, authorize the use of force against a transgressor. The problem was that the League had no mechanism to compel member states to enforce its authorized actions. Rather, all it could do was to call for volunteers—issue the hue and cry. If members chose to let someone else do the enforcing, which was often the case, then League sanctions had no effective teeth; deterrence failed.

Change Agents

The interwar period was a turbulent time. The rising appeal of fascism provided an ideological basis for political conflict within states, replacing monarchism as the alternative to democracy or to communism, as found in the new Soviet Union. In one form or another, right-wing authoritarian (fascist) regimes took hold in Germany, Italy, Japan, Spain, Portugal, and a number of Eastern European states. Communist parties joined the political debate throughout Europe.

Economically, all states, but especially Germany, were convulsed by the abrupt collapse from the prosperity of the 1920s to the worldwide Great Depression of the 1930s and its accompanying economic nationalism (in which steep barriers were placed on the importation of goods and services in order to protect depression-ravaged domestic industries). As noted earlier, reparations payments left the German economy extremely fragile, subject to rampant inflation in the early 1920s and then especially vulnerable to the depression; Germany was hit hardest by the downturn. In the economic chaos, Adolf Hitler, whose appeal in better times had been marginal, swept into power.

The rise of fascism was a social phenomenon as well. Many core supporters of the Nazi and Italian fascist regimes were members of the lower middle class and the working class (many of the latter were communists). In Germany the lower middle class had been the group most affected by the hyperinflation of the early 1920s, which wiped out their savings, and they had long felt disenfranchised and put upon by their economic and social superiors. The appeal of fascism, including its racism, was partly a populist one, aimed at them.

Internationally, the response to the rise and spread of fascism was tepid, at best. As the fascists consolidated their holds on domestic power and began to expand outward, the defenders of the status quo stood by and watched. This unwillingness of the western democracies to act is crystallized in British Prime Minister Neville Chamberlain's trip to Munich on the eve of Nazi occupation of Czechoslovakia in 1938, where he declared that Hitler had promised him "peace in our time" and an end to German expansion.

Critical Events

The progressive failures of that part of the system dedicated to the status quo to act when the status quo was threatened emboldened the states that became the Axis powers (Germany, Italy, and Japan) to behave in ways that eventually made war inevitable. Although these failures were numerous, the unwillingness to act decisively against each individually constituted the period's critical events.

Some analysts argue World War II really began in 1931, when Japan invaded and conquered the industrial heart of China, Manchuria. It proceeded to rule brutally through a puppet figure descended from the Chinese Manchu dynasty, who was placed on what Japan called the new Manchukuo throne (to make it seem a popular return to the Manchus, whose rule had ended with the establishment of the Chinese republic in 1912). The western response to the rape of Manchuria was decidedly restrained. For example, the United

A mass march by young German Nazis in 1934 reflects the widespread appeal of fascism between the world wars. The international system based on the League of Nations proved powerless in the face of fascist aggression in the 1930s, encouraging the fascist states to launch World War II.

States issued the Stimson Doctrine of Non-Recognition (named after Herbert Hoover's Secretary of State, Henry Stimson), which simply declared that it was American policy not to recognize any state that came to power by force. The declaration was unaccompanied by sanctions against Japan.

Italy's turn came in 1935, when it launched an invasion of Ethiopia from its adjacent colony, Eritrea. As advancing Italian tanks rumbled against horse-mounted Ethiopian troops armed in some cases with spears, the Ethiopian leader, Emperor Haile Selassie, made his famous plea to the League of Nations to come to his country's aid. The League merely passed voluntary sanctions (members were not compelled to obey them) forbidding trade in war materials to Italy, but excluding petroleum, motor oil, and lubricants, upon which a modern armed force is almost totally reliant.

The Impact of Technology
The Pearl Harbor Raid

The Japanese air attack on the U.S. Pacific Fleet at Pearl Harbor, Hawaii, on December 7, 1941—the "day of infamy," as President Franklin D. Roosevelt described it in his message asking Congress for a declaration of war against Japan—has been described as one of the most tactically brilliant and strategically stupid military ventures of all time. It was an event made possible by technological innovation between the world wars—and one that would be utterly unthinkable in an age of global telecommunications.

The tactical brilliance of the attack was that the Japanese fleet, incorporating aircraft carriers developed after World War I and fighter-bomber aircraft with considerably greater range than American intelligence recognized, was able to traverse the Pacific Ocean and launch its aircraft without detection. The attack virtually decimated the American fleet, but the strategic stupidity of the raid was that it put Japan into a war its military leaders knew it could not win once the United States mobilized.

Modern telecommunications would make even the contemplation of such an attack out of the question. The Japanese fleet could not steam out of port today without a phalanx of electronic

media observing, recording, and transmitting the scheme in full detail via telecommunications satellites. Even if the fleet could somehow be launched without media attention, military satellite reconnaissance would track its every movement, thereby removing any chance of surprise. Technology made such an attack possible in 1941 and makes it quite impossible today.

The *U.S.S. Arizona*, ravaged by Japanese bombs and torpedos, sinks in Pearl Harbor. More than 1,000 crew members were trapped in the ship's hull and drowned.

Germany acted in 1936. Against the advice of his military leaders (who believed their forces no match for those of France), Hitler ordered the occupation by German troops of the Rhineland area along the French border, which had been demilitarized under the terms of the Versailles Treaty. Hitler timed the move to coincide with a crisis in the French government (a cabinet had fallen and not yet been replaced). By the time any official reaction could occur, German forces were in place, presenting a fait accompli. Britain and France decried the action, but they took no forceful steps to reverse it.

These inactions by the democratic states simply emboldened the Axis powers to further aggression. The League, now weakened by these powers' formal withdrawal, could not or would not act. Finally, Germany stepped over the line by invading and conquering Poland, which was allied to Britain. The British were forced to declare war. The largest, bloodiest conflict in human history ensued.

The Cold War System

World War II was war on a scale previously unseen and unconceived. Its sheer extent was so great that estimates of its effects vary greatly and are only approximations, but some authorities estimate that about 80 million participated as combatants; as many as 20 million combatants, and about an equal number of civilians, were killed. (Official estimates of casualties for the major participating states are listed in Table 3.3.) The fighting was concentrated in Europe and East Asia, but no continent except unpopulated Antarctica was spared combat of some sort. World War I had been a European war with ancillary theaters; World War II was truly a global affair.

Of all parts of the globe, no country was as affected as the Soviet Union. Much of the German onslaught took place on Soviet territory, and the results were devastating. As many as 20 million civilian and military personnel died; when this figure is added to the 8 to 10

Table 3.3 World War II Casualties (major participating states)		
	Killed*	**Wounded**
Allies		
Britain	305,800	277,100
China	1,400,000	1,800,000
France	122,000	335,000
Poland	110,000	146,700
United States	405,400	670,800
USSR	11,000,000	?
Axis		
Germany	3,250,000	4,606,000
Italy	226,900	?
Japan	1,740,000	94,000

*Includes missing
Source: John Ellis, *World War II: A Statistical Survey*. New York: Facts on File, 1993.

million Soviet citizens killed in the Stalinist purges of the 1930s, upwards of one in seven Soviets alive at the beginning of the purges was dead by the war's end (by comparison, total American dead in the war numbered slightly more than 400,000). The Soviets called the conflict the Great Patriotic War; that they would be obsessed by its memory and the prevention of its recurrence is hardly surprising.

Context

The outcome of World War II shattered the European-dominated international system in two distinct ways. First, it left the principal players in the old balance of power prostrate and incapable of providing leadership. The Axis states (particularly Germany and Japan) were defeated, devastated, and occupied, and they would require considerable rehabilitation and development before they became major actors again. The victorious European allies, Britain and France, were physically and financially battered and effectively reduced to regional-power status.

In addition, the war led inevitably to the end of European colonial subjugation of much of the rest of the globe. The colonial powers had been forced to turn to their colonies for troops and laborers during the war, and the colonies, for their part, hatched independence movements in the process. (It is almost axiomatic that you cannot ask a group to engage in the ultimate sacrifice of war and then return to bondage.) The economic losses and overall exhaustion of the major European colonialists—France and Britain—were such that when independence movements asserted their claims, the colonialists lacked the wherewithal successfully to resist or, in many cases, even to try.

Summary ━━━━━━━━━━━━━━━━━━━━━━━━━━

The Cold War System

Context

- Change: end of World War II and of European-dominated system
- Better state of the peace: United Nations system

Distribution of Power

- Major powers: United States, Soviet Union
- Relationship: bipolar (powers divided)
- Stability: unstable to 1962; increasingly stable thereafter

War and Peace System

- Organizational base: collective security and collective defense
- Formality: formal (United Nations, alliances)
- Purpose: deterrence and defense

Change Agents

- Domestic
  1. Political: nationalism in Third World
  2. Economic: impact of Cold War spending, technology
  3. Social: weakening of communist system
- International: nuclear competition, competition for influence in Third World

Critical Events

- Suez crisis, Hungarian rebellion, Cuban missile crisis, revolutions of 1989

The changes in the structure and composition of the international system and its center of gravity were the most profound since the Westphalian state system came into existence. Not only did the war end the 100-year competition between Germany and France for domination of Europe inconclusively; it swept the anchor of the system from its historic moorings.

The mechanism that was to recreate order was the nascent United Nations system. Largely drafted in the U.S. Department of State during the war in anticipation of its eventual outcome, the new organization had to deal with several highly significant unknowns, one of which was the composition of the postwar balance of power.

The triumph of Mao Ze-dong's communists in China in 1949 presented the West with a daunting prospect: if China joined the Soviet Union in a hostile communist alliance, western democracies would confront an enemy consisting of nearly one-third of mankind occupying two-thirds of global land space. In its first years of existence, China did precisely this, and incantations of the evil of the "Sino-Soviet bloc" reverberated throughout the West. China soon came to wonder what kind of ally it had: China fought the Americans in Korea between 1950 and 1953, and the Soviets sold rather than gave them weapons. In 1957, Mao rocked the Kremlin by rejecting Soviet-style central economic planning, setting them into economic rivalry. Matters reached their low point in 1969 when the traditional rivals engaged in warfare over control of an island in the Ussuri river that forms their boundary. In response, China began to open itself to the West (President Nixon visited in 1972) and began its entrance into the world economy.

Japan's direction in the world was simple: follow the Americans. As we will see in Chapter 7, Japan has been a reticent actor on the international stage since its shattering defeat in World War II. During the Cold War, it was important to the United States to link Japan securely to the West so that its talented workforce and strategic location would not fall into communist hands. Likewise, it was important to Japan's conservative leaders to secure an American guarantee of their security from nearby communist states China, North Korea, and the Soviet Union.

Distribution of Power

Only two states emerged from the war with significant residual power, although that power was of different kinds. The United States was the only clear winner in the war: the Americans suffered the least damage and relatively light casualties, had the world's only major functioning economy (which had been rescued from the Great Depression by the war effort), and was the sole possessor of the world's most powerful weapon, the atomic bomb. In retrospect, the U.S. power advantage in 1945 was at a height not reached again until the dissolution of the Soviet Union in 1991. The Soviet Union still possessed its huge Red Army of over 12 million, much of which was an occupation force in Eastern Europe and Korea.

Within a few years, beginning in 1949, the Soviet Union also acquired nuclear power to rival that of the United States, thereby coming to share in the designation of superpower. In 1945, however, how this configuration of power would work was not immediately obvious. One uncertainty was the question of whether the two superpowers could continue their wartime harmony and thus create a cooperative international system based in collective security. In the West there was not much official optimism about continued comity, but its possibility could not be ruled out.

Another uncertainty was the new variable in the power equation, the role of nuclear weapons. By 1946, two remarkable books had been published that laid out the possibilities about nuclear weapons that framed the debate thereafter. The better-known book, Bernard Brodie's edited compilation of essays called *The Absolute Weapon,* argued that in the future these weapons could serve no other purpose than deterrence. A less well-known work, William Liscum Borden's *There Will Be No Time,* argued conversely that since atomic weapons were available, they would be used in future wars as they had in World War II.

Both uncertainties were resolved in the course of time. The U.S.-Soviet military collaboration was dissolved in the competition between two opposed but equally evangelical ideologies and worldviews, a situation basically known and recognized by 1947. George F. Kennan's article "The Sources of Soviet Conduct" correctly set forth the nature of the competition, which was put into operation early on by actions such as the provision of U.S. military aid to Greece and Turkey to resist communist incursions. That deterrence would be the role of nuclear weapons in the Cold War was an evolving realization accepted by some only after the collapse of the Soviet Union.

Thus, what emerged in the early postwar years was a bipolar system, but one whose nature evolved through time. In the early days, it was classified as a tight bipolar system, which meant that each superpower could order and enforce its authority over those states drawn to its "pole." The chief Soviet instrument was its army of occupation in Eastern Europe; the main American instrument was the power to give or withhold assistance to war-ravaged Western European economies. The result was a European map largely divided into two opposing military alliances, the U.S.-sponsored North Atlantic Treaty Organization (NATO) and the Soviet-led Warsaw Pact. (A few states maintained official neutrality, and a few others did not formally affiliate with either alliance.) In the words of British Prime Minister Winston Churchill, an "Iron Curtain" had fallen across the continent.

By 1989, when its final dissolution began, the Cold War system had evolved to one of loose bipolarity, where the two superpowers continued to be the dominant states (at least in the military realm), but their ability to control the system, including members of their own blocs, had decreased. Any point chosen as the transition from tight to loose bipolarity is somewhat arbitrary, but we will argue that 1956 is as plausible a year as any. It followed the Bandung Conference of 1955, the first meeting of African and Asian states and the first point at which a split emerged between the Soviet Union and the other major communist power, China. In addition, 1956 was the year of the Suez crisis and the Hungarian rebellion; as explained later in this chapter, both helped to diminish the superpowers' control over their blocs.

The system also evolved from one of instability to stability. In the early period, when the Soviets were establishing their physical domination over Eastern Europe in ways the West viewed as violating wartime agreements and anticommunism was at its zenith in the West, there was a series of confrontations with considerable escalatory potential. The most tense occurred in 1962, when the Soviet Union attempted to install nuclear-tipped missiles in Cuba but was forced to abandon the effort in response to a U.S. ultimatum, an episode known as the Cuban missile crisis.

The missile crisis is generally considered the closest the two sides came to war—including nuclear war—and it frightened and sobered both sides into a vision of the reality such a conflict could produce. After the missile crisis, both sides came progressively to recognize the absolute unacceptability of war between them and to take positive steps in areas such as nuclear arms control to lessen the likelihood of war. The result was an

Map 3-6 **Europe in 1989**

©1996 by St. Martin's Press, Inc. From: *Contours of Power*, by Snow/Brown. Reprinted with permission of Bedford/St. Martin's Press, Inc.

increasingly stable, nonconfrontational relationship, the dynamic of which was a necessary peace between the superpowers (peace born of the necessity to avoid war) that eventually contributed to the termination of the Cold War, as we argue at greater length in Chapter 6.

Peace Mechanisms

The new United Nations was to be the centerpiece for reorganizing the peace in the post–World War II environment. The organization's charter provided for a new collective-security system designed to remove the deficiencies that undermined the effectiveness of the League of Nations (which officially ceased to exist when the UN Charter took effect).

The UN Charter is a remarkable and flexible document that has outlasted its numerous critics of the Cold War period. Its collective security provisions are contained in Chapter VII of the document, whose text appears in the box "Amplification: Chapter VII of the UN Charter." Articles 39–44 establish the authority of the UN to take a series of progressively more punitive actions, up to and including the employment of force. Up to this point, the Charter resembles the League Covenant. In Articles 45–50, however, the Charter goes further, improving on the League's method of force recruitment with a permanent standing force commanded by the UN Military Staff Committee and coming from the permanent members of the Security Council: the United States, the Soviet Union (whose seat is now held by Russia), Great Britain, France, and China. This force, in theory, would help deter would-be aggressors, tipping their calculation of success in a negative direction.

Such a force has never come into being, and during the Cold War the provisions were never utilized. The reason was that not all the conditions for collective security were met. Notably, there was no agreement between the United States and the Soviet Union on what peace to enforce, especially since most violent conflicts involved clients or friends of one side pitted against clients or friends of the other.

The power of the permanent members of the Security Council to veto any proposal considered by the Council disabled efforts at collective security when unanimity was impossible. The framers of the UN have often been criticized as utopians for having failed to anticipate the East-West rift and thus for creating an unworkable system. This criticism could hardly be farther from the mark. The framers did not expect the wartime collaboration to continue; rather, they provided a collective-security mechanism if cooperation could occur. In the event of noncooperation, Article 51 states, "Nothing in the present Charter shall impair the inherent right of individual or collective self-defense."

Thus, the Charter provided for both collective security and collective defense. Which principle would be activated depended on the relations between the major powers. Through the Cold War, ideological opposition left collective security moribund. (Technically, the UN effort in the Korean War was a collective-security operation, but it was possible only because the Soviets, who would have vetoed the action, were boycotting the Security Council in protest against the UN's refusal to seat the communist Chinese government as the rightful representative of China.) When the Cold War ended, the collective-security provisions could be reactivated, as we shall explain.

Change Agents

While it was ongoing, the Cold War system seemed permanent and immutable. The two sides were in a kind of zero-sum game where one side could only win what the other lost. The political chasm between East and West seemed unbridgeable; the economic systems of capitalism and communism were diametrically opposed; and the Third World countries, many of which had just shed their colonial yokes, were treated largely as just another venue for the Cold War competition.

East-West, communist-anticommunist confrontation was the principal political reality of the Cold War. It defined the foreign policies of the major actors; the dictates of the "national security state"—in which the military aspects of confrontation overrode other

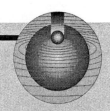

Amplification
Chapter VII of the UN Charter

Article 39
The Security Council shall determine the existence of any threat to the peace, breach of the peace, or act of aggression and shall make recommendations, or decide what measures shall be taken in accordance with Articles 41 and 42, to maintain or restore international peace and security.

Article 40
In order to prevent an aggravation of the situation, the Security Council may, before making the recommendations or deciding upon the measures provided for in Article 39, call upon the parties concerned to comply with such provisional measures as it deems necessary or desirable. Such provisional measures shall be without prejudice to the rights, claims or position of the parties concerned. The Security Council shall duly take account of failure to comply with such provisional measures.

Article 41
The Security Council may decide what measures not involving the use of armed force are to be employed to give effect to its decisions, and it may call upon the Members of the United Nations to apply such measures. These may include complete or partial interruption of economic relations and of rail, sea, air, postal, telegraphic, radio and other means of communication, and the severance of diplomatic relations.

Article 42
Should the Security Council consider that measures provided for in Article 41 would be inadequate or have proved to be inadequate, it may take such action by air, sea, or land forces as may be necessary to maintain or restore international peace and security. Such action may include demonstrations, blockades, and other operations by air, sea, or land forces of Members of the United Nations.

Article 43
1. All Members of the United Nations, in order to contribute to the maintenance of international peace and security, undertake to make available to the Security Council, on its call and in accordance with a special agreement or agreements, armed forces, assistance and facilities, including rights of passage, necessary for the purpose of maintaining international peace and security.
2. Such agreement or agreements shall govern the numbers and types of forces, their degree of readiness and general location, and the nature of the facilities and assistance to be provided.
3. The agreement or agreements shall be negotiated as soon as possible on the initiative of the Security Council. They shall be concluded between the Security Council and Members or between the Security Council and groups of Members and shall be subject to ratification by the signatory states in accordance with their respective constitutional processes.

Article 44
When the Security Council has decided to use force it shall, before calling upon a Member not represented on it to provide armed forces in fulfillment of the obligations assumed under Article 43, invite that Member, if the Member so desires, to participate in the decisions of the Security Council concerning the employment of contingents of that Member's armed forces.

Article 45
In order to enable the United Nations to take urgent military measures, Members shall hold immediately available national air-force contingents for combined international enforcement action. The strength and degree of readiness of these

Chapter VII of the UN Charter *(continued)*

contingents and plans for their combined action shall be determined, within the limits laid down in the special agreement or agreements referred to in Article 43, by the Security Council with the assistance of the Military Staff Committee.

Article 46
Plans for the application of armed force shall be made by the Security Council with the assistance of the Military Staff Committee.

Article 47

1. There shall be established a Military Staff Committee to advise and assist the Security Council on all questions relating to the Security Council's military requirements for the maintenance of international peace and security, the employment and command of forces placed at its disposal, the regulation of armaments, and possible disarmament.
2. The Military Staff Committee shall consist of the Chiefs of Staff of the permanent members of the Security Council or their representatives. Any Member of the United Nations not permanently represented on the Committee shall be invited by the Committee to be associated with it when the efficient discharge of the Committee's responsibilities requires the participation of that Member in its work.
3. The Military Staff Committee shall be responsible under the Security Council for the strategic direction of any armed forces placed at the disposal of the Security Council. Questions relating to the command of such forces shall be worked out subsequently.
4. The Military Staff Committee, with the authorization of the Security Council and after consultation with appropriate regional agencies, may establish regional sub-committees.

Article 48

1. The action required to carry out the decisions of the Security Council for the maintenance of international peace and security shall be taken by all the Members of the United Nations or by some of them, as the Security Council may determine.
2. Such decisions shall be carried out by the Members of the United Nations directly and through their action in the appropriate international agencies of which they are members.

Article 49
The Members of the United Nations shall join in affording mutual assistance in carrying out the measures decided upon by the Security Council.

Article 50
If preventive or enforcement measures against any state are taken by the Security Council, any other state, whether a Member of the United Nations or not, which finds itself confronted with special economic problems arising from the carrying out of those measures shall have the right to consult the Security Council with regard to a solution of those problems.

Article 51
Nothing in the present Charter shall impair the inherent right of individual or collective self-defence if an armed attack occurs against a Member of the United Nations, until the Security Council has taken measures necessary to maintain international peace and security. Measures taken by Members in the exercise of this right of self-defence shall be immediately reported to the Security Council and shall not in any way affect the authority and responsibility of the Security Council under the present Charter to take at any time such action as it deems necessary in order to maintain or restore international peace and security.

concerns—were supreme. Both sides built impressive military coalitions to confront and deter, and if necessary to fight, one another.

On the economic level, the battle was over the ascendancy of one economic philosophy or the other. It was a competition between apostles who sought aggressively to export their beliefs, especially to the Third World, and to demonstrate the inherent superiority of their economic system.

The clash of philosophies and systems brought a remarkable order and predictability to events. Both sides knew who the enemy was, what it proposed to do in most instances, and what actions were necessary to counteract it. Indeed, the Cold War construct became, over time, so intellectually comfortable that even professional analysts of international relations failed to see the signs of its implosion.

The causes of the end of the Cold War are discussed in detail in Chapter 6. For the moment, it is sufficient simply to list the three most prominent ones. First was the increasing irrelevance of the conflict in most of the world, notably the Second Tier. For most countries emerging from the bonds of colonial rule and struggling for political and economic well-being, the Cold War was little more than instrumental, an opportunity to extort resources from one side by threatening to align with the other. As more Second Tier countries became independent, the rhetoric of the Cold War lost its meaning in ever greater parts of the globe.

Second, the economic rot of the socialist system was undermining its vitality at the very time that economic expansion was occurring in the First Tier. As the 1970s gave way to the 1980s, the gap in economic performance between the capitalist and socialist worlds became a chasm that, thanks to the far-seeing eye of global television, could not be hidden from the populations of socialist countries. Unless something was done, the chasm could become unbridgeable.

Third, the military burden of competition became unbearable. The Cold War was expensive: as much as 60 percent of the American defense budget was devoted to NATO, and estimates of Soviet defense spending were as great as 15 to 25 percent of gross national product (GNP).

These realities gradually dawned on the leadership of both sides. The key instigator of change based on these perceptions was Mikhail Gorbachev, who emerged in 1985 from the succession process begun by the death of Soviet leader Leonid Brezhnev. Gorbachev instigated a process of introspection and change that resulted in the implosion of the Soviet Union and hence in elimination of the reason for a bipolar world. What is remarkable about this transition is that it occurred without a major shooting war, as had marked the other transitions from one system to another.

Critical Events

The Cold War was an eventful period, and it goes beyond our current purposes to reiterate the things that happened to make it what it was. Instead, we will highlight several events of special importance: the Suez crisis and the Hungarian rebellion, the Cuban missile crisis, and the revolutions of 1989.

As has been noted, the Suez crisis and the Hungarian rebellion, which both occurred in 1956, marked the beginning of the end of the tight bipolar system. The Suez crisis was precipitated by a joint British, French, and Israeli invasion of Egypt; Britain and France occupied the Suez Canal Zone, which had been nationalized by Egypt's President Gamal Abdel Nasser the previous year, while Israel occupied the Sinai peninsula.

In systemic terms, the crisis was important in two ways in demonstrating the United States' slipping grip on its bloc. First, the Americans were not fully informed nor consulted in advance, a show of independence by their closest allies (who chose to ignore what they knew to be American opposition). Second, in the aftermath of the invasion, the United States and the Soviet Union cosponsored a UN resolution condemning the invasion and demanding withdrawal of the forces. Britain and especially France felt betrayed by the action and never fully trusted the United States afterward.

The Hungarian case is more complex. In late 1956, demonstrations and street fighting brought back to power the communist government of Imre Nagy, who had announced his intention to declare a neutrality similar to that of Austria and to continue reforms aimed at extending personal liberties. (His earlier reforms had led to his overthrow by more orthodox communists within Hungary.) The Soviet reaction was swift and brutal, as Soviet tanks rumbled into the country, quickly crushing Nagy's supporters and overthrowing his government. The lesson appeared to be that any Warsaw Pact leader opposing Soviet desires would be stopped, that Soviet control of Eastern Europe was as iron-fisted as ever.

Worldwide reaction to the invasion, fanned by the United States, was swift and condemnatory, especially damaging to a Soviet Union portraying itself as the peaceful supporter of self-determination in the Third World. The Eastern Europeans learned that the Soviets could not use force with impunity against them, for fear of another public relations disaster. Rather, as long as basic Soviet territorial security was not threatened (a mistake made by Czechoslovakia in 1968), there was considerable autonomy.

As Suez and Hungary loosened bipolarity, the aftermath of the Cuban missile crisis of October 1962 was the first crack in the hard lines of the Cold War competition. Previously, both sides had assumed that competition was pervasive and all-consuming; that they possessed no common interests. "The missiles of October" taught them otherwise; they quickly realized they did have a mutual interest in avoiding nuclear annihilation. The result was the opening of a dialogue on nuclear arms control. After Cuba, the Cold

Hungarians wave the national flag from an army tank during the country's brief rebellion against Soviet domination in October 1956. Although Soviet troops quickly crushed the insurgency, the resulting international criticism led in the long run to a loosening of the Soviets' control over their Eastern European satellites.

War started to unravel. To cite two examples, ongoing arms control negotiations gradually improved Soviet-American relations, and the United States and communist China established diplomatic ties in the 1970s, thus reducing another risk of confrontation. Ultimately, the succession crisis of the 1980s in the Soviet Union began the dissolution of the Soviet state.

The final critical event was the revolutions of 1989. In the last three months of that year, first Poland, then Hungary, Czechoslovakia, East Germany, and Romania overthrew the communist governments that had been imposed on them by the Soviet Union. The Soviet leadership had warned the regimes in advance not to expect military assistance if their peoples rose up against them, and the tanks did not rumble as they had in 1956 and 1968; instead the process was allowed to proceed.

The conclusion of the process was the peaceful dissolution of the Soviet Union at the end of 1991. With these events, half of the bipolar confrontation literally evaporated. The Warsaw Pact had already voted itself out of existence in 1991; all that was left was a western alliance—NATO—facing a suddenly nonexistent adversary.

Case Study: Beyond the Cold War

The international system has been in a process of adjustment since the dissolution of the remnants of the Soviet "empire" (the Soviet Union and the communist governments of Eastern Europe). The transition has been more difficult than the restructuring of the system after World War II, for at least three reasons that constitute the context of the transition.

Context

Adjustment to the post–Cold War system has been difficult first of all because the end of the previous system was so swift and largely unanticipated. When Gorbachev ascended to power in 1985, hardly anyone expected anything unorthodox from him. That he would oversee the peaceful undoing of the Soviets' primary defense arrangement, preside over his own country's breakup into 15 parts, and lose power to a more thorough reformer was not a scenario for which anyone had planned. The unexpectedness of change lengthened the process of system reconstruction. The absence of a shooting war from which to recover also made the restructuring seem less urgent. After a major war, there is an urgent need to reach accord on the terms of the peace and to set people's lives back in order. It may be important to reinforce the Soviet successor states' movement into the international mainstream and attempt to see that those states do not revert to their authoritarian pasts, but that task has not been as pressing as the reconstruction of Europe after World War II. The virtual implosion of the Russian economy in 1998 makes the wisdom of that lack of urgency questionable.

Finally, the broad contours of the new order were not initially as clear as they are at the end of systemically traumatic wars. At the end of World War II, it was clear who were the victors and who were the vanquished, and that fact provided guidance and direction to the process of restructuring. That clarity was at first lacking as the Cold War ended because the Cold War was not really a war, so that there are no victors and vanquished in the normal sense of those words.

This ongoing process of adjustment, of thinking through the new order, which would normally begin during war, is the context in which a new international system is being shaped. Although the precise shapes of the future remain murky, certainly the changing contours are becoming clear.

Distribution of Power

Two things are clear about the distribution of power in the new system. First, it is more complex than it was in the past. Clearly, the amount of military power a state possesses is now a less important measure of its ability to shape events in its favor. Second, the multiple sources of power make the description of power more difficult.

At its simplest, one can think of the distribution in terms of the instruments of power, where military and economic power contribute to political/diplomatic success or failure. In terms of military power, the world is effectively unipolar. The United States stands alone in possessing both massive—if reduced—thermonuclear power and especially the conventional military power needed for projection of force globally. Russia remains a major power by virtue of its residual nuclear power, and countries such as Britain and France retain some projection capability. Only the United States has both.

This condition of comparative American strength is accentuated by the technological gap between the major countries of the First Tier and those of the Second Tier. In Operation Desert Storm, the United States gave an example of the enormous technological advantages

---

Summary ———————————————————————
Post–Cold War System

Context
- Change: collapse of Soviet Union and Eastern European communism
- Better state of the peace: ongoing process of adjustment

Distribution of Power
- Major powers: United States (military); United States, EU, Japan, others (economic)
- Relationship: multipolar and multilevel (powers like-minded)
- Stability: stable (First Tier); unstable (Second Tier)

War and Peace System
- Organizational base: collective security
- Formality: formal (United Nations)
- Purpose: deterrence

Change Agents
- Domestic and international
   1. Political: democratization, national self-determination
   2. Economic: globalization
   3. Social: exclusionary nationalism

Critical Events
- (tentative) Operation Desert Storm, Bosnian civil war

it has in firepower, intelligence gathering and analysis, and command and control over the military of Second Tier Iraq. The same asymmetry exists between major western states and other Second Tier countries. Even the cutbacks attendant to the end of the Cold War do not greatly erode this relative advantage.

Economic power, on the other hand, is clearly multipolar. At a minimum, it is tripolar: the United States, Japan, and the European Union stand far above the rest of the world by any measure of production. If consumption is the indicator, then China enters the picture, with the world's second largest economy measured by total consumption (see the discussion in Chapter 9). Moreover, this gap between the First and Second Tiers is widening as the increasingly interdependent countries of the First Tier are propelled through the high-technology revolution that undergirds economic growth.

The stability of this new multilevel, multipolar system is a major question yet to be answered. At one level, it appears quite stable. The major political and economic actors of the First Tier have only minor political divisions among them, sharing common economic and political philosophies that produce a sameness of basic worldview unseen since the eighteenth-century system. Unless some drastic unforeseen event occurs, it is difficult to conceive of major conflict with military potential arising among them. For the First Tier, traditional realist frameworks of international affairs are not entirely appropriate.

The same is not true within and among Second Tier states. Internal conflicts, often in the form of large-scale religious and ethnic violence, have become commonplace now that the ideological competition of the Cold War period has disappeared. At the same time, simmering regional conflicts in places such as South Asia are exacerbated by the emergence of advanced military capabilities such as nuclear, biological, and chemical weapons and ballistic-missile delivery capability. The testing of nuclear bombs by India and Pakistan and an intermediate range missile (800 mile range) by Iran, all in 1998, exemplifies the problem.

Peace Mechanisms

The dissolution of the Soviet military bloc has rendered irrelevant the system of static alliances that marked the Cold War. Cooperation on most issues between the United States and Russia has removed the Security Council veto as a major block to UN collective-security actions, except in extreme instances where deeply held interests are at stake. A major task of the evolving system is determining how the collective-security system will operate.

The conditions for collective security, although not totally met, are closer to actuality than at any other time in the history of the state system. At least when consideration of China is put aside, it appears that a tranquil world is desired (support for the status quo) and that overwhelming force is available to deter those who would disturb that tranquillity (preponderance of power). Two major questions, however, remain to be resolved. Both relate to the other condition for collective security, the willingness of the major powers to commit themselves physically to defense of the status quo.

First is the question of how the forces for collective security will be made available. Two options are the hue-and-cry method of the League of Nations and the permanent forces authorized by the UN Charter. Almost all observers agree in broad principle that it would be most effective to have a standing force under permanent UN control, or at least to have national forces earmarked and available for international duty. However, this goal is extremely difficult to achieve in practice.

The key to this problem is the United States. If a UN-based force large enough to deal with difficult missions involving active combat (as opposed to passive peacekeeping) is to be formed, the Americans, with their unique projection capabilities, must participate. But here the pull of state sovereignty reenters the calculus: American politicians, military leaders, and citizens refuse to see the fate of American forces determined by foreigners. Until that issue can be (if it can be) resolved, the hue-and-cry method will continue to prevail, as it did in the recent interventions in Kuwait, Somalia, Croatia, and Bosnia.

The second question is where and how collective security will be applied. Specifically, since a large portion of the ongoing violence is internal to states, is it appropriate to commit international forces into civil wars? Moreover, the bases of these conflicts are often extremely complex, intractable, and poorly understood by outsiders who may feel the urge to "do something" to end suffering. The effectiveness of these efforts has not yet been demonstrated; it may be that such attempts fail because outsiders cannot solve internal problems. It may also be the case that the major First Tier powers will conclude that they do not have sufficient interests in these conflicts to put their forces at risk.

UN-sponsored or organized operations do not represent the only options available. In cases such as Bosnia, collective action may be organized by some other mechanism such as NATO (in the Bosnian case with UN blessing, and in Kosovo as well). Although the imprimatur of the UN officially backed the U.S. "intervasion" (part intervention, part invasion) of Haiti in 1994, the action was essentially unilateral by the United States, as was Russian intervention in Georgia in 1993 to help the government put down the attempted Abkhazian secession.

The centrality of the United States in this process cannot be overstated, for two reasons. First, the United States not only possesses the world's most powerful military forces, but it is also among the most trusted as peacemaker and hence is in great demand when the peace is breached. Moreover, the United States has the world's only logistics capability that can rapidly insert forces and equipment into conflicts worldwide, meaning U.S. support is necessary for the system to mount a sizable response in much of the world.

U.S. Marines search a building in Mogadishu for suspected snipers during the UN intervention in Somalia in the early 1990s. Formation of a UN military force able to carry out missions involving actual combat would require the participation of the United States, the only country with the necessary military projection capabilities.

Third, the emerging role of the United States, buttressed by its military might, has become that of peacemaker. It is commonplace for the United States to act as a broker for dissenting parties to negotiate their differences in places as physically and intellectually diverse as the Arab-Israeli conflict in the Middle East, Northern Ireland, and Bosnia. A major reason for this is the ability of the United States to act as a guarantor of peace settlements it helps to reach, including, in cases like Bosnia, a military guarantee.

This discussion of the limits on collective security leads to a final preliminary question about the system: what is its deterrent value? Collective security is supposed to prevent and or at least moderate violent changes to the status quo. But given the evolving world situation, can it do so?

A preliminary assessment must be mixed. The two types of violence prevalent in the Second Tier are differentially amenable to deterrent threats. Regional conflicts involving cross-border invasions are the kind of conflicts with which collective security is designed to deal; and the prevention of forcible alterations of the political map, such as Saddam Hussein's attempted annexation of Kuwait, may be effectively deterred by international action. Indirect evidence that such a dynamic is at work is the fact that regional conflicts have become dormant. Since the Iraqi invasion of Kuwait, the only cross-border fighting has been the rather minor action between Ecuador and Peru over disputed territory. (The evidence is indirect because we cannot demonstrate conflict would have occurred in the absence of some deterrent force.) On the other hand, there is little—or no—evidence to suggest that groups within countries are dissuaded from violence by the prospect of international action, especially when the form of that action is itself uncertain. In these cases, military intervention will almost always face uncertain prospects.

Despite these flare-ups in the Second Tier, the problem of maintaining reasonable peace in the emerging system seems less daunting than it did in the Cold War. Current Second Tier instabilities pale in comparison with the problem of preventing nuclear war between the superpowers; and for the time being at least, the problem of global war and peace has moved off center stage.

Change Agents

Domestically and internationally, a new set of dynamics born in the latter stages of the Cold War and contributing to its demise has emerged to help shape the future. Each of these dynamics is discussed in some detail in subsequent chapters. For present purposes, they can simply be introduced.

The dual political phenomena sweeping larger and larger parts of the globe are democratization and national self-determination. Both arise from the gradual demise of authoritarian regimes in the former communist world and the developing countries. Once given a voice, people clamor for one or the other or both. However, these goals are not the same and not always compatible.

Democratization, with people freely participating in their governments and expressing their views, has been a hopeful sign where it has appeared, for instance in Eastern Europe and much of Latin America. Unfortunately, however, freedom of expression has proved to have a darker side in some places, manifested in the demands of national groups to make nation and state coterminous, often at the expense of other groups alongside whom the dominant group had existed for long periods of time. Bosnia and Kosovo reflected this phenomenon at its most nightmarish; there are also numerous prospects for new or continued ethnic strife elsewhere—in parts of the former Soviet Union (such as Armenia and Azerbaijan) and in Africa and Asia.

This social phenomenon is exclusionary nationalism, and it is a major problem with which the evolving system must come to grips. First, the resulting conflicts are one of the major threats to overall systemic stability. Arguably, such conflicts in Second Tier countries are more irritants than anything else to the First Tier, but their solution would add to tranquillity. Second, as discussed in Chapter 2, the rise of global television makes these phenomena, especially the most garish, blood-soaked atrocities associated with them, extremely public wherever the ubiquitous camera wanders. Ethnic cleansing in Sudan may not affect the daily lives of people in upstate New York, but it may be hard to ignore if it is graphically displayed on the evening news. In addition, a new breed of internal conflict, which we will call new internal war, has emerged, where violence lacks overt political purpose and is directed at civilian populations either to destabilize the political order or to promote systematic criminal behavior. These criminal insurgencies and narco-insurgencies will be discussed in Chapter 5.

Economically, the growing globalization of the economy is a phenomenon poorly understood but with an extreme dynamism. Economic activity no longer merely occurs within a national context, certainly not for the states of the First Tier. Whether the interdependence that results is good or bad is debatable; whether it exists is not. Moreover, it is important to consider what an economy for which national boundaries are largely meaningless implies for the structure of the state system.

Internationally, the relationship between the First and Second Tiers will be critical to the future of the system. The Second Tier will remain unstable at least until it begins to share in the general prosperity of the First Tier, if it ever does. Historically, the Cold War overlay meant that the superpowers could exercise some restraining influence on possible destabilizing developments in client states. The nature of the new relationship between the First and Second Tier states, and the importance that will be attached to it, remains uncertain.

Critical Events

If there have yet been defining events in the new order, they and their meanings have not been obvious. We have chosen two possible defining events to mention in passing. Operation Desert Storm may be a harbinger of how the system will react to international challenges of the future. Analysts of international affairs continue to debate whether that intervention was a last act of the old order or the first act of the post–Cold War order. The Bosnian war, on the other hand, represents the darker side of the new system. One hopes that the precedent set by the forcible Serbian and Croatian annexation of much of Bosnia will not be the one that is followed in the future.

Changing Contours of the World Order

The process of change that has been described in this chapter continues as the post–Cold War system continues to evolve and form. For the greater part of the 1990s, the theme was overwhelmingly positive, as authoritarian governments disappeared and representative governments with vibrant market economies took their place. Nowhere was this more evident than in the western Hemisphere. In 1994 and 1998, the Summits of the Americas were attended by the heads of states of all the democratically elected governments of the Hemisphere; of all the states of the region, only Cuba was excluded using that criterion.

Events in 1998, however, demonstrated that the evolution to a world of market democracies is neither linear nor inevitable. As noted earlier, Russia found itself in an economic and financial crisis that threatened the vitality of the political system as the value of the ruble free fell and the savings of Russians evaporated. Some analysts saw this as the beginning of the end of the spread of market democracy: if a country as consequential as Russia could not make the transition to the values of market democracy, was it really a universal trend? Others, more hopeful, believed the crisis would eventually work itself out. The ultimate resolution will have an impact on the structure, and stability, of the system.

At the same time, the financial crisis that began in eastern Asia in 1997 and spread to places such as Japan and even the United States in 1998 punctured some of the optimism about the continuing growth of the globalizing economy. If nothing else, the crisis in Asia revealed financial systems that were generally underregulated and in need of sharper limits on how money was handled and spent. The question of whether the adoption of American-style or some other form of oversight would evolve is a major concern. As it eventually spread to and affected the U.S. stock market, the crisis also revealed that the world's economies are interconnected in negative as well as positive ways.

The effects of these crises dampened some of the general optimism about world politics that has been a dominant theme of the "go-go" 1990s. What does the future hold as we enter the new millennium? Will we rebound to the growing prosperity of the 1990s, or do the 2000s have a dimmer prospect? It is a contour of change that we will watch with great interest.

Review

This chapter provided a framework and examination of the historical evolution of the modern international system. In the process, the following points were made:

1. The international system based on state sovereignty emerged from the settlement of the Thirty Years War in 1648 and in its original form lasted until the French Revolution of 1789. This was a period dominated by absolute monarchies that had few political disagreements and few military resources. As a result, wars were infrequent and less bloody than in subsequent times.

2. In 1815, following the Napoleonic wars, the Concert of Europe sought to recreate the old system for the nineteenth century. The spread of nationalism, the industrial revolution, and great social change made the period turbulent domestically but thereby discouraged international conflict, at least initially. The Concert system effectively came to an end in the Franco-Prussian War of 1870, after which Germany and France could no longer align. Each organized its own military alliance, and the two eventually clashed in World War I.

3. The system between the world wars was also one of considerable instability. The punitive peace settlement imposed on Germany ensured that universal support for the status quo was not present and helped to make the collective security system of the League of Nations ineffective. A series of provocations by Japan, Germany, and Italy created the momentum for World War II.

4. The outcome of World War II left only two states, the United States and the Soviet Union, with residual power to reorganize the system. Because their wartime collaboration could not be sustained, the result was a bipolar Cold War system wherein superpower competition was the major feature. The growing irrelevance of the Cold War in the Third World, the high cost of military competition, and the economic failure of the communist world led to its breakup and thus to the end of the system, culminating in the peaceful dissolution of the Soviet Union at the end of 1991.

5. The post–Cold War world is in a state of flux as new patterns emerge. In some ways, two subsystems, the First and Second Tiers, are the dominant features of the new system. The First Tier is composed of the wealthy, technologically advanced, market-based democracies, whereas the old Second and Third Worlds constitute the Second Tier. A major question is how the tiers will interact with one another.

Suggested Readings

Alperowitz, Gar, and Kai Bird. "The Centrality of the Bomb." *Foreign Policy* 94 (spring 1994): 3–20.

Bialer, Seweryn. "The Passing of the Soviet Order?" *Survival* 32, 2 (March/April 1990): 107–120.

Borden, William Liscum. *There Will Be No Time: The Revolution in Strategy.* New York: Macmillan, 1946.

Brodie, Bernard. *The Absolute Weapon: Atomic Power and World Order.* New York: Harcourt, Brace, 1946.

—. *War and Politics.* New York: Macmillan, 1973.

Claude, Inis L., Jr. *Swords into Plowshares: The Problems and Progress of International Organization,* 4th ed. New York: Random House, 1971.

Deibel, Terry. "Internal Affairs and International Relations in the Post–Cold War World." *Washington Quarterly* 16, 3 (summer 1993): 13–36.

Fukuyama, Francis. *The End of History and the Last Man.* New York: Free Press, 1992.

Gaddis, John Lewis. *The United States and the End of the Cold War: Implications, Reconsiderations, Provocations.* New York: Oxford University Press, 1992.

Gorbachev, Mikhail S. *The Coming Century of Peace.* New York: Richardson and Stierman, 1986.

Haass, Richard N. "Military Force: A User's Guide." *Foreign Policy* 96 (fall 1994): 21–36.

Kaplan, Morton A. *System and Process in International Politics.* New York: John Wiley, 1957.

Kissinger, Henry A. "Reflections on Containment." *Foreign Affairs* 73, 3 (May/June 1994): 113–30.

Krauthammer, Charles. "The Unipolar Moment." *Foreign Affairs* 70, 1 (1990/91): 23–33.

Laqueur, Walter. *The Long Road to Freedom: Russia and Glasnost.* New York: Charles Scribner's Sons, 1989.

Rosecrance, Richard. *Action and Reaction in World Politics.* Boston: Little, Brown, 1963.

Snow, Donald M., and Dennis M. Drew. *From Lexington to Desert Storm: War and the American Experience.* Armonk, NY: M. E. Sharpe, 1994.

—. *The Shape of the Future: The Post–Cold War World,* 2nd ed. Armonk, NY: M. E. Sharpe, 1995.

Stoessinger, John G. *Why Nations Go to War,* rev. ed. New York: St. Martin's Press, 1985.

Foreign Policy: Decision-Making

PREVIEW

This chapter examines the decision-making process in international affairs. It begins with an idealized model of rational decision-making, focusing on the clear specification of state objectives at hand, a realistic appraisal of existing threats to those interests, and a careful assessment of the types and amount of power needed to counter those threats. Next, we examine a series of human pitfalls that frequently lie between decision-makers and the ideal model of rationality. We conclude with a case study analyzing the details of foreign policy decision-making in the international relief effort in Somalia in the early 1990s.

KEY CONCEPTS

groupthink
false analogy
cognitive dissonance
personality idiosyncrasies

cultural factors
Deputies Committee
Operation Restore Hope

OUTLINE

In Chapters 2 and 3 we established the historical and systemic context within which international relations occur. While acknowledging the growing role of nonstate actors such as multinational corporations and intergovernmental organizations, we believe that the state will continue for the foreseeable future to retain its position as the principal wellspring of action in international affairs. We need, then, to provide some insights into the ways that states establish their foreign policy goals, the ways their leaders make decisions intended to attain those goals, and the array of psychological and organizational factors that all too often prevent leaders from basing those crucial decisions on accurate perceptions and ordinary standards of rationality.

Foreign Policy-Making: The Rational Ideal

While clearly much in human affairs is irrational, or at least nonrational, rationality remains an ideal, both a goal toward which human beings aspire and a yardstick by which they measure their current performance. In the field of foreign policy-making, it is possible to stipulate the elements of an ideal, rational policy process. First, decision-makers must translate the vague concept of the national interest into more clearly articulated policy objectives. Second, once they have determined interests and objectives, they must continually maintain a sophisticated understanding of existing threats to those interests and objectives. Third, they must maintain and apply in a disciplined way the appropriate means to protect against those threats.

Summary

The Three Elements of Rational Foreign Policy-Making

1. Clear specification of the policy objectives being sought
2. Accurate reading of existing threats to attaining goals
3. Disciplined maintenance and use of the instruments of power needed to counter those threats

Defining Objectives

Regarding the clear specification of precise national interests and objectives, we acknowledge the debt owed by foreign policy analysts to Donald Nuechterlein, whose books and articles have done much to promote greater clarity about the various types of national objectives and the relative priority to be accorded to them. Nuechterlein's well-known national interest matrix is reproduced in Table 4.1.

In the left-hand column, Nuechterlein takes the vague concept of the national interest and divides it into four distinct components. "Defense of the homeland" is, of course, the bedrock of all national interests; once the national territory is lost, all other interests are rendered moot. "Economic well-being" is similarly a self-evident aspect of national interest. By "favorable world order," Nuechterlein means that it is very much in the self-interest of the United States, or any other state, to help promote a stable global order in which violence and aggression are less likely to occur. As a practical matter, doing so entails maintaining a balance of power in key regions, assisting the developing world in climbing out of poverty

Table 4.1 National Interest Matrix				
Basic Interest at Stake	**Intensity of Interest**			
	Survival	Vital	Major	Peripheral
Defense of the homeland				
Economic well-being				
Favorable world order				
Promotion of values				

Source: Donald E. Nuechterlein. *America Overcommitted: United States National Interests in the 1980's.* Lexington: University of Kentucky Press, 1985.

and desperation, and promoting greater support for international law and international institutions such as the United Nations. Finally, "promotion of values" acknowledges that it is indeed a legitimate interest for states to want to promote their cherished domestic values abroad. For the United States, this includes encouraging respect for human rights, encouraging freedom and democracy, and promoting the precepts of market economics.

A key point is that Nuechterlein has arranged these four constituent ingredients of the national interest in a hierarchical order of priority. While defense of the homeland is always a necessity whenever it is threatened, the promotion abroad of one's own values is an interest that is legitimate but not of such compelling necessity.

The top row of the matrix usefully points out that the four objectives of foreign policy specified in the left-hand column are experienced in varying degrees of seriousness from one circumstance to another. The most serious degree of intensity is clearly one that threatens the survival of the state, such as a major armed attack upon its territory and population. A "vital" interest is one whose vindication does not entail the survival of the state per se, but is of sufficient importance that states will ordinarily use force to protect it. In contrast, an interest deemed to be "major" in a given situation calls for a vigorous utilization of national resources to protect it, but those measures would stop short of the use of force. "Peripheral" interests, finally, are those whose loss would not entail serious harm to the state.

When one combines the four horizontal and four vertical categories, a certain clarity about the national interest in specific situations is attained. For example, the German threat to British territory—its homeland—in World War II presented British policy-makers with a survival issue. By contrast, when in 1983 Argentina attacked and seized the Falkland Islands, a British possession located off the eastern coast of South America, Britain's survival was not affected, but its credibility was. The successful British counterattack arose from the conviction that a vital interest was at stake.

Later in the chapter, we will examine in some detail a case study of national decision-making by many states in the face of the vicious Somalian civil war and subsequent mass starvation in the late 1980s and early 1990s. While animated by an admirable impulse to "do something," the United States proved unwilling to stay the course in Somalia once its soldiers sent there on a humanitarian relief mission became entangled in the complex web of clan violence that had created the mass famine in the first place. In part, the sudden change of heart of most Americans from an initial pride in the U.S. effort to bring relief to a starving people to a demand that the troops be withdrawn as soon as possible reflected the inability of either President Bush or President Clinton to articulate a persuasive case for a continued U.S. presence—a case grounded in a plausible argument that U.S. national interests in this situation would justify the deaths of American troops.

Neither the military security of the United States nor its economic well-being was remotely affected by Somalia's agony. A modest case could be made that the viability of United Nations multinational missions to international hot spots would be irreparably harmed by a precipitous withdrawal of U.S. forces, but that involved at most the rather vague objective of forging a more favorable world order. In the Somalian instance, the degree of U.S. interest at stake was certainly never more than "major."

Understanding Threats

As to the second requirement of a rational foreign policy—maintaining a sophisticated understanding of existing threats to the state's interests and objectives—we will explore more fully below how national policy-makers frequently misperceive the intentions of other states. For example, throughout the 1920s and 1930s the Western democracies consistently underestimated the threat posed by the emerging totalitarian regimes in Germany, Japan, Italy, and the Soviet Union. World War I had been waged at immense physical, emotional, and financial cost to Europeans, and neither the publics nor the leaders of Great Britain or France were inclined to believe that the ghastly experience of modern warfare might have to be undertaken once again. As late as 1939, Europe's democracies still sought to persuade themselves that Adolf Hitler's ambitions were limited in scope and could be satisfied by a policy of appeasement. In fact, of course, Hitler's ambitions were limitless. By the time that realization had sunk in across Europe, Hitler's neighbors were woefully unprepared to counter his aggression.

As for the United States, it had suffered much less in World War I but had interpreted the postwar settlement as a cynical reversion to traditional European power politics, devoid of moral content in its indifference to such cherished U.S. ideals as national self-determination and democracy. Viewing itself as a fortress protected on both sides by vast oceans, and the outside world as corrupt and unworthy of American sacrifice, the United States retreated into isolationism. As a result, when the Japanese attack on Pearl Harbor, followed quickly by Hitler's declaration of war on the United States, demonstrated that Americans could not remain aloof from the global struggle against totalitarian aggression, they were caught almost entirely unprepared for war. The point, once again, is that rational foreign policy-making depends critically on decision-makers' maintaining a sophisticated and realistic comprehension of threats to their country's goals and interests.

It is as dangerous to overestimate the dangers one confronts abroad as it is to underestimate them. In the early 1980s, for example, the Iranian regime led by the Ayatollah Khomeini shared a pervasive conviction that the outside world was determined to destroy Iran's newly installed Islamic theocracy. Fear of the world beyond their borders helped Iran's leaders to justify their support of international terrorist groups aimed at striking out against the perceived foes of Iran in particular and of Islam in general. Iran's support of terrorism led to its growing isolation from ordinary international economic, cultural, and political dealings and thus helped to create the very hostility its leaders had feared. Together with the lengthy and ruinous war with neighboring Iraq in the 1980s—in which most of the rest of the world sided with the Iraqis—this isolation devastated the Iranian economy.

Overestimating the danger posed by the outside world can harm a country's interests as much as underestimating it. The Islamic theocracy established in Iran by the Ayatollah Ruhollah Khomeini was so fearful of foreign threats to its existence that it became a sponsor of terrorism aimed at its supposed enemies. This policy only increased Iran's international isolation and contributed to the devastation of its economy.

Maintaining and Applying Means

Third and finally, a rational foreign policy requires the disciplined maintenance and application of appropriate means to counter the threats facing the state's interests. In Chapter 2 we discussed in detail the instruments of power in international relations. As noted above, the western democracies were unprepared for World War II because their leaders badly underestimated the aggressive intentions of the Germans and the Japanese. In that instance, the pertinent policy instrument was military capability, and its absence at the outset of the war resulted in needless Allied losses.

However, not all threats to a state's interests involve physical force, and thus the threatened or actual use of force is not always an appropriate response. This generalization is becoming ever more applicable today in the relations among the industrial democracies that make up the First Tier. Certainly Japan's economic well-being has been harmed by a renaissance of U.S. scientific, technological, managerial, investment, and manufacturing capability. However, it is difficult to imagine a scenario under which Japanese leaders, alarmed by their loss of global market share in critical industries, would contemplate an armed assault upon U.S. territory, assets, or citizens. Similarly, the enormous advantage that the United States enjoys in military capability over the Japanese has little relevance in trade talks aimed at persuading Japan to open its markets further to foreign goods and capital. The Japanese simply know that whatever the Americans' economic frustrations, they are not about to attack Japan as an element of economic diplomacy.

Which types of policy instruments are most useful? Generally speaking, they are those that fit into the same category as the threat they are intended to counter. Military threats are best countered by maintaining and employing appropriate levels of military power. Economic challenges are usually best met through economic countermeasures. In the case of states that refuse to allow foreign competitors fair access to their markets, for example, an effective and nonviolent policy often involves imposing prohibitive tariffs or quotas against the products of the offending states. In a world of multiple and multiplying threats—ranging from arms proliferation to terrorism to economic rivalries to environmental degradation to disease epidemics—the states that will be best equipped to vindicate their interests are those that possess both the resources and the political will to maintain and employ a diverse and balanced repertoire of policy tools, including military, economic, and political instruments of power.

Barriers to Rationality in Foreign Policy Decision-Making

We have looked in some detail at the intellectual foundations on which foreign policy decisions should ideally be built. In practice, though, our rather lofty standard of rationality is clearly not always met. Some foreign policy decisions seem downright irrational, while others are merely obtuse. A part of our job as analysts is to try to identify the things that get in the way of policy-making rationality. In doing so, we not only will gain a good deal of personal clarity but also might promote greater policy rationality in the future by alerting decision-makers to the potential pitfalls that we have uncovered. In this spirit, then, we look now at five distinct barriers to rationality in the foreign policy-making process.

Summary ━━━━━━━━━━━━━━━━━━━━━━━━
Barriers to Rational Foreign Policy

1. Groupthink
2. False analogy
3. Cognitive dissonance
4. Personality idiosyncrasies
5. Cultural factors

Groupthink

The first barrier to rationality is what the psychologist Irving Janis termed "groupthink" in his famous book *Victims of Groupthink*. Janis, who had done considerable work in the study of social group dynamics, first began thinking about the possible relevance of his findings to the understanding of foreign policy failures while reading an account of the Bay of Pigs invasion, the Kennedy administration's disastrous 1961 attempt to topple Cuba's Fidel Castro. "How could bright, shrewd men like John F. Kennedy and his advisers be taken in by the CIA's stupid, patchwork plan?" asked Janis. "I began to wonder whether some kind of psychological contagion, similar to social conformity phenomena observed in studies of small groups, had interfered with their mental alertness."

Case in Point

MacArthur and the Missing Chinese

A classic example of the consequences of group-think in foreign policy was the failure of U.S. policy-makers to anticipate the entry of China into the Korean War. In the fall of 1950, U.S.-led allied forces under the sponsorship of the United Nations were pressing northward in North Korea, whose troops had invaded South Korea but then had been driven back into their own territory. As the allies advanced, they came ever closer to Chinese territory, which is separated from North Korea by the Yalu River. The allied commander, U.S. General Douglas MacArthur, supremely confident of his own abilities and wisdom, was persuaded that the Chinese would never enter the war, given that (1) MacArthur had no intention of crossing the Yalu into China and (2) the Chinese, after years of foreign invasion and civil war, were thought to be too weak to mount a serious offensive against the technologically superior Americans.

To the Chinese, however, the available evidence seemed to point towards an allied military drive into China itself. Accordingly, the Chinese army began preparations to cross the

General Douglas McArthur in South Korea in 1950.

Once aroused, his curiosity led to a work that has made a major contribution to understanding why policy-makers are too often deflected away from the path of rationality. While Janis's work focused on the U.S. foreign policy-making process, there is every reason to believe that the distorting effects of group dynamics on the decision-making processes are potential traps for policy-makers in every country.

Janis defines groupthink as "a mode of thinking that people engage in when they are deeply involved in a cohesive in-group, when the members' striving for unanimity override their motivation to realistically appraise alternative courses of action." This phenomenon is something that everyone has undoubtedly encountered; it is simply natural to want to remain on good terms with one's own "in crowd," and so one is subtly influenced to go along with the group's prevailing beliefs and behaviors, even to the point, sometimes, of setting

MacArthur and the Missing Chinese *(continued)*

Yalu and defeat the coalition, before it could reach Chinese soil.

Why did U.S. intelligence fail to detect China's preparations to enter the war? In large part, the pernicious effects of groupthink were at work. Given MacArthur's belief that China would never take on the Americans militarily and his towering stature and influence within his command, his intelligence agents confined their efforts largely to looking for evidence of large-scale, conventional massing of Chinese forces just north of the Yalu. When reconnaissance failed to detect such evidence, U.S. policymakers felt assured that MacArthur had been right: the coalition could safely conduct armed operations against North Korea right at China's doorstep without fear that the Chinese would intervene.

The Chinese, however, had positioned their forces in small, dispersed units not easily detected by the intelligence capabilities of the day. When they did cross the Yalu in mass late in 1950, they caught the allied forces by surprise, succeeded in driving them back to the 38th parallel (the border between North and South Korea, where the war had begun), inflicted heavy casual-

ties, and transformed what had appeared to be a quick allied victory into a bitter stalemate that would last until 1953 and would poison U.S.-Chinese relations for the next two decades.

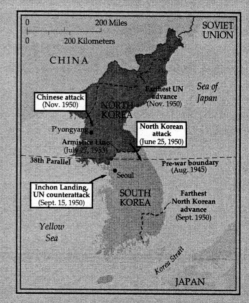

The Korean War

aside doubts about their wisdom. To speak out would undermine the solidarity of the group, thus marking the dissenter as something of an "outsider."

While this familiar syndrome may be harmless enough in shaping the clothing tastes of adolescents, it can, in the world of foreign policy, lead to genuine tragedy. Janis believes that this is precisely what happened not only in the Bay of Pigs fiasco but also in other U.S. foreign policy blunders—the ill-considered 1950 decision to drive North Korean forces not only out of South Korea but to the Chinese border, the failure to prevent the Japanese attack on Pearl Harbor in 1941, and the escalation of the Vietnam War in 1965. In each case, he argues, otherwise intelligent and responsible people led the country into disaster because they allowed the normal human desire for solidarity within their small decision-making circle to override their capacity for independent and critical judgment.

Apparently, the greater the cohesiveness of a group, the greater is the risk of groupthink and its attendant distortions. Since it is unrealistic to expect decision-makers to give up the psychological comfort afforded by a congenial, supportive circle of colleagues, those seeking to minimize this risk must look instead at reforming the way in which group members interact. According to Janis, there are a number of things that decision-makers can consciously do to avoid the negative effects of groupthink. In particular, he urges policy-makers to do three things: they should (1) not only tolerate but actively encourage each group member to think critically and freely voice any objections or doubts, (2) remain impartial—or at least appear to be impartial—when initiating a policy-making process, and (3) assign several separate groups to work on the same topic, each independent of the others.

False Analogy

A second source of misperception and irrationality in foreign policy-making is false analogy. Reasoning by analogy—that is, trying to analyze one situation by falling back on the "lessons" learned in another—is something everyone does at times. Properly done, it can be helpful by alerting policy-makers to possible dangers and opportunities ahead of time. Sometimes, though, the "lessons" are more hindrance than help, obstructing rational decision-making more than assisting it. When insights drawn from one occasion are applied to another that is quite different, the ability to interpret the situation at hand and act appropriately in it is undercut.

One of the best accounts of this phenomenon in the field of foreign policy is historian Ernest May's book *Lessons of the Past: The Use and Misuse of History in American Foreign Policy.* May argues that "policymakers ordinarily use history badly. When resorting to an analogy, they tend to seize the first that comes to mind. These habits can have important consequences, for they can affect the way statesmen understand their situations and problems." In his case studies of World War II, the Cold War, Korea, and Vietnam, May shows how important leaders were sometimes influenced by their simplistic references to the past. As a result, he believes, U.S. foreign policy decision-making often suffers from an insufficient grounding in reality.

An interesting question in this context is how U.S. leaders will use the experience of the Vietnam War as a guide to future actions. In light of the bitter divisions and disillusionment it caused in American politics and society, all would agree that "another Vietnam" must be avoided at all costs. But what, precisely, does that mean? Except in the most literal sense that U.S. leaders are not about to send 500,000 soldiers to fight for an uncertain cause in a distant land called Vietnam, is it really clear what lessons should be drawn from that painful, humiliating experience?

Thoughtful analysts who have tried to salvage some practical wisdom from the wreckage of that war have been unable to agree on the meaning of the evidence. To some, the lasting lesson of Vietnam is that the United States should not commit its forces, funds, and national reputation to armed conflict in distant lands in the absence of clear and immediate threats to U.S. vital interests. Others conclude that whenever the United States does commit itself to military operations, it must do so from a position of decisive superiority. Overwhelming U.S. force must be brought to bear against adversaries, they argue, so as to shorten the conflict and limit American casualties.

What the American public will not tolerate, all agree, is another protracted war that consumes the lives of the country's young, diverts vast amounts of its wealth away from productive investment, and has at best only a vague relationship to the vindication of U.S. national interests. In that sense, U.S. leaders will surely go to great lengths to avoid "another Vietnam."

A classic example of a political leader couching policy decisions in false analogies is found in President Clinton's March 24, 1999, address to the American people. The purpose of the speech was to announce the initiation of NATO air strikes against Yugoslav Serbs engaged in a brutal campaign of "ethnic cleansing" against the Muslim ethnic Albanians who had for centuries lived in the Yugoslav province of Kosovo. In truth, the NATO campaign was neither more nor less than a humanitarian effort by prosperous western democracies to prevent the brutish Yugoslav leader, Slobodan Milosevic, from conducting a campaign of terror and genocide against a vulnerable minority. But President Clinton, perhaps believing that the American people would not support an armed intervention in a distant land of no strategic significance to the United States, chose to couch his policy in the imagery of gruesome geostrategic catastrophes. "Sarajevo, the capital of neighboring Bosnia, is where World War I began," he intoned gravely. Furthermore, "World War II and the Holocaust engulfed this region." Two devastating world wars and the Holocaust are powerful analogies indeed.

The problem with the President's rhetoric is that the events in Yugoslavia in 1999 bore no relation whatever to Europe's twin catastrophes of the twentieth century. In a rebuttal in *Newsweek* soon after Clinton's remarks, Henry Kissinger stated that "World War I started in the Balkans not as a result of ethnic conflicts but for precisely the opposite reason: because outside powers intervened in a local conflict." Moreover, "The Second World War did not start in the Balkans," Kissinger wrote, "much less as a result of ethnic conflicts."

While Clinton's rhetoric succeeded in its short-term goal of winning the support of the American people for the policy that the United States and its NATO allies were embarking on, it did all too little to provide the nation with a sustainable, long-term rationale for staying the course in an ethnic conflict in which hopes of a lasting victory through air power would inevitably prove illusory. Six times in his speech, Clinton invoked the concept of America's "interests" in Yugoslavia whose vindication required military action, but nowhere did he attempt a serious explanation of just what precisely those interests are. However one judges U.S. participation in a NATO campaign on behalf of a persecuted minority in Yugoslavia, the truth of the matter is that America's interests, strictly speaking, were tangential at best. Nothing that might transpire in Yugoslavia would touch remotely on American security and economic well-being. By casting a defensible humanitarian effort in the grandiose false analogy of yet another world war emanating from Europe, President Clinton did little to help the American people understand the true significance of the armed undertaking he was summoning them to support.

Did Clinton and his policy-making team base their decision-making on the false analogies contained in the emotional speech? To answer that question, we will have to await the appearance of Clinton's memoirs, along with those of National Security Advisor Sandy Berger, Secretary of State Madeleine Albright, and Secretary of Defense William Cohen.

Cognitive Dissonance

In his classic work *A Theory of Cognitive Dissonance,* psychologist Leon Festinger demonstrated the natural tendency of the human mind subconsciously to minimize cognitive dissonance, or conflict between its existing beliefs and new information it encounters.

Festinger summarizes his central hypotheses as follows: "1. The existence of dissonance, being psychologically uncomfortable, will motivate the person to try to reduce dissonance and achieve consonance. 2. When dissonance is present, in addition to trying to reduce it, the person will actively avoid situations and information which would likely increase the dissonance."

For example, imagine citizens of the former Soviet Union who held deep-seated beliefs in Marxist-Leninist theory. When confronted with clear evidence that Soviet society was dysfunctional, as evidenced by widespread alcoholism, alienation, and poverty, they would have a difficult time reconciling the evidence of Marxism in practice with their cherished attachment to Marxist theory. They might, for example, attribute the symptoms of social decay to forces not related to Marxism (such as the sinister efforts of capitalist states to destroy the cradle of communism) or persuade themselves that the problem was a failure by Soviet leaders to apply Marxist theory stringently enough to the running of Soviet society.

A similar process makes it difficult for Americans to hold rational discussions about issues such as gun control. Given the inherent tension between a broadly shared belief in maximum individual freedom and the all-too-apparent evidence of the devastating consequences of such freedom in the form of a permissive gun policy, many resolve the cognitive dissonance they experience by attributing the high rate of firearms violence to causes other than the extreme ease by which virtually anyone in the United States can acquire a gun. "Permissive judges," they may conclude, are the root of the problem, or perhaps the disintegration of traditional values in inner cities. By whatever mental path, they—like virtually everyone—unconsciously seek to reduce the dissonance, or tension, between a deeply held preexisting belief on the one hand, and incoming information on the other.

In the making of foreign policy, the subtle workings of cognitive dissonance often hamper the attainment of policy rationality by distorting decision-makers' perceptions of evidence, sometimes with fateful consequences. A recent example of this phenomenon was provided by the decision of Iraq's President Saddam Hussein to invade Kuwait in 1990. His belief that the United States would be paralyzed by the memory of its disastrous intervention in Vietnam as well as his discussions with U.S. Ambassador April Glaspie before the invasion had led him to believe that the United States would not act against his aggression. His belief was so firm that he dismissed repeated later U.S. warnings against such an action. Moreover, Saddam downplayed other evidence that his aggression would not succeed. Virtually every other country in the region was on record as opposing an Iraqi seizure of Kuwait. Saddam also failed to recognize the significance of the end of the Cold War, which allowed the formation of a large international coalition to oppose aggression under UN auspices. In the event, of course, the coalition drove Iraq out of Kuwait and back into its own territory.

Personality Idiosyncrasies

Yet another barrier to foreign policy rationality lies in personality idiosyncrasies, or unique traits of individual policy-makers. A classic example was Soviet leader Joseph Stalin. At the onset of the Cold War in the late 1940s, whatever strategic and ideological differences existed between the Soviet Union and the West were greatly exacerbated by the fact that Stalin was a deeply disturbed man whose grasp of reality was at best tenuous. Stalin's chronic paranoia and brutality have been amply documented. Persuaded that enemies were everywhere—at home and abroad—and that the best way to deal with those enemies was

Case in Point

Secretary of State Madeleine Albright

Personality characteristics do not, of course, always inhibit rational foreign policy-making. A case in point is the Secretary of State in the second Clinton presidency, Madeleine Albright. A Czech-born refugee and survivor of a devastating divorce, Albright rose through the foreign policy ranks, first as a professor at Georgetown and then as U.S. Ambassador to the United Nations. Her candor is refreshing: "I'm not that smart," she says, "but I work very hard."

Albright is known for her bluntness. When Cuban fighters shot down two unarmed anti-Castro civilian planes, she uttered a memorable line involving the Spanish curse word for testicles: "frankly, this is not *cojones*, this is cowardice." Many United Nations delegates received her remark negatively, arguing that it was unbecoming for a woman to use the language of men in the locker room. Despite her idiosyncra-

cies, many in the Clinton administration think highly of Albright's performance as Secretary of State.

through brute force or the threat of force, he contributed greatly to the atmosphere of mutual suspicion and misperception that characterized both sides during the Cold War years.

Another example of the effects of personal idiosyncrasy on foreign policy was the case of the late Achmad Sukarno of Indonesia. A person of immense charisma, Sukarno led the nationalist movement that in 1945 forced the Dutch to grant independence to the vast Indonesian archipelago, made up of 14,000 islands and 300 different ethnic groups. From 1945 until he was formally deposed in 1968, Sukarno served as the new state's first president. The diversity of ethnic, regional, and ideological forces within Indonesia meant that Sukarno's grip on power was tenuous, and many of his political maneuverings, including those in foreign policy, can be explained as rational responses to these divisions and the lack of a clear national identity. But many were also a reflection of Sukarno's idiosyncrasies, especially his famously moody temperament and his grandiose dreams of thrusting his new state onto center stage in world affairs.

These two forces converged in Sukarno's policy of confrontation against the newly created neighboring state of Malaysia from 1963 to 1966. The policy involved some high-stakes moves by Indonesia, including provocation of a series of border incidents,

Indonesian President Achmad Sukarno (*left*) with the country's army chief of staff in 1965. Sukarno's mercurial temperament and grandiose self-image led him to conduct a dangerous war of nerves with newly independent Malaysia in the mid–1960s.

intimidation of Malaysian fishermen by Indonesian vessels, and landings of Indonesian troops on the Malaysian coast for missions of harassment and intimidation. Sukarno sought to justify these actions by arguing that Malaysia represented a pro-western British creation that would serve as a strategic wedge against Indonesian interests.

Given his chronic need to shore up his domestic base, provoking a foreign crisis with Malaysia was in some sense a rational action; he could rally his people and call for restraint by opponents on the grounds that a national crisis was at hand. The greatest factor explaining Sukarno's policy, however, was his own personality. He led his state to conduct a dangerous game with Malaysia because, as a strong anticolonialist, he was personally offended by its creation. Also, he was looking for a dramatic foreign undertaking because he believed that presiding over his state during a foreign crisis would enhance his own personal (as opposed to political) reputation among Indonesians. Sukarno's policy was thus a mix of rational domestic political calculation and nonrational personality forces that included grandiose egoism and emotional volatility.

Sukarno's tolerant attitude toward the Indonesian Communist Party ultimately led to his downfall. In 1965 the Communists attempted a coup, killing a number of key military officers in the process. In turn, the military launched its own successful coup. Once their power was consolidated in 1966, the military leaders decided to call off Sukarno's policy of confrontation with Malaysia, a policy they concluded had been more damaging to Indonesia than to its supposed enemy.

As for Sukarno, he had to bear the indignity—made all the worse by his grandiose view of himself—of being demoted in 1966 and dismissed from the government altogether in 1968. Indonesia's leaders since then have been less quixotic, and so have been able to lead their country on a policy of regional cooperation.

Cultural Factors

In referring to cultural factors as barriers to rational perception and decision-making, it is worth stressing that we are not arguing that a country's culture per se necessarily undercuts the rationality of its foreign policy. The point, precisely, is that cultural differences sometimes lead to misperceptions that in turn hamper the ability of policy-makers to develop appropriate and rational policies to deal with other peoples.

Even if Stalin had been blessed with a more serene and lucid nature, for example, it is likely that his cultural conditioning while growing up in the Russian Empire would have left him deeply suspicious about the intentions of outsiders, especially the western powers. Lacking natural geographic barriers, Russians throughout history have endured immense suffering at the hands of a succession of foreign invaders, ranging from the Mongols in the thirteenth century through Napoleon's forces in the nineteenth century to two German armies in the twentieth century. The "lessons of history" incorporated into Russian culture are that the outside world is a fearful source of predators out to take over Russia and the corollary that Russia can best maintain its security by surrounding itself with buffers backed by massive armed might. While both sides must ultimately accept some share of responsibility for the outbreak of the Cold War, the combination of Stalin's advanced paranoia and the traditional Russian cultural view of the outside world as a place of lurking dangers clearly made post–World War II cooperation between the Soviets and the West much more difficult.

By becoming more fully knowledgeable about and appreciative of foreign cultures, policy-makers and their advisers are less likely to misperceive the "odd" behavior of others and thus are more likely to be able to remove one barrier to foreign policy rationality. For example, many Africans and Asians are highly sensitive to any real or imagined racial slight in international relations, particularly by Americans or Europeans. The reason is simple: throughout much of the last 500 years, westerners have exploited, dominated, and demeaned the peoples and cultures of Africa and Asia. Many Japanese, for example, believe that Japan is not fully accepted as an equal by western states because the Japanese are not Caucasians. As we will see in Chapter 7, Japanese foreign policy is influenced by racial considerations not only in this suspicion of the West but also, ironically, in the disdain of Japanese themselves for darker-skinned peoples.

In another example, the rationality of a country's policy toward China may suffer if policy-makers fail to take into account the traditional Chinese sense of superiority to the rest of the world. Throughout much of its long history, China regarded itself as the "Middle Kingdom" in its dealings with other Asian states; though a step below heaven, China was seen as clearly superior to its Asian neighbors. As the historian Daniel Boorstin put it, the Chinese have historically viewed theirs as "the one and only center of civilization" (quoted in Frank Gibney, *The Pacific Century*). Their characteristic attitude is captured in the famous reply made by China's emperor in 1793 to the British official who was seeking European-style trade and diplomatic relations. "Our celestial empire," he said, "possesses all things in abundance and wants for no product within its borders. There is, therefore, no need to import the manufactures of outside barbarians" (quoted in Gibney).

The emperor's attitude put China squarely within the sights of the rising Europeans, who in the eighteenth and nineteenth centuries experienced a dramatic surge of military and economic power due to the first industrial revolution. Between the mid-nineteenth and mid-twentieth centuries, China underwent the humiliation of foreign domination, political and social collapse, warlordism, civil war, invasion by Japan, and more civil war before the communist triumph and consolidation of authority in 1949. This bitter century only intensified China's traditional ethnocentrism and desire to withdraw from the outside world. Only since the political ascension of Deng Xiaoping in 1978 has China exhibited a wish to conduct normal trade and attract foreign tourism and investment. Beneath Deng's policy, however, was a profound sense that China is a special state to whom international norms do not fully apply. When they defy international standards of human rights or copyright and patent protection, China's leaders are influenced, in part, by a conviction that China is not obligated to follow the wishes of the westerners, who have been disproportionately influential in establishing such standards.

Case Study: *Somalia and the Do-Something Syndrome*

The response of the international community to the specter of mass starvation in the East African country of Somalia in the early 1990s serves as an intellectually useful—if depressing—case study of foreign policy decision-making. The case illustrates the complex welter of personal, ideological, and organizational factors that shape the various ways that key actors defined their respective interests, and hence their appropriate policies, amid the unfolding tragedy.

Certainly the magnitude of the tragedy can scarcely be exaggerated. Over 400,000 Somalis perished in what was essentially an artificial rather than a natural catastrophe. At the worst point, in late 1992, as many as 95 percent of Somalis suffered from some degree of malnutrition and more than 70 percent from severe malnutrition, according to the International Committee of the Red Cross. Hardest hit were the young: in the most affected regions, three-fourths of the children under five years old were lost to the ravages of hunger. In effect, an entire generation was decimated or profoundly debilitated.

The Making of a Tragedy

Somalia, an impoverished land of 4.5 million people, wraps around the peninsula known as the Horn of Africa, on the continent's eastern coast. It has yet to develop a mature sense of national self-identity that permeates the thinking of its citizens. Instead, most Somalis are accustomed to thinking more in terms of their clan affiliation than of the more abstract notion of the state. It is within these traditional boundaries of clan affiliation that much of ordinary Somali politics occurs, and the country's political dynamics are often driven by the ever-shifting rivalries and alliances among clan leaders.

The overthrow of the dictator Siad Barre in January 1991 opened the door to a nightmare of declining internal order, chronic violence, and growing hunger, sickness, and mass misery. Somalia's dozen clans increasingly resorted to the coercive capabilities of their own militias as the jostling among them grew in the face of a nationwide power vacuum. By late 1991, the two most powerful clan leaders—a wealthy Mogadishu businessman, Ali Mahdi Mohammed, and a shrewd military tactician, General Mohamed Farah Aidid—each sought to establish personal primacy over the entire country via the militias under their commands. The fighting between the two clan leaders soon plunged Somalia into an all-out civil war.

Meanwhile, the vagaries of nature conspired to make the lives of ordinary Somalis even more dangerous and miserable. Drought had once again returned to northeast Africa, and as its toll began to mount, more and more Somalis fled their parched homelands and villages in a desperate search for food, thus exposing tens of thousands of them more directly to the effects of the war.

A Somali mother and daughter at an international aid agency feeding center in 1992. Over 400,000 Somalis starved to death in the early 1990s, a disaster caused largely by political forces rather than a shortage of food.

The International Community's Passivity

By 1990 the consequences of drought were unmistakable throughout much of Somalia. Television images of starving children with distended bellies and sunken eyes bore testimony to the unfolding human misery. As the horrors became apparent, there was a broad expectation among international relations specialists around the globe that the United Nations would mobilize its institutional capabilities and its moral leadership on behalf of a large-scale relief effort. The 1984–85 Ethiopian famine had galvanized international sensibilities to the specter of mass starvation, and by the early 1990s it was widely assumed that the UN had absorbed the lessons of its widely criticized ineffectuality in the Ethiopian case. What of the major powers who possessed both the material wherewithal and the international leadership responsibility to restore order in Somalia and to mount a relief effort to alleviate the immediate threat of mass starvation? Throughout the critical period of 1990 to late 1992, it was painfully clear that the major powers, particularly the five permanent

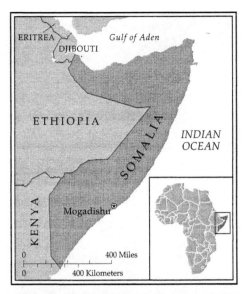

Map 4-1   **Somalia**

©1996 by St. Martin's Press, Inc. From: *Contours of Power*, by Snow/Brown. Reprinted with permission of Bedford/St. Martin's Press, Inc.

members of the UN Security Council, had little appetite for adding a peacekeeping and humanitarian relief project to an already crowded international agenda. Iraq and the Balkans were the preoccupying issues of the day. Whether one chooses to interpret the passivity of the major powers generously ("they can't solve all the world's problems all at once") or more harshly ("starving Africans affect neither the security nor the prosperity of the rich states"), there is no denying the timidity of the world's richest and most powerful countries as the Somali tragedy ballooned into catastrophic proportions.

Perhaps most telling, throughout most of 1991 tiny Cape Verde consistently advocated within the UN a more aggressive plan of action for pacifying Somalia and feeding its starving population than did the United States. In the absence of U.S. leadership, none of the other major industrial democracies was willing to pick up the banner. The Somali crisis illustrates once again the criticality of leadership in a decentralized international system; and it remains the case that other countries look to the United States to provide a disproportionate share of that leadership because of its position as the globe's leading political, military, and economic power.

The U.S. Assertion of Leadership

By late 1992 conditions had deteriorated further throughout much of Somalia. Fighting between the forces of Aidid and Mahdi had driven nearly half of the country's population from their lands. The chaos of civil war made the relatively mild drought into a nightmare of human survival. Farmers were unable to plant their crops. Much of the country's livestock perished amid the war's upheavals. In November 1992 relief officials estimated that fully one-third of Somalia's people could die within six months if regular access to food and water was not soon restored.

By this point, the international community was responding generously to Somalia's plight. Large amounts of food and medical supplies were being shipped to Somalia by numerous governmental and private donors. But getting the relief supplies to the people who needed them was another matter altogether. By that same fateful month—November 1992—fully 80 percent of donated food was being stolen by armed militias, who deliberately withheld it from starving members of rival clans. The militias were also attacking relief convoys and distribution centers in order to inflict further suffering on their enemies. Clearly, if left to their own devices, Somalia's contenders for political supremacy were willing to use starvation as an instrument of their political objectives.

In late November, President George Bush surprised many by approving a major U.S. initiative to avert further mass starvation in Somalia. At the heart of Bush's policy was the politically sensitive decision to dispatch a large contingent of American armed forces to Somalia to prevent the competing militias from stealing and withholding food as a political tactic. Ever since the Vietnam debacle, the American people and most of their elected representatives have been instinctively cautious about sending U.S. armed forces to distant hot spots in the absence of a clear and compelling threat to U.S. national interests. What, then, can explain Bush's decision to undertake a major overseas military deployment to a region where no apparent U.S. interests were threatened?

Four other factors were decisive. First, the purely personal perceptions, emotions, and reasoning of George Bush in late November 1992 must not be discounted. Only weeks before, in his bid for a second term, he had suffered a humiliating defeat in a campaign debate at the hands of a much younger candidate, Bill Clinton, who was inexperienced in international matters. Though the wounds of the bitter campaign were still raw, Bush's policy deliberations proceeded in large part from a genuine determination to take politically difficult steps in the waning months of his term in order to spare the new President the burden of tackling a complex and divisive international issue at the outset of his administration.

Summary ━━━━━━━━━━━━━━━━━━━━━━━━━━━━━

Factors Influencing U.S. Intervention in Somalia

1. Bush, in final months of presidency, seeking crowning accomplishment
2. Belief that in post–Cold War world, only the United States can provide global example and leadership for other states
3. Mounting violence threatening multi-national force
4. General Aidid's temporary cooperation
5. U.S. bureaucratic politics

For Bush, who prided himself on his grasp of international affairs but had long been lambasted at home for his difficulty in articulating a clear and consistent set of policies ("the vision thing," Bush once called it), Somalia presented him with an occasion to show, in the autumn of his presidency, that he did indeed have a vision for the kind of international order he had hoped to help shape in the aftermath of the Cold War. Central to that vision was the requirement that a steadily growing community of states cooperate under UN auspices to stem aggression and alleviate suffering around the globe. Assembling the needed multilateral coalitions requires, in the first instance, a few key states that are willing to take the lead. To Bush, it remained an article of faith that the United States was both uniquely equipped and historically destined to play a critical leadership role during the historical transition from the Cold War to the uncertainties of the post–Cold War era. So Bush's own mix of intellectual conviction and sense of historical responsibility played a key role in his decision to vastly alter the U.S. role in Somalia.

Fortifying Bush's strong impulse that the United States must "do something" was a second factor, mounting evidence that the situation within Somalia was deteriorating rapidly and in a manner that threatened the future of the precise policy instrument that Bush regarded as central to constructing a stable post–Cold War order: the multinational coalition dispatched to trouble spots under UN authority. By November 1992 over a dozen countries had agreed in principle to dispatch armed units to safeguard the distribution of food and medical supplies to the Somali people. Only Pakistan had actually done so, however, and its 500-man contingent, sent to safeguard the Mogadishu airport, was badly outnumbered by the Somali militias. The imminent danger that the Pakistani contingent would be overrun and massacred sent a palpable chill up the collective spine of George Bush's foreign policy-making team. Such a disaster would severely diminish, if not end altogether, the willingness of many countries to commit their own forces to UN-sponsored peacekeeping and humanitarian relief missions.

A third factor shaping Bush's decision was the uncharacteristically cooperative stance being taken at the time by one of the two principal Somali warlords. General Aidid had recently experienced setbacks on the battlefield and sensed power gravitating away from him amid the ever-shifting clan alliances within Somalia. A continuation of the "no holds barred" civil war held out the very real prospect that his own forces would be defeated and that his personal bid for national primacy would be doomed. In a cynical, though thoroughly rational, bid to buy time to regroup his political and military position, he stepped forward to announce his support of the U.S. plan then under discussion to send U.S. forces to protect relief columns and food storage and distribution sites. By donning the costume of humanitarian statesman, Aidid had positioned himself to win both new international backing and broadened support within Somalia.

A fourth and final reason explaining Bush's decision is the fact that the bargaining process over Somalia within the U.S. foreign policy bureaucracy produced a policy option that was in harmony with Bush's personal beliefs as well as those of his most influential associates. In the three weeks preceding Bush's December 4 unveiling of the U.S. plan, this process was operating in high gear to generate options reflecting the institutional views of the key foreign policy agencies, especially the State and Defense Departments. Most of the policy development work occurred at the level of the Deputies Committee of the National Security Council. The Deputies Committee is made up of relatively senior officials, including the undersecretary of state for political affairs, the undersecretary of defense for policy, the deputy director of the Central Intelligence Agency, and the vice chairman of the Joint Chiefs of Staff.

In its early deliberations, the Deputies Committee did not contemplate the dispatch of U.S. combat forces. By late November it had developed two policy options. One would have essentially continued the existing UN operation for shipping food to Somalia's principal cities but with more UN involvement to secure the shipments. A second option envisioned a multilateral coalition of noncombat ground, air, and naval armed forces, organized by the United States but placed under UN command, to strengthen the logistical, communication, and sealift capabilities of the relief effort.

Critical to the bureaucratic bargaining process was the position of the Defense Department, which would have to bear any operational responsibilities. Initially, there was strong sentiment in the Pentagon to avoid any direct U.S. military role in the Somali imbroglio. By November 19, however, Admiral David Jeremiah, then vice chairman of the Joint Chiefs of Staff, advanced the position in a Deputies Committee meeting that any realistic plan of safeguarding and distributing food to Somalis would require the introduction of a substantial U.S. land expedition. The committee did not endorse Jeremiah's "third option," but forwarded it along with the other two options to senior decision-making levels.

The crucial decision-making regarding U.S. policy in Somalia occurred at a meeting of the National Security Council held on November 25 in the White House. Persuaded by the urgency of the situation on the ground in Somalia, Bush decided to offer U.S. forces to the UN, but with the following conditions attached: they would be large enough to discharge their humanitarian mission without unduly endangering American lives, they would remain under U.S. control, they would be part of a larger multilateral effort, and they would be supported by a UN Security Council resolution approving of "all necessary means" to accomplish the mission.

For UN Secretary General Boutros Boutros-Ghali, the U.S. offer was a mixed blessing. On the one hand, firm U.S. leadership meant that other countries would be more likely to take decisive steps to alleviate the mass misery in Somalia. On the other hand, the conditions attached by the Americans meant that the UN per se would play a secondary role in this crucial test of forging a stable post–Cold War international order. Whatever his reservations, Boutros-Ghali kept them to himself and urged the UN Security Council to embrace the American offer. Once it did so on December 3, the Bush administration proceeded to dispatch a force that would eventually number nearly 30,000. President-elect Clinton weighed in with his strong endorsement of the undertaking, code-named Operation Restore Hope, and pledged that his administration would continue the policy set in motion under Bush.

Operation Restore Hope: Successes, Failures, and Lessons

Although the U.S. policy seemed straightforward enough—send sufficient U.S. forces to ensure that tens of thousands of Somalis would not die of starvation—it was in fact predicated on blurring a distinction whose significance would not become clear until the spring of 1993. On the one hand, there was the immediate task of securing Somalia's cities and countryside so that food and medicine could be safely distributed. An estimated 100,000 Somalis were saved by the humanitarian rescue mission. On the other hand, given the absence of a viable Somali government and the presence of heavily armed rival militias, there was a longer-range need to foster a peaceful resolution of Somalia's civil war so that the immediate aid effort would not be quickly undone once the foreign troops went home.

Bringing peace to Somalia, however, would be an enormously ambitious undertaking. At a minimum, it would require physically suppressing and disarming the most violent clan militias, especially that of Aidid. Necessary too would be sufficient political reconciliation to permit the establishment of a stable government, which could then tackle the massive tasks of rebuilding Somalia's shattered economy and infrastructure. Humanitarian relief was one thing; nation-building is an entirely different enterprise.

Within the United States, there was an initial wave of enthusiastic approval from Congress and the public over the humanitarian mission being carried out, efficiently and quite successfully, by U.S. forces. Only later would it become apparent that neither the American people nor their elected leaders had the will to commit American lives and American money to the more treacherous and thankless long-term challenges of nation-building in a distant land of no apparent strategic significance to U.S. interests.

By March 1993 the inherent tension papered over by U.S. policy was becoming apparent. That month, the UN Security Council passed a series of resolutions that essentially expanded the UN mission in Somalia to one of nation-building. The restoration of civil order and the reconstruction of Somalian political structures were the avowed objective. Inherent in achieving that objective was the disarming of the competing warlords, especially Aidid, who was seen as the principal obstructionist to the peace process and whose militia posed the greatest threat to the UN presence in Somalia.

U.S. policy-makers seemed oblivious to the increasing disparity between the ambitious UN agenda for Somalia and the narrowly defined humanitarian relief mission that served as the sole justification for the large U.S. military contingent. By late summer 1993 the U.S.-led effort had largely succeeded. The specter of mass hunger had been turned back. Most Somalis were regularly receiving adequate food and water. As the summer wore on, the bulk of the U.S. force was withdrawn. The lightly armed troops remaining were placed under UN command.

In September and October 1993, U.S. forces were increasingly drawn into UN military operations against Aidid. On September 9, U.S. and Pakistani forces searching for Aidid's militia opened fire on a hostile Somali crowd, killing 100 civilians. This ugly incident triggered the first expressions of major congressional opposition to the new direction of U.S. policy. On September 18, President Clinton—untested and largely unknown internationally—affirmed that U.S. forces would not be withdrawn in the face of Somali hostility. To do so, said Clinton, would mean that Somalia would soon be plunged back into chaos, thus undoing the successful work of Operation Restore Hope.

Back in Somalia, meanwhile, Aidid increasingly saw foreign forces as obstructing his prospects for ruling all of Somalia. Aidid calculated that if the costs of the U.S. presence were raised, American public opinion and congressional sentiment would force Clinton to lead an ill-concealed retreat from his country. On October 3, Aidid's forces mounted a savage counterattack on a U.S. Ranger unit that was participating in a raid on one of Aidid's strongholds. Lacking adequate heavy equipment with which to defend themselves or adequate backup forces, the Rangers were easily overrun, and 12 lost their lives. Television viewers around the world witnessed grisly scenes of Aidid's followers dragging the bodies of dead U.S. soldiers through the streets of Mogadishu.

The gruesome spectacle set off a chorus of criticism within Congress and among the American public at large. Polls showed strong support for an early withdrawal of all U.S. forces from Somalia. Clinton, too, wanted out; on September 20, Secretary of State Warren Christopher had sent a letter to Boutros-Ghali urging a political strategy to facilitate an early exit of foreign forces from Somalia rather than continuing to seek a military defeat of Aidid. On the other hand, Clinton did not want to be seen as weak. It was important to not act in such a way as to create the impression that all that foreign powers had to do to scare the United States away would be to send a few Americans home in body bags. Clinton's position was made more difficult by Boutros-Ghali's continued insistence that a U.S. withdrawal would destroy the entire UN peacekeeping mission, an undertaking that, he pointed out, the United States had supported by voting for the March 1993 Security Council resolutions.

Faced with multiple, and clearly conflicting, objectives, Clinton devised a political strategy aimed at conveying several messages at once. First, he ordered the rapid dispatch to Somalia of 5,000 more U.S. soldiers, along with greater firepower capability through armored personnel carriers, M1A1 tanks, heavily armed helicopters, and AC–130 gunships. This action was meant to send two signals. To the American people, it was designed to demonstrate that, as Clinton put it, "we are doing everything we can to protect the young Americans that

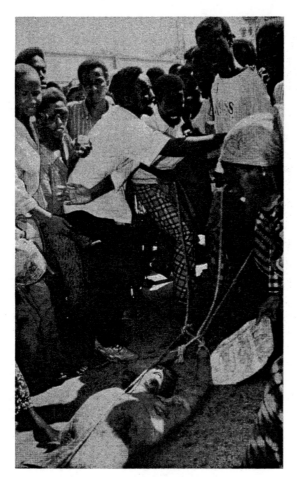

Televised images of the body of an American soldier being dragged through the streets of Mogadishu in October 1993 played a large part in turning American public opinion against the U.S. military intervention in Somalia.

are putting their lives on the line so that hundreds of thousands of Somalis can stay alive." To Aidid in particular and any potential foreign challengers of Clinton's political toughness in general, it was designed as a tangible, highly visible demonstration of the kind of U.S. might that could be deployed against any others who would threaten American interests or lives.

Yet along with this public display of toughness, Clinton simultaneously announced an early exit date for all U.S. forces in Somalia. By April 1, 1994, he declared, the U.S. mission would be completed and the forces sent to accomplish that mission would be brought home. Again, Clinton was attempting to communicate two messages to two distinct audiences. To the Somali warlords, he was signaling that the United States harbored no long-term designs on Somalia and posed no protracted threat to the designs of any particular clan leader. U.S. troops, therefore, were the enemy of no one in Somalia and ought not be subject to armed assault. To the American people, and especially to Congress, Clinton was making it as clear as possible that Somalia would not bog down into another Vietnam. By setting an early exit date, Clinton calculated that he would avoid a looming showdown with Congress that would have challenged his authority to direct American foreign policy and would have diverted attention away from what he saw as his all-important domestic legislative agenda.

Clearly, Clinton was trying to make the best of a politically perilous situation. In his October 7, 1993, speech, President Clinton made clear the risks inherent in his policy. "If we were to leave today," he said, "we know what would happen. Within months, Somali children again would be dying in the streets. Our own credibility with friends and allies would be severely damaged. Our leadership in world affairs would be undermined at the very time when people are looking to America to help promote peace and freedom in the post–Cold War world. And all around the world, aggressors, thugs, and terrorists will conclude that the best way to get us to change our policies is to kill our people. It would be open season on Americans."

Read casually, Clinton's comments bear a striking resemblance to the repeated rationales offered by the Kennedy, Johnson, and Nixon administrations as to why the United States must not permit itself to be driven from the field of battle in Vietnam, no matter that Vietnam was of no greater strategic significance to U.S. interests in the 1960s and 1970s than was Somalia in the 1990s. But note Clinton's artful construction of his argument: "If we leave today," he said, then terrible consequences could follow. Left unstated, but clearly implied, was that if the United States simply waited another six months, a withdrawal then would bring down the curtain on a successful mission and none of the dreaded consequences of "withdrawing now" would follow.

In many ways, Clinton's strategy succeeded. A politically costly struggle with Congress was indeed averted. The American public was sufficiently reassured by the precise exit date that its attention soon wandered onto other matters. Somalia's warlords did see the wisdom of permitting the Americans to make a graceful exit; there would be no more major attacks on U.S. forces. Finally, through sheer good luck, the situation in Somalia gradually became less chaotic and deadly as the various combatants grew wary of the benefits to be gained by continuing the vicious fighting of the previous three years. Through sheer war-weariness, as much as anything else, Somalia gradually settled into an uneasy condition of routinized disorder, which, while far from an ideal settlement, was infinitely preferable to what had preceded it.

The bitter aftertaste of the Somalian misadventure has left the United States reluctant to commit its forces in humanitarian interventions. The death of the Army Rangers led directly to the Clinton Administration's refusal to suppress the genocide in Rwanda in 1994. According to Walter Clarke and Jeffrey Herbst, "In Bosnia, UN peacekeepers under fire or taken prisoner by Serb forces over the last two years were expected to turn the other cheek for fear of 'crossing the Mogadishu line'" ("Somalia and the Future of Humanitarian Intervention," *Foreign Affairs,* March/April 1996).

Review

In this chapter we examined the decision-making process in international politics. The following points were made:

1. In an ideal, rational foreign policy-making process, leaders would (a) be able to articulate precisely their policy objectives, (b) keep a vigilant eye on threats to those objectives, and (c) maintain and use appropriate instruments of power to counter those threats.

2. In the real world, there are a number of barriers to attaining that ideal image of rational foreign policy-making. Among them are (a) groupthink, (b) false analogy, (c) cognitive dissonance, (d) personality idiosyncrasies, and (e) cultural factors.

3. The United States entered Somalia on a humanitarian mission for generally altruistic reasons divorced from calculations of the national interest. When its mission changed from food relief to combat against the forces of General Mohammed Farah Aidid, public and congressional support for the undertaking quickly shrank. President Clinton's decision to withdraw U.S. forces in 1994 was an acknowledgment that (a) peacekeeping and nation building are virtually impossible in a state lacking a central government, where hostile groups are fighting each other rather than reconciling, and (b) the American people will not long tolerate a military mission unrelated to key U.S. national interests.

Suggested Readings

Allison, Graham. *Essence of Decision: Explaining the Cuban Missile Crisis.* Boston: Little, Brown, 1971.

Beard, Charles A. *The Idea of National Interest.* Chicago: University of Chicago Press, 1962.

Brown, Seyom. *The Faces of Power: Constancy and Change in United States Foreign Policy from Truman to Reagan.* New York: Columbia University Press, 1983.

Buzan, Barry. *People, States and Fear: An Agenda for International Security Studies in the Post–Cold War Era.* Boulder, CO: Lynne Rienner Press, 1991.

Clark, Jeffrey. "Debacle in Somalia," *Foreign Affairs* 72, (1992/93). 109–123.

Festinger, Leon. *A Theory of Cognitive Dissonance.* Stanford: Stanford University Press, 1957.

George, Alexander L., and Robert Keohane. *Presidential Decision-Making in Foreign Policy: The Effective Use of Information and Advice.* Boulder, CO: Westview Press, 1980.

George, Alexander, and Juliette George. *Woodrow Wilson and Colonel House: A Personality Study.* New York: Dover Press, 1964.

Hartz, Louis. *The Liberal Tradition in America: An Interpretation of American Political Thought Since the Revolution.* New York: Harcourt Brace, 1995.

Janis, Irving. *Victims of Groupthink.* New York: Houghton Mifflin, 1972.

Jervis, Robert. *Perception and Misperception in International Politics.* Princeton, NJ: Princeton University Press, 1976.

Kissinger, Henry. *A World Restored: Europe After Napoleon.* New York: Grosset and Dunlap, 1964.

Klineberg, Otto. *The Human Dimension in International Relations.* New York: Holt, Rinehart, and Winston, 1966.

May, Ernest R. *Lessons of the Past: The Use and Misuse of History.* London: Oxford University Press, 1973.

Morgenthau, Hans. *Politics Among Nations: The Struggle for Power and Peace,* 6th ed. New York: Knopf, 1985.

Snyder, Richard C., et al. *Foreign Policy Decision-Making: An Approach to the Study of International Politics.* New York: Free Press, 1962.

Truman, Harry S. *Memoirs: Year of Decisions.* New York: Doubleday, 1955.

Walker, Stephen, ed. *Role Theory and Foreign Policy Analysis.* Durham, NC: Duke University Press, 1987.

5

The Functions, Origins, and Forms of War

PREVIEW

In this chapter, we will examine the problem of war and its effects on the nature of the international system. Because war has been an enduring part of international relations, we will begin by looking at the functions it serves for international actors and how its scope and purposes have evolved over time. A major aspect of war's evolution has been its increased deadliness. Nuclear weapons, in fact, may have made some kinds of war too deadly to contemplate. Because many people through time have sought to reduce or eliminate war, we will examine various theories about the causes of war and how the problem might be "cured." We will then turn to the contemporary system and the nontraditional kinds of war it features. The chapter will conclude with a case study of how the United States recently envisioned responding to possible calls for military intervention in the context of the post–Cold War system.

KEY CONCEPTS

better state of the peace	social contract
total purposes	frustration-aggression hypothesis
total means	feminism
limited purposes	game theory
limited means	prisoner's dilemma
civil (internal) war	insurgency
asymmetry of objectives	terrorism
lethality index	internationalism
nuclear allergy	neoisolationism
state of nature	

OUTLINE

A"rmed violence directed by one politically defined group of people against another, or war, is as old and enduring an institution as contact between human groups. In a world divided into sovereign states, war becomes the ultimate arbiter when conflicts of interest can be resolved in no other manner; war is the most dramatic, extreme instrument of power. When the political purposes that motivate states and even groups within them can be achieved in no other way, then the "dogs of war" (to borrow Shakespeare's phrase from Julius Caesar) may be unleashed.

Understanding why groups go to war, as well as alleviating those causes if possible, has been a central concern of many students of international relations. The ultimate goal of these concerns and efforts, which some adherents call "peace studies," is to eliminate war as a recourse of groups. This orientation also characterizes much feminist theory, which claims that the prevalence of war stems from male dominance of both the conduct of international relations and the way it is studied.

Despite such efforts—and the end of the Cold War—war continues to be a major force in the world. With the central problem of East-West confrontation and its consequent danger of society-destroying nuclear war between the superpowers largely eliminated, the spotlight moves to the less pressing—yet troubling—problem of more or less organized violence in the Second Tier. From the standpoint of the First Tier, war seems, for the time being, to have moved to the peripheries—the edge of Europe, Africa, Asia. It nonetheless persists.

This chapter will explore the question and problem of war. We will begin by examining the function of war within international politics. We will then look at trends in warfare, especially at the pervasiveness and deadliness of the modern military instrument of power. This in turn will lead to an examination of some views of the causes of war and prospects for its elimination. We will then move to some contemporary and nontraditional manifestations of warfare. The chapter will conclude with a case study of the American debate about how force should be used in a non–Cold War environment.

The Functions of War

The first and most fundamental observation we must make is that war has traditionally been thought of as a political enterprise, in at least two distinct ways. First, the reasons one goes to war are politically defined: the objectives for which one decides to go to war are a set of political conditions one deems necessary to bring about (the better state of the peace). Second, victory and defeat in war are ultimately defined not by whether military battles are won, but by whether political objectives were achieved. The outcome of military action will, of course, affect the achievement of objectives, but the two things are not necessarily the same.

The nineteenth-century Prussian strategist Carl von Clausewitz summarizes the conventional functions of war best in his epic work *On War,* written as a reflection on the Napoleonic wars (in which he had participated as a member of the Prussian general staff): "War is not merely a political act, but also a political instrument, a continuation of political relations, a carrying out of the same by other means." Mao Ze-dong, who led the successful Chinese communist revolution and himself was a student of Clausewitz, voiced much the same philosophy when he said, "War cannot be divorced from politics for a single moment."

This relationship follows from the way the operation of the international system was described in Chapters 1 and 2 (the realist paradigm). If the international system is one of anarchy where states' vital interests require that they impose power on others, then military force, in its various manifestations, is an instrument of power to which recourse will sometimes be made.

This Clausewitzian view of war, which forms an important pillar of the realist paradigm of the international system, is not universally accepted. Some observers, including most feminists, find the Clausewitzian formulation a self-fulfilling justification for a status quo in which war is an important system element. Others, such as the military historian John Keegan, find the realist paradigm a transitory rather than permanent description that may fit the Napoleonic era through World War I but does not capture the function of war as a self-fulfilling act, as he argues it was during the pre-Napoleonic period. (This dynamic is described in the Coming to Terms box, "The Return of Non-Clausewitzian Warfare?") At the same time, the post–Cold War era is witnessing an outbreak of a new form of violence—new internal war—for which the Clausewitzian framework is also quite inadequate.

The purposes for which war is pursued and the means employed to achieve its ends have changed across time. There is every indication that those purposes and means will continue to evolve in the post–Cold War system, as part of the war and peace mechanism of that system, and that the current technological changes sometimes described as a revolution in military affairs will further alter war and its conduct (see the Impact of Technology box "The New Revolution in Military Affairs" on page 149).

Purposes and Means

At this point, we need to review two fundamental distinctions made more briefly in Chapter 3. The first deals with the political purposes for which war is fought: wars can be fought by either side for total purposes or for limited purposes. A total political purpose,

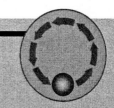

Coming to Terms

The Return of Non-Clausewitzian Warfare?

The discussion of purposes and means of conducting warfare in the text highlights the Clausewitzian/realist way of dealing with the role of armed violence in the international system. Implicit in this analysis is the presumption that the Clausewitzian model is universal in its application. This view is not universally accepted either by scholars with a primary interest in eliminating war or by some observers who believe there are exceptions to the Clausewitzian paradigm.

Among the latter group, two objections are notable. The military historian John Keegan argues, for instance, that the Clausewitzian formulation is an historical oddity reflecting the fact that *On War* was, to a large degree, a history of the Napoleonic wars, where the political goal of spreading the ideals of the French Revolution predominated. Rather, Keegan maintains warfare before the Napoleonic wars was typically divorced from politics and fought for other purposes, including war for its own sake—the warrior ethic. Moreover, Keegan contends that many modern wars are barely explainable in Clausewitzian terms.

Edward N. Luttwak picks up on this latter theme as it applies to contemporary internal warfare—the new internal wars. Luttwak argues that the Clausewitzian paradigm contains implicit Napoleonic assumptions that suggest that military force is only justifiable for large, sweeping purposes such as those for which the Napoleonic campaigns were fought. Because there are very few contemporary conflicts for which Napoleonic-sized purposes are realistic, clinging to the Clausewitzian criteria can paralyze the use of force for useful, but less than grand, purposes. He calls these applications "post-heroic warfare."

The most obvious category of examples on non-Clausewitzian wars are the new internal wars. These conflicts often occur without any overt political purposes at all, making the Clausewitzian analysis in terms of purposes and means of dubious applicability in understanding and dealing with them. These wars may not invalidate the Clausewitzian framework for most wars, but they do represent a return to non-Clausewitzian principles for *some* wars.

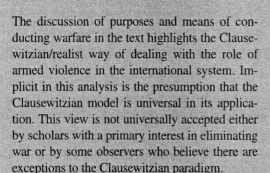

as we have defined it, is one for which a sweeping political condition—normally the overthrow of the enemy government—is a prerequisite for accepting a peace. The better state of the peace for the Allies in World War II, the overthrow of the fascist regimes of the Axis, was such a purpose. A limited political purpose does not require such a sweeping outcome. In the Persian Gulf War, the coalition objective of restoring Kuwaiti sovereignty was a limited one: the removal of the Iraqi armed forces from Kuwait and the restoration of the Kuwaiti government did not require the overthrow of the Iraqi government headed by Saddam Hussein.

The second distinction deals with the military means employed in war; once again, each side may employ either total means or limited means. In a war of total military means, all of the available weapons and other resources are employed to achieve the political objective. The Allied effort in World War II, which included "saturation" bombing of German cities and nuclear bombing of Japanese cities, is again illustrative. In a war of limited means, less than the total available resources are utilized.

This latter distinction may be initially puzzling. Why would a country at war not use all its weapons? Why would it, in effect, fight with one hand tied behind its back? The answer can be approached by examining how the two sets of distinctions interact with one another.

Interaction of Ends and Means

Because war is a political enterprise, the achievement of political goals is the overriding criterion by which the war effort is measured. As Clausewitz put it, war has its own grammar (or language) but not its own logic. By this, he meant that the physical conduct of hostilities has its own rules but not its own purposes. When those come into conflict, the political objectives of war (the ends for which it is fought) must override its language (the means used to achieve those ends). At the same time, means can limit ends. A state with very small, weak forces cannot successfully attack and conquer a larger, more powerful neighbor.

This may become clear by example in Table 5.1. The diagram juxtaposes the concepts of purposes and means into a matrix, as was done in Chapter 3, this time covering a wider range of examples. An examination of each cell demonstrates the relationships involved.

Most wars fit into the cells where ends and means are both total or both limited. Thus, a total war aim such as the overthrow of fascism in World War II required using all means available. Civil (internal) wars aimed at the overthrow of governments are similar: since one side must physically destroy (or capture) the other's leadership to gain or maintain power, these wars are total in purpose and warrant total means.

However, most civil wars are fought in the countries of the Second Tier, which generally have only modest weapons. Would not such wars, therefore, involve only limited means? The answer is no, because the definition of total means includes the word available. In Bosnia and Herzegovina, for instance, hand-carried weapons, some mortars, and archaic artillery were the only weapons used, but they represented the totality of weaponry available to the combatants.

Wars of total purpose tend to be particularly desperate, thereby justifying the use of all means available. When you know that your defeat means your total capitulation and subjection to an enemy, possibly including your own death, this knowledge tends to increase your resolve and the measures you are willing to contemplate in its service.

The other "pure" combination in the matrix covers wars of limited purpose and means. In most cases, wars are fought for reasons that do not require the replacement of the enemy government. The removal of the Iraqi army from Kuwait did not require either the total

Table 5.1	Ends and Means in War	
Means	**Ends**	
	Total	**Limited**
Total	World War II, most civil Wars	Weak state against strong state
Limited	A conventional World War III (?)	Most other wars

destruction of that body or the overthrow of the Iraqi government of Saddam Hussein, as already noted. The military objective could be accomplished short of employing all military means (nuclear weapons, for example).

It is true that in the aftermath of the war against Iraq, many Americans and others thought overthrowing Saddam Hussein should have been the objective. President Bush, for instance, rued the failure to remove Hussein in a 1998 interview. But if the objective had changed to overthrowing Saddam, then the conduct of the war would have been changed as well. The coalition would have had to invade and occupy Iraq, something which almost none of the member states—and especially the Islamic members of the Joint Task Force under Saudi command—was willing to do. Moreover, the Iraqis would almost certainly have fought more resolutely in that circumstance. Limitation makes sense if the expansion of either ends or means would transform the nature of the war in undesirable ways.

The hybrid combinations in the matrix can be treated quickly, because they are less plausible and occur infrequently. A war of limited purpose fought with all means will occasionally be necessary or tempting for a state whose opponent has considerably more strength. An example is Argentina's unsuccessful effort to seize the Falkland Islands from Britain in 1982. Similarly, during the Cold War it was possible to envision a World War III between the Soviet-led and the American-led coalitions that might remain at the conventional (nonnuclear) level while being aimed at a sweeping military objective (although many rejected the plausibility of such a scenario).

Evolution and Asymmetry

Two further points need to be made about these issues of ends and means in warfare. The first has to do with how the prevalence of total or limited war has evolved through the history of the state system, especially as it has affected the major members. The second deals with the situation where one or both sides in a war have total purposes and use total means while an intervening outsider's purposes and means are limited, a particular problem for the contemporary system.

The evolution of tendencies toward total or limited wars has been affected by the ways that ends and means relate to one another. That relationship is depicted in the Summary box "Evolution of Ends-Means Relationship in War."

Summary ———————————

Evolution of Ends-Means Relationship in War

Period	Dynamic	Change Event
1648—1789	Limited war (means limit ends)	French Revolution, first industrial revolution
1789—1861	Moving toward total war (ends and means expand)	American Civil War
1865—1945	Total war (total means and ends)	Development of atomic bomb
1945—Present	Limited war (means limit ends)	

The state system came into being as a result of the total nature of the Thirty Years War. The relatively tranquil period between the peace of Westphalia and the outbreak of the French

Revolution was one in which, as noted in Chapter 3, monarchs had relatively small armies capable only of being used for modest purposes: France could not, for instance, think of conquering England. That is, available means limited ends.

The French Revolution and the first industrial revolution began to change that situation. The new French nationalism allowed the recruitment of much larger forces than previously, and those forces could be and were employed for larger purposes, such as conquest of another country. By the time of the American Civil War, thanks to the results of the first industrial revolution, means had expanded as well (as discussed in the next section of this chapter). The American Civil War did not begin as a war of total means, but in its final stages it involved a virtually complete mobilization of the human and economic resources of Southern society (which were much smaller than those available to the North). The North responded by "bringing the hard hand of war to the Southern people": troops under the command of William T. Sherman and Philip Sheridan embarked on wholesale destruction of crops, livestock, and other civilian property in Georgia, South Carolina, and Virginia. The American Civil War thus became the prototype of modern total war, in which the extensive engagement of a civilian society in the war effort makes it a target for equally extensive enemy hostilities.

A near century of total war, culminating in the world wars, ensued. Its end, ironically, came with the invention and use of the ultimate means for conducting total war, nuclear weapons. As the Cold War competition evolved and the nuclear arsenals expanded to

General William Sherman's 1864 "march to the sea," in which Union troops swept across Georgia destroying everything in their path. The American Civil War marked the transition in warfare from the limited means of the eighteenth century to the total means used in World Wars I and II.

globe-threatening dimensions, it became questionable whether there was any political purpose for which nuclear weapons could be employed. In other words, the effect of general nuclear weapons exchange between the superpowers would clearly overwhelm any end for which they might be used. Since a total war involving the major powers could become a nuclear World War III, excessive means restricted purposes.

A major complication to be considered in analyzing ends and means is the situation where one or both sides in a conflict are fighting a total war, but an intervening outsider has limited purposes and is willing to use only limited means. This condition, which can be called asymmetry of objectives, most often occurs in civil wars where the outsider is supporting one side or the other (usually the besieged government). Vietnam is the prototype of this situation. In that war, North Vietnam and its Viet Cong allies were fighting a total war, the purpose of which was the forcible reunification of Vietnam (which required overthrowing the South Vietnamese government). South Vietnam and its ally, the United States, were fighting for the limited purpose of causing the North to cease its campaign in the South. Because of fears that escalation of fighting might lead to an all-out war involving the major world powers (both the Soviet Union and China had mutual defense treaties with North Vietnam that the United States wanted to avoid being activated), the means employed were also limited.

In such a situation the total purpose of one side is almost always more important to its members than the limited purpose of the other. As a result, the resolve of the side fighting totally will almost always outlast the other, as was apparently the case in Vietnam, where the importance of the outcome to the North Vietnamese contributed to their willingness to continue against all odds, and ultimately to prevail.

The contemporary relevance of this pattern is that a large number of the peacekeeping and peace enforcement situations in which the United Nations and others are being asked to become involved (Somalia, Bosnia and Herzegovina, Rwanda, Kosovo) share the dynamics of asymmetry. UN interveners are neutral and have even more limited objectives than an intervener who is taking sides. The UN's resolve in these situations thus will not match the ferocity and determination of the combatants, and this may be the real way that such situations resemble Vietnam (an analogy always made when intervention is suggested).

The Deadliness of War

The resort to war has become increasingly problematic as warfare has become gradually more expensive and lethal because of the successive industrial revolutions that have been applied to it. The epitome of this increase in deadliness is, of course, the development of thermonuclear weapons. The nuclear arsenals of the United States and the Soviet Union were the militarily defining characteristics of the Cold War competition; the possession of a large number of nuclear weapons was the membership card of the superpower club.

The rise in the deadliness of war and its impact on international relations are complex issues. We will begin by looking at the evolution of weaponry and other technological changes in the way warfare came to be conducted. We will then briefly survey the special role of nuclear weapons in a post–Cold War environment. Finally, we will look at the role of weaponry in the relationship between the First and Second Tier states.

Technological Developments

Especially as a result of the first industrial revolution (the development of the factory-based industrial production system) and the great growth in science and technology during the twentieth century, the history of warfare has been one of gradual, sometimes spectacular, increases in the pace, destructive ability, and variety of physical locales in which it is conducted. War today would be virtually unrecognizable to those who practiced it 100 or even 50 years ago.

Consider for a moment war in the eighteenth century, which we have already described. At that time, the only way to get to the battlefield was to walk, meaning that armies were normally tired when they fought or required considerable rest before engagement. Soldiers were armed with smooth-bore muskets that could be fired only a couple of times a minute and were accurate to a range of 50 yards or less, and available cannons shared this inaccuracy. Moreover, the powder for these weapons was vulnerable to moisture, effectively eliminating battle during rainy weather or winter. Soldiers were normally aligned in tight linear formations (usually three deep); thus, the obvious places for land battles were open fields where there were no obstacles that could break up the ranks. As noted, the armies were small, and since muskets were also used as spears (if they had bayonets) or clubs, the clash of the linear formations would often produce casualty rates that are quite high by modern standards.

The industrial revolutions gradually changed these conditions. By the time of the Crimean War and the American Civil War, the telegraph had increased the ability of forces to communicate with one another and their national leaderships, larger armies could be transported over distances to fight wherever there were rail lines, and the introduction of rifled weapons had considerably increased the range of effectiveness of hand-held weapons. Later, the internal combustion engine made possible truck transport, the tank, and the airplane. The storage battery made the submarine practical, and the helicopter meant troops could be transported to battle anywhere a helicopter can hover—which is virtually anywhere.

In the eighteenth century, armed forces could fight in open fields and on the high seas. Today, they can clash on the ground anywhere, on the sea, under the sea, and in the air. The only frontier is space, which has been militarized with reconnaissance satellites but not yet "weaponized." The high technology of the late twentieth century has produced weapons of incredible accuracy, as well as the ability to collect intelligence and bring force to bear with precision and deadly efficiency heretofore unimaginable. The image of the minuteman at the North Bridge in Concord, Massachusetts, has been replaced by the cruise missile with a television camera in its nose following an Iraqi soldier through a bunker door (although media images at the time overrated the technological impact).

This trend has had at least three discernible effects. First, it has greatly increased the efficiency of killing and destroying in war—the lethality index. Nuclear weapons illustrate this point in the extreme, but "conventional" (non-nuclear) forms of munitions do so as well. Second, modern weaponry has become enormously expensive; generally speaking, the more sophisticated it becomes, the more expensive it is. Third, the application of the most sophisticated technologies has created an enormous gap between those who possess them and those who do not, a factor of great import for the balance of military power between the countries of the First and Second Tiers.

The Impact of Technology
The Battle of First Manassas and the Transition to Total War

Just as the American Civil War marked the transition from eighteenth-century limited war to twentieth-century total war, it also demonstrated dramatically the impact of new technologies on military affairs. Although the impact was largely unanticipated, it was evident in the first major encounter of that war, the Battle of First Manassas (the Confederate name) or First Bull Run (the Union name). The new technologies were the telegraph and the railroad. Both had seen limited service in the Crimean War a decade earlier; their maturation as a part of war began at this battle on July 21, 1861.

The battle's location reflected the importance of the railroad. Manassas Junction, Virginia, was (and still is) a major rail junction, where east-west and north-south rail lines intersect. Of special importance was the fact that the junction contained a line running directly to the Confederate capital in Richmond. Union strategists believed that if their forces could capture Richmond and the Confederate government, the rebellion would collapse, a belief apparently shared by the Confederates who came out to block Union capture of the junction.

The railroad combined with the telegraph to affect the ensuing battle's outcome. The Union force under General Irvin McDowell that marched out of Washington, D.C., was consid-

erably larger than the Confederate force under General P. G. T. Beauregard that it encountered. As a result, Beauregard telegraphed for reinforcements to the Confederate army in the Shenandoah Valley, on the other side of the Blue Ridge Mountains. General Joseph E. Johnston's troops boarded a train, rode to Manassas, and entered the battle fresh and rested late in the morning, arguably turning the tide and preventing a Confederate loss that might have ended the war much sooner.

Although the railroad helped to save the Southern cause at the First Manassas, as the American Civil War went on the North's significant advantage in the new technology became increasingly decisive. Here, a Union military train crosses a bridge hastily thrown up by soldiers in Northern Virginia.

The Nuclear Case

The New Mexico sky was suddenly and violently set ablaze before dawn on July 16, 1945, as the international scientists involved in the Manhattan Project detonated the world's first atomic bomb at the Trinity Site at White Sands. As the quotations in the Amplification box "The Birth of the Nuclear Age" suggest, the assembled scientists knew they were witnessing the most awesome weapon yet to be devised. The nuclear age was born.

Three weeks later, on August 6 and 9, atomic weapons were exploded over Hiroshima and Nagasaki in Japan to convince the Japanese government of the futility of continuing its

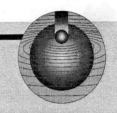

Amplification

The Birth of the Nuclear Age

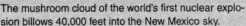

The mushroom cloud of the world's first nuclear explosion billows 40,000 feet into the New Mexico sky.

The awe-inspiring nature of nuclear weaponry was captured in comments by two of the principal members of the team that exploded the first atomic device at the Trinity Site. Robert Oppenheimer, the physicist considered the "father" of the bomb, said later, "There floated through my mind a line from Bhagavad-Gita ...'I am become death, the shatterer of worlds.' I think we all had this feeling, more or less." General Leslie Groves, who supervised the project, declared, "This is the end of traditional warfare."

Source: Quoted in Ronald W. Clark, *The Greatest Power on Earth: The International Race for Nuclear Supremacy from Earliest Theory to Three Mile Island.* New York: Harper and Row, 1980, pp. 199, 200.

war effort and hence to avoid what had been projected to be a very bloody invasion of the Japanese home islands. The explosions represented the only times that nuclear weapons have been employed against human targets.

The existence of nuclear weapons raised at that time and continues to raise basic questions about their role in war. Do they represent a qualitative difference from other kinds of weapons in terms of the destruction they cause, or only a quantitative one? Can they be used to achieve political goals that would not be overwhelmed by their sheer ferocity? (We have already answered this question negatively.) Could their use be measured and limited, or would their introduction so impassion the combatants as virtually to guarantee escalation to a general exchange that would destroy all the combatants? Do nuclear weapons have any military utility beyond deterring an enemy from using them against you?

Rational discussion about nuclear weapons is clouded by at least two factors. First, feelings about them tend to be highly emotional; nuclear weapons are, after all, weapons of massive destruction whose primary use is to kill large numbers of people or destroy large things. As such, they inspire a kind of terror that produces what might be called a "nuclear allergy." People are repelled by the thought of them and are reluctant to regard them as having any possible value.

Second, military analysts know very little about the dynamics of deterrence and war with nuclear weapons, for the simple reason that there has never been a war in which more than one party had and used them. Where is the nuclear threshold (the point in a conflict where nuclear weapons are used)? No one knows. Does a nuclear war, once started, inevitably escalate? Once again, no such war has been observed; no one knows. What would a postnuclear world look like? Same answer. Moreover, whatever nuclear "theory" exists was developed almost exclusively to deal with the U.S.-Soviet confrontation. Very little of it clearly applies to the post–Cold War problem of discouraging nuclear proliferation (the spread of nuclear weapons to states that do not possess them) and dissuading possessors from using these weapons.

The situation of a heavily nuclear-armed world defined both the Cold War and the period succeeding it. Efforts to reduce the number of such weapons significantly after the dissolution of the Soviet Union were slowed by the fact that three successor republics in addition to Russia (Ukraine, Belarus, and Kazakhstan) retained them; by early 1994, however, agreements had been reached to place all former Soviet strategic weapons under Russian control.

During the Cold War, the nuclear balance was of critical importance because the overall antagonism between the superpowers created plausible scenarios wherein nuclear weapons might be employed. Those conditions have dissolved with the end of the Soviet Union, and the demise of communism; there is little if any reason why the United States or Russia would want to destroy one another. Meanwhile, nuclear arsenal sizes have been decreased as a result of arms control agreements, and there has been a general reduction of armaments among the Cold War antagonists

The question of what roles nuclear weapons will fill is part of the overall uncertainty of the contemporary environment. While their continued existence is a source of anxiety to some who believe international security requires a nuclear-free world, at least three points can be made in support of their continued utility. First, the maintenance by Russia and the United States of arsenals larger than those possessed by any other states provides a hedge against a deterioration of relations between them. If, for instance, an authoritarian government should come to power in Russia, the nuclear balance could prevent relations from becoming too negative, since preserving peace would be essential.

Second, maintaining the arsenals is probably good for Russian self-esteem. Russia lost much power and prestige when the Soviet Union disintegrated, and may be, as some have argued, a "Third World country with nuclear weapons." As a matter of prestige, that is better than being a Third World country without nuclear weapons, and it may help control impulses toward authoritarian nationalism within Russia and aggressive actions abroad.

Third, large nuclear arsenals may have some deterrent value in dealing with Second Tier countries, and especially those with nuclear, biological, and chemical weapons and ballistic missiles. This is especially a Russian problem, since many of these countries are along the periphery of the old Soviet Union or within missile range of its borders.

Two events in 1998 raised international awareness about the continuing relevance and problem nuclear weapons create. The explosion of nuclear devices by Indian and Pakistan reminded us that the spread of these weapons to former nonpossessors remains a dynamic of international relations and makes the Indian subcontinent a potentially much more deadly place. The political crisis in Russia also reminded the world of the possibility that the Russian arsenal could fall into the hands of a hostile regime.

First Tier–Second Tier Military Relations

As new international relationships have begun to order themselves in the aftermath of the Cold War, a distinctive pattern of violence has begun to emerge as well, in which warfare occurs largely within and occasionally between countries of the Second Tier. In the immediate aftermath of the fall of communism in Eastern Europe and the Soviet Union, it was concentrated in that area. Recently, it has begun to spread elsewhere.

Although these conflicts may be peripheral to the central concerns of the major actors of the First Tier, they have come to demand increased public attention. Rooted in ethnic, religious, and historical animosities, they tend to give rise to gruesome atrocities that are graphically illustrated on global television, and they appear quite beyond resolution by the parties involved. The early response was to let the United Nations work out solutions, but that organization's resources and capacities were rapidly overwhelmed. How should the First Tier states, which alone possess the military wherewithal, deal with these problems?

. The response has at least three aspects. The first has to do with the imbalance in technologically based capability between the most advanced and the less advanced militaries of the world. The second has to do with the question of arms transfers to the Second Tier and the effect they have on evolving conflict. The third involves the willingness of First Tier publics to become involved in Second Tier conflicts.

The Persian Gulf War revealed vividly the gap in military capabilities between the major western members of the coalition (notably the United States, Britain, and France) and a very large and what was believed to be a highly capable Second Tier conventional armed force in Iraq. The gap proved to be a wide chasm: Iraq's army was outgunned and outperformed by all measures, and the enormous gap in air and naval resources gave the coalition an instant monopoly on the seas and in the skies that was put to deadly effect.

The conclusion seems clear: Second Tier armed forces do not stand a chance against a concerted effort by First Tier forces in anything resembling conventional warfare. It is an open question whether the technology gap also extends to guerrilla warfare, a strategy that has in the past negated technological advantage or the chaotic military situation that often typifies new internal wars; this is an issue taken up later in the chapter. The overall military superiority of the First Tier is manifested in such things as reconnaissance capabilities, data processing and interpretation, and precision firepower over ranges outside the lethal ranges of Second Tier militaries. The relentless, 24-hour-a-day air campaign in Operation Desert Storm, against which Iraq was powerless to respond, illustrates these capabilities.

The lesson is mixed for the First Tier, as we shall see in the case study at the end of the chapter. The high-technology gap between the tiers will broaden, not shrink. Among its positive consequences for the First Tier is the ability to conduct very precise, surgical warfare that minimizes casualties—especially to First Tier forces. Televised pictures of body bags, which in the past haunted public opinion in western democracies, should become less of a problem. At the same time, high-technology weapons are very expensive at a time defense expenditures are declining. Even if the will is there, will the resources be? Will public opinion create a situation analogous to that in the eighteenth century, where the lack of public support limited military capabilities?

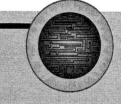

The Impact of Technology

The New Revolution in Military Affairs

The high-technology revolution is creating a new Revolution in Military Affairs (RMA) that may prove as profound as the technological revolution in the nineteenth century that was first manifested in the American Civil War. The basis of this RMA is a great increase in capabilities for information collection and processing, sensing of enemy targets, and precision strikes on such targets. According to one recent study by Michael J. Mazaar, the new RMA represents a postnuclear phenomenon, embodying a renewed emphasis on nonnuclear warfare. Its bases include "an interdependent world economy, and the dramatic effects of new military and civilian technologies."

According to the study, the RMA is likely to have four principal characteristics:

1. An emphasis on information, focusing on the idea of information "dominance" or superior intelligence. This means the possessor can learn the location of and target an enemy that has neither counterpart capability or the ability to thwart the intelligence collection.
2. An emphasis on synergy or jointness between the services in conducting military operations because of technological progress allowing common weapons designs and communication links to conduct joint operations. This capabil-

ity is seen as a "force multiplier" (something that gives the force greater effectiveness).

3. Disengaged combat, or fighting over long distances where opposing forces do not come into direct contact with one another. This characteristic was first seen in the Persian Gulf War, where coalition tanks and artillery could attack counterpart Iraqi systems from outside the range of those Iraqi weapons.
4. Civilianization, meaning that as technologies with both civilian and military applications develop, the gap between civilian and military expertise will narrow. This will be especially true in the realm of information warfare, which emphasizes conversion of enemy populations rather than killing enemy troops, thereby lowering casualties in future wars.

The exact contours of RMA are currently unknown, but there are likely to be profound effects on the conduct of warfare. Of particular interest is the fact that the RMA is almost exclusively a product of the technologically advanced First Tier. It is therefore likely to broaden the considerable military gap between the tiers, already so evident in the Persian Gulf War.

Source: Michael J. Mazaar, *The Revolution in Military Affairs: A Framework for Defense Planning.* Carlisle Barracks, PA: Strategic Studies Institute, 1994.

Another aspect of this intertier comparison is the extent to which the First Tier will prove willing to share advanced military technologies with Second Tier countries through arms transfers. During the Cold War, it was not uncommon for the most advanced equipment to be sold to important client states or to whatever states could afford it—Iran, Saudi Arabia, and Israel being among the biggest purchasers. There is rhetorical consensus that this practice is undesirable, because it simply fuels arms competitions, makes conflicts more deadly, and could decrease the advantage First Tier militaries currently enjoy. The

other side of the coin is that arms transfers can be lucrative sources of foreign exchange for countries like the United States that are experiencing balance-of-payments problems.
The other aspect is the extent to which First Tier publics will support missions to Second Tier countries embroiled in, normally, internal wars without easy solutions. Generally speaking, few U.S. or other First Tier interests are involved in these situations, making activism based on vital interests difficult to sustain. The experience in Haiti and Bosnia suggests that involvement will be tolerated if casualties are avoided. It is not clear what happens if involvement results in indigenous resistance and sustained casualties. The Somali experience offers a cautionary note to such situations.

The Causes and "Cures" of War

The kinds of concerns raised in the first two sections of this chapter largely reflect the descriptive realist approach to the study of international relations, which basically says certain problems and dynamics exist and does not offer solutions or criticisms. Students of international affairs from other perspectives, however, find the situation appalling or descriptively inaccurate, in need of basic change. Those who seek to reform the system to ameliorate or eliminate war are a prominent, if not the only, source of theorizing about why war occurs. Students of international relations have long been fascinated by this question, often hoping that with better understanding it might be possible to "cure" the system of its violent propensities.

People from diverse backgrounds have looked at war from different points of view: philosophers and psychologists concerned with human nature and the roots of violent behavior, anthropologists studying the link between humans and other species, sociologists considering the connection between war and social structure, and political scientists examining the nature and structure of the international political system, to name a few types of specialists. A number of these inquiries explicitly adhere to the goal of a future in which there is no war. Benjamin Franklin captured this sentiment with his famous observation in a letter written in 1773: "There never was a good war or a bad peace."

The number and variety of potential theories and explanations of the causes of war are too extensive and complex to deal with here; some guidance for those interested in pursuing the subject further is provided in the Suggested Readings list at the end of this chapter. For our purposes, we will identify what are, at least arguably, the major schools of thought and briefly summarize what they suggest about why humans organize to fight and kill in war. Recognizing that the boundaries between them are somewhat arbitrary, we will distinguish four approaches: philosophical/structural, Marxist, microcosmic, and macrocosmic.

Philosophical/Structural Theories

Some of the earliest musings on the causes of war were concerned with basic human nature and what led humans to create social structures of which organized violence seemed an integral part. The heart of this approach is thus a dual question: Is there something about human nature that makes us act violently? Is there something about the social organizations humans devise that impedes or promotes violent behavior?

Analysis of human nature goes back to the ancient Greeks, is expressed in the Christian belief in the fall of humanity from grace, and crystallized in the social contract debate of the seventeenth and eighteenth centuries. The two lightning rods in this debate were

Thomas Hobbes and John Locke, whom we encountered in the discussion of sovereignty in Chapter 2. Both viewed the essence of human beings through the allegory of an original state of nature that was followed by a social contract, an implicit agreement about how humans would live together in groups.

To Hobbes, the original state of nature, reflecting the nature of human beings as such, was cruel and forbidding, involving "continual fear and danger of violent death," and human life was "solitary, poor, nasty, brutish, and short." In the natural state, Hobbes believed, the "condition of man . . . is a condition of war of everyone against everyone." In the Hobbesian view, humans agree to a social contract out of fear, giving up their unlimited—if tenuous—freedom in exchange for a commonwealth governed by a strong sovereign who can impose order. In this view, which was shared by many of the early realists, the function of societal structure is to constrain humanity's violent nature.

Locke was more optimistic about human nature. His state of nature was one of considerably greater cooperation and comity amongst its members, who are guided to some extent by natural reason. According to Locke, the social contract by which humans entered society was a trade-off wherein people gained the advantages of group association—such as division of labor—partly in exchange for the danger that tyranny and other social imperfections might force them to act unnaturally, which is to say to engage in war.

If one starts from the philosophical position that human beings have an inherent nature that impels them one way or the other—either to act or not to act violently (a third possibility is that humans have no fundamental nature at all), then it is important to decide which way they are inclined. If they are inherently violent (the Hobbesian position), war is probably inevitable, and attempts to reduce it substantially or eliminate it are ultimately futile. If one accepts the Lockean notion that social structures force people to act violently, then it is reasonable to think about ways to restructure society to overcome the problem.

Marxist Theories

The Marxist theory of war is the most prominent, but by no means the only, explanation of international violence based on economic factors. The heart of these explanations is the notion of economic exploitation and inequality as a basic structural flaw of society that divides states or groups within states from one another, thereby leading to hostilities that end in war. Implicit in this approach is the tenet that the removal of economic inequities could lead to the elimination of war.

The original Marxist explanation of war is embedded in an economic theory of history, the historical dialectic, and in the milieu of the first industrial revolution in which this theory was fashioned by Marx and Engels. The dialectic maintains that history is a process of struggle to reconcile conflicting economic and political realities and to adjust the relations of conflicting groups and societies. Thus, in the Marxist view feudalism gave way to the state system because feudal organization created political units too small to accommodate the growing mercantile economic system, which relied on the free movement of goods, at least within countries. In the nineteenth century, when Marx was writing, the central conflict was over the industrial system; it was a clash between the bourgeoisie (owners) and the proletariat (workers) that would eventually end in the victory of the latter and finally in the highest form of economic and political organization, communism. In the communist utopia, history (in the sense of social change) would end, classlessness would produce social harmony, and war would disappear. First, however, capitalism had to be dislodged wherever it clung to power (although not necessarily by war).

Vladimir Ilyich Lenin added to this analysis the idea of international imperialism as the last, fitful stage of capitalism. According to this theory, western colonization of Africa and Asia was the culmination of a system of economic exploitation that would eventually engulf the capitalist world in self-destructive warfare. From the ashes of that conflagration, communism would produce utopia.

The Marxist vision may seem quaint from the contemporary vantage point, since its prophecies have proven so incorrect. However, the description above does not do it complete justice. Basically speaking, it represents a vision of the causes of war as embedded in a sociopolitical and economic system. The major contemporary advocates of such a vision are the interdependence theorists first introduced in Chapter 1. They are not Marxist; they do not start from the premises that mark the Marxist analysis. They do, however, share the belief that economic imperfection, which is correctable, underlies much of the violence in the world. It is an optimistic view in that it suggests that war can be controlled.

Microcosmic Theories

In contrast to those philosophically and economically based theories, a number of anthropologically and psychologically based inquiries have tried to determine why individual humans, and by extension groups and states, act violently. Once again, the field is complex and too varied even to be surveyed here. What we can do is provide at least a taste of these approaches by looking briefly at three variations.

Karl Marx, the co-founder of communism with Friedrich Engels, included in his theory a unique explanation of the causes of war based in conflict between classes. Given the fate of operational communism, his analysis is of primarily historical interest.

One line of inquiry seeks to extrapolate the behavior of other species to human behavior. Two of the leading twentieth-century names associated with this approach are Konrad Lorenz, whose most well-known work is *On Aggression,* and Robert Ardrey, author of *The Territorial Imperative* and *The Social Contract.* Each used different methods and arrived at different conclusions.

Lorenz studied aggressive behavior in animals, trying to see if there was any pattern to when animals of the same species or different species attacked one another. He differentiated between intraspecies and interspecies violence. Interspecies violence, he concluded, was done not to hurt or kill, but to survive by gaining food. He found, however, that within many species members often attack and kill one another without apparent outside motivation. Since the problem of war is one of intraspecies aggression, the latter finding particularly interested Lorenz. He concluded that some species, including Homo sapiens, possess an aggressive instinct, which could become acculturated within human groups and thus passed along. Since the underlying triggering mechanism is an innate characteristic, Lorenz concluded that it could not be eliminated. Although "instinct theory" has since been assailed, his work remains seminal.

Ardrey, an amateur anthropologist, also used the observation of animals to extrapolate the basis of human aggressive behavior. Starting from no particular first premise about inherent characteristics of humans, Ardrey observed that there were species of animals that exhibited aggressive behavior, including organized violence, when the territory they inhabited was intruded upon by other species or members of their own species.

Extrapolating from animals exhibiting this trait, Ardrey identified what he called the territorial imperative, the idea that violent behavior is impelled by territory-acquiring and territory-protecting instincts on the part of certain species. Ardrey included humans within the list of animals governed by the territorial imperative.

The second thread of microcosmic inquiry into war, in some ways a reaction to the anthropological approach and to instinct theory, comes from psychology. It again begins with the notion of aggression, asking in what circumstances individual humans and groups of humans act aggressively.

The central concept in this approach is something called the frustration-aggression hypothesis. According to this notion, a key variable in predicting aggressive behavior is prior frustration—the blockage of goal attainment. In simpler terms, when people want something and it is denied to them, the result is frustration, which will in some circumstances result in aggressive behavior.

Quite obviously, not all frustration results in violent aggression; if it did, Hobbes's war of all against all would be literally true. In some cases, acting aggressively against what frustrates one would be counterproductive: hitting the police officer who gives you a ticket, for instance. In that case, the frustration may instead be sublimated (stored) and blamed on someone else (displaced). These are well-established principles of individual behavior, but other aspects of the question are less settled.

The relationship of frustration to aggression can be said to be one of necessary (but not sufficient) causation. This means that whenever aggression occurs, there necessarily was prior frustration, but that not all frustration is sufficient to induce aggression. When, then, is sufficiency achieved? In particular, to what extent is frustration-aggression a learned as opposed to a biologically determined response? For some psychologists, such as B. F. Skinner, all behavior is learned, and thus one can condition people when to be

and when not to be aggressive. For other psychologists, there may be underlying geneti-
cally or biologically based conditions that dispose people to aggression; these, while
subject to some controls, could not be entirely altered short of chemical manipulation or
genetic engineering.

A third emerging strand of inquiry that focuses basically on the microcosmic level of
studying war is represented by the various schools of thought associated with feminism
and gender studies. Some feminists, sometimes called essentialists, emphasize what they
believe are the distinctive qualities of women as opposed to men and generally conclude
that men are more prone to war and women to peacemaking and cooperation. This difference is variously attributed to biology (such as hormone levels) or culture (such as child-
rearing practices) or both. But essentialist feminists largely agree that male domination of
international relations (and its study) over time has resulted in structures and perceptions

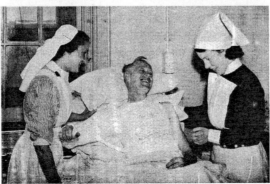

Different schools of feminist thought
disagree about the relationship between women and warfare. "Essentialist" feminists see men as more prone
to conflict and women to cooperation;
many of them argue that child-rearing
practices, such as encouraging boys to
play with guns and girls with dolls, play
an important part in creating gender
differences in adults. Other feminists
dispute claims of "essential" differences between the sexes, and feminists influenced by postmodernism
have explored what they see as the
role that military nurses, wives, and
prostitutes play in sustaining warfare
by male combatants.

about the "normality" of war that would be changed by greater female participation. In general, essentialists see feminism as a means of achieving a more peaceful world.

Essentialism has been criticized on various grounds. Many feminists simply argue that there are no significant differences between the sexes; they advocate more female participation in international relations but are not convinced that it would result in a more peaceful world. A more complex critique comes from feminists influenced by postmodernism, who contend that both the traditional realist understanding of war and the essentialist feminist view of it are too limited in their intellectual scope. The intellectual approach known as postmodernism rejects the possibility of arriving at a universally valid, "objective" explanation of war (or any other phenomenon); instead, it accepts—or even celebrates—the existence of a multitude of conflicting and overlapping perspectives on reality, none of which can be regarded as the "true" one. With intellectual roots in the school of literary criticism known as deconstructionism, postmodernists try to "deconstruct" language and other "constructions" of human thought to uncover hidden meanings and perspectives within them.

In applying this technique to studying the causes of war, feminists have particularly noted the sexual connotations of much of the language and imagery used in connection with weapons, such as the use of words like potency and penetration to refer to the capacity of weapons and the use of attractive female models to market them. Such words and images suggest to these scholars that the sexual drives of male political and military leaders may play a part in their decisions to go to war or use particular weapons.

Macrocosmic Theories

The behavioral revolution in political science and sociology spawned yet another approach to the study of war, one that considers groups—whether states or contending groups within states—as the basic unit of analysis. Those following this approach attempt to examine the interactions of these groups abstractly through constructs from other fields or through quantitative analysis.

Once again, we can proceed only by example. The attempt to look at complex processes through constructs from other fields is demonstrated vividly in the study of arms races. One of the early pioneers in this area was a mathematician, Lewis Fry Richardson, who began producing mathematical representations of the action-reaction phenomenon involved in arms competitions in 1926 and whose work culminated in 1960 with the publication of *Arms and Insecurity.*

Richardson's reaction processes were widely studied and criticized, largely on empirical grounds of oversimplification. A major outgrowth of his approach was the application of game theory to the topic. Game theory describes the relationship between two competing parties in a particular situation by assigning various values to outcomes. This approach examines how rational actors will perform in situations with different possible outcomes.

The best-known game used in analyzing the arms race is known as "the prisoner's dilemma." In it, one prisoner in a cell shared with two others is found murdered, and the problem is for each of the remaining prisoners to decide whether to turn in the other to the warden or keep quiet, in an atmosphere where they are separated after the murder, cannot communicate, and thus cannot trust one another. This game's extrapolation to arms races was based on the idea that both sides during the Cold War were led to continue arming themselves (turning in the other) because failing to arm (keeping quiet) could lead to disadvantage (the worst outcome for each prisoner is if he or she fails to talk and is implicated by the other). The game is explained in more detail in the Amplification box "The Prisoner's Dilemma."

The heart of the second group-based approach to the study of war is to develop large data banks of statistical characteristics of states—called indicators—and then to attempt to see how they are statistically correlated to state actions, notably the likelihood of engaging in war or warlike behavior. Possibly the most famous of these efforts is the "correlates of war" project conducted by J. David Singer, Melvin Small, and others. Based at the University of Michigan, this project involved collecting a massive amount of quantitatively defined information about states: political (such as frequency and openness of elections), economic (gross national product per capita), sociological (distribution of wealth and status), communications (number of letters mailed across national boundaries), and military (expenditures on and size of the military), to cite a few examples from a few categories.

These independent variables (conditions occurring independently or prior to change in the object of study) are then statistically tested across time against a series of dependent variables (conditions in which change may depend on changes in the independent variables). The most common dependent variable under scrutiny has been the inclination toward or actual participation in war.

Nontraditional Forms of War

Much of the analysis of war and its causes that we have surveyed in this chapter was done during the period between the world wars and during the Cold War, when the major powers were in opposition and the prevention of systemic war was thus an important priority. It is not entirely clear that these analyses are adequate to describe current patterns of war.

One of the defining characteristics of the contemporary international system is that the states of the First Tier lack ideological division. Despite some cultural differences that are the basis of the "clash of civilizations" idea raised by Samuel P. Huntington and discussed elsewhere in the text, they are all political democracies with market-based economies. The same cannot be said of the two other big powers, Russia and China. Russia has a tentative democracy but only the chaotic hint of a market economy, while China has a growing market economy in parts of the country but hardly a political democracy. If Russia and China make the transition to "normalcy" as defined by the First Tier, then ideological harmony will prevail among all the major powers.

This observation is important because one of the few generally accepted hypotheses about international relations is that political democracies rarely go to war with one another. The idea that any of the major powers—except possibly Russia or China if they resist the transition—would go to war with another in the near to medium term is almost beyond the imagination. This is the position of those who argue for the "democratic peace," which asserts that democracies do not fight one another. Critics argue that may—or may not—be true, but it does not mean democracies are less likely to fight—presumably against nondemocracies—than other polities. War, as already noted, has moved to the periphery of the international system, to the countries of the Second Tier.

War and violence in the developing world are different in structure and purpose from the kinds of war we have previously discussed. Adjusting to this difference is a major part

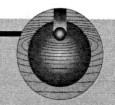

Amplification

The Prisoner's Dilemma

In game theory, the prisoner's dilemma is an example of a game whose structure leads a "rational" person to engage in noncooperative behavior. A prisoner who shares a cell with two others is found murdered. The two are then separated so that they cannot communicate, and each must then decide whether to accuse the other or to refuse to talk. The verbal structure of the game may be pictured like this:

		Player B	
		Don't Talk	Talk
Player A	Don't Talk	0, 0	+100, −5
	Talk	+5, −100	+10, −10

The numbers in each cell indicate outcomes from different actions (by convention, the outcome for Player A is always listed first). In the upper-left cell, neither turns in the other, the warden has no case against either, and they get no additional sentence (0, 0). If Player A keeps quiet and is turned in by Player B (upper-right cell), Player A is convicted of murder and gets life (−100), and Player B gets a reduced sentence for turning state's evidence (+5). The outcomes are reversed when Player A talks and Player B remains silent (lower-left cell). If each implicates the other, however, both are convicted of a lesser crime (manslaughter, for instance), and get a relatively short additional sentence (+10, −10), as shown in the lower-right cell.

What should each do? In game theory the answer lies in the *minimax principle,* which says that in any single play of a game, a rational player should minimize his or her maximum loss. Applying that logic to the player's choice, the outcome is determined. If a player remains silent, the outcome could be no additional sentence (0) or life (−100). Talking can yield a reduced sentence (+5) or an incremental additional sentence (−10). The maximum possible loss is thus −100 for not talking and −10 for talking. Applying minimax, each player will implicate the other, thereby getting the additional sentence. If the two could trust one another, they would both remain silent; in the absence of trust, rational behavior drives each to a mutually negative outcome.

The prisoner's dilemma is often applied to arms races between states. In these constructions, remaining silent translates into not continuing to arm (not building more weapons), and talking is the equivalent of continuing to arm. Discontinuing arming (upper-left cell) saves money, but if one side quits and the other does not, great military advantage may accrue to the arming party. Thus, both sides will continue to arm without gaining an advantage, and effectively wasting the money spent. As we explain in Chapter 11, the advent of satellite reconnaissance helped overcome the problem of lack of trust and thus allow for solutions to the arms race.

of the task of the post–Cold War international system as it devises structures and strategies for a peace mechanism. For summary purposes, the types of violence involved include internal wars (both traditional insurgencies or low-intensity conflicts, and new internal wars), regional conflicts, and terrorism. Our purpose here is simply to identify them as part of the systemic struggle with the problem of war.

Internal Wars

As we have discussed earlier, with the waning of the Cold War, resurgent nationalism in Second Tier states has opened a Pandora's box of old, simmering rivalries and hatreds, which often manifest themselves in violence intended either to oppress dissident parts of the population or to gain independence through secession. The result is internal war in far-flung places: Tamil uprisings in Sri Lanka, ethno-religious violence in the Sudan, and similar violence in Armenia (the Azeri enclave of Nakichevan) and Azerbaijan (the Armenian enclave of Nagorno-Karabakh), to name a few trouble spots. In addition, criminal insurgencies in a number of African countries (Sierra Leone, Liberia) and narco-insurgencies (Colombia, Peru) are an increasingly important variant.

Lacking great military resources, the movements that arise usually generate insurgencies, either traditional or new internal wars. The distinctions are vague, used to cover a number of phenomena, and the dynamics vary between traditional insurgencies and new internal wars. For present purposes, traditional insurgency can be defined as military action by a political group within a country seeking to overthrow and replace a government and employing unconventional strategies and tactics. This definition suggests two characteristics that differentiate insurgency from other forms of warfare and frame the problem of dealing with it. New internal wars, on the other hand, often lack the political goal of overthrowing or replacing governments.

Summary

Defining Characteristics of Insurgencies

1. They are internal or civil conflicts.
   - This makes them particularly desperate.
   - Atrocities are often committed.

- Outside interference is rarely conclusive.
2. They are conducted using unconventional means.

The first defining characteristic is that insurgencies are internal or civil conflicts. As such, they are typically wars of total political purpose and total means (although, as noted earlier, those means may appear modest when compared to the forces of advanced powers). This internal nature and totality of means and purposes creates certain complications, especially for the international community if it seeks to involve itself.

Insurgencies are particularly desperate affairs. Since gaining or maintaining control is the objective, they are rarely amenable to compromise. One side wins; the other loses. Often, the losers end up dead, in prison, or in exile. Compromise solutions reached in El Salvador and Cambodia in recent years are exceptions to the rule caused by mutual exhaustion of the parties or withdrawal of outside assistance; normally the totality of effort means that it is difficult to reach negotiated settlements in these kinds of wars.

Desperation is often accompanied by atrocities in the conduct of insurgencies. The purpose of insurgency is to convert as much of the population as possible to your side. Some means of conversion are positive; Mao Ze-dong, one of the original architects of modern insurgent practice, urged his forces to treat the people better than did the Chinese government he was seeking to overthrow. Sometimes, however, conversion is accomplished through terror and atrocities. This tendency toward atrocity is especially pronounced in the new internal wars; the absence of a positive political appeal removes much of the inhibitions against bloody violence.

Efforts by outsiders to affect the outcomes of insurgencies are rarely conclusive. Insurgencies are internal affairs that ultimately must be solved internally. Especially at the level of military intervention, outside involvement, no matter how high-minded it may be, inevitably will be resented. Interveners who are racially distinct from the combatants are especially likely to be ineffective. Since World War II, there has not been a single instance in which a racially distinct intervener succeeded against an insurgency that had substantial popular support. American intervention in Vietnam between 1965 and 1973 stands out as the most extreme example of this rule.

❋The second defining characteristic of insurgencies is their unconventional means of conduct. As a strategy (plan of action to accomplish goals) and set of tactics (military actions to implement strategy), insurgent warfare is designed to give a militarily weak movement a chance to succeed against a militarily superior opponent. In fact, insurgency is often referred to as "warfare on the cheap."

We cannot detail the strategy here (for an extensive overview, see Snow, *Distant Thunder*). The basic idea, however, is for small bands of fighters, called guerrillas, to act against government units whenever, but only when they have superior force at the point of contact. When government forces are superior, insurgents simply fade into the population. Mostly part-time fighters, they generally do not wear regular military uniforms.

This style of fighting is based on attrition and patience. The insurgents win by not losing decisively, gradually increasing their support as small successes accumulate and the balance of power turns against the opponent. The government becomes frustrated, its armed forces gradually lose their superiority, and eventually the insurgents are able to topple it.

This style is also tailor-made to frustrate the tactics and strategies employed by technologically advanced military forces. The doctrine of "overwhelming force" adopted by the U.S. military and applied in places such as Panama and Kuwait is nullified by insurgents. When overwhelming force enters the field, the insurgents simply disappear and wait for a small unit to come along that they can ambush (a favorite tactic). This is sometimes known as technology-negating strategy.

The end of the Cold War altered the pattern of insurgency. During the 45 years of its duration, insurgent wars typically pitted a force supported by the United States against one sponsored by the Soviet Union. Generally, insurgencies featured American-backed governments fighting Soviet-backed insurgents espousing nominally Marxist intents. In the 1980s, U.S. President Ronald Reagan began to support anticommunist insurgents, notably in Nicaragua, Afghanistan, and Angola, a policy that became known as the Reagan Doctrine. With the collapse of Soviet communism and the end of ideological competition, sponsorship became more problematical for traditional insurgents, because there is no incentive to arm opposing sides.

The end of the Cold War has stimulated the development of new internal wars. Criminal insurgencies existed in places like Liberia (whose civil war broke out in 1989) and narco-insurgency had found a home in Colombia while the Cold War raged. With the end of the Cold War, the superpowers withdrew from competition for influence in the Second Tier. As the Cold War dissolved, so too did whatever restraints they placed on internal violence. In that vacuum, the phenomenon of internal war has spread and intensified.

During the Cold War most insurgencies pitted Soviet-backed insurgents against American-supported governments. In the 1980s, however, the administration of President Ronald Reagan offered U.S. support to anti-communist insurgents like this 13-year-old contra in Nicaragua.

Regional Conflicts

Another problem altered by the end of the Cold War is regional conflicts, animosities between neighboring countries, often with long histories of rivalry. The most extreme of these exist in Asia: between India and Pakistan, India and China, North and South Korea, Vietnam and Cambodia and Thailand, Iran and Iraq, and Israel and its neighbors, to cite the most obvious examples.

Events since 1989 have changed these conflicts in three potentially insidious ways. First, constraints have been loosened. During the Cold War, the typical pattern was for the United States to supply one partner with weaponry and the Soviets the other, with each power creating in the process a source of influence over the assisted government. However, open warfare between their client states could possibly draw the superpowers into direct confrontation, even war, which neither wanted. Consequently, the superpowers sought to moderate conflict by using techniques such as threatening to cut off arms flows (for example, spare parts or ammunition) to the client state in the event of hostilities.

That ability to restrain has evaporated as the superpowers have reduced their involvement. Their departure has led to a second problem: the flow of arms has not abated. Arms are still desired by these Second Tier countries locked in rivalry; while Russian and American government sources may not be so forthcoming, others have replaced them. A number of Second Tier countries, ranging from China to North Korea, have entered the market as armorers. These new sources include in their inventories NBC

Contours of the Future?

Rebels Without a Cause

The phenomenon of new internal war has emerged in several African states in recent years: the insurgency with no political ideology or political aspirations. The insurgents seem motivated only by their ability to enrich themselves by terrorizing the population. As the information minister of Sierra Leone, Arnold B. Goodling, put it, "They don't control anything. But they wreak havoc. They kill innocent villagers, kidnap young boys and force them into service, burn down rice farms, and even shoot the cows."

In Sierra Leone the government seemed incapable of controlling the violence, at least partly because the country's military is so corrupt that it is feared nearly as much as the rebels, who call themselves the Revolutionary United Front. There have been widespread accusations that government troops pursuing the insurgents routinely loot the countryside of whatever the insurgents have failed to steal. Although a cease-fire and elections took place in early 1996, the potential for new breakdown persists, as was the case in Liberia, where a cease-fire dissolved only months after taking place.

The apparent prototype for this style of what one can call criminal insurgency is Liberia, which a similar war left on the verge of joining the failed states of the region until a tentative peace was reached in 1995. Sierra Leone, whose mineral riches make it one of the few countries in the region with the apparent potential for prosperity, seems poised for a similar fate.

Source: New York Times (national edition), February 17, 1995, p. A5.

weapons (nuclear, biological, and chemical) and ballistic missiles, a problem discussed in Chapter 11. Indigenous efforts to up the lethality index, such as Indian and Pakistani development of nuclear weapons, only add to the problem.

The third consequence of the end of the Cold War is that regional conflicts have emerged or resurfaced in the wake of the breakup of the communist world. In a sense, this problem is parallel to the loosening of the Cold War restraints. As the Soviet Union broke apart, ancient rivalries resurfaced, notably in those areas where Islam and Christianity have collided in the past. Armenia and Azerbaijan represented the first clash, but conflicts between Moldova and Ukraine, Chechnya and Russia, and a number of other uneasy neighbors may emerge. The breakup of Yugoslavia also has rekindled old conflicts, such as those between Serbia and Macedonia, Macedonia and Greece, and Serbia and Albania (over Kosovo).

The record has not been entirely negative, however. The emergence of the United States as the lone superpower and global peacemaker has meant that a number of regional conflicts—Israel and its neighbors, and Northern Ireland, for instance—have moved significantly toward resolution, at least partially due to U.S. goading. Although this phenomenon is too new to constitute a permanent feature of the new order, it does represent a hopeful trend.

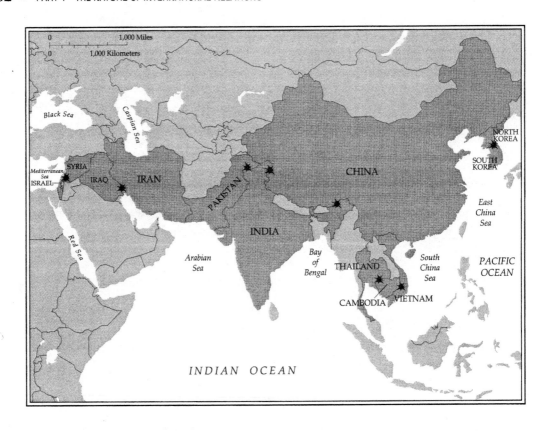

Map 5-1 **Regional Conflicts in Asia**

©1996 by St. Martin's Press, Inc. From: *Contours of Power*, by Snow/Brown. Reprinted with permission of Bedford/St. Martin's Press, Inc.

Terrorism

Few international phenomena evoke as much emotion and reaction as does terrorism. As an international phenomenon, terrorist acts peaked during the latter 1980s and have steadily declined since. Terrorist groups continue to exist, however, sustained by clandestine support, and each individual terrorist act attracts attention and stirs concern. For Americans, the bombings of the World Trade Center in New York City in 1993 and the Murrah federal office building in Oklahoma City in 1995 were disturbing evidence that terrorism could strike close to home (although the following discussion will focus on international rather than domestic terrorism); the bombing of the American embassies in Nairobi, Kenya, and Dar es Salaam, Tanzania, in 1998 were reminders it does not disappear.

What exactly constitutes terrorism is a source of considerable disagreement, even among those who specialize in its study. For our purposes, however, it can be captured in six characteristics:

1. Terrorism involves committing criminal acts to achieve political ends. Classification of terrorist law-breaking as criminal points to a central focus of the controversy about

Web Sitings: Terrorism

Several sources of information on patterns of terrorism are readily available on the world wide web. The U.S. State Department produces an annual report, *Patterns of Global Terrorism,* which can be accessed through the home page of the State Department (http://www.state.gov). Its appendices, which are included, provide various statistical reviews of patterns over time, chronologies, and lists of terrorist groups. Amnesty International also provides a more expansive list of global terrorism through its annual report, which is available at www.amnesty.org. (If you use a search engine such as AOLFind, a search under the heading Amnesty International will include home pages for AI chapters around the world.

terrorism. Terrorists maintain that the political basis of their actions makes them acts of war, not common crimes, which is how the victims tend to view them. To Scotland Yard, Irish Republican Army (IRA) terrorists have always been common criminals; to their supporters, they are "freedom fighters."

2. Terrorist acts are random in nature. The purpose of terrorism is to frighten (or terrorize) a population to the point where members of the population conclude it is better to comply with terrorist demands than to continue to resist. Fear is best induced if the population can never guess when, for instance, the next poison-gas attack will occur in a Tokyo subway or the next automobile will explode on a Middle Eastern street.

3. Terrorist organizations aim to influence government actions, not to gain control of governments. At most, terrorists seek to force governments to do things: to release political prisoners, to force the Israeli government to grant Palestinian autonomy. Sometimes, their goals are less coherent (for instance, no concrete political motive appears to have underlain the bombing of the World Trade Center in New York other than that the perpetrators hated Americans). It should be noted that groups seeking to overthrow governments (insurgents) occasionally engage in terrorist acts to achieve their ends; for terrorist groups, however, terror is the principal or only method employed.

4. Terrorism is a tactic of the weak. The political positions that terrorists take are, by definition, minority positions that could not be achieved through normal political processes; usually the terrorists themselves represent the positions of only a tiny fragment at the political extreme that cannot attract a broader following. Terrorist acts fit this condition. They normally require only a small number of people to carry them out. It might be said that, as a rule, the larger the proportion of a group's actions that are terrorist, the smaller the group's appeal and strength.

5. Terrorists are sponsored and financed by governments and private interests. By far the largest number of terrorist organizations, especially those in the Middle East, are aided, trained, financed, and often created by national governments. Following the Iranian Revolution in 1979, the U.S. Department of State identified Iran as the world's major terrorist sponsor; Syria, Iraq, Sudan, and Libya have also been on the U.S. government's list of sponsors, and the former Soviet Union and East Germany were frequent sponsors. On the other hand, the IRA is not sponsored by the Irish government and receives most of its financing from private donations (notably in Boston and New York). The shadowy figure of Osama bin Laden, the self-professed sponsor of the 1998 embassy bombings,

illustrates private sponsorship. Identifying sponsors is important in dealing with terror. It is often impossible to deter terrorist groups directly; they are hard to infiltrate, and their fanaticism does not lend itself to easy dissuasion. However, it may be possible to identify and target sponsors and take action against them. This was done in 1986 in an air raid against Libya's Mu'ammar Qaddafi, following an allegedly Libyan-sponsored attack on a Berlin disco that killed two members of the American military; after the raid, Libyan-sponsored terrorism decreased. The same intent underlay aerial attacks against terrorist training camps in Afghanistan sponsored by bin Laden.

6. There is disagreement about what causes terrorism. Two broad arguments are made about what causes terrorist groups to come into being. One view stresses the role of adverse social, economic, and political conditions. In this view, for instance, the Palestinian refugee camps surrounding Israel produced such wretched living conditions that their residents had literally nothing to lose by sacrificing themselves as terrorists. The other view stresses that terrorism's appeal is closely related to particular cultures, religions, and political ideologies.

The problem of terrorism is anomalous. On the one hand, attempts to suppress terrorists through counterterror (active attempts to prevent acts of terror, such as infiltrating terrorist organizations or capturing or killing their leaders) or antiterror (making targets more resistant to terrorists, such as installing metal detectors at airports) have met with rather limited success. On the other hand, terrorists have been spectacularly unsuccessful in gaining their ends most of the time (which may explain the decline in terrorism better than the effectiveness of counterterror), unless their ends are the sheer commission of terrorist acts. The problem of countering these random acts of terror are well illustrated by the series of bombings against U. S. targets in 1996.

Case Study: The U.S. Response to Global Violence

Because the United States is the world's remaining superpower and the only country with the global "reach" to project military power nearly anywhere, how it participates in global military affairs affects how the entire system responds to violence. As early post–Cold War events have shown, American leadership or its absence can be critical. In 1990, the United States took the lead in forming the Desert Storm coalition, and the system followed. Until December 1995, the United States had not taken the same kind of resolute action toward Bosnia and Herzegovina; the system acted ineffectually until the United States took the lead in negotiating and implementing the Dayton accords.

What the United States should do in response to violence abroad remains a matter of debate within the country and in the world at large. The American debate begins with the general issue of how active the United States ought to be abroad (internationalism versus neoisolationism). How much attention should the United States give to maintaining order in the world, especially in light of its priorities at home (playing "globocop" versus meeting domestic needs)? The extent of foreign involvement the United States chooses may also depend on the nature of the situation and the projected efficacy of different actions ("doability"). Finally, there is the question of how important a favorable outcome would be to the United States (vital interests versus humanitarian interests).

Internationalism Versus Neoisolationism

The extent to which the United States should involve itself in external affairs has historically been a matter of debate. George Washington in his Farewell Address and Thomas Jefferson in

Contours of the Future?

Dhahran and the Future of Terrorism

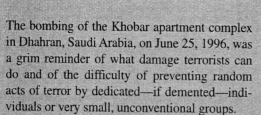

The bombing of the Khobar apartment complex in Dhahran, Saudi Arabia, on June 25, 1996, was a grim reminder of what damage terrorists can do and of the difficulty of preventing random acts of terror by dedicated—if demented—individuals or very small, unconventional groups.

The Dhahran incident killed 19 U.S. service personnel assigned to Operation Southern Watch (the mission to protect Iraqi Shiites in southern Iraq from assault by the Saddam Hussein government) and wounded 80 more. The incident was connected to an earlier car bombing that killed five Americans and resulted in the execution of four Saudis who committed the act (there was initial suspicion that the apartment bombing was in retaliation for the executions, as had been warned by anonymous sources).

The Dhahran bombing, along with a series of incidents including the attack on the Atlanta Olympic Village and the assault on TWA flight 800 provided a potentially chilling prospect in at least two ways. First, it was an apparently random act committed by a person or group that made no claim to the act nor tied it to any political purpose. Traditional terrorist acts have been carried out by various Middle Eastern and other groups (such as the IRA) that were identifiable, thereby assisting in surveillance and apprehension. The Dhahran incident, on the other hand, appeared to be a case of "freelance terrorism," for which the terrorist groups are very small, obscure, and hence difficult to detect in advance.

Second, the bombing pointed to the extreme difficulty of sustaining effective antiterrorism against dedicated perpetrators. Although precautions had been taken to make the complex less vulnerable, the sheer force of the explosion left a scene reminiscent of the Murrah building in Oklahoma City. As a frustrated State Department official, John Dinger, put it, "The bombing in Dhahran indicates once again that a determined terrorist can do a lot of damage regardless of your best security efforts."

Source: James Kitfield, "Freelance Terrorism Hard to Halt," *National Journal* 28, 27 (July 6, 1996), 1483-1484.

his first Inaugural Address both warned against binding political ties with Europe (the effective international system of the time); the immigration patterns of the nineteenth and twentieth centuries have been a tale of people fleeing, first from Europe and then from around the globe, to escape political or economic oppression. The desire to be what Ronald Reagan called the "shining house on the hill," gleaming but slightly aloof, is a central part of the American self-image.

In the twentieth century, the tradition of aloofness broke down. The United States embarked on a World War I crusade to "make the world safe for democracy," only to retreat to "splendid isolationism" afterward. World War II drew in the Americans once again, and as one of the two superpowers after the war, the United States had no real option to retreat from the world.

The end of the Cold War inevitably reopened the debate. With the United States being the one remaining superpower, neoisolationism could not mean a total retreat, but it could mean a scaling back of the extent of involvement. The rationale for such a retreat included the felt need to devote resources hitherto expended on the Cold War competition to domestic priorities—reviving the infrastructure and improving education, among others—and the belief that it was time for others, notably the countries of the European Union and Japan, to bear a larger share of the global load.

The internationalist side of the argument held that a retreat was both irresponsible and impossible as a practical matter. It was irresponsible, the argument went, because the United States was the only country with the resources, standing, and prestige to provide global leadership—a position broadly echoed by foreign leaders. It was impractical, the internationalists argued, because global interdependence is so great—especially but not exclusively in the economic realm—that no real retreat could be sustained.

Much of this debate reflects an assessment of America's relative standing in the world. How much does the world need the United States, and how much does the United States need the world? The answer has to do with what it means to be the only pole in a unipolar world: how powerful a pole is the United States compared with other countries?

Globocop Versus Domestic Priorities

The degree to which the United States should attempt to lead the international system's efforts to maintain order and stability—to be the world's police officer or, as Newsweek termed it in 1993, "globocop"—has been a source of much domestic debate. No one has argued the extremes: that the United States should become involved either all of the time or not at all. The question is the extent to which U.S. resources should be engaged in keeping order, especially in the Second Tier.

Three arguments, two of which are discussed in the next two sections of this case study, are commonly made against extensive involvement. The first is that most of the sources of instability are none of the United States' business, occurring in places where there are few, if any, important interests. The second is that most of these sources of instability are domestic in origin and hence not susceptible to solution by force of U.S. arms.

The third and most politically compelling argument is that the United States needs to concentrate its resources on remedying domestic problems that have accumulated over the last couple of decades, notably the federal budget deficit the debate over which has dominated the domestic agenda and continues despite a balanced budget in 1998. Given the difficulties associated with that problem, expending additional dollars on such items as UN peacekeeping missions continues to be a tough political sell.

The globocop debate is enlivened by a sense of moral obligation. The United States is the only power both capable of global leadership and, at least to an appreciable extent, willing to provide it; reactions by Europeans and others to crises in places like Bosnia and Herzegovina clearly indicate that if the United States does not lead, no one else will. With the knowledge that one cannot react everywhere, the question is how to choose.

Vital Interests and Humanitarian Interests

The most obvious way that states choose international action is by considering the extent to which their interests are affected. As noted in Chapter 2, those vital interests on which states do not willingly compromise are the triggering mechanism for the instruments of national power. Thus, an analysis of when vital interests are and are not involved can—many would argue must—form a basic criterion for action.

The difficulty in a system that demands U.S. leadership is that, in most cases, vital or even important interests are only questionably at stake. From a geopolitical, hardheaded (some would add hard-hearted) viewpoint, there is little way that the United States or its citizens are measurably affected by any outcome in conflicts in the Second Tier. What are U.S. interests in Bosnia? Sudan (other than stemming possible terrorist sponsorship)? Cambodia? Sri Lanka? Kosovo? From a traditional realist perspective, the answer is that there are no interests engaged, and hence there is no reason for American involvement.

This perspective is obviously not universally accepted. A sizable part of American opinion, based in the Wilsonian tradition of American idealism, views it as callous and out of tune with the contemporary system. The representatives of this viewpoint argue that the realist, interest-driven paradigm, even if it was appropriate for the Cold War, is not appropriate to a new system more driven by systemic concerns, with the UN and other mechanisms with global interests more prominent and relevant. The realist paradigm, in other words, does not always fit current circumstances.

In addition, they argue that embodied in the new system are what are often called humanitarian interests or even humanitarian vital interests—interests in the well-being of the whole human race and in the promotion and protection of human rights around the world. Former UN Secretary General Boutros Boutros-Ghali has been a prime proponent of this approach. Many Americans, however, concur, contending that the failure to honor such interests dehumanizes Americans in the process.

Whether Americans believe that there are humanitarian interests that should trigger military or other responses in given situations will largely define the extent of U.S. activism in the new system. A traditional vital-interests analysis results in a very modest degree of activism. If humanitarian concerns are added to the list of things deemed vital (in effect expanding what a vital interest is), then the list becomes longer than can be implemented or contemplated, and the additional criterion of effective involvement becomes significant.

"Doability"

The post–Cold War debate within the U.S. military over the contrast between American action in Kuwait and Iraq and inaction in Bosnia and Herzegovina before the Dayton accords spawned the curious term "doability," which means roughly that a major criterion for the insertion of U.S. forces, and especially ground forces, must be whether such forces can be effective in solving the problem at a cost acceptable to the American people. As a number of wags put it in contrasting the two experiences, "The Army does deserts (Kuwait); it doesn't do mountains (Bosnia)."

This criterion of doability is raised primarily by the military itself, and it is a serious concern. The U.S. military remains in a state of ambivalence. On one hand, it is buffeted by force reductions made possible by the withering of the Soviet threat; these create a need and desire for new missions. On the other hand, the military also remains obsessed by the memory of Vietnam and the determination not to allow itself to be involved in another Vietnam-style "quagmire."

This concern is closely associated with Colin Powell, former chairman of the Joint Chiefs of Staff. As discussed in Chapter 4, he has been the chief publicist of the doctrine of "overwhelming force" for employing American forces. The doctrine holds that Americans should be placed in harm's way only if the situation is amenable to inserting massive force that can rapidly bring about a military victory accomplishing the clear

Marines wade ashore on the coast of South Vietnam in 1965, in the early stages of the massive American military buildup in Southeast Asia. Ten years later the United States lost the Vietnam War, and 30 years later the U.S. military remains determined not to become involved in any mission that could turn into a Vietnam-like "quagmire."

political objective for which it is being utilized. This doctrine was applied with success against Panama in 1989 and against Iraq in 1991. It stands in contrast to the idea, presented in Chapter 2, that in the future modest applications of force for modest purposes may become more common.

The problem—and the U.S. armed forces are well aware of it—is that internal wars are rarely amenable to the application of maximum force. In Bosnia, for instance, it has never been clear against whom such force should be used or to what effect. In Somalia in the winter of 1992, the United States had considerable force that it did not have to employ; but once that force was withdrawn, the situation deteriorated. Overwhelming force, like geopolitical vital interests, is very much a limiting condition.

What makes all these calculations difficult is the transitional nature of the times. No clear rules dictate how the peace will be enforced; there is instead a debate. That debate is global, and its outcome will define the war and peace system of the new order. The shape and outcome of that debate in the United States are important because the United States is the only pole in the unipolar system.

The Changing Contours of Violence

The discussion in this chapter has raised three significant ways in which the pattern of war has changed since the end of the Cold War. Each has emerged against the backdrop of a basically tranquil, prosperous international setting. Whether they will continue into the new millennium, where global conditions may change, is a question worth pondering.

The first major change has been the virtual disappearance of interstate wars (conflicts between countries). Since the Iraqi invasion of Kuwait in 1990, there has been exactly one interstate war in the world through 1998, a 1994 border clash between Peru and Ecuador. Among the political democracies of the First Tier, the prospects that this will continue are great, particularly if you accept the "democratic peace" hypothesis. During this period, international energies have been more closely associated with the growing globalism of the world economy. In 1998, however, that economy took its first sizable downturn of the decade. Will this be reflected in the pattern on violence?

The second trend has been the emergence of what we have called the new internal wars. This phenomenon has been geographically isolated to those places generally outside the global economy—Africa and parts of central and southern Asia in particular. The anomaly

Osama bin Laden, one of the private supporters of terrorism.

WEB SITINGS: The National Security Strategy

By law, the U.S. administration is required to submit annually to the Congress a document known as "The National Security Strategy of the United States." This report, which discusses, among other things, general policies toward foreign military involvements, is available by accessing the website of either the White House (www.whitehouse.gov) or the Department of Defense (www.dtic.dla.mil/defenselink).

---

of these conflicts is enormous. They tend to be bloody, even gruesome, in their conduct, with nearly all the victims being unarmed civilians who happened to be in the wrong place at the wrong time. Because they occur well outside the international mainstream, however, there has been little orderly, predictable systemic response to them, although the formation of a permanent War Crimes Tribunal may be a first step. If these continue to dominate the pattern of organized violence, will the system be forced to respond?

The third trend is the return of terrorism to the forefront. This is particularly a novel problem for Americans, because prior to the early 1990s, they had been largely immune from the terrorists' wrath, unless they were victims of international acts, such as blowing up airliners or kidnapping in places like Beirut. The last half-decade, however, has personalized the problem. The bombing of the Trade Center in New York, the terrorist attack on the Murrah Building in Oklahoma City, and the capture and conviction of the Unabomber demonstrated it can happen here. The attack in Dhahran and the embassy bombings in Africa provided evidence that there are indeed fanatics like Osama bin Laden for whom hating and wanting to kill Americans form an obsession. Whether this will lead to more effective efforts to thwart international terrorism will be interesting to observe.

Review

This chapter has provided an examination of the nature and dynamics of war. In the process, the following points were made:

1. War is a political act, success or failure at which is measured in terms of achieving the political ends for which it is fought. Ends may be either total or limited, as may the means employed. The relationship between ends and means has changed over time.

2. The deadliness of war has increased over time, largely through the application of technological advances to weaponry. This is seen most dramatically in the evolution of nuclear weaponry, from the atomic (fission) bomb, to the thermonuclear (fission-fusion) bomb to the intercontinental ballistic missile (ICBM) and the multiple independently targetable reentry vehicle (MIRV).

3. There have been a number of approaches to explaining war. Philosophical and structural approaches key in on human nature and the development of social structures. The Marxist approach focuses on the imperfections of capitalist society. Microcosmic approaches examine characteristics of humans (such as gender) that may influence warlike behavior. Macrocosmic approaches look at system-level dynamics and causes.

4. In the contemporary system, nontraditional forms of war are becoming dominant. The most prominent form is internal or civil wars for the control of a country's government. Somewhat less frequent are regional conflicts between states and terrorism.

5. American policy response toward the emerging pattern of violence is in the midst of a debate with four interrelated parts. The first, between the internationalists and the neoisolationists, is about how heavily the United States wants to be involved in international affairs. This leads to the second point: to what extent the United States should adopt a major policing role in the world, especially considering the urgency of domestic priorities. How activist the United States will be depends on whether it acts out of a traditional assessment of vital interests or expands policy to embrace "humanitarian vital interests." Finally, the level of activity will be influenced by the extent to which American action is expected to be effective or ineffective.

Suggested Readings

Ardrey, Robert. *The Territorial Imperative: A Personal Inquiry into the Animal Origins of Property and Nations.* New York: Dell, 1968.

Burk, James, ed. *The Military in New Times: Adapting Armed Forces to a Turbulent World.* Boulder, CO: Westview Press, 1994.

Clark, Ronald W. *The Greatest Power on Earth: The International Race for Nuclear Supremacy from Earliest Theory to Three Mile Island.* New York: Harper & Row, 1980.

Clausewitz, Carl von. *On War.* Princeton, NJ: Princeton University Press, 1976 (originally published 1832).

Hobbes, Thomas. *Leviathan.* Cambridge, UK: Cambridge University Press, 1991.

Keegan, John, *A History of Warfare.* London: Hutchison, 1993.

Locke, John. *Second Treatise on Government, 3d ed.* Oxford, UK: Blackwell, 1966.

Lorenz, Konrad. *On Aggression.* New York: Harcourt, Brace and World, 1966.

Luttwak, Edward N., "Toward Post-Heroic Warfare." Foreign Affairs 74, 3 (May/June 1995), 109–122.

Megargee, Edwin I., and Jack E. Hokanson. *The Dynamics of Aggression: Individual, Group and International Analyses.* New York: Harper & Row, 1970.

Marx, Karl. *Capital: A Critique of Political Economy.* New York: Vintage Books, 1977.

Richardson, Lewis. *The Statistics of Deadly Quarrels.* Pittsburgh: Boxwood Press, 1960.

Rothgeb, John M., Jr. *Defining Power: Influence and Force in the Contemporary International System.* New York: St. Martin's Press, 1993.

Singer, J. David. *The Correlates of War.* New York: Free Press, 1979.

Snow, Donald M. *Distant Thunder: Patterns of Conflict in the Developing World, 2d ed.* Armonk, NY: M.E. Sharpe, 1997.

—. *UnCivil War: International Security and the New Internal Conflicts.* Boulder, CO: Lynne Rienner Publishers, 1996.

— and Dennis M. Drew. *From Lexington to Desert Storm: War and Politics in the American Experience.* Armonk, NY: M. E. Sharpe, 1994.

Sylvester, Christine. *Feminist Theory and International Relations in a Postmodern Era.* Cambridge, UK: Cambridge University Press, 1994.

Tickner, J. Ann. *Gender in International Relations: Feminist Perspectives on Achieving Global Security.* New York: Columbia University Press, 1992.

Waltz, Kenneth. *Man, the State, and War: A Theoretical Analysis.* New York: Columbia University Press, 1959.

Wright, Quincy. *A Study of War, 2d ed.* Chicago: University of Chicago Press, 1983.

Ze-dong, Mao. *Selected Works (4 vol.).* Beijing: People's Publishing House, 1965.

Contemporary International Patterns

PART 2

6

A System in Transition

PREVIEW

In this chapter, we will examine the transition from the Cold War to the post–Cold War world. We will begin by examining the causes of the end of the Cold War, emphasizing both the military and economic dynamics that underlay the change. We will then turn to the effects the end of the Cold War has had on the international system, including both short-term and longer-term effects. This will lead to a discussion of the emerging rules of the new international system, including the changing importance of economic and military power. The chapter will conclude with a case study examining the struggle for change in the formerly communist countries of Eastern Europe and their transition to the post–Cold War era.

KEY CONCEPTS

necessary peace
high-technology revolution
Potemkin village
nuclear allergy
Cuban missile crisis
escalation
Cold Warriors
era of stagnation
nomenklatura
perestroika
glasnost
Commonwealth of Independent States
  (CIS)

North Atlantic Treaty Organization
  (NATO)
Warsaw Pact
Partnership for Peace (PfP)
United Nations system
selective activism
northern states of Eastern Europe
southern states of Eastern Europe
Western European Union (WEU)
Organization on Security and
  Cooperation in Europe (OSCE)

OUTLINE

For more than a generation, the Cold War was an immutable, pervasive, and encompassing reality. The global struggle between communism and anticommunism was the first premise of the foreign policies of states and set the tenor of international relations. Domestic politics, and people's ways of thinking, were affected by the competition: Americans, for instance, became used to the idea of a "national security state," whose first purpose had to be to provide a buffer against "godless communism." Compulsory loyalty oaths to the government and "witch hunts" to uncover and prosecute alleged communist subversives were natural consequences of this mindset.

Moreover, the Cold War was enduring. The international system created around it seemed, at least in fundamental terms, unchanged and unchanging. This was reality; since the only way the system appeared likely to change was through the inferno of a nuclear World War III, war had to remain "cold." The Marxists talked vaguely of the "withering away of the state" in the final approach to the communist millennium; no one considered the withering away of communism as the way in which the impasse might be broken.

The Cold War system became intellectually comfortable. Everyone knew whose side everyone else was on and what the rules of the competition for conversion were. The dictates of national policies flowed naturally and deductively from the "rules of engagement" of that competition. Whether it was a question of countering an armaments buildup or giving aid to a friendly insurgent movement, the system provided the rationale for whether and when to act.

Since it was unaccompanied by a great war, the aftermath of which would necessitate planning and change, the sudden collapse of communism in Europe left the international system in a conceptual and intellectual vacuum. Leaders and scholars simply had not thought much about the possibility of a post–Cold War world and so had not planned for it. The alternative to the familiar landscape was uncharted territory.

Even after it should have been clear that basic change was under way in 1988 and 1989, many still distrusted their perceptions of what was going on. Evidence of change in the Soviet Union and in Eastern Europe was apparent to the naked eye, but the idea of

Case in Point

Mink Wars

During the last two decades of the Cold War, the Swedish navy regularly reported detecting the clandestine movement of Soviet submarines around the long coastlines of Sweden, Norway, and Finland. Although the Soviet Union consistently denied the accusations, its claims were generally disbelieved in the West, and Swedish naval vessels dropped depth charges into the fjords of the three countries in an attempt to flush out the suspected intruders.

In 1992, however, the Swedes discovered that minks swimming in the fjords emit a sound very similar to that of a submarine, and reviews of audiotapes of the supposed Soviet intrusions revealed that the stealthy "invaders" were in fact schools of minks. Swedish Prime Minister Ingvar Carlsson admitted the mistake on February 10, 1995, stating, "It's a sad fact that what [were] originally stated to be intrusions into our waters have proved to be minks." Carlsson said he did not believe that Sweden needed to issue a formal apology to Russia, and added that there had been no reports of submarine activity since 1992. The minks, presumably, appreciate being able to swim in Scandinavian waters without fear of being attacked with depth charges.

Source: New York Times, February 12, 1995, p. 10.

fundamental change was too incongruous to fit into people's mental constructs. "Is it real?" they asked themselves at each instance of apparent change, "or is it merely a particularly clever instance of Soviet disinformation?"

In this chapter, we will examine the process of transition. We will begin by looking at the dynamics leading to the decision—mostly emanating from Moscow under the more or less witting stewardship of Soviet President Mikhail S. Gorbachev—that the Cold War competition had become too expensive and self-defeating to continue. Our basic argument will be that a stalemated military situation combined with a stagnating economy and progressive technology-based economic competition to force the Soviets, and especially Gorbachev, to conclude that the Cold War had to end. In the process of making this argument, we will raise the question of whether scholars in the field of international relations (again including ourselves) should have seen the changes sooner than they did.

Next, we will look at the actual changes that occurred, viewing in kaleidoscopic fashion the events beginning in September 1989, as the Polish electorate voted out its communist leaders amid Soviet acquiescence, and culminating in the final, peaceful dissolution of the Soviet Union itself at the last moment of 1991. This will lead to examining the effects of the changes, first in Eastern Europe and then for the world more generally. That discussion will be followed by a look at evolving rules for the new system. We will conclude with a case study examining the struggle of states within the former Warsaw Pact bloc to find their place in the new order.

Causes of the End of the Cold War

While recognizing that it is always easier to predict the past than it is the future, scholars of international politics are still flagellating themselves over their inability to foresee the Cold War's demise. With the more than considerable assistance of hindsight, however, it is possible to discern dynamics that, if viewed within the framework of the possibility of change, make some sense of the process.

For present purposes, we will identify three related factors that, in combination, apparently induced the Soviet leadership—with the American leadership largely in its trail—to conclude that the Cold War competition was no longer sustainable and that it must be terminated. These factors were: (1) the existing nuclear stalemate, and the resulting stalemate in the overall military relationship; (2) a growing gap in economic performance between the noncommunist and communist worlds that was undermining the socialist system and its global competitiveness; and (3) a widening gap in competitiveness in the high-technology revolution—a factor with direct relevance to both the other causes.

Although history may well treat him as a transitional figure, the role of Mikhail Gorbachev is pivotal in all the discussions that follow. The factors that caused the Gorbachev regime to call off the Cold War probably would have forced any Soviet leadership group eventually to conclude something like what Gorbachev and his colleagues concluded. Gorbachev's role was to recognize the problem at a point when others did not, and to facilitate the idea of change. His failing was that he was unable to harness or control the process once it began.

It is apparent in retrospect (though it was not at all apparent at the time) that Gorbachev inherited a very difficult set of circumstances, which cumulatively defined a not very palatable set of priorities. A list of these circumstances is presented in the Case in Point box "Gorbachev's Potemkin Village." Individually and collectively they suggested a superpower in serious trouble—a power in the kind of decline described by Paul Kennedy and other declinists and discussed in Chapter 7.

The term "Potemkin village" refers to a false front, or facade, that is erected to obscure real conditions; it was inspired by the story that a Russian prince, Grigori Potemkin, had a series of false facades of towns built for a tour of the Crimean peninsula by Tsarina Catherine the Great, to fool her into believing that the region was much more prosperous than it was. As it happened, this image turned out to be a particularly appropriate one for the Soviet Union when Gorbachev came to power in the mid-1980s. The Soviets had grown, especially in military power, to the point where they appeared to have achieved equality with—by some measures even superiority to—the United States. The show of military might, however, was a false front hiding a deeper poverty that could not be obscured forever. The combined weight of military stalemate, economic uncompetitiveness, and the technology gap knocked the false front to the ground.

Nuclear Stalemate and Necessary Peace

The first factor leading to recognition that the Cold War competition was unsustainable involves nuclear weapons and military competition. That nuclear weapons would themselves ultimately lead to a stabilization of the relationship between the Cold War rivals, and hence contribute to the peaceful end of their rivalry rather than to the fiery end of the world, was

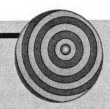

Case in Point

Gorbachev's Potemkin Village

When Mikhail Gorbachev came to power in the mid-1980s, he was faced with a number of serious problems that were, individually and certainly collectively, not widely appreciated in the West. In combination, they revealed a Soviet Union that was increasingly a hollow power, a mere facade of the superpower it was represented to be—in other words, what is sometimes called a "Potemkin village." Soviet woes included:

1. Economic ruin—a progressively deteriorating economy, featuring economic stagnation by most measures of growth and declining productivity in virtually all industrial sectors.
2. A growing military technology gap with the West—with prospects that the gap would widen.
3. Domestic political inertia—the government and ruling party controlled by cronies of former president Leonid Brezhnev and by the entrenched management class of state-owned enterprises (nomenklatura).
4. Social discontent—a lack of quality consumer goods, and the absence of any meaningful service industries.
5. An increasing burden of military spending—an outgrowth of Cold War competition, especially manifested in the confrontation with a heavily armed, hostile NATO.
6. An expensive external empire—in Eastern Europe, with few benefits to the Soviet Union.
7. Expensive international overcommitments—in Afghanistan, Angola, Cuba, the Horn of Africa (Ethiopia), and Nicaragua.
8. A growing minorities problem—Russians outside the Russian republic, non-Russians inside it.
9. Exacerbating distractions—an Armenian earthquake that killed thousands, the Chernobyl nuclear plant disaster.

To buy imported meat from a state-owned store, these customers in Moscow in 1991 endured long lines and surly salesclerks—perhaps only to learn that the store was sold out. Growing consumer discontent with chronic shortages and the low quality of goods and services provided a strong base of popular support for Mikhail Gorbachev's reforms. At the time this picture was taken, shortly before the Soviet Union broke up, Soviet media were reporting that hungry people in some areas of the country were raiding farms to steal sheep and cattle.

not an idea widely embraced during the Cold War, nor is it universally accepted today. Certainly a part of the reason is what we have already called a nuclear allergy, a repugnance toward nuclear weapons and hence an inability to think dispassionately about them. The launching of nuclear weapons against the Soviet Union that was depicted in the satirical 1964 movie *Dr. Strangelove* never occurred in reality; in many quarters, neither did rational thinking about nuclear weapons.

Our thesis here can be stated clearly. Beginning with the aftermath—or aftershock—of the Cuban missile crisis, a growing realization emerged within policy-making elites that the consequences of nuclear war were such that it had to be avoided at all costs. Beyond the simple recognition that there was indeed a common interest in avoiding nuclear war, the resulting necessary peace between the Cold War antagonists spread to their entire military relationship. When defense spending became so onerous to the Soviets that they feared it threatened their overall international position, they moved to defuse the competition, thereby contributing to the winding down of the Cold War.

As we discussed in Chapter 3, the Cuban missile crisis was a key event in changing the dynamics of the nuclear relationship. Previously, there had been widespread public belief in the West in the absolute incompatibility of the two blocs and in the likelihood—to some observers, even inevitability—of nuclear war as the climactic event of the Cold War. In combination, these beliefs bred a morbid popular culture that debated whether a society was "better Red than dead" or "better dead than Red." The temper of the times is well illustrated by the motion picture *On the Beach* (adapted from a novel by Nevil Shute), which ends with the radiation clouds of a nuclear holocaust reaching Australia, where the last survivors await their deadly fate.

During the missile crisis, nuclear war seemed likely until, as American Secretary of State Dean Rusk put it, "The other guy blinked" and the danger subsided. In coming as close as the human race had to nuclear Armageddon (although the possible physical dimensions of a nuclear war increased steadily for the next 20 years as arsenal sizes grew on both sides), the two superpowers took a sobering look into the abyss and backed away.

In addition to sowing the seeds that would lead to Nikita Khrushchev's removal as Soviet leader in 1964, the crisis gave rise to two related dynamics that grew in importance across time. The first stemmed from the realization that the superpowers had a mutual interest in avoiding annihilation. What emerged was a nuclear arms control process, the common theme and rationale of which was to try to make nuclear war less likely. This progression is captured in the Amplification box "Major Arms Control Agreements, 1963–1979." In the beginning, the spirit of cooperation between the two superpowers was limited to nuclear relations. This spirit did not spread to sustained broader cooperation until the 1980s and especially the rise of Gorbachev. The whole trend is, nonetheless, traceable to the Cuban crisis.

The second, related dynamic set in motion by the Cuban missile crisis was the growing realization that nuclear war between the superpowers was not merely undesirable but actually intolerable. This understanding eventually led to a loss of faith in the military buildup on each side and in the idea even of conventional warfare between the two powers.

In the heat of the time, this dynamic was hardly recognized from the outside, and sizable proportions of the intellectual and policy-making communities continued to debate drearily the likelihood of nuclear war and the inherent instability of the nuclear balance. The simple fact was that the nuclear balance, especially as arsenals grew to over 10,000

Amplification

Major Arms Control Agreements, 1963–1979

The aftermath of the Cuban missile crisis created a window of opportunity within which a number of arms control agreements were reached. This "Golden Age of arms control" lasted from 1963 to the Soviet invasion of Afghanistan in December 1979. The precedent for this activity had been set in 1961 when the Antarctic Treaty, which banned nonpeaceful activities in Antarctica, went into force (it was negotiated in 1959). In the following list of agreements, the earlier date is the year when heads of state initialed it. The agreement does not enter into force until it is approved by signatory states through their constitutional processes (for instance, Senate ratification in the United States).

1. The Limited Test Ban Treaty banned nuclear weapons testing in the atmosphere, in outer space, and underwater (everywhere except underground). It was signed and went into force in 1963.
2. The Outer Space Treaty set forth principles for use of outer space, including the moon, such as nonweaponization of space. It was signed and entered into force in 1967.
3. The Latin American Nuclear-Free Zone Treaty prohibited nuclear weapons in Latin America. It was signed in 1967 and entered into force in 1968.
4. The Non-Proliferation Treaty prohibited non-nuclear signatory states from acquiring nuclear weapons and nuclear states from aiding in such acquisition. The treaty was signed in 1968 and entered into force in 1970.

5. The Seabed Arms Control Treaty banned the placement of nuclear or other weapons of mass destruction on the ocean floor. It was signed in 1971 and went into force in 1972.
6. "Accidents Measures" and "Hot Line Modernization" Agreements between the United States and the Soviet Union improved procedures for defusing nuclear crises. They were negotiated and took effect in 1971.
7. The Biological Weapons Convention prohibited the development, production, and stockpiling of biological and other toxic elements and called for destruction of existing supplies. It was signed in 1972 and came into force in 1975.
8. The first Strategic Arms Limitation Talks (SALT I) between the United States and the Soviet Union resulted in two agreements, an antiballistic missile (ABM) Treaty that limited defenses against nuclear attacks and an interim agreement freezing offensive arms. These agreements were signed and entered into force in 1972. The ABM Treaty was modified by protocol in 1974.
9. Subsequent Strategic Arms Limitation Talks (SALT II) proposed further limits on superpower nuclear arsenals. An agreement was signed in 1979 but was never ratified by the U.S. Senate. Its provisions were, however, followed until it lapsed.

Source: Arms Control and Disarmament Agreements: Texts and Histories of Agreements, 1980 ed. Washington, DC: United States Arms Control and Disarmament Agency, 1980.

nuclear warheads aimed at one another on both sides (the result of formerly single-warhead rockets being converted to multiple warheads), actually became more stable. In this condition of mutual societal vulnerability, the deadliness of war, as it turned out, was inversely related to its likelihood: the more consequential the prospect of war became, the more it had to be avoided.

Policy-making elites, particularly the leaders of both superpowers, understood this truth. American leaders at least as far back as Dwight D. Eisenhower in the 1950s and Soviet leaders as far back as Khrushchev voiced the sentiment that the prospect of nuclear war was "inadmissible," as the Soviets put it in the 1970s. One of the more obscure Soviet leaders and Gorbachev's immediate predecessor, Konstantin Chernenko, stated the case in 1983 with particular clarity: "In a nuclear war, there can be no victors and no political aims can be achieved by means of it. Any attempts to use nuclear weapons would inevitably lead to a disaster that could endanger the very existence of life on Earth."

Chernenko's observations, repeated in similar words by Gorbachev when he achieved power, and the words of other leaders seem so obvious that one can only wonder why they were not more carefully noted at the time and entered into nuclear calculations. In the expert community, only a few analysts argued the stabilizing role of nuclear balance. Robert Jervis did conclude, in his 1985 study *The Illogic of American Nuclear Strategy,* that the prospect of an assured destruction outcome created a deterrent effect, a view expressed by one of the current authors in 1987 (Snow, *Necessary Peace*).

What hardly anyone seemed to see, however, was the extension of nuclear stalemate beyond the nuclear balance to the overall military balance between East and West. That relationship follows logically from certain premises. First of all, any war between the United States and the Soviet Union (or their close allies) was potentially a nuclear war. The key concept here is escalation, the idea that even a small clash involving nonnuclear weapons could widen (or escalate) to the point that nuclear weapons might be employed, with uncertain consequences for further escalation. In any given circumstance, it did not matter how much probability there was of such an escalation, because the possibility always existed. Second, it was recognized by the leaderships that nuclear war was unacceptable and that its avoidance was a matter of the very highest priority. Given such premises, the conclusion is that all war between the superpowers was unacceptable. The Summary box "Unacceptability of Conventional U.S.-Soviet War" captures the logical sequence involved in reaching this conclusion.

Summary ——————————————
Unacceptability of Conventional U.S.-Soviet War

The argument regarding the unacceptability of conventional war between the superpowers can be reduced to a simple logical construction—a syllogism:

1. Conventional war creates the possibility of nuclear war.

2. The possibility of nuclear war is unacceptable.

3. Therefore, conventional war is unacceptable.

When one accepts this logic, then the entire arms competition between the superpowers begins to lose its meaning. The costly preparations for war, the endless practicing and exercising that marked the preparation for World War III, are reduced to ritual behavior in which both sides continue to prepare for a war they are committed to avoid at all costs. This being the case, the military competition, especially its very expensive conventional dimension, becomes progressively an economic albatross around the necks of both superpowers.

The contribution of large, robust nuclear forces to this calculus cannot be overestimated, because they made uncertain the ability of either side to gain from interbloc military action. With enormous nuclear arsenals that if used would produce only losers, then the assessment of any action is negative; it is difficult, even impossible, to calculate a great enough likelihood of success to warrant military action. At the same time, this very calculation suggests the efficacy of changing that part of the balance that is most debilitating economically, the conventional balance.

The recognition that both sides were spending a great deal of money preparing for a war they were absolutely dedicated not to fight combined with the Soviet, and then the American, economic crises of the 1980s to prod leaders to end the Cold War. For the Soviets, the situation was more compelling. As we shall explain in the next section, the economic crisis of the Soviet Union became public in the early 1980s, and remedying it became very high-priority business. The huge Soviet defense effort was an obvious drain on resources, human and otherwise. At the same time, a prominent aspect of Soviet uncompetitiveness was the cutting edge of science and its applications (the high-technology revolution); if the Soviets were to keep up in high technology, they needed to join the West. As long as military confrontation existed, they would be excluded from the information and knowledge base on which technology exists.

Several years removed from the Cold War experience, these conclusions may seem unexceptional and lead one to ask why they were not recognized nor embraced at the time. For they were not. Had the analysis put forward above been expounded even as late as 1989 or 1990, it would have been the subject of widespread derision and disbelief. There are no totally satisfactory explanations for this skepticism (which undoubtedly still exists in some quarters); on the basis of our own experience and observations, we would suggest three interlocking explanations.

The first is an atmosphere of suspicion and distrust that bred conservatism. The Cold War was, after all, a long and difficult period during which levels of mutual antagonism engendered a high degree of suspicion. When Americans first heard Gorbachev talk about turning the Soviet state into a "normal" member of the international system, they did not believe him. When he published his blueprint of the future (to which he closely adhered), entitled *Perestroika: New Thinking for Our Country and the World,* it was initially dismissed by many as disinformation intended to lull the West into lowering its guard.

Given the deadly potential consequences of misstepping, of engaging in actions that might produce a Soviet advantage in the overall conflict, the result was an overall conservatism. The Cold War had a heavily military content, and the military profession has an inherently cautious, conservative outlook that is a necessary part of its obligations. The U.S. national security establishment (like its Soviet counterpart) was thus reluctant to accept "liberal" interpretations of peaceful overtures from the other side of the divide.

The second explanation for the widespread failure to recognize this dynamic was the Cold War mindset of both leaderships. When the warning signs of the end of the Cold War

Case in Point

Gorbachev's "Disinformation"

The following statements by Mikhail S. Gorbachev were widely dismissed as "disinformation" when he wrote or said them. The first two are from his book *Perestroika: New Thinking for Our Country and the World*, published in 1987. The third is from a speech given in 1989. Compare them with what he subsequently did:

> The fundamental principle of the new political outlook is very simple: nuclear war cannot be a means of achieving political, economic, ideological, or any other goals. This conclusion is revolutionary, for it means discarding the traditional notions of war and peace....Nuclear war is senseless; it is irrational. There would be neither winners nor losers in a global nuclear conflict; world civilization would inevitably perish.

> And we do not want simply to conduct negotiations....It's good that talks are going on. But it is essential to move toward something so as to make progress, to arrive at agreements and let the Soviet and American people and the whole world get, through the Geneva accords, the solution to the outstanding problems that will remove the nuclear threat and pave the way to disarmament.

> European states belong to different social systems. That is a reality. Recognition of this historical fact and respect for the sovereign right freely to choose a social system constitute the major prerequisites for a normal European process....Change is the exclusive affair of the people of [a] country and is their choice. Any interference in domestic affairs and any attempts to restrict the sovereignty of states—friends, allies, or any others—are inadmissible.

This last excerpt is from a speech delivered two months before the beginning of the revolutions of 1989.

Sources: Mikhail S. Gorbachev, *Perestroika: New Thinking for Our Country and the World,* New York: Harper and Row, 1987, pp. 140–141 and 249; Mikhail S. Gorbachev, "The International Community and Change: A Common European Home," *Vital Speeches of the Day* 55, 23 (September 5, 1989): 707.

Mikhail S. Gorbachev, who oversaw the transfer-nation and ultimate disembling of the Soviet Union, also foresaw the need to modify East–West relations.

began to arise, the people in military and decision-making positions and in the academic community were themselves very much products of the Cold War. Some had been born prior to 1945 and some after, but they all shared common reference points, whether they had learned them from academic sources or from practical experience in the foreign policy community. Their intellectual roots and constructs were those of the Cold War.

Probably the most persistent assumption about the Cold War was its endurance. Short of a cataclysmic nuclear war or some highly dismissible utopian schemes, few had thought of ending the Cold War. A few thinkers like George Kennan, the father of the American policy of containment (which sought to contain communism within the boundaries it had achieved in the late 1940s), had suggested the possibility of Soviet collapse; but in the terms we have used here, there was hardly any sense of systemic change, no speculation about what change agents might be at work, not to alter the way the Cold War worked (there was an abundant amount of speculation about a changed Cold War), but to end it. Insensitive to the prospects for fundamental change and acculturated to believe it would not happen, people looked at it and did not see it happening.

Moreover, many policymakers and academics had a real stake in the Cold War. These Cold Warriors had developed whole careers based on their ability to understand or manipulate international relations within a Cold War context. Loss of the old premises threatened them with the intellectual equivalent of the fate of the dinosaurs, so the Cold War was a hard thing to give up.

A third and final reason for failure to recognize what was coming is that nuclear allergy made it difficult for analysts to think about a positive role for nuclear weapons. To a large part of the policy-making elite, and especially of the academic community, nuclear weapons were simply bad, dangerous artifacts needing to be controlled or eliminated. That they could serve the positive purpose of placing boundaries on permissible U.S.-Soviet interactions and even lead to the realization that continued competition was untenable was simply unacceptable to these people.

The Economic Performance Gap

In inducing the end of the Cold War, the changes in the dynamics of the military relationship shared intellectual billing with a second factor—the realization in the Soviet Union that the socialist system was losing the economic competition with the capitalist West by a large and steadily increasing margin. The basic nature of the problem is by now well known. Beginning in the early 1970s, economic growth ceased in the Soviet Union; not only did output by any measure other than the production of vodka flatten, but in some sectors it actually declined. As it happened, the latter 1970s and early 1980s were a period of unprecedented growth of the economies of the First Tier, thereby accentuating the differences.

This performance problem went largely unnoticed in the West, mostly because it coincided with an unrelenting buildup of Soviet arms that spurred a similar program within the United States under the leadership of President Reagan. Within the Soviet Union, however, there was a growing recognition of what would later be called the "era of stagnation."

Those who recognized the problem were largely Soviet intellectuals, and especially economists. This group communicated with one another, often by writing articles in academic journals; the articles were presumably as impenetrable as those of their American counterparts, meaning that the censors could not understand them even if they read them.

What the Soviet reformers needed was a political sponsor, and they found one in Gorbachev. Although the details have never been fully disclosed, the apparent point of contact was his wife, Raisa, a faculty member at Moscow State University. When Gorbachev succeeded Chernenko in 1985, this group was positioned to act as advisers in planning economic reform.

The heart of the perceived problem of stagnation was the *nomenklatura,* the class of managers of the state-owned production system, which owed its position and loyalty to the Communist Party and to longtime Soviet leader Leonid Brezhnev, rather than to indications of economic success. The reformers, and especially Gorbachev, recognized this fact but, as committed Marxists, they still believed that socialist economics could accomplish its goals if properly managed. As they saw it, what needed to be done was to make Marxism work correctly—not to abandon it, as Boris Yeltsin would seek to do later.

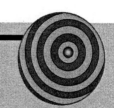

Case in Point

George Kennan on the Soviets

In addition to suggesting that the Soviet Union, especially as it extended itself to a broadening empire, might fail of its own internal contradictions, the scholar and policy-maker George F. Kennan made several other observations about Soviet power that were considered unorthodox at the time but that proved largely true. In the so-called "long telegram" of early 1946, for instance, he suggested:

> The Russians don't want to invade anyone. It is not their tradition....They don't want war of any kind....They prefer to do the job politically with stooge forces. Note well: when I say politically, that does not mean without violence. But it means that the violence is nominally domestic, not international, violence. It is, if you will, a political violence...not a military violence.
>
> The Soviet leaders, formidable as they were, were not supermen. Like all rulers of all great countries, they had their internal contradictions and dilemmas to deal with. Stand up to them, I urged, manfully but not aggressively, and give the hand of time a chance to work.
>
> Soviet power, unlike that of Hitlerite Germany, is neither schematic nor adventuristic. It

does not work by fixed plans. It does not take unnecessary risks. Impervious to the logic of reason, it is highly sensitive to...force.

Source: George F. Kennan, *Memoirs, 1925-1950.* Boston: Little, Brown, 1967, pp. 361, 364, 557.

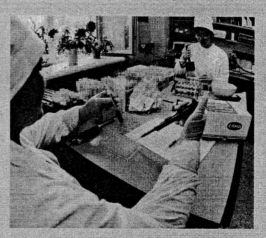

The primitive state of scientific laboratories like this one, in which donated blood is being tested for HIV antibodies, reflected the widening technological gap between the Soviet Union and its capitalist rivals in the 1980s.

The reform program called for fine-tuning the system, and internally it had three elements. The first was *uskeronie* (acceleration), which aimed simply at getting notoriously unproductive Soviet workers to work harder and thus more productively. In recognition of their historically high rates of alcohol-related absenteeism and nonperformance, *uskeronie* focused on a cutback in the production and availability of vodka and other alcoholic beverages, which was resisted so strongly by Soviet workers that it was ultimately abandoned.

The second prong of the economic reform program was *perestroika* (restructuring), a term originally associated with Lenin. Given that the *nomenklatura* had become a privileged class—a virtual new tsarist elite—the aim of *perestroika* was to restructure state enterprises (not to eliminate them) so as to circumvent the managers, thereby revamping the incentive system and presumably aiding productivity.

The third feature of this reform program, also aimed at the *nomenklatura,* was *glasnost* (openness or criticism): if the managerial class was the problem, then these people should be publicly identified as such and properly criticized. As a result, many of the constraints of censorship were lifted. The result was a flood of criticism—not only of the target group, but of the system as a whole.

The combination of these initiatives unleashed forces that would get beyond the control of the Soviet leadership and contribute to the demise of the Soviet state and hence the Cold War. The top leadership did not recognize these possibilities in 1985 when they instituted the process of change; had they been able to foresee the outcome, they probably would have taken a different course.

It is clear in retrospect that this conceptual framework doomed the effort from the start, in at least five ways. First, the individual reforms were tentative and timid, reflecting the attitude that there was nothing fundamentally wrong with the key aspects of the system. In attempting to stimulate agriculture, for instance, the Law on State Enterprise allowed farmers to lease or buy parcels of land but so restricted the conditions of land tenure as to make the prospect unappealing for the majority. Similarly, provisions were instituted to allow private enterprise, but profits were taxed at such a high rate (originally 85 percent) that it hardly made sense to open a business.

A second drawback was that the reformers underestimated the inertial drag in the system. Except for the party elite, people realized the system did not work well for them, but that realization did not necessarily translate into dedication to change. One might not do terribly well under the old system, but one was guaranteed a job from which it was almost impossible to be dismissed, and the extensive social welfare system ensured a reasonable existence. Furthermore, there was no tradition of peasant land ownership, so that many farmers associated with collective and government-owned farms were leery of the idea and derided the new kulaks, or prosperous private farmers (the original kulaks had been eliminated by the Communists during the 1920s and 1930s). Similarly, the new capitalists charged market-driven prices for their wares, rather than lower state-subsidized prices, and were thus viewed by many as gougers.

A third factor dooming the reform effort was that ideological blinders kept the leadership from understanding that the heart of the problem was the system itself. A socialist economy, that is, did not provide the individual incentives to work and innovate competitively with the rest of the world, and a state-controlled bureaucracy could not manage efficiently an economy of the size and complexity of the Soviet economy. Moreover, the Communist Party of the Soviet Union (CPSU) had become irremediably corrupt and flabby, more concerned with ensuring the well-being of its elite members than with managing the government or fostering the well-being of the population. Making these basic institutions better could not solve the problem; they either needed to be swept aside entirely or reformed to such an extent as to be unrecognizable.

A fourth obstacle to success was that the reformers made many tactical mistakes that made matters worse than they had to be. This should not come as a surprise. The reformers were, by and large, trained as Marxist economists, and they were being asked to make the transition to a market economy, about which they knew little. Moreover, the task was unprecedented. The conversion of a command to a market economy had never been undertaken on such a scale before; there was no "textbook" to act as a guide.

The fifth and final problem with the reform program was that meaningful change required becoming part of the world economy. Economic growth in the West was more than the sum of growths in national economies, because of the increasing interdependence of these economies. As they intertwined, their interactions stimulated greater growth. For years, however, insulation from the global economic system had been part of Soviet policy—a prime example was Soviet persistence in keeping the ruble inconvertible to other currencies so as to avoid its being weakened. This sort of isolation prevented the Soviet Union from taking part in the surge of economic growth occurring in the West and continues to dog the Russian economy.

The High-Technology Imperative

A third factor in inducing the Soviet leadership to abandon the Cold War was the growing technology gap between the Soviets and the West. Military and economic problems came together in Soviet nonparticipation in the high-technology revolution—the current ongoing explosion in knowledge generation (the result of advances in computing), knowledge dissemination (the result of advances in telecommunications), and a number of derivative technologies (such as fiber optics, new materials science, and biotechnology) that contributed to knowledge generation and dissemination.

This revolution has several distinctive characteristics, of which four stand out. First, it is international, the result of collaboration among scientists in the First Tier countries, whose cooperative efforts generate scientific advances much more significant than could be produced in isolation. Second, it is interactive. Advances in computing trigger discoveries in, for instance, fiber optics, which in turn increase the ability to transmit more data faster across boundaries and between scientists.

Third, participation in this revolution is progressive. This means that one must be a part of the process to benefit from it. Yesterday's computing ability, for instance, is inadequate to compete in today's high technology. Since the accumulation of new technology is geometric, the farther outside one is, the farther behind one falls.

Fourth, the high-technology revolution is critical to a country's status, because applications of high technology to commercial endeavors and military development represent the cutting edge of competitiveness. Superpower status in economic terms is largely defined by a country's scientific-technical status and its ability to translate scientific-technical knowledge into commercially viable products.

The Soviets stood clearly outside this process. Although Soviet science was renowned for its broad theoretical advances, the highly centralized scientific community had fallen far behind the West in the areas that constitute high technology. For instance, Soviet computers were fully two generations behind their western counterparts. Not only were Soviet telephone lines so antiquated that data could not be transmitted over them, but the whole idea of fiber-optics transmission, so much in vogue in the West, was no more than a wishful thought.

The nature of Soviet society contributed to this gulf. By bureaucratic fiat, the Soviet Academy of Sciences had disbanded its computer division in 1960 to free more Soviet scientists for developing weapons, a totally self-defeating move. The Soviet system thrived on secrecy and control of access to information (Soviet computer laboratories, for instance, seldom had more than one printer); scientific advance requires openness. Moreover, the kinds of people willing to do the very hard work involved in technology are often motivated by the ability to reap great personal gain for their endeavors. A society that bragged that the earnings gap between its highest-paid and lowest-paid workers was only three to one is hardly likely to produce a Bill Gates.

In addition, the Soviets were deliberately excluded from much of the technological revolution because of the military rivalry with the West. Most of the technologies involved are dual-use; they have applications in the civilian and military sectors. Thus, an advance in computer-chip technology may be applied to improving a hand-held calculator or the electrical system of an automobile; that same chip may also form the heart of the guidance system on Tomahawk cruise missiles (the pilotless missiles used to great effect by the United States against Iraq in the Persian Gulf War of 1991).

Gorbachev understood his society's disadvantage in technology (for a summary, see Snow, *The Shape of the Future*) and the need for the Soviets somehow to become part of the high-technology loop. The alternative was to fall hopelessly further behind the West economically and militarily. The military recognized this prospect, which is why they supported the reform efforts. As long as the Soviet Union remained excluded, the problem would persist.

Solution: End the Cold War

If the analysis to this point has been cogent, Gorbachev and the Soviet Union faced dual economic-technological and military crises in 1989. First, they were locked into a military competition that was ruinously expensive and ultimately meaningless. Second, they were falling progressively behind the West economically and technologically. Moreover, the problems were related to one another: bloated military expenditures stunted investment in the civilian economic sector and in research and development of new technologies, and a faltering economic system and outmoded technology were becoming progressively unable to supply the military with competitive weapons. Continuing things as they were would only make the problems worse.

Military competition and economic problems also plagued the United States, if not in quite such dramatic form. Beginning in 1979, the administration of President Jimmy Carter had initiated a major military spending campaign to compensate for investments that had been deferred after the Vietnam War. When Ronald Reagan assumed office in 1981, he accelerated the program to erase what he called the policy of "unilateral disarmament" of his predecessor, which he alleged had resulted in military disadvantage for the United States in the face of relentless continuing Soviet armament. In addition, some Reagan advisers hoped that the buildup would stimulate an arms race with the Soviets that they would eventually conclude they could not win. Many of these same analysts see the collapse of the Cold War as a vindication of their position, a view for which there is increasing evidence.

By the middle 1980s, it was apparent to many that the U.S. arms buildup was contributing to difficulties in the country's economy. Along with tax reform that reduced federal revenues and especially entitlement programs whose cost continued to burgeon, defense spending was a leading contributor to growing annual budget deficits that would quadruple the national debt between the beginning of the Reagan presidency in 1981 and the end of the Bush administration in 1993. Many felt that the government borrowing necessary to cover deficits was robbing the private sector of funds necessary for investment, and hence contributing to a decreasing American competitiveness in the global economy.

Thus, both superpowers had some incentive to engage in a process of change. In the end, the Soviets were first to realize this—in their case, that their only chance (and it was no more than a chance) was to join the world system as a normal, rather than as a rogue, state. The West was not going to embrace its enemy and share knowledge with it. The only way for that to happen was for the military rivalry to end; the Cold War had to go.

One of the first elaborated signs of the Soviet intent occurred with the 1987 publication of the book we have mentioned by Gorbachev. Apparently written during his mysterious eight-week disappearance from public view in 1986, *Perestroika* was divided into two parts: the first half dealt with the internal reform program, and the second put forth a new Soviet view of international relations that suggested Gorbachev's intent to transform the Soviet Union into a wholly normal state. Among other things, the book denounced the idea of interference in the internal governance of states, including rebellious socialist states (the Brezhnev Doctrine that had been invoked to justify Soviet intervention in Afghanistan, among other places).

Perestroika was greeted by great caution and skepticism; as we mentioned, the West had been so conditioned to Soviet perfidy as to expect any suggestions of normalization to be no more than disinformation and propaganda. Subsequent Soviet initiatives in other areas such as arms control (including a summit in Reykjavík, Iceland, where Gorbachev and Reagan came close to agreeing to complete nuclear disarmament without their aides realizing it) were not enough to overcome Western suspicions. Only when Warsaw Pact communist governments began falling, with no Soviet reaction, and change became apparent within the Soviet Union itself did the West begin to get the wake-up call.

What specifically led Soviet leaders to act when and as they did to end the Cold War, thereby setting in motion a process of fundamental systemic change? Any judgment must remain somewhat incomplete. The entire decision-making record is not available; moreover, those leaders, notably Gorbachev and his entourage, no longer in official positions implementing the processes they began, have not publicly explained their motives in detail.

Nevertheless, one can draw some inferences based on the public record and what has happened since the initial decisions were made. The first and overarching reason for the Soviets to take the initiative is that the leadership concluded they had no real alternative. The Soviet empire (the Soviet Union always had the structure more of an empire than of a normal state) was crumbling in full public view. Glasnost had quickly turned to basic criticism of the communist system and the first calls for secession in the Baltic states (Estonia, Latvia, and Lithuania). Economic deprivation was widespread, and costly international commitments—in places like Cuba—were indulgences for a faltering system that could no longer afford the luxury.

All the trend lines were negative. As reforms began, they created predictable interruptions in economic activity that made Soviet performance worse, at least in the short run. These shortcomings were most clearly apparent in consumer goods and services, long a matter of neglect and indifference, but now important because of the increased freedom of speech accorded Soviet citizens. The reinforcing aspects of military spending and economic failure could only snowball, resulting in the decline of the Soviet Union.

The only hope lay in gaining access to western capital and technology, a need openly acknowledged by the Gorbachev regime. Verbal assurances of change in Soviet international behavior had not been enough to overcome the Soviet image as the adversary. Too many of the symbols of the Cold War remained: the opposing alliance systems, Soviet-imposed communist governments in Eastern Europe, the Iron Curtain of barbed wire keeping "enslaved" peoples in, and—of greatest symbolic importance—the Berlin Wall.

The Gorbachev decision to let the Cold War unravel was apparently made and transmitted to Eastern Europe in the summer of 1989. Between them, Gorbachev and his foreign minister, Eduard Shevardnadze, visited the capitals of all the Eastern European satellite states. Their apparent message was "Come to terms with your populations. If you do not, there will be no Soviet tanks to save you this time." When the Poles exercised the option of voting out the Communist Party and there was no adverse reaction from Moscow, the floodgates opened. The process of transformation had begun.

Literally playing in the ruins of the Cold War, a girl balances on the rubble of the Berlin Wall. From 1961 to 1989 the wall stood as the paramount symbol of Soviet repression, preventing escape from the eastern to the western sector of the city. The building on the left is the Reichstag, home of the German parliament.

At this point the Soviet leadership did not yet perceive the need to restructure fundamentally the Soviet system. By ending their 45-year-old adversarial relationship with the West, the Soviets did become eligible for at least modest amounts of western economic assistance and the infusion of some western technology. However, the process of change was not rapid enough or successful enough either to keep the Soviet Union intact or to maintain Gorbachev in power. He had been a catalyst necessary to begin change; it would fall to Boris Yeltsin and other successors to carry the process forward in the direction of more fundamental change.

Effects of the End of the Cold War

The fallout from the end of the Cold War is still being felt years after the process began, as suggested in the case study at the end of Chapter 3. What we can distinguish is some of the short-term impacts (those occurring more or less from the last quarter of 1989 through the end of 1991) and some medium-term effects that have emerged since the end of 1991 and may grow into long-term effects.

Short-Term Effects

The end of the Cold War and the fall of communism in Europe were, of course, simultaneous and intertwined events; the fall of communist regimes undercut the rationale for the Cold War competition. The rapidity with which change occurred is captured in Table 6.1. When the progress of events is set forth in this manner, it shows an apparent flow and continuity that was less obvious at the time the events were occurring. Retrospect, in other words, makes the progression altogether more orderly and planned than it either appeared or probably was at the time. This series of events, however, defines the end of the Cold War and hence the beginning of the post–Cold War world—which, for convenience sake—we can regard as having begun on January 1, 1992.

Table 6.1	The End of European Communism
1985	Gorbachev becomes CPSU General Secretary, ending succession process in Soviet Union.
1987	Gorbachev publishes *Perestroika*.
1988	Soviets complete withdrawal from Afghanistan. Gorbachev is elected President of Soviet Union and shifts political power from CPSU to Soviet government.
1989	Gorbachev and Shevardnadze warn Eastern European leaders to come to terms with their populations. Revolutions of 1989 occur: Communist government falls in Poland *(September)*. Reform government comes to power in Hungary; Iron Curtain is breached *(October)*. Velvet Revolution occurs in Czechoslovakia; East German government is imprisoned; Berlin Wall falls *(November)*. Romanian government falls *(December)*.
1990	Multiple parties are authorized in Soviet Union; Bulgarian government falls; German reunification occurs.
1991	Warsaw Pact dissolves; attempted coup fails to overthrow Gorbachev; Soviet Union dissolves.

The immediate effects of the revolutionary process were felt most strongly in the Soviet Union and Eastern Europe. These include the breakup and reconstitution of the Soviet empire, the beginnings of reorientation of the formerly communist countries of Eastern Europe, and the breakdown of the security system that had both divided and structured Europe politically and militarily.

The first and most dramatic short-term effect of the breakdown of the Cold War was the dissolution and reconstitution of the Soviet Union itself. In a remarkable political act, the country ceased operation without bloodshed at the end of 1991, an event without precedent in the modern state system (any number of states, of course, have been forcibly dissolved). In the immediate sense, the former "republics"—equivalent to U.S. states or to provinces in many other countries—became independent countries, with the same boundaries they occupied as republics. Retaining these borders was a source of ongoing problems, discussed below.

Eleven (eventually 12) of the 15 former republics reconstituted themselves into a loose political entity called the Commonwealth of Independent States (CIS). The members include the four largest and potentially most important states—Russia, Ukraine, Belarus (formerly known as White Russia or Byelorussia), and Kazakhstan—as well as the states of the Caucasus and the other Asian republics. The three Baltic states did not join, and Georgia was persuaded to join in 1994 after Russia intervened there to help put down Abkhazian separatists seeking to bring down the government of Shevardnadze.

The idea underlying the CIS was to maintain some associational institution among the former Soviet states to facilitate the common defense, to continue economic ties, and to coordinate general relations among the states. The CIS continues to exist, but only as a limited actor. It has no officials or offices of note, the common military command has engaged only in limited peacekeeping activities within member states, and economic warfare, not cooperation, has been the norm among its members. The republics operate as sovereign entities. Russia, by virtue of size (about three-quarters of the former Soviet Union) and population (about half of the old empire), remains the most important successor state, and some view the CIS as a way for Russia to maintain influence in the other successor states. In any event, Russia occupies the permanent UN Security Council seat formerly held by the Soviet Union, has become an active member of the Group of Seven (now Group of Eight) conference of world economic giants, and is still by far the largest country in the world physically.

The second major short-term effect of the demise of the Cold War has been the restructuring of the formerly communist states of Eastern Europe. All six of the states allied with Moscow overturned their communist regimes, as did Albania and Yugoslavia, which itself was dismembered into warring parts. All of the states involved have made their first, tentative steps toward a market economy and, to some extent, political democracy (see the case study at the end of this chapter for an assessment).

What was and is remarkable about the transformation of Eastern Europe is the relative ease with which it occurred. As already noted, communist regimes toppled in a matter of months, although it took until 1992 for Albania to denounce the communist system. In some countries, communists calling themselves something else remain prominent in politics (Serbia/Yugoslavia is an example), but avowedly communist governments have simply disappeared from the European continent, leaving Europe with no sharp political divisions among regimes for the first time since the Congress of Vienna briefly reinstalled absolute monarchism at the end of the Napoleonic wars.

Map 6-1   **Members of the Commonwealth of Independent States**
©1996 by St. Martin's Press, Inc. From: *Contours of Power*, by Snow/Brown. Reprinted with permission of

•The third short-term effect was the breakdown of the security system in Europe. The North Atlantic Treaty Organization (NATO), created in 1949, and the Warsaw Pact, formed in 1955 in response to the rearmament of West Germany, had dominated the security "architecture" of the continent and, by extension, the overall international system. With the collapse of the competition, the alliances became increasingly hollow. The Warsaw Pact formally ceased to exist in 1991 when its members voted its demise; NATO remains an active, functioning organization, but one with far smaller troop commitments and nagging questions about its long-term mission, much of which is tied to the longer-term success of the Partnership for Peace (PfP) process that is also discussed in the case study at the end of this chapter.

Probable Long-Term Effects

In a sense, the end of the Cold War is too recent to have produced more than the beginnings of trends or effects that may become long-term. We can, however, identify four such effects: the end of the East-West military competition, the consequent end of major-power competition in the Second Tier, emerging cooperation between Russia and the United States, and the evolution of the former Soviet Union toward a more normal place in the world.

The first change that may become long-term is the end of East-West military competition. In the wake of the end of the Cold War, both former sides moved quickly to cut back their forces. Within NATO, all major states rapidly drew down their active-duty forces; within the former Soviet Union a draw-down took place more slowly because of the inability of Russia in particular to find alternate sources of livelihood for soldiers in uniform. In the other republics, former Soviet forces were converted to new national forces and were, by and large, reoriented toward a new potential adversary, Russia itself. At the same time, most of the republics sold off large stocks of arms to gain hard currency necessary for economic development.

The result of these cutbacks has been a major military realignment. Russia remains a nuclear superpower, but its conventional forces have been reduced drastically (its navy, for instance, is only about half its 1992 size) and probably cannot be projected effectively beyond the boundaries of the former Soviet Union—a limitation underscored by the difficulty its forces have had in subduing the Chechen rebellion within Russia. Indeed, Russian military doctrine now emphasizes defense and projection into the other successor states on behalf of Russian minorities there. Although the United States has also cut back active-duty forces, by about a third (from a little over 2 million to an estimated 1.4 million at the end of 1995 with cuts continuing), it remains the only country in the world capable of global power projection—a fact that helps to define the unique U.S. position and responsibility in the new order.

A second possible long-term effect of the end of the Cold War is the apparent end of superpower competition for influence in the old Third World (the Second Tier). Overextension into parts of the world like Angola and Nicaragua was, to repeat, one of the factors militating toward Soviet abandonment of the overall Cold War competition. As the Russians have moved out, so too have the Americans. The implications of this trend for the Second Tier are evolving and ambiguous. On the positive side, the artificial overlay of communist-anticommunist conflict onto Second Tier problems is removed, leaving the possibility that the real problems of political and economic development can be addressed directly and without distortion. On the other side of the coin is that there is less motivation for the United States and Russia to provide resources as a way of currying influence.

A third long-term effect of the Cold War's end is the emergence of Russian-American cooperation on international issues. It was suggested during the Cold War that it was a good thing that the chief antagonists were the Russians and the Americans (rather than, say, the Russians and the Germans), because they would not have been enemies except for their ideological differences. The truth of that observation is reinforced by the rapidity with which the animosity between the two peoples and their governments has virtually evaporated since the demise of ideological confrontation.

This U.S.-Russian cooperation has spread to and included the military sector. In fact, military officers from Russia and other Soviet successor states now freely travel in the United States and even attend war colleges whose previous purpose revolved around how to defeat them. The Russians have reciprocated with an open hand to the West. The joint participation of the United States and Russia in the Bosnian IFOR/SFOR (Implementation/ Stabilization Force) operation shows how far cooperation has come.

Another ramification of the new U.S.-Russian cooperation has been the resuscitation of the United Nations system. Before the end of the Cold War, the veto power residing in the permanent members of the UN Security Council (the United States, Soviet Union, China,

Views from Abroad

The Suppression of Chechnya

Russia's ongoing attempt either to crush or negotiate away the secessionary movement in its autonomous southern republic of Chechnya has
raised many questions. Does Chechnya have a
"right" to national self-determination through the
creation of a sovereign Chechen state, or is Russia's action a proper expression of its sovereign
control of Russian territory? In any event, was it
necessary for the Russian military virtually to
level the center of the Chechen capital of Grozny,
killing an estimated 22,000 people? The Moscow
newspaper *Pravda* argued that the regime of
President Boris Yeltsin had committed "a number
of transgressions against the Chechen people
[that] lie on the consciences of Russia's leaders."
Moskovskiye Novosti, a Moscow weekly maga-
zine, was blunt in assessing blame: "The big
president [Yeltsin] did not meet with the little one
[Chechen President Dzhokhar Dudayev] and instead sent in tanks and soldiers: Let them die, but
I have nothing to talk about with Dudayev."

The Chechen incident was also widely seen by
newspapers in Russia and abroad as a test of
Russian democracy. Moscow's *Izvestia,* for instance, argued that "Chechnya has become a test
of the maturity of [Russia's] democratic institutions, just as Chernobyl [the 1985 disaster at a
Soviet nuclear power plant, which Soviet officials at first tried to cover up] once served as a
test of glasnost, public access to information, and
the openness of society. That time, the test
yielded a negative result. What will Chechnya
show?" Outside Russia, *The Independent* of London argued that Russians "seem to understand
that there is a direct connection between the
amount of liberty Russia allows its weaker neighbors and the amount of freedom they themselves
will enjoy." Germany's *Frankfurter Rundschau*
argued that democracy had been compromised

because Russia had chosen to join "the ranks of
those countries for which the preservation of state
power is worth a small or even a big war against
parts of their own populace."

A solution remains elusive. Although Yeltsin
and the Chechen leadership agreed to a cease-
fire before the 1996 presidential election (which
some Yeltsin detractors argued was no more
than a cynical ploy to boost his reelection
chances), violence continues to flare up periodically, and the Russian military remains unable
to repress it altogether, a problem that a 1996
study blames partially on the enormous supply
of illegal arms available to the Chechens from
Russian organized crime sources.

Source: World Press Review, February 1995, p. 6; Graham
H. Turbiville Jr., *Weapons Proliferation and Organized
Crime: The Russian Military and Security Dimension* (US
Air Force Academy, CO: Institute for National Security
Studies), 24–26.

Russian tanks ride past a mural depicting a Caucasian
mountain warrior near the Chechen border in late 1994,
in the early stages of the conflict over Chechnya's
attempted secession.

Britain, and France) meant that the world body was paralyzed from acting in any situation where the Soviets and United States were in disagreement. Since they were in disagreement on almost all issues of importance, the UN could not be a central actor on the world stage; it functioned merely as an observer and as a forum for venting contrary opinions.

The great symbolic act breaking the bottleneck was the Soviet-American cooperation in sponsoring the UN's participation in the Desert Shield/Desert Storm effort to evict Iraq from Kuwait in 1990–91. During the Cold War, the Soviet Union, a putative sponsor of the Iraqis, probably would have vetoed any such action; freed of its client-sponsor relationship, the Russians willingly joined the broader effort.

The fourth long-term effect of the Cold War's end involves the evolution of the former Soviet Union toward a more normal place in the world. Two aspects of this evolution stand out. The first involves the changing situation within the various republics as they struggle with economic development and political self-determination. Almost all the republics are striving—with widely varying success—to move from socialism toward a market basis for their economies. In all cases, progress is tortuous, uncertain, and reversible, since a transformation of this nature is unprecedented. Moreover, some of the republics have more resources and a better chance than others. The fact that these now-separated 15 states were formerly part of a single, integrated (if inefficient) economy makes matters more difficult.

There is also a political struggle within the successor states. Although there are no avowed, openly communist regimes in the successor states of the Soviet Union, many of the old leaders remain in power, and progress toward some approximation of western-style democracy is highly differential and by no means certain. The victory of Boris Yeltsin over communist Gennadi Zyuganov in the 1996 Presidential elections (the effects of which are discussed in the Contours of the Future? box) eased some worries about a Russian reversion to the old regime. At the same time, the Soviet policy of ethnic migration—especially of Russians to the non-Russian republics—has created serious minority problems within many republics.

The second aspect in the evolution of the former Soviet Union involves relations between Russia and the other republics. In this case, very little progress toward international standards of normality appears to have occurred. As noted, the CIS format has not facilitated cooperation, and the formerly integrated economy creates economic weapons that are used by all parties. Thus, the Russians have withheld energy from the Baltic states in order to influence their policies regarding their sizable Russian minorities. The Ukrainians similarly have used wheat and other foodstuffs to extort cheaper oil and natural gas from Kazakhstan and Russia.

The treatment of minorities, however, is the most basic problem in relations among the republics. Over 25 million ethnic Russians live outside Russia and are now minorities against whom many have grievances. Artificial republican boundaries created by Stalin have contributed to there being an even larger number of non-Russians living outside their "nations." The process of adjustment between majorities and minorities, whether by peaceful accommodation, migration, or violence, remains a core concern. As noted, Russian military doctrine now directly confronts this problem. At the same time, Ukrainian war games now feature planes, tanks, and the like with Russian markings as the adversary.

Contours of the Future?

Russia After the 2000 Presidential Election

Although there was a visible sigh of relief in much of the world at Boris Yeltsin's successful reelection as Russian president in July 1996, the aftermath left a number of questions about the future of Russian democracy unanswered. Some of the questions were structural, dealing with problems of democratization of the Russian political system. Others dealt more personally with the likely future of Yeltsin, who has a history of health problems. The 1998 economic and political crisis and calls for Yeltsin's resignation have only intensified speculation.

The fact that a reasonably orderly election without major accusations of corruption or malfeasance could be held in Russia is not the same thing as an indication of the flowering of democracy. There are still widespread evidences of official corruption within Russia, and the rule of law in any western sense has not visibly taken over. As Yuri Shchekochkhin, a Russian parliamentarian, puts it, "I have not seen any sign in the country of what is most essential to the development of democracy—that those in authority are subject to the law." Further evidence of authoritarian trappings include the overwhelming support for Yeltsin in the Russian press before the election and the fact that Yeltsin ruled by decree—including dispensing pork barrel favors to selected constituencies.

There has been great concern about Yeltsin's ability to serve a second term. His disappearance from the campaign trail before the election stirred concerns about his health. At age 65, he had already exceeded the life expectancy of Russian males by seven years (Russia is one of a relative handful of countries where life expectancies are in decline), and his absence fueled speculation over his health problems, including heart disease and alcohol-related ailments. Following his heart bypass surgery, this speculation intensified; his apparent return to better health in 1997 at least temporarily quieted such discussions. In 1998, he even began talking of running for reelection in 2000.

Source of quote: U.S. News and World Report, July 15/22, 1996, 82.

Rules of the Game in the Emerging System

The major impacts of the end of the Cold War on the international system involve security aspects, since the Cold War was decidedly a military competition. The evolving economic realities (discussed especially in Chapter 9) were not greatly affected. The old Soviet economy operated outside the economic system of the rest of the world, and although the successor states desire full participation in the global economy, that has yet to occur. The nonmilitary aspects of change consist mainly of greater political cooperation between former adversaries, some loosening of the security concerns of major economic powers (for instance, the United States and Japan), and the prospect that reduced military spending by the former superpowers and other states may free up funds for other priorities.

In relation to security, at least three trends that constitute changing rules of the game can be identified. These are the changing role of the UN in shaping international security, the decline of the national security state as the focal point of major-power concern, and the increased importance of the Second Tier states in the war and peace system.

The United Nations System

Because the United Nations was the principal means for forming and legitimizing the coalition that conducted the highly visible Persian Gulf War in 1990–91, there were initial expectations that the world body would therefore assume a major, possibly the major, role in managing global security. Authorization of UN roles in Somalia and elsewhere seemed to reinforce that new position. At the beginning of 1993, for instance, there were 13 United Nations peacekeeping missions in the field, out of a total of 27 similar missions in the whole history of the organization. Bolstered by the promotional efforts of Secretary General Boutros Boutros-Ghali, the UN was riding high as the legitimizing agent of choice for the new system.

Some of the enthusiasm for this expanding mission began to fade in 1993, chiefly for three reasons. First, euphoria over the UN's supposed ability to settle difficult internal problems was dampened by failures in places such as Somalia, where the international rescue mission went sour after the United States withdrew and handed over command to the UN itself. As we shall argue in Chapter 13, this lack of success was probably not altogether the UN's fault, as the organization was being thrust into civil wars, where successful outside interference is often impossible. At any rate, however, it served to take some of the bloom off the rose.

The second reason for the decline of enthusiasm is financial. Money problems have plagued the UN throughout its existence but have been particularly acute in recent years. For military actions such as peacekeeping, the UN has always relied on a system of assessing the members beyond their normal annual dues or asking for voluntary contributions to cover such costs. The problem is that some members—notably the United States—do not meet these obligations all of the time. The more missions the UN mounted, the larger the bills grew, and the greater the inability of the organization to meet its financial obligations became. Clearly, the world body is only financially capable to the extent its members are willing to dig into their pockets. That extent is not great enough to cover the growing number of world crises where the UN may be called on.

The third problem for the UN, the availability of military forces committed to UN duty, is similar. For a relatively modest number of small peacekeeping operations, commitments from countries such as Norway, Canada, and Morocco, to name a few of the most frequent participants, were adequate; but as the number of missions expanded, the UN outgrew its resources. In the case of the United States and other major powers, a particularly vexing problem was the UN's desire that national troops be placed under UN command, as was suggested for Somalia; such an arrangement is politically unacceptable in the United States.

While the UN's role in keeping the peace has expanded from the Cold War (when it had practically no role), the old realities still hold. As an intergovernmental organization whose members are sovereign states, the UN will have a restricted role, conditioned by the desires of the important states who must pay the bills. As an entity independent of those states, the

UN has limited power and legitimacy. Many idealists find this situation unfortunate, and many realists find it comforting. Regardless, if the United Nations occupies a more prominent position in managing world peace, it is mostly because the world's principal players have assigned it a larger role.

Decline of the National Security State

The Cold War required that the most basic foreign policy concern of the major powers had to be the military competition between them. Because of this priority, a phenomenon known as the national security state emerged, in which defense and foreign policy essentially merged; the result was that in their foreign policy, states were primarily concerned with the development and maintenance of those aspects of national power relevant to military concerns.

The end of the Cold War has permitted the powers to begin rearranging their national priorities and the way in which they view systemic problems. One of the central realities of the new international system is that there are essentially no potential military confrontations that are system-threatening. During the Cold War, a conflict between the United States and the Soviet Union could have threatened the entire international system; there are no likely conflicts of the same magnitude today. Granted that Russia and the United States maintain the nuclear ability to evaporate a large part of the human race, it is now farfetched to consider circumstances in which they would commit that act (even if it was not farfetched before). The decline of former Soviet conventional forces also means that the wherewithal for a massive conventional war in Europe is missing. The possibility of nuclear war in some form (such as between members of the Second Tier) may actually be on the increase, but it is not clear that such a war, fought with limited numbers of nuclear weapons, would escalate to the point of threatening the overall international system. India and Pakistan, through the public testing of nuclear weapons in 1998, are the major testing ground of this dynamic.

This does not mean the new system lacks conflict and violence. Quite the contrary. The new system is punctuated by military conflicts that are numerous, highly visible, and responsible for large-scale misery. What is equally true is that they essentially all occur outside the core of the international system (the First Tier); it is hard to imagine how even the worst possible outcome of any such conflict could escalate and engulf the system. We will revisit this phenomenon and its implications in Chapter 11.

How does this shift in the focus of conflict change things? First, it causes the major players to reassess their foreign policy, including military, priorities. Granting that the unforeseeable could still occur, traditional military power is depreciated; the kinds and quantities of arms and preparation necessary for a major war on the northern European plain are clearly irrelevant under current and predictable future scenarios. Particularly as the Revolution in Military Affairs transforms warfare, arsenals containing large stocks of things like heavy tanks and artillery may become obsolete. This does not mean that concerns about and preparations for military conflict will disappear or recede very far. What it does mean is that the relative emphasis on military force as an instrument of power will shrink and that different forms of the military instrument will become more important.

In this circumstance, a second, related effect of the changed security situation is a reorientation of the instruments of power that states employ for various ends. Among the First

Haitian President Jean-Bertrand Aristide waves to supporters after returning to his country in 1994, three years after he was driven into exile by a military coup. Although the United States imposed economic sanctions to try to force the military from power, it took the diplomatic efforts of former U.S. President Jimmy Carter and a peaceful occupation by American troops to achieve Aristide's restoration.

Tier countries, the economic instrument has already become supreme, and it is increasingly dangled before (or held over) Second Tier states as well—for example, most-favored-nation status as a primary U.S. tool to influence Chinese human rights performance, or economic sanctions to force Haiti's military government from power. Given the questionable relevance of military force in ending Second Tier ethnoreligious conflicts, diplomatic tools may become more prominent as well.

Third, with this shift of military focus, new instruments of power may well arise. As an offshoot of the economic instrument, technological superiority may emerge to define the economic competition and thus become an instrument of power in itself (see discussion in Chapter 9). The great-power "warfare" of future years may be fought over preeminence in efforts such as the production and utilization of telecommunications equipment, or the processing and disseminating of information.

A fourth change in a system not so clearly dominated by military matters will be a turning of governments' attention more toward other concerns, such as environmental degradation, population control, and women's rights. Such topics have recently been made focuses of international concern through events such as the Rio de Janeiro Earth Summit of 1992, the 1994 UN population conference in Cairo, Egypt, and the 1995 conference on women held in Beijing, China. It has become common to talk about concerns like the environment in terms of national security and economic competitiveness.

Fifth, there is an apparent shift in the patterns of associations between states in the new order. During the Cold War, military associations such as NATO were clearly supreme, relegating other forms such as economic ties through international forums such as the General

Agreement on Tariffs and Trade (GATT) and even the European Union (EU) to a more secondary role. In the post–Cold War world, NATO and other military associations have diminished in importance (but have certainly not disappeared) while economic forms have either flourished (GATT expanded to the World Trade Organization, the EU intensified by the Maastricht Treaty) or come into existence (the North American Free Trade Area and the Asia-Pacific Economic Cooperation).

The Second Tier Security Problem

In contrast to the essential military tranquility to be expected among the major powers of the First Tier, sporadic violent conflict can be expected within and between countries of the Second Tier. Occasionally such conflicts will draw in First Tier countries. The conflict arises both from relations between the First and Second Tiers and from intra–Second Tier problems. The systemic question is what can or should be done to alleviate destabilizing conditions in the Second Tier, a number of which are legacies of the Cold War competition. This question reflects the long-standing disagreement between the tiers about First Tier obligations to assist in Second Tier development.

The First Tier–Second Tier (or what has been called First World–Third World or North-South) conflict arises from contrasting levels of economic development and wealth, gaps in technology, and cultural differences. From the vantage point of much of the Second Tier (see Chapter 8), the cause of its problems is the legacy of European colonial rule, which systematically retarded Second Tier growth and development. (The contrasting view is that colonialism merely made manifest the preexisting developmental advantage of Europe over what is now the Second Tier.) The overwhelming desire of almost all Second Tier states is to join the general prosperity of the countries of the First Tier, and many link this prosperity with the attainment of political democracy.

An argument that has been popular in the First Tier is that development in its various senses is the prerequisite for the emergence of stable political conditions in the Second Tier. The premises of that argument are a matter of debate. If one accepts part or all of the argument, however, then aiding Second Tier development is in the enlightened self-interest of a First Tier that values peace and stability. From a Second Tier perspective, the First Tier, whether or not its self-interest is involved, has an obligation to assist in that development as partial compensation for the deleterious effects of colonial rule.

The intra–Second Tier bases of conflict largely have to do with developmental problems (such as vast differences of wealth within countries), adjustments of state boundaries or relations among ethnoreligious groups within states, or the reemergence of old rivalries unregulated by Cold War restraints. While any or all of these sources of conflict have the potential for considerable localized carnage and may even upset regional stability, there is very little escalatory potential beyond the regions involved. The largest and historically most explosive regional conflict is on the Asian subcontinent, between India and Pakistan. During the Cold War, when the Soviet Union served as a sort of patron for India and the United States for Pakistan, there was fear the two superpowers could be dragged into a confrontation. In contemporary circumstances, Russia and the United States might become involved as mediators, peace seekers entering side by side.

Three possibilities, with nuances between them, stand out as candidates for systemic solutions to these problems. The first is simply to leave the Second Tier alone to work out its own problems, an approach of benign neglect. This approach has two signal advantages.

One is that it may be the only realistic approach that can be taken. It is not at all clear either that the resources are available in the First Tier to make much difference in Second Tier development or that their application can work beyond the margins of Second Tier problems. The Second Tier may simply have to work its way through development just as the First Tier did in the nineteenth century. A second reason for benign neglect is that there is little support for anything else among First Tier publics. The negative side of benign neglect is that it assures a continuation of instability and friction between the First and Second Tiers, at least for the near future.

A second alternative, at the opposite end of the spectrum, is massive involvement, seeking to facilitate and maximize the pace and extent of developmental activity within the Second Tier. The advantages and disadvantages of this approach are virtually the flip sides of the arguments for neglect. Such an approach would obviously be very popular in the Second Tier, because it would respond to claims that the First Tier owes developmental assistance. If the resources could be absorbed and used to maximum effect, the process of development could be accelerated. However, there is relatively little systematic evidence to buttress theories of development, put forth originally in the 1950s, that call for massive intervention. Rather, especially given the lack of expertise and the existence of massive corruption in many Second Tier countries, there is considerable risk that massive infusions of assistance would mostly be wasted and would move Second Tier countries forward only marginally, as has apparently occurred in a number of Asian countries leading to their financial crises. Moreover, First Tier publics would not stand for the levels of resource diversion necessary for the attempt.

The third alternative in relations with the Second Tier is selective activism, involvement either where vital interests (such as petroleum) are clearly engaged, where massive human tragedy would be the result of inaction (perpetual natural disasters in places like Bangladesh, or human-created disasters in places like Somalia), or where involvement is mutually advantageous (development of Pacific Rim countries as manufacturing centers). Selective activism represents the current approach and is probably the only sensible and possible way for the First Tier to deal with the Second Tier. Benign neglect and massive intervention are impractical and of dubious effect: the First Tier can neither ignore nor take care of everyone. Selective activism represents a broad range of possibilities between the fringes of these extremes. The questions of how much activism should be employed and what criteria should be used to decide when and where to act have yet to be clearly answered. How these issues eventually are worked out will, of course, have a great impact on how the Second Tier contributes to the general peace and prosperity or its absence.

The pattern selective activism will take remains conjectural. Given the negative outcomes of some major interventions so far and general dissatisfaction with them within the First Tier, Somalia-style military interventions will probably be infrequent at best. A more intriguing possibility (discussed in Chapter 9) is to broaden the general prosperity of the Second Tier through economic associational structures such as the North American Free Trade Association (NAFTA).

Case Study: *The Struggle for Change in Eastern Europe*

The world was rightly astounded at the pace and vigor with which the countries of the former communist bloc in Eastern Europe threw off the shackles and rejected the leadership

Map 6-2　**Eastern Europe**

©1996 by St. Martin's Press, Inc. From: *Contours of Power,* by Snow/Brown. Reprinted with permission of Bedford/St. Martin's Press, Inc.

of their former system. Although there had been roots of dissent in most Eastern European countries for more than a decade before the revolutions began in 1989, the way that populaces promptly shrugged off their devotion to the communist "utopias" for which they had so long toiled illustrated the depth of their rejection of the system.

Vestiges of the old system remain and play a role in the ongoing struggle. Transforming an economic system based almost entirely on state ownership into a market-based, private entrepreneurial system is not easy, especially when there is limited expertise in capitalist business procedures and philosophy. At the same time, 40-plus years of socialism have created work habits (not working very hard) and expectations (high levels of government welfarism) that make the transition difficult.

The problems and their prospects are not uniform across the various Eastern European states, because despite the gray, lifeless facade of communism, there are distinctly different cultures and levels of development. The most basic differentiation is between the northern states of Eastern Europe (former Warsaw Pact members Poland, East Germany, Slovakia, and the Czech Republic and Hungary, plus the Yugoslav successor states of Slovenia and Croatia) and the southern states of Eastern Europe (former Warsaw Pact members Romania and Bulgaria, plus Albania and Yugoslav successor states of Serbia, Bosnia and Herzegovina, and the Former Yugoslav Republic of Macedonia). The northern states are generally more prosperous and culturally western and are hence given the best short- to medium-term chances of entry into the general prosperity already enjoyed in Western Europe; the process of change in the southern states will be longer and its outcome more problematical.

The process of integrating these Eastern European states into the world system has internal (domestic) and external (international) dimensions. Internally, the problems are political, economic, and nationalist; the formerly communist states must become more like the First Tier to be accepted by the system. Externally, the concerns focus on developing a security system superceding the Cold War mechanisms of which Eastern Europe was a part and on joining the global economic mainstream, which eventually will require integration into the European Union.

The Internal Dimension

The three aspects of internal development—political, economic, and nationalist—are, of course, intertwined and are part of the general debate over proper strategies of change. Should economic development precede political development (democratization) or vice versa—or should there be equal emphases on both? What has happened in China suggests the first strategy (economic, then possible political development), the Russian case implicitly promoted political freedom first, and there is evidence of the third approach in some Eastern European countries.

Democratization in Eastern Europe is hampered in two ways. First, very few of these countries—most of which were parts of various empires during the nineteenth century—have democratic traditions (histories of democratic rule and adherence to democratic political ideas). Both the Czech Republic and Poland have some democratic tradition (from the period between the world wars) on which to build; by contrast, there is almost none in countries such as Bulgaria, Romania, Serbia, Slovakia, or, for that matter, most of the former Soviet republics. Second, banned communist parties have reemerged under other names in most of these countries and continue as a drag on democratic development. The success of former communist leader Slobodan Milosevic in clinging to power in Serbia has been a prime example of this problem. The free election of former communists to lead governments in Poland and Hungary in 1994 also suggests some frustration at the pace of development.

As one might guess, the "report card" on democratization has been differential. Poland and the Czech Republic not only have elected governments but also have experienced the healthy sign of elective governmental transitions, including in the Czech case the peaceful dissolution of Czechoslovakia. Hungary has made progress, and despite the emergence of neo-Nazi groups in former East Germany, progress is evident there as well. Most of the southern states, by contrast, have made only feeble attempts at a democratic transition.

Economic performance has been similarly differential, with the northern states outperforming their southern neighbors. By 1993, many observers were talking openly of the Polish "economic miracle." Regarded earlier as one of the economic weak links in the transition, Poland had a private sector that accounted for almost half the country's gross domestic product (GDP, the value of all internally produced goods and services), and both industrial output and GDP were growing. A stable political environment and very attractive business climate have made Hungary the most popular country for foreign investment,

Views from Abroad

Four Ways of Looking at Post-Communism

The return of former communists to center stage in many East European countries and the successor states to the Soviet Union has raised concerns about the resurgence of the old communist system, a prospect viewed with differing levels of dismay. An Indian commentator, Sumer Kaul (reported in the *Hindustan Times* of New Delhi), blames the phenomenon on a "snowballing rejection of the largely imported philosophy of the market as the sole deity of their post-communist destiny." Among the pitfalls of this conversion, he lists the fall of Russia from a superpower to a "toothless mammoth," rampant criminality, the destruction of social guarantees, and the loss of savings due to hyperinflation. He suggests the need for a distinct alternative to pure capitalism: "call it social democracy, controlled capitalism, or socialism with a human face."

Zhelyu Zhelev, president of Bulgaria (writing in *Le Monde* of Paris) attributes part of the problem to natural causes: "Revolutions, even 'velvet revolutions,' are rarely capable of fulfilling the hopes they have raised." While he argues that "the traditional version [of communism] is incapable of reestablishing its power," he fears the effects of "the consolidation of post-communism," including the return of the "state, omnipresent and omnipotent," and growing citizen apathy. Polish journalist Adam Michnik, writing in Moscow's *Izvestia*, catalogues the tactics of the post-communists. In his view, they use "the language of political cynicism," block decentralization and broader powers for local government, and impede privatization.

Russian novelist Vassily Aksyonov, also writing in *Izvestia*, issues the strongest warning against the post-communists, equating them with Rumpelstiltskin, the Brothers Grimm dwarf who terrorizes the population until his real name is revealed. "The evil dwarf is roaming around again, this time in a parliamentarian's sports jacket," he writes. He argues the return of the post-communists is intolerable, because "democracy cannot tolerate in its midst a party that rejects democracy. Either they ban democracy or democracy bans them."

Source: World Press Review, February 1996, 10-11.

another sign of conversion to a market base for the economy. By contrast, the southern countries lag behind, with continuing large governmental participation in the economy and little privatization or outside investment.

The third internal problem is the adjustment of ethnic, religious, and nationalist conflicts within and between the Eastern European states, conflicts that were previously suppressed by Austrian and Ottoman despotism and then by communist authoritarianism but have resurfaced with the lifting of the communist veil. These struggles have been evident in a number of areas, with differing outcomes. The bloodiest and most notorious conflict, of course, has resulted from the unraveling of "old" Yugoslavia and centers on Bosnia and Herzegovina and more recently Kosovo. The existence of a large Hungarian minority within the Romanian province of Transylvania and of a Romanian majority within the Soviet successor state of Moldova suggests other potential trouble spots.

Goulash to go may be still to come, but Hungarians with a hankering for burgers and fries can now indulge themselves at a variety of outlets of American fast-food chains. Since the fall of communism, Hungary has attracted the most foreign investment of any Eastern European country.

The External Dimension

For the former communist countries of Eastern Europe to fully make the transition from their prior status to full-fledged members of Europe, they must also become part of the web of international relationships on the continent. Two aspects are involved: becoming part of whatever security system supersedes the Cold War arrangement and becoming part of the economic system that is defined by the European Union (EU).

A clear strategy for association has emerged among the formerly communist states, most of whom desire both forms of attachment. The first step is through participation in one or both of the security arrangements as a way to "get a foot in the door." Once that has been accomplished, then the hope is that collaboration will make it increasingly difficult to deny access to the greater economic prosperity represented by EU membership.

These are two very different problems. Joining a security system would be relatively simple (there would be few objections to it) if a structure suitable for the purpose existed. There are two possible candidates for this role: NATO, expanded through the Partnership for Peace (PfP) initiated by President Bill Clinton in 1994 and the Organization (formerly Conference) on Security and Cooperation in Europe (OSCE). Both can be pursued simultaneously and without contradiction due to highly overlapping memberships.

A number of the Eastern European states have pursued the NATO alternative through the PfP program, a loose, vaguely defined form of association that was intended to allay Russian objections to full NATO membership for these countries. NATO has the advantage of being a functioning military mechanism with an experienced bureaucracy. The membership, listed in Table 6.2, includes most EU states, as well as the United States, Canada, Iceland, and Turkey. However, NATO was conceived and structured against those very states that now seek admission, and it has a current mission crisis of its own, since its opposition no longer exists. For NATO to become a security blanket covering all of Europe, in other words, would require a fairly fundamental restructuring of the organization, both politically and militarily. The major question is whether PfP can provide the mission that will revitalize the alliance. Impatience with the PfP structure is indicated by the fact that nine members of PfP, indicated in Table 6.2, had applied for full NATO membership by

Table 6.2 Membership in NATO (Including PfP), WEU and OSCE

NATO	WEU	OSCE
Belgium	Belgium	Albania
Canada	Denmark	Armenia
Czech Republic	France	Austria
Denmark	Germany	Azerbaijan
France	Great Britain	Belarus
Germany	Ireland	Belgium
Great Britain	Italy	Bosnia
Greece	Luxembourg	Bulgaria
Hungary	Netherlands	Canada
Iceland	Total: 9	Croatia
Italy		Cyprus
Luxembourg		Czech Republic
Netherlands		Denmark
Norway		Estonia
Poland		Finland
Portugal		France
Spain		Georgia
Turkey		Germany
United States		Great Britain
Total:19		Greece
		Hungary
		Iceland
PfP		Ireland
Albania		Italy
Azerbaijan		Kazakhstan
Bulgaria		Kyrgyzstan
Estonia		Latvia
Finland		Liechtenstein
Georgia		Lithuania
Kazakhstan		Luxembourg
Kyrgyzstan		Macedonia
Latvia		Malta
Lithuania		Monaco
Moldova		Netherlands
Romania		Norway
Russia		Poland
Slovakia		Portugal
Slovenia		Romania
Sweden		Russia
Turkmenistan		San Marino
Ukraine		Slovakia
Uzbekistan		Slovenia
Total:19*		Spain
		Sweden
		Switzerland
		Tajikistan
		Turkey
		Turkmenistan
		Ukraine
		United States
		Uzbekistan
		Vatican
		Yugoslavia**
		Total:53

*As of July 31, 1998

**Membership suspended July 1992. Italicized PfP members have applied for
full NATO membership.

Web Sitings: Keeping Up with Nato

The status, including membership, of NATO and its member states is undergoing almost constant change. Fortunately, the organization maintains a comprehensive website that facilitates updating information. The NATO home page can be found at http://saclant.nato.int/nato.html. For more specific information on the roster and status of members of the PfP, contact http://www.nato.int/pfppartners.htm. Alternatively, one can reach these sites by using one of the search engines such as AOLFind and simply calling up NATO.

---

mid–1995; in July 1997, Poland, Hungary, and the Czech Republic were granted membership effective in 1999, while the applications of Slovenia and Romania were deferred.

The other and most inclusive alternative would be the OSCE—created by the Helsinki Final Act of 1975—whose primary advantage is that the members of NATO, the formerly communist states or their successors, and the historically neutral states of Europe are all members. Hence, every state needing to be part of a European security system already belongs. On the other hand, the size of OSCE—53 members since early 1995—makes it arguably unwieldy in an organizational sense, and it only began to develop a small secretariat, and hence a permanent structure, in 1991. OSCE may develop a security architecture, but it clearly has a long way to go.

The Yugoslavian crisis clearly points to the need for a security system that can regulate the transition in Eastern Europe. Systemic impotence in that case was at least partially a matter of jurisdiction: there was no security organization except OSCE of which Yugoslavia or its successor states was a member, and mechanisms to intervene were unavailable through that institution. The deputization of NATO (including members of the PfP and others such as Russia, which was not a member of PfP at the time IFOR was formed) to monitor the Dayton accords on Bosnia through the IFOR is positive indication that the organization may emerge as the security system. If that is the case, however, it will be a far different NATO than that of the Cold War.

We can now turn to the economic aspect of European integration that is, for most formerly communist states, their ultimate goal. The general tranquillity would clearly be aided by integration of Eastern Europe into the European economic system. Poland, Hungary, the Czech Republic, Slovakia, Romania, Bulgaria, and Albania have already applied for and received associate status within the EU; Estonia, Latvia, Lithuania, and Slovenia have signed cooperation agreements with the Union. According to EU sources, twelve countries will be considered for membership under the so-called "fifth enlargement" (the fifth time new members will be admitted): Bulgaria, Cyprus, the Czech Republic, Estonia, Hungary, Latvia, Lithuania, Malta, Poland, Romania, Slovakia, and Slovenia.

Web Sitings: Questions and Answers About EU

The European Union (EU) headquarters has a comprehensive website that is easily accessible. For basic information (such as the roster of states that will be considered for membership, contact http://www.eubasics.allmansland.com.

There are two barriers to expansion of the European Union. The first is an internal debate within the EU about the future direction of the organization, the poles of the debate being "deepening" and "widening" the organization. Those favoring deepening suggest that the EU's energies should be channeled toward the fuller economic and political integration of the existing membership. Additional members would make more difficult the forming of deeper bonds. Those favoring widening the EU prefer to expand the membership as a way to integrate the newly noncommunist countries into Europe. Some existing members, such as the British, also favor widening precisely because of the obstacles it poses to deeper integration, of which they are wary. That debate will not be resolved quickly.

The second barrier to EU admission for the Eastern European states has to do with meeting the criteria for membership. All members of the EU are functioning, stable democracies with basically market economies (although the European definition allows what is by American standards an extensive degree of government involvement in the economy). As new members have been admitted, they have had to pass the test of meeting the political and the economic criteria. This test was particularly applied to Spain and Portugal, whose membership was delayed until there was a clear demonstration of a commitment to the market and stable democratic governance. Moreover, the relative poverty of Spain and Portugal, as well as Greece and Ireland, has already created a need for economic assistance to those countries from the other members, which have little desire to take on an additional burden.

A 1993 study by the EU clearly stated that both political and economic criteria would apply to membership applications from Eastern European countries, which are poorer than any of the existing members. (These criteria also remain a barrier to the membership of Turkey and, to a lesser extent, Cyprus and Malta.) Until their economic transition is complete and the durability of their democratic institutions is demonstrated, most Eastern European states will have to remain outside EU. While no precise schedule has been established for demonstrating eligibility, it is generally conceded that it will be after 2000 before such a demonstration can be made.

The Changing Contours of the Transition

As the previous discussion of change in Eastern Europe should indicate, the transition in the formerly communist world is by no means complete, and the Eurasian landmass on which the Cold War was largely contested remains in a state of flux that will undoubtedly continue into the twenty-first century. What should one look for in terms of the way that transition will occur?

Obviously, the most important sources of change and the most serious challenges to a smooth transition reside in Russia. The 1998 economic collapse of the Russian economy, which triggered demands for political change in Moscow (up to and including demands for President Yeltsin to resign), represent major questions about the timing—even the feasibility—of Russian transition to the "circle of market democracies" that the United States and others have sought to nurture since the fall of communism. The glittering prosperity of Moscow (largely at the expense of the rest of the country's economic well-being) proved to be a Potemkin village, easily as obfuscatory as that of the early 1980s. As the financial structure of Russia imploded in 1998, there was even talk of the collapse of the globalizing economy and the universal triumph of the western system.

It is premature to speculate on how this will all turn out, but there are things to look for that will help define the continuing evolution of the transition. The first is the rocky economic road between now and the Russian presidential election scheduled for 2000. Can the virtual panic that has seized Russia be steadied by Russian governmental policy changes or by outside assistance? If so, will Russia return to a more centralized, managed economy, including state reinvolvement in the production and distribution system and more aggressive action against its new class of "robber barons" (very rich entrepreneurs who have, for instance, almost entirely evaded the tax system)?

Then there is the 2000 election. Will Boris Yeltsin try to run again? and if he does, will the voters reject him as a failure? If Yeltsin is out of the picture, to what kind of leadership espousing what kind of philosophy will the population turn? Clearly, the answer will depend to some extent on the handling of the financial crisis. The outcome, in turn, will affect whether the process of making Russia a normal state begun by Gorbachev in the 1980s will continue or be derailed.

Review

This chapter provided an examination of the dynamics of the transition from the Cold War to the post–Cold War world. In the process, the following points were made:

1. The end of the Cold War was the result of both military and economic factors. Militarily, the necessary peace resulting from large nuclear arsenals made war between the superpowers unthinkable and the competition meaningless. Economically, the Soviets faced a large and growing technological gap with the West that would worsen as long as the Cold War continued.

2. The end of the Cold War has had both short-term and long-term effects. Among the short-term effects are the end of communism in Europe, the dissolution of the Warsaw Pact and hence of the security structure of the Cold War period, and the peaceful dissolution of the Soviet Union into a series of successor states struggling to join the new international system.

3. Long-term effects of the end of the Cold War are also beginning to emerge. These appear to include an end to the East-West military competition that dominated the Cold War period (including its extension to the old Third World); growing U.S.-Russian cooperation on a range of issues, including the resuscitation of the United Nations; and the continuing attempt of the states that were part of the Soviet Union, especially Russia, to achieve the status of normal members of the international community.

4. The rules of the international game are undergoing change and adaptation as well. Among those changes are a revived interest in the United Nations as a prime component in the international security system, a decline in the importance of the "national security state" and the military instrument of power, and an ongoing debate over the maintenance of Second Tier stability.

5. One major question for the system is how Eastern Europe will evolve from socialism to some form of political democracy and market economy. The prospects are clearly brighter for the more prosperous northern states (Poland, Hungary, and the Czech Republic) than they are for the southern states like Bulgaria, Romania, Albania, and most of the successor states to Yugoslavia. Questions remain about how much emphasis should be put on economic, as opposed to political development; how ethnic, religious, and other forms of conflict can be controlled; and what the relationship will be between the Eastern European states and Western institutions such as NATO and the EU.

Suggested Readings

Abshire, David. "Strategic Challenge: Force Structures, Deterrence." *Washington Quarterly* 15, 2 (spring 1992): 33–42.

Asmus, Ronald D., Richard L. Kugler, and Stephen F. Larrabee. "Building a New NATO." *Foreign Affairs* 72, 4 (September/October 1993): 28–40.

Bowers, Stephen R. "East Europe: Why the Cheering Stopped." *Journal of Social, Political, and Economic Studies* 15, 1 (spring 1990): 25–42.

Brzezinski, Zbigniew. "The Premature Partnership." *Foreign Affairs* 73, 2 (March/April 1994): 67–82.

Deudney, Daniel, and G. John Ikenberry. "After the Long War." *Foreign Policy* 94 (spring 1994): 21–36.

Doder, Dasko. "Yugoslavia: New War, Old Hatreds." *Foreign Policy* 91 (summer 1993): 3–23.

Gorbachev, Mikhail S. *Perestroika: New Thinking for Our Country and the World.* New York: Harper and Row, 1987.

Jervis, Robert. *The Illogic of American Nuclear Strategy.* Ithaca, NY: Cornell University Press, 1984.

Kennan, George F. ("X"). "The Sources of Soviet Conduct." *Foreign Affairs* 25, 4 (July 1947): 566–82.

Kennedy, Paul. *The Rise and Fall of the Great Powers.* New York: Random House, 1987.

Kissinger, Henry. "Reflections on Containment." *Foreign Affairs* 73, 3 (May/June 1994): 113–130.

Mearsheimer, John J. "Why We Will Soon Miss the Cold War." *Atlantic Monthly* 266, 2 (August 1990): 35–50.

Nagorski, Andrew. "The Intellectual Roots of Eastern Europe's Upheaval." *SAIS Review* 10, 2 (summer/fall 1990): 89–100.

Nye, Joseph S. Jr., "Peering into the Future." *Foreign Affairs* 73, 4 (July/August 1994): 82–93.

Pipes, Richard. "Why the Soviet Union Thinks It Can Fight and Win a Nuclear War." *Commentary* 64, 1 (July 1977): 21–34.

Porter, Bruce D., and Carol R. Saivetz, "The Once and Future Empire: Russia and the 'Near Abroad.'" *Washington Quarterly* 17, 3 (summer 1994): 75–90.

Rogov, Sergei. "International Security and the Collapse of the Soviet Union." *Washington Quarterly* 15, 2 (spring 1992): 16–28.

Snow, Donald M. *The Necessary Peace: Nuclear Weapons and Superpower Relations.* Lexington, MA: Lexington Books, 1987.

—. *The Shape of the Future: The Post–Cold War World,* 2d ed. Armonk, NY: M. E. Sharpe, 1995.

—. "Soviet Reform and the High Technology Imperative." *Parameters* 20, 1 (March 1990): 76–87.

7

The First Tier: Democracy and Affluence

PREVIEW

This chapter examines the countries that constitute the First Tier. After first reviewing the defining criteria for First Tier membership, we look in some detail at the three principal centers of the First Tier: the United States, Western Europe, and Japan. In each instance, historical forces that condition contemporary behavior are examined, current issues confronting the First Tier states are assessed, and prospects for the continued maintenance of wealth and power are discussed. The chapter concludes with a case study of a Second Tier state that may well join the ranks of the First Tier early in the next century: China.

KEY CONCEPTS

G–7, G–8
classical liberalism
submerged Lockean consensus
isolationism
mood theory
Truman Doctrine
Marshall Plan
European Coal and Steel Community
  (ECSC)
European Union (EU)

European Commission
Western European Union (WEU)
Maastricht Treaty
Greater East Asian Co-Prosperity
Sphere
Yoshida Doctrine
re-Asianization
Four Modernizations
Special Economic Zones (SEZs)

OUTLINE

The collapse of the Cold War and the defeat of communism mean that today, for the first time since the French Revolution shattered the eighteenth-century international system, all of the world's most important powers share similar social, political, economic, and ideological characteristics. Those powers, which we refer to as the First Tier, are located principally in North America, Western Europe, and East Asia. As explained in Chapter 1, politically, all are functioning democracies, with civil liberties to protect dissenting views, broad public access to information, liberal voting rights, competition between two or more political parties, and free and competitive elections to choose key political leaders. Economically, all have structurally and technologically advanced economies organized along some variant of the capitalist model, ranging from Japan's tradition of a strong governmental coordinating role to the more laissez-faire tradition of the United States.

Of the world's nearly 200 sovereign states, no more than 30 could be classified as belonging to the First Tier. Among them they contain about 15 percent of the world's population but account for over half of its wealth. In addition, members of the First Tier marshal large and modern military capabilities that can be deployed around the world on behalf of the members' policy objectives. By any measure, then, the First Tier enjoys a commanding international position. Its sophisticated science and technology, industrial and military might, mass affluence, and democratic freedoms make it the most powerful—and emulated—bloc of the world's states.

What is striking about the First Tier's international position is that it faces no centrally directed, large-scale threat to its safety or its democratic way of life. The twentieth century's industrialized totalitarian aggressors have been successively defeated, from the fascism of Japan, Italy, and Germany to the communism of the Soviet Union. Not only does the First Tier lack a significant external enemy, but its members are also unlikely to go to war with one another. Each is heavily bound up with the others through an intricate array of trade, investment, travel, cultural, and security ties. This complex web of interdependence among them makes war less likely, but more important is the fact that all First Tier states are securely democratic. History offers no precedent for two modern democracies waging war against one another.

It appears, then, that the world is on the brink of an unprecedented international system dominated by the advanced industrial democracies of the First Tier, whose mutual relations will consist more of managing complex interdependence than of coping with security threats arising from their midst. The First Tier is not, of course, a homogeneous unit capable of speaking with a single voice. Nor are its members in full agreement on the leading international issues of the day. Yet the members seem likely to perceive their shared stake in working cooperatively to resolve global issues. Leaders of the seven countries with the largest economies, called the Group of Seven or G–7 (referred to as the Group of Eight or G–8 when Russia also participates), hold annual meetings aimed at coordinating their policies on key economic and political issues. In the future, it is likely that First Tier states will establish a more inclusive consultative body to serve as a forum for fostering cooperation, policy coordination, and common approaches to the other, more troubled states that constitute the Second Tier.

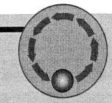

Coming to Terms
The G-7 and G-8

Since 1987 the leading industrial democracies (the United States, Canada, Japan, Great Britain, France, Germany, Italy) have held annual summit meetings designed to foster closer coordination of economic policies among them. The highly publicized meetings of the Group of Seven, or G-7 for short, vary in effectiveness from year to year. In 1998 Russia was given membership as a reflection of support for Russia's hoped-for democratization. Thus G-7 is now frequently referred to as G-8. Sometimes G-7 or G-8 meetings are little more than elaborate photo opportunities. On other occasions, meaningful agreements are reached on economic and political issues. Yet nothing can paper over the fact that the annual meeting is a mere consultative forum made up of sovereign states. For example, there is a predictability to some states' positions. For the Japanese, advocacy of growth and policies that enhance Japan's export opportunities is a given. To the Germans, no matter how sluggish the intertwined economies of the industrial states, high interest rates must be maintained to prevent a recurrence of the devastating German inflation of the 1920s. The G-8 meeting serves as a useful sounding board for the views of its rich members, but the group's declarations should not always be taken as reliable guides to the policies that the member states will actually follow.

President Clinton addresses his counterpart leaders of the G-8 at a 1998 meeting in Denver, Colorado.

In this chapter we examine the principal members of the First Tier: the United States, the European Union, and Japan. We conclude the chapter with a brief case study of the rise of a potential major member of the First Tier—China.

The United States: The Preeminent Superpower

Just as individuals in their adult lives think and behave in ways that are heavily shaped by their formative years, so too do countries acquire distinct characteristics that reflect their historical conditioning. In foreign affairs this tendency often leads to identifiable national styles of viewing the outside world and defining the country's place in the international system. The U.S. national "personality" in foreign affairs was molded by its formative experiences in the eighteenth and nineteenth centuries. Once established, this diplomatic style greatly affected the way the country conducted itself when it reached the status of global superpower in the twentieth century. Here we examine the distinctive American approach to international relations and then consider the prospects of America as a global power in the years ahead.

Summary ──────────────────────

Influences on America's Global Role and Their Effects

Two principal conditioning influences on the U.S. approach toward the outside world:

1. A pervasive consensus on Lockean values at home
2. A historical pattern of isolationism

Two principal effects of those conditioning influences:

1. A strong streak of idealism in foreign policy
2. A pattern of oscillation between periods of introversion, or isolationism, and periods of extroversion, or foreign policy activism

America's International Style

America's foreign policy style was principally shaped by two influences. The first is the country's distinct set of political beliefs. As Louis Hartz argued in his classic book *The Liberal Tradition in America,* the U.S. political culture is unusual in that it has always reflected a massive, underlying consensus on the core values of classical liberalism. As a body of formal doctrine, classical liberalism was developed beginning in the seventeenth century by British philosophers such as John Locke, Adam Smith, and John Stuart Mill. Championing then radical notions of individual rights, equality, limited government, democracy, and free-market economics, the intellectual founders of classical liberalism were protesting the political and socioeconomic realities of the Europe of their day: authoritarian rule by a hereditary elite, rigid social class stratification, limited opportunity for individual social and economic mobility, and few if any safeguards against the monarch's intervention in political and economic life. In eighteenth- and nineteenth-century Europe, classical liberal ideals voiced the aspirations of a small middle class that was sandwiched between a conservative aristocracy bent on preserving the inherited order on the one hand, and a proletariat looking for its radical overturn on the other.

The United States, by contrast, had no feudal heritage and thus never developed a European-style conservatism devoted to perpetuating monarchical rule, aristocratic privilege, class stratification, and extensive governmental control of economic life. Largely for this reason, it also never developed a genuinely radical left bent on the violent destruction of the old order. Instead, from its founding the United States was molded by an implicit, pervasive consensus on the Lockean values of personal liberty, equal opportunity, economic freedom, limited government, and political democracy. Early settlers left behind the rigid, repressive societies of Europe and sought economic success amid the political freedom and opportunity provided by a thinly settled continent.

So thoroughgoing has been this agreement on a set of core values that Americans lost any self-consciousness about their most bedrock beliefs. Hartz's reference to America's "submerged Lockean consensus" captures both the near unanimity of popular sentiment in support of classical liberal values and the notable absence of intellectual self-awareness about this sentiment, a lack that is the natural consequence of a political culture with virtually no experience of fundamental ideological divisions.

The second influence that shaped America's diplomatic style was its historical isolationism. As a state born in the European-dominated eighteenth century, early America was isolated from ordinary international relations by the elementary facts of its location: the Atlantic Ocean to its east, the Pacific Ocean to its west, and the absence of strong power centers to the north and south. Beyond these important geographical influences, however, isolationism reflected the conscious choice of the new country. Preoccupied with rounding out its continental dimensions and persuaded that their new democracy was morally superior to Europe's authoritarian regimes, early Americans looked upon European-style balance-of-power politics as the corrupt, war-prone plaything of unaccountable monarchs. George Washington, in his famous Farewell Address as president, exhorted Americans to avoid foreign entanglements that would, he feared, threaten the country's peace and democratic system and its citizens' pursuit of individual economic advancement.

These two factors—a broad consensus on liberal ideology and a history of isolationism—together have given the United States much of its enduring approach to international relations. Among their effects, two stand out. First, U.S. foreign policy has often reflected a pronounced idealism. Americans have long believed that theirs is, as Lincoln put it, "a nation committed to a proposition." That proposition—classical liberalism and its affirmation of freedom, equality, and democracy—is what defined the United States from its infancy, and it was the country's ideals that guided its constitutional formulation of limited government and individual liberty.

Throughout their history Americans have been suspicious of political power; their ideology told them that freedom, democracy, and limited government are the natural state of human beings, and their memories and observation of Europe told them that centralized political power equates to capriciousness, coercion, and despotism. To Americans, democracy is an inherently peaceful form of governance. Since foreign involvements have the unwanted effect of strengthening the power of government—particularly the military—Americans have ordinarily insisted that such interventions be conducted only in the name of promoting the country's domestic ideals. If war is caused by autocratic rule, one of the few justifications for expending American blood and treasure is to convert today's enemy into a democratic, peace-loving society.

The strong influence of its domestic ideals on its foreign policy has proven to be a mixed blessing for the United States. On the one hand, the values that Americans have stood for have broad appeal around the world. The principal ideological challengers to America's cherished norms have all ended up discredited and cast into history's dustbin. In steady succession the doctrines of monarchical rule, fascism, and communism have seen their moral legitimacy evaporate, and their collapse has left classical liberalism virtually alone as a set of secular values capable of igniting hope and idealism worldwide.

To put the point differently, the central thrust of twentieth-century U.S. foreign policy has been the use of American power to confront totalitarianism, militarism, and imperialism and to extend the international realm of freedom, democratic rule, and market economics. What is remarkable about America's foreign policy record in this century is less its failures than the extent to which its core objectives have been obtained. That record is due in no small measure to the perception that the United States stands for something beyond its own narrow interests. The power of its ideals has thus contributed greatly to the power of the United States in international affairs.

However, devotion to the ideological values of Lockean liberalism has at times distorted U.S. perceptions of global realities and diminished Americans' capacity to think and act pragmatically on the basis of the national interest. American moralism can easily shade into a crusading zeal that transforms foreign policy into contests of good versus evil. While such an impulse can lead to altruistic acts on behalf of other peoples, it can also lead to misbegotten ventures abroad. In many respects, the Vietnam War illustrates the kind of tragedy that an excessively ideological foreign policy can lead to. Apart from a laudable wish to oppose the spread of totalitarian communist ideology, U.S. policymakers could point to few concrete American interests in Vietnam. The point is not that America's domestic values have led its foreign policy astray, but rather that a zeal to propagate these values abroad has sometimes done so because it was divorced from prudent calculations of power and interest.

The second effect of America's historical conditioning has been a pattern of oscillating between periods of strenuous foreign activism and periods of extreme withdrawal from the rest of the world. European states have been conditioned by centuries of uneasy proximity to each other to think in terms of power, concrete national interest, and the inevitable, continuous demands imposed by an anarchic state system. Americans, by contrast, until recently enjoyed the luxury of geographic isolation from countries that could harm them, and so viewed themselves as having the choice either to act on behalf of their beliefs abroad or, when the world proved unreceptive to their maxims, to retreat into domestic preoccupations. Little in their formative national experience conditioned Americans to think in terms of the impersonal necessity of constantly balancing the power of potential adversaries.

The result has been a recurring shift of the country's mood and behavior between periods of introversion and periods of extroversion. Historically, periods of introversion have lasted an average of two decades and share these traits: (1) a diminished public interest in foreign affairs and an increased emphasis on domestic matters, (2) a general scaling down of foreign political and military involvements and a reluctance to take on new ones, and (3) a shift in political power from the executive branch to Congress. By comparison, periods of extroversion have lasted, on average, nearly three decades and have been marked by (1) mounting public interest in international matters, (2) a marked upswing in the overall level of political and military engagement abroad, and (3) dominance of the policy-making process by the President, with Congress deferring to his leadership.

As the pendulum has swung repeatedly, first in one direction and then in the other, policy makers have tended to follow the shifting national mood beyond the point of prudence.

After World War II broke out in Europe, many prominent Americans opposed joining the war. In this picture, Charles Lindbergh, who gained fame in 1927 by making the first successful solo flight across the Atlantic, is shown addressing a rally of the America First Committee opposing U.S. participation. Like most America Firsters, his opposition was doused by the Japanese attack on Pearl Harbor.

Historically, periods of foreign policy activism persist until either a policy fiasco brought on by needless overcommitment or sheer public exhaustion with foreign exertions triggers a swing in the pendulum toward retrenchment. That shift, in turn, sooner or later leads to the neglect of looming international danger until a clear crisis is reached. For example, U.S. engagement in World War I was followed by a wave of disillusionment triggered by Europe's resistance to Wilsonian idealism. The resulting period of national introversion persisted until the worldwide threat of fascism was brought home with clarity at Pearl Harbor. So thoroughly had the United States renounced foreign policy activism after World War I that in 1933, the year that Adolf Hitler came to power in Germany, it maintained a smaller army than that of Romania! Even if American policy makers had had the clarity of mind and will to nip Hitler's aggression in the bud, they lacked the armed might to do so. According to the so-called mood theory, then, the United States has historically had difficulty steering a steady course in its dealings abroad.

The United States as a Superpower

At the conclusion of World War II in August 1945, the United States towered, intact and exuberant, over a world devastated by the war's protracted violence. Alone among the major countries, it had been spared the physical destruction of modern warfare, and its immense industrial prowess promised a new age of American prosperity. Americans' traditional instinct for withdrawing from the world led to a rapid demobilization of the armed forces. Within two years of the silencing of the guns of World War II, however, the United States confronted the specter of a new totalitarian challenge to the democratic West, as the hoped-for continuation of the wartime alliance with the communist Soviet Union foundered in an unbridgeable gulf of mutual suspicions, incompatible strategic interests, and ideological differences. By 1947 President Harry Truman concluded that the Soviets must be prevented from expanding their political and ideological domain. Apparent Soviet support for communist insurgents in Greece, Stalin's refusal to remove his forces from northern Iran, his intimidation of Turkey over control of access to the Black Sea, and his efforts to fan the flames of communist sentiment amid the desperation of devastated Europe—all convinced Truman that the Soviets must be contained.

Doing so would clearly require the United States to take the lead, since the only other possible candidates, the British and the French, were severely weakened by the war. But to sustain a protracted U.S. geostrategic undertaking in the absence of an armed attack on U.S. territory or interests meant that Truman would have to arouse the American people from their postwar slumber. He did so through a campaign to persuade them that the Soviets posed as great a threat to American values and interests as had the dictators of Germany, Italy, and Japan.

His speech of March 12, 1947, outlining what became known as the Truman Doctrine, depicted a world divided into the free and the unfree, and he argued that only the United States was capable of offering assistance to free peoples threatened by the new totalitarian challenge. The following year saw the unveiling of the Marshall Plan, an ambitious program of economic assistance to help the war-torn countries of Europe rebuild and offer their people hope for the future so that they would be less vulnerable to the siren song of communism. In 1949 the third leg of America's Cold War strategy was formed. The North Atlantic Treaty Organization (NATO) institutionalized U.S. defense of Western Europe, the first time the United States had undertaken such an arrangement during peacetime. With the ideological, economic, and military components of containment in place, the United States began a 45-year-long period of leadership of the world's anti-Soviet, anti-communist forces. (The origins of the Truman Doctrine are discussed in more detail in the Amplification box.)

It is not our purpose here to recount in detail the history of the Cold War, but three points need to be stressed. First, it was unprecedented for the United States to undertake such vast and protracted international activities during peacetime. The magnitude and duration of America's Cold War exertions can be explained in part by the importance that Americans have historically attached to ideological and moral preferences. If the necessity of maintaining a favorable balance of power against the Soviet Union and its allies seemed abstract to ordinary Americans, the struggle between totalitarian communism and liberal democracy was not. Instinctively, the American people detested communism and thus permitted their leaders to undertake ambitious international efforts to contain it.

A second point to be noted is that once engaged in the Cold War, U.S. efforts expanded in response to the globalization of the communist challenge. The triumph of Mao Zedong's communist forces in China in 1949 and the outbreak of the Korean War in 1950 showed that the conflict had spilled beyond its European origins and would require a truly global effort.

A third important point about the U.S. role in the Cold War is that the necessity of maintaining a favorable balance of power against the hostile Soviet Union and China too easily

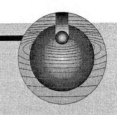

Amplification

The Truman Doctrine

In his *Memoirs* President Harry Truman claimed to have realized as early as 1946 that the hoped-for post—World War II cooperation with the Soviet Union would not materialize. To Truman, Soviet pressures on Iran and Turkey were threats to the larger global balance of power. As Truman's pessimistic views took hold throughout much of the executive branch in 1946 and early 1947, it became apparent that Congress and the public as a whole would have to be mobilized around the new objectives of curbing the expansion of Soviet influence. The problem was that the American people were still weary from the rigors of World War II, were enjoying their hard-won peace, and would likely be difficult to mobilize once again around ambitious international exertions.

In February 1947, Truman assembled a bi-partisan group of congressional leaders at the White House to hear briefings laying out the administration's new perceptions and logic. The lead presentation, by Secretary of State George Marshall, went badly. Marshall's arguments for assisting Greece and Turkey were couched in humanitarian terms, hardly a compelling argument to politicians interested in cutting taxes.

Undersecretary of State Dean Acheson saved the day by painting the emerging struggle with the Soviets in stark strategic terms. "Not since Rome and Carthage has there been such a polarization of power on this earth," he argued. In this struggle between the forces of freedom and the forces of dictatorship, Acheson declared, "We have the choice of acting with energy to meet this situation or losing by default."

One congressman, captivated by Acheson's dramatic presentation, said to President Truman: "By God, if you'll come and make that argument to Congress, you'll get whatever funding you need." The stage was thus set for the delivery of the historic Truman Doctrine speech. On March 12, 1947, Truman stood before Congress and proclaimed a new crisis of universal proportions:

> At the present moment in world history nearly every nation must choose between alternative ways of life....One way is based upon the will of the majority, and is distinguished by free institutions, representative government, free elections, guarantees of individual liberty, freedom of speech and religion and freedom from political repression.

shaded into an indiscriminate anticommunism that was only vaguely connected to prudent calculations of national interest. Confronted with a seemingly implacable communist foe bent on challenging western liberal democratic values and interests in a worldwide contest for supremacy, the United States settled in for what John F. Kennedy called a "long twilight struggle." That struggle saw the country assume an ever-expanding array of economic, political, military, and cultural programs intended to strengthen its own position and undercut the Soviet capacity to add new clients, especially in the newly independent states of Africa, the Middle East, and Asia. But with the passage of time, the inherent U.S. stake in preventing a hostile Soviet Union from dominating the Eurasian land mass became transformed into a more general insistence that communism per se must be opposed wherever it threatened the established order.

The Truman Doctrine *(continued)*

The second way of life is based upon the will of a minority forcibly imposed upon the majority. It relies upon terror and oppression, a controlled press and radio, fixed elections and the suppression of personal freedom.

Amid such global competition, Truman argued that it must be U.S. policy to

help free people to maintain their free institutions and their national integrity against aggressive movements that seek to impose upon them totalitarian regimes. This is no more than a frank recognition that totalitarian regimes imposed on free peoples, by direct or indirect aggression, undermine the foundations of international peace and hence the security of the United States.

Note the emotional tone of Truman's famous speech. He reasoned that only a dramatic depiction of a worldwide struggle for freedom would arouse the somnolent Americans. In this, the seminal U.S. document of the Cold War, Truman set an ideological tone that would color many later American perceptions and actions, including, most tragically, in Vietnam, where "containing communism" divorced from prudent calculations of national interest led to a

protracted national nightmare for Americans and Vietnamese alike.

Sources: Seyom Brown, *The Faces of Power* (New York: Columbia University Press, 1968), pp. 39–43; Forest L. Grieves, *Conflict and Order* (Boston: Houghton Mifflin, 1977), pp. 157–159.

President Truman proclaims to a joint session of Congress in 1947 the need for U.S. resistance to Soviet expansionism. His formal declaration of the Cold War became the basis for American foreign policy for the next four decades.

This essential logic spawned America's most tragic international undertaking: Vietnam. What began as a limited policy of providing material assistance and advisers to the South Vietnamese became transformed into a major U.S. land war. As the United States took over the fighting from its wobbly clients in Saigon, it became ever more deeply mired in stalemate. As the U.S. commitment mushroomed to 500,000 troops, so too did U.S. casualties rise steadily. By 1968 the war had become deeply divisive at home. Seeing neither a compelling justification nor an end in sight, growing numbers of Americans pressured their leaders to terminate the misbegotten venture. President Richard Nixon finally did so in 1973, but within two years the communists had overrun Cambodia and Laos as well as South Vietnam, thus handing the United States its most humiliating international defeat.

For those who did not live through the period, it is difficult to comprehend the bitterness, disillusionment, divisiveness, and cynicism that the Vietnam War spawned among many Americans. So great were the corrosive effects that recent Presidents have felt the need to limit major international commitments to situations where public support can definitely be sustained. That limitation, in turn, has meant avoiding becoming involved in potential quagmires, such as in the former Yugoslavia until the very late 1990s (in Kosovo). So long as the ghosts of Vietnam linger, we expect that U.S. interventions will be confined to situations that meet three tests, the substance of which is reflected in the ideas of Colin Powell and the Weinberger and Clinton Doctrines. First, there must be a clear rationale for the undertaking, such as the specter of an anti-western tyrant gaining a chokehold over critical oil supplies in the Persian Gulf or the moral imperative of offering relief from "ethnic cleansing," as in Kosovo in 1999. Second, there must be a reasonable prospect of quick success with few U.S. casualties. Finally, there must be broad international support. All three criteria were met to some degree in the U.S.-led efforts to drive Iraq's forces out of Kuwait in 1990–91 and to stave off mass hunger in Somalia in 1992–93. Arguably, only the first of them was met in the case of the U.S.-led NATO intervention in Yugoslavia in 1999.

The Europeans: Problems and Prospects for Unity

Western Europe's historic influence on the modern world is incalculable. From the sixteenth to the mid-twentieth century, Western Europe was the unrivaled world center of economic innovation, intellectual creativity, and political power. The modern state system was a European innovation, as were the first industrial revolution, the political theories of democracy, fascism, and communism, and the competitive acquisition of worldwide colonial empires. By the early twentieth century, Europe towered over the rest of the globe. It was, in the memorable phrase of the historian Barbara Tuchman, the "proud tower."

However, Europe's old vices of power politics and nationalism led it into two destructive wars between 1914 and 1945. What was in effect a protracted European civil war reduced the once proud tower to ashes and provided convincing proof that the Europeans would have to address the most fundamental questions regarding their political organization and traditional methods of dealing with one another. From the rubble of wartime defeat, then, arose Europe's greatest contribution to international politics in the twentieth century: the effort to intertwine the economic fates of historic national enemies so thoroughly that a resort to war among them would become unthinkable.

Europe's Need to Unify

Four factors are particularly important in explaining Western Europe's drive to unify after World War II. First, as noted, there was the unmistakable lesson taught in the cruel classroom of the war itself. For the second time in 30 years, the countries of Europe had been drawn into total war with one another. Advances in military technology and the deliberate targeting of enemy factories, transportation facilities, and urban concentrations meant that the war exacted a horrible physical and psychological toll. When the guns fell silent in 1945, Europe's cities lay in ruins and much of its population was destitute, often without housing, jobs, or public services. Many of the war's survivors thus came to accept through bitter experience what philosophers like Immanuel Kant had long argued: competitive nationalism leads to conflict and suffering, while cooperative union means peace and well-being.

A second factor encouraging cooperation was the onset of the Cold War, which meant that the states of Western Europe were confronted by a common threat from the armies of the Soviet bloc. The dawning perception of mutual vulnerability gave a new urgency to the search for ways for Europeans to think and act in broader regional terms.

Summary ━━━━━━━━━━━━━━━━━━━━━━━━━━━━━━━━━━

Forces Behind European Unification

1. Desire to avoid another war
2. Common threat to Western Europe from Soviet Union
3. Marshall Plan's encouragement of economic cooperation
4. Necessity in superpower-dominated world for smaller states to coalesce into a bloc to make their voices heard

---

The initiative unveiled by U.S. Secretary of State George Marshall in June 1947 provided further impetus towards European unity. The Marshall Plan, as it came to be known, was an unprecedented offer of U.S. funds to aid the rebuilding of Europe's cities, factories, and economic infrastructure. Though aid was offered to all of Europe, the Soviet Union forced its Eastern European client states to spurn the offer. Inadvertently, then, the Marshall Plan deepened the Cold War division across Europe even while strengthening the unity of its Western European participants. A key feature of the U.S. program was that it went beyond a series of bilateral transfers of economic aid and instead triggered, in Marshall's words, "a joint recovery program based on self-help and mutual cooperation." In 1948, 16 Western European nations agreed to continue economic cooperation beyond that required by the Marshall Plan itself. To facilitate that cooperation, they formed the Organization for European Economic Cooperation, a crucial early building block in forging European unity.

A fourth and final impetus toward European union was the growing realization that in a new era dominated by two nuclear-armed, continental-size superpowers, the relatively small states of Europe would be relegated to diminished international roles unless they could coalesce into a bloc. In terms of land area, for example, France and Britain together amounted to less than four percent of the Soviet Union's vast expanse. In terms of population, France, Britain, Italy, and West Germany combined had fewer people than the United States. Perhaps more disturbing than population and land measures, however, was that the countries of Western Europe could not begin to compare with the United States or the Soviet Union in their endowment of natural resources. Except for coal, most of the mineral resources necessary for Europe's industrial economies had to be imported, mostly from the Middle East, Africa, and Asia. The United States and the Soviet Union, by contrast, were richly endowed with an abundance of raw materials.

Further diminishing the status of postwar Europe was the loss of overseas colonial empires, long a source of power, prestige, and wealth, but no longer able to be held against a rising tide of nationalism. In the late 1940s the Dutch were forced to relinquish Indonesia, while the British granted independence to India, Pakistan, and Burma.

Europe's retreat continued throughout the 1950s and 1960s, as the French were forced out of Indochina, Belgium lost the mineral-rich Congo, the British relinquished what are now Malaysia and Singapore, and French and British alike withdrew from their vast colonial holdings in Africa.

The Path to Unity

Europe's evolution towards unity has proceeded along two separate tracks: economic integration and defense cooperation. In time both tracks would generate momentum toward greater political convergence as well. However, advocates of a formal European political union, known as federalists, have had relatively modest influence to date.

Economic Unification. Europe's resounding success in achieving its current economic integration began quite modestly. In 1950 two Frenchmen—Jean Monnet, a civil servant regarded as the intellectual father of European unity, and Robert Schuman, France's foreign minister—proposed forming a limited common market for coal and steel. Their proposal to allow these materials to be shipped between the Western European countries without trade restrictions such as tariffs or quotas was intended to foster mutually beneficial cooperation in a narrow, specialized segment of national economies and was fashioned to generate as little controversy as possible while holding out the promise of concrete economic benefits. In narrowly economic terms, such an arrangement would create an expanded internal market—that is, a market surrounded by but not divided by import barriers—which would stimulate expanded economic activity.

More important, though, would be the political benefits. If implemented, the pact would provide a framework for cooperation between France and West Germany, would end the historic Franco-German struggle over the coal- and steel-rich Saar region, and would allow the West Germans to begin the long process of reentering the international community. In 1951 Monnet and Schuman's plan to create the European Coal and Steel Community (ECSC) was approved by six countries: France, West Germany, Italy, Luxembourg, Belgium, and the Netherlands. (Notably absent from the group was Great Britain, which continued to aspire to a major independent global role through its still vast overseas colonies and its perceived "special relationship" with the United States.) More than a mere trade pact, the ECSC created supranational institutions with substantial authority, including a High Authority, a Council of Ministers, a Parliament, and a Court of Justice.

Within its limited policy domain, the ECSC proved a stunning success. Trade in coal and steel among its six members more than doubled within five years, and under Monnet's prodding the ECSC countries agreed to proceed toward broader economic union. In 1957 they signed the historic Treaty of Rome, which created the European Economic Community (EEC), better known as the Common Market; it later became known as the European Community (EC) and, more recently, the European Union (EU). Monnet and his fellow "functionalists" believed that by phasing out national barriers on the movement of goods, labor, and capital, the Common Market members would create a large internal market that would ignite economic growth for all of them.

Nearly three decades later, adoption by EC members of the Single European Act in 1986 provided the political and legal impetus for finally achieving a barrier-free Europe. The Treaty of Rome had focused on the free movement of goods among its member states. In 1986, by setting a timetable for the elimination of restrictions on the free circulation of people, capital, and services as well as goods, the Europeans hoped to pull themselves out of their economic doldrums and regain their economic competitiveness with the United States and Japan. The principal architect of Europe's intensified drive toward a borderless market was Jacques Delors, the president of the European Commission, the executive and administrative organ of the EU. Under Delors's prodding, EC members focused on a single goal—economic union—and a firm date for attaining it—January 1, 1993. (See Table 7.1.) Without the energizing effects of such clarity of purpose, Delors argued, Europe would merely continue to muddle along, inspiring little optimism among its own people or respect internationally.

In addition to achieving its original purpose of economic integration, the EU has evolved in two other important ways since its founding. First, its membership has grown from the original 6 to the current 15 with the addition of Britain, Denmark, Ireland, Greece, Spain, Portugal, Austria, Sweden, and Finland. In population, EU states total 400 million, compared with the United States' 270 million and Japan's 126 million. Economically, EU members annually produce $7.5 trillion in goods and services, compared with $6.5 trillion for the United States and $3.8 trillion for Japan. By nearly any measure, then, the EU appears as a dazzling constellation of wealth and potential international political power.

The second change since 1957 has been the growing influence of community-wide institutions. The identity and functions of the EU's four principal institutions—the Commission, the Council of Ministers, the European Parliament, and the Court of Justice—can be described simply enough, as is done in the Amplification box "The Key Institutions of the EU," but their inherent political character is rather difficult to grasp. On the one hand, they are more than mere intergovernmental agencies, since in some areas they are authorized to create laws and regulations that are directly enforceable on individual European citizens,

Table 7.1	Evolution of the European Union

1951 Following a proposal by French Foreign Minister Robert Schuman in 1950, a treaty regulating the production and trade of coal, coke, iron ore, and steel by several countries under a common authority, the *European Coal and Steel Community (ECSC)*, is negotiated and signed. The members are West Germany (now Germany), France, Italy, the Netherlands, Belgium, and Luxembourg (known as the Six). The ECSC becomes a precedent for other economic and political integration.

1957 The members of the ECSC sign the Treaty of Rome, creating the *European Economic Community (EEC)* and the *European Atomic Energy Community (EC)*.

1958 The ECSC, EEC, and Euratom are merged into one organization, the *European Economic Community (EEC)*.

1973 Denmark, Ireland, and Great Britain join the EC, raising its membership to nine.

1981 Greece becomes the tenth member.

1986 Spain and Portugal are admitted, bringing the membership to 12.

1991 The EC and the seven members of the *European Free Trade Association (EFTA)* agree to form the *European Economic Area (EEA)*, a single market of 19 countries.

1993 The ratification of the 1992 Maastricht Treaty creates the *European Union (EU)*.

1995 Three states (Austria, Finland, and Sweden) are added to the EU, raising its membership to 15.

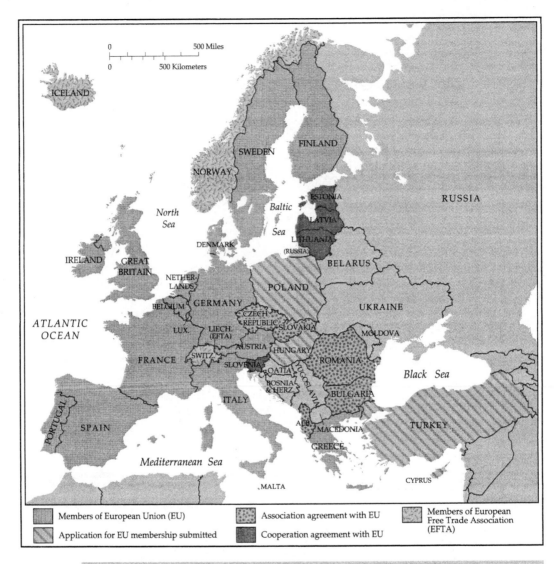

Map 7-1 **The European Union**

©1996 by St. Martin's Press, Inc. From: *Contours of Power,* by Snow/Brown. Reprinted with permission of Bedford/St. Martin's Press, Inc.

corporations, and other organizations. On the other hand, they do not amount to a full sovereign state, since the member states retain individual national prerogatives over defense, foreign policy, and key aspects of domestic law. Operating somewhere between the definitive authority conferred by sovereignty and the institutional frailty characteristic of intergovernmental bodies, the EU is a collection of independent states that have granted important social, economic, and legal powers to the community's supranational institutions but are unwilling to surrender their own sovereignty to a federal European state.

Amplification

The Key Institutions of the EU

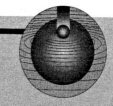

The four essential institutions of the European Union are the European Commission, the Council of Ministers, the European Parliament, and the Court of Justice. Of the four, the most important is the Commission, whose 20 commissioners (two from Spain, Germany, France, Britain, and Italy, and one from each of the other member states) preside over the Union's executive machinery. As such, they administer EU policy, initiate legal action to enforce compliance with EU regulations, and take the lead in proposing new Union policies.

If the Commission is the Union's engine, the Council of Ministers acts as a regulator on the engine. Composed of one cabinet-level official from each of the member states, the Council has the authority to approve or reject the Commission's policy proposals. Note that the Council ordinarily serves a reactive function; the critical power to define the policy agenda and formulate policy initiatives is effectively dominated by the Commission.

The European Parliament, despite its grandiose title, wields little real power. Its 518 members are directly elected for five-year terms, but the legislature as a whole meets only about one week each year and then does little beyond conducting general discussions about issues confronting Europe.

The final institution, the Court of Justice, adjudicates disputes involving EU law and regulations. In those policy areas where the Treaty of Rome permits the EU legislative authority, its laws supersede conflicting national laws, and hence rulings by the Court of Justice are binding on all members of the Union.

Despite the inherent problem of disentangling the policy-making sphere of the EU on the one hand and that of its member states on the other, the Union's institutions have emerged as important centers of policy-making power in today's Europe.

Defense Cooperation. Western Europe's economic integration has been paralleled by growing defense collaboration. Regional cooperation on security matters has proceeded along two tracks. The North Atlantic Treaty Organization (NATO), formed in 1949, was formed under U.S. leadership to erect a shield against Soviet military designs against Western Europe. Consisting originally of 12 European countries plus Canada and the United States, NATO eventually expanded to its present 19 members.

NATO was undoubtedly a key link in the U.S.-orchestrated effort to contain the Soviets worldwide. Similarly, there is no denying NATO's beneficial effects in providing an institutional framework for the development of routine cooperation among Europeans on such matters as strategic planning, standardizing equipment, and conducting regular joint exercises. Behind NATO's shield, its European members were developing the common bonds of worldview and defense policy among themselves.

On the other hand, three factors somewhat reduced NATO's ability to knit deeper ties among the Western Europeans on nondefense issues. First, from its inception, NATO was very much a U.S.-dominated enterprise. In its early years, the European members were not strong enough to resist the overwhelming U.S. role in their continent's defense even if they had wanted to do so. Second, France's prickly national pride, so shrewdly manipulated and given voice by Charles de Gaulle (French president from 1959 to 1969), led to his 1966 decision to pull French forces out of NATO's integrated command structure. Though still a member of the treaty itself, France would remain aloof from the day-to-day military activities of the other members that were aimed at fostering a common regional response to the Soviet threat. Third, as the Cold War atrophied and the Soviet Union itself disintegrated, NATO's institutional identity became less clear. Lacking a common enemy, its members were less inspired to rally around NATO's banner. Its 1999 "out of area" intervention in Yugoslavia on behalf of the persecuted ethnic Albanians in Kosovo eventually revealed deep political differences among NATO's members.

A second track towards European defense cooperation is the Western European Union (WEU). Virtually dormant for many years and overshadowed by the U.S.-dominated NATO, the WEU is today acquiring new significance as the principal institutional vehicle for a purely European defense organization. Founded in 1954, it was originally planned to provide a European framework for West Germany to rearm and join NATO. During the decade between France's 1963 veto of British entry into the EC and Britain's admission in 1973, the WEU served as a useful common institution linking its more continental-minded members and the U.S.-oriented British. Its nine members (Belgium, France, Germany, Italy, Luxembourg, Netherlands, Portugal, Spain, and the United Kingdom) all participate in NATO as well, but they have recently begun using the WEU to present a common European voice on security issues. In 1987, for example, the British, French, Belgian, Italian, and Dutch navies dispatched a coordinated naval force to the Persian Gulf to escort oil tankers threatened by the war between Iran and Iraq.

In 1992 the WEU Council of Ministers formally called for the creation of a standing WEU force that could serve as a distinctly European rapid-reaction force to be deployed for humanitarian, peacekeeping, or crisis-management operations. Among the plan's strongest boosters are the Germans and the French, who see it as a key step in establishing the WEU as the formal defense component of the European Union. Not all Europeans are enthusiastic, however, about elevating the WEU as the paramount European defense institution. The British, for example, continue to insist that NATO—and with it, America's armed might and political influence—should remain the keystone of European defense cooperation, with the WEU continuing to play a secondary role.

Europe's Future

Today Europe confronts four critical issues regarding its future identity and role in the world. These issues all relate to the debate over "deepening" or "widening" the EU that was discussed in the case study in Chapter 6.

The first question is, who is allowed inside the EU tent? The dramatic success of the EU, coupled with the collapse of communism in Europe, has generated a queue of countries wanting to link their fates to the Union's rising star. In 1991 the EU agreed to form an economic union with the seven members of the European Free Trade Association (EFTA): Austria, Sweden, Finland, Iceland, Liechtenstein, Norway, and Switzerland. The resulting European Economic Area will comprise a rich market of 380 million people who together account for 40 percent of global trade. The union will be a limited one, since the EFTA states will not participate in the EU's governing bodies. In 1994, however, national referenda in Austria, Sweden, and Finland approved full EU membership for those countries.

Summary ————————————————————

Three Questions About Europe's Future

1. Who should be permitted to join the EU?
2. How far should unification be pursued?

3. Can Europe develop a coherent international role? If so, what should it be?

To its east, the EU confronts the formerly communist states of Eastern Europe and the western or European successor states of the Soviet Union, who hope to gain access to the EU's market and, eventually, be admitted as full members of a greater European Union. As explained in the case study in Chapter 6, Eastern Europe is undergoing a painful adjustment to the postcommunist world of market economics, an adjustment that will bar even the most prosperous countries from full membership until the turn of the century. Perhaps, as former French President François Mitterrand has proposed, some form of confederation will emerge among the former communist countries that could serve as a transitional link to the democratic and more prosperous EU. For now, however, the EU faces instead the prospect of being inundated by waves of refugees from the east. It is thus in Western Europe's own self-interest to help devise economic and institutional arrangements that will help lift its eastern neighbors out of their poverty, social unrest, and ethnic conflict.

The second question confronting the EU is, how far should unification be pursued? As noted earlier, the EU is essentially an economic union administered by a hybrid political arrangement, whereby certain specialized powers are vested in Union-wide institutions while control over such matters as criminal codes and the critical domains of foreign and defense policy remain in the hands of the sovereign member states. Plans for a more ambitious union were agreed to by the EU states at a 1991 meeting held in Maastricht, the Netherlands. The resulting Maastricht Treaty called for the creation of a single European currency and a central European bank by 1999 as well as the development of common EU foreign and defense policies. If fully implemented, therefore, the Maastricht Treaty will lead to a Europe that is not only economically integrated but also effectively a single political and military unit in international affairs. Should it come to pass, Europe's single voice would carry immense weight abroad, given the enormous economic, political, and military power that its states could mobilize behind common policy objectives.

While the Maastricht Treaty has been ratified by the member states of the EU, it is doubtful that its bold vision of political unity will be fully realized. Shortly after the agreement was reached, a popular reaction against the centralized EU bureaucracies headquartered in Brussels, Belgium, swept across Europe. Whereas "Brussels" had earlier served as shorthand for the Union's dramatic success in spurring regional economic growth, many Europeans now associate it with distant bureaucrats, intrusive regulations, and the erosion of local autonomy. Prior to Maastricht, European integration had left national sovereignty largely intact and had earned enormous popular support for restoring Europe's economic dynamism and international competitiveness. By the mid–1990s, however, Europe's economy was in the doldrums, its national leaders commanded little popular support, and its governments seemed paralyzed in the face of ethnic violence in the former Yugoslavia and Soviet Union. The consequent loss of enthusiasm for the ideal of a united Europe meant that the heads of Europe's governments would have to proceed toward greater unity with caution. While political unification around a common European foreign and defense policy might seem to be a logical step beyond economic union, prominent commentators began to voice their doubts that the supranationalist interdependence that had worked so well in spurring economic growth would be well suited to the rather different tasks of foreign and defense policy.

A third question is, how is Europe to define its international role? Although the Maastricht Treaty calls for the development of a unified foreign and defense policy, it establishes no supranational mechanism for either formulating or carrying out such a policy. That means that despite Maastricht's bold talk of a united EU front to the outside world, the reality will be a continuation of separate foreign policies arrived at by Europe's national governments. On some issues, those policies will be coordinated and will thus be backed by Europe's combined strength. In other instances, however, the Europeans will be unable to agree among themselves, with the result that their independent international efforts will be in conflict with one another and will be unable to marshal the greater authority and resources of a truly European policy.

For example, on some foreign economic issues, the EU has maintained a unified policy. Under a series of conventions, for example, 70 former colonies in Africa, the Caribbean, and Asia enjoy preferential access to EU members' markets for their exports, and most also receive direct economic assistance channeled through the EU. On other foreign economic issues, however, EU unity appears shaky. The Union's high tariffs on non-EU imports and its generous subsidies to European farmers have come under sharp attack in the WTO negotiations on trade liberalization; and other countries, including the United States and Japan, have sought to exploit the barely muted tensions between the ardent French supporters of these protectionist policies and the British and German advocates of free trade. As pressures for global trade liberalization grow, the facade of EU unity behind a wall of protectionism is likely to crumble.

Similarly, the EU states face endless opportunities for division among themselves amid the ethnic conflicts, social instabilities, and economic privations in the formerly communist countries of Eastern Europe and the old Soviet Union. The Balkan crisis that began in 1992, for example, cast into sharp relief the EU's inability to act in concert in its own backyard. Germany, with historical and economic ties to the Yugoslavian republics of Croatia and Slovenia, favored strong action against Serbia, including air strikes against Serb positions within Bosnia. France, on the other hand, retained historical links with Serbia and initially favored preserving a Serb-dominated Yugoslav federation. When that option was overtaken by events, both the British and the French introduced peacekeeping forces into Bosnia and, fearing for their safety, strenuously opposed the Germans on the issue of air strikes—but eventually gave in and approved strikes by NATO beginning in 1995. The EU's appearance of weakness, indecision, and lack of leadership on the Balkan crisis cast a pall over earlier hopes that Europe was about to present a strong and united front to the world.

Finally, in the late 1990s Europe was shaken by division over its earlier commitment to adopt a common currency, the euro, by January 1, 1999. The protocols adopting the euro also stipulated stringent budget and debt policies for EU members. Budget deficits, for example, could run no more than an austere 3 percent of GDP. The prospect of such tight budgets, and the unemployment believed to accompany them, was widely believed to account for the defeat of Gaullist Jacques Chirac's parliamentary elections and the victory of the Socialists headed by Lionel Jospin, who became prime minister. By 1997 France and Germany were recording the highest unemployment levels since World War II. Amid such circumstances, it was not at all evident that the twin pillars of Europe would be able to meet the demanding goal of 3 percent by the end of 1997.

Sometimes lost amid the political squabbling is that the common European currency is designed to ease trade among European nations and improve Europe's ability to compete worldwide, especially with the American dollar.

Japan: Wealth Versus Influence

Japan represents an interesting phenomenon for students of international relations. Its economic stature alone places it among the leading countries of the world; however, for the past 50 years it has neither sought nor accepted the international leadership role that is the traditional hallmark of major-power status. Particularly in international political and security issues, Japan's has been a hesitant voice. It is this anomaly, this phenomenon of an emerging power that bears little resemblance to traditional major powers, that has recently sparked so much interest among scholars of international relations. Will this "incomplete superpower" acquire the full array of instruments of power—including military power—that will catapult it into the status of "complete superpower"? And how might a newly powerful Japan wield its new influence? Can a country whose culture and history set it apart from the dominant western powers truly rise to the challenge of sharing leadership of a world in which it often seems ill at ease?

Summary ━━━━━━━━━━━━━━━━━━━━━━━━━━━━━

Key Elements of Japan's Self-Concept

1. Belief that it is small and vulnerable
2. Exaggerated sense of its own uniqueness
3. Desire for the approval and respect of the West

As a basis for answering these questions, we start by examining some broad themes of how Japan relates to the international community, paying particular attention to three aspects of Japan's own self-concept that do much to condition its overall approach to world affairs. First is the pervasive belief that Japan is a small and vulnerable country, chronically threatened by outside forces over which it has little control. This self-image, which is a standard teaching in Japanese schools and is routinely reinforced by the country's leaders and in the national media, is easier to understand if one looks at a world map, where Japan appears between the vast expanse of the Pacific Ocean to the east and the massive land powers of Russia and China to the west. Set amid such immense land and maritime dimensions, Japan does indeed, at first glance, seem small and vulnerable.

However, several comparative measures put a rather different light on Japan's size and strength. First, in terms of land area, many people are surprised to learn that Japan's four main islands add up to an area larger than Italy and 50 percent larger than Great Britain, two states that are seldom thought of as being "small and vulnerable." Second, Japan's population of about 130 million is the seventh largest in the world, hardly an indicator of national diminutiveness. Third, if economic production is used as a comparative measure, Japan does not look small and vulnerable at all. It has the second-largest economy in the world (behind only the United States); and by some measures, such as savings rates, capital investment, and trade balances, Japan's has been arguably the healthiest economy in the world until recently.

It is only in terms of a fourth comparative measure, natural resources, that the Japanese self-concept of vulnerability to outside forces takes on some obvious validity. Japan is a very resource-poor country, having virtually none of the mineral wealth essential for an industrial economy. Apart from coal, it must import virtually all the raw materials needed for its world-famous manufacturing operations. It is especially dependent on foreign suppliers of energy; over 80 percent of Japan's energy is imported. Virtually all of its petroleum is imported, 70 percent of it from the politically volatile Persian Gulf region. An experience that hit Japan especially hard and reinforced its exaggerated sense of vulnerability to outside

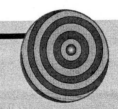

Case in Point

Japan's Plutonium Ordeal

Japan's tendency to take unilateral steps to hedge against its fear of outside forces, as well as the tendency of such steps to draw international criticism, was illustrated by the notorious plutonium shipment of 1992–93. In order to lessen its dependence on imported petroleum, Japan generates one-fourth of its electricity from nuclear reactors, a proportion exceeded only by France. In the late 1960s the government decided to develop breeder reactors. Unlike conventional reactors, which are fueled by uranium that must be replaced as it is depleted, breeder reactors are fueled by plutonium. Plutonium is produced by converting spent uranium; when burned in breeder reactors, it generates even more plutonium, thus holding out the tantalizing possibility of greater energy self-sufficiency for the Japanese. Since the Japanese lacked the capacity to convert their own uranium to plutonium, however, they contracted with the British and French to do so. By late 1992 the first shipment of plutonium was ready to be sent back to Japan.

The problems in this scenario soon became apparent. For one thing, the plutonium was nearly of sufficiently high grade to be used in making nuclear weapons, thus making it a tempting target for hijacking by an international terrorist group. Furthermore, the convoy of ships transporting the deadly element was lightly guarded, "protected" only by Japan's equivalent of the Coast Guard. Finally, plutonium is one of the most toxic substances known; a single drop can induce cancer in humans. Transporting it from Europe to Japan thus represented a serious threat to the international environment. The shipment did indeed arrive safely on Japan's western coast, but the international criticism triggered by the voyage proved highly embarrassing to the Japanese. In 1994 the Japanese government decided to abandon the breeder reactor, which had turned out to be uneconomical as well as controversial.

forces was the 1973 oil boycott by the Organization of Petroleum Exporting Countries (OPEC), in which the principal oil-producing states withheld their oil from the market in an effort to drive up prices and to coerce the West to force Israel to withdraw from territory it had occupied in wars with Arab countries.

The chronic anxiety produced by this sense of vulnerability partly explains the pattern of self-regarding behavior that in recent years has begun to generate international opposition to Japan. For example, in the 1980s the Japanese were very slow to grasp the worldwide anger caused by their country's large and chronic trade surpluses. To the Japanese, the documented unfair trading practices that help to produce these surpluses are necessary elements of a national security strategy. To outsiders, those practices look like little more than grasping attempts to enrich Japan at the expense of countries that follow international norms of trade reciprocity.

The second factor in Japan's self-image that conditions its approach to the outside world is its exaggerated sense of its own uniqueness. Through most of its history, Japan was an unusually isolated society because of its island location and its distance from Asian trading routes. It was not until the U.S. naval expedition led by Commodore Matthew Perry forcibly "opened" the country in 1853 that Japan reluctantly cast off its instinctive isolationism and truly joined the international community.

Japan thus entered the global stage quite late, having spent over 2,000 years living apart from the ordinary interactions of international dealings. This exceptionally long phenomenon of isolationism has had two lasting effects: (1) the Japanese are a strikingly homogeneous people, and (2) they retain a deep sense of psychic separateness from the rest of the world. Physically and culturally, the Japanese are the most homogeneous large nation in the world, resembling in many ways a large tribe. Growing up, young Japanese have much less personal experience dealing with people who are different from them than do, for example, people growing up in the United States or in Great Britain. This pronounced "we-they" mentality creates a distinct cultural and psychological wall between Japan and the peoples of other cultures. It is perhaps axiomatic that all peoples are somewhat ethnocentric, but it is certainly true that the Japanese are unusually ethnocentric.

The greatest challenge that Japan faces internationally may be learning how to interact with diverse cultures as equals. The hierarchical thinking deeply embedded within Japanese culture, whereby personal interactions are shaped by an acute sense of being either above or below others in social rank, carries over into Japan's often awkward dealings with other countries. To this day the Japanese, more than most other countries, view the world through the lens of hierarchical thinking. They feel either inferior or superior to other peoples, according deference in the former case and ill concealing their contempt in the latter. Little in their history or their contemporary culture equips them to deal with a pluralistic world in which diverse peoples expect to be accorded equal respect.

The third aspect of Japan's view of itself that affects its approach to international affairs is its deep desire for the approval and the respect of the West, a desire that for almost 150 years has prompted a drive to catch up with the West. Its forced opening by the United States in 1853 prompted an intense campaign of national modernization, with the strategic objective of matching the West's industrial and military strength in order to avoid the fate of other Asian countries. As it happened, Japan's self-imposed period of isolation, from 1639 to 1853, had sealed it off at a particularly critical period in world history. During this time the Europeans were inaugurating an extraordinary new age of scientific and technological capability.

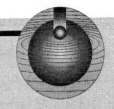

Amplification

Japanese Ethnocentrism

Most scholars of Japan have commented on the unusual degree of ethnocentrism among the Japanese. Like all things in a modern, dynamic society, this characteristic is gradually changing. Today's young Japanese are more attuned to the world beyond Japan's borders than are their elders, and they tend to be more accepting of and comfortable with the diversity of the world's lands and peoples.

As recently as the 1980s, however, a spokesperson for a Japanese trade delegation was able to say to the press, with a straight face, that Japan could not accept the importation of American beef because Japanese intestines are different from other peoples' intestines. Soon after, one of his colleagues declared that Japan could not import American skis because Japanese snow is different from other countries' snow.

These examples of a sense of exceptionalism shading into garden-variety ethnocentrism are probably not terribly harmful and, to many non-Japanese, are a source of amusement. Less benign, and not at all amusing, was the utter racist contempt harbored by Japanese leaders toward other Asians during World War II. In the language of one key report, Japan's design for its Greater East Asian Co-Prosperity Sphere was to create "an economic structure which would ensure the permanent subordination of all other peoples and nations of Asia to Japan." It was Japan's mission to do so, the report said, because the Japanese were clearly the "leading race" of Asia. The legacy of its brutal treatment during World War II of Koreans, Chinese, Filipinos, and other Asians whom it considered inferior has left an abiding suspicion of Japan throughout much of Asia that will not soon be erased.

Source: Kenneth B. Pyle, *The Japanese Question* (Washington, DC: AEI Press, 1992), pp. 18–19.

Young Japanese today, like these tourists in Paris, are more open than their elders to foreign influences, but Japanese society remains an extremely inward-looking one.

Together with organizational skill, military power, and the political will to spread western power into the less developed parts of the world, this capability left the Japanese, like their Asian neighbors, highly vulnerable. By the mid-nineteenth century European states had colonized all of South Asia and most of Southeast Asia and had virtually carved up China, historically the cultural and political center of East Asia, into European spheres of influence. Russia was extending its land empire eastward and with the conquest of Siberia was now facing Japan. From the other direction, the young United States expanded steadily westward, first across the North American continent and then into the Pacific. The appearance of Commodore Perry's fleet showed Japan that it must join the world, rapidly modernize, and emulate the more powerful West in education, science, technology, industry, and military strength.

In the late nineteenth century Japan's leaders concluded that they would also have to mimic the western practice of seeking overseas dominions. In quick succession Japan fought and defeated China (1894–95) and Russia (1904–05), acquiring Taiwan, portions of Manchuria, and Korea. Then, during the Great Depression of the 1930s, economic desperation, weak civilian rule, and a rising sentiment of ultranationalism created a climate in which the Japanese army effectively slipped the bonds of civilian control and dragged the country into a campaign of conquest that, by the summer of 1941, included most of China.

Japan in 1928	Occupied by 1941	→ Japanese attacks
Occupied by 1933	Under Japanese political influence	* Independence movements supported by Japan

Map 7-2   Japanese Expansion, 1928–1941

©1996 by St. Martin's Press, Inc. From: *Contours of Power,* by Snow/Brown. Reprinted with permission of Bedford/St. Martin's Press, Inc.

As it became apparent that Japanese aggression was aimed at conquering all of East and Southeast Asia, including the oil-rich Dutch holdings in what is now Indonesia, the United States increasingly pressured Japan to halt its expansionist drive. Unwilling to back down, however, Japan bombed the American naval fleet concentrated at Pearl Harbor, Hawaii, on December 7, 1941. Its reasoning was that the United States, mired in one of its characteristic moods of isolationism and preoccupied domestically with the effects of the economic depression, would be neutralized militarily while Japan completed its conquest of East and Southeast Asia. By the time the Americans could respond, the Japanese believed, Japan's so-called Greater East Asian Co-Prosperity Sphere would be an accomplished fact whose reversal the decadent and isolationist Americans would have little inclination to undertake.

Japan's fatal miscalculation of U.S. will led to its defeat in 1945 and occupation by U.S. forces that lasted until 1951. In the wake of this disastrous attempt to compete with the West in the military arena, post–World War II Japan embarked instead on a single-minded drive for domestic economic development, the Yoshida Doctrine. The Japanese government played a strong role in this effort by nurturing new industries and erecting stiff import barriers against foreign manufactured goods in order to allow Japanese businesses to get fully established. From the late 1940s until the present, Japan has pursued its own global economic advancement with an intensity and success unrivaled by any other country. Its steady progress up through the ranks of the major industrial states was widely chronicled: in the late 1960s its gross national product surpassed in turn those of Italy (in 1966), Britain (1967), France (1968), and West Germany (1969). For the last quarter century only the United States has remained as a challenge to Japanese economic prowess.

Taken together, these three enduring elements of Japan's national self-concept give the Japanese a set of attitudes that shape their approach to the outside world: their chronic feeling of national insecurity, their wish to maintain large trade surpluses in order to offset that insecurity, their difficulty in connecting psychologically with other countries, their exceptional degree of self-serving behavior, their ethnocentrism, their feeling that international norms aren't entirely applicable to Japan, and their difficulty comprehending that Japan has arrived at the head table of world powers and that its success carries responsibilities for helping maintain the international system as a whole.

Can Japan Be an International Leader?

As its economic stature has risen, Japan has found itself increasingly expected to take a leading role in addressing the multitude of global political, security, economic, and environmental problems. Certainly it has the wealth to wield the kind of clout traditionally associated with major powers, but does it have the political will? Japan must overcome four impediments before its global leadership role can truly match its economic stature.

Summary ————————————————————————

Impediments to Japan's Becoming a Global Leader

1. Its difficulty in coming to terms with its past aggression
2. Its inability to articulate values with broad global appeal
3. Its need to overcome its insular worldview
4. Its need for political reform to create a center of decisive leadership

First, Japan must fully, if belatedly, come to terms with its past. Japanese aggression and colonialism during the first half of the twentieth century caused immense suffering to the country's Asian neighbors, especially the people of China and Korea. Even by the standards of wartime behavior, Japanese soldiers were uncommonly cruel to the people they defeated. The wanton rape and killing of civilians in Nanking, China, claimed 300,000 lives; Korean women were kidnapped and forced into serving as prostitutes for Japanese soldiers throughout the Japanese Empire; captured American soldiers in the Philippines were subjected to starvation and torture during the infamous Bataan Death March, during which many lost their lives.

Yet to this day, neither the government nor the people of Japan have fully confronted the question of their country's wartime guilt. The contrast with Germany, which has squarely addressed its behavior under Nazism and which keeps the memories of this past alive by teaching them to each new generation of schoolchildren, is strong. Japan's Ministry of Education, which must approve all textbooks, has systematically downplayed Japan's record of aggression and the suffering it created, and Japanese schoolchildren read only brief references to the "Nanking incident" and learn nothing at all of the horrors perpetrated by Japanese soldiers during the 1930s and 1940s. They are, however, taught in great detail about the U.S. nuclear bombings that ended the war, with the result that they see Japan more as victim than as villain in World War II. Though the events happened many years ago, the issue of how contemporary Japan interprets them matters a great deal today, for the countries of Asia that suffered so greatly at Japan's hands will not trust it to play a greater international role until they can conclude that contemporary Japanese have fully come to terms with their country's past and have learned the lessons it contains.

In addition to dealing with the unsavory aspects of its history, Japan will have difficulty exercising international leadership until it can articulate values with broad global appeal. Unlike the United States, to cite the most extreme example of the opposite characteristic, Japan is not associated in the minds of foreigners with abstract ideals capable of sparking the hopes and aspirations of people in distant lands. This characteristic is rooted in Japanese culture, which with its philosophical relativism and group-defined situational ethics has placed less weight on moral absolutes and abstract concepts than has been the case in western societies. Lacking fixed principles of right and wrong grounded in religious or secular tradition, Japanese culture conditions its members to focus on the shifting requirements of their immediate group. "Right" behavior springs from one's appreciation of his or her position within the group and desire to be perceived as a team player who goes along with the group's consensual views. "Wrong" behavior arises from individualistic impulses to follow one's own beliefs when they diverge from group-defined norms. The key point is that among the major countries, Japan stands apart in its relative absence of transcendent principles of right and wrong.

In foreign policy, this trait has given Japanese leaders broad latitude in making decisions pragmatically on a case-by-case basis, but to Japan's critics it is seen as evidence of an unprincipled opportunism that leaves Japan incapable of acting on behalf of transcendent, universal values. Though Japanese leaders speak of their country's commitment to democracy, market economics, and human rights, many outside observers conclude that Japan remains unwilling to take a firm stand on contentious international issues in the name of any principle higher than "stability" or Japan's own immediate self-interest. In another age, Japan's reputation for amorality might have made little difference. Today, however, its lack of ideological appeal, along with its insular culture, has put Japan at a disadvantage in projecting a clear vision of its national purpose. As Joseph Nye has pointed out, in an increasingly interdependent world, "hard" instruments of power such as military or economic coercion are becoming less useful, while "soft power," such as a country's cultural and ideological appeal, takes on greater significance.

For Japan to assume a leading role in world affairs, its people will also need to overcome their insular worldview. As noted above, Japan's strikingly homogenous population and its long history of isolation have left an indelible imprint on the country's character. The absence of ethnic and cultural diversity at home and the traditionally minimal contacts with the outside world have given rise to an uncommonly inward-looking society which values above all else internal harmony and stability. To a degree unusual among citizens of leading industrialized countries, the Japanese tend to view the world beyond their borders as a giant market for their own manufactured exports but otherwise see it as a threatening maelstrom of alien ways and chronic strife. The stark contrast between the chaos scattered across the international landscape and the orderly and safe society of Japan is often noted in Japanese media. Although more Japanese than ever before are now traveling, studying, and working abroad, the cultural gap between Japan and the rest of the world remains vast and will change only very gradually. Despite their affluence, a far smaller percentage of Japanese travel abroad than do Europeans, and Japanese who live in other countries have earned a reputation for clannishness, often remaining aloof from foreign ways and retaining maximum Japanese control over overseas business ventures by minimizing the number of non-Japanese elevated to key management positions.

Japan's insular mentality easily shades into a sense of national, racial, and cultural superiority. A poll conducted in the mid–1980s found that 80 percent of Japanese respondents believed that they were among the world's "superior races." Racial bias against darker-skinned peoples is a given among Japanese, and they also harbor an ill-concealed contempt for Asian neighbors, such as China and the Koreas, that were once conquered by Japan and now lag behind it economically.

Such attitudes undercut the ability of Japanese leaders to step up to the responsibilities of global leadership commensurate with their country's wealth. While public opinion polls rarely determine foreign policy specifics in any democracy, broadly held public attitudes do set the outer boundaries within which democratically elected governments can safely operate. The insularity and prejudiced attitudes characteristic of the Japanese people create a general sense that the messy conflicts and challenges of the outside world are truly foreign worries and thus require little or no contribution from Japan. Polls showed, for example, that most Japanese regarded the Persian Gulf war, in which much of the world united to turn back Iraq's Saddam Hussein from his invasion and annexation of Kuwait, as simply another instance of *taigan no kaji*, "a fire on the other side of the river." Until Japan's leaders, educators, and media instill a greater internationalization of popular attitudes, Japan will be hampered in its efforts to play an international leadership role commensurate with its economic stature.

Finally, Japan will have to undergo significant political reform before it is capable of exercising the influence of a major power. Japan's political institutions have not created a center of decisive authority that would permit the state to act firmly and promptly on international matters. Members of the Diet, Japan's parliament, have had fewer political incentives to develop foreign policy expertise than their counterparts in other leading democracies. When they do turn to international issues, their ability to initiate policy is constrained by the Diet's weak committee structure and the absence of strong professional staff. Japan's prime ministers, chosen by the Diet, have seldom been commanding leaders with strong foreign policy credentials. Rather, during the long period that Japanese politics was dominated by the Liberal Democratic party (1955–1993; 1999–present), prime ministers were generally bland consensus builders whose greatest political talent lay in mediating differences among the party's factions rather than in defining a clear sense of purpose for the nation. Their rapid turnover (since 1972, only Yasuhiro Nakosone has served longer than two years) coupled with their lack of an independent source of political authority severely hampered their ability to chart a new path for Japan in international affairs.

By default, then, the career bureaucracy has played a much more powerful role in shaping foreign policy in Japan than have its counterparts in other major democracies. Japan's professional diplomatic corps is an elite repository of foreign policy expertise whose quality rivals that of any other major state. But the Ministry of Foreign Affairs is severely understaffed (Japan has fewer professional diplomats than Great Britain, France, or Germany, and far fewer than the United States), and so its talented men and women are constantly "putting out fires" of daily details, with precious little time for policy planning and analysis. This problem, coupled with a lack of domestic political support, means that the ministry, while the principal shaper of Japanese foreign policy, is seriously hampered in charting a long-term international course for the country and in marshaling the domestic political backing to enact its internationalist outlook.

Four Questions for Japan's Future

As Japan contemplates its place in the post–Cold War world, four fundamental issues confront it. The first question is, does its future lie with the East or the West? For the past century, Japanese elites have identified more with the educational, scientific, technological, and industrial prowess of the West than with their less economically advanced neighbors in Asia. In recent years, however, Asia has emerged as an economically dynamic region that now attracts huge amounts of Japanese investment. The countries of Southeast Asia, especially Malaysia, Thailand, and Singapore, are gradually being transformed into cogs in Japan's industrial juggernaut; they provide critical resources and, perhaps more important, low-wage off-shore sites for Japanese manufacturing firms, helping offset labor shortages caused by a declining birthrate in Japan itself.

Summary ———————————————————

Four Questions About Japan's Future

1. Does its future lie with Asia or with the West?
2. Will its relationship with the United States be close and cooperative or strained and competitive?
3. What will its national security strategy be?
4. How can it best contribute to world order?

Some Japanese commentators are now calling for Japan's "re-Asianization," suggesting that Japan should seek to organize the workforce and resources of Asia around Japanese strategic objectives rather than continuing to identify with the "white" western world. However, lingering mistrust of Japanese motives in the region—a function of Japan's failure to come to terms with its legacy of militarism and colonialism—and the fact that contemporary Japan more closely resembles Europe or the United States in the social, economic, educational, and political consequences of affluence mean that Japan's future is necessarily inseparable from that of the industrial democracies of the West.

A second critical question Japan faces is, will its relationship with the United States, which has loomed so large in its national life for the past half-century, be close and cooperative or strained and competitive? Over this period, the relationship has evolved from that of bitter enemies in World War II to the dominant-subordinate relationship of the postwar U.S. occupation and then to a strategic Cold War alliance in which the United States was the unquestioned superior partner and in many ways Japan's patron as it sought to gain rehabilitation from the stigma of its past and readmission to international society. With the end of the Cold War, U.S.-Japanese relations are being reassessed by both sides. Today's Japanese retain less of their elders' gratitude for the benevolence of the U.S. occupation policies and for American protection of Japan and sponsorship of its reentry into the international community. Chronic wrangling over trade issues has left both sides exasperated, with Americans often perceiving a selfish, mercantilistic Japan that aggressively seizes every opportunity to enrich itself in the more liberalized global trading environment that was largely established and maintained by the United States in the post–World War II era, while at the same time denying other countries equal access to its own markets. Many Americans wonder aloud why they continue to contribute heavily to the costs of defending Japan when the latter has benefited so handsomely by avoiding most of the defense burdens ordinarily borne by major countries.

As for the Japanese, constant American pressure to alter long-established Japanese relationships among businesses and between business and government is seen as an unwarranted intrusion on a national system that has contributed so much to Japan's postwar economic resurgence. The Japanese increasingly see the United States as a bully that blames the Japanese for its own self-inflicted economic ills. Many Japanese resent what they see as a condescending American attitude and believe that the United States refuses to accept the new reality of Japanese stature, in part, they suspect, because of western racism. Japan's chronic insistence that it is the object of western racism is ironic, given the pervasive racism of Japanese society. In the late 1980s, two Japanese prime ministers publicly attributed U.S. economic woes to the presence of large racial minorities in the American population. Both later apologized for their remarks, but it is certain that they merely verbalized the conventional wisdom of most Japanese.

Strains in the Japanese-American relationship are to be expected. Given the profound differences between the two countries' cultures and the transformation in their relative stance from that of victor and vanquished to the contemporary reality of greater equality in strength, certain frictions and misunderstandings are simply inherent. While Japan will cultivate a broad array of bilateral relationships and gradually assume greater independence, however, the U.S. link will retain its critical centrality for Japan for many years. The U.S. market is still essential to Japan in a way that the Japanese market is not to the United States.

The security relationship between the two countries continues to reassure Japan's neighbors that it will not soon embark on a return to militarism and conquest. Finally, whatever irritations the Japanese experience in their dealings with the Americans, the United States still holds Japan in higher esteem than do the other major powers. Japan remains a broadly unpopular country, widely disliked and mistrusted. More than any other country, the United States has developed an intricate web of interdependence with the Japanese, and it remains Japan's most important strategic partner and closest friend.

The third question for Japan's future is, what will its national security strategy be? Throughout the Cold War, Japan relied on the United States to protect it against strategic nuclear threats while gradually building up its conventional defensive capabilities with U.S. encouragement to do so. Today, the United States continues to extend its strategic protection to Japan under the terms of the 1960 Mutual Security Treaty, but its rationale for doing so is now greatly altered. Rather than protecting Japan against a much-diminished threat from the former Soviet Union, the U.S. nuclear shield is intended to maintain regional stability in Asia and to undercut Japan's incentive to remilitarize and, specifically, to acquire its own nuclear capability. Some Japanese believe that Japan must develop an independent nuclear armory, not only to ensure its continued security but to establish itself as a genuinely major world power. So long as it remains in the shadow of the American nuclear umbrella, they argue, Japan will remain subservient to the United States and remain a second-class power.

For now, however, Japanese leaders decline to pursue the nuclear option, though they stress that Japan could build a nuclear device within six months. They understand that the specter of a nuclear-armed Japan would set off alarm bells among its heavily armed neighbors, all of whom retain historical antagonisms against Japan. A bid for nuclear status by Japan would stimulate a dangerous round of arms races and alliance restructuring among China, Russia, the Koreas, and much of Southeast Asia. Absent a dramatic new threat to Japan's security (the most likely scenario would be a nuclear-armed North Korea) or the collapse of the security relationship with the United States, Japan is unlikely to risk the destabilizing consequences of pressing for an independent nuclear capability. Its continued reliance on the United States for strategic deterrence, however, will continue to cramp its quest for an independent identity in international affairs.

The fourth and final question confronting Japan as it seeks to chart its new international role is, how can it best contribute to world order? Given domestic attitudes toward the outside world and the residual suspicion in Asia of an independent Japanese military role, neither the Japanese public nor most of Japan's neighbors would tolerate a militarized Japan unilaterally intervening in trouble spots outside its borders. Yet the international community will remain in constant need of multilateral peacekeeping operations mounted by the United Nations, and the Japan that has benefited so much from the post–World War II order will increasingly be expected to play its part to help establish and uphold order in the post–Cold War era. In 1992 the Diet approved landmark legislation authorizing elements of the Self-Defense Forces, as Japan's armed forces are officially known, to participate in UN peacekeeping operations. Forces dispatched will be few in number, lightly armed for self-protection only, and confined to noncombat support roles, such as transportation, medical care, and election monitoring. The measure represented an important step, yet there remain sharp limits to Japan's ability to contribute to international order via military means.

Perhaps the most promising route for Japan is to become what journalist Yoichi Funabashi has termed a "global civilian power." Working through international institutions, principally the UN, Japan can channel its considerable financial and human resources to promote Second Tier development, democracy, market economics, and environmental protection. While any expansion of Japan's international role will generate some resistance, both at home and abroad, activities such as providing developmental assistance, assisting refugees, and promoting educational and scientific advances provide the least threatening and hence least controversial channel for Japan to discharge the responsibilities of international leadership commensurate with its economic stature.

Case Study Will China Join the First Tier?

Studying China's current rise in economic, military, and political power provides useful insights into the underlying basis of major-power status in the modern world. In many respects, China appears well poised to vault into the First Tier sometime in the twenty-first century. Its people are heirs to the world's oldest continuous civilization, one long noted for its political, cultural, and intellectual innovations. Its population of 1.25 billion is by far the world's largest, accounting for one-fifth of the globe's population. and in area it ranks third, behind only Russia and Canada. China is one of the five permanent members of the UN Security Council, and its possession (since 1964) of nuclear weapons adds to its stature. Despite these impressive claims to great-power status, however, China stands apart from the elite ranks of the First Tier by virtue of its poverty and its authoritarian government. As we will explain, the first of these conditions is being altered, while the second shows no sign of changing anytime soon.

China's communist rule was established in 1949, when revolutionaries led by Mao Zedong triumphed in a long and bitter civil war. Once in power, Mao set out to accomplish two objectives. First, he restored China's unity, strength, and pride following a humiliating century of internal decay, dynastic collapse, and domination by the Europeans and the Japanese. Second, he sought to radically transform Chinese society into a "utopia" of egalitarianism. Since much of China's population did not share his vision of redemption through communal life, Mao instituted a thoroughgoing police state to crush dissidents and ensure compliance with his ambitious attempt at social engineering.

As Mao's campaigns to remake Chinese society became increasingly radical, so too did their toll of victims increase. From 1960 to 1962, more than 40 million Chinese starved to death from famine brought on by ill-conceived social programs. Amid the Cultural Revolution of the late 1960s, which was aimed at re-igniting Maoist ideological zeal among the young, another 500,000 Chinese lost their lives. Mao's legacy, then, was a decidedly mixed one. When he died in 1976, he did leave behind a centralized regime that had brought China back to much of its past vigor and international stature. However, his obsessive and totalitarian quest for egalitarian communism left the Chinese mired in poverty, their country ranking among the poorest in the world in per capita wealth.

Following Mao's death, Deng Xiaoping effectively consolidated his authority over China's political system. As soon as his power base was secure, Deng announced his famous campaign of Four Modernizations. Of the four, three were economic in nature: scientific and technological advancement, greater industrialization, and improved agricultural productivity. The fourth goal, military modernization, received the least emphasis until recently.

Map 7-3   China and Its Neighbors

©1996 by St. Martin's Press, Inc. From: *Contours of Power,* by Snow/Brown. Reprinted with permission of Bedford/St. Martin's Press, Inc.

Deng's reforms were begun in the agricultural sector, where peasants were permitted to sell much of what they produced for their own profit. The introduction of market incentives spurred a dramatic growth in entrepreneurial behavior, agricultural productivity, and rural prosperity. Deng then began a gradual phasing in of market structures in the urban, industrial sectors of the economy. Especially important were the four Special Economic Zones (SEZs) created in southeastern China in 1979. The SEZs were designed as laboratories of economic reform, deliberately set apart from the broader economy. Their laws encouraged the establishment of export-oriented manufacturing industries that could earn badly needed foreign currency. Foreign investment was courted for the SEZs, and with it China gained advanced foreign technology and managerial expertise. While China's traditional communists detested the SEZs on ideological grounds, the experiments have proven to be economic dynamos that have helped ignite a nationwide economic boom. Though not pure oases of capitalism, the SEZs operate much more according to the laws of the market than to the laws of communism. Deng's highly publicized visit to the Shenzhen SEZ in 1992 sent a clear signal that this was the direction in which he intended to lead China.

China's dramatic economic growth—averaging ten percent per year—is due principally to the steady expansion of the nonstate sector. In 1980 there were about 1,500 private firms in all of China; today there are nearly half a million. Agriculture is now almost entirely decollectivized, and industrial production is shifting rapidly away from the Maoist state monopoly. Whereas in the early 1980s nearly 80 percent of China's industrial production was by state-owned enterprises, by the early 1990s the state-owned share had shrunk to about 50 percent, while collectives and private firms account for the other half. By the end of the decade, the state will account for less than one-third of China's industrial production.

By introducing market mechanisms, including private property, profit incentives for workers and entrepreneurs, and the acceptance of income differences, Deng has unleashed the energies of the Chinese people and ignited an economic boom. That boom is fed by China's high personal savings rate, which has been averaging 40 percent—a striking contrast with the U.S. rate of five percent. Such savings create a large pool of capital to finance the frenetic construction of new roads, power facilities, and factories. China's per capita output is now doubling every ten years, and between 1984 and 1990 China's average annual growth rate was a whopping ten percent, much higher than Asian countries such as the Philippines, Indonesia, or Thailand. Of Asia's major economies, only South Korea grew at a faster rate during the same period. Calculating the full effects of Deng's reforms is difficult, but in May 1993 the International Monetary Fund released a report concluding that China's economy is four times larger than suggested by previous measures, making it the third largest in the world, behind only the United States and Japan.

Despite their dramatic rise, Chinese living standards still lag far behind those in First Tier countries. Per capita income in China is only about one-tenth that of the United States, Japan, or Germany. University enrollment remains low, a reflection of the Communist Party's long-standing suspicion of intellectuals. But literacy rates have risen steadily, as has the quality of medical care, especially that provided to infants and children.

The question naturally arises as to why the Chinese were able to spur economic growth while the Soviets' attempt at reform in the 1980s failed spectacularly, as we discussed in Chapter 6. Two reasons stand out. First, when China embarked on market reforms in 1978, there was a group of entrepreneurs—and an entrepreneurial culture—that had survived under communism's relatively brief reign of less than 30 years. By contrast, Russia had never been known for its entrepreneurial spirit; and in any case, by the time Gorbachev came to power in 1985, communism had ruled Soviet life for nearly 70 years, virtually destroying any vestige of the capitalist spirit. Second, the Chinese had never regarded themselves as the Vatican of communist faith. That dubious distinction belonged to the Soviets, and it injected into Soviet life a degree of rigidity on ideological adherence that inhibited pragmatic innovation. The Chinese, by contrast, enjoyed a certain freedom in matters of ideology, thus permitting them more readily to bend communist doctrine to fit the circumstances at hand.

The contrast between China's communist heritage and its modernizing economy is captured as soldiers of the People's Liberation Army march past the Hard Rock Café in suburban Beijing.

China's pell-mell drive towards economic modernity has left a large number of casualties in its wake. For example, more than 100 million workers have fled the countryside to seek better opportunities in the cities. This is not surprising, since the agricultural growth is currently about 3 percent while urban areas are growing at about 20 percent. Still, the 100 million rural workers who have fled to the cities typically bring with them few skills needed in an industrializing economy. Most wind up as day laborers in construction, with none of the social, housing, and medical benefits enjoyed by Chinese with a steady, full-time position.

Another new issue for industrializing China is environmental degradation. 90 percent of China's cities fail to meet Chinese air-quality standards. Some scholars believe that by the year 2025 China will spew out three times the amount of greenhouse gases as the United States does.

China's economic rise has been accompanied by a new assertiveness in foreign policy and an enhancement of the country's military capability. While other major states are reducing military spending, China has posted double-digit annual growth in its military budget throughout the 1990s. The most significant aspect of its rapid military modernization campaign is the new posture of Chinese forces. Traditionally, their training, equipment, and deployment were oriented toward providing a defense against external threats. Increasingly, however, the Chinese military is acquiring power-projection assets, such as bombers, oceangoing ships, and long-range fighter planes such as the Soviet SU–27 and MIG–31.

Alongside the acquisition of modern force-projection capability, the Chinese have become more assertive in the numerous territorial disputes in Asia and the Pacific to which they are a party. In the South China Sea, for example, seven countries have staked out various claims to the Spratly Islands, which are widely believed to contain oil and natural gas deposits. In 1988 China used force against Vietnam to enforce its own claims to all of the Spratlys, and in early 1992 China alarmed the rest of Asia by promulgating the Territorial Waters Law, which asserts China's sole right to all of the Spratlys and its right to use force, if needed, to vindicate its claim. In light of China's newly acquired naval and aerial force-projection capabilities, countries such as the Philippines, Vietnam, Malaysia, and Indonesia are understandably wary over the appearance of a newly confident China that seems bent on reclaiming its historical position as the dominant power in the Asia-Pacific region.

China's economic growth appears to make it a strong candidate to join the ranks of the First Tier in the foreseeable future. However, there is one major storm cloud hanging over its otherwise bright horizon: the issue of how it is governed, and the related issues of freedom, democracy, and human rights. The growing influence of China's private sector inevitably raises questions about the continued viability of the country's authoritarian one-party system. Notably absent from Deng's goals was the "fifth modernization" of greater freedom and, eventually, political democracy. Deng has insisted that China's transformation is to be a highly compartmentalized one, with greater freedom in economic matters but the maintenance of the Communist Party's monopoly of centralized state authority. History teaches that rising levels of education, prosperity, contact with foreigners, and economic autonomy will inevitably generate mounting pressures for political liberalization as well. However, as the brutal suppression of pro-democracy demonstrators in Beijing's Tiananmen Square in June 1989 graphically demonstrated, political reform will have to await the passing of China's current generation of rulers.

Even in economic terms, we believe that China's continued advance will require a degree of freedom that the current one-party police state cannot permit. To move beyond the middle levels of industrialization requires a self-sustaining capacity for scientific and technological innovation. That capacity for innovation, in turn, requires a broader climate of intellectual and personal freedom, which is antithetical to authoritarian rule. Until China undertakes the "fifth modernization" of political liberalization and democratization, it seems likely to remain outside the elite circle of the First Tier.

The death of Deng Xiaoping in February 1997 created fears and opportunities for China. The fears arose from the loss of the leader who had given China its prosperity and stability unheard of in modern times. On the other hand, Deng's decade-long enfeeblement meant that his passing opened the door for younger, more vigorous leadership. By the time of Deng's death, power in China had been effectively consolidated in the hands of President Zhang Zemin. Zhang brought to office three principal goals. First, he was determined to continue the drive for economic growth begun by Deng. Secondly, he was resolute in his goal to increase China's national strength by modernizing its armed forces. Finally, under Zhang the force of nationalism was unleashed in order to promote unity among the populace.

The phenomenon of a China rising inevitably stimulates debate as to its international intentions. The January/February 1999 issue of the prestigious journal *Foreign Affairs* succinctly captures the division of First Tier policy elites and officials. Journalists Richard Bernstein and Ross Munro write that "Since the late 1980s, Beijing has come to see the United States not as a strategic partner but as the chief obstacle to its own strategic ambition." The authors predict boldly that "China and the United States will be adversaries in the next major global rivalry." Taking the opposite stance is the scholar Robert Ross, whose article is entitled "Beijing as a Conservative Power." Ross argues that China's armed force projection is today modest at best, and he sees China doing little to join the ranks of the military superpowers. China's armed forces are configured in heavily defensive posture, and Ross sees little to change that crucial factor anytime soon.

The 1999 crisis in Kosovo revealed a yawning gap in international thought between the West and China. In intervening militarily in a sovereign state—Yugoslavia—to protect ethnic Albanian Kosovars from the brutal "ethnic cleansing" campaign of the Serbian leader Slobodan Milosevic, NATO's members were saying, in effect, that the old rule of the inviolability of a sovereign state is an idea whose time has come and largely gone. Many leading western scholars of international relations believe that the greatest threat to the security and well-being of the world's peoples lies less in aggression by outside states and more from the unbridled cruelty of national leaders toward their own vulnerable citizens. Sovereignty, then, is now believed by a growing number of western thinkers to be a concept in decline, less a nearly absolute barrier to outside intervention than a tattered cloak behind which dictators mistreat their own population.

China, by contrast, is perhaps the world's leading advocate of the traditional concept of state sovereignty and its corollary doctrine of noninterference in the internal affairs of sovereign states. This is due largely to China's historical conditioning. The nation's bitter "century of humiliation," which lasted from the 1840s to the 1940s, saw a frail China under the corrupt and reactionary Manchu Dynasty endure relentless humiliation at the hands of western imperialists, the most egregious of which was the British-waged Opium Wars of the 1840s. Within years, westerners had carved the nation into spheres of exploitative privilege which a weak China could not resist. During the first half of the twentieth century, China experienced the brutality of Japanese conquest and foreign intervention in its longrunning civil war. When Mao Ze-dong's communist forces finally prevailed in the civil war, Mao exulted to a cheering throng in Beijing that "China has stood up." He meant, of course, that a unified and strengthened China would no longer tolerate foreign interventions in its internal affairs.

It is not difficult to understand why China would cling relentlessly to the doctrine of national sovereignty. Doing so, however, places it at odds with a profound emerging line of reasoning that is today taking root in much of the rest of the world.

Review

In this chapter we have examined the major countries that constitute the First Tier of the contemporary international system. In the process, the following points were made:

1. The members of the First Tier are all market-oriented, affluent, technologically advanced democracies that face no centrally directed threat to their security. Geographically, they are found in Western Europe, North America, and East Asia.

2. The United States is a relative latecomer to the ranks of the major powers. Its approach to the rest of the world is heavily shaped by its domestic ideology of Lockean liberalism and its historical isolationism. These forces have frequently given its foreign policy an idealist strain and a tendency to oscillate between periods of international introversion and extroversion.

3. While the United States confronts many domestic ills, those who see it as a declining power have generally not made a persuasive case.

4. After World War II Western Europe began to unify, a movement prompted by (a) the lessons of two wars in this century, (b) the onset of the Cold War, (c) the effects of the Marshall Plan, and (d) the realization that in a world of nuclear-armed superpowers, the medium-sized states of Europe would become internationally marginal.

5. Beginning with the European Coal and Steel Community, Europe's unification has grown steadily, although political integration has lagged behind economic union.

6. Japan's self-concept is shaped by (a) a belief that it is unusually small and vulnerable, (b) a conviction that it is unique and thus cannot be understood by outsiders, and (c) an intense desire to be accepted or respected by the West.

7. There are impediments to Japan's becoming a true world leader: (a) its need to come to terms with its past, (b) its inability to articulate values with broad global appeal, (c) its need to overcome its insular worldview, and (d) its need for political reform that creates a center of decisive authority.

8. Four issues for Japan's future involve (a) its orientation toward Asia versus the West, (b) its relationship with the United States, (c) its national security strategy, and (d) the best means for it to contribute to world order.

9. China's economic liberalization, begun in 1978 by Deng Xiaoping, has ignited dramatic economic growth, but China will not become a member of the First Tier until it undertakes a comparable political liberalization and permits democracy and human rights.

Suggested Readings

Akaha, Tsuneo, and Frank Langdon, eds. *Japan in the Posthegemonic World*. Boulder, CO: Lynne Rienner, 1993.

Blaker, Michael. *Japanese International Negotiating Style*. New York: Columbia University Press, 1977.

Brown, Seyom. *The Faces of Power*. New York: Columbia University Press, 1968.

Curtis, Gerald L., ed. *Japan's Foreign Policy After the Cold War*. New York: M. E. Sharpe, 1993.

Hartz, Louis. *The Liberal Tradition in America*. New York: Harvest Books, 1955.

Heywood, Robert W. *The European Community: Idea and Reality*. San Francisco: EM Text, 1990.

Inoguchi, Takashi. *Japan's International Relations*. London: Pinter, 1991.

Kennedy, Paul. *The Rise and Fall of the Great Powers*. New York: Random House, 1987.

Kristof, Nicholas D., and Sheryl WuDunn. *China Wakes: The Struggle for the Soul of a Rising Power*. New York: Random House, 1994.

Linter, Valerio. *The European Community: Economic and Political Aspects*. New York: McGraw-Hill, 1991.

Lodge, Juliet. *The European Community and the Challenge of the Future*. London: Pinter, 1989.

Nau, Henry. *The Myth of America's Decline: Leading the World Economy into the 1990s*. Oxford: Oxford University Press, 1990.

Nye, Joseph S. *Bound to Lead: The Changing Nature of American Power*. New York: Basic Books, 1990.

Oksenberg, Michel, and Robert B. Oxnam, eds. *Dragon and Eagle: United States-China Relations*. New York: Basic Books, 1978.

Pyle, Kenneth B. *The Japanese Question*. Washington, DC: AEI Press, 1992.

Segal, Gerald. *Rethinking the Pacific*. London: Oxford University Press, 1990.

Urwin, Derek. *The Community of Europe: A History of European Integration Since 1945*. New York: Longman, 1991.

The Second Tier: Diversity and Development

PREVIEW

In this chapter, we will examine the dynamics of the group of states that constitute the Second Tier and consider how the First Tier can and may interact with them. We will begin by analyzing the political and economic dynamics of the Second Tier and how these may retard democratization and economic development. In the process, we will evaluate the argument that the Second Tier's problems are a legacy of the colonial experience and the process of decolonization. The plight of the Second Tier will be examined in terms of strategies for and barriers to development. We will then turn to the question of what the First Tier might do to assist in Second Tier progress, including the developmental agenda for the 1990s and beyond. The chapter will conclude with a case study looking at the Association of Southeast Asian Nations (ASEAN) as a strategy for promoting economic development.

KEY CONCEPTS

First World
Second World
Third World
Fourth World
legitimacy
industrial revolutions
Four Tigers
Second Tier subtiers
colonialism
multinationalism

relative deprivation
infrastructure
developmental assistance
Group of 77
New International Economic Order
   (NIEO)
privatization
Association of Southeast Asian Nations
   (ASEAN)

OUTLINE

As we discussed in Chapter 1, students of international relations have long had difficulty devising language to distinguish between the wealthiest and most technologically advanced democratic states of the world, constituting what we have called the First Tier, and the rest, constituting what we have termed the Second Tier. Finding appropriate designations is difficult for a number of reasons, which include the geographic and economic diversity of the Second Tier and the difficulty of finding designations that are not offensive to its people.

A basic problem, of course, is that no single geographical region or group of regions can be marked off as constituting the Second Tier. Rather, the states that compose the Second Tier cover most of the world, including most or all of Africa, Asia and the Pacific, and Latin America and the Caribbean, as well as the parts of Europe that formerly belonged to the communist world. Although most First Tier countries are in Europe and North America, some are within these other regions—Japan and Australia and New Zealand in Asia and the Pacific, for example, and, arguably, South Africa on the African continent.

One possible, and inoffensive, approach to this topic has been to use the terms "North" and "South." Most of the First Tier states are indeed located north of most Second Tier states; but First Tier states Australia and New Zealand, and some states along the Pacific Rim that might soon qualify as First Tier states are exceptions to this rule. In addition, people tend to equate "South" with the Southern Hemisphere, which is misleading because many Second Tier states are in the Northern Hemisphere.

Another terminology that has been used distinguishes among four economic worlds. The First World is composed of the most economically developed countries, essentially the same group of states that we have identified as the First Tier. The Second World is the communist states, a category that has virtually vanished as most of these states have abandoned communism. The largest group of states is the Third World, the so-called developing states largely concentrated in Latin America, Asia, and Africa. Finally, there is the Fourth World, a category reserved for the very poorest states, those that have little realistic prospect of achieving economic prosperity in the near to middle term.

There are three difficulties with this terminology as applied to the contemporary situation. The first, and most obvious, is that the Second World has disintegrated with the end of the Cold War, leaving a gap in the sequence, unless there is to be a whole category for the few remaining communist countries. The Second World category perhaps could be retained to include former communist countries, but this leads to a second problem. These designations suggest a hierarchy that may have made some geopolitical sense in the 1950s when the scheme was devised (the First World was certainly wealthier than the Second, some of which was wealthier than the Third) but no longer reflects reality very accurately. Brazil, a Third World country, is clearly wealthier than Romania—which, as formerly communist, could be considered Second World— and many Third World countries are better off by any measure than is formerly communist Albania. A third problem is that the categories lump together very disparate countries. This problem also arises with "tier" terminology; we will, as suggested in Chapter 1, offer some hopefully useful subcategories to deal with the key distinction within the Second Tier.

As has been indicated, a major problem in finding an appropriate terminology is that almost all of the schemes so far devised appear either patronizing or otherwise offensive to what we have called the Second Tier. It clearly sounds better to be part of the "first" rather than the "second" or "third" world. Likewise, it is better to be part of the "developed" world (another traditional descriptor) than the "less developed" or "underdeveloped" world, and, in fact, most Second Tier states would prefer to be part of the First Tier. Moreover, since these terms have been devised and generally applied by western scholars, development tends to be defined largely in terms of how closely a state approximates the West, and especially the United States. As we will see in the case study at the end of the chapter, this tendency often upsets relations among states when approaching developmental issues. With the understanding that no terminology is completely satisfactory, we have adopted a terminology of tiers and subtiers, distinguished on the basis of levels of political and especially economic development.

The Second Tier: Basic Distinctions

The First and Second Tiers are generally distinguishable on political and economic grounds. The criteria for admission to the First Tier are not unlike those for joining the European Union, as discussed in Chapter 6: a stable political democracy and a wealthy, technologically advanced market-based economy. To the extent that states possess both characteristics, especially the second, in ways that approximate the First Tier, will allow them to approach or enter it. National political and economic traits will generally converge in time (political democracy and wealth, authoritarian rule and poverty), but during the transition one form of development often occurs more rapidly than the other, making classification more difficult. In developing the idea of the Second Tier, we must examine the political and economic dimensions of the Second Tier that have a bearing on their status, as well as the relationship between these dimensions. It should also be noted that our analysis is done from a particular standpoint; characteristics used here to distinguish members of the First Tier from those of the Second Tier reflect the political and economic values that the First Tier shares. This means the scheme may be culturally biased by classifying countries on the bases of values they do not hold. Many of these characteristics were considered in some briefer form in Chapter 1, but the following breakdown is more detailed.

The Political Dimension

Recognizing that no scheme will entirely cover all individual cases, we can tentatively lay out a group of related characteristics that tend to differentiate First and Second Tier states in the political dimension. These characteristics include societal strength or weakness, perceived economic well-being, political legitimacy, need for coercion, and political stability. While not all Second Tier states fall "below" all First Tier states on all criteria, the overall intertier contrasts help define the essential differences.

Summary ────────────────────────────────────

Political Characteristics Differentiating the Tiers

1. Societal strength or weakness
2. Degree of perceived economic well-being
3. Degree of legitimacy enjoyed by government

4. Degree to which the state must use coercion to enforce order
5. Regime stability

The first characteristic, societal strength or weakness, refers to the degree to which the state's citizens share basic values about their society, the way it operates, and their place in it. Societal strength is closely related to common nationality. Societies tend to be weak in multinational states where nationalism is exclusionary rather than inclusionary, as we defined these terms in Chapter 2, or where state boundaries divide national groups, creating irredentist tendencies. Such societies seem to require strong coercive state mechanisms to suppress differences. Where coercion is absent and shared values have not been widely accepted, the result can be instability and violence—leading in the most dramatic cases to the disintegration of the state. Several central African states undergoing new internal wars, such as Rwanda and Liberia, are examples.

A second characteristic distinguishing the tiers politically is the degree of economic well-being in the society as perceived by its members. Wealth is the most obvious aspect of economic well-being and thus the most important in this perception, but the idea embraces other aspects, including equality of opportunity and prospects for betterment. As we shall explain in a subsequent section, the economic difference between the First and Second Tiers involves more than just gross measures of wealth and extends to a variety of measures such as income distribution and social benefits.

The importance of perceived economic well-being is its contribution to overall stability. Generally speaking, a population that sees itself as economically well-off and becoming better off will exhibit a stronger attachment to its political system than one that does not. In fact, most theories of development start implicitly or explicitly from the assumption that perceived economic well-being and stability are directly related; that is the rationale for development. On the other hand, there are enough exceptions to suggest that a sense of economic well-being is only one of the necessary conditions for stability. Economic advancement that manifests itself in culturally offensive consumption, as in

Iran under Shah Mohammad Reza Pahlavi, or is unmatched by expanded opportunities for political participation, as in South Korea until recently, can lead to instability or even (as in Iran) to revolution.

These exceptions suggest a third political distinction between the tiers, the degree of legitimacy the government enjoys. As previously noted, legitimacy refers to the extent that the population willingly submits to the rule of law and regards the political system as correct or proper. This concept is closely related to societal strength and inversely related to the need for coercion, because legitimacy suggests the existence of shared values about governance. Thus, a major aspect of societal strength is agreement on the justice of the political system, and a sense of political legitimacy contributes to societal strength. In turn, both factors contribute to political stability.

Societal weakness and the absence of a shared sense of legitimacy also have common roots. Societies that include competing nationalities, for instance, will often be politically configured in such a way that one nationality benefits at the expense of others. The oppressed national groups are unlikely to confer legitimacy on a political system that causes them to suffer. If legitimacy is sufficiently absent and cannot be compensated for by coercing the population into obedience, the result is often instability and violence.

This latter observation leads to the fourth characteristic distinguishing the two tiers politically: the degree to which the state must use coercion, or force, to maintain order. If a population—or a significant portion of it—does not willingly agree to be governed by a system, then the regime, if it is to remain in power, must possess and exercise sufficient force to compel order. The alternative is chaos. The need to rely on the instruments of coercion is, however, a sign of weakness in the social and political fabric, stemming from a variety of problems already identified. Strong societies with legitimate governments do not require military or paramilitary force to enforce order; unpopular, unjust regimes require such authority.

The transition from a political system based in coercion to one based in legitimacy is one of the major problems facing large parts of the Second Tier. The wave of democratization that has accompanied the end of the Cold War has involved the loosening of authoritarian, coercive rule. However, the removal of coercion may reveal a weak, fractured society underneath. In such cases, chaos may result. Somalia on the eve of the American intervention in December 1992 is emblematic of this combination; the Somalis had been capable of overthrowing the authoritarian regime of Muhammad Siad Barre, but they were incapable of bestowing legitimacy on a successor.

The final distinguishing characteristic in the political dimension, reflecting the others, is regime stability, the extent to which the political system is capable of incorporating change, including governmental succession, in an orderly, nonviolent manner. Stable regimes possess a high degree of legitimacy. Some indicators of that stability and legitimacy include fair, free, and frequent elections; broad citizen participation in political affairs; the government's ability to collect and distribute revenues from its citizens in a manner deemed equitable; active or tacit support of social institutions; and a fair and independent judicial system (this list is derived from Manwaring's *Uncomfortable Wars*).

Clearly, these characteristics are related to one another and to the economic dimension. For instance, political contentment produces a more highly motivated workforce, and affluence is likely to result in support for and participation in the political system.

The Economic Dimension

As in the case of political development, there are no universally accepted criteria for economic development, and there is no generally accepted measure that differentiates levels of such development. A common approach is to use statistical indicators such as gross national product per capita, industrial output, or energy consumption as a means of categorizing. Sometimes these indicators are accumulated into indices such as the Overseas Development Council's Physical Quality of Life Index (PQLI), which combines various measures of the pleasantness of existence, such as life expectancy and literacy rates. We believe, however, that the degree to which states of the Second Tier approximate those of the First is better illustrated in a more structural approach, where the economic dimension is viewed in terms of a progression through the process of economic development. This is the approach we will take.

We will begin by examining structural development through the various industrial revolutions, as a means of pinpointing differing levels. The stages of development are listed in order from least to most advanced. Normally (but not always) economies progress through the list one "revolution" at a time.

Summary ─────────────────────

Industrial Revolutions

Industrial Revolution	Primary Economic Activities
Preindustrial	Subsistence agriculture, extraction, cottage industry
First	Heavy industry, basic consumer goods
Second	Sophisticated consumer goods, services
Third	Knowledge, research, new processes and products

The most structurally advanced economies today are those that have entered the third industrial revolution, also called the high-technology revolution. While such economies maintain characteristics of all the other structural models (they produce goods and services and engage in agricultural production, for instance), what makes them distinct and forms the basis of their prosperity is their mastery of knowledge production and dissemination, and mastery of the application of knowledge to commercial production. The most notable aspect of this mastery is possession of the most advanced computing capability. Entry into the high-technology revolution differentiates the highly interdependent economies of the First Tier from the Second Tier.

At the next level are those states that have entered the second industrial revolution. In this echelon, heavy and basic industry, such as steel production, is gradually replaced by the production of specialized consumer goods and especially by a large and active service component to the economy. With sophisticated and differentiated economies, second industrial revolution states resemble those of the third industrial revolution. The main difference is that these second industrial revolution states are more typically consumers rather than producers of high technology.

Some of these states undergoing a second industrial revolution stand at the boundary between the First and Second Tiers. The Four Tigers of Asia—South Korea, Taiwan, Singapore,

A glittering shopping mall in Singapore displays the growing affluence of this city-state in Southeast Asia, one of the leading candidates to advance from the Second Tier to the First in the near future. A key reason for its success is Singaporeans' favorable perception of their economic condition, a perception enhanced by massive government housing programs; these help to ensure the stability of a regime many Westerners find overly coercive.

and Hong Kong—are typical examples. South Korea, for instance, has already become the world's leading shipbuilding state and the third-largest producer of computer chips, and it is challenging for leadership in other areas, such as electronics and automobiles. Certainly prior to the East Asian financial crisis of 1997 and 1998, a strong case could be made that South Korea was a First Tier state in economic terms.

At the next lower level are the states that have entered the first industrial revolution. States in this category have entered the factory age of manufacturing, with effects such as urbanization and class restructuring (development of an industrial working class and a middle class). These states specialize in the more basic forms of industrial activity, such as steel and textile production and food processing. In cases such as China, India, or even Russia, there will be vestiges of second industrial revolutionary activity in the country that is contrasted by regions that have not yet entered the first industrial revolution.

At the least advanced level are those countries that are preindustrial. Generally the poorest states, they typically have economies based on agriculture, especially subsistence

Map 8-1 **The Four Tigers**

©1996 by St. Martin's Press, Inc. From: *Contours of Power*, by Snow/Brown. Reprinted with permission of Bedford/St. Martin's Press, Inc.

farming, and on the extraction of natural resources, such as mining, oil production, and fishing. These states also tend to rate low on objective indicators such as the PLQI.

Four comments need to be made about these economic categories. First, each incorporates a wide range of development. Among those countries of the third industrial revolution, for instance, the United States, Japan, and certain EU members such as Germany clearly stand above the rest in knowledge production. At the other end of the scale, some preindustrial countries are on the verge of entering the first industrial revolution while others (Bangladesh and Mali are often cited in this regard) have little resource base that can be employed in industrialization (these are the states that have sometimes been referred to as the Fourth World).

Second, the categories are not entirely discrete. Third industrial revolution states retain some vestiges of preindustrial status, such as a small subsistence agricultural group, while states that have largely not been industrialized at all may produce some sophisticated goods or services. The predominant characteristic is the criterion for placing a country at one level or another.

Third, not all movement between categories takes the form of an orderly progression. A number of states, particularly in Asia, skipped the first industrial revolution and went immediately into the second. Singapore is a good example. At the same time, economies can deteriorate to a lower category. It is uncertain, for instance, whether the financial crisis that began in a number of East Asian states in 1997 and which has weakened their economies will not cause some reversion.

Finally, there are anomalies that cannot readily be fitted into any category. The major group of states that "fall between the stools" are the oil-rich states of the Middle East. By virtue of sheer wealth, they rank with the most advanced economies of the third industrial revolution; by most measures of economic structure, they rank nearly at the bottom.

Subtiers

This set of structural characteristics helps us to form categories within the Second Tier. We will make use of the same four Second Tier subtiers introduced in Chapter 1: the three hierarchical subtiers of developed, partially developed, and developable and the important if anomalous category of resource-rich. Table 8.1 displays the number of states in each category by geographical region. (A complete list of states of the Second Tier and an explanation of their classifications are found in the Appendix.) As the table suggests, the vast majority of Second Tier states remain within the less developed subtiers, and the geographic distribution by region is far from uniform.

A word of warning about these classifications is necessary. The basic rationale for putting a country in one category or the other was its degree of economic development. Operationally, this means looking both at the composition of the economy—whether the country has a sizable industrial output that indicates first industrial revolution status, for instance—and at measures of wealth, such as per capita income. Thus, into which industrial revolution a country has progressed—or not progressed—is a critical concern in its classification. The process was made more difficult by the fact, which we have already noted, that states that have achieved advanced economic status by some criteria, such as developing a large service sector, normally retain some vestiges of more primitive economic activity, such as mineral extraction. Progress up the development ladder must thus be measured by the degree of concentration on more advanced economic activities. The association between the industrial revolutions and the tiers and subtiers is summarized in Table 8.2. Political development—how much progress toward democratization has been made—was then assessed as a second criterion for classification. Inevitably, some states were on the

Table 8.1 Second Tier Distribution by Geographic Region	Developed	Partially Developed	Developable	Resource Rich
Asia and Pacific	4	8	18	1
Middle East	2	6	2	7
Latin America and Caribbean	5	19	8	1
Former Soviet Union and Eastern Europe	1	8	19	0
Africa	1	11	37	4
Total	13	52	84	13

Table 8.2 The Industrial Revolution and the Tiers	
Industrial Revolution Country Has Begun	**Tier or Subtier**
Preindustrial	Developable
First	Partially developed
Second	Developed
Third	First Tier

borderline, so that one could argue that not all of them were properly placed. Our experience, however, was that relatively few states were close calls; thus, the general scheme of classification is reliable.

The first subtier is the developed states. Generally speaking, the 13 states in this category have highly developed economies and at least fragile democratic political systems—democratically elected governments but not enough experience with democracy (such as a series of free elections) to guarantee a long-term commitment. Their economic development is demonstrated by a highly developed service sector (second industrial revolution) and some indication they are becoming producers rather than simply consumers of technology (progress toward the third industrial revolution). South Korea is an outstanding example of this latter capability. In most of these countries, the development of a robust and stable democracy is likely only a matter of time. In a few places like Singapore, however, a commitment to western-style democracy is apparently quite weak or even lacking.

States of the developed subtier vary in their proximity to joining the First Tier. As we have seen earlier, the Four Tigers of Asia—Hong Kong, Singapore, South Korea, and Taiwan—are economically closest. (The absorption of Hong Kong into China in 1997 could change its status, of course.) The five Latin American states that are included in this subtier—Argentina, Brazil, Chile, Mexico, and Venezuela—are not as economically advanced (and all share fragile democratic forms). Their prospects of movement into the First Tier, however, have been enhanced by reductions in and restructuring of their foreign debts—the amounts owed foreign governmental and private lenders—which have been a major obstacle to their economic progress. These prospects may also be stimulated by the implementation of the Free Trade Area of the Americas, which was approved in principle at the November 1994 meeting of heads of Western Hemisphere countries in Miami (discussed in the Introduction and Chapter 9) and reiterated at the second summit in 1998 in Santiago, Chile. The other members of this subtier are Israel and Cyprus in the Middle East, South Africa (assuming the continuing progress of multiracial democracy there), and Slovenia in Eastern Europe.

The next subtier is the partially developed states. Membership in this subtier is defined by the development of heavy industry and the manufacture of basic consumer goods (first industrial revolution), at least in some parts of the country. As noted, states in this category typically have large sectors of the economy or geographical regions that are preindustrial, with economic activity confined to forms like subsistence agriculture and cottage industry. The existence of such conditions in much of the interior of China, for instance, explains why that country, which has one of the most dynamic economies in the world in its Special Economic Zones (SEZs), remains in the partially developed category.

Most of the states in this category also lack democratic political systems, the prerequisite for the highly motivated workforce typical of the First Tier. There are, of course, exceptions. India maintains a democracy and has a growing middle class approaching 100 million, yet as in China sizable parts of the country remain at the subsistence agricultural level of economic activity. A number of the Caribbean states are idiosyncratic as well: countries like Jamaica and the Bahamas have long-standing, stable democracies but economies that rely almost entirely on tourism.

The partially developed states are broadly distributed geographically. Their largest concentration is in Latin America and the Caribbean, and especially South America. Examples include Bolivia, Colombia, and Ecuador in South America and Grenada (in addition to Jamaica and the Bahamas) in the Caribbean. Elsewhere, states in this category include Indonesia, Malaysia, and Thailand (as well as China and India) in Asia; Egypt, Turkey, and Lebanon in the Middle East; Russia, the Czech Republic, Hungary, and Poland among the Soviet successor states and Eastern European countries; and Cameroon, Botswana, Nigeria, and the Ivory Coast in Africa. Like the developed states, the states in this category vary widely in their prospects for moving up the developmental scale.

The third subtier that fits within a developmental hierarchy is the developable states. As Table 8.1 shows, this is the largest subtier: 84 of the total of 162 states included in the Second Tier. By definition, the countries in this subtier have not undergone systematic development toward the first industrial revolution.

As in the partially developed subtier, there is a broad range of geographical location and developmental prospects within this subtier. A number of states, like the Philippines, Peru, and Belarus, have large enough industrial sectors that one can make an argument for their inclusion in the partially developed category, but their overall level of wealth or distribution of wealth leaves them wanting (for close calls on categorizing, we chose an annual per capita income of $1,000 as the breakpoint between this subtier and the partially developed subtier). At the same time, desperately poor states within this category include many for whom short-term or even medium-term prospects of meaningful economic progress are virtually nil. Countries at the lower end of the development ladder generally have annual per capita incomes of $200 or less, few if any natural or human resources to exploit, and dim prospects for those conditions to change. States with these conditions are particularly evident in Africa, where 37 of the 83 developable states are located. Examples include Ethiopia, Sudan, Somalia, and Eritrea in the Horn of Africa; Rwanda, Burundi, Liberia, and the Democratic Republic of the Congo (formerly Zaire) in Central Africa; and Burkina, Chad, and Mali in the Sahel region of western Africa. Concentrations of developable states are also found in Asia and the Pacific (Afghanistan, Burma/Myanmar, Nepal, Pakistan, Sri Lanka) as well as Latin America and the Caribbean (Haiti, Cuba, El Salvador), and in the former Soviet Union and Eastern Europe (many of the southern successor states to the Soviet Union, such as Tajikistan and Armenia, and the states of the Balkans).

The final, anomalous subtier is the resource-rich states. The states in this category are generally quite wealthy as the result of exploiting natural resources (normally, but not always, petroleum), but they normally do not have democratic political forms (Trinidad and Tobago is the notable exception) and have structurally undeveloped economies other than a financial sector to process oil revenues. What is notable about these countries is that they would fall into the partially developed or, more likely, the developable category if resource-derived income were removed.

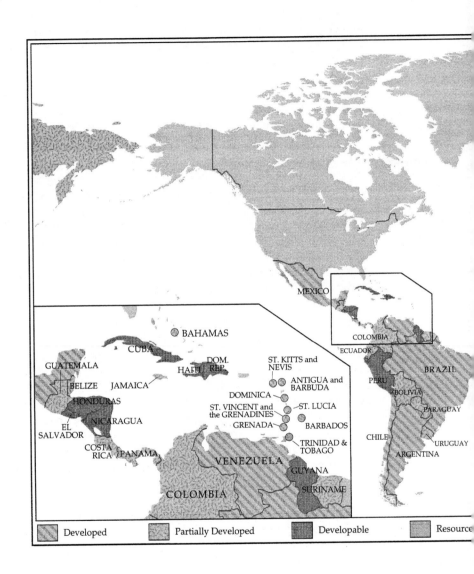

Map 8-2   **The Second Tier**

©1996 by St. Martin's Press, Inc. From: *Contours of Power*, by Snow/Brown. Reprinted with permission of Bedford/St. Martin's Press, Inc.

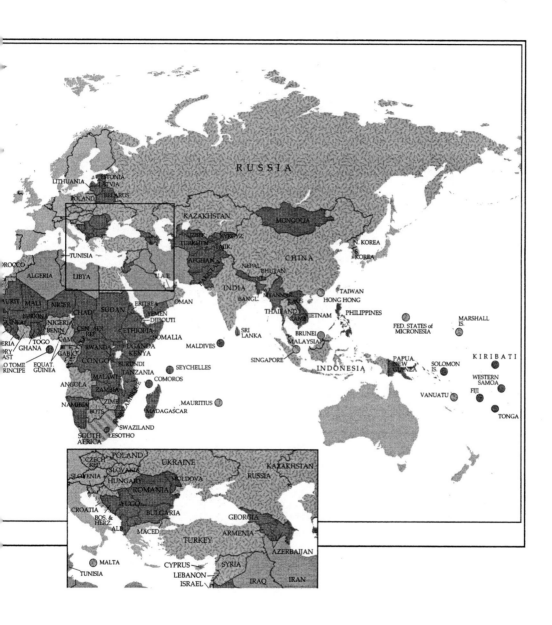

RUSSIA

LITHUANIA ESTONIA
LATVIA
POLAND BELARUS

KAZAKHSTAN

MONGOLIA

N. KOREA

UZBEK.
TURKMEN. KYRGYZ.
TUNISIA TAJIK.
AFGHAN.

KOREA

CHINA

MOROCCO
ALGERIA LIBYA U.A.E.

NEPAL
BHUTAN

INDIA

TAIWAN
HONG KONG

BANGL.

MAURIT. MALI NIGER CHAD SUDAN ERITREA OMAN
YEMEN
DJIBOUTI

MYANMAR
LAOS
THAILAND

VIETNAM
CAMB.

PHILIPPINES

MARSHALL
IS.

GUINEA BURKINA
NIGERIA CEN. AFR.
BENIN REP. ETHIOPIA
SOMALIA

SRI
LANKA

BRUNEI
MALAYSIA

FED. STATES of
MICRONESIA

NIGERIA TOGO
GHANA GABON
IVORY CONGO
COAST RWANDA UGANDA
O TOME EQUAT. BURUNDI KENYA
PRINCIPE GUINEA TANZANIA

MALDIVES

SINGAPORE

INDONESIA

KIRIBATI

ANGOLA MALAWI
ZAMBIA SEYCHELLES
COMOROS

PAPUA
NEW
GUINEA

SOLOMON
IS.

WESTERN
SAMOA

NAMIBIA ZIMB.
BOTS. MOZAM.
MAURITIUS
MADAGASCAR

VANUATU

FIJI

TONGA

SWAZILAND
SOUTH LESOTHO
AFRICA

CZECH
REP. POLAND
SLOVENIA SLOVAKIA
HUNGARY
CROATIA YUGO.
BOS. & BULGARIA
HERZ. ALB. MACED.

UKRAINE

MOLDOVA
ROMANIA

KAZAKHSTAN

RUSSIA

GEORGIA

ARMENIA

TURKEY

AZERBAIJAN

MALTA
TUNISIA

CYPRUS
LEBANON
ISRAEL

SYRIA

IRAQ

IRAN

With 13 members, this category matches the developed subtier as the smallest. It is concentrated, unsurprisingly, in the oil-rich Islamic world: the Persian Gulf littoral (Bahrain, Iran, Iraq, Kuwait, Qatar, Saudi Arabia, and the United Arab Emirates) and northern Africa (Algeria, Libya, and Tunisia). Gabon, Trinidad and Tobago, and Brunei complete the category. Map 8-3 shows the resource-rich subtier as well as other countries that are major oil exporters. Azerbaijan, a Soviet successor state in the developable subtier, will likely join this category when the exploitation of the Caspian Sea oil and gas fields that it controls (the world's second largest known reserves after the Persian Gulf) occurs.

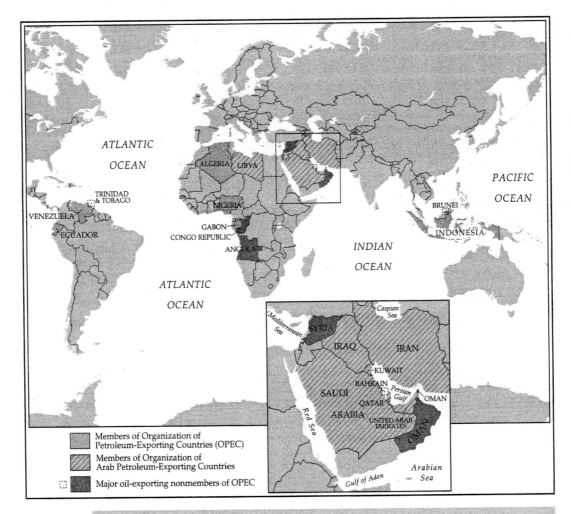

Map 8-3   **Oil-Exporting Countries**

©1996 by St. Martin's Press, Inc. From: *Contours of Power,* by Snow/Brown. Reprinted with permission of Bedford/St. Martin's Press, Inc.

The developmental problem can be thought of as a matter of whether and how strategies can and should be devised to facilitate movement by Second Tier states upward through the subtiers, since the categories (with the exception of the resource-rich) represent levels of increasing structural development and affluence. To focus that debate, we need first to look briefly at possible roots of Second Tier problems in the emergence of much of the Second Tier from colonial rule after World War II. We will then examine some of the deep social and economic barriers to development before finally turning to the question of outside responsibility for aiding development efforts.

The Colonial Legacy

The colonial experience and the post–World War II process of decolonization form the backdrop against which current conditions and claims for the future must be viewed. The movement toward independence experienced by most of the countries of Africa and Asia and parts of the Caribbean after World War II began the third and most massive of four phases of response to external rule in various parts of the world in the last two centuries. In the nineteenth century, the Spanish and Portuguese empires in Central and South America crumbled, leaving only minor colonial enclaves (the Guianas) in that region along with some island colonies in the Caribbean basin. In the wake of World War I, the collapse of the Ottoman and Austro-Hungarian Empires allowed self-determination for most of Eastern and Central Europe, as well as part of the Middle East. The collapse of the Soviet empire brings the last vestiges of imperial rule to an end.

The breakup of the European empires in Africa and Asia has defined much of the relationship between the First and Second Tiers in both political and economic senses. The manner of colonization and of decolonization has a bearing on the extent of legitimacy and violence in many Second Tier states. In the minds of Second Tier representatives and advocates, the economic gulf between the tiers is the direct consequence of the colonial period. There is strong disagreement about this latter point, however. That the European colonial powers did not make a major effort to raise the economic standards of the colonies to their own level is indisputable; what is disputed is whether colonialism (colonial rule) impeded development or whether preexisting disparities would have continued, possibly even widened, in the absence of the colonial experience.

The Colonial Experience

European colonial rule in Africa and Asia lasted anywhere from four centuries or longer to less than a century, depending on the exact location. By the beginning of World War II, however, that rule extended to most of the two continents, as the map of the colonial world shows. Even where Europeans were not formally in charge—in China, for instance—their influence (along with that of the United States) dominated the globe outside of the Western Hemisphere. The century before World War II was very much the European century.

Imperial motives need not be considered at length here, but it can be said that the motives of the European colonizers had both economic and political bases. Economically, the Europeans were always interested in making profits and in benefiting the

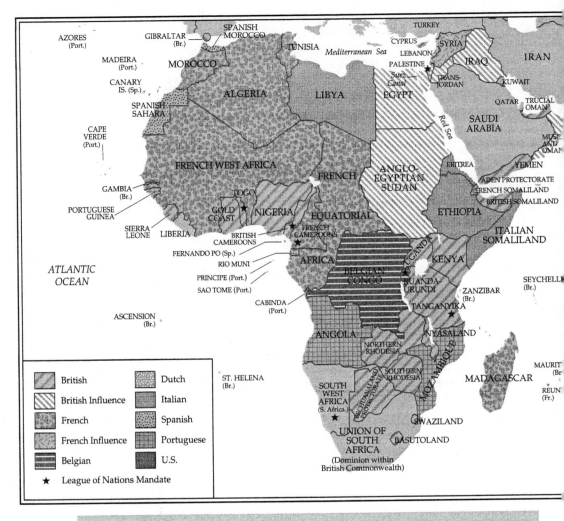

Map 8-4   The Colonial World in 1939

©1996 by St. Martin's Press, Inc. From: *Contours of Power*, by Snow/Brown. Reprinted with permission of Bedford/St. Martin's Press, Inc.

economy of the mother country. Whether the lure was the exotic spice trade of the South Pacific, the mineral wealth of southern Africa, or the huge market for British textiles represented by the population of India, the promise of fortune played a key role. Politically, colonialism became a competition among European states, in which great-power status was equated with imperial possession. This competition eventually drew in the United States as well; one of the reasons advanced by "jingoists" for the U.S. war with Spain in 1898 was to capture Spain's remaining colonies and thus to achieve great-power status.

Except possibly for missionaries, colonialism was never aimed at "uplifting" the native population and preparing them for political or economic independence at some point in the

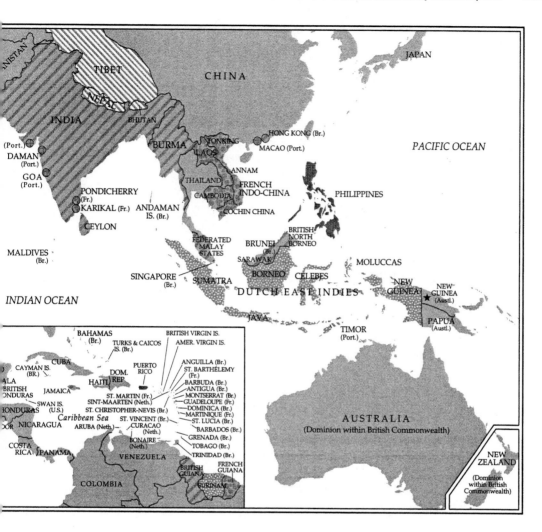

future. Preparing people to assume increased political or economic power and perhaps eventually to overthrow their rulers or compete with them economically would have violated the basic purposes of colonial rule: to make money, benefit the economy of the mother country, and maintain status.

From the vantage point of the colonized, the colonial experience was profoundly disorienting and humiliating. When the Europeans arrived, they upset traditional patterns of habitation and political and economic organization that often dated back centuries, even millennia, replacing those patterns with arrangements that suited their purposes. The experience was also likely to be quite brutal; the cruelty of colonial rule is captured in a particularly harsh glare by the writer George Orwell in his often overlooked classic *Burmese*

Days, based on his experiences as a member of the British police force in Burma from 1922 to 1927.

By the middle of the period between the world wars, movements to seek independence had begun to form in many colonies. These movements were most developed in Asia, which had generally been colonized earlier than much of Africa. The real impetus for the drive for independence, however, was World War II.

The global reach of the war served as a catalyst in several ways. In some places, such as Burma, natives fought alongside their European rulers as coequals. In others, such as Indonesia, the Europeans sponsored or aided independence movements in their attempts to oust the Japanese. In French Indochina (Vietnam, Cambodia, and Laos), the population had the instructive experience of seeing their French rulers subjugated by the Japanese, which pierced the myth of European invincibility. Many Africans and Indians were also commandeered to serve in the factories of Britain and elsewhere to substitute for workforces that had gone off to war. In all of these ways, and especially where the colonized fought on behalf of their masters, the experience of war changed relationships; a group cannot be expected to sacrifice and then return willingly to bondage. Just as African American participation in World War II (and Korea) helped doom racial segregation in the United States, so too was European domination of Africa, Asia, and the Caribbean a victim of the war.

The Process of Decolonization

At the end of the war, the colonialists nevertheless expected things to return to their prewar condition, but that was not to be. Achmad Sukarno and his followers used the infrastructure built to expel the Japanese from Indonesia to prevent a Dutch return. The Vietnamese leader Ho Chi Minh used the anti-Japanese underground movement that had been nurtured by the West—including the United States—to evict the returning French. Mohandas (Mahatma) Gandhi's Indian Congress and Mohammed Ali Jinnah's Muslim League cooperated long enough to force Britain to retreat from India and Pakistan in 1947. After having seen the material bounty of Europe, Africans like Jomo Kenyatta of Kenya were not about to return to their economic or political bonds.

Besides the effects already mentioned, the war contributed to the success of the colonial independence movements in another way. The economic and psychological exhaustion of Europe after the war was such that the colonial powers, notably Britain and France (which between them had the vast bulk of colonies) simply lacked the financial resources and moral will to resist successfully. France tried resistance for a time in Indochina and Algeria; the British just attempted to remove themselves from their colonies as gracefully as they could. The process of decolonization began in Asia in the 1940s, spread to Africa in the 1950s, reached the Caribbean in the 1960s, and essentially concluded in the middle 1970s when Portugal withdrew from its African colonies.

Decolonization was largely unplanned because it was unanticipated and because it violated the basic purposes of colonial rule. When anticolonial movements arose, the colonialists scrambled to control them, usually with limited success. As the process unfolded in the 1950s, it almost seemed that the British foreign minister traveled from colony to colony with copies of an independence treaty, where he simply had to fill in the blank for the name of each new country and find someone to sign it. When the inevitability of decolonization became apparent, some belated efforts at reform were made; they were usually too late to be of much help. In these circumstances, the retreat of the Europeans left behind a political and economic mess somewhat like the backwash left after a major flood.

The Colonial Legacy

There remains the question of whether conditions were worse after colonial rule than they would have been without it. Joining the global economic system of the late twentieth century required the transformation of formerly colonized societies. Whether changes would have occurred faster or slower or not at all in the absence of colonialism is an interesting question, but one that is hypothetical and ultimately cannot be answered.

Politically, there were two underlying problems. The first was the physical shape of the new political units granted independence. The rule was that the old colonial administrative unit became the new state. But the boundaries of these units generally had borne no resemblance to precolonial divisions. Instead, as we explained in Chapter 2, the colonial units cut across and rearranged the old political and ethnic units, trapping together historical adversaries and dividing ethnic groups. (The same phenomenon existed in the Soviet Union and Yugoslavia at the time they dissolved, but in that case Stalinist and Titoist policies aimed at ethnic integration had created the artificial boundaries.) Little had been done to integrate different population groups or to reduce antagonisms during the colonial period; in fact, keeping them apart served to aid a "divide and rule" strategy for the British.

The result was that most countries emerging from colonial rule suffered from multinationalism in the sense explained in Chapter 2: they contained multiple national groups, and political loyalty attached to the more parochial group rather than the state. After independence, the new leaders could have tried to create an inclusionary process of nationalism that would gradually shift primary loyalties to the new state. In most cases, however, they were neither prepared for nor predisposed toward such a task. The situation was even worse where state boundaries also divided groups, resulting in irredentist movements as well as purely internal dissension.

The second underlying problem impeding the transition from colonial rule was the lack of preparation of new governments. Because the colonialists had not educated native populations to be politically sophisticated, there were very few people within the new states with the expertise necessary to manage large governmental institutions. As an example, most colonial armies had exclusively European officers, with natives at no higher ranks than noncommissioned officer (sergeant). When the Europeans left, so did the commissioned officers, and the scramble was on as to who would be the new generals.

Thus, the new governments generally did not rule very well; they could not administer programs efficiently and could not master the levers of economic development. In some cases, the cause was simple ineptitude born of inexperience, lack of education, and underestimation of the depth and complexity of problems. In others, the situation was made worse by corruption, often rooted in traditional customs. For example, payments to officials for favors, as in the Latin American tradition of *la mordida* ("the bite"), reflect longstanding social practices. Whatever the reasons, the democratic institutions established at independence often rapidly deteriorated, and the politics of the new state became a struggle between variously defined groups. In such circumstances, the goal of political power came to be the ability of one's own group to rule at the expense of others.

As for the economies of the new states, they usually suffered from the same ills that afflicted politics, and the incompetence, corruption, and intergroup conflict in each sphere exacerbated those in the other. The economies also had other problems. As noted earlier, to the extent that economic development had occurred during colonial rule, it was intended to exploit the native economy to the benefit of the colonialists. If there were mineral resources to be extracted, development was geared toward that result, with attention paid to whatever enterprises supported the industry (producing food to feed the miners, building rail lines between the mines and ports). Very little effort was made to create a diversified, technologically advanced, or self-sufficient economy—one directed toward achieving the first industrial revolution and able to stand on its own.

The extent and impact of these structural economic problems has historically been underestimated in assessing the developmental problem, but the Asian financial crisis has brought them home. Much of the crisis, discussed more systematically in Chapter 9, has resulted from attempting to graft western institutions onto societies that have neither the cultural values nor institutions—such as fiscally responsible and accountable banking practices—to absorb the western system. The failure of the colonial experience to inculcate such values can thus be "blamed" for some of the current morass.

In this circumstance, most of the new states were artificial economic units just as they were artificial political units. They contained elements of traditional economic structures (subsistence, village-based agriculture and herding) as well as more modern components such as mining and light manufacturing. They also remained economically undiversified and dependent on the former colonial ruler for many goods and services. That dependence had been intentional during the colonial period; its implications as a malady requiring First World attention have been analyzed by the *dependencia* (dependence) theorists.

The Plight of the Second Tier

Throughout the Second Tier, there is the universal cry for development in the economic and political senses. In the least developed countries, because of the misery and wretchedness of life in so many quarters, the call for economic development is the stronger one; as one moves toward the higher categories of economic development, demands for political democratization also abound.

The Second Tier states are progressively disadvantaged, and they increasingly perceive the gap. The overall economic gap between the First and most of the Second Tier is gradually widening in absolute terms, as measured by such things as an increasing gap in standards of living, wealth, and GNP between them. In most countries in the lower subtiers of the Second Tier, the gap between rich and poor within the country is similarly wide and growing. This situation is creating increasing frictions within Second Tier states and between the tiers. That is, both the Second Tier as a whole and poorer people within Second Tier countries feel increasing relative deprivation, a term coined by political scientist Ted Gurr to refer to the extent to which people perceive themselves to be disadvantaged (deprived) relative to others and the extent to which they view this situation as unjust. A major reason is access to television and the Internet, which makes the disparities very evident and their tolerability a shrinking commodity.

How development in its political and economic aspects can occur is a problem not only for those countries seeking to develop internally, but also for the international system generally. The system's obligations are examined in the next section; in this section we will look at the internal problem, dealing both with strategies of development and with factors that frustrate development.

Developmental Strategies

While economic and political development are the overwhelmingly shared values of the Second Tier, there is disagreement about the strategies to pursue to achieve the goals. These disagreements are exacerbated by incompatibilities between pursuing one aspect or the other.

Summary ──────────────────────────────────

Second Tier Developmental Strategies

1. Economic reforms first; political later (China)
2. Political reforms first; economic development later (former Soviet Union)
3. Simultaneous economic and political development (Poland)

There are three basic approaches to attacking the developmental problem, which were briefly introduced in Chapter 6 in connection with the former communist world. Countries may pursue economic development before turning to political reform, reverse the order, or push for both forms of change simultaneously. Each approach has been tried within both the former Second World and the traditional Third World. Each has advantages and disadvantages, successes and failures. Whichever approach is taken, however, a conflict emerges between the two forms of development.

The first model, economic before political development, is essentially the Asian model. It is the approach taken, for instance, by countries such as South Korea, Taiwan, and Singapore, all of which have now gone most of the way through both forms of development. The same model is also being implemented by China. Its feasibility in the Asian context may reflect the absence of a western democratic tradition, which allows these societies to hold demands for political reform in abeyance longer than might be possible in western societies.

The major advantage of this model is the flexibility it provides to manage economic development in ways that may be economically sound but politically unpopular. Considerable frugality by individuals and spending by government on basic infrastructure (schools, roads, rail lines, utilities) rather than social welfare are necessary as an underpinning for industrial development, as well as for maintaining a political order that makes investment appear safe. The beneficial effects of such austerity are not immediately obvious to ordinary citizens, who are being asked or forced to delay improvements in their standard of living to defray these underlying costs of development. Nowhere are such frugal policies popular over the long term; in a democratic political environment, they may be impossible.

The financial crises of 1997 and 1998 in East Asia have revealed a potential weakness in this approach. Before development occurs in most Second Tier countries, they are essentially closed societies where most transactions, including financial ones, occur in private, not subject to public accountability. If political democratization does not occur parallel to economic development, economies can remain opaque rather than becoming transparent.

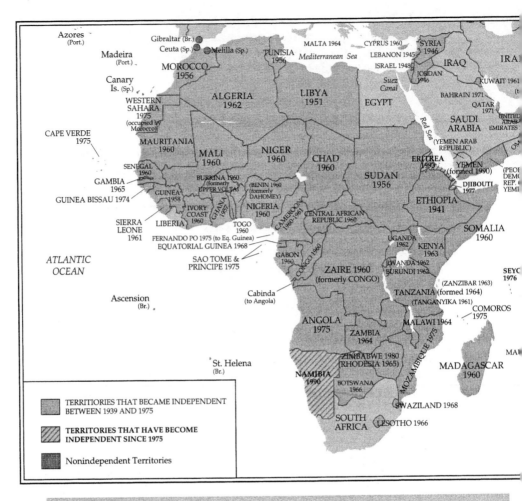

Map 8-5   The Postcolonial World, 1975

©1996 by St. Martin's Press, Inc. From: *Contours of Power*, by Snow/Brown. Reprinted with permission of Bedford/St. Martin's Press, Inc.

If the transparency of accountability does not occur, the result can be the continuation of bad, even corrupt practices that can undermine the developmental process.

A prominent example of the second developmental approach, in which political reform precedes economic change, was begun in the Soviet Union under Mikhail Gorbachev and has been partially continued in Russia under Boris Yeltsin. In the original Gorbachev conception, the goal was to unleash public support for economic change under the banner of glasnost as a way to force modernization. A major advantage of such an approach is its low initial cost: all that is needed is a declaration plus the removal of whatever mechanisms stifled political participation.

The problem, however, is that the developmental process requires a period of sacrifice when economic conditions worsen, at least to some extent; and such sacrifices are unwelcome to a populace that embraced reform as a means of improving, not contracting, the

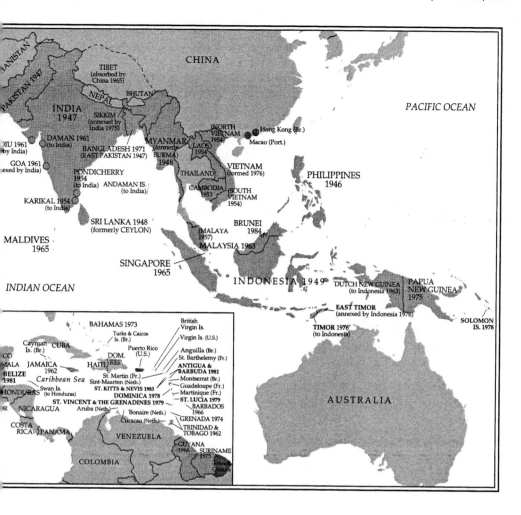

standard of living. In a system like Russia's, where the need for basic structural economic and financial reform is as pervasive as it is, the process of reform may be so extensive as to undermine support for it and result in the economic chaos so evident in 1998, which may explain why few other countries are adopting the Russian approach.

The Polish experiment probably most closely exemplifies the third developmental model, in which extensive economic reform is pursued along with political democratization in the hope that the two will be mutually reinforcing. If the economy indeed improves with some rapidity, this approach can work. If it does not, this approach is prone to the same weaknesses as the second model: political support may evaporate before economic reform produces tangible benefits. Aside from Poland, support for this approach has largely been limited to proposals in some other formerly communist countries.

The debate over which approach to take reveals the basic tensions among them. Stated simply, the relationship is this: economically responsible developmental actions may be politically suicidal and destabilizing, whereas politically popular actions may be economically and developmentally irresponsible. Given that the governments of most Second Tier states already have only tenuous legitimacy, they are left with a serious dilemma as to what approach to follow. Much of this dilemma centers on government-provided services and entitlements that, if provided generously, drain developmental resources. The First Tier also suffers from this problem to some extent, but in the First Tier entitlements came after development had occurred, rather than simultaneously.

The Barriers to Development

In addition to the hazards of which developmental strategy to select and other problems already discussed—managerial inexpertise, corruption, conflict between groups—achieving economic and political progress in most Second Tier states is made more difficult by a number of other economic and social factors: rapid population growth, inadequate food supply, maldistribution of wealth and capital flight, disease, and debt service. Although not all Second Tier states have all of these problems (which are discussed more fully below), most have at least some of them. Some of these problems (AIDS and debt service, for example) are also shared by some First Tier countries, but these countries generally have greater resources to deal with them.

Summary ———————————————————————————

Barriers to Development in the Second Tier

1. Rapid population growth
2. Inadequate food supply
3. Maldistribution of wealth and capital flight
4. Disease
5. Debt service

Rapid Population Growth.   As we will discuss in greater detail in Chapter 10, the Second Tier states are experiencing the bulk of population growth on the planet. A world population of 4.4 billion in the year 1980 will grow to over 6 billion by the year 2000, an increase of about 1.8 billion. Of that total, 1.6 billion will reside in countries of the old Third World (First Tier population will increase by a little under 200 million in the same period).

Many factors influence the high population growth in the Second Tier. In the most traditional and least developed countries, having a large number of children is considered a sign of a man's virility or of a woman's success as a wife; in many countries, children are valued for their contribution to family income and the support of elderly family members; and, in general, the prospect of a number of children dying young often influences attitudes toward pregnancy.

The heart of the problem, however, is that people are living longer. Population growth for any country is represented by the difference between the birthrate and the death rate. In most of the world, birthrates are static or declining; where population growth is occurring, it is because of an even faster decline in death rates (more people are living longer). Most of this decline is in infant and small child mortality, meaning that the population is not only growing but also, on average, becoming younger. It is not unusual in Second Tier countries for half or more of the population to be in their teens or younger. The chief "culprit" in this problem is modern medicine and sanitation, which facilitate survival. A reduction in death rates from childhood diseases alone can ultimately have a strong effect on population.

The effect of population growth is that resources that might otherwise be devoted to development must be used to support the additional population—or, in the many Second Tier states where the population growth rate exceeds the economic growth rate, to prevent the declining standard of living from falling even further. Perhaps the best way to reduce population growth, ironically, is development: there is a direct and strong relationship between wealth accumulation and birthrate reduction. But since development itself is impeded by population growth, the result is a kind of vicious circle.

Because fathering many children is a means by which men maintain social and political control over women in many Second Tier societies, population issues (notably access to contraception and abortion) are high on the agendas of most feminists and most First Tier states. As the 1994 Cairo population conference and the 1995 Beijing women's rights conference clearly demonstrated, however, this agenda has met with considerable opposition on moral, religious, and cultural grounds in some Second Tier societies.

Inadequate Food Supply. One major way in which the population growth problem is manifested is in the difficulty of supplying adequate food to Second Tier populations. At the global level, the "green revolution" in agricultural production that occurred in the 1960s and 1970s has resulted in an adequate total amount of food for the world's population (although there is some concern about when the carrying capacity—the maximum sustainable limit of agricultural productivity—will be reached). The major food problem is distribution. Not all parts of the globe are equally suitable for agriculture: the Sahel region and Horn of Africa, for instance, often cannot grow crops adequate to feed their populations and must rely on imports. The main reasons for this are inadequate rainfall and desertification—the gradual spread of deserts, mostly because of overfarming or overgrazing marginal agricultural land. Even when imports are available in sufficient quantity, primitive transportation facilities in many countries impede distribution to those in need.

Food supply is a developmental problem in two ways. First, countries that must spend considerable resources on food imports do so at the expense of investing in development; this is a prominent way in which population growth impedes development. Second, the inability in many cases to provide a qualitatively adequate diet debilitates the population and makes people less productive. For instance, many small children in the Second Tier receive inadequate protein in their diets, a deficiency that stunts mental development.

Maldistribution of Wealth and Capital Flight. Beyond the sheer lack of economic resources in many Second Tier states, whatever wealth exists is often concentrated in the hands of a small elite unwilling to contemplate redistribution of any of that wealth to the masses. The result is an endemic tension where the wealthy fear that the poor will rise up and seek to expropriate their property. That emotion in turn triggers capital flight, the investment of wealth in First Tier countries in order to protect it from possible governmental confiscation at home. Even where confiscation is not a threat, a general unwillingness to invest internally simply makes even less resources available for developmental efforts. In some cases, like El Salvador in the 1980s and more recently Haiti, economic conflict may lead to a political alliance between the wealthy and the military whereby the military protects the elite's wealth in return for a privileged place in the government and society.

Disease.   Although improvements in the provision of basic health services have helped to trigger population growth, adequate medical care remains the preserve of the wealthy and privileged throughout most countries of the Second Tier. Diseases long eradicated in the First Tier, such as child blindness preventable by simple vitamin dosages, still prevail in many regions and, like nutritional deficiencies, act as a chronic long-term drag on economic progress.

In recent years, the Second Tier, and especially Africa, has experienced a rash of sexually transmitted diseases, especially AIDS. Partly, this is the result of having a youthful population that tends to be more sexually active and insufficiently knowledgeable about prevention of these diseases. Although estimates are notoriously unreliable (in some cases because governments either do not know or do not want to know the dimensions of the epidemic), a high proportion of the youthful population of many African states carry the virus that causes AIDS, and experts suspect that the proportion is still growing. The problem is especially serious in sub-Saharan Africa, as the accompanying map (8-6) indicates. Infection rates of 10

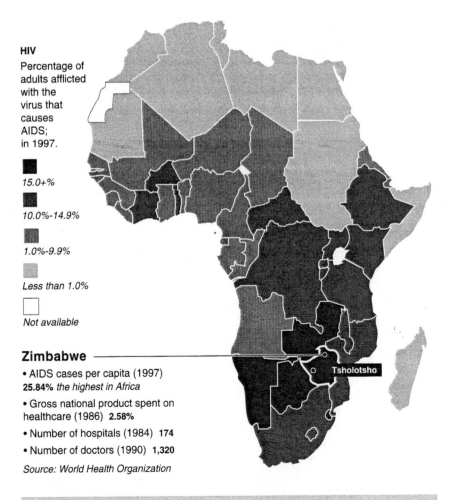

HIV

Percentage of
adults afflicted
with the
virus that
causes
AIDS;
in 1997.

■ 15.0+%

■ 10.0%-14.9%

■ 1.0%-9.9%

▨ Less than 1.0%

☐ Not available

Zimbabwe

• AIDS cases per capita (1997)
25.84% *the highest in Africa*

• Gross national product spent on
healthcare (1986) **2.58%**

• Number of hospitals (1984) **174**

• Number of doctors (1990) **1,320**

Source: World Health Organization

Tsholotsho

Map 8-6   **Africa's Health Crisis** Kris Goodfellow/NYT Graphics

percent of the adult population are not uncommon. The most dramatic case is Zimbabwe, with an HIV infection rate of 25.84 percent. To get some idea of the consequences of the epidemic, life expectancy in Zimbabwe was 61 years in 1993; thanks to AIDS, it is expected to be 49 years in 2000 and could decline to 40 years in a decade. In the absence of a cure or sharp curtailment of the behavior that increases the risk of AIDS, some countries face the prospect of a lost generation of leaders cut down by the disease. In addition, the inability to provide adequate sanitation, as described in the Amplification box "Global Urbanization," will add to the burden. More recently, the large number of refugees uprooted by wars (upwards of 23 million in 1996) and forced to live in wretched conditions has led to outbreaks of numerous diseases, some of which had virtually been eradicated.

Debt Service. The problem of inadequate resources for development is made even worse in many Second Tier countries by the burden of debt service, the amount of

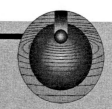

Amplification
Global Urbanization

Global population is not only growing rapidly; it is being concentrated in urban areas. Fifty years ago, only about one-third of the world's population lived in cities. By early in the twenty-first century, that proportion will be one-half; by the year 2025, when worldwide population will be 8-9 billion, two-thirds will be urban dwellers. To discuss the problems that are and will be created by this trend, the United Nations convened the second UN Conference on Human Settlements (the first was held in Vancouver 20 years ago) in Istanbul in June 1996 as the capstone of a series on international meetings on the human condition that began with the Earth Summit in Rio de Janeiro in 1992 (the intermediary conferences were in Vienna in 1993 on human rights, in Cairo in 1994 on population, and in 1995 in Copenhagen on poverty and in Beijing on women's rights).

Among the problems the conferees had to confront were the following:

- By the turn of the century, many areas in both the First and Second Tiers, will be unable to provide basic public services such as security,

sanitation, water, and transportation. The World Bank estimates that 1.4 billion people will live without safe water and sanitation by 2010, with unknown but undeniable negative health consequences. The provision of many basic services will likely by privatized.
- Urbanization, especially in Africa, will occur in places without basic infrastructure that will produce, in the words of U.S. deputy assistant secretary of state Melinda Kimble, "villages of 200,000 to 300,000."
- Sanitation will become an increasing concern. Ninety percent of raw sewage produced in developing world cities is released untreated into streams and oceans. More specifically, India has only eight full treatment plants to service more than 3,000 cities and towns.
- Currently, 600 million people (out of a global population of slightly less than 6 billion) are homeless. Almost 100 million of these are women and children.

Source: Barbara Crossette, "Hope, Pragmatism for UN Cities Conference." *New York Times* (national edition), June 3, 1996, A3.

money that a country must pay to public and private foreign lenders in interest on previous loans. In the Second Tier this amount often approaches, and in a few cases exceeds, the amount the country earns from foreign trade. Until this problem can be solved, there will always be inadequate capital available within many Second Tier states to aid in development. The inability to service debt on loans is a basic barrier to solving the Asian financial crisis.

What Does the First Tier Owe the Second?

Very few (Islamic fundamentalists being a partial exception) seriously debate the desirability of moving the countries of the Second Tier through the developmental process and hence upward through the various categories of Second Tier status. For the reasons already discussed, however, the resources for economic development are generally unavailable within the affected countries, meaning that they must be generated, at least in part, from external sources. The question is who (if anyone) should provide developmental assistance and why.

This section will explore the question of whether the First Tier states have some moral or legal obligation to assist the Second Tier. With that discussion in mind, we will then examine the various forms assistance can take.

An Obligation to Assist?

During the Cold War, Second Tier states were often able to extract some levels of developmental assistance from the West by threats of consorting with the Soviets. With the Cold War motivation gone, that leverage has disappeared. But there may be other reasons for the First Tier to render assistance. A major source of contention between the countries of the two tiers involves the claim that the First Tier countries, having colonized, dominated, and exploited most of Africa, Asia, the Caribbean, and Latin America, are obliged for that reason to help raise the economic condition of Second Tier countries to something like parity with the First Tier.

This issue is contentious in several ways. The assertion of obligation suggests former wrongdoing in a legal or ethical sense, the foundations of which are not established in traditional international relations or international law. Furthermore, as noted earlier, the claim that colonial oppression creates a responsibility can be countered by the assertion that without colonial "tutelage" former colonies would be even farther behind. Neither claim is indisputable. Finally, if obligation is accepted, to what level is the First Tier obliged to raise Second Tier countries: to First Tier status or to something less?

The concerted demand for developmental assistance has its roots in the early 1960s or, arguably, even earlier (the Bandung Conference in 1955 produced the beginning of a united front among Second Tier states). In the early 1960s, the United Nations held its first Conference on Trade and Development (UNCTAD), and an organization of Third World states, called the Group of 77 (after the number of states attending the initial meeting), came into being. Both UNCTAD and the Group of 77 declared it the duty of the world's wealthier states to assist the development of poor ones.

The demand for large-scale capital transfers came into focus in the form of calls for a New International Economic Order (NIEO). Largely the work of *dependencia* theorists, who argued that only movement toward economic equality would dissolve the relationship of dependency of the Second Tier on the First, the NIEO scheme demanded that the rich states (more or less the members of the Organization of Economic Cooperation and Development, the same states that form the First Tier) transfer one to three percent of their gross national product (GNP) annually for developmental programs. For the United States today, one percent would amount to about $60 billion; the actual U.S. foreign economic aid budget was around $13 billion for the 1994–95 fiscal year, and the entire concept of developmental assistance is under continuing assault within the U.S. Congress.

NIEO has gradually faded from the international agenda for a number of reasons. First, its specific demands substantially exceeded any amounts that the governments of most developed states could realistically (in political terms) commit. Whether the full amounts called for were needed for developmental purposes or not, there was simply no domestic consensus within most donor countries that could allow such levels to be achieved.

A second reason for the fading of NIEO is that, as previously noted, the Second Tier has very little leverage with which to pressure the First Tier. The instruments of national power simply cannot be brought to bear, especially in a post–Cold War environment in which the threat to align with one side or the other cannot be invoked.

A third factor has been the notable number of countries that have managed to develop without help on the scale of the NIEO. The "economic miracles" of the Pacific Rim appear to give the lie to claims that development requires large-scale outside assistance. Moreover, one of the chief bulwarks of Second Tier claims, China, has also begun moving toward successful competition in the global economy without massive infusions of aid.

Organized opposition has been a fourth barrier to NIEO. The most notable opponent was the United States during the 1980s; the Reagan administration was philosophically opposed to foreign assistance, in accordance with its general orientation toward privatization, the turning over of formerly governmental activities to the private sector. The fact that many *dependencia* theorists have a basically Marxist orientation also did little to endear them to the Reaganites. Without active American involvement, resources to fund NIEO were too meager.

A fifth and final obstacle is the belief of many analysts that until developing countries reform themselves both economically and politically, developmental assistance will be misused and wasted. The prescription that these countries must begin by adopting the values of the First Tier is a major point of contention, because the kinds of reforms proposed are of the economically sound but politically suicidal nature described earlier. Lacking the political leverage to obtain aid otherwise, many Second Tier states face the unpalatable alternatives of no assistance or assistance with numerous financially constricting conditions attached (such as those imposed by the International Monetary Fund).

This situation presents a grim set of prospects for the future. There currently is a net flow of resources between the tiers, but it is from the Second Tier to the First. Although precise figures are hard to verify, the estimated annual net flow is between $35 and $45 billion. The chief sources of flow from the Second Tier to the First are debt service and capital flight. The effect is that the developing world is contributing to the continued development of the already wealthiest countries, rather than the other way around.

The Sources of Development

If resources for development in the Second Tier are to become available, from what sources can they come? Broadly speaking, the possible sources may be public or private, and may be domestic or foreign. These distinctions are combined in Table 8.3 in matrix form to indicate four possibilities.

As indicated in the table, public domestic sources include tax revenues and net foreign earnings (what is left after foreign obligations are paid off). These sources can be used for expenses such as infrastructural projects, which do not attract private money but are prerequisite to attracting foreign capital. These are limited sources, however. Developing countries typically have narrow tax bases (the privileged and the poor generally pay little, if any, taxes) and competing priorities (often the military) for what tax moneys there are. The debt service burden often makes net foreign earnings a small or nonexistent commodity.

Private domestic funds come from entrepreneurs or members of the traditional moneyed elite who are willing to invest their wealth in domestic business enterprises that generate jobs and income. Governments can offer inducements for investment through such devices as tax and incorporation laws and regulations. The problem that must be overcome is the fear of unstable governments and economies, a fear that has resulted in capital flight.

Within the foreign public sector, there are two basic forms of so-called foreign aid, bilateral and multilateral. By far the larger source is bilateral assistance, the direct transfer of money or other resources (food, technical experts) from one country to another. Within the United States, the organization responsible for such assistance is the Agency for International Development (AID), a part of the U.S. Department of State.

States give aid for different reasons. Within the Cold War context, foreign aid was primarily an instrument of power either to gain favor or to deny favor to the adversary. In some cases, aid was the payment for security arrangements or other Cold War–related benefits. Some assistance has also been extended, during and after the Cold War, on a humanitarian basis, such as disaster relief. During the Cold War, assistance was rarely justified in purely developmental terms. Its purpose was only indirectly developmental: more developed countries were believed to be more resistant to the appeal of communism, for instance.

The basic multilateral public sources are those international organizations that provide developmental assistance. The most prominent of these is the International Bank for Reconstruction and Development (IBRD or World Bank) group, which includes both the bank itself and the International Development Agency. The bank is a specialized agency of

Table 8.3 Developmental Resources		
	Public	**Private**
Domestic	Tax Revenues	Entrepreneurs
Foreign	Foreign earnings	Elite Investment
	Bilateral aid	Capital Investment
	Multilateral aid	Corporate Investment

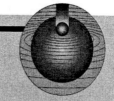

The Impact of Technology

Can the High-Tech Revolution Help the Second Tier?

Can, or will, the high-technology revolution extend to the Second Tier, adding to the developmental process and assisting the Second Tier in attaining the general prosperity of the First Tier? The answer is not entirely clear, and it would seem to vary between subtiers, with the most developed countries being most likely to benefit.

One positive impact of technology is that it reduces the remoteness of some parts of the Second Tier that were previously unpromising developmentally by virtue of location. Television satellites allow instantaneous communication with the most remote places, and projected breakthroughs in avionics and maritime technology mean that products made in previously out-of-the-way locations can now be shipped to markets in a much more efficient manner than before.

At the same time, the attractiveness of Second Tier locales to high-technology-based concerns will depend on developed infrastructures even more than before. While computer-based factories can be imported to Second Tier countries to take advantage of low labor costs, the operation of high-tech business requires basic infrastructure features such as an educated and well-motivated workforce, abundant power, an efficient transportation system, and a reliable and stable government. The provision of these items explains the success of many Pacific Rim countries in their approach to the First Tier and suggests that other states will succeed to the extent they can emulate the Asian "model."

As for other results of high technology, clearly improvements in the ability to grow crops, to treat disease, and to manage pollution and waste will all be beneficial. As argued throughout the text, however, the whole phenomenon of high technology is so dynamic and vibrant as to make future developments difficult if not impossible to predict.

New technology, such as the satellite dish on the roof of a colonial-era church in Guatemala, may aid in Second Tier development by making formerly remote areas more accessible to the outside world.

the United Nations and acts as an agent of its members, all of which are states. In addition, the International Monetary Fund provides indirect assistance by guaranteeing currencies and providing credits to states.

The World Bank devises standards of economic performance for developing states and then makes loans and grants to those states that meet them. These standards are generally more stringent than individual donor states could exact on their own. Many countries will give aid only to countries approved by the bank, making it a convenient structure for forcing economic responsibility. In some cases, as a matter of efficiency and convenience, the bank coordinates the bilateral assistance going into a country that has multiple donors, such as India.

The final source of funding for developing countries, private foreign investment, basically comes in two forms: loans from private financial institutions and investment by multinational corporations. Direct loans from private banks in First Tier countries are largely an artifact of the 1960s and 1970s, when a sizable number of financial institutions "discovered" the Third World (and especially Latin America) and determined that there were great potential profits to be made there. In many instances these banks lacked an adequately sophisticated understanding of international affairs and of the politics of the countries in which they were investing, and they made two mistakes: they loaned more funds than Third World governments could profitably absorb, and they failed to place adequate safeguards on how the funds could be used. As a result, many of the funds were poorly invested in ways that did not produce profits with which to repay interest and principal on the loans. Corruption and misappropriation were also problems. The current debt service burden of many Second Tier countries is largely the result of these problems, and the flood of private funds into underregulated east Asian economies contributed to the crisis of 1997–98.

Investment by multinational corporations (MNCs) is of a different nature. As the name implies, MNCs do business in more than one country; their involvement in Second Tier countries generally takes the form of setting up agencies or factories, either individually or through joint ventures with governments or local private firms. Currently, much of this activity is occurring in Eastern Europe and the former Soviet Union, but there is also considerable activity by Japanese and other companies in the countries of the Pacific Rim and southern Asia.

The benefit of MNC participation is that it creates jobs and tax revenues that can be used for further development. The major drawback is that MNCs are mainly attracted to those countries that already have well-developed infrastructures capable of supporting their enterprises—that is, to Second Tier countries in the two subtiers nearest the First Tier. Conversely, they are least attracted to those countries that are in the greatest need of developmental assistance.

The Developmental Agenda for the Future

How the Second Tier will fit into the evolving international system remains to be seen. The altered geopolitical environment means that the situation will be different; there is no ideological competition involved. The possibility that the Asian financial crisis could become global further muddies the prospects. Three sets of questions can be used to frame the debate about the role of the Second Tier. The first is how important the Second Tier will or can be. The second is whether public or private mechanisms should play the leading role in helping establish that position, especially for those states in the lower rungs of the Second Tier. The third, reflecting a recognition that developmental resources are scarce, is what the most fruitful strategies are for organizing whatever level of effort emerges.

Marginalization or Centrality?

In the Cold War system, the old Third World was a basically marginal, instrumental participant rather than a central one. The Third World was marginal because it had little intrinsic importance to the central operation of international relations. It was instrumental because it served as a tool (or instrument) of the central East-West competition. Lacking central importance, the Third World could, for most purposes, be ignored by the more developed states. Decolonization and development were nearly sideshows in the greater circus of world affairs.

Will a restructured international system leave the Second Tier (or parts of it) at the margins, safely ignorable, or will the system pull the Second Tier toward the center? A case can be made for either scenario. Marginalization is a possibility for two main reasons. First, it can be (and is) argued that politically the Second Tier is actually less important than it was before. Its concerns remain at the margins of overall systemic dynamics both economically and politically, and the end of the Cold War has removed its instrumental value. Ignoring the Second Tier no longer creates the risk that one Cold War competitor or the other will gain; there is no competition among suitors.

The other major reason marginalization might be anticipated is that the problems of the Second Tier, especially within the lower subtiers, are so enormous that they appear to be beyond remediation. The available developmental resources are inadequate even to make a dent in countries like India (with its population of close to 1.1 billion); the effort can only be frustrating. Moreover, it may be that even the greatest of efforts will not speed change much. It took the First Tier a century or more to go through the process of development, after all.

On the other hand, there are arguments suggesting a more central, or at least expanding, role for the developing world in the future. For one thing, the global economy is becoming so intertwined that it is virtually impossible to ignore any state any longer. The tags in clothing sold in America are a veritable roll call of the Second Tier; the trinkets formerly "made in Japan" have long since moved to South Korea, and from South Korea to South and Southeast Asia and China. It is possible to speculate, as we will in the next chapter, about a kind of economic "trickle down" effect, where different kinds of economic activity permeate downward through the categories of developmental status that will incorporate the Second Tier and thus be beneficial to all.

A further argument for the likelihood of inclusion can be made. Granted that the early stages of development are usually destabilizing, there appears to be a positive relationship between economic prosperity, the emergence of participatory democracy, and eventual stability. A system whose primary source of instability is the Second Tier may simply find it to be in its enlightened long-term self-interest to move the Second Tier into the more general prosperity of the First Tier—to centralize rather than to marginalize. This is particularly true of the Pacific Rim and much of Latin America. Institutions such as Asia-Pacific Economic Cooperation (APEC) and the North American Free Trade Association (NAFTA) (both discussed in Chapter 9) and ASEAN (the subject of the case study in this chapter) may serve as vehicles to facilitate such a transition.

Privatization or International Welfare?

When development first became an international agenda item in the 1950s and 1960s, it was thought of as a government-to-government, or public, problem. The debate was over whether bilateral or multilateral assistance was most appropriate. This orientation reflected the positive view of government characteristic of the time and the fact that the modern global economy as we know it and its primary private creature, the MNC, were in their infancies.

The 1980s, by contrast, was the decade of privatization. Conservative governments in many First Tier states, notably the United States and Great Britain, professed the goal of "getting government off people's back" and the belief that the private sector uniformly makes better economic decisions than do governments, a conviction that extended to development. Governments' economic job was to reduce restrictions on the private sector. Considering the great economic prosperity within the First Tier during the 1980s, it was a difficult argument to counter.

The perspective of the 1990s is not so clear. As world economic growth flattened in the early part of the decade, some of the momentum behind the trend toward privatization declined as well. Changes in government and sharp falls in the approval ratings for governments of the Group of Seven states contributed to this decline. In the United States, the 1992 election of Bill Clinton, a proponent of free trade in the economic realm, has provided an impetus toward the development of a global economy the roots of which were planted in the 1980s. The resulting "go-go 1990s" in the world economy brought an optimism about the growing prosperity that the crises of the late 1990s have served to dampen somewhat.

In the area of developmental aid and investment, what is likely to emerge from these trends is a mixture of resources from public and private sources—to the extent that First Tier support for Second Tier development is forthcoming at all. Domestic economic difficulties in the First Tier will place sharp limits on the amount of public funds available for foreign developmental aid; the emphasis on budget deficit reduction, competing priorities, and tax reduction in the United States, for example, has produced pressures for a decline in funding for USAID, the major source of American public assistance. It is also unlikely that foreign aid budgets will increase elsewhere.

Private funding increases will come mostly from corporate investment. Other private sources, notably banks, are just now recovering from the bad loans they had previously made, and they are unlikely to venture aggressively into Second Tier lending again, for fear of investor retaliation.

The dynamics of the global economy, on the other hand, suggest that corporate investment will continue to expand, as more and more MNCs move their manufacturing operations into the cheap labor markets in developing countries, although the crises of 1997–98 have at least temporarily slowed that trend. The primary sites will be the most developed of the developing countries, where infrastructure development and other strategies for enticing foreign investment are most advanced.

An electronics factory in Taipei, the capital of Taiwan. Formerly the recipient of massive foreign economic aid and investment, Taiwan has developed to the point where its businesses now invest in other Asian Second Tier countries.

Strategies for Development

For private firms, the question of where to invest is not difficult; they will go where there is the best prospect of the greatest profit and the least risk that political or economic turmoil will interfere with making profits. Within the Second Tier, those conditions exist only at the upper rungs, in the countries that have made the most progress toward economic and political development. General Motors may build an automotive parts plant in Malaysia; it is unlikely to do so in the Sudan.

The way public funds may be spent in the Second Tier is more problematical. As noted, the end of the Cold War made the old geopolitical criterion irrelevant. The guiding principle in the future is likely to be the contribution to stability, defined both in terms of the general geopolitical tranquility of the system and of the creation of a stable environment in which the private sector can do increasing business.

In general, funds will probably not be widely dispersed. In the early days of developmental assistance, funding tended to be spread out, with small amounts going to a large number of states. The economic results of this strategy were marginal, and in the late 1960s the emphasis shifted to concentrating assistance on a smaller number of important states. The rationale was that if these states could be pushed through the developmental process rapidly, they would then become sources of assistance for the rest. A prime example of the success of this approach is Taiwan, where massive external assistance and private investment produced near First Tier status, followed by Taiwanese firms' investment in other Asian Second Tier states.

Case Study: *ASEAN as a Development Strategy*

Given the clear and likely continuing scarcity of external funding for developmental purposes, one approach to maximizing the amount of development is through regional cooperation among Second Tier states. The organization that most clearly represents that method is the Association of Southeast Asian Nations (ASEAN).

ASEAN was originally established on August 8, 1967, in Bangkok, Thailand, with the signing of the Bangkok Declaration. The states that attended and were charter members were Indonesia, Malaysia, the Philippines, Singapore, and Thailand. The Bangkok Declaration committed the members to a joint effort to promote economic cooperation and regional welfare; underlying the declaration were three common objectives for the region: economic, social and cultural development, political and economic stability in the face of superpower rivalry, and resolution of intra-regional differences. In addition, there was the political goal of providing a united front to avoid being drawn into the Vietnam war.

Over time, ASEAN has grown and changed in two basic ways. First, its membership has gradually been extended within the area. In 1984 Brunei (technically Brunei Darussalam) joined, in 1995 Vietnam was added to the rolls, and at the 1997 summit conference, Burma/Myanmar and Laos were added. The addition of Cambodia was suspended in 1997 pending the outcome of the civil war in that country.

The second basic change in ASEAN is that the purposes of the organization have expanded. In 1976 the organization established a secretariat in Jakarta, Indonesia, to oversee its common efforts, including the enhancement of economic activity between ASEAN members and in ASEAN's relations with the rest of the world. The increasing economic ties were formalized in 1992 under the guise of the Singapore Declaration, which called for setting up the ASEAN Free Trade Area within 15 years; the major instrument to create this free trade area is something called the Common Effective Tariff (CEPT) Scheme. In 1995 ASEAN went one step further in expanding its purposes by signing the Southeast Asia Nuclear Weapon-Free Zone Treaty.

The ASEAN arrangement is interesting and important for at least three reasons. First, the organization, especially as it has expanded, represents a very diverse group of Second Tier states, as depicted in Table 8.4. As the table shows, the organization's membership is extraordinarily diverse. In terms of size, it encompasses one of the world's most populous countries (Indonesia) and one of its least populated (Brunei). Singapore and Brunei are two of the Second Tier's most prosperous countries, but very marginal economies such as those of former French Indochina (Vietnam, Laos, and eventually Cambodia) and Burma/Myanmar are included. All subtiers of the Second Tier are included.

Second, ASEAN is contiguous to arguably the world's most vibrant economic area, the Pacific Rim, and it is actively pursuing economic relations with Pacific Rim countries that

Web Sitings: ASEAN on the Web

To demonstrate the practical utility of using the Internet to do research, most of the information from which this case study was constructed came directly off the web. For information on ASEAN, one can contact the ASEAN home page (which was specifically established by act of the organization at its 1995 summit meeting to promote knowledge and understanding of it): http://www/asean.org.id/. If you did not know that address, you could easily get to the page by using one of the several search engines (Netscape Navigator, Yahoo, AOLFind) and simply typing in the organization's name.

For information on individual countries, an easy source of up-to-date information is the CIA's *World FactBook*. It is available at http://www.odci.gov/cia/publications/nsole/wfb-all.htm. A number of servers feature this document in their political reference sections.

Table 8.4	Characteristics of ASEAN Members			
State	Year Joined	Population	GDP/Capita	Second Tier Subtier
Indonesia	8/67	212,941,810	3,770	Partially Developed
Malaysia	8/67	20,932,901	10,750	Partially Developed
Phillipines	8/67	77,225,862	2,600	Developable
Singapore	8/67	3,490,356	21,200	Developed
Thailand	8/67	60,037,366	7,700	Partially Developed
Brunei	1/84	315,292	15,800	Resource-Rich
Vietnam	7/95	76,236,259	1,470	Developable
Burma	8/97	47,305,319	1,120	Developable
Laos	8/97	5,260,842	1,150	Developable
Cambodia	Pending	11,334,562	710	Developable
U.S.	No	270,311,758	28,600	First Tier

Source of figures: *World Almanac and Book of Facts*, 1999. Mahwah, NJ: World Almanac Books, 1999.
The United States is not a member. Figures are provided for comparative purposes only.

will facilitate the movement of ASEAN members through the tiers into the greater prosperity. The first six members admitted to ASEAN are also members of the Asia-Pacific Economic Cooperation (APEC) that encompasses all the major economic powers around the Pacific Ocean littoral (including the United States). Vietnam was invited to join APEC in 1998, suggesting that ASEAN membership may serve a "gatekeeper" function for new membership into APEC.

Third, the ASEAN area is already economically important, and is becoming more so. The ASEAN area includes a population of over 500 million people, and it has become a major producer of consumer goods imported into the United States and elsewhere. Collectively, the ASEAN area now ranks as the United States' fourth largest trade partner. Relations with ASEAN are considered important enough that Secretary of State Madeleine Albright personally attended the 1997 Summit in Kuala Lumpur, Malaysia (the U.S. and several others major states—such as Japan and China—attend these meetings by invitation as observers).

The recent evolution of ASEAN also demonstrates the close relationship between the economic and political aspects of development. One of the major characteristics of the membership is that most remain basically authoritarian regimes: the Philippines is an exception, as is the benign monarchy in Brunei. At the same time, ASEAN members such as Malaysia and Singapore have been among the loudest proponents of the cultural relativity of human rights and even the need to revise documents such as the Universal Declaration of Human Rights to reflect Asian values (a suggestion Secretary Albright dismissed at Kuala Lumpur, saying the United States "would be relentless in its opposition" to any attempt to water down the declaration). Burma and Cambodia have, at various times, topped the State Department's list of human rights violators.

Some young entrepreneurs see associations such as ASEAN as ways to tie member countries into the global economy and hence promote democratization by tying the hands of authoritarian governments to international standards. One particular example is in Indonesia, described in the Contours of the Future? box "The Globalutionaries."

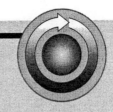

Contours of the Future?

The Globalutionaries

Reporting for the *New York Times* on the movement in Indonesia that helped subvert the authoritarian control of the 30-year old Suharto regime, Thomas L. Friedman noted that the strategy is to tie Indonesia increasingly into the global economy, thereby imposing on the Indonesian society the kinds of rules and restrictions that apply in the advanced market democracies. As one Indonesian source put it, "The global market will force upon us business practices and disciplines that we cannot generate internally," including restrictions on corruption that permeate the regime.

The strategy consists of two parallel activities. First, the "globalutionaries" promote Indonesian participation in as broad a range of international economic associations as possible, including the World Trade Organization (WTO) and APEC, in addition to ASEAN. The second prong of the strategy is to promote as much foreign investment as possible, since foreign investors will serve as role models for Indonesian firms and will insist on business practices that will restrict corrupt and authoritarian government practices, the kinds of practices that contributed to the financial collapse in Indonesia in 1997.

A similar line of argumentation has been used as a way to bring about change in China, and that has been less than a total success. What sets Indonesia's globalutionaries apart from their Chinese counterparts, according to Friedman, is its explicit political intention: to democratize the society by undercutting the authoritarian structure. How much influence this group had on Suharto's resignation remains conjectural. To the extent it did contribute, it could write a new chapter in the developmental debate.

Source: Thomas L. Friedman, "The Globalutionaries," *New York Times* (national edition), July 17, 1997, A15.

Indonesians discontented with the alleged corruption of the Suharto regime protest for reforms. The demonstrations were a factor in Suharto's 1998 resignation.

The other form of politicization regards the involvement of ASEAN in the domestic politics of its members. Historically, ASEAN has followed the position that internal policies are only the concern of the states involved (a strict sovereignty interpretation), which was practical given the nature of some its regimes already described. In the case of Cambodia, however, ASEAN was put under great pressure both to delay Cambodian membership and to act in a proactive manner to insure that the Hun Sen government conforms to international standards of behavior. At the considerable urging of the United States at Kuala Lumpur, ASEAN agreed reluctantly to a mediating role in the internal Cambodian crisis.

Review

This chapter provided an examination of the dynamics and problems of the Second Tier. In the process, the following points were made:

1. The Second Tier can be divided into four subtiers of states on the basis of economic and political criteria: the developed, the partially developed, the developable, and the resource-rich. Factors affecting political stability include regime legitimacy, democratization, and the need for coercion. Economic factors are related to the progress of Second Tier states through the various industrial revolutions.

2. There is disagreement about the impact of colonization and decolonization on the Second Tier, but almost all agree that the colonial powers did little to prepare their colonies for political independence or economic prosperity. Moreover, many were granted independence with colonial borders that include many nationalities or split up national communities between more than one state.

3. The all but universal cry of the Second Tier is for economic development; democratization is widely demanded as well. There is disagreement about the best order in which to pursue these goals.

4. Among barriers to development are rapid population growth, inadequate or maldistributed food supply, maldistribution of wealth within society and capital flight, disease (prominently including AIDS), and debt service.

5. There is disagreement about whether or to what extent the First Tier has an obligation to assist in Second Tier development, and it is uncertain whether Second Tier concerns will remain marginal to the First Tier or become a central part of the overall system.

6. ASEAN represents one way that Second Tier states attempt to improve their developmental status through joint action. Recent controversies over membership expansion demonstrate the interconnection between economics and politics in the globalizing economy.

Suggested Readings

Apter, David. *Rethinking Development: Modernization, Dependence and Postmodern Politics.* Beverly Hills, CA: Sage, 1987.

Bhagwati, Jagdish, ed. *The New International Economic Order: The North-South Debate.* Cambridge, MA: MIT Press, 1977.

Burton, Daniel F. Jr. "Competitiveness: Here to Stay." *Washington Quarterly* 17, 4 (autumn 1994): 99–110.

Carothers, Thomas. "Democracy and Human Rights: Policy Allies or Enemies?" *Washington Quarterly* 17, 3 (summer 1994): 109–20.

Dessouki, Ali E. Hilial. "Globalization and the Two Spheres of Security." *Washington Quarterly* 16, 4 (fall 1993): 109–17.

Gurr, Ted Robert. *Why Men Rebel.* Princeton, NJ: Princeton University Press, 1973.

Huntington, Samuel P., et al. *The Clash of Civilizations: The Debate.* New York: Foreign Affairs Press, 1993.

—. *The Third Wave: Democratization in the Late Twentieth Century.* Norman, OK: University of Oklahoma Press, 1991.

Manwaring, Max G., ed. *Uncomfortable Wars: Toward a New Paradigm of Low-Intensity Conflict.* Boulder, CO: Westview Press, 1991.

Moran, Theodore H. *Multinational Corporations: The Political Economy of Foreign Direct Investment.* Lexington, MA: Lexington Books, 1988.

Ohmae, Kenichi. "The Rise of the Region State." *Foreign Affairs* 72, 2 (spring 1993): 78–87.

Orwell, George. *Burmese Days*. New York: New American Library, 1960.

Overholt, William H. *The Rise of China: How Economic Reform Is Creating a Superpower*. New York: W W. Norton, 1993.

Peng, Ernest H. "Who's Benefiting Whom? A Trade Agenda for High Technology Industries." *Washington Quarterly* 16, 4 (fall 1993): 17–34.

Schwartz, Herman M. *States Versus Markets: History, Geography, and the Development of International Political Economy*. New York: St. Martin's Press, 1994.

Singer, Max, and Aaron Wildavsky. *The Real World Order: Zones of Peace, Zones of Turmoil*. Chatham, NJ: Chatham House, 1993.

Sullivan, John D. "Democracy and Global Economic Growth." *Washington Quarterly* 15, 2 (spring 1992): 175–86.

Vernon, Raymond, ed. *The Promise of Privatization: A Challenge for American Foreign Policy*. New York: Council on Foreign Relations, 1988.

Zakaria, Fareed. "A Conversation with Lee Kuan Yew." *Foreign Affairs* 73, 2 (March/April 1994): 109–26.

The New Agenda: International Political Economy

PREVIEW

This chapter will examine the increasingly important role of economic factors in the operation of the international system. We will begin by looking at some ways in which international economics and politics are interrelated. From there, we will go on to describe the international system from an economic angle, beginning with the Bretton Woods arrangement after World War II and contrasting it with the structure of the present world economy. The present is and the future almost certainly will be marked by global interdependence and an increasingly global economy, and we will discuss these characteristics and then another primary feature of the new system, high technology, preeminence in which is the mark of competitiveness. The chapter will conclude with a discussion of one wave of the future, the stateless corporation.

KEY CONCEPTS

international political economy (IPE)
multinational corporations (MNCs)
Group of Seven (G–7)
Bretton Woods system
International Monetary Fund (IMF)
World Bank
General Agreement on Tariffs and Trade
   (GATT)
World Trade Organization (WTO)
hard currency
global economy
high-technology revolution

privatization
economic internationalization
European Union (EU)
North American Free Trade Association
   (NAFTA)
Asia-Pacific Economic Cooperation
   (APEC)
interdependence
economic intertwining
economic competitiveness
industrial policy
stateless corporation (SC)

OUTLINE

O ne way all observers agree that the new international system is different from the Cold War system is the extent to which economic aspects of international affairs have increased in importance and the impact this change has had on national and international politics. The beginnings of this shift actually date back to the Cold War era, but in public attention they were somewhat overshadowed at the time by the overwhelming concern with life-and-death issues that the Cold War demanded. Some of the key international economic features of today, such as the Group of Eight (G–8), are Cold War artifacts that may evolve, both economically and politically, in the new geopolitical environment. Post–Cold War phenomena such as Asia-Pacific Economic Cooperation (APEC) reflect a newer set of economic and political realities and may become increasingly important in the future.

A number of analysts saw signs of this shift as far back as the middle 1960s, and others at least saw evidence of it before the Cold War was over. Viewing the increased level of international economic activity and the degree to which countries were becoming economically intertwined and dependent on one another, political scientists Robert Keohane and Joseph Nye, Jr. laid out an analysis of what they termed "complex interdependence" in their 1977 book *Power and Interdependence: World Politics in Transition* (a concept they have widened to include the information revolution). Together with the parallel work of a number of other analysts, all of whom emphasized the complex ways in which political and economic factors affect one another, the Keohane-Nye study gave rise to a new approach to studying international relations, called *international political economy* (IPE).

At the risk of oversimplifying a complex set of theoretical assumptions and debates, we will attempt to summarize this approach. IPE theorists contend that traditional international relations scholarship invested too much effort in studying the political—including military—aspects of international relations at the expense of exploring how economic concerns affected the economic and political operation of the international system. In their view, the emergence of a strong global economy, cutting across national boundaries and making those boundaries irrelevant for certain economic purposes, means that scholarly neglect of economic factors has led to increasing distortion of the reality of international relations. Moreover, IPE theorists stress that economic developments are strongly influenced by political decisions within the major countries, especially policies for encouraging (or limiting) foreign investment, trade, and the like.

Politics and economics are, of course, closely related. If politics is about how conflicts of interest over scarce resources are resolved, then clearly one of the categories where conflict resolution is called for is that of economic resources. Moreover, economic decisions are often politically driven, and economic policies are the result of political processes. The economic and political aspects of international relations may be as closely intertwined as are domestic and international aspects of a country's foreign affairs, the connection between which led to the coining of the term "intermestic policy."

The rising prominence of IPE concerns reflects important changes in the structure of the international system. Any list of these changes will be partially subjective; by way of introduction, however, we can identify five reasons that the international economic system has increasingly come to the fore in thinking about and describing international relations.

Summary ――――――――――――――――――

Reasons for the Rise of IPE

1. Declining importance of military factors with end of Cold War competition
2. Movement of the United States from dominance to more equal participation in international economic system
3. Evolution of international economic structures
4. Declining role of state in directing or controlling international economic behavior
5. Emergence of new centers of international power based in economic strength

---

The first change is the declining importance of military factors because of the breakdown of East-West military competition. Important economic developments, such as the rise of the multinational corporations, were beginning to occur during the Cold War era, but they did not get into the spotlight. With the central importance of military competition reduced (especially among the states of the First Tier), economic concerns have moved toward center stage.

A second influential change in the structure of international relations has been the movement of the United States from a position of overwhelming dominance to one of more equal participation in the international economic system. This factor, which was discussed in Chapter 7 in connection with the "declinist" thesis about U.S. power, has had a bearing on political debate and academic studies throughout the First Tier. With respect to practical policy, the commanding position of the United States from the end of World War II until at least the middle 1960s (different observers cite different benchmarks for change) meant that during these years, there was little need for politicians or voters to think much about the general nature of the international economic system. That system was, in essence, whatever the United States said it would be; the United States dictated international economic policy and could and did put that advantage to political use. More recently, however, international economic policy has become a matter of wide public concern, and notions of IPE have entered the political debate. Bill Clinton, for instance, is the first U.S. president to talk about a global economy, where there is no clear-cut distinction between domestic and international aspects of the system.

Meanwhile, in the academic world, the movement of the United States from being the overwhelming force shaping the world economy to merely being a dominant force created a "market" for those interested in studying the economic aspects of international relations and the impact of economic aspects on political developments. Since most international relations analysts—including IPE scholars—are American (largely because of the domination of the social sciences generally by scholars working in American universities), the changing fortune of the United States in the world economy is an area of particular interest and concern to them.

The third important change in the international system has been the evolution of international economic structures. The true internationalization of the world's economy is actually a rather recent phenomenon. Although multinational corporations (MNCs) existed in the 1960s, they were generally corporations having their headquarters and primary operations in one country while doing business in a number of others. As technology and other factors changed in the 1970s and 1980s, however, the very structure of how such firms do business began to change rapidly. Encouraged by governments in the West, which gave relatively free rein to corporations headquartered or doing business in their jurisdictions, these businesses became truly international in ways we will describe in the pages that follow. Another aspect of economic international-ization was the emergence or growth of international intergovernmental arrangements of greater (EU, NAFTA) or lesser (G–8, APEC) formality.

A fourth, and as yet not entirely understood, change in the system has been the declining role of the state in directing or controlling international economic behavior. In earlier times, governments directly and effectively monitored economic activities crossing their borders, often on national security grounds or for domestic political reasons. A

Traders on the floor of the Tokyo Stock Exchange. The ability of investors today to buy and sell on an exchange somewhere in the world around the clock has helped to undercut national governments' control of economic activity.

country would, for instance, limit the importing of certain goods such as automobiles or trucks, thereby protecting domestic industries manufacturing those goods, on the grounds that the industries would need to be healthy if the country were to go to war. Domestically, the health of the automobile industry was important in gaining political support in American states like Michigan.

Such monitoring is hardly possible any longer, and it may be that the loss of state control over economies is the single most important current issue of international relations, the structural issue that may impel the creation of new international mechanisms to maintain some degree of public control. In the automobile industry, for instance, countries have some residual ability to limit imports of vehicles, but since automobile components come from all over the world, distinguishing what constitutes one country's cars from what constitutes another's has become a complex and bewildering task. This phenomenon is discussed as part of the case study at the end of the chapter. Financial transactions are another example, with a stock exchange now operating somewhere in the world 24 hours a day and investors having the electronic capability to move enormous sums of money across the globe almost instantaneously. The net result of these and other trends in economics and business is that states are much less capable of regulating economic activity (where they are interested in doing so) either within their jurisdictions or between themselves and other states.

A fifth change is the emergence of new centers of international power based in economic strength. The most important and obvious example is the Group of Seven (G–7) meetings, which began formally as a secret meeting among representatives of France, Britain, Germany, Italy, and the United States at New York's Plaza Hotel in 1985. (Finance ministers of these countries had been meeting occasionally since the 1970s, notably to deal with the global recession of 1975–78.) It began to expand at the Tokyo Summit of 1986, and became a public forum in 1987 with the formal addition of Canada and Japan. It has become a force to stabilize economic relations among states within the First Tier; by the early 1990s, it was reaching further afield, involving itself in such matters as coordinating economic assistance to Russia. In 1997, Russia was granted a kind of associate membership reflecting its importance in the international system, if not the strength of its economy. It became, as noted, a full member in 1998, thus necessitating the renaming of the forum as the Group of Eight (G–8).

What all those developments suggest is the growing importance of economic factors on the international political agenda, especially after the end of the Cold War. Partly this is a matter of default. With the First Tier in general political harmony, with the likelihood of great destabilization that might lead to war among First Tier countries reduced virtually to nothing, and with instability relegated to the periphery of the international system, the system has less concern with geopolitics, or traditional power politics. Instead, the new geopolitics may be "geo-economics," a term coined by analyst Edward Luttwak to suggest that future international competition will increasingly be economic in nature.

With this base in mind, we will first describe the emergence of a U.S.-controlled international economic system after World War II and its evolution into a new form no longer so strongly controlled by the United States. Next, we will examine that new form, with particular emphasis on global economic competitiveness as the new basis of international political competition, on the emergence of new international structures for defining and guiding the competition, and on the notion of interdependence. We will then discuss the role of technology in defining change and status in the system. We will conclude by analyzing the most dramatic example of change, the stateless corporation, which has come on the scene especially in the automobile and electronics industries.

The Emerging International Economic System

The international economic system has gone through at least two distinctive phases since the end of World War II. The first phase lasted until 1971. This period, under the aegis of an international agreement that created what became known as the Bretton Woods system, saw the economic recovery of all the participants in the war (including the defeated states) and the promotion of freer trade among states, in the context of an economic system managed largely by the United States. The period concluded with President Richard Nixon's August 15, 1971, announcement of the U.S. intention to renounce the gold standard.

The second phase emerged from this American change of course. As other economies became more competitive with that of the United States, this phase saw increases in interdependence and competition at the economic level, for a time accompanied by an essential political unity among First Tier states because of their geopolitical commitment to the West in the Cold War. As the Cold War ended, the new global economy emerged more conspicuously as a factor independent of traditional geopolitical constraints.

The Bretton Woods System

Western planners for the post–World War II peace had as one of their major organizing assumptions the belief that the economic warfare of the 1930s had been a major contributor to the outbreak of military conflict. That economic warfare had been fueled by a lack of monetary regulation, which resulted in wild fluctuations in the value of currencies against one another, and had taken the form of prohibitively high tariffs that effectively stifled international trade. Germany had been a particular victim of these conditions, which were believed to have contributed to the appeal of Nazism. Moreover, many U.S. officials believed that the failure of the United States, as the world's largest economy, to provide economic leadership had made matters worse.

These convictions meant that when representatives of 44 countries, under British and American leadership, convened at the tiny New Hampshire resort town of Bretton Woods in July 1944 to devise a postwar international economic order, the result was a system whose major goals were to stabilize national economies by producing reasonable guarantees of the comparative values of currencies and to promote freer trade among states, as well as to assist in the economic recovery of Europe. The first two functions were to be performed by a newly created agency known as the International Monetary Fund (IMF), which could advance credits of funds to promote trade and to bolster and thereby stabilize currencies. The third was to be performed by the International Bank for Reconstruction and Development, commonly called the World Bank, which was authorized to grant loans to assist reconstruction in Europe and later to assist development in the Third World. Parallel discussions sought to create an International Trade Organization (ITO) to promote free trade, but these failed on political grounds until recently. The General Agreement on Tariffs and Trade (GATT) was approved in

Amplification

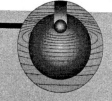

The International (World) Trade Organization

The attempt to create an organization in the field of trade parallel to the International Monetary Fund in the field of finance demonstrates some of the constancy of international and domestic politics. The original International Trade Organization was proposed in the late 1940s as a result of an American effort to stabilize and promote international trade. It failed to come into existence because of developing congressional opposition in the United States from disparate groups: Republicans who believed in high tariffs, other protectionists, liberals who considered the ITO proposal too timid, and business leaders. A Truman administration seeking a free-trade policy was thus stymied by a coalition of strange bedfellows.

When the ITO proposal was resuscitated in the early 1990s under the name World Trade Organization (WTO), as part of the Uruguay Round of negotiations on the General Agreement on Tariffs and Trade (GATT), a similar opposition emerged. Once again, a Democratic administration promoting freer trade and seeing WTO as an organization that would promote that end faced a more diverse opposition, this time composed of (according to *U.S. News and World Report*) "U.S. environmentalists, state

and local governments, protectionists, and followers of Ross Perot." These groups opposed it because of various feared effects, ranging from diluted environmental standards to the overturning of state and local laws restricting trade to the famous "great sucking sound" (that is, a massive loss of American jobs to other countries) that Perot, the billionaire political activist, warned would be the result of NAFTA.

The major difference is greater international support for the WTO than was true, for a variety of reasons, of the ITO in the 1940s. In fact, the WTO did win U.S. approval and formally came into existence in 1994. It first gained widespread public attention in 1995 when Japan threatened to have it investigate alleged American violations of GATT obligations after the United States threatened to raise tariffs on Japanese luxury cars. The dispute was settled, however, without resort to the WTO, which was still in the process of formation at the time.

Sources: Joan Edelman Spero, *The Politics of International Economic Relations* (New York: St. Martin's Press, 1985), pp. 46–51; Susan Dentzer, "Global Trade Meets James Bond." *U.S. News and World Report,* July 25, 1994, p. 45.

1947 as a more diluted version of ITO. A stronger version, the World Trade Organization (WTO), was finally approved in 1993 as part of the Uruguay Round of periodic negotiations for implementing GATT, and is discussed in the Amplification box "The International (World) Trade Organization."

The United States alone could enforce the new system, because its economy was the world's sole truly functioning major economy. The American dollar was the only hard, or fully convertible, currency: no other currency was convertible to gold and thus universally acceptable in trade. Moreover, the U.S. Treasury was the only real source of funds to finance global recovery, which the American government was willing to do to fight the appeal of communism. By 1947, it was clear that the management of the Bretton Woods system would be an American enterprise. The permanent headquarters of the IMF and the World Bank were located on the same city block in downtown Washington, DC; the American governors on both boards were, in effect, given veto power; and, in the case of the bank, it was presumed that the president would be an American.

This system proved durable and was a useful tool of American policy for some 20 years. A supply of American dollars as the unit of international trade meant stable exchange rates and facilitated greater levels of trade. At the same time, until interdependence developed among other members of what became the First Tier, the United States was essentially a hegemony (leading or paramount power) dominating the global economic system. This meant that between 1945 and the middle 1960s, the United States could and did wield the economic instrument of power to gain compliance with its policies.

This position of overwhelming U.S. strength gradually eroded. One reason for the change was the economic recovery of the First Tier, in large measure thanks to American assistance. By the middle 1960s, for instance, the Japanese economic miracle was beginning to take shape, and the European Economic Community (later called the European Community, and known since 1993 as the European Union) was helping to produce a vibrant European economy increasingly competitive with the United States. Of symbolic importance was the return to convertibility of a number of European currencies. By the beginning of the 1970s, American predominance was beginning to end, although it would continue into that decade.

American difficulties contributed to the process of erosion. The decision by President Lyndon Johnson to finance the Vietnam War and his Great Society social programs without raising taxes created the first sizable American budget deficits since World War II, which initiated a trend of declining confidence in the U.S. economy. Because of inflationary policies that devalued the dollar, the promise that the currency in circulation could be redeemed for gold was obviously empty, and by 1970, the dollar was so terribly overvalued against other currencies as to keep U.S. goods from being competitive against foreign goods (it cost too many units of foreign currency to buy enough U.S. dollars to buy American goods).

It was against this backdrop that President Nixon made the fateful decisions that ended the Bretton Woods system by abandoning an unsustainable American dominance. His decision to renounce the gold standard (to state that American dollars could no longer be converted to gold) and instead allow the dollar to "float" (have its value against other currencies set by market forces) meant that the dollar would no longer be the single currency acceptable in trade. Gradually, a series of other countries' currencies would achieve the status of hard currencies. The reign of the dollar had ended. Along with dropping the gold standard, the United States also decided to place a 10 percent surcharge on foreign goods entering the country, in what amounted to an assault on the principle of free trade. The decision was a tactical one, meant to reduce overvaluation and allow a freer flow of U.S. goods overseas.

The reaction to the U.S. announcements was gradual. Before thoroughgoing movement toward an altered system could occur, an additional stimulus was needed. That stimulus came with the oil shocks of the 1970s, when the price of petroleum soared worldwide. Because postwar recovery in Europe and Japan had been based on the assumption of cheap petroleum as an energy source, the increased prices charged by the Organization of Petroleum Exporting Countries (OPEC) created a serious problem there. In the developing

During the oil shortage of the 1970s, it was not uncommon for service stations to be forced to close because of inadequate amounts of gasoline caused by Middle East states restricting the flow of oil to drive up prices.

world, the burden was even worse, as funds to pay inflated oil prices were simply unavailable. The oil shocks caused a massive flow of resources from the First Tier to the oil-producing states (the resource-rich subtier of the Second Tier), the funds for which had to come from somewhere. The source was found through increased competition between the developed countries.

Interdependence and Competition

The American decline in the world market during the 1970s and 1980s was gradual, but it ranged over a wide spectrum of products. The Amplification box "Market-Share Fluctuations" lists 15 product areas in which the United States lost 50 percent or more of its share of the global market between 1960 and 1988. What is notable about nearly all these product areas is that the basic technologies and discoveries that underlay them all were American, yet other countries—especially Japan—were better able to market commercial applications and thus capitalize on them. The success or failure of different countries in this type of commercialization has much to do with their relative competitiveness and future economic prospects, a matter taken up later in the chapter.

How can one describe the nature of the changes since the early 1970s that produced a world economic structure so utterly different from anything that preceded it? For present purposes, we can introduce three basic observations. First, the process was technologically driven, as the countries of the First Tier hurtled through the third industrial revolution, a phenomenon its enthusiasts say was greatly aided by the privatization and deregulation of economic activity during the 1980s. Second, the result was a situation of economic tripolarity within the First Tier between the United States, Japan, and the European Union. Third, despite some exaggerated accounts of what took place, the competition was actually a restrained one, embodying some elements of cooperation and collaboration. These three circumstances help explain the development of the interdependent global economy that now exists.

The first factor, the high-technology revolution or third industrial revolution, which was introduced in the last chapter, affected almost all aspects of life because the increases in knowledge generation and dissemination quickened the pace of change at an unprecedented and accelerating rate, as described in the Coming to Terms box "The Structure of

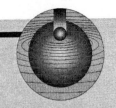

Amplification
Market-Share Fluctuations

In recent years, the health and relative standing of the American economy in the new global era have become matters of intense discussion and analysis. During the period between 1960 and 1988, the U.S. market share of the following types of products fell by over 50 percent, largely because of Japanese and other Pacific Rim competition: automobiles, cameras, stereo equipment, medical equipment, hand tools, radial tires, electric motors, food processors, microwave ovens, athletic equipment, computer chips, industrial robots, electron microscopes, machine tools, and optical equipment.

This is an impressive list, but does it indicate a permanent decline of American competitiveness? The answer is, probably not. In the early 1990s, there was a clear American resurgence in several basic areas that may signal a reversal of this trend.

The American share in automobiles was on the rise, the once nearly moribund computer chip industry revived, and American telecommunications companies rebounded greatly. Moreover, the unfolding North American Free Trade Association was intended to increase demand for American-made high-technology products.

If there are lessons in all these developments, two stand out. First, one should treat with suspicion any long-term economic projections based on "snapshots" of data at any particular point in time, because the situation is too changeable for such linear projections to be reliable. Second, the dynamism of the international economic competition is such that no state's industries dare rest on their laurels; technological breakthroughs can alter the situation quickly and dramatically.

High Technology." During the 1970s and 1980s, discoveries across the board made possible a staggering array of activities with economic consequences, ranging from computer-integrated manufacturing processes to genetic engineering.

In addition to the impact that such discoveries have for the quality of the human experience, they have obvious commercial benefits for the firms and states that master them. Breakthroughs in waste management, for instance, have enormous economic potential for cleaning up environmental disasters, and preeminence in this area for the United States was an early priority of the Clinton administration. The transportation revolution is on the verge of generating technology capable of producing a very fast commercial cargo ship that could revolutionize international trade—especially among the states of the Pacific Rim, whose trade is almost entirely ship-borne. The country that is first to master production of this technology will obviously have a huge and lucrative market. The list of advances in various fields is virtually endless, with new possibilities occurring all the time.

According to enthusiasts for technology like Tom Forester, the high-technology revolution was greatly aided by policies of privatization and deregulation pursued by the major industrial democracies during the 1980s. The removal of governmental restrictions allegedly encouraged a high level of entrepreneurial activity, in places like Silicon Valley in California and the Route 128 complex around Boston, Massachusetts, that accelerated the rate and heightened the quality of technological change. Whatever the validity of this argument, the

Coming to Terms

The Structure of High Technology

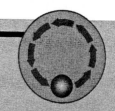

The high-technology revolution can be thought of as a reciprocal relationship between three elements:

The first element, knowledge generation, refers to the creation of knowledge through technology that rapidly processes and analyzes massive amounts of complex information. The revolution in this area was the invention of the computer chip, which allowed for the tremendous expansion of computing capability. Digitization (the technique of reducing all data to intervals of zero and one) enables information to be processed by rapid electronic means.

The second element, knowledge transmission, refers to the instantaneous sharing of large amounts of information among scientists and technologists through telecommunications technology. This is made possible through such innovations as fiber optics, satellites, modems, facsimile machines, and the like. The result is a level and efficiency of scientific intercommunication inconceivable a decade or less ago.

The third element, derivative technologies, refers to scientific innovations resulting from knowledge generation and transmission, which in turn may feed back into the process of generating or transmitting knowledge. The application of laser technology to fiber optics as a way of increasing the speed and volume of data transmission is one example. Breakthroughs in new materials science that can dramatically decrease the amount of energy necessary for computation is another.

The three areas are thus highly interactive. Increases in computing power (the backbone of knowledge generation) make possible new telecommunications and derivative technologies; increased telecommunications capability speeds the generation of knowledge; and derivative technologies benefit from and contribute to advances in the other two.

Source: Donald M. Snow, *The Shape of the Future: The Post–Cold War World,* 2d ed. (Armonk, NY: M. E. Sharpe, 1995), pp. 65–71.

pace of technological change in recent decades has been such that governments could not keep up with it or adequately regulate its outgrowths, even if they wanted to. The science that underlies technological growth represents national assets where it occurs, and states in a competitive environment naturally are inclined toward proprietary control over that science. Science, however, is inherently international in nature, and modern technology, through devices such as modems and the Internet, allows the international distribution of scientific information beyond any effective control governments might wish to impose—presuming policies for such aims were in place (which they generally are not).

A noneconomic example may illustrate the point. When the Chinese government cracked down on the Democracy Movement in China, focusing on demonstrations held in Beijing's Tiananmen Square in the summer of 1989, one of the first things it ordered was strict censorship and restriction of information, especially communications between student groups within China and groups outside China. But this policy failed. The reason was that Chinese students in the United States who supported the movement continued to distribute newsletters throughout China. Their weapon was the facsimile (fax) machine, against which the Chinese government had no defense short of shutting down the Chinese telephone system.

The second basic characteristic of change in the world economy during the 1970s and 1980s, the emergence of tripolarity among the major economic powers, was largely manifested in three respects: scientific/technological preeminence, productive capacity and adaptability, and market size and stability. Within these areas, each of the three "poles" brought special advantages and disadvantages to the competition.

The United States has the world's largest, most sophisticated scientific base and the world's largest consumer market. The EU also has a huge market, and the prospect for expansion by "widening" its membership to places such as Eastern Europe and beyond. Japan has led in the commercialization of technology, although the Japanese advantage in that area is on the wane. Conversely, structural problems (for example, chronic budget deficits and a decaying infrastructure) and lack of commercial innovations have until recently been the major American weaknesses. Nationalist barriers toward cooperation in scientific research have been a problem for the EU, while a relatively small market and weakness in basic science have been disadvantages to the Japanese.

The third basic characteristic of global economic change during this period, the generally restrained nature of the competition among states, had four prominent causes. The first was the continuing existence through the 1970s and 1980s of the Cold War. The First Tier (then First World) countries shared, through treaty obligation and common political systems and ideology, an opposition to communism and its expansion. To the extent that competitive behavior could be expected to interfere with common efforts against communist expansion, such competition tended to be avoided.

The second restraint on competition, related to the first, is that all the major poles were essentially similar in economic philosophy and political ideology. The countries involved were industrial and market-based democracies. While they may have differed in cultural detail, they shared the same basic values and supported the same world order. Moreover, they all tended to pursue policies that nurtured their economic and political interaction, if with differing degrees of enthusiasm.

A third constraint was the growing economic interdependence among the major powers. For example, investment across national borders expanded throughout the period. The Japanese invested heavily in a wide array of American businesses, in ways that often went to considerable lengths. Japanese private corporations, for instance, were the single greatest source of post-doctoral fellowships at the Massachusetts Institute of Technology (MIT) in 1990. States also became increasingly dependent on one another for products and for markets. As a result, the realization slowly arose that the prosperity of any member of the system critically depended on the economic health and prosperity of them all. There are, for example, no longer any purely national boom or bust periods; they are systemic. The recession that began in the late 1980s and continued into the early 1990s was systemic; it could not be relieved by the policies of any single state, but required international action. Whether the Asian crisis can be contained and reversed will affect global prosperity at the millennium.

The fourth restraint on competition, related to interdependence, was increasingly obvious economic internationalization, especially within the private sector. On the organizational level, multinational corporations became increasingly international in character, and firms have interpenetrated one another across national boundaries by buying stock in one another. All three of the major American automobile firms, for instance, have had significant financial and working relationships with Japanese automobile companies with which they coproduce cars (currently General Motors with Toyota and Ford with Mazda). More dramatically, Daimler-Benz and Chrysler merged in 1998 to become a single automobile giant, Daimler Chrysler.

These corporate relationships have been accompanied by the emergence of international production. At the forefront of this phenomenon were the electronic and, as discussed earlier, the automobile industry. Like cars, pieces of stereo equipment, whatever their identification by nationality or brand name, often contain components manufactured in a variety of different countries and assembled in yet another country. In many cases, one country or firm has a virtual monopoly on a particular component—the Japanese firm Canon, for instance, produces 85 percent of the world's imagers for copying machines—and this fact acts as a further restraint on competition.

Emerging International Economic Structures

A number of international institutions have emerged or are emerging as mechanisms to promote the greater extension of the global economy, both within the First Tier and between the tiers. The oldest and most established of these are European-centered: the European Union (EU) and the G–7 or G–8, which serve as models for emerging entities.

With its roots in the 1957 Treaty of Rome and its future laid out in the 1992 Maastricht Treaty, the EU is not only the oldest but also the most highly institutionalized of these structures. Despite uncertainty about implementation of the more ambitious political and security provisions of the Maastricht Treaty and about extending its membership and benefits to the formerly communist countries of Eastern Europe, the EU remains a major force and source of European economic and political leverage.

The EU is the model on which a more recent institution, the North American Free Trade Association (NAFTA), is based. Originally negotiated among its three charter members (the United States, Canada, and Mexico) in 1991, NAFTA was approved by the legislatures of each country in 1993. A complicated arrangement, it calls for a series of implementation steps over a 15-year period, at the end of which all trade barriers among the three countries are to have been removed and common economic policies are to be in place. The purposes include the promotion of trade among the member units and creation of a stronger bargaining bloc in world trade.

A unique property of NAFTA is that it extends an economic hand from the First Tier to the Second Tier, providing a mechanism by which Second Tier Mexico (and future prospective members) may move toward the greater prosperity of the First Tier members. As noted in Chapter 8, increased trade will likely reduce the debt service burden in Mexico that has kept that country in the Second Tier, possibly raising it eventually to First Tier status. NAFTA (doubtless under some other name such as the Free Trade Area of the Americas) may eventually encompass the entire Western Hemisphere and extend its benefits hemisphere-wide, a goal agreed to in principle in 1994 by all Western Hemisphere states except Cuba, a prospect raised in the Introduction.

Although receiving relatively little publicity, the Summit of the Americas meetings in Miami in 1994 and at Santiago, Chile, in 1998 that authorized negotiation of the Free Trade Area of the Americas (FTAA) have potentially revolutionary implications. The 34 participating states agreed to create a hemisphere-wide free trade zone by the year 2005;

should it come into being (negotiations are currently underway), its size would eclipse the EU and create the world's largest trading bloc, depending on the evolution of the APEC (see below).

The G–8 meetings have become institutionalized as a series of economic summits among the bigger economic powers of the First Tier, convened annually, or more often as the need arises. In addition to discussing economic issues and attempting to coordinate economic policies, G–8 has also ventured into political and security areas—for instance by sponsoring the Missile Technology Control Regime (MTCR), an attempt to prevent the proliferation of ballistic missiles to Second Tier states that is discussed in Chapter 11. The association of Russia with the group (creating the G–8 from the earlier G–7) provides a vehicle for coordinating assistance to Russia.

There have been some indications that G–8 may begin to lose focus in the absence of a common menace. Such a problem does not attach to a younger emerging institution, Asia-Pacific Economic Cooperation (APEC). Like G–8, APEC is an informal arrangement involving regular conferences, in this case among the countries of the Pacific Rim. It was instituted in 1989 at the suggestion of the Australian prime minister and has been growing in membership and visibility ever since.

APEC came into the international public eye in September 1993 when President Bill Clinton and the heads of government of most other members attended a highly publicized meeting near Seattle to discuss common economic policies. At that time the membership encompassed 17 countries—Australia, Brunei, Canada, China, Hong Kong, Indonesia, Japan, Malaysia, Mexico, New Zealand, Papua New Guinea, the Philippines, Singapore, South Korea, Taiwan, Thailand, and the United States. By the November 1994 meeting in Djakarta, Indonesia, the membership had increased to 18 with the addition of Chile. After a moratorium on new members expired at the end of 1997, Russia, Vietnam, and Peru were elected as new members in 1998.

APEC could become an extremely important institution. Its members produce 55 percent of world gross domestic product at $13 trillion (based on 1995 APEC figures), and trade among them already amounts to over $1 trillion a year (46 percent of total world trade). The addition of a South American state suggests expansive capacity for the future, especially as advances in naval transportation expand the efficiency of sea-based trade. Moreover, the Pacific Rim contains most of the world's most rapidly expanding, vibrant economies. Since most countries of near First Tier status are members of APEC, it could provide a vehicle to facilitate their admission to the First Tier. Further, APEC has the advantage of providing a forum for the interchange of views among the economic giants of the region—the United States, Japan, and China.

The declared purpose of APEC is to promote greater trade among the members. For example, the group has asked the International Monetary Fund (IMF) to study ways to increase cross-border private investment within the region, a further sign of the growing intertwining of this part of the global economy. The members agreed in principle at their 1994 meeting in Bogor, Indonesia, to remove all trade barriers between them; the so-called Bogor Declaration charges the industrialized economies with the goal of free trade and investment by the year 2010, and developing economies by 2020.

Particularly in combination, the progress of APEC and the FTAA toward their stated goals could revolutionize the structure of the global economy in ways that have hardly been considered. Should both mature, it is likely that they might formally or informally merge, since four states (the United States, Canada, Mexico, and Chile) belong or will

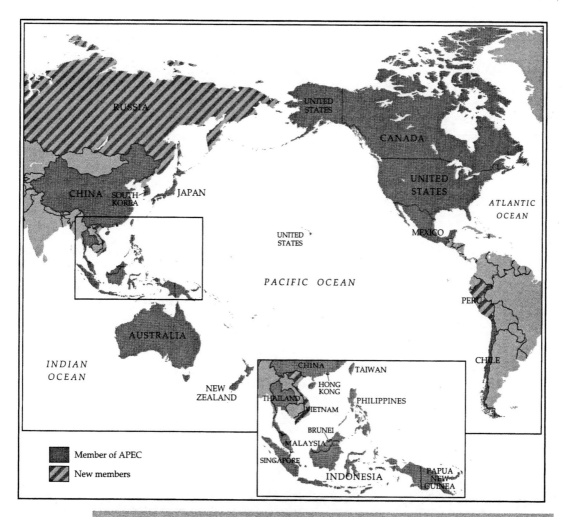

Map 9-1   **Members of Asia-Pacific Economic Cooperation**
©1996 by St. Martin's Press, Inc. From: *Contours of Power*, by Snow/Brown. Reprinted with permission of Bedford/St. Martin's Press, Inc.

likely belong to both. A free trade area encompassing both areas would capture most of the world's economic activity and would probably force the EU into some form of collaboration, thereby creating an effective global free trade condition.

Interdependence and the Global Economy

Which of the trends that began during the 1970s and 1980s remain operative in the contemporary environment? More specifically, what constraints do and do not exist on the competition for preeminence in the global economy of the 1990s?

Web Sitings: Profiling APEC

As the discussion in the text suggests, APEC is rapidly becoming a very prominent part of the globalizing economy, yet it is seldom in the public eye (about the only time it receives any publicity is at the picture-taking ceremony when the heads of state of the members conclude the annual meeting), and there is very little in the journal or scholarly literature that allows you to learn more about it. To do research in this circumstance was very difficult before there was a world wide web. If you would like more information about APEC, the place to go is the Internet. APEC can be found by "surfing," for instance typing the organization's full name into one of the search engines on the net, or by going directly to the official home page at http://www.apecsec.org.sg/. Most of the information about APEC in this chapter was obtained directly from files within the home page.

The ready answer is that most of the factors remain basically the same. Preeminence in high technology remains the benchmark of economic superpower status, the requirement for being at the top rung of the First Tier. Tripolarity remains the basic structure of the world economic system, with slight modifications. The nature of the European pole is being altered with the implementation of the Maastricht Treaty, and the implementation of NAFTA is transforming the U.S. pole into a North American pole that would be visibly strengthened by the flowering of the FTAA. The form APEC will eventually take remains conjectural, as does the future role of G–8.

Most of the restraints on competition also remain. The big difference is that the major powers no longer must maintain the same national security front; now they debate how and to what extent to aid the successor states to their old adversary. Their political and economic philosophies remain the same; interdependence has, if anything, grown, as has the internationalization of corporations and production.

These restraints are too often undervalued in the heat of debate over the emerging system. Cries of economic "warfare" are occasionally sounded by politicians and analysts alike, but they are mostly empty rhetoric. The simple fact is that interdependence is creating a global economy where everybody is in it together; as with the Three Musketeers, it is "one for all and all for one." To understand this, it is necessary to look at the meaning of interdependence and the shape of the global economy.

Interdependence

The term interdependence became a prominent part of the academic debate about the changing international system in the years after American renunciation of the gold standard and torpedoing of the Bretton Woods system. With the age of American economic dominance ended, there had to be a new way to describe the international economic and political system. Interdependence refers to the intimate connection between economics and politics at the global level and in the relationship among the states of the First Tier—the heart of IPE. Thus, interdependence describes how politics and economics combine to define the relationship of First Tier states with one another.

At its most generic level, the term means mutual economic and political dependence—that the economic and political actions of one member of the international system affect other members. This, of course, is a specific form of one of the general characteristics of a system, as was discussed in Chapter 1. To this basic idea, most IPE analysts would add the element of vulnerability—that the members of an interdependent system can consciously affect one another in negative ways that the affected parties cannot entirely control. Joan Edelman Spero, the author of a standard text in the IPE field, defines interdependence as a relationship in which "actors or events in one part of the [international economic] system have the ability to influence actors or events in another part of the system." As a consequence, "individual countries' economic policies and events are increasingly sensitive to the economic policies and events of other members."

Extending the notion of systems to the economic realm is hardly a revolutionary idea. What makes it noteworthy is that traditional analyses of international relations have often overlooked or underemphasized the economic dimension of interdependence (this oversight is the central IPE critique of the international relations scholarship generally) and the increasing importance that economic interdependence has on international politics. The notion of interdependence is also useful because it allows us to draw attention to three concepts or phenomena relevant to the contemporary international economic system: the notion of economic intertwining, the relations between the First and Second Tiers, and the movement toward intermestic politics.

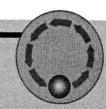

Coming to Terms

International Politics and Economics

The separation of international relations into discrete categories of international politics and economics distorts the close ties between them: much of international politics is a contest over economic values, and the state of international economics is largely the result of political processes reflecting political values and agendas. Joan Edelman Spero captures the fundamental relationship with three statements:

1. "The political system shapes the economic system", in the sense that the political system creates most of the rules under which economies operate. In the Cold War, for example, a political structure created two isolated economic systems with hardly any economic relationship between them.

2. "Political concerns often shape economic policy," because economic policies are often subservient to political interests. An example is trade policy, which may be tied to various political agendas, including promotion of human rights or other noneconomic values (as in U.S. policy toward Iraq, Cuba, or China).

3. "International economic relations are themselves political relations," in the sense that both areas have as their problem and goal the management of conflicts of interest. An example of this fundamental similarity is the use of instruments of power: forms of the economic instrument such as embargoes or trade restrictions may be used to promote geopolitical interests, and geopolitics may strongly influence the tenor of economic relations among states.

Source: Joan Edelman Spero, *The Politics of International Economic Relations,* 4th ed. (New York: St. Martin's Press, 1990).

When the idea of interdependence first entered the lexicon of international relations, it was used largely—but not exclusively—to refer to the ways in which national governments, through their economies, were becoming dependent on one another. A model was the European Coal and Steel Community (ECSC), discussed in Chapter 7, in which the steel-producing capabilities of the original members (France, West Germany, Italy, Belgium, Luxembourg, and the Netherlands) were pooled in such a way that no single member had the ability to produce steel independently of the others—and hence independently produce the weapons of war. A key idea was to make the two biggest traditional enemies, Germany and France, physically unable to wage war against the other. Implemented in 1952, the ECSC became the model for the European Union.

In the early IPE literature, the basic idea behind the ECSC was extended as a model for promoting international economic growth and reducing violent conflict in the system. As states generally became more economically dependent on one another, the hope was that political relationships would solidify and that both the desire and the ability for warfare would sharply diminish. This early vision, which liberally mixed description and prescription, gave way to a more sophisticated analysis as the international economic system became transformed in the 1970s and 1980s.

What necessitated this rethinking was recognition of what we will call economic intertwining, the intermingling of private economic concerns across national boundaries (multinational corporations), producing a more global economy in which political boundaries become less important or relevant (see Snow, *The Shape of the Future,* for a fuller discussion). Intertwining adds to the basic notion of interdependence the idea that many of the ties that link the economies of the major countries together result from private corporate and entrepreneurial activity quite outside the purview and control of national governments, as well as from governmental policies promoting greater economic ties. The implications of this phenomenon for the global economy will be taken up in the next section.

The second notion or phenomenon to which interdependence draws attention is the nature of economic relationships between the tiers. If Spero's definition is adapted to our categories, interdependence describes the relationship among the countries of the First Tier, and especially its most prominent members. At the same time, she uses the term dependence to describe the relationship between members of the First Tier and members of the Second, although the dependence obviously varies in degree according to what category of Second Tier state is involved. Moreover, Spero argues, independence described the relationship between the old First World (First Tier) and the Second (socialist or communist) World, since their economic relationships were minimal at most.

These distinctions provide a useful framework for analyzing change in the system. The absence of First Tier–Second Tier interdependence, for instance, suggests a way to discuss how those relations could, or should, evolve. Those states on the verge of moving from the Second to the First Tier (the Four Tigers) will achieve the higher status when their mastery of technology places them in a position of interdependence with those on whom they were formerly reliant. When Japanese industries depend on Korean suppliers for critical components, for instance, dependence will become interdependence. APEC, with its emphasis on the promotion of trade, may provide the engine for this conversion.

This language also suggests possible value judgments. As the *dependencia* school of thought emphasizes, the dependence of the Second Tier on the First was a result of conscious policies on the part of First Tier countries. As part of the debate over future roles, it

Much of the Second Tier remains economically dependent on the First, as is evident from the labels of British and French cigarettes and American evaporated milk at a market in the African country of Burkina. Given that dependence was deliberately encouraged during the colonial period, is the First Tier now obliged to assist the Second toward greater independence?

might be asked whether the First Tier should seek to replace dependence with interdependence systematically for all the categories of the Second Tier. This is another way to frame the alternatives, discussed in Chapter 8, of Second Tier marginalization (continued dependence) or centrality (movement toward interdependence).

Further, this dependence relationship provides a way to analyze the outcome of transition from the old Second World. A major reason for the overthrow of socialist economies was to replace independence, which produced inferiority, with participation in the world economy. The question of whether former Second World states will become part of the First Tier or remain in the Second can be rephrased as a question of whether they will achieve interdependence or fall into dependence—a determination that will vary from country to country.

The third notion or phenomenon suggested by the concept of interdependence is that of the connection between economic activity in one country and in another—such that it is difficult, if not impossible, to make meaningful distinctions between domestic and international aspects of economic policy or activity. The bruising debate over U.S. congressional approval of NAFTA was illustrative of how directly an international economic arrangement can affect individual livelihoods and suggested strongly the need for a sophisticated analysis of the impact of international economic change.

Views from Abroad

Recognizing Vietnam

The end of the Cold War was no better exempli-fied than by the decision of the United States to extend full diplomatic recognition to Vietnam (technically the Socialist Republic of Vietnam) in 1995, almost exactly 20 years after the last Americans left that country at the end of the Vietnam war. From a U.S. viewpoint, the move had several advantages. A number of Vietnamese Americans wished an easing of restrictions on their ability to travel back to the country (includ-ing some who wished to emigrate), and a num-ber of Vietnam veterans wanted to be able to return to the land over which they had fought two decades ago or more.

The largest motivation, however, was commer-cial. Following the Chinese lead, Vietnam had opened itself to outside investment, and the United States lagged in pursuing business in the coun-try. According to *Liberation* of Paris, "the U.S.

figures in a lowly 15th place" among investing countries. *The Hindu* of Madras, India, is more specific, stating that "the motivations for the U.S. to establish diplomatic relations with Viet-nam are simply the promises that the country is offering for investment." Particularly given Viet-nam's 1996 membership in the Association of Southeast Asian Nations (ASEAN), the applica-tion for which was pending when the article was written, "Vietnam is seen as a glittering prospect by other countries in Europe and Southeast Asia." A derivative hoped-for benefit of the recognition, according to *Hong Kong Standard*, is that "normalization of ties with the U.S. will provide an added incentive for the boat people stranded in Hong Kong and in camps in Southeast Asia to return home."

Source: World Press Review, September 1995, p. 5.

The evolution of G–8 may be a logical extension of the emergence of international eco-nomics as an intermestic policy area. The states between which interdependence is greatest are essentially those of the G–8 membership. Interdependence theory suggests that these states are so entwined that they cannot individually shape policy that controls their indi-vidual destinies. In that regard, G–8 could evolve into an informal policymaking body for the "domestic economy" of the member states; in other words, if the G–8 countries really represent something like a single economy, then the G–8 organization may become some-thing like its legislature.

There has always been some controversy about whether interdependence is beneficial or pernicious. This issue may be irrelevant from a practical viewpoint, because interdepen-dence exists, whatever valuation one may place upon it. Moreover, efforts either to nurture or to discourage further interdependence within the system may be largely beyond the ca-pacity of governments. Indeed, the attempt to impose controls would reverse fundamental intergovernmental efforts in areas such as trade and investment that have helped promote and create the current situation.

In large measure, interdependence and sovereignty are competing concepts: the degree to which interdependence affects the economic affairs of a state is a measure of the degree to which the state's sovereignty is diluted. If one believes that sovereignty is a pernicious influence on the international system (leading, most prominently, to war), then interdependence is good at least partly because it reduces sovereignty. On the other hand, to the extent that sovereignty is valued (as a decentralizing force or an expression of nationalist feelings, for instance), the value of increased interdependence is to be questioned, especially when national control is eroded with no clear compensating national benefits.

The phenomenon of interdependence and the questions it raises—especially whether governments can control it and how the international system is affected by it—are a direct result of the emergence of a truly global economy. Understanding the dynamics of that economy is thus crucial to comprehending international relations.

The Global Economy

The idea that the world may be moving toward something like a single, encompassing economic structure is a relatively new one. In one sense, it suggests an interdependent, if possibly hierarchical, economic system of which virtually all states are—or can become—a part. Such a globally interdependent system is not yet—and may never be—a reality. It is, however, a construct about which one can now meaningfully talk.

Several elements of what could evolve into a truly global economy are already in evidence. The first of these is the modern multinational corporation. The original MNCs, as

An IBM facility in Berlin, Germany. IBM was among the prototypes of the multinational corporation, which some observers suggest is essentially becoming the central political as well as economic unit of the future.

noted, were generally concerns based primarily in one country but doing business (selling or making things) in several other countries. The modern MNC, by way of contrast, is typically a global entity, often with subsidiaries around the world coordinated from a central headquarters located somewhere in the First Tier. Such corporations can conduct business wherever the best terms can be found; geography is decreasingly an object. The prototype, discussed in the case study at the end of the chapter, is the stateless corporation.

The development of truly international MNCs was to a great extent the result of conscious political actions, notably deregulation, both within and between states of the First Tier. In addition, modern technology has made it feasible. Before the high-technology revolution and especially its telecommunications aspect, it was meaningless to talk about truly global business operations; the mechanisms for control and coordination were unavailable or so inefficient that it was impossible to think of operating such a firm profitably. Telecommunications has overcome such barriers: it is no longer difficult to think, for instance, of a board of directors meeting with members literally on several different continents by the device of teleconferencing through satellite hookups. CNN reporters talk live to one another across continents all the time; why not leaders or managers of corporations?

A global economy would feature any number of truly global corporations conducting business around the world in ways bounded almost exclusively by the imagination. Assembling a complex product in one country from components built in several countries on multiple continents (wherever comparative advantage accrues) and then shipping the finished product around the world would have been unimaginable a decade ago; modern computing, telecommunications, and transportation advances make it a highly conceivable possibility today.

Who benefits in such an economy? Potentially, all who have something to contribute could benefit. Notions like First and Second Tier, or developed and less developed economies, could give way to a new conceptual scheme, a hierarchy of productivity, where the currently least developed countries provide contributions at the lower end of the production scale and those at the top of the scale direct and innovate. This system would be different from the current one primarily in that all would have some stake in it and in its outcomes.

Such a system would not be without its drawbacks. One is that it is a hierarchical system with no one in charge. If the system is entirely a privatized effort, where the Sonys and the IBMs are the effective political as well as economic powers of the future, then one form of sovereignty will have effectively given way to another, possibly more feudal form. Such a form will simply replicate the anarchy of the state-based system.

The role of government in such schemes has hardly begun to be addressed. For instance, a pure capitalist economic system is quintessentially Darwinian: it is a competition for "survival of the fittest," in which there is no "social safety net" for the losers. Governments have traditionally provided such a net in the form of welfare programs. What happens to a country such as Bangladesh if it turns out to have no role whatsoever in a privatized international economic system? Who takes care of the international losers?

Is the idea of such a system merely a fantasy? Certainly, such a system does not currently exist, at least partially because it could not have existed up until now. Have the conditions now come into being that would allow it to develop? Are there prototypes for such an eventuality? The international economic environment is an extremely dynamic system, where change is constant. Many in the international business community do maintain that conditions for the genesis of a "borderless economy," wherein national boundaries are irrelevant

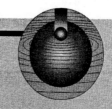

Amplification

Two Views of a Global Economy

From an international businessman:

Outmoded, nationalistic chauvinism and geocentric thinking have no place in the one-world economy...where competition will be even more intense and universal...and where a global perspective will increasingly be needed to compete and win. The global economy of the 90s approaches the world as if it were one, single market.

Source: Donald K. Peterson (Northern Telecom executive), "Globalization and Telecommunications Leadership: The Future Ain't What It Used to Be." *Vital Speeches of the Day* 56, 17 (June 15, 1990): 529.

From an academic:

The fundamental challenges posed by the age of globalization are how to make economic actors accountable to political communities and how to modernize government so it can protect the public interest in the territory it is expected to govern....Global corporations, whatever flag they fly, have outgrown national laws and national cultures, and the world has not yet begun to address the problem.

Source: Richard J. Barnet, "Reflections (on the Age of Globalization)," *New Yorker,* June 16, 1990, p. 59.

as regulators of economic activity, already exist. If one examines the pace of change in recent years and extrapolates that pace into the future, the prospect that yesterday's science fiction will be tomorrow's fact does not seem farfetched.

The motor of change in the international economy is high technology, which opens up possibilities for the future and defines the nature of future economic competition. At the same time, a prototype of the future is available in the form of the stateless corporation. These two phenomena will be taken up in the final sections of this chapter.

Downside? The Asian Crisis

The discussion to this point has been overwhelmingly positive, depicting the growing globalizing economy as a major contributor to the general prosperity of most of the 1990s. Beginning in 1997 with a series of stock market runs in major Asian financial stock markets such as Hong Kong and virtually wiping out markets in places like Indonesia and Thailand, a major economic and financial crisis seized Asia in 1998 and threatened to spread an economic Asian flu to the rest of the world. How the globalizing economy reacts to this series of setbacks will largely define the vibrancy of the system as it moves to the twenty-first century.

Although the overall dynamics are matters of debate, several underlying problems contributed to the crisis. One was overheating of a number of economies, largely caused by the influx of more foreign investment capital seeking to maximize profits than could reasonably be absorbed by the countries. A result was investment in a number of projects the economic soundness of which was questionable (empty office buildings in a number of Asian capitals are a visible sign of this practice).

The problem was exacerbated by questionable banking procedures in a number of countries. When investors began to panic in the wake of stock market downturns, they made runs on banks that had more or less systematically misused investor funds and hence lacked the reserves to meet demands. Part of the reason was a practice that has become known as "crony capitalism," where financial transactions are made out of the public eye behind closed doors on criteria other than financial soundness. This kind of practice (known as opaqueness) reflects traditional oriental practices that have come under serious question as the system attempts to react and restructure the problem.

A major fear of the crisis is its larger effects. Will the American and European economies be affected? By one measure, they cannot avoid it. As currencies in a number of Asian countries depreciated to near worthlessness, potential consumers were left with inadequate funds to buy, for instance, dollars with which to purchase American goods, thereby limiting demand. This is particularly a problem in industries such as automobiles, where global production already outstripped demand before the downturn.

A major outcome of the crisis was to recognize the structural problems of Asian economies and create demands for change. The most obvious source of difficulty was the obvious lack of transparency and openness in Asian financial practices that allowed the problems of cronyism and favoritism to evolve and erode the economies without outside scrutiny. This has led to demands for fundamental reforms, including major doses of accountability and openness from agencies such as the International Monetary Fund. Because such demands contrast with traditional practices in a number of countries, the implementation of reforms is likely to be slow and, in turn, to depress recovery from the crisis.

Technology and the Changing Economic Map

The leading role of technology has been a recurring theme throughout this book. For instance, technological deficiencies helped impel the Soviet Union into the process of change leading to its dissolution, and technological prowess is a prime indicator of First Tier status. This role will not recede in the future; if anything, it will broaden and become more prominent. High technology is and will be both the motor of change and the indicator of competitive advantage and disadvantage.

These latter concerns define the subject matter of this section. First, we will discuss the consequences of high technology. Our emphasis will be on the overall international economic impact, but the effects in such related areas as telecommunications and national security cannot be ignored. We will then look at the relationship between high-technological prowess and economic competitiveness, an area in which national efforts appear to remain relevant.

Impacts of High Technology

The impacts of high technology on international relations are complex, not yet fully understood or analyzed, and in a state of constant change. For present purposes, however, we can examine three major areas where technology has had and will have a major impact: economic status, telecommunications development, and national security.

Technology has an impact on the relative economic status of states partly because it places a premium on education. The scientific underpinning of technology is itself an economic product; and the education of young scientists is a growth industry of enormous proportions, in which the United States—thanks to possessing the best graduate education complex in the world—maintains a substantial advantage. American universities remain powerful magnets for scientific aspirants globally; the extent to which more American students are attracted into these programs will help to determine future American technological and hence economic competitiveness, as discussed in the following section. More generally, the importance of technology means that any country's economic status will depend in large part on its ability to attract and educate scientific and technical talent.

Technological capability is also vital to the efficient production of attractive products, and this is a key to the economic status and development level of modern societies. In the 20 years after World War II, much of American economic strength was based on global demand for American goods and services, which were viewed as the best in the world. After a period of perceived decline in the quality of American products, that technological superiority has been reestablished, especially in products such as high-definition television (HDTV) and other forms of electronics and telecommunications that have become the key to contemporary American economic strength. Developments in these areas will dominate not only home entertainment but also computing and knowledge generation capabilities well beyond the turn of the century.

This leads to a second point—the growing importance of telecommunications. The development of telecommunications is actually a contributing part of the high-technology revolution, in that advancements in telecommunications allow the dissemination of information around the globe in ways hitherto unimaginable. For example, 20 years ago scientists communicated with one another largely by presenting papers at conventions and other meetings and publishing those papers in journals. Today, scientists can communicate vast bodies of information instantaneously worldwide thanks to digitization of information, modems, fiber optic transmission cables, and possibly satellite links. The result is a quantum leap in scientific and technological productivity; it also means activity largely beyond the control of governments.

At the same time, telecommunications benefits from technology; for instance, fiber optic technology is one of the major outcomes of scientific research. As a result, telecommunications, computing, and entertainment are all merging into one gigantic field. When HDTV systems become economically accessible to large numbers of people, they will become part of the typical computerized workplace (replacing conventional monitors with much clearer images); serve as centers for communications activities such as teleconferences; and, through fiber optics, serve as entertainment centers from which viewers can choose among literally hundreds of program options. It is little wonder that major American-based MNCs such as AT&T and IBM are coming into competition with Japanese and other non-American electronic/communications firms for the huge market that may be available. Because of this phenomenon, telecommunications is sometimes referred to as a strategic industry: whoever is ahead in telecommunications will have a sizable advantage in technological competition generally.

Summary

Effects of Technology on National Security

1. Loss of national economic control
2. Improved crisis management
3. Loss of control of propaganda
4. Loss of control of sensitive technologies
5. The technological battlefield
6. Greater difficulty of strategic surprise and covert action

Finally, high technology affects more traditional national security concerns, often with an indirect economic impact. A list of these effects might include the following:

1. *Loss of national economic control.* As economic activity increasingly internationalizes, the ability to harness and convert national economic structures to national security ends becomes more problematical. This is the effect of interdependence most hoped for by many IPE advocates: it is now virtually unimaginable that internationalized and intertwined economies could be torn asunder and reconstituted to enable members of the First Tier to go to war with one another (even assuming they might have such a desire).

2. *Improved crisis management.* In the past, many international conflicts were allowed to fester into full-blown crises because the parties had incomplete, differing views both of the situation and of the intentions of other parties. The process leading to World War I is a classic example of failed communication, notably between Tsar Nicholas of Russia and his cousin, Kaiser Wilhelm of Germany. Neither used available means to communicate with the other and thus dampen the mounting crisis, and the media of that era were neither large nor powerful enough to force them to talk. With modern global television, such situations are more difficult to imagine. Outlets such as CNN and ITN ensure that all parties have generally the same information about situations as they begin to unfold, providing a greater ability to solve problems before they escalate.

3. *Loss of control of propaganda.* One of the prerequisites of authoritarian rule is the control of information, both of what the domestic population knows and what other societies know about the country. Modern telecommunications make it hard either to lie to or about one's country or to use the classic method of telling the domestic population one thing and the world something else. The 1989 uprising in Beijing's Tiananmen Square is a dramatic example; with television present the Chinese government could not conceal the incident, as, of course, it would have liked.

4. *Loss of control of sensitive technologies.* During the Cold War, keeping knowledge of dual-use technologies from the adversary (and sometimes from allies) was an important way in which military advantage could be secured. Although the need is not so great now that the Cold War has ended, the issue of what to share and what to try to hold close remains—albeit largely as an economic matter. Many analysts argue, for instance, that depriving other countries of cutting-edge technology is an important component of competitiveness. However, the effects of contemporary telecommunications on the international flow of science and technology make such an effort difficult.

5. *The technological battlefield.* A major "theater" of Soviet-American military confrontation was the sophistication of their arsenals, and the fear of falling behind helped motivate the Soviet military to support Mikhail Gorbachev's reforms, as noted in Chapter 6. While that motivation has disappeared, the cutback in military spending by most First Tier powers has meant they have smaller forces, whose effectiveness must be augmented by technological superiority on the battlefield, especially against more numerous but less sophisticated Second Tier forces. The Persian Gulf War illustrates the successful use of this strategy.

6. *Greater difficulty of strategic surprise and covert action.* These traditional national security tools have been especially undermined by telecommunications technology. The

Japanese navy in 1941 was able to steam undetected out of Japan's home islands to within several hundred miles of Hawaii to launch its attack on Pearl Harbor—a strategic surprise inconceivable today, given modern surveillance technologies. In general, covert actions by governments are also more difficult to accomplish without discovery than before. In 1954, for instance, the CIA helped orchestrate a covert action to overthrow the Guatemalan government of Jacobo Guzman Arbenz (because of alleged communist ties). Its tool was to plant a false story that a large armed force was approaching the capital, Guatemala City; in fact, the force numbered about 50 people on four trucks. In the absence of accurate coverage, the government panicked and fled. A president more sympathetic to American interests, Carlos Castillo Armas, assumed office. Modern television would have revealed the hoax almost immediately.

Economic Competitiveness

The need for economic competitiveness has become a political catchphrase of the 1990s. It is a classic example of an intermestic issue. Success in international competition depends, as has been noted, on domestic conditions such as the educational level of the population and the development of technology; and the results of competition are felt at home in terms of jobs, prosperity, and the like. Manifestations of national competitiveness—wealth and economic well-being—are increasingly replacing military measures as the symbols of international status. Economic policies such as those governing terms and balances of trade are among the most divisive issues affecting the relations among the top layer of First Tier states.

The Young Commission, established by the Reagan administration, provided a working and workable definition of competitiveness as "the degree to which a nation can, under

Modern telecommunications technology has made it much harder for governments to carry out covert actions, such as the CIA's orchestration of a 1954 coup that overthrew Guatemala's President Jacobo Guzman Arbenz, who was believed to have communist ties, and replaced him with Carlos Castillo Armas.

free and fair market conditions, produce goods and services that meet the test of international markets while simultaneously maintaining or expanding the real incomes of its citizens." There are two major concepts embedded in this definition. The first involves the rules of the game within which it is said that competition should occur. Reflecting classic capitalist economic thinking, these rules are that "free and fair market conditions" must prevail. Freedom refers to the absence of artificial barriers to entry of a country's goods and services into a market, and fairness refers to equity in the treatment of foreign and domestic goods and services.

The imposition of tariffs (unit taxes on imports) or quotas (limits on how many units can be imported) and the practice of dumping (selling goods in foreign markets at prices below those in domestic markets, including selling at prices below the cost of production) are all examples of restrictions on international trade. For competition to be based solely on the comparative merits of one country's goods and services versus another's (so-called comparative advantage), all of these restrictions should be removed. That was the official goal of the General Agreement on Tariffs and Trade (GATT), the international arrangement in which all major countries participate and which succeeded in lowering most tariffs in the Uruguay Round of discussions in December 1993. Implementing a global free trade environment is the institutional goal of the WTO.

Agreement on across-the-board elimination of restraints on trade has nevertheless remained elusive, so that rules of the game acceptable to all (free and fair) are not yet in place. The agreement in principle among the APEC members at their 1994 Bogor meeting to eliminate all trade restrictions by 2020 is a regional first step in that direction, as are parallel activities in the EU and NAFTA.

The second key concept in the Young Commission's definition involves the measurement of success. According to the definition, a state is competitive when it "meet[s] the test of international markets" and "maintain[s] or expand[s] the real incomes of its citizens." In one sense, this combination of criteria suggests that the international economic competition is akin to a zero-sum game, in that success is attained when one country's goods and services are bought rather than another's. In that circumstance, the "winner" can gain only at the expense of the "loser."

What such a notion fails to take into account is that the competition takes place within the context of a system of interdependence. The economies of the major states rise and fall together in significant ways. As noted, the recession of the late 1980s and early 1990s was a systemic recession. Intertwining suggests that the competition can also be conceived as a positive-sum game, where all can profit through adopting a fair and free set of rules that promote a systemic expansion of world trade from which all can benefit. Moreover, measuring winning and losing is not a simple matter in the global economy. Which country "wins," for instance, when an American decides to buy a Toyota produced in Ohio rather than a Ford built in Mexico or an Oldsmobile built somewhere in the United States?

Conceptualizing competitiveness in sheerly national terms, that is, distorts reality to some extent. The competitiveness question, rather, is about narrow fluctuations in relative positions within the First Tier or subtiers of the Second Tier or, at its most radical, about movement from one tier or subtier to another. Within that context, however, there are two side issues that have dominated the 1990s debate, especially but not exclusively within the United States.

One of these issues has to do with the government's role in promoting competitiveness and centers on the controversial question of industrial policy. As noted, in most countries of the First Tier, the 1980s were marked by privatization and minimal governmental involvement in economic activity. On the other hand, in some countries, notably Japan, government continued to intervene actively in the economy, guiding economic ventures for national ends. Accusations of lagging competitiveness in the United States caused a backlash there among those favoring governmental activism in helping the private sector to become and remain more competitive, a position associated with a vigorous national industrial policy.

The other side issue has to do with national infrastructures, of which educational opportunity and attainment are the most important. Since future success will go to those who continue to master high technology, the argument goes, the countries that produce the most and best scientists and engineers will likely be most competitive. Critics in the American

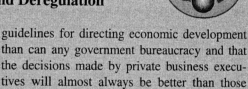

Coming to Terms
Industrial Policy Versus Privatization and Deregulation

Whether, or to what extent, national governments should involve themselves in the private sector has for some time been a highly charged political issue, basically separating liberals from conservatives. Industrial policy, defined as "an economic strategy that calls for the national government to strengthen the competitive position of...firms through cooperation among management, labor, and the government" as well as research centers, operates from two premises. First, government is often the only institution capable of convening the major groups (labor, management, researchers) in one place to discuss areas of possible mutual interest so they can cooperate, and government research contracts may provide the necessary "grease" to get the process going. Second, this kind of intervention may be necessary to focus and direct private-sector activity in an increasingly competitive international economy.

Privatization (the conversion of government-run enterprises to private ownership) and deregulation (the removal of governmental regulations on economic activities) became the springboard for a movement toward greater private-sector autonomy during the 1980s. Its advocates argue that the marketplace provides a far better set of

guidelines for directing economic development than can any government bureaucracy and that the decisions made by private business executives will almost always be better than those made by bureaucrats.

In the American context, the 1980s was the decade of deregulation, which extended to much of the First Tier. The major exception was Japan, where the Ministry of Industry and Trade (MITI) was quite successful in its traditional sponsorship of industrial policy, as noted in the text. In the United States, the election of a Democratic President in 1992 added a spirited advocacy of free trade to the mix. Moreover, it happened at a time when MITI was under attack in Japan for its failure to anticipate a number of emerging technologies, including digitized high-definition television (which was developed in the United States without government prompting), adding to the allure of governmental "hands-off" policies. By 1998, the industrial policy concept had largely fallen into disrepute.

Source of definitions: Jack C. Plano and Milton Greenberg, *The American Political Dictionary*, 9th ed. New York: Harcourt Brace Jovanovich, 1993, pp. 429, 436.

debate point to wretched scores on standardized science and mathematics tests by American students compared with those of other national groups as evidence of a competitiveness malaise.

Case Study: *The Stateless Corporation*

Very few phenomena capture the dynamics of change in the international political economy better than the emergence of the stateless corporation (SC). Outgrowths of the multinational corporations that began to appear in the 1960s, the SCs are largely the products of the 1980s and 1990s. They encapsulate the trends we have discussed: they transcend national boundaries, which have little meaning for their activities; their existence and expansion have been made possible by the high-technology revolution, and especially the telecommunications and transportation revolutions. Moreover, they are a leading force in the economic interdependence that has produced an evolving global economy.

The stateless corporations are such a rapidly developing phenomenon that it is difficult to capture them in a verbal "snapshot." We will try to do so, however, by offering a definition and description followed by some examples. The global automobile industry will be examined as an area where the SC is rapidly emerging. Finally, we will conclude with a brief discussion of the political implications of the phenomena of which the SC is a defining example.

What Is a Stateless Corporation?

A stateless corporation can be defined as a business enterprise so international in ownership, management, workforce, product composition, and areas of operation that it is effectively impossible to identify it with any single state. SCs transcend the traditional MNCs, which often share many of their characteristics but are still identifiably grounded in one country; they are truly international rather than merely multinational. Their impact, which is maximized because they are among the largest and most important corporations in the world, adds dramatically to the internationalization of the global economy.

Most of the more prominent SCs began as MNCs and have gradually transformed themselves as they became more and more involved in foreign countries in which they do business. One way they have done so is by buying into foreign firms, thereby internationalizing their workforce and management. The SCs often promote these acquired employees and integrate them into the corporate structure. Japanese automobile companies engaged in joint ventures in the United States, such as the joint General Motors–Toyota operation in Fremont, California, are primary examples. Many argue that the operationalization of the merger between Daimler-Benz and the Chrysler Corporation will be a model for the next century.

As telecommunications, transportation, and other capabilities expand, the production systems become more global as well. As noted earlier, one of the difficulties that the U.S. government has in determining the national origin of automobiles—how to define an "American" car—is that the typical automobile is made up of parts manufactured by companies all over the world and owned by corporations that are not necessarily based in the country in which the part is manufactured. In fact, the automobile is an ideal example of statelessness in production.

The Stateless Automobile?

The production and sale of automobiles, once an American redoubt, has come to be a major symbol both of the global economic competition and, at least until fairly recently, of American decline in the world economy. A quarter century ago the "Big Three" American auto makers (General Motors, Ford, and Chrysler) sat atop the automotive world as the symbols of American productive superiority. Japanese cars were viewed as little more than tinny challengers to the cult of the Volkswagen Beetle. How times change!

One can think of the global automotive industry as having gone through two distinct phases since 1970. The first, during the 1970s, was one of challenge to American dominance, especially in the American market itself. The major challengers were Japanese, first at the cheaper end of the product spectrum and gradually moving upward to the luxury end. In the process, American and European shares of markets gradually declined, and protectionist sentiment (much stronger in Europe) arose against the Japanese.

The second, and ongoing, phase in automobile production since 1970 has been the gradual internationalization of the industry, a process that began in the 1980s and continued into the 1990s, manifesting itself in three different ways. First, the automotive companies have bought into one another's stock, hence internationalizing ownership. The interpenetration of American and Japanese ownership (GM-Toyota, Ford-Mazda) has already been noted. U.S.-European examples include Jaguar, which is owned totally by Ford, and Swedish Saab, now completely owned by General Motors.

Internationalization has also manifested itself in the joint development and production of whole automobiles by manufacturers in different countries. The most dramatic instances of this are between American and Japanese auto makers. The Toyota Corolla and GM's Geo (now Chevrolet) Prizm are essentially the same car, manufactured on the same California assembly line but given different external features to make them appear different. The Ford Probe and Mazda MX–6 likewise differed only in external appearance, as do the

Since 1993 the Toyota Corolla and General Motors Geo (Chevrolet) Prizm have been essentially the same car, each produced on this assembly line in Fremont, California, but given different external features and a different brand label. The joint venture, known as New United Motor, is among the most dramatic examples of the internationalization of industrial production.

Ford Explorer and Mazda Navajo. Through the 1994 model year, Chrysler's Eagle Talon and Plymouth Laser rolled off the same assembly line as the Mitsubishi Eclipse, with only different decals applied at the end of the line to distinguish them. In addition, Toyota and British Rover combined to design the Sterling, built in Britain in a factory designed to Japanese specifications.

The third manifestation of internationalization is in the manufacturing and assembly of components. The typical automobile built today is made up of components from any number of countries. Because of this, for instance, the U.S. government's criterion for calling a car American is that a minimum percentage (75 percent) of its components be manufactured in the United States, not that the brand name or place of assembly be American. Thus, a 1993 Mazda 626 built in Japan is considered American, because of the source of most of its components, whereas a Toyota Camry built in Ohio is considered a foreign car, because the total of all Camrys sold in the United States (some built in Japan, some in the United States) had less than 75 percent American-made parts.

As mentioned, there is also the question of where automobiles are assembled. Chrysler, for instance, accomplished "the renaissance of the American automobile"—its advertising theme for its models introduced in 1993—by assembling its LH series cars in Canada from parts manufactured in numerous countries. Ford produces automobiles in Mexico (the Mercury Tracer and Marquis and the Ford Crown Victoria), and the Dodge Colt is produced exclusively in Japan, where its clone is the Mitsubishi Mirage.

Political Implications

The dynamics of internationalization we have described have strong potential political implications with which both practitioners and theoreticians within the IPE community are only beginning to come to grips. Overall, the result is an international economic system so intermestic as to make specification of separate domestic and international elements almost impossible.

With this in mind, we can tentatively describe a number of ways in which economic change linked to phenomena such as technological advances and how the rise of stateless corporations is having an impact on political structures and functioning. It must be recognized that this list is suggestive rather than exhaustive.

Summary ━━━━━━━━━━━━━━━━━━━━━━━━━━━━━━━━━━━

Political Implications of Economic Internationalization

1. Its pace is outrunning state regulatory abilities.
2. National sovereignty is being diluted.
3. National control of technology and economic resources is eroding.
4. Economic nationalism is becoming less possible.
5. New actors like MNCs and SCs are effectively beyond state control.
6. Public involvement will require economic units coterminous with international activity.
7. These trends will continue and accelerate.

1. The pace of economic change is outrunning the ability of national decision structures. The high-technology revolution and its international economic artifacts are very new phenomena, and ones with which national governments are only beginning to deal. It is axiomatic that governmental regulation of science and technology will always lag behind innovation and change: you cannot foresee and regulate conditions that do not exist and cannot be predicted. The pace of recent change in private enterprise of which the SCs are a cutting edge is so rapid that national political structures are simply being overwhelmed. The laissez-faire attitude of major governments toward economic activity in the 1980s served to widen this gap, in effect creating the atmosphere in which the SCs came into existence.

2. In economic terms, national sovereignty means less than before. People in the private sector have noted this simple reality for some time, and have been quite frank in stating the irrelevance of national authority in economic activity. This may mean that government-to-government economic negotiations could become little more than sideshows to negotiations within and among the MNCs and SCs.

3. National control of technology, the flow of monetary resources, and hence economic activity is eroding. The economic instrument of power is often pointed to as the replacement, in international relations, for military might; and economic incentives may, indeed, assume increasing importance in the post–Cold War world. But if governments decreasingly control the economic bases within their countries, how usable is the economic instrument? If the process of assisting the development of the successor states of the Soviet Union is any indication, achieving this goal will require resources of significant magnitude from private investment funds rather than intergovernmental grants, whose availability must compete with domestic priorities.

4. The practice of economic nationalism is becoming less and less possible. Decreased national control of economic activity makes the use of tariffs and other restrictive economic practices by one state against others more difficult to engage in. This reality reinforces the assertion by IPE advocates that interdependence can lead to more peaceful international relations. It contradicts the notion that economic "warfare" will be conducted between the major powers; the economic "bullets" are simply unavailable.

5. The new actors, notably the MNCs and SCs, are essentially beyond effective state regulation. This can, of course, be overstated. These businesses do pay taxes in the countries in which they operate and where they are headquartered, are subject to antitrust and other forms of regulation, and must comply with quality standards in the products they produce and sell. At the same time, international commercial law and enforcement regulations dealing with the increasingly numerous transactions they undertake across national borders are much less developed.

6. Public involvement in regulating and influencing the new economic structures will require economic bodies coterminous with international activity. If governments cannot effectively regulate economic activity in accord with some notion of public interest, it is because those interests sprawl beyond the jurisdictions of individual states. One does not have to adopt a Marxist dialectic approach to suggest that new structures representing broader jurisdictions will have to emerge and, through intergovernmental agreements, develop regulatory mechanisms. G–7 is already attempting to perform some of these functions among its membership, and the same dynamic may extend to APEC as well. As the global economy becomes broader in its reach, wider forms of control will likely have to evolve as well.

7. These trends will continue and will accelerate. There is no reason to assume or conclude that the high-technology motor of economic change, or structural consequences like
the SC, have reached any developmental plateau or begun to decline in importance. Forms
and types of economic activity inconceivable a decade ago are commonplace. The changes
are geometric in progression; adaptation, especially by governments, has been arithmetic
at best. If one views the trends as good, one can expect times to get better. If one views
them unfavorably, it will seem that the worst is yet to come.

The Changing Contours of the Global Economy

The great global economic expansion of the "go-go" 1990s created an atmosphere of optimism that was heady wine for many caught up in it. Those relatively sanguine analysts
who reminded us that business "cycles" are indeed cyclical were widely derided for their
pessimism by those who extolled globalization and speculated that possibly the business
cycle had been overcome and supplanted by a condition of virtually perpetual prosperity.

The events in Asia and Russia in 1997 and 1998 vindicated the pessimists. The widely
held view that international economic affairs were a positive-sum game where everyone
could gain was replaced, in some quarters, with the image of negative-sum games where
all or most were losers coming to the fore. As the bottom fell out on East Asian economies
like Indonesia and Thailand, threatened countries like Malaysia, and even sent tremors
through a Japanese economy in recession for the first time in decades, there was increasing
talk of the Asian economic flu spreading across the Pacific and infesting the Western
Hemisphere. The virtual collapse of the Soviet economy under the weight of uncollected
taxes to finance government raised concerns of a return of Russia to its authoritarian past.

Just as the optimists were probably too expansive about the good times, probably the pessimists overplay the bad times as well. Will the economic woes of Asia result in a long decline,
or will they instead spawn the kinds of reforms that will align traditional Asian values and
practices with the principles of western capitalism? Likewise, will the crisis in Russia result in
long-term chaos where the Russian people reach a Faustian bargain with their past, or will it
spur real economic reform that will turn things around? The answers to these questions will
help define how the global economy moves smoothly or lurches toward the new millennium.

Review

This chapter provided an overview of the international political economy. In the process, the following points were made:

1. The international economy, in its economic and its political influences, is becoming increasingly
   important to understanding international relations. Among other areas, it has an impact on how
   power is conceptualized and used and on the limits of effective national sovereignty.

2. Following World War II, the Bretton Woods system stabilized the international economic system.
   After the United States renounced the gold standard in 1971, the system became more fluid.

3. A new global economy is emerging, marked by growing interdependence between national
   economies and by the increased impact of structures like the European Union, the North American

Free Trade Association, the Group of Seven and Group of Eight, and Asia-Pacific Economic Co-operation, all of which transcend national boundaries. This economy is also characterized by the influence of multinational corporations and of their new outgrowth, the stateless corporations.

4. A major motor of the global economy is the competitiveness of national economies. At the root of competitiveness is high technology. States that lead in the development and application of high technology have significant economic and national security advantages.

5. An important new phenomenon is the stateless corporation, a business organization so international in ownership, management, workforce, and products that it cannot effectively be associated with any single state. The development of stateless corporations has particularly important implications for national politics, because these corporations increasingly find national boundaries and governments irrelevant to their concerns.

Suggested Readings

Bergsten, C. Fred. "APEC and World Trade." *Foreign Affairs* 73, 3 (May/June 1994): 20–26.

—. "The World Economy after the Cold War." *Foreign Affairs* 69, 3 (summer 1990): 96–112.

Burton, Daniel F., Jr. "High-Technology Competitiveness." *Foreign Policy* 92 (fall 1993): 117–32.

Finkelstein, Joseph, Jr., ed. *Windows on a New World: The Third Industrial Revolution.* Westport, CT: Greenwood Press, 1989.

Forester, Tom. *High-Tech Society: The Story of the Information Technology Revolution.* Oxford, UK: Basil Blackwell, 1987.

Holstein, William J. "The Stateless Corporation." *Business Week,* May 14, 1990: 98–105.

Inman, B. R., and Daniel F. Burton Jr. "Technology and Competitiveness: The New Policy Frontier." *Foreign Affairs* 69, 2 (spring 1990): 116–34.

Keohane, Robert O., and Joseph S. Nye, Jr. *Power and Interdependence: World Politics in Transition,* 2d ed. Glenview, IL: Scott Foresman/Little, Brown, 1989.

—. "Power and Interdependence in the Information Age." *Foreign Affairs* 77, no. 5 (September/October 1998): 81–94.

Krugman, Paul. "Competitiveness: A Dangerous Obsession." *Foreign Affairs* 73, 2 (March/April 1994): 28–44.

LaPalombara, Joseph. "International Firms and National Governments: Some Dilemmas." *Washington Quarterly* 17, 2 (spring 1994): 89–99.

Luttwak, Edward. "From Geopolitics to Geo-economics: Logic of Conflict, Grammar of Commerce." *National Interest* 20 (summer 1990): 17–24.

Malmgren, Harald M. "Technological Challenges to National Economic Policies of the West." *Washington Quarterly* 10, 2 (spring 1987): 21–33.

Ohmae, Kemichi. "Beyond Fiction to Fact: The Borderless Economy." *New Perspectives Quarterly* 7, 2 (spring 1990): 20–21.

Reich, Robert B. "The Quiet Path to Economic Preeminence." *Scientific American* 261, 4 (October 1989): 41–47.

Snow, Donald M. *The Shape of the Future: World Politics in the New Century,* 3d ed. Armonk, NY: M. E. Sharpe, 1999.

Spero, Joan Edelman. *The Politics of International Economic Relations,* 4th ed. New York: St. Martin's Press, 1990.

Sullivan, John D. "Democracy and Global Economic Growth." *Washington Quarterly* 15, 2 (spring 1992): 175–86.

Wriston, Walter B. "Technology and Sovereignty." *Foreign Affairs* 67, 2 (winter 1988/89): 63–75.

Young, John A. *Global Competition: The New Reality.* Washington, DC: The Report of the President's Commission on Industrial Competitiveness, 1985.

The New Agenda: Transnational Issues

PREVIEW

This chapter focuses on an emerging array of transnational issues, a topic that has become increasingly prominent in international relations in recent years. Three of these issues will be examined in detail: human rights, population control, and environmental protection. Each issue has a significant First Tier–Second Tier component to it, with the policy preferences of First Tier countries frequently opposed to those of the numerically greater Second Tier. The chapter concludes with a detailed case study of the 1992 Earth Summit held under UN auspices in Rio de Janeiro, Brazil.

KEY CONCEPTS

transnational issues
Amnesty International
Convention on the Prevention and
   Punishment of the Crime of Genocide
Universal Declaration of Human Rights
Bangkok Declaration
population explosion

greenhouse effect
global warming
Montreal Treaty
Earth Summit
sustainable development
G–77

OUTLINE

As the twenty-first century approaches, the lands and peoples of the world increasingly find themselves bound together in a web of complex interdependence. Produced by technological advances in manufacturing, communications, and transportation, the growing reality of interdependence means that progressively fewer policy domains are now regarded as being purely domestic in nature, and progressively more issues are understood to affect and to be affected by events outside a state's borders. In an age of growing global interconnectedness, a host of transnational issues are rising to the top of the global agenda. Defined as issues that transcend international borders in ways over which governments of individual states have little control, transnational issues are coming to be recognized as central to the well-being of people in diverse locales.

That well-being, in turn, is increasingly understood as being less divisible than in the past. Environmental protection, for example, is an issue that lies beyond the competence or the responsibility of any one state. Acid rain originating in the United States may kill marine life in Canada, while the destruction of Malaysia's carbon dioxide—absorbing tropical forests may contribute to the global problem of altered climate patterns. Similarly, the security of all states seems to be enhanced by the spread of democratic practices, which in turn both depend on and enhance the protection of elemental human rights.

In this chapter, we will look at some of the principal transnational issues of our time. We begin with the promotion of human rights, then turn to population explosion and the global environmental crisis, and conclude with a case study of the 1992 Rio de Janeiro Earth Summit.

Human Rights

The Emergence of Human Rights as a Transnational Issue

Since the dawn of history, the wishes of ordinary citizens have been regarded as secondary to the claims of political rulers. The concept of *raison d'état,* or the requirements of the state, was invoked to justify the supremacy of the rights of rulers over those of their subjects. While benign rulers used their exalted authority to pursue the common good, at least as they defined it, others have arbitrarily imprisoned, tortured, and murdered their opponents or critics and even slaughtered entire ethnic and religious groups. This harsh imposition of the rulers' will upon their subjects has been the dark consequence of the centuries-old doctrine of the priority of the state over its people.

The idea that individuals possess certain inherent rights that their rulers cannot violate is a comparatively recent one. Throughout most of recorded history, challenges to rulers arose from such things as personal rivalries, mass discontent over economic conditions, or rebellion against unpopular wars. Only within the past two centuries have notions of individual freedom and inherent natural rights entered the realm of mass political belief, and ordinary people rebelled because of a shared sense that these rights were being violated. Today the power of the ideal of human rights is such that millions of people around the world are now willing—on their own behalf and that of others—to challenge practices that in earlier times would have been passively accepted as simply "the way things have always been."

Amplification

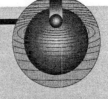

When Culture and Human Rights Collide

For centuries, hundreds of African tribes—both in Islamic North Africa and in sub-Saharan Black Africa—have practiced an initiation ritual for young girls known as female circumcision. Intended to insure a woman's fidelity to her husband, the rite involves removing with a knife a girl's clitoris (a procedure known as a clitoridectomy), and sometimes her labia as well. Performed without anything to dull the pain, the ritual cutting is extremely painful. Its consequences, at a minimum, is to render the tribes' females unable to enjoy ordinary sexual pleasure. In more dire instances, the procedure leads to life-threatening infections and bleeding.

Archaic and cruel as it may seem to outsiders, the ritual is deeply embedded in the culture of many of Africa's peoples. It is today practiced in 28 African nations. Ninety percent of the women in Egypt, Eritrea, Mali, and northern Sudan have undergone a clitoridectomy. One hundred thirty million women worldwide have suffered genital mutilation, and an additional two million girls are forced to submit to it every year.

In recent years, numerous human rights and women's rights groups have launched a vigorous campaign to end the practice. The United Nations has named the Somalian-born model, Waris Didie, as its special ambassador on female mutilation. Recounting her own ritual clitoridectomy at the age of 5, she says, "I really didn't think I was going to survive it. I remember thinking, after they tied me down on my back flat and left me there completely hopeless, in agony, Why? What have I done to deserve such a thing?"

Other African leaders have responded to the mounting chorus of international condemnation of ritual female mutilation. G.W. Cheborian is chairman of the Elders Association, a council of clan leaders and chiefs of the Sabiny people of eastern Uganda. His grassroots efforts to end the clitoridectomy ritual and replace it with a symbolic ritual which declares a girl to be a woman without maiming her sexually earned him a special United Nations award in 1998. At the national level, eight African states have recently passed laws that make ritual female sexual mutilation illegal. However, a ritual so steeped in the cultural identity of peoples largely outside the Western tradition of rationalism and the rule of law will yield to international standards very slowly.

Thus, while the contemporary world displays many continuities with the brutalities of the past, there are also signs of the emergence of more humane standards of permissible behavior by governments toward those they govern. Many of the world's peoples continue to be vulnerable to arbitrary legal proceedings; the denial of rights of expression, worship, and property ownership; torture; slavery; and even genocide. But alongside these grim realities, something new is occurring. This change is primarily one of people's consciousness and worldview. It is thus less vivid and harder to depict graphically than other momentous changes in human affairs, such as the devastation of war or the misery of mass starvation. Yet the rise of the doctrine of human rights promises to bring about a profound change in modern international life. What begins as "merely" changes in attitude becomes a powerful engine of radical and widespread changes in human behavior.

Summary ─────────────────────────────────

Forces Promoting Human Rights

1. Publicity given by media to rights abuses
2. Efforts of prominent individuals, such as Jimmy Carter and Pope John Paul II
3. Activism by private groups, such as Amnesty International
4. U.S. promotion of Lockean ideals as part of foreign policy

Many factors have contributed to the rising international salience of human rights concerns. Among them are the attention of the modern media, the influence of several outstanding individuals, and the activism of private groups committed to advancing human rights worldwide. Another factor, which we will shortly discuss in some detail, is the movement's philosophical underpinnings in the theories of John Locke. As we explained in Chapter 7, Locke's theories have come to constitute the consensual ideology of the United States. With its rise as a world power, the United States often marshaled its vast might on behalf of global objectives that were influenced heavily by its own domestic creed.

Although descriptions of state brutality against citizens have long been reported by the traditional media, the advent of an electronic "global village" in which people throughout the world see live televised images of political persecution has given human rights issues a heightened vividness and reality for millions of people. Iraq's mistreatment of its Kurdish minority becomes more real to outsiders—and thus evokes deeper sympathy—when CNN brings live pictures of anguished Kurdish mothers and their terrified children into living rooms worldwide. Similarly, the otherwise remote protests by Chinese students in 1989 took on a sickening immediacy to millions watching around the world as television instantaneously documented their massacre by forces loyal to China's communist rulers. From the standpoint of oppressed people themselves, radio and television reports of freedom abroad and oppression at home—reports that authoritarian governments are increasingly unable to control—have helped to bring about the changes in mass consciousness that were mentioned earlier.

Individual leaders have also done much to spur the world's awareness of human rights. U.S. President Jimmy Carter won the admiration of oppressed people, particularly those in Second Tier countries, for his elevation of human rights to the top of the U.S. foreign policy agenda. As he notes in his memoir *Keeping Faith,* "whenever I met with the leader of a government which had been accused of wronging its own people, the subject of human rights was near the top of my agenda....At least they were confronting a question they had not been forced to address before." Pope John Paul II electrified the people of his native Poland during visits there in 1979 and 1983. In rallying behind his call for religious freedom, the people began to sense the sheer strength of their numbers. Their escalating demands for freedom sped the demise of Poland's communist system in 1989.

A third influence in moving human rights to the top of the international agenda has been nongovernmental groups such as Human Rights Watch and Amnesty International, which

The cause of human rights in Eastern Europe took on new life when a Polish cardinal was elected pope in 1978. Visiting his native country the next year, Pope John Paul II set off a wave of popular enthusiasm with his call for religious freedom; 10 years later Poland became the first Eastern European country to abandon communism.

are dedicated to spreading awareness of rights abuses. Amnesty International, the best-known group, helps to keep the world's attention on human rights through its annual, country-by-country report on abuses. Careful research, plus the organization's considerable public relations skills, makes the report an influential document whose findings are widely reported by the world's media.

Because of this attention from the media, individual leaders, and organized groups, human rights issues seem certain to remain a central concern in future international relations. As mentioned earlier, another major cause of their rise to prominence has been their promotion by the world's most powerful state, whose ideology they represent. For both of these reasons, therefore, we need to explore more fully the philosophical underpinnings of contemporary human rights debates. That understanding, in turn, will help explain why some Second Tier officials insist that there is no such thing as a universal standard for human rights and that current human rights doctrines and policies are cultural reflections of the West's political and economic supremacy in recent centuries.

America's Lockean ideals of individual liberty, equal opportunity, economic freedom, and limited government are reflected in the country's two founding documents: the Declaration of Independence and the Constitution. Thomas Jefferson, the author of the Declaration, had read Locke's *Second Treatise on Government* and virtually lifted some of its key passages to justify the American colonists' bid for independence from Britain. Locke's theory that natural rights take precedence over the artificial creation of government was captured in the Declaration's ringing assertion that "all men are created equal, that they are endowed by their creator with certain unalienable rights, that among these are life, liberty, and the pursuit of happiness—That to secure these rights, governments are instituted among men, deriving their just powers from the consent of the governed."

No one could have known in 1776 that Jefferson's words, drawn from an obscure philosopher to justify the independence of an assortment of remote and backward colonies, would two centuries later embolden ordinary people around the globe to stand up to violators of their "unalienable rights." The spirit of the Declaration of Independence was given practical expression in the new country's Constitution, particularly its Bill of Rights, which specified then radical boundaries of individual freedom that government could not violate.

If a belief in individual freedom created America, it is little exaggeration to say that America shared in the creation of the global standard of human rights. As the first modern democratic society, the United States inspired countless social movements against oppressive regimes, the first and perhaps most dramatic being the French Revolution. We do not mean to suggest that the United States alone has promoted global human rights, nor that its behavior has always been consistent with its own ideals. Among other countries, Sweden, Canada, Austria, and Switzerland, to name a few, have been consistently active since World War II in promoting an international awareness of human rights abuses. As for U.S. inconsistency, during the Cold War the United States often actively supported highly repressive regimes on the grounds that doing so served the "greater cause" of containing the Soviet Union and communism. In the 1960s and 1970s, for example, U.S. support for the Shah of Iran grew steadily even as his treatment of dissidents in his strategically located country grew ever more brutal. Similarly, the United States participated in the overthrow of over a half-dozen democratically elected governments in the Second Tier on the grounds that they were veering intolerably far to the political left. However, despite the important role played by other states and the blemishes on the U.S. record, it remains the case that the United States has played some part in the global advancement of human rights.

Summary ——————————————————————

Six Core UN Human Rights Documents

1. Charter of the United Nations
2. Convention on the Prevention and Punishment of the Crime of Genocide
3. Universal Declaration of Human Rights
4. International Convention on the Elimination of All Forms of Racial Discrimination
5. International Covenant on Economic, Social, and Cultural Rights
6. International Covenant on Civil and Political Rights

Turning Rights into Rules

Efforts to establish a formal body of international human rights have intensified since World War II. In some ways, the war itself served as a catalyst for the postwar emphasis on human rights. The U.S.-led Allied powers fought the German-Italian-Japanese Axis not only out of self-preservation, but also in the name of freedom, a goal spelled out most famously in Franklin Roosevelt and Winston Churchill's Atlantic Charter. Once the fighting ended in 1945, the revelation of Hitler's campaign of genocide against the Jews intensified the broad desire to rebuild a more humane world atop the ashes of the old.

In June 1945, representatives of 51 countries assembled in San Francisco to sign the Charter of the United Nations. In doing so, they—and the nearly 150 states that have since joined the UN—affirmed their "faith in fundamental human rights [and] in the dignity and worth of the human person." Thus, as Jimmy Carter would argue three decades later, all member states must be held accountable for its human rights practices because "all signatories of the United Nations Charter have pledged themselves to observe and to respect basic human rights."

Building on the foundation provided by the UN Charter are five other key documents that together with the charter constitute the heart of the international human rights regime. The first was the Convention on the Prevention and Punishment of the Crime of Genocide, adopted by the General Assembly in 1948 as a direct result of the international revulsion toward Nazi Germany's systematic extermination of Jews. The Convention establishes legal mechanisms for punishing those guilty of acts "committed with intent to destroy in whole or in part, a national, ethnic, racial or religious group." The United States did not ratify the Convention until 1988 because of congressional concern that the document's requirement of automatic jurisdiction by the World Court on genocide cases could undermine U.S. national sovereignty.

Also in 1948, the General Assembly adopted the Universal Declaration of Human Rights, a major milestone in the emergence of an international set of norms protecting the rights of ordinary citizens against the coercive capabilities of states. The Declaration stipulates a broad array of freedoms that are declared to be the inherent rights of every person. They include the right to life, to due process of law, and to freedom of thought and worship; the right not to be tortured or enslaved; and "the right to a standard of living adequate for the health and well-being of himself and his family." Critics have charged that the Declaration is so sweeping that it can be made to mean as much, or as little, as a particular interpreter wants it to. But its defenders hail it as constituting a new and universal standard for evaluating the performance of states.

The remaining three pillars of the international human rights regime are a series of treaties approved by the General Assembly in the 1960s: the International Convention on the Elimination of All Forms of Racial Discrimination; the International Covenant on Economic, Social, and Cultural Rights; and the International Covenant on Civil and Political Rights. In some ways the UN's principal convention on human rights, the Covenant on Economic, Social, and Cultural Rights was passed by the General Assembly unanimously in 1966. Although the United States was a leader in drafting the Covenant, it did not sign the document until 1977, after Carter became President. For complex reasons, it then took another 15 years for the U.S. Congress to ratify the Covenant. The delay was due principally to congressional sentiment that the U.S. Constitution, particularly its Bill of Rights, contained stronger protections for human rights than the Covenant, thus rendering its ratification superfluous. Regardless of the legal merits of Congress's hesitation, the fact that the United States had not joined 100 other countries in ratifying a major human rights treaty proved a liability to U.S. leadership on the global promotion of human rights. That liability was finally removed by congressional action in the final months of the Bush administration.

Clearly, a substantial gap exists between the soaring language of the UN documents and the everyday experience of millions of oppressed people. But note that the international human rights regime has come into being only since World War II. Even though much work remains to be done to close the gap between the rules and the reality, the very existence of international human rights norms represents an important step.

Unresolved Issues

Among the human rights issues unresolved by the international system, two fundamental issues in particular stand out. The first is the absence of reliable enforcement mechanisms, a problem that human rights standards share with other evolving international norms. The second is disagreement over whether there is indeed a single, universally applicable standard of human rights; this debate often pits the First Tier against much of the Second Tier.

As we will discuss in Chapter 13, international law often founders on the fact that there is no international police force to corral offenders. The 1948 Universal Declaration of Human Rights was adopted only by the UN General Assembly; it is not a treaty legally binding on its signatories. As noted above, four legally binding human rights treaties entered into effect in the 1970s; but again, in the absence of a global police force, violators need not fear the collective wrath of the global community.

That leaves national and multilateral means of enforcement, which are better than nothing but can be—or are—applied only selectively. Donors such as the World Bank are now insisting on progress toward democracy and human rights as conditions for granting development assistance, but this means little to the repressive but oil-rich governments of states like Kuwait, which do not need foreign aid. Unilateral efforts can be of help, but sometimes they are held hostage to other political agendas. The United States has been generous in granting political asylum to refugees from communist Cuba, for example, but has been much less hospitable to those who fear persecution by authoritarian noncommunist regimes elsewhere.

The issue of disagreements over the universality and the nature of human rights was cast into bold relief in 1993 when the UN held a two-week conference in Vienna on human rights issues, the first global meeting in 25 years devoted exclusively to that topic. In preparation for the June event, regional meetings were held in Thailand, Tunisia, and Costa Rica from Asian, African, and Latin American and Caribbean countries, respectively. What emerged from these regional meetings were declarations arguing that different cultures create different concepts of rights and thus should not be held to a single, universal standard. Some Second Tier leaders argued that the Universal Declaration of Human Rights was merely a cultural expression of the First Tier states that had the greatest role in its creation. In 1948, they noted, most Asian and African countries were still European colonies and thus were excluded from participating in the Declaration's construction.

The tone of many Second Tier governments' assault on the principle of universality was set by the Bangkok Declaration signed by 40 Asian governments. The statement argued that notions of justice and freedom are contingent upon "regional particularities and various historical, cultural and religious backgrounds." To insist on the universal applicability of human rights standards, some Asians argued, was simply one more expression of

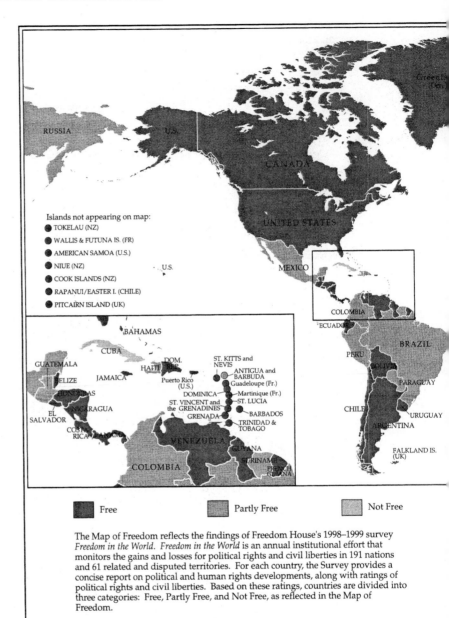

Islands not appearing on map:
- TOKELAU (NZ)
- WALLIS & FUTUNA IS. (FR)
- AMERICAN SAMOA (U.S.)
- NIUE (NZ)
- COOK ISLANDS (NZ)
- RAPANUI/EASTER I. (CHILE)
- PITCAIRN ISLAND (UK)

■ Free   ■ Partly Free   ■ Not Free

The Map of Freedom reflects the findings of Freedom House's 1998–1999 survey *Freedom in the World*. *Freedom in the World* is an annual institutional effort that monitors the gains and losses for political rights and civil liberties in 191 nations and 61 related and disputed territories. For each country, the Survey provides a concise report on political and human rights developments, along with ratings of political rights and civil liberties. Based on these ratings, countries are divided into three categories: Free, Partly Free, and Not Free, as reflected in the Map of Freedom.

Data from *Freedom in the World* can be accessed at our website: *www.freedomhouse.org*.

Map 10-1   **The Map of Freedom**

Copyright © Freedom House.

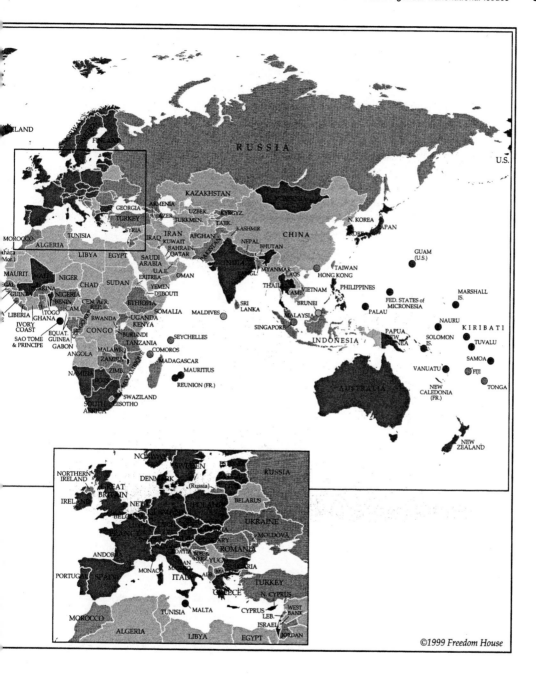

©1999 Freedom House

western imperialism toward Asian peoples. At the African meeting, the delegates argued that rather than focusing on First Tier concepts of individual political and legal freedoms, the human rights agenda should be redefined in terms of the economic and social needs of poor people. In their declaration, the Africans claimed for themselves an absolute right to receive development aid from wealthy states, even as they sought to weaken the concept of absolute rights in the political sphere.

Indeed, on the eve of the Vienna meeting, First Tier–Second Tier divisions over the questions of the universality and the nature of human rights appeared so deep that the conference seemed doomed to failure. In preparatory meetings, Second Tier delegates were so intent on equating "universality" with "western" that they could not even agree on a draft declaration condemning torture. Some observers feared that the divisions would prove unbridgeable, and thus the cause of human rights itself might be dealt a grave setback by perceptions of a retreat from the lofty standards of the 1948 Declaration.

Despite such gloomy prospects, the conference delegates ended up adopting by consensus a declaration that, if implemented by UN bodies, promises to strengthen international human rights, not undermine them. Three provisions in the Vienna Declaration are particularly important. First, the conference backed a U.S. proposal for stronger UN efforts in rectifying abuses, including specifically a call for establishing a new position of High Commissioner on Human Rights. In addition, the conference expanded the definition of human rights by calling for special efforts on behalf of women, children, and minorities. Finally, for reasons explained in the Amplification box "Bridging the Tiers at the Vienna Conference on Human Rights," the conference strongly endorsed the obligation of all states to protect human rights "regardless of their political, economic and cultural systems." So as to erase all ambiguity, the final declaration affirmed that "the universal nature of these rights and freedoms is beyond question."

Thus, although problems remain, the cause of international human rights has clearly come into its own in recent years. Transnational forces have undermined the traditional claim that whatever states do within their own borders is their own business. The expansion of human rights ideals has shifted the balance of standards of international legitimacy. Governments that persist in ignoring emerging global norms and committing abuses against their people will find themselves increasingly isolated—and hence weakened—in an interdependent world.

The Problem of Overpopulation

A second transnational issue of great concern to the contemporary world is the swelling ranks of the earth's population. As in the case of human rights, this issue has significant implications for relations between the tiers. In one sense, the problem principally affects the Second Tier. As noted in Chapter 8, it is among the poorer countries that population growth is occurring at the greatest rate, and bringing with it a wide assortment of economic, environmental, social, and political pressures on already strained national systems. But in an age of interdependence, First Tier states correctly perceive that they cannot remain insulated from the population explosion and related political and environmental pressures originating elsewhere. That perception, in turn, has led members of the First Tier to adopt policies aimed at curbing Second Tier population growth, policies that have frequently put the two tiers at odds with one another and thus exacerbated the already wide gulf between them.

Amplification

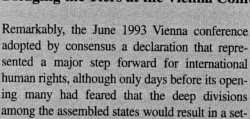

Bridging the Tiers at the Vienna Conference on Human Rights

Remarkably, the June 1993 Vienna conference adopted by consensus a declaration that represented a major step forward for international human rights, although only days before its opening many had feared that the deep divisions among the assembled states would result in a setback for the cause. What explains the turnaround? Three factors were particularly important.

First, there was an informal but highly effective campaign by nongovernmental supporters of universal international standards of human rights to attack the logic and motives of Second Tier opponents of the principle of universality. Nearly 1,000 nongovernmental human rights groups, along with influential media, joined in the effort to rebut the opponents' relativistic argument. Echoing the admonition by UN Secretary General Boutros Boutros-Ghali that "forces of repression often cloak their wrongdoing in claims of exception," supporters of human rights argued that authoritarian rulers try to characterize universal standards as mere "western imperialism" in order to escape international accountability for their mistreatment of their own subjects. The *New York Times,* for example, weighed in with an editorial entitled "Ending Torture Isn't Colonialism." Similarly, many regional nongovernmental organizations argued that African rulers who claim an "absolute right" to receive western aid are all too often tyrants who steal aid intended to help their own poor.

A second factor in the turnaround was that the United States and its allies were able to erode the political influence of those Second Tier regimes most determined to weaken the principle of universality. Despite the apparent solidarity expressed at earlier regional meetings of Second Tier states in Asia, Africa, and Latin America and the Caribbean, the reality was that the effort to dilute human rights standards had been led by only a handful of governments, who not coincidentally were the ones with the worst human rights records and who enjoyed only lukewarm support among their neighbors. During the Vienna negotiations, U.S. officials adopted a tactic dubbed "identify and isolate," which meant that the United States threatened to issue what amounted to a "human rights enemies list"; candidates for the list included China, Cuba, the Sudan, Libya, North Korea, Iran, and Iraq. The tactic worked. Fearing international isolation and condemnation, the obstructionist authoritarian regimes quietly backed away from much of their effort to dilute the standards.

A third and final contribution to the success of the conference was the U.S. decision to win Second Tier support for its emphasis on legal and political rights by backing Second Tier arguments on behalf of recognizing economic and social rights as well. In doing so, the Clinton administration reversed prior U.S. policy, which had insisted on defining rights almost exclusively in political and legal terms, while acknowledging economic and social rights as less compelling "goals." In accepting an expanded concept of human rights, however, the United States insisted that political and legal rights must be enforced at all times, while social and economic rights will evolve gradually, "in step with development."

The Population Explosion: Predictions Versus Reality

To begin to convey the magnitude of the population problem, we must necessarily use a lot of statistics. In using so many numbers, as indeed we must, it is important to keep in mind the face of humanity that lies behind them. We begin by noting that a study of the population explosion that began shortly after World War II and continues unabated today should give scholars a healthy sense of humility about their ability to predict human patterns. In 1945, world population stood at about 1.5 billion. Writing that year, Frank Notestein, one of the most prominent demographers of his day, predicted that by the year 2000 the ranks of humanity would swell to 3 billion. The prospect of a doubling of the world's population in only half a century seemed astounding to Notestein and his contemporaries.

What proved to be truly astounding, however, was that the 3 billion mark was reached by 1960. What Notestein thought would take over 50 years to occur had in fact arrived in just 15 years. By the year 2000 the planet will be shared by more than 6 billion

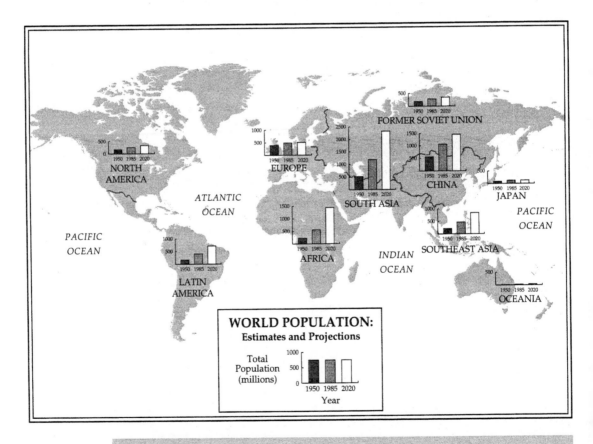

Map 10-2   **World Population by Region**

people, not the "mere" 3 billion that so alarmed Notestein and his contemporaries. Our purpose in noting his underestimate is certainly not to belittle a distinguished demographer—no one else knew what was coming, either—but rather to underscore both the magnitude of the population explosion of the past half-century and to remind ourselves that, as Casey Stengel once pointed out, predictions are risky things, especially those dealing with the future.

Before looking at the causes and consequences of the post–World War II population boom, we need first to give a fuller sense of its extraordinary dimensions. To do that, we will have to wade through more of those impersonal numbers. We might begin by noting that humans have walked the earth for about 150,000 years. It took almost all of those 1,500 centuries for total population to reach 1 billion, which it did by about the year 1800. Adding the second billion took only a bit over one century, until 1927. The 3 billion mark was reached by 1960, only 33 years later. The fourth billion had arrived by 1974, within a mere 14 years; and by 1987—only 13 years later—global population had reached 5 billion. This means that while human population has been growing for the past 150,000 years, most of that growth has happened in just the past four decades.

In the mid–1990s, about 5.5 billion people shared the planet with you. At current growth rates, 1 billion more are added every 11 years. Most demographers believe that by the year 2020, global population will reach 8 billion. This means that in the next 25 years, 2.5 billion people will be added to the ranks of an already crowded planet, a figure equal to the total world population as recently as the mid–1950s. We will discuss the problems that this kind of exponential population growth creates, but at its most elementary level, the problem is self-evident. Too many people competing for scarce resources threaten the environmental, economic, social, and political well-being of us all. In the words of the environmentalist Russell Peterson, "The quality of all life on earth is increasingly threatened by a powerful and growing ecological force. We humans are that force, ever more of us using ever more materials, assaulting the environment with ever more machines, chemicals, weapons, and waste."

Case in Point
The Growth of the World's Cities

At the turn of the twentieth century about 5 percent of the world's people lived in cities larger than 100,000. Today about 45 percent—more than 2.5 billion people—live in cities. The most dramatic urban growth has been in the Second Tier. From 1950 to 1995 the number of million-plus cities in the Second Tier grew from 34 to 213. According to the United Nations, by the year 2025 5 billion people, or 60 percent of all mankind, will be living in cities. Some of the mega-cities are Mexico City (15.6 million), Karachi (9.5 million), and Sao Paulo (13 million). Rio de Janeiro, Beijing, and Kinshasa also join the list of mega-cities.

Causes of the Population Explosion

The reasons for the global population explosion are rooted in that cluster of factors together known as modernity. Leaps in human knowledge, especially in the fields of science and technology, have made it possible to prevent disease and cure afflictions that were previously thought of as simply humans' "natural" plight. Some diseases, such as polio, have been virtually eradicated altogether through inexpensive and readily available vaccinations, while many others can now be successfully treated with advances in medicines and surgical techniques. Improved diet and sanitation have also contributed to the sharp drop in death rates—the number of deaths per unit of population—that is one of the early symptoms of modernity.

As two centuries of accelerated modernization has shown, however, societies caught up in the complex throes of becoming modern tend not to reduce their fertility rates—the number of births per woman of childbearing age—until well after the steep drop in death rates is an accomplished fact. Modernizing societies do eventually undergo sharp declines in fertility rates as well, as people come to realize that large families are no longer needed to do the manual labor of pre-industrial, agrarian times, or to ensure the survival of two or three children out of six or eight. But such societies typically require several generations of falling death rates before displaying a similar decline in fertility rates.

More than any other single factor, it is this time lag between falling death rates and falling fertility rates that accounts for the extraordinary surge in global population in recent decades. Until the gap is closed between these two great demographic curves, the population boom will continue to pit humanity in a perilous race with the earth's ability to sustain ever-growing numbers of people.

Feminist scholars and activists have long noted what they see as a significant but under-recognized cultural basis for the population explosion: the pervasive lack of power on the part of women in issues such as family planning and the concomitant belief of many men that fathering as many children as possible is evidence of their virility. Until broader cultural, social, political, and legal changes grant women around the world equal authority over reproductive choices and, more generally, economic freedom comparable to that enjoyed by men, feminists argue, efforts to control population growth will be treating the symptoms rather than the root causes. Table 10.1 seems to support the feminists' claim. At

Table 10.1 Are Men the Source of the Population Problem						
	Average Number of Desired Children of Men and Women			Average Number of Living Children of Men and Women over 50		
Country	Men	Women	Percentage by Which Male Rate is Higher	Men	Women	Percentage by Which Male Rate is Higher
Cameroon	11.2	7.3	53%	8.1	4.8	69%
Niger	12.6	8.5	48	6.7	4.9	37
Ghana	7.6	5.3	43	8.5	7.4	15
Kenya	4.8	4.8	0	9.6	7.9	22

Source: *World Watch*, April 1994, pp. 15,17.

least in sub-Saharan Africa, it indicates, the average man both wants and has more children than the average woman.

Effects of the Population Explosion

Since rapid population growth is closely correlated with low levels of industrialization, it follows that most of the recent surge in global population has occurred in the Second Tier. The altered composition of the world's population is starkly captured in the fact that whereas the areas that are now Second Tier countries accounted for two-thirds of global population in 1950, by 1985 the proportion had risen to three-fourths. Of the 2.5 billion people expected to be added to the world population by the year 2020, 95 percent will be in the Second Tier. Africa alone is projected to grow by over 700 million people, a figure roughly equal to the current combined total populations of North America, Europe, and Japan.

Clearly, the earth cannot indefinitely absorb such vast increases in the number of people it sustains. As we will discuss in a later section on environmental issues, there are growing concerns that the earth's carrying capacity may be nearing its outer limits.

In addition to the mounting strains it imposes on the environment, continued population growth threatens to ignite large-scale international population flows as large numbers of people seek to flee the poverty and strife endemic throughout much of the Second Tier. The U.S.-Mexican border—one of the few places where the First and Second Tiers directly adjoin one another—provides a picture of what will likely become a much more common international occurrence. By the mid–1990s, U.S. officials had all but lost control over their own borders, as hundreds of thousands of Mexicans illegally entered the United States in search of better economic opportunities. States like Texas and California were nearly overwhelmed by the growing demands for schooling, health care, and social services generated by the illegal aliens.

The United States and the Development of Global Population Policy

As evidence has mounted in recent decades of both the magnitude of the global population boom and of its deleterious economic, political, and environmental effects, the international community slowly began to organize itself to address the issue. From the 1950s through the 1970s, the United States was in the forefront of international leadership on the issue. In 1969 the Nixon administration led in the creation of the United Nations Fund for Population Activities (UNFPA), which conducts studies, disseminates information, and promotes greater global awareness of the population crisis. Having played the key role in UNFPA's founding, the United States readily agreed to contribute the largest share of its operating budget.

Similarly, Nixon pressed for convening the UN's first conference on global population. At the meeting, held in Bucharest, Romania, in 1974, the U.S. delegation pressed an activist agenda to curb population growth, including sharp increases in aid for national birth control campaigns. Most Third World countries reacted negatively to the U.S. proposals, arguing instead that the United States and other First World states should sharply increase foreign aid, not worry about the Third World population explosion.

During the 1980s, however, the Reagan and Bush administrations, committed to the "pro-life" agenda that had become so prominent an issue in domestic American politics,

Case in Point

The Cairo Population Conference

In September 1994, 20,000 people converged on Cairo, Egypt, for a nine-day United Nations Conference on Population and Development. Among the 20,000 were delegates from more than 170 states and a large number of lobbyists for nongovernmental organizations. In many ways the conference, the third such meeting sponsored by the UN, proved to be a significant event. While only time will tell if its proclamations will translate into progress on worldwide population control, it appeared to produce four significant results.

First, the conference produced a 113-page document that explicitly acknowledged legal abortion as part of a population control strategy. Although the Vatican, some Islamic states, and several heavily Catholic Latin American states had campaigned vigorously against including approval of abortion and birth control in the document, once they had lost that battle nearly all of them granted some degree of approval for the final document as a whole.

Second, the conference marked a watershed in the way that population issues are framed and addressed. Feminists and their allies succeeded in having the phrase "empowering women" become virtually the informal slogan of the meeting, as speaker after speaker argued that runaway population growth in poor states cannot be addressed apart from the larger problem of the subordinate status of women in most societies. Only when women become empowered worldwide, the feminists argued, can real progress be made on population control. Symptomatic of the recurring theme of women's rights was a dramatic presentation to the delegates by a female Islamic physician on the horrors of ritual female genital mutilation, which remains a widespread practice in much of the Middle East, Africa, and South Asia.

Third, the Cairo meeting provided a showcase for a number of highly successful population control programs launched by Second Tier states. Bangladesh, for example, though terribly poor, has managed to cut its population growth rate in half in the past 20 years through vigorous government efforts. Thailand cut its fertility rate from 6.5 to 2.1 in 25 years, while Indonesia's birthrate dropped from 5.6 to 3.0 between 1971 and 1991. The publicity given to such exemplary programs served to demonstrate that the Second Tier is by no means doomed to runaway population explosions.

Fourth and finally, the Cairo meeting highlighted the fact that most of the Second Tier requires outside financial assistance if it is to meet the population control objectives of the conference's final report. The conference calculated that spending on population policies will need to increase from the current $5 billion per year to about $17 billion by the year 2000. Several First Tier states used the Cairo meeting to announce increases in their population aid, as did the World Bank. Still, it is difficult to see where the full additional $12 billion will come from. The Cairo conference assumed that about half would come from the First Tier, while the Second Tier itself will be expected to come up with the remaining $6 billion—an unlikely prospect given the poverty that does so much to define Second Tier status.

Source: New York Times, September 2, 5, 6, 7, 11, 12, 13, and 14, 1994.

reversed earlier U.S. policies on global population programs. At the 1984 UN International Conference on Population held in Mexico City, the U.S. delegation startled their fellow conferees by proclaiming population growth to be "a neutral phenomenon" in economic development and dismissing as an "overreaction" existing policies aimed at curbing it. Henceforth, they announced, U.S. assistance for international population programs would be held to the test of opposition to abortion: organizations and governments supporting abortion as one option in family planning would be denied U.S. financial aid. A year later, the U.S. government announced that it would no longer contribute any funds to UNFPA, the very organization that an earlier Republican administration had done so much to create.

On taking office in 1993, the Clinton administration soon set about reversing the population policies of the Reagan and Bush years. In preparation for the UN's third population conference—held in 1994 in Cairo, Egypt—Timothy Wirth, the State Department's senior official for population policy, announced that U.S. funding for family planning organizations and the UNFPA would be restored, foreign aid programs would be restructured to encourage family planning, and increased amounts of family planning aid would be requested of Congress. On the issue that had figured so prominently in the Mexico City policy, Wirth announced that "our position is to support reproductive choice, including access to safe abortion."

By the mid–1990s, then, the United States was once again in the forefront of international efforts to curb the explosive population growth of the post–World War II period. Clearly, today's policies will affect the international system well into the next century. Even if present birth rates are lowered, the doubling of the world's population since the 1950s means that large net additions will continue to occur for some time. Progress in raising per capita income in the Second Tier will be thwarted by continued upward population pressures, and the prospects for mounting political turmoil and swelling refugee flows are made worse by runaway population growth.

Preserving the Earth's Environment

We turn now to consider a third transnational issue, which is closely bound up with the population problem. Increasing human mastery of nature has had many beneficial effects, including the rising affluence accompanying industrialization, breakthroughs in the treatment of diseases, and previously unimagined opportunities for personal fulfillment through education, communications, and travel. But the same advances in science and technology that have been life-enhancing have also allowed human beings to affect their natural environment—and increase their numbers—in ways that threaten the life-sustaining capacity of the planet. Clearly, the environment is another transnational issue that will loom ever larger in international dealings. In this section we will focus on two aspects of the international environmental crisis: (1) the threat of global warming and ozone depletion, and (2) the effects of harmful environmental practices on the earth's oceans, forests, and farmland.

Global Warming and Ozone Depletion

One correlate of industrialization is the greater use of fossil fuels, such as oil and coal. When burned, these fuels produce carbon dioxide (CO_2), most of which enters the atmosphere. As CO_2 accumulates in the upper atmosphere, it joins with other gases such as methane to trap solar radiation and other heat sources inside the atmosphere, producing the so-called greenhouse effect. Over time, most scientists believe, the greenhouse effect will alter the earth's climate by producing what has become known as global warming. Researchers have painted alarming scenarios of the devastating consequences of an increase in the earth's average temperature. A rise of even two or three degrees would alter world rainfall patterns, turning large areas that once produced bountiful crops of food into arid, hostile moonscapes. If global temperatures rise by eight or nine degrees, the earth's climate will be profoundly altered. Polar ice caps will melt, sea levels will rise, and large coastal areas and even entire island countries will sink beneath the waves.

As we will discuss in the case study at the end of the chapter, the topic of "greenhouse gas" emissions was a point of bitter controversy at the 1992 Earth Summit held in Rio de Janeiro. Most Second Tier states want the First Tier states, which in general are more industrialized, to take aggressive steps to curb their high CO_2 emissions. Within the First Tier, the Japanese and Europeans are prepared to formally commit themselves to reducing CO_2 emissions to 1990 levels by the year 2000. The United States, however, under the Bush administration, succeeded in watering down the global warming treaty adopted at the summit, so that signatories agree to make progress in reducing greenhouse gas emissions but are not committed to specific targets and timetables.

A second air pollution issue of international concern is the depletion of the ozone layer in the upper atmosphere. Naturally occurring ozone there blocks cancer-causing ultraviolet rays from the sun, but this protective shield has been eroded by a group of chemicals called chlorofluorocarbons, or CFCs, which until recently were widely manufactured for use as aerosol propellants and as coolants in refrigerating equipment. CFCs rise to the upper atmosphere and react with the ozone there, reducing its concentration and thus its protective effect.

In response to the clear link between ozone depletion and rising incidences of skin cancer, the international community has moved aggressively to curb CFC emissions. Nearly half the world's countries have signed the Montreal Treaty of 1987, negotiated under UN auspices, which commits its signatories to slash CFC use by the end of the century. There is already evidence that the rate of ozone depletion has declined, with the result that tens of thousands of cases of skin cancer that would otherwise have occurred will be averted.

What the Montreal Treaty shows is the ability of states to arrive at constructive environmental solutions in cases where (1) the scientific evidence is compelling as to environmental cause and effect, and (2) all can readily see their common stake in adopting environmentally sensible solutions. In contrast to the issue of CO_2 emissions, there is virtually no dispute about the adverse effects of CFCs, and the issue does not contain a built-in First Tier–Second Tier fault line. Moreover, substitute gases are available as aerosol propellants and coolants. For these reasons, significant progress has been made in reversing the depletion of the protective ozone layer, while the world still lacks a global warming treaty with real teeth in it.

Protecting the Earth's Oceans, Forests, and Soil

With the combination of ever-mounting population and expanding industrialization, the earth's oceans, forests, and food-producing farmlands have come under severe environmental strain. We will examine each of these three problems in turn.

The oceans, which cover more than two-thirds of the earth's surface and are home to thousands of species, have been threatened in recent decades by two problems. The first is that of pollution caused by indiscriminate dumping of waste, much of it toxic. The second problem is overfishing of international waters, which has threatened the world's supply of edible fish.

Central to the problem of protecting the oceans is the fact that they do not belong to any state or group of states, but rather exist in a twilight zone of sovereign authority. Therefore, there is little to prevent even the most rapacious abusers of ocean ecosystems from pursuing their own self-advantage, while the broader interest of the international community in the preservation of healthy oceans goes largely untended. For example, the practice of drift-net fishing—which indiscriminately harvests everything in its path, including dolphins—is an efficient way for any one country to gather needed food. When practiced by a large

Case in Point

The Law of The Sea Treaty

In 1982 the decade-long United Nations Conference on the Law of the Sea (UNCLOS III) produced a treaty aimed at codifying an expanded concept of territorial waters. The treaty went into effect in 1994, having received the necessary ratification by 61 states. Under treaty rules, the sovereign authority of coastal states extends seaward for 200 miles for commercial endeavors such as fishing and 12 miles for the regulation of shipping activities. By extending, and making uniform, the commercial zone, the treaty sharply reduced the number of states in control of the principal ocean resources, thus increasing the likelihood that cooperation can be reached among them on behalf of both the ocean environments and the landlocked states.

For more than a decade after it was negotiated, the effectiveness of the treaty was placed in doubt by the refusal of the Reagan and Bush administrations to sign it or to commit the United States to abide by its terms. This refusal arose from the belief that the United States would be the country with the most to lose by the treaty's provision on deep-seabed mining. U.S. firms have pioneered advanced techniques, including remote-guided submersible vehicles, for mining the rich nodules of manganese and other minerals that lie on the oceans' floors. The United States also leads the world in sophisticated technologies for off-shore drilling of natural gas and oil. In establishing a mechanism for regulating the commercial exploitation of the oceans' resources beyond the 200-mile national limit, the UN treaty ran afoul of the Reagan administration's commitment to free-market economic principles.

In 1994, however, the Clinton administration announced that it had succeeded in negotiating the seabed provisions into a more market-oriented agreement and hence would sign the agreement. With this U.S. backing, the UNCLOS treaty promises at least limited protection for the world's ocean environments, particularly from the damaging activities that formerly occurred within what are now the 200-mile coastal economic zones and that can now be more readily prevented or controlled by adjacent states.

number of countries, however, it has a devastating effect on marine life, and thus undermines the interests of all countries.

Because of its well-documented ravages, drift-net fishing has come under mounting attack by environmentalists. While some countries, like Japan, have responded to international pressure and banned the use of drift nets by their fishing fleets, others, like Taiwan, refuse to do so. In the absence of reliable international enforcement mechanisms for environmental controls, the oceans remain vulnerable to the most self-regarding members of the international community.

The world's forests represent a second area of environmental concern. While forests are scattered throughout the world, particular attention has been given to the tropical rain forests, found principally in Latin America, especially in Brazil, and in Southeast Asia, especially in Indonesia and Malaysia. Unlike the world's oceans, its forests lie within national boundaries and thus are subject to the control, for better or worse, of national governments.

Protecting forests is critical to the broader protection of the environment, for three reasons. First, they provide natural habitat for thousands of species that would become endangered if deprived of their native environment. Preserving forests is thus inseparable from the need to protect the planet's biodiversity. Second, forests produce oxygen, thus contributing to the maintenance of nature's balance. Third, and most critically, forests act as natural "sinks" for greenhouse gases. By absorbing these gases, especially carbon dioxide, their trees and other plants remove it from the earth's atmosphere and thus dilute the harmful effects of industrial air pollution.

Clearly, then, from the perspective of the earth's overall well-being, it is essential that the wholesale deforestation of recent decades be halted and adequate safeguards adopted to assure the preservation of these vital links in the environment. The problem in doing so is, precisely, the conflict between sovereign authority and planetary necessity. While major CO_2 producers within the First Tier depend on the environmentally cleansing effect of the tropical rain forests, Second Tier governments in whose territory the forests are principally located are under immense pressure to improve their peoples' living standards. Frequently the drive to develop economically has been interpreted as requiring a frontal assault on the rain forests. Their role as CO_2 sinks seems all too abstract to people mired in poverty, who see instead the commercial potential of clearing the forests in order to gain the concrete benefits of wood harvests, new farmland, and access to untapped mineral resources.

In some countries, most notably Brazil, progress has been made in protecting the rain forests through "debt-for-nature swaps," whereby large amounts of Brazil's huge debt owed to First Tier countries is canceled in exchange for assurances that the forests will be preserved. The technique represents a novel and altogether constructive instance of international environmental activism that benefits all parties. Debt-for-nature swaps work, however, only where Second Tier countries are swayed by the burdens of heavy foreign debts. For less indebted countries, such as Malaysia and Indonesia, there is much less incentive to accept such arrangements. As we will explain in the case study of the 1992 Earth Summit, the Malaysians in particular have taken a hard-line stance against First Tier appeals to preserve their forests. Malaysia continues to insist on the principle that all natural resources lying inside the boundaries of states are to be regarded as subject only to the sovereign prerogatives of national governments.

The third aspect of environmental vulnerability we will examine is the steady loss of agricultural land. The problem is particularly acute in dry regions of the Second Tier, especially in sub-Saharan Africa. Prompted by mounting population pressures, too many African farmers are grazing too many livestock and raising too many crops on soil that is chronically vulnerable to erosion due to dryness.

One-fourth of Africa is classified as "dryland," and much dryland that has historically been used for productive agriculture is at risk of being lost in a process known as desertification. As noted in Chapter 8, desertification involves the transformation of life-sustaining agricultural land into virtually useless deserts. According to UN studies, 60 percent of the Second Tier's dry croplands and 80 percent of its dry pastures are producing a declining amount of food because of overuse. On current evidence, as much as 15 million acres of dryland could be irreparably lost to desertification.

Such a loss of agricultural land raises the specter of mass hunger, starvation, disease, and social and political upheaval among affected peoples. Hence, it is essential to assist African countries to adopt agricultural practices that do not deplete the very soil on which their survival depends. In the long run, however, the only practical hope for avoiding the immense suffering accompanying desertification is to bring under control the swelling population growth that has overtaxed Africa's drylands in the first place.

Case Study: The Earth Summit

In June 1992, 35,000 people descended upon Rio de Janeiro, Brazil, to participate in a milestone event popularly known as the Earth Summit. The magnitude of the two-week conference was reflected in a host of "biggest ever" statistics that it spawned, including (1) participation by 172 countries, the most ever to take part in an international conference; (2) the attendance of 110 heads of state, the largest such convergence of world leaders in history; and (3) the presence of 15,000 representatives from hundreds of nongovernmental organizations from around the world, representing a record outpouring of citizen activists at an international event.

The conference's key product, a 1,000-page document known as Agenda 21, spells out the actions required to achieve "sustainable development" in the twenty-first century. Among the massive document's topics are the familiar environmental concerns of loss of biodiversity, global warming, soil erosion, desertification, and ozone depletion, as well as steps needed to protect the world's poor against the afflictions of disease, illiteracy, malnutrition, and infant mortality. Breathtaking in its sweep, Agenda 21—like the Earth Summit that produced it—mirrors the broad sense of global danger posed by environmental and developmental issues, but it also reflects the immense international political divisions over how best to tackle those issues.

The Earth Summit's formal name was the United Nations Conference on Environment and Development. The name is revealing, for it captures two significant points about contemporary efforts to address international environmental matters. First, like smaller international environmental conferences in 1972 and 1982, the summit was conducted under UN auspices. As we have seen in previous chapters, the post–Cold War order holds out the hope that the UN can more fully realize its original promise as an inclusive institutional framework within which otherwise divergent countries can address a host of problems afflicting people around the world. The Earth Summit of 1992, then, was meant in part to continue—and in some ways revive—the UN's role as the principal forum for focusing the world's attention on environmental issues and facilitating common policies.

A second point to note is that the Rio Earth Summit was formally the United Nations Conference on Environment and Development. When the 1992 conference was proposed in 1989, Second Tier countries had urged linking the environmental issues preoccupying the prosperous members of the First Tier to the broader array of social, population, health, and economic needs afflicting the poor countries. The United States, Britain, and France had initially opposed linking the two agendas, on the grounds that adding development to the agenda would detract from a clear focus on environmental concerns. The Japanese, however, in a rare act of political independence from their western allies, weighed in with support for the Second Tier. Gradually, other First Tier states softened their opposition to expanding the agenda, so the Rio conference had as its mandate the development of a plan, supported by as much of the international community as possible, to both promote the economic development of the poor Second Tier countries and foster stronger measures to address the mounting global environmental crisis.

The two-week conference was the culmination of nearly three years of preparatory work by countless diplomats, bureaucrats, and private citizens who met in four earlier sessions to hammer out a workable framework for the summit itself. Chaired by Singapore's Tommy Koh, the conference's Preparatory Committee—better known as PrepCom—labored mightily to ensure that the Rio summit would not degenerate into a bitter spectacle of finger-pointing and denial of responsibility that would actually set back rather than advance the cause of international environmental cooperation.

First Tier–Second Tier Differences

The biggest fault line was that separating the First Tier from the Second Tier. As we will explain, there were also sharp divisions within the two groupings, but those paled in comparison with the profound gulf between the interests and worldview of the rich, developed First Tier states and the poorer, developing states of the Second Tier.

Reduced to its essentials, the division reflected the divergent attitudes toward environmental preservation that accompany industrialization. Having already industrialized, the First Tier countries consume a disproportionate share of the earth's resources, produce most of its solid waste, and generate most of the CO_2 that, as we have seen, is the principal human-generated source of the greenhouse gases believed to cause global warming. While First Tier states differ among themselves over such issues as regulating the level of future CO_2 emissions that they produce, none is prepared to accept a reduction of its own level of industrialization and consumption, which gave rise to the problem in the first place; furthermore, all insist that Second Tier states must help remedy the global effects of the First Tier emissions of greenhouse gases. Principally, this means that Second Tier members must do two things: (1) protect the carbon dioxide–absorbing tropical rain forests within their borders and (2) commit themselves to pursue their dreams of industrialization in environmentally sensitive ways.

The Second Tier countries see things quite differently. As far as they are concerned, the rich First Tier states are asking them to pay a heavy cost to protect an environment ravaged largely by First Tier excesses. To poor countries, the overriding issue is poverty, not the environment per se, and they regard industrialization as the principal means to overcome the ancient afflictions of poverty. If the First Tier insists that the Second Tier participate in expensive worldwide efforts to avert further environmental deterioration, they reason, then the First Tier owes the Second Tier much greater levels of aid to pay the surcharge for environmentally sensitive development.

The Second Tier states have a point. The rich countries, they note, spew out far more pollution, including specifically CO_2, than Second Tier forests can absorb. If the citizens of the First Tier are serious about the global environment, they reason, then let them take the lead in reducing their high-consumption, environmentally damaging lifestyles before lecturing the struggling poor of the Second Tier about their responsibilities for maintaining the global biosphere. If the people of Peru, Jamaica, Chad, Oman, and Bangladesh attained industrial-based affluence anywhere comparable to that enjoyed by the citizens of Western Europe, North America, or much of East Asia, the planet would soon choke on impossibly high levels of resource overconsumption, solid waste production, and air and water pollution.

It was thus immensely significant that in early PrepCom deliberations key Second Tier states accepted the First Tier's concept of "sustainable development." The phrase is today so routinely invoked that many people have lost sight of both its meaning and, more fundamentally, the significance of Second Tier acquiescence to its logic. As we have seen, sustainable development means that future efforts to transform poor, low-technology, agrarian societies into affluent, urbanized, high-consumption ones must be done in ways that protect

In a not uncommon summer scene, a smoggy blanket obscures the New York City skyline. Although—or because—it produces a fourth of the world's carbon dioxide emissions, the United States led the resistance at the Rio summit to a treaty that would lower the risk of the greenhouse effect and global warming.

an already polluted environment. Single-minded industrialization, as practiced by the Europeans, Americans, and Japanese since the eighteenth century, is no longer viable amid a damaged global ecosystem, argue the proponents of sustainable development. This means, then, that today's Second Tier states that accept the logic of sustainable development implicitly agree to pay an additional overhead cost, in the form of environmentally benign technology, in their efforts to industrialize. In eschewing a "development only" model, key Second Tier states have signaled their awareness that their own chances for a better material life are irreparably intertwined with global efforts to maintain the earth's natural well-being. Essential to their acceptance of the First Tier's concept of sustainable development, however, is their insistence that it must provide substantially higher levels of aid to pay for the Second Tier's adoption of environmentally sensitive technologies.

Diversity Among Second Tier States

Once this "grand bargain" was in place, the stage was set for the conflicting interests within each tier to assert themselves. The cacophony of Second Tier voices was channeled principally through the G–77, a loose coalition of developing countries (now numbering more than 125) that grew out of a group of 77 Third World countries formed during the heyday of the Cold War. Within the ranks of the G–77, divergent regional and national interests soon surfaced.

As suggested earlier, many Asians—most notably the outspoken Malaysians—resent what they see as First Tier efforts to order poor countries about on environmental issues, particularly the preservation of forests. The Malaysians were joined by the equally outspoken Indians, who, although their own deforestation is almost entirely their own doing, are quick to blame the rich First Tier for India's environmental problems, including deforestation. Another key Asian country at the Earth Summit was China, whose leadership is determined to double the country's gross national product within the next decade. Given China's huge population, its vast reserves of "dirty" soft coal, and its low levels of energy efficiency, it is being watched closely for the immense impact its drive to modernize will have on the global environment.

Malaysia's hard-line opposition to any binding treaty to protect the world's forests on the grounds that the national sovereignty of Second Tier states would thereby be compromised was gradually adopted by other G–77 members. In the end, the Rio summit was unable to produce anything stronger than a tepid, nonbinding resolution calling on all countries to take into account the impact of developmental efforts on their forests—this despite the fact that the Bush administration had made global forest preservation its number one priority at the Rio summit.

Other Second Tier regions pressed different priorities. African leaders stressed developmental issues over environmental ones, though many have learned the human cost of losing fertile land through desertification. To many African leaders, soil erosion and other agricultural issues are the principal environmental concerns in an otherwise poverty-focused worldview. The major oil-producing states of the Middle East resisted PrepCom efforts to restrict CO_2 emissions, out of fear that diminished demand for their oil by the energy-rapacious First Tier states would be economically detrimental to them. Some Latin American countries, most notably Brazil, the summit host, felt singled out for criticism because of their vast rain forests. Beyond a broad acquiescence to the First Tier's insistence on sustainable development and its unanimous view that the rich countries must provide more developmental assistance to help the poor acquire environmentally benign technology, then, the Second Tier at the Rio summit was a heterogeneous cluster of diverse and some-times conflicting interests and outlooks.

First Tier Splits

The members of the First Tier were as divided among themselves at the summit as were their Second Tier counterparts. Particularly notable was the U.S. resistance to emerging in-ternational environmental norms and its impact in undermining the adoption of strict and binding standards. Aside from its interest in preserving the world's forests, the United States was conspicuously at odds with the overwhelming majority of other countries, First and Second Tier alike.

As noted earlier, it was the United States, more than any other country, that was respon-sible for watering down a proposed treaty on global warming. Similarly, the United States was one of the few major countries to object to the so-called biodiversity treaty, aimed at protecting the habitats of endangered species. In both instances, U.S. officials offered ra-tionales for their stance that contained some plausibility. The adoption of strict limits on greenhouse gas emissions, they said, could handicap First Tier economies already mired in recession, and thus wind up costing precious jobs. In the case of the biodiversity treaty, they contended that the treaty language threatened the legal protection of U.S. patents in the emerging field of biotechnology.

But beneath these arguments lay the distinctive political and ideological proclivities of the United States in general and the Bush administration in particular. In the first place, Americans produce one-fourth of the world's CO_2, due in no small measure to their famed love affair with the automobile and the fact that 60 percent of their electricity is produced by coal-burning generators. As the world's most voracious energy consumer, the United States thus had the most to lose by the adoption of strict international CO_2 standards.

Moreover, the Bush administration, despite its early rhetoric, accorded low priority to environmental issues. Bush's head of the Environmental Protection Agency, William Reilly, was widely admired as a committed environmentalist, but his voice was often drowned out by those of powerful White House officials, some of whom were positively scornful of environmentalists and their agenda. Much of the White House hostility toward environmental issues reflected the combative John Sununu, Bush's first chief of staff, and Richard Darman, the President's budget director. In a 1990 speech, Darman went so far as to proclaim that "Americans did not fight and win the wars of the twentieth century to make the world safe for green vegetables."

A third and final reason for the U.S. stance was that the Earth Summit occurred in the midst of the 1992 presidential election. Bush's electoral support in coal- and oil-produc-ing states in the Sun Belt and Rocky Mountains was essential to his reelection plans, and he calculated that Americans cared more about preserving jobs at home than protecting obscure species in distant lands or cleaning up air that the Chinese threatened to pollute in any case.

Against this background, it is little wonder that the United States was widely regarded as the principal laggard of the Rio Earth Summit. Its strong stand against deforestation was undercut by its refusal to sign the biodiversity treaty and its successful efforts to take the teeth of concrete goals and timetables out of the global warming treaty. Even the gesture of providing $50 million in new environmental aid for Second Tier states was revealed as a political shell game when it was learned that the money was simply transferred out of the Environmental Protection Agency's existing budget and thus did not represent any new

U.S. commitment. Bush's eleventh-hour decision to attend the Rio meeting served only to underscore America's estrangement from prevailing international environmental norms. In an interview with a Brazilian newspaper, a defiant Bush was reduced to arguing that "I'm president of the U.S., not president of the world....I can't do what everyone else does." This from the President who only the previous year had resolutely, and masterfully, orchestrated the complex international coalition assembled to reverse Iraq's invasion and annexation of Kuwait.

Most members of the European Community entered the PrepCom sessions supporting strict caps on CO_2 emissions and substantial increases in First Tier aid to help the Second Tier acquire sustainable development technologies. The northern European countries of Denmark, Germany, and the Netherlands were particularly "out front" of the United States, in no small measure because of the greater political clout of environmental groups and parties in their domestic politics. By the time the summit arrived, however, the Europeans had largely backed away from their advanced positions. They deferred to the U.S. insistence on taking the strict emission standards out of the global warming treaty, reasoning that a treaty on greenhouse gas emissions that was not supported by the United States would be virtually worthless. Signaling their continued belief in their earlier principles, however, the 12 EC members signed an agreement pledging that they would reduce their own CO_2 emissions to 1990 levels by the year 2000, even though the Rio global warming treaty did not obligate them to do so. At the insistence of the British and the Dutch, the Europeans also retreated from earlier expressions of support for substantial increases in aid to Second Tier states. Like the United States, the Europeans were feeling the pinch of recessionary pressures, and so in 1992 wound up accepting positions on global warming and on aid that were closer to those of the Americans than would have been predicted earlier.

Perhaps the most interesting First Tier positions developed in preparation for the Rio Earth Summit were those of the Japanese. As a resource-poor manufacturing country, Japan had pioneered new technologies in areas such as energy efficiency and air and water cleanup. For the past quarter century, Japan's government had enforced strict air and water quality standards and had provided Japanese corporations with generous incentives to develop and install pollution control measures. By the early 1990s, Japan's energy efficiency was double that of the United States, and its environmental technology was widely regarded as a full generation ahead of that developed by the Europeans or the Americans and thus a lucrative potential export.

Added to their economic motives for environmental activism was the fact that the Japanese were looking for some big international project they could lead. Sensitive to charges of being international "free riders" on trade and security arrangements and looking to shed their reputation for "checkbook diplomacy," they wanted to exercise real leadership on a global issue of great significance. The environment seemed to provide Japan with the perfect opportunity it had been looking for.

As we explained in Chapter 7, however, the Japanese remain chronically uncomfortable about getting too far ahead of their U.S. strategic patrons on contentious international issues. Despite their earlier avowals of support for strict CO_2 controls, by the time of the Rio Earth Summit the Japanese had lost their nerve: they were unwilling to challenge the United States publicly on greenhouse gas emissions. In the end, they did precisely what they had set out not to do: deferring to the Americans on larger policy issues and quietly contributing the one thing that constitutes Japan's claim to major-power status—money.

Japanese officials announced plans to increase environmental aid to Second Tier countries from the $800 million a year it had spent between 1989 and 1991 to $1.4 billion a year from 1992 to 1997. Symptomatic of the deflation of earlier expectations that Japan would emerge as a global leader on the environment was the fact that Prime Minister Kiichi Miyazawa, citing pressing domestic concerns, was one of the few national leaders who did not even show up at the Rio summit.

Effects of the Earth Summit

After years of preparation, countless speeches, elaborate political maneuvering, and lavish press attention, did the 1992 Earth Summit actually change anything? A good case can be made that it did. For one thing, the immense attention focused on environmental issues further promoted global awareness of the interconnectedness of the earth's lands and peoples. Heightened awareness of the need to tend to environmental deterioration does not itself solve the problem, of course, but it is a necessary element in persuading people to make the sacrifices necessary to protect the biosphere.

Second, the Earth Summit gave a new legitimacy to the concept of sustainable development. As the Second Tier acknowledges the necessity of pursuing its dreams of economic advancement in tandem with environmental preservation, so too is the First Tier more fully grasping its obligation to help provide the aid essential to this process.

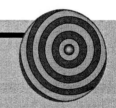

Case in Point
The Kyoto Summit

Spurred by the Rio summit, most of the states of the world met in Kyoto, Japan, in December 1997 to tackle the single issue of global warming. Since Rio, emissions of greenhouse gases, such as carbon dioxide, methane, nitrous oxide, and chlorofluorocarbons, had been reduced, but not anywhere near the levels pledged at Rio. It soon became apparent that a deep schism separated the First Tier from the Second Tier.

First Tier nations were generally serious about bringing their greenhouse gas levels to 1990 levels. Too, the First Tier countries committed themselves at Kyoto to a stringent set of emission standards that would last well beyond the year 2010. However, the heart of the problem of reducing greenhouse emission is the reluctance of most of the Second Tier to limit their economic growth and their voracious appetites for energy in order to advance their economies. To leaders of many Second Tier countries, the requirement of economic growth—along with the unregulated emission of greenhouse gases that it brings—is an immediate and compelling need, while curbing global warming is a distant and abstract goal. First Tier countries, they argue, are rich and can afford to absorb the average of 7 percent of greenhouse gas emissions by the year 2010. Second Tier states, by contrast, regard their poverty as the defining feature about them. Anything that threatens to curb the economic growth of Second Tier States is unlikely to win the support of the Second Tier. It is thus unlikely to succeed on a global scale in dealing with a truly global problem.

Third, the adoption of Agenda 21 represented a step forward in the creation of a shared international commitment to protect the planet. Though not a formal treaty and thus not legally enforceable, Agenda 21 nonetheless constitutes a positive political declaration of environmental objectives acceptable to as many of the world's states as is politically possible. The meeting also led to the creation of the Sustainable Development Commission, a United Nations agency that will review how closely states are adhering to the pledges they made in Agenda 21.

Fourth, the Earth Summit did indeed result in two new treaties signed by 153 states. As noted, pressure from the United States prevented the treaty on global warming from containing concrete standards of greenhouse gas emissions, but it does commit signatories to be more attentive to the need to reduce such emissions. The biodiversity treaty was signed by a majority of the conference participants despite the U.S. rebuff. Within months of taking office in 1993, the Clinton administration did sign the treaty, though it attached reservations designed to protect U.S. patent rights in the field of biotechnology.

Fifth, and finally, the conference provided the impetus for First Tier countries to announce some increase in environmental aid for Second Tier states. Maurice Strong, the Canadian who chaired the Rio summit, estimated that First Tier contributions announced at the meeting would total $6 to $7 billion, though some environmentalists insisted that only about $2 billion of this sum represented new commitments.

Clearly, protecting the earth's environment will require ongoing international efforts. A single meeting, even a dramatically successful one, cannot definitively resolve such complex and continuing issues. In light of the profound differences of worldview and economic interest that were evident during the elaborate preparations for the Rio meeting, however, the actual summit must be judged a moderately successful step forward for an international system struggling to come to terms with new, complex, and profound transnational issues.

Review

In this chapter we have examined some of the principal transnational issues of our times, focusing on human rights and democracy, the population explosion, and environmental protection. In the process, the following points were made:

1. Given the growing global technological and economic interdependence, transnational issues are increasing in importance. These are issues that transcend international boundaries in ways that individual states have little control over.

2. Human rights have risen to the top of the global agenda because of (a) the role of the media, (b) the influence of several outstanding individuals, (c) the role of private groups such as Amnesty International, and (d) the spread of Lockean values of individual freedom as a result of the large international presence of the United States.

3. The principal UN human rights documents are (a) the UN Charter, (b) the Convention on the Prevention and the Punishment of the Crime of Genocide, (c) the Universal Declaration of Human Rights, (d) the International Convention on the Elimination of All Forms of Racial Discrimination, (e) the International Covenant on Economic, Social, and Cultural Rights, and (f) the International Covenant on Civil and Political Rights.

4. Rapid population growth rates reflect principally declining death rates. The greatest growth is occurring among the poor states of the Second Tier.

5. Greater international cooperation will be needed to address the global environmental crisis. For example, First Tier states are responsible for most of the carbon dioxide emissions that many scientists fear will produce catastrophic results through global warming caused by the greenhouse effect; most of the tropical rain forests, necessary to help absorb carbon dioxide, lie in the territory of Second Tier states, many of which are under severe economic pressure to cut them down.

Suggested Readings

Brown, Lester. *World Without Borders*. New York: Random House, 1972.

Caldwell, Lynton K. *International Environmental Policy,* 2d ed. Durham, NC: Duke University Press, 1990.

Carroll, John E. *International Environmental Diplomacy*. New York: Cambridge University Press, 1988.

Cline, William R. *The Economics of Global Warming*. Washington, DC: Institute for International Economics, 1992.

Diamond, Larry, and Marc F. Plattner, eds. *The Global Resurgence of Democracy*. Baltimore, MD: Johns Hopkins Press, 1993.

Donnelly, Jack. *Universal Human Rights in Theory and Practice*. Ithaca, NY: Cornell University Press, 1989.

Hass, Peter M., Robert O. Keohane, and Marc A. Levy, eds. *Institutions for the Earth*. Cambridge, MA: MIT Press, 1993.

Korey, William. *The Promises We Keep: Human Rights, the Helsinki Process and American Foreign Process*. New York: St. Martin's Press, 1993.

Matthews, Jessica Tuchman, ed. *Preserving the Global Environment*. New York: Norton, 1991.

Porter, Gareth, and Janet Brown. *Global Environmental Politics*. Boulder, CO: Westview Press, or Lynne Reinner, 1991.

Sanger, Clyde. *Ordering the Oceans: Making of the Law of the Sea Treaty*. Toronto: University of Toronto Press, 1987.

Sebenius, James K. *Negotiating the Law of the Sea*. Cambridge, MA: Harvard University Press, 1984.

Shute, Stephen, and Susan Hurley, eds. *On Human Rights: The Oxford Amnesty Lectures, 1993*. New York: Basic Books, 1993.

Young, Oran R. *International Cooperation: Building Regimes for Natural Resources and the Environment*. Ithaca, NY: Cornell University Press, 1989.

Young, Oran R., and Gail Osherenko. *Polar Politics: Creating International Environmental Regimes*. Ithaca, NY: Cornell University Press, 1993.

Security Issues in a Post–Cold War Environment

PREVIEW

In this chapter, we will describe how the pattern of conflict and violence among and within states has changed since the end of the Cold War and how those changes affect the problem of security in the world. After reiterating an earlier point, that the only serious security threats are found within the Second Tier, we will analyze the pattern of Second Tier conflict and instability. We will begin with regional conflicts involving Second Tier states. One way the First Tier can affect these conflicts is by discouraging arms proliferation—especially of the most deadly weapons capabilities—through arms control processes, and we will consider the dynamics and degree of success of these efforts. The discussion will then turn to a more prevalent and highly publicized phenomenon in the Second Tier—internal wars arising from the disintegration of so-called failed states—and how media coverage affects public perceptions of these tragedies. The chapter will conclude with a case study of the civil war in the Democratic Republic of the Congo (formerly Zaire) and what it may portend for the future.

KEY CONCEPTS

national security	N+1 problem
international security	arms freeze
collective defense	arms reduction
collective security	disarmament
NBC (nuclear, biological, and chemical) weapons	Limited Test Ban Treaty (LTBT)
	Nuclear Nonproliferation Treaty (NPT)
internal war	Missile Technology Control Regime (MTRC)
regional conflict	
weapons states	secession
proliferation	national self-determination
arms control	do-something syndrome

OUTLINE

A s we have often noted in earlier chapters, war, its avoidance, and its containment within as narrow limits as possible are central problems with which individual states and the international system must constantly come to grips. There is, however, a tension between two levels of concern. The individual state is the principal political unit of the international system that has existed since the end of the Thirty Years War in 1648, and the primary concern of each state has been its own safety, or what is called national security. However, one state's security can be—or appear to be—another state's insecurity; when one state arms itself for protection against a neighbor, for instance, the latter may consider itself threatened by the action, even if no threat was intended. This is known as the security dilemma. Therefore, actions taken to increase national security may decrease international security—stability of the system as a whole. Conversely, actions taken in the name of international security, such as intervention in a civil war, may threaten the security of a particular state.

Debate over such issues is carried out among academic analysts of international relations and among policymakers and diplomats, but in general it tends to divide the two groups. As we noted earlier, a reduction in the frequency and carnage of war, even its elimination, is a goal that attracts many scholars to the field. Since wars often, though by no means always, involve conflicts between states, from this perspective the very existence of a system of sovereign states, each concerned with its own security, may be the key obstacle to peace. Many academics, thus, prefer to think in terms of international rather than national security.

Government officials with a responsibility for protecting their populations typically view such thinking as a luxury they can seldom afford. National security must be the focus of those charged with overseeing vital national interests; international security and related concerns are considered relevant when, and only when, they also serve (or at least do not harm) national interests. This contrast in perspective explains much of the gap in attitudes toward security between those who practice international relations and many who study the field.

This debate relates to our earlier discussions about systems of war and peace. The idea that national security must override a primary concern for the system tends to occur at times of systemic division and rivalry; rivals view one another with suspicion, and each state seeks to safeguard its safety through some form of what was classified in Chapter 3 as collective defense—a banding together of states with similar interests, as in a military alliance. The Cold War period certainly was of that nature, as were the periods leading to the world wars. For a heightened concern with international security to arise, the member states must agree on systemic values; in such cases, a system of collective security may develop, where all or nearly all powers agree to promote peace and act against any state seeking to break the peace.

Framing the issues in this way leads to a consideration of the evolving international system. With the old structure dividing the major players now destroyed, what will replace it? We will look for answers to this question, which we raised initially in Chapter 3, in terms of two sets of alternatives: national security–collective defense on the one hand, and international security–collective security on the other.

Summary ━━━━━━━━━━━━━━━━━━━━━━━━━━━━━━━━━━

Characteristics of the New International System

1. Absence of ideological divisions among the major actors (First Tier plus Russia and China) that will lead to war
2. Major source of instability and violence in system concentrated in Second Tier
3. Alternative security systems: dual collective-security (First Tier) and collective-defense (Second Tier) systems or a First Tier—imposed collective-security arrangement
4. A concentration of internal wars within the Second Tier

We will begin by presenting what we view as four apparent and relevant characteristics of the new post–Cold War system. First, there are no fundamental ideological divisions among the major actors in the system (essentially the First Tier states plus Russia and China) that will lead to military conflict among them in the foreseeable future. This basic agreement means that preparation for a central systemic war for the time being is less necessary than it used to be. As more Soviet successor states and former members of the Warsaw Pact affiliate with NATO, through the Partnership for Peace program and eventually as full members, any rationale for a collective-defense system evaporates. Instead, a collective-security arrangement stressing international security among the major actors becomes not only possible but attractive, since sharing the responsibility for peacekeeping reduces the individual burden of each state. Whether such an arrangement can be effective is another question, however; the belated NATO response to the violence in Bosnia—where NATO's Implementation Force (IFOR), later renamed the Stabilization Force (SFOR), essentially acted in a collective security manner—may presage the future of the transition of historically collective defense to collective security mechanisms.

What might happen that could change this basic situation of agreement? One possibility is for an ideological or other schism caused by an economic depression or some other traumatic event to drive a wedge between states of the First Tier. As the argument in Chapter 9 suggested, First Tier economies are so intertwined as to make this eventuality highly unlikely; however, since the same arguments about interdependence were made before World War I, one must concede that such a rift is not inconceivable.

A more likely—or less unlikely—cause of deterioration would be from a major state at the periphery, that is, Russia or China. A reversion of Russia to authoritarian, antiwestern rule amid economic chaos and collapse is a policymaker's nightmare, roughly analogous to the rise of Nazi Germany. Fears of such a scenario, of course, have energized efforts to promote Russian movement to political and economic normalcy, particularly in light of the collapse of the Russian economy in 1998. A China of growing economic and military magnitude is the only other state outside the First Tier that is large and potentially powerful enough to challenge systemic stability. Any attempt to do so would be an act of political desperation by China's transitional leadership. Despite their differences with First Tier states, Chinese leaders are committed to joining the world's capitalist economy and adhere to the traditional Chinese policy of keeping the "barbarians" out rather than expanding to conquer and include them. Tying itself more closely to the global economy is clearly a high priority of the Jiang Zemin government. Nevertheless, a destabilizing move by China at some point cannot be totally ruled out.

A second characteristic of the post–Cold War system is that the major source of instability and violence will continue to be conflicts among and particularly within states of the Second Tier. This is also an unexceptional statement to which allusion has been made previously. The sources of instability are numerous; they include tensions associated with development and with its absence, historical rivalries among states now given freer rein by the collapse of the Cold War, and similar feuds and hatreds among groups within states. All of these circumstances afford a potential for violence.

Fortunately, the resulting conflicts should be localized. They may, as in the Balkans or even on the Asian subcontinent, have the potential to draw in close neighbors, but in general they do not have much prospect of threatening the overall system through escalation to general war. The single exception is the unknown escalatory potential should NBC (nuclear, biological, or chemical) weapons be exchanged in Second Tier conflicts, for instance, between India and Pakistan. As we shall explain, it is the fear of escalation in such circumstances that motivates the First Tier to eliminate or control the deployment of such weapons. Otherwise, however, Second Tier conflicts remain peripheral to the overall system's stability, and, for the most part, dealing with these conflicts remains optional for the major powers.

Second Tier states argue officially and publicly for broad collective-security arrangements to preserve the peace. But such rhetoric belies their real interest, which is for collective defense. In some instances, the existence of outside enemies and internal rivalries creates an "us versus them" mentality for Second Tier governments that makes agreement on a common peace seem impossible. Furthermore, a truly systemic collective-security system in the world would have the Second Tier as its object; that is, peace enforcement (to use a current term to which we will return in Chapter 13) would be directed against Second Tier states—in ways that individual states or groups would likely oppose.

Speaking more generally, another characteristic of the post–Cold War era is that there are two alternatives for organizing the peace: a dual-tiered system of collective security and collective defense or a collective-security system largely imposed by the major powers. The choice of which system will prevail is largely at the discretion of the First Tier and becomes a matter of what the major states believe to be within their national and international security self-interests.

This assertion is harsh and may suggest a paternalistic view of international relations; it is also realistic. The gap in economic and military capability between the tiers is sufficiently wide and growing that military threats to the First Tier from the Second will effectively be limited to acts of terrorism, which it will be in the best interests of Second Tier states to prevent, for fear of economic or military retaliation.

The stability of this relationship between the tiers will depend on how the First Tier treats other consequential states within the system. States with the military potential to be system-threatening, such as Russia, China, and possibly India, represent one category; whether the system provides for their well-being will determine their interest in joining the collective-security system. The other category comprises those states poised economically on the boundary between the tiers, such as the Four Tigers and some former members of the Second World. A flexible, inclusionary strategy by the First Tier will maximize stability. The final general characteristic of the post–Cold War era is that most Second Tier violence now takes the form of internal war. A survey in mid–1996 tallied 32 ongoing wars in the world; all were internal wars. This spate of warfare has been an unanticipated outgrowth of the end of the Cold War, and no consensus has emerged about what the system can or should do about these conflicts.

What kind of orientation toward Second Tier violence and instability will the First Tier adopt? The record on this matter is unclear. Most of the post–Cold War involvements that have occurred have been coordinated by the system's major structure for collective security, the United Nations, which is currently in a curious position. During the Cold War, the UN, especially the General Assembly, was the bastion of the developing world, a forum where Second Tier states could vent their anger at systemic indifference to their plight. As the UN has become more active, however, those same states find themselves the objects of actions proposed by the First Tier–dominated Security Council.

The First Tier states may continue to act through the UN to a greater or lesser extent. In any case, either through informal precedent or through the formal enunciation of principles, a set of rules of engagement will eventually emerge, determining when the system will respond with joint action and when it will not.

There are two major questions about what the First Tier may do. The first has to do with what kinds of forces may be employed. The options are UN forces, either a standing force (as discussed in Chapter 13) or forces recruited for particular occasions; forces provided by NATO or other regional organizations; or individual intervention by states with a particular interest in a given country, such as a former colonial relationship. Each has a problem: the UN's resources are too limited for more than a few applications, regional organizations other than NATO in Bosnia have yet to demonstrate their effectiveness in these kinds of situations, and individual interventions such as that by the United States in Haiti lack predictability and thus cannot be counted on to occur. The other question about intervention is how often it will occur. The options, as defined in Chapter 8 regarding developmental assistance, include comprehensive engagement, selective engagement, and benign neglect. Some form of selective engagement is most likely.

To understand how the pattern of security may be expected to evolve, in the rest of this chapter we will analyze the various forms conflict is likely to take, with an obvious emphasis on the Second Tier. We will begin by discussing international problems, so-called regional conflicts. We will then explain the unique problems posed for the system when regional rivals possess nuclear, biological, and chemical (NBC) weapons and ballistic missiles capable of delivering them. The discussion will then move to internal sources of violence and the question of systemic involvement in those situations.

Regional Conflicts and the Weapons States

Regional conflicts are situations of rivalry among neighboring states, usually with a historical basis reflecting national differences, that either have already erupted into violence or may do so in the future. The end of the Cold War has strongly affected the relationship between the major powers and those parts of the Second Tier beset by such conflicts.

Before the end of the Cold War, most of these conflicts had been suppressed, first by colonial rule, which imposed order for the benefit of the colonialists, and later by the Cold War rivalry between the superpowers, who competed for influence in regions emerging from colonial rule. The common currency of their competition was economic and military assistance, and they found willing customers for military aid in places where ancient rivalries created fear and a perceived need for military security. Although this flow of arms sometimes fueled such rivalries and increased the deadliness of the resulting warfare, it occurred within defined rules that produced certain advantages in terms of containing regional conflicts geographically and in terms of the decisiveness of the outcomes, containing rather than letting them spread in ways that might result in direct superpower confrontation.

The rules flowed from the nature of the superpower competition, the purpose of which was instrumental: to gain influence, to protect influence already gained, and to deny influence to the other side. In most instances, there were no vital or even major interests involved (petroleum resources in the Middle East are an exception), and the outcomes of the engagement produced only a modest advantage or disadvantage to the superpowers. Therefore, they sought to manage conflicts so as to keep them within limits and avoid any direct confrontation between themselves with escalatory potential. The tool for this conflict management was the modulation of assistance so there would be little risk of one's "client" either winning decisively (thereby embarrassing or threatening the interests of the other superpower) or of losing decisively (thereby embarrassing oneself). Since regional conflicts tended to pit a Soviet against an American client, they both could be controlled fairly easily.

This arrangement had at least two direct benefits. First, the superpowers were able to restrain the intensity with which conflicts could be pursued. Second, regional balances of power tended to be maintained—not for their own sake, but because imbalance could destabilize relations between the superpowers. Therefore, the arrangement served to restrain the efforts of regional hegemons, states that seek to gain a significant power advantage within a region. The most extreme examples are the weapons states that are described later in this chapter.

The end of the Cold War has negated this system of constraints. As the Soviet Union came to recognize its unacceptably costly overextension in Second Tier areas, it began to pull back, withdrawing economic and military aid and thereby forfeiting influence. The removal of Soviet interest meant that the United States could back away as well. To some extent, this mutual withdrawal was useful: it meant the elimination of East-West, communist-anticommunist rivalries that the competition had superimposed on regional conflicts having no inherent meaning in those terms. The conflict between India and Pakistan, for example, is about many differences, notably in religion; Cold War rivalry was an artificial overlay that could only make an ultimate resolution more difficult by distorting perceptions of the reality of the situation.

As noted in Chapter 6, the results of this withdrawal have been mixed. Although most of the geographic regions of the Second Tier lack effective regional organizations or structures around which to fashion a viable regional order, there have not been a rash of regional conflicts regardless of the existence of regional organizations. Latin America, a reasonably peaceful region, for instance, benefits from the effective Organization of American States. In Africa, on the other hand, the Organization of African Unity has a history of failure in dealing with conflict between its members. Other regions do not even have such structures encompassing all states within the region.

The end of the Cold War has also exacerbated existing rivalries. As the major powers have reduced their military forces, their need for weapons has declined, and most of them find themselves with excess arsenals they wish to dispose of. This is particularly true of Russia and the other principal Soviet successor states, which also desperately need the hard currency for developmental purposes that weapons sales can bring. Virtually all these countries agree in principle that they should not fuel Second Tier conflicts with an influx of more arms. The economics of arms sales, however, have impelled some to act otherwise, and the result has been a flood of new weaponry into the regions.

Major Regional Conflicts

The problems posed for the system by regional rivalries vary considerably from region to region. When one surveys the Second Tier, five conflicts stand out as particularly serious: the Arab-Israeli conflict in the Middle East and conflicts in the Persian Gulf region, South Asia, Southeast Asia, and the Balkans. Each will be discussed briefly.

The Arab-Israeli conflict, pitting Israel against a varying coalition of states that has included Egypt, Syria, Jordan, and Iraq at different times, was an active, simmering conflict for more than three decades beginning with the birth of the Israeli state in 1948. In that year, a disorganized coalition of Islamic states unsuccessfully attempted to prevent the establishment of an independent Jewish state in Palestine. The war created several million Palestinian refugees, who have pursued the goal of an independent state of their own under the leadership of the Palestine Liberation Organization (PLO). There followed a long period of tension and violence, punctuated by three full-scale wars: the Suez War of 1956, in which Israel joined Great Britain and France to attack Egypt and occupy the Sinai Peninsula and the Suez Canal zone (from which international pressure forced the three countries to retreat); the Six Day War of 1967, in which Israel prevailed over Egypt, Syria, and Jordan and occupied the areas of Sinai, the Gaza Strip, the Golan Heights, East Jerusalem, and the West Bank of the Jordan River; and the Yom Kippur War of 1973, in which Israel defeated Egypt after suffering early setbacks. In addition, Israel intervened in the Lebanese civil war in 1982 in order to destroy the military arm of the PLO.

This conflict has become in large part dormant; with the Cold War over, a revitalized peace process has shown promise of resolving many lingering differences between Arabs and Israelis. In the wake of the Yom Kippur War, into which the superpowers came close to being drawn, an American-led peace process began between Israel and Egypt. It culminated in 1978 in a formal peace treaty, the Camp David Accords engineered by American President Jimmy Carter. With its western front stabilized, no other

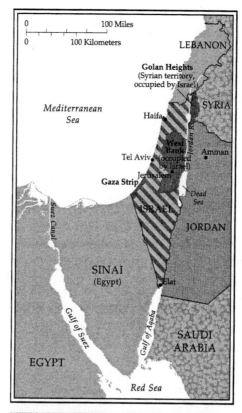

Map 11-1   The Arab-Israeli Conflict

©1996 by St. Martin's Press, Inc. From: *Contours of Power*, by Snow/Brown. Reprinted with permission of Bedford/St. Martin's Press, Inc.

combination of states thus posed a deadly threat to Israel. The defeat of Iraq in the Persian Gulf War (1991), mutual Israeli-PLO recognition and the sporadic granting of increasing Palestinian autonomy in parts of the occupied territories (beginning in 1993 and expanding in 1995), a formal peace agreement between Jordan and Israel (1994), and Syrian-Israeli talks on the Golan Heights (1994) have all contributed to the greatest approximation of stability in this area since the independence of Israel was declared. Although the defeat of Labor leader Shimon Peres (who succeeded assassinated Prime Minister Yitzhak Rabin in late 1995) raised concerns about the future of the peace process, the conservative Likud government of Benjamin Netanyahu continued to negotiate, as has his successor, Ehud Barak. Palestinian and Israeli extremist factions opposed to a final peace settlement in which both sides coexist continue to attempt to undermine the process periodically. A new Labor government in Israel and the succession of King Abdullah in Jordan promises to add new vitality to the peace process.

The Persian Gulf conflict became a prominent regional problem after the fall of the Shah of Iran in 1979. Previously, the Shah's regime had been a bulwark of western interests, ensuring continued western access to the two-thirds of the world's known oil reserves that are located in the area. After the Shah was overthrown by radical Persian Shiite Muslims (Shiism being one of the two major sects of Islam), Iran came into conflict with the other states of the region, which are predominantly Sunni (the other major Islamic sect). The result was a prolonged war between Iran and Iraq from 1980 to 1988; this was followed by the Persian Gulf War of 1990–91, in which Iraq invaded and occupied Kuwait but was expelled by an American-led coalition under UN auspices. Iran and Afghanistan have more recently nearly come to blows over alleged excesses by the Afghan Taliban regime against Iranian citizens.

For several reasons, the Persian Gulf conflict remains a source of instability. The first is the underlying antagonism between ethnically Persian, religiously Shiite Iran and ethnically Arab Iraq, where Sunnis dominate though they are a numerical minority. Within Iraq, Saddam Hussein remains an intransigent leader, in large part defying international pressure to reduce his belligerence toward Iraq's neighbors and his violations of international standards of behavior. Moreover, since the Gulf War, the Kurdish minority in northern Iraq has existed as a semiautonomous "state," protected from Iraqi authority by American, British, and French forces. This arrangement, originally called Operation Provide Comfort and renamed Operation Northern Watch in 1997, is an irritant that Saddam Hussein would like to eliminate (the Shiites of extreme southern Iraq are aided by a similar arrangement called Operation Southern Watch).

In South Asia, the Indian subcontinent is also the center of a number of potential regional conflicts. Muslims and Hindus have been rivals in the area for about a thousand years, ever since Muslims first entered it. Their conflict was muted under British colonial rule but broke out into widespread violence when the subcontinent was partitioned into predominantly Hindu India and predominantly Muslim Pakistan in 1947 and millions fled from one state to the other. India and Pakistan also fought wars in 1965 and 1971, the latter eventuating in the secession from Pakistan of East Pakistan (Bangladesh), with Indian assistance.

The situation within the region remains potentially volatile. India and Pakistan have major territorial claims against each other, focusing especially on the Indian-held province of Kashmir, which has a Muslim majority and has sustained a Pakistani-backed rebellion for years. Fighting over Kashmir continued in 1999. The ongoing ethnic conflict in Sri Lanka between the ruling Sinhalese majority and the Tamil minority also engages India, which has a Tamil population of about 60 million. On the periphery of the region, the rivalry between India and China, the world's two most populous countries, remains a latent but potential source of conflict. The possibility of interstate warfare in this region is of particular concern because India, Pakistan, and China are all openly nuclear states since India and Pakistan publicly tested these weapons in 1998.

The Southeast Asian conflict involves a triangular dispute among the three major countries of the peninsula, Vietnam, Cambodia, and Thailand. It is a long-standing ethnonational conflict that was interrupted when the French colonized Indochina (Vietnam, Laos, and Cambodia). With decolonization, and especially the end of the Vietnam War, it erupted into active regional war.

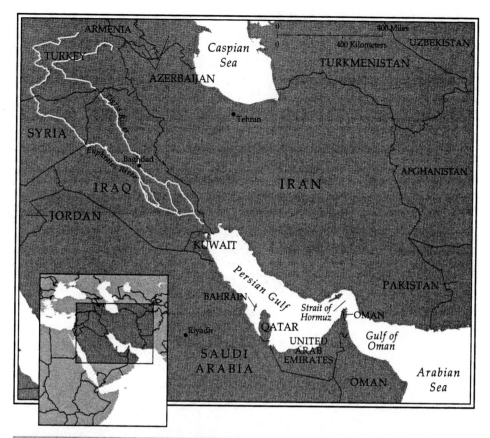

Map 11-2 The Persian Gulf Region

The stimulus to this regional war was the Cambodian civil war, itself an outgrowth of the Vietnam conflict. The communist Khmer Rouge won the internal war in 1975 and embarked on a policy of murdering large elements of the population it viewed as politically intransigent. The atrocities stimulated a massive flight, primarily into Thailand, where the refugees were not especially welcome, and the intervention of the Vietnamese armed forces, who occupied and pacified much of Cambodia. The fact that the Vietnamese and Cambodians are traditional deadly enemies added to the tension of occupation.

The conflict in Southeast Asia is, for the moment, latent. The government of Thailand has remained strong enough to ward off expansionist desires by its neighbors; the Vietnamese have adopted a less confrontational posture toward the First Tier and their neighbors as a means of gaining greater international respectability (making overtures for investment toward Europe, North America, and the Pacific Rim and gaining full diplomatic recognition by the United States); only Cambodia remains a point of major

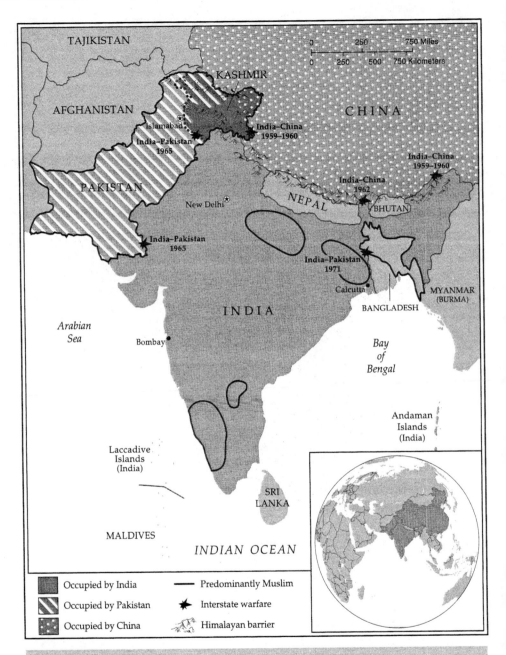

Map 11-3   Regional Conflicts in South Asia

©1996 by St. Martin's Press, Inc. From: *Contours of Power,* by Snow/Brown. Reprinted with permission of Bedford/St. Martin's Press, Inc.

contention. Although UN-supervised elections were held in 1993 and appeared to create stability for a time, the country continues to limp along, buffeted by periodic outbreaks of political violence.

The fifth and final regional conflict, in the Balkans, is located along one of the major boundaries between the First and Second Tiers. The violence in the region has centered on Yugoslavia, and notably on the republic of Bosnia and Herzegovina, whose three-sided civil war was discussed as the case study in Chapter 2. The area of Kosovo within Serbia, which has a heavily Albanian population, erupted into secessionist violence in 1997 that escalated in 1998 and greatly intensified in 1999, when a Serbian campaign of ethnic cleansing and a NATO air campaign against the Serbs resulted in a massive flight of Kosovars into neighboring countries. Moreover, there is a real prospect that the conflict could spread within the region. A Serbian advance to reclaim the Former Yugoslav Republic of Macedonia could draw Greece, and possibly Bulgaria, into the conflict.

Farther north, there are other similar cases of ethnic mixing in the region—for example, the population of Transylvania, in Romania, is ethnically Hungarian, and the population of the Soviet successor state of Moldova (formerly Moldavia) is largely Romanian. In fact, there are numerous parallels between the situation in Yugoslavia and that in the Soviet successor states. As discussed earlier, Yugoslavia was modeled after the Soviet Union, including the intermixing of ethnic populations. Many former Soviets, especially Russians, are anxiously watching events in the Balkans; the methods of "ethnic cleansing" by which groups were driven out of areas of Bosnia and Kosovo could, in some instances, be attempted against Russian minorities in a number of the successor states, a condition that would certainly activate the Russian military.

The Weapons States

Regional conflicts have been exacerbated by the rise of what political columnist Charles Krauthammer, in an article in *Foreign Affairs,* called "weapons states." He defined these as "small, aggressive states armed with weapons of mass destruction and possessing the means to deliver them." The weapons have some combination of NBC capability; the delivery means are ballistic missiles.

The quintessential weapons state is Iraq, for which the term was basically coined. After the end of the Iran-Iraq war in 1988, Iraq engaged in a program of massive armament, collecting in the neighborhood of $50 to $60 billion worth of arms. It accelerated an active chemical weapons capability (having already used chemical weapons against Iran and its own Kurdish minority in 1987), as well as a clandestine nuclear weapons program. It also continued to acquire Soviet Scud B missiles, which it used against Iranian cities in 1988 and against Israel and Saudi Arabia during the Persian Gulf War.

What helps define the weapons state is that it is an otherwise rather minor part of a region. The population of Iraq, for instance, is about 14 million (including the Kurdish and Shiite populations that are in rebellion), as compared with an Iranian population of about 65 million. In terms of sheer numbers, Iran should be the dominant power of the two, as it was under the Shah. With the Shah's overthrow, much of Iran's professional military was broken up; then the Iraqi military build-up made it the clear rival of Iran and a major power in the region.

Weapons states create a number of specific regional and systemic problems. First, controlling proliferation of some of the advanced military capabilities possessed by these states is very difficult. The easiest and cheapest capability to develop is chemical weaponry (also known as "poor man's nuclear weapons"). These can be produced from commonly available materials that can be purchased legally, and a chemical plant can be readily converted to chemical weapons production. To make matters worse, any number of Second Tier states—weapons state North Korea being a prime example—have been willing to build chemical weapons plants for a price. Similarly, an impressive list of countries, including China, are or have been in the business of building and selling ballistic missiles. Easily accessible chemicals can also be fashioned into crude but highly effective bombs, such as those used in Oklahoma City in 1995 and against the Khobar apartment complex in Dhahran, Saudi Arabia, in 1996.

A second problem is that these capabilities are becoming increasingly sophisticated and increase the deadly potential of regional conflicts. One of the lures of NBC or missile capability is that it can turn a militarily inconsequential country into one of great military importance. When one side in a regional conflict possesses one or more of these capabilities and its adversary does not, then the possessor may hold a critical advantage. NBC weapons

In the Persian Gulf War, Iraq never used the chemical weapons it had launched a few years earlier against Iranian troops and Kurdish separatists. But with the anti-Iraqi coalition forces fearful of such attacks, many of the Saudi Arabian soldiers and other Muslims shown here were taking no chances, wearing protective masks as they prayed in a hotel basement being used as a bomb shelter.

and ballistic missiles can rapidly and decisively make the prospects of war more deadly in a preexisting regional balance.

This point leads to a third problem posed by weapons states: the entry of these capabilities into a region can lead to a measures-countermeasures arms spiral. If one side gains any of the NBC capabilities, it is not unreasonable for its adversary to attempt to gain a like capability, either as a deterrent or for offensive use. A missile acquisition program in one country can stimulate an arms spiral involving offensive missiles and defenses against missiles.

A fourth and final problem is that weapons states pose a direct threat to First Tier states and create the possibility that they could be drawn into Second Tier conflict. Apart from isolated incidents of terrorism, few Second Tier states currently have weapons that can directly attack any First Tier state (because of limits on missile range); a major exception is Japanese vulnerability to Chinese and North Korean capabilities. However, First Tier forces scattered around the globe may be subject to attack in or outside war zones—as was the case when 27 American soldiers were killed in an Iraqi Scud attack in their barracks in Dhahran, Saudi Arabia, during the Persian Gulf War, again at the Khobar complex in 1996, and again when American embassies in Kenya and Tanzania were bombed in 1998. If personnel of a First Tier state were attacked directly by, say, chemical weapons, how would First Tier armed forces react?

Such questions lead to the more general issue of involvement by the First Tier in conflicts within the Second. While it is true that for the most part First Tier states' interests are not sufficiently engaged in most Second Tier conflicts to make intervention appealing (the obvious exception being situations where petroleum resources are involved, as in the Gulf War), the use of NBC, especially nuclear, weapons could change that calculus. There is absolutely no empirical evidence (evidence based in observation) to suggest if or how the escalatory process is engaged when nuclear weapons are used, because nuclear war at any level—war in which more than one state had nuclear weapons—has never occurred. This problem was especially acute during the Cold War. What would have happened if a Soviet client had used nuclear weapons against an American client? Although the dynamic of superpower involvement on opposing sides has vanished, the use of NBC weapons would qualitatively change things. Could the First Tier sit idly by if a weapons state used nuclear weapons against a helpless, defenseless state? What if two rivals like India and Pakistan both escalated to the exchange of nuclear weapons? Or would the prospect, however remote it might seem, of involvement in a war with NBC weapons potential cause First Tier states to conclude they should not become engaged?

Although we lack the knowledge needed to answer these kinds of questions, the very fact that they can be asked and that there are scenarios in which escalation might occur predisposes many to seek ways of curbing access to the weaponry that characterizes the weapons state. A primary vehicle for doing so is arms control.

Arms Control and Proliferation

The acquisition of a military capability by more and more countries that did not previously possess it (proliferation) and the use of means to prevent such acquisition or curb such capabilities (arms control) are opposite goals normally dividing countries that already have

Contours of the Future?

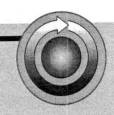

The Conventional Arms Trade

During the Cold War there was a concerted competition, principally between the superpowers, to supply arms to the Third World. The motives were sometimes complex but were reducible to two basic ones. The first was to gain influence in Third World countries or to deny influence to the other side. Since if one superpower refused to provide weapons the other probably would provide them, this was a lively motive. The second motive was profit: the sale particularly of large items such as airplanes provided revenue for defense industries, lowered fixed costs for research and development by amortizing such costs over larger production runs, aided a country's overall balances of payments with the rest of the world, and in the case of the Soviets, occasionally provided a source of badly needed hard currency.

Conventional (nonnuclear) arms sales peaked worldwide at $61.5 billion in 1988, the year before the revolutions in Eastern Europe, and have declined since then except in 1990, when preparations for the Persian Gulf War caused the figures to rise. In 1992 the global figure was $26.2 billion,

and it dropped by 22 percent to $20.4 billion in 1993, about one-third the level of the peak year.

The United States remains the Second Tier's principal armorer. In 1992 the American share of the total global trade was $14.6 billion, about 56 percent of the total; in 1993 the figure was $14.8 billion, about 73 percent of a smaller total. Eighty percent of that total was accounted for by two large arms sales: McDonnell Douglas Corporation sold 72 F-15 fighter jets valued at $9.5 billion to Saudi Arabia, and Kuwait bought 256 M1A1 main battle tanks worth $2.2 billion from the General Dynamics Corporation.

The trend continues. The Congressional Research Service, which produces an annual report on arms sales, reports that in 1997 the United States remained the leading arms supplier, selling $15.2 billion worth. Britain was second with a volume of $5.9 billion, France was third at $4.9 billion, and Russia was a distant fourth at $2.4 billion. The U.S. share was 44 percent of the global figure.

Source: New York Times (national edition), August 4, 1998, A5.

a capability from those that do not. During the Cold War, the emphasis was on regulating the nuclear arsenals of the superpowers in such a way as to minimize the likelihood of nuclear war between them. Now there is a new emphasis.

The record of arms control in the past and prospects for it in the future are decidedly mixed. The clear intent of states favoring arms control is to stabilize a situation (normally one from which they benefit) by containing either the amount of weaponry, the number of parties possessing such weaponry, or both. States that resist such restriction generally do so because they feel disadvantaged by the status quo. In the contemporary system, the countries of the First Tier mostly favor arms control, while most proliferation occurs in the Second Tier. As long as international violence remains a threat in the Second Tier, there will be some resistance to arms control measures, especially if they appear to be imposed by the First Tier (which they often are).

The nuclear balance between the United States and Russia, which inherited the Soviet arsenal after negotiations with Ukraine, Belarus, and Kazakhstan (the other republics in which Soviet weapons were stationed), continues to cause some concern: the weapons remain even if the intent to use them does not. In the new international system, arms control will likely be an issue debated between the First and Second Tiers, but at a lower level of urgency than during the Cold War and centered around possession of NBC weapons and ballistic missiles.

Dynamics of Arms Control

In its broadest sense, arms control is a technique by which states seek to enhance their individual national security or the security of the international system. When a given arms control proposal is perceived as increasing the security of those party to it, it is likely to succeed. If, however, some or all parties believe an arms control treaty will increase their insecurity, they are likely to reject it. To put the point a slightly different way, the key to arms control is convincing potential parties that they are better off under an arms control regime than they would be without it.

Since different individuals and groups have different perceptions of what constitutes security, there will always be disagreement about whether particular arms control proposals contribute to security or to insecurity. Some believe that a key element in successful arms control is to alter expectations by changing the way security is viewed; for instance, by defining security less in military terms.

These different perceptions are largely a matter of differences in vantage point, especially in the First Tier–Second Tier context. This point is captured in a construct derived from analysis of nuclear weapons proliferation during the Cold War: the N + 1 problem. In this formulation, N represents the number of states that currently possess nuclear weapons and +1 the addition of one more nuclear state.

The basic problem is that N and 1 have different perspectives. As far as the current possessors are concerned, the size of the nuclear "club" is acceptable as it is, while an addition (+1) creates additional problems. Would-be possessors, of course, disagree. If a state gains nuclear weapons and becomes part of N, however, it may then see additional potential possessors (new "1's") as a problem. In the current context, the First Tier states that are urging Second Tier states to eschew NBC or ballistic-missile capability are, by and large, possessors of these capabilities and not interested in seeing other states follow suit.

A state's perspective on and attraction to arms control also depends on the kind of control being proposed. Agreements sought by arms controllers can be placed into three types: arms freezes, arms reductions, and disarmament. (The last type, however, is not technically a form of arms control, since control implies there are some remaining arms in whatever category of weapons is under consideration.)

The definitions of the three forms are straightforward. In an *arms freeze,* a category of weapons is frozen at some predetermined time and normally in some predetermined numbers for all parties. It is the least difficult and least controversial form of arms control, and may also be the least effective. It is easiest for national security bureaucracies to accept because it does not entail destroying deployed weapons that those who authorized them felt were needed. If the level of existing arms is itself the problem, however, arresting the numbers is also the least effective method.

The second form of arms control is *arms reduction,* in which a category of weapons is shrunk from an existing level to a lower level. In traditional nuclear arms control parlance, this type was further divided into what were called shallow-cut and deep-cut reductions, according to the degree of reduction involved. Although there was no real consensus about the exact distinction between those subtypes, a 50 percent reduction marks the approximate dividing line.

The deeper the cuts are, the more controversial arms reductions are. Since arms control agreements typically are made between adversaries rather than friends, there is always the possibility that one or both parties might attempt to cheat by hiding excess stocks of controlled weapons. Therefore, it is necessary to have some means to monitor, or verify, compliance. Adequate means of verification can allow distrustful adversaries to enter into and implement agreements that serve their individual and collective security interests, something that was impossible to accomplish without monitoring capability. (The role of reconnaissance satellites in this process is discussed in the accompanying Impact of Technology box.) However, monitoring is never perfect; some amount of cheating (hopefully small) will normally be possible. A relevant question then would be, is the structure of the agreement

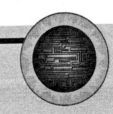

The Impact of Technology

Satellites and Arms Control Verification

A technological innovation was largely responsible for breaking the prisoner's dilemma (discussed in Chapter 5) that had blocked completion of agreements between the United States and the Soviet Union to limit their nuclear arsenals. The dilemma was the inability to trust the other side not to build weapons in excess of agreed numbers. Since "cheating" might provide a distinct military advantage to the side that went over the limits, this distrust was a formidable problem.

The reconnaissance satellite, which came into use in 1960, swept away the problem; by taking progressively sharper pictures of Soviet (and American) territory, it enabled each side to observe what the other was doing. Satellites produced what was called "national technical means of verification" of an adversary's behavior.

Satellites cannot see everything, however, and their limitations affected the nature and extent of agreements. Since they could not take pictures of the insides of scientific laboratories or other facilities, details that could only be verified thereby were excluded from agreements. What could be verified, and usefully made part of arms control agreements, were large weapons systems such as ICBMs (and especially their permanent silos) and submarines newly commissioned (or, for that matter, under construction).

The contribution of the satellite to breaking the impasse in Soviet-American relations cannot be overstated. Prior to development of this means of verification, relations were uniformly negative and confrontational, and there was little belief in the possibility of cooperation. With satellites taking detailed pictures of the ground below, it became possible to reach a whole series of arms control measures, promoting a dialogue that helped make ending the Cold War possible.

such that cheating would make sense? The answer is directly related to the size of residual weapons stocks negotiated in an agreement.

Generally speaking, the larger the arsenals after arms reduction, the less incentive there is to cheat; the reason, simply put, is that small increments of advantage provided by cheating make less difference to overall balances after shallow cuts than after deeper ones. If, for instance, the number of nuclear warheads of each superpower were reduced from 12,000 (close to the real Cold War number) to 9,000 (a shallow cut), then hiding 500 additional weapons would offer little advantage and would hardly be worth the potential embarrassment of disclosure. If those smaller arsenals were further reduced to 3,000 apiece (a deep cut), however, a residue of 500 hidden weapons might confer an advantage to the cheater that would warrant the risk of getting caught.

These numbers illustrate another important point. The first, shallow-cut reduction (from 12,000 to 9,000) was close to the outcome of the Strategic Arms Reduction Talks I (START I), negotiated between the United States and the Soviet Union before the Cold War had totally dissolved. The deep cut (from 9,000 to 3,000) was negotiated between the United States and Russian President Boris Yeltsin in 1992 as START II after the Cold War competition had ended. The point is that it is far easier to negotiate deeper reductions in an atmosphere of relative comity than in an atmosphere of tension and conflict—when arguably the reductions are more necessary.

The third form of arms control, *disarmament*, is the agreement to eliminate a whole category of weapons. Normally such an action will occur when both or all parties agree that a

Web Sitings: Searching for Start

Although the START II Treaty has been signed by both governments and given positive advice and consent by the U.S. Senate, it had not been ratified by the Russian Duma (Parliament) as of middle 1999 because of the continuing political confrontation between Russian President Yeltsin and the Duma.

What if you wanted to know the most up-to-date information on START II and its status? Where would you go? In most of the Web Sitings to this point, the path through the web has been pretty straightforward. But is that the case with arms control agreements? The answer is, not so obviously.

In that case, it may be time to surf the web, to use a little imagination. Since the State Department negotiates treaties, that would seem a logical place to start. How do you get to the home page? If you know the site (http://www.state.gov), you can go directly. If not, use the find mechanism on one of the available search engines and type in "State Department." Once you get to the home page, scroll down until you come to arms control (it is under the International Policy directory), and call up START.

There is an easier alternative, and that is to go directly to the U.S. Arms Control and Disarmament Agency, which is the repository for arms control agreements entered into by the U.S. government. Either type "Arms Control and Disarmament Agency" into the search engine, or call up the site (http://www.acda.gov). Or if you want another path, simply call up "Strategic Arms Reduction Treaty" on the search engine and sample the menu the engine provides.

category is either inherently destabilizing or of no remaining military utility. The 1987 Intermediate Nuclear Forces (INF) Treaty between the superpowers was of this nature; it eliminated categories of weapons that were designed to support conventional combat activities but that would have devastated large parts of the territories of NATO and Warsaw Pact countries if they were ever used.

Most of the existing theory and experience related to arms control comes from the efforts to regulate the nuclear competition between the United States and the Soviet Union—that is, efforts with the explicit purpose of reinforcing deterrence in a bilateral relationship between heavily armed, technologically advanced powers. If our analysis to this point has been cogent, this form of arms control will recede in importance in the evolving international system. The two principal Cold War antagonists are no longer adversaries—one of them no longer even exists in its Cold War form—and the likelihood of arms competitions between Russia and the United States or within the First Tier is small. After the transition it is likely that the United States and Russia will remain the world's premier nuclear powers, if with much reduced arsenals (about 3,000 warheads each). As we have argued earlier, the remaining arsenals serve to promote a stability in their relationship that may be expected to survive any interruption in the democratizing process in Russia.

Arms Control and the Second Tier

The major arms control efforts of the evolving order are likely to focus on limiting the introduction of highly lethal capabilities into Second Tier regions and regional conflicts. Such efforts raise issues of national security for Second Tier states that confront one another; arms control will also have an intertier dimension because the First Tier will likely see the problems as systemic, international security concerns.

The fear of nuclear weapons spreading to and within the developing world is by no means new, and experience offers some precedent for arms control interaction between the tiers. Direct and indirect efforts whose success or failure may be relevant to the future were attempted during the Cold War era.

The indirect attempts at preventing horizontal proliferation (the spread of weapons to previously nonpossessing states) came in the form of test bans—treaties banning nuclear testing in different media. The first and most significant was the Limited Test Ban Treaty (LTBT) of 1963. The first nuclear arms control treaty successfully negotiated by the superpowers, LTBT banned testing in the atmosphere. In addition to its obvious benefits for areas downwind from atmospheric testing, the treaty also had an explicit antiproliferation purpose on which the Soviets and Americans could agree: given the technology and state of science of the time, it was unlikely that any developing country could produce a nuclear device in which it would have any confidence unless the device could be tested in the medium where it would be used in war—above ground in the atmosphere. LTBT was followed by a series of treaties banning tests everywhere but underground, and restricting the nature and scope of underground testing. All were aimed at countries with nascent nuclear weapons programs.

The more direct attempt to prevent the spread of nuclear weapons to the Third World came through the Nuclear Nonproliferation Treaty (NPT) of 1968. Negotiated under the leadership of the United States, the Soviet Union, and Great Britain, the NPT attempted to create a nuclear weapons caste system. Nuclear weapons possessors who sign it can maintain their weapons, but cannot share weapons technology with nonpossessors and are obliged to work toward nuclear disarmament. The nonpossessor signatories agree not to attempt to gain nuclear weapons. States in the second category come in two varieties. Some have joined the treaty simply because they had no desire to build nuclear weapons (Germany and Sweden); others have joined because, whatever they might like, they are unlikely to be able to produce such weapons (most African states other than South Africa). The list of states that have not signed the treaty includes nuclear or near nuclear states such as India, Pakistan, and Israel.

The NPT has been a mixed success. No state has ever exercised its right to withdraw, although North Korea threatened to do so in the summer of 1993. Those states that have joined the treaty have, by and large, abided by their obligations. Saddam Hussein's Iraq, with its clandestine nuclear weapons program that created so much controversy following the Persian Gulf War, is a clear and challenging exception, as was North Korea in its unwillingness to submit to full International Atomic Energy Agency inspections required under the treaty in 1994 (this situation was resolved by a U.S.-negotiated agreement to supply North Korea with modern nuclear reactors from which nuclear weapons–grade material cannot be extracted). The successful outcome of the treaty's five-year review in 1995 (it must be renewed every five years) was expected to reinforce concern about the continuing problem of proliferation. Reactions to that renewal are included in the accompanying Views from Abroad box.

The NPT and other attempts at avoiding nuclear proliferation have always been based on efforts to restrict the availability of weapons-grade nuclear material. The Nuclear Suppliers Group—an informal grouping of the major First Tier suppliers of nuclear energy materials—has acted as a kind of coordinating device to maintain safeguards on the export of plutonium of a quality that can be converted to bombs. A significant development along these lines is the Missile Technology Control Regime (MTCR). This agreement began as an informal coalition initiated by G–8 countries to prevent the export of ballistic missiles and their supporting technologies from the major First Tier states and Russia to Second Tier countries. MTCR has expanded to include over 20 countries, including Argentina and Brazil, which previously were missile exporters. A major novelty is the fact that it is a product of G–8, suggesting that the group's economic summits are evolving into something broader.

Has MTCR been effective? As with NPT, the answer is mixed. The members of MTCR—and it should be noted that MTCR is a gentleman's agreement, not a treaty—have been vigilant in upholding the ban on missile exports. The problem has been how to widen the list of participants to include more Second Tier states. In 1994, for instance, one of the major conditions of American continuation of China's most-favored-nation status was that China honor the ban on missile exports—in essence, join MTCR, which it has subsequently done.

What is the future of arms control? Clearly its major rationale involves regulating activity within the Second Tier, where the proliferation of NBC and ballistic-missile capabilities poses the major military threat to regional balances and stability. For Second Tier states, these are national security problems as long as there are no effective mechanisms for containing proliferation systemically and providing adequate security assurances to these states. Potential new weapons states must be prevented from reaching that status if Second Tier violence is to be moderated.

Second Tier states caught in regional conflicts probably cannot do this themselves. In a regional context, there is too much volatility to promote the kind of deep-cutting or elimination

Views from Abroad

The Nuclear Nonproliferation Treaty

The Nuclear Nonproliferation Treaty (NPT), the extension of which was negotiated in 1995, remains one of the most ambitious yet controversial arms control measures. This controversy is evidenced by global press reactions during the negotiation period that reflect long-standing disagreements about the rights and obligations of signatories and nonsignatories.

A leading newspaper in a nonnuclear signatory country, *Suddeutsche Zeitung* of Munich, Germany, gave reasonably high success marks to the treaty, saying it has been "relatively effective" in keeping "the circle of atomic powers as small as possible," and that under the regime "the shrinking process" of states abandoning nuclear weapons programs has made notable progress. In signatories that do possess nuclear weapons, concern was expressed about the obligations possessors have under the treaty. Moscow's *Izvestia* publicly speculated that the five admitted nuclear powers (the United States, Russia, Britain, France, and China) "are clearly going to have to explain how and when they are planning to...completely dismantle their nuclear stockpiles, prohibit nuclear testing, and cease the production of weapons-grade nuclear materials." In the view of the *Financial Times* of London, this concern argued for a limited but renewable extension (which was the approach eventually approved) for the purpose of "leaving nonweapons states with some influence and for keeping weapons states' feet to the fire."

In the wake of the renewal, France and China announced their intentions to carry out a series of underground nuclear tests, producing much criticism that these actions violated the spirit of the NPT. *The Hindu* of Madras, India, condemned both countries, saying they "have declared that they will perfect their arsenals and then stop testing altogether." It added that "China added insult to nuclear injury by citing the fact that, of the five [admitted nuclear powers], it had conducted the fewest explosions."

France, which proposed and subsequently carried out the most extensive tests, received the most criticism. *The Hindu* called the decision "a definite slap in the face of the 174 nonnuclear countries that voted for the indefinite extension of the NPT." *The Guardian* of London deplored "the contemptuous timing of the announcement, only a month after France and the other nuclear addicts pledged to exercise 'utmost restraint.'" Toronto's *Globe and Mail* argued that the actions of French President Jacques Chirac "confirmed his country's reputation as a haughty and insensitive loner," while Paris's *L'Humanite* (the Communist Party newspaper) asserted Chirac "takes the enormous risk of relaunching the arms race." Finally, the semi-official *Al Ahram* of Cairo asks, "What will prevent [non-NPT] nuclear countries such as Israel and India from conducting nuclear tests? If the superpowers can betray their commitments..., what is the value of such treaties?"

Source: World Press Review, June 1995, p. 6, and August 1995, p. 4.

of deadly arsenals that is necessary for stability. Unrestrained, the incentives will sometimes favor the emergence of would-be hegemons that seek to obtain regional ascendancy by developing deadly capabilities.

Only the First Tier has the capacity to provide the leadership needed for a system of deterrence that could stabilize weapons proliferation. The possible forums through which this can occur, singly or in combination, include the UN Security Council (especially if the permanent membership is expanded to include Germany and Japan); the G–8 membership as in the case of Russia; or NATO expanded through the Partnership for Peace.

Summary ━━━━━━━━━━━━━━━━━━━━━━━━━━━━

Deterring Arms Proliferation

Acquisition deterrence
1. Persuasion
2. Coercion

Employment deterrence
1. Retaliatory threats
2. Defense/denial

How can the proliferation of deadly capabilities be discouraged? We will examine a sequence of options involving two kinds of deterrence: acquisition deterrence and employment deterrence. The definitions of these terms are intuitive. *Acquisition deterrence* refers to attempts to prevent countries from gaining undesirable capabilities, by getting them to join control regimes such as NPT. This could be accomplished by offering positive incentives as NPT does—such as guaranteed fuel supplies for nuclear power reactors. For those countries not so easily persuaded, coercive actions may be attempted, such as the economic sanctions against Saddam Hussein and North Korea's Kim Il-Sung and his son and successor, Kim Jung Il, because of their failure to cooperate with UN inspection of suspected nuclear facilities. For these nonproliferation efforts to be satisfying to the range of regional actors, some mechanism, such as the UN, needs to be available to monitor compliance.

If states cannot be induced to eschew deadly capabilities, a next step is *employment deterrence*—actions to discourage possessors from using them. Steps that may be taken include threats of retaliation and the erection of defenses rendering the capability ineffective; those are familiar constructs from the period of nuclear deterrence between Cold War rivals.

Whether any of these methods of deterrence is feasible depends on First Tier resolve—which leads back to questions about how the Second Tier fits into the new international system. If the First Tier decides to marginalize the Second Tier (or at least its most volatile areas), in effect turning away from regional problems because sufficient interests are not engaged, then arms control structures adequate to the task are unlikely to be developed. If, on the other hand, the First Tier adopts the attitude that linkages between it and the Second Tier require the adoption of an international security posture, then it may be possible to develop effective mechanisms.

Internal Violence, National Disintegration, and the Media

By no means all, or even most, of the violence and instability in the Second Tier is generated by conflicts between states, which are limited to a few areas. Of greater frequency and concern in the post–Cold War world are some very intensive and highly publicized wars within states of the Second Tier.

Internal conflict is nothing new to the Second Tier. Much of the violence has its roots in the decolonization process; for instance, long-standing conflict between the Hutu and Tutsi groups gave rise to the process leading to the bloody breakup of Rwanda and Burundi in the 1960s and continued intermittently until it erupted into massive slaughter in the early 1990s (as discussed in the Case in Point box "The Rwandan Tragedy"). In fact, some of the conflicts that preceded the end of colonialism were bloodier and more atrocious than some of those that have gained attention in recent years. What is different about the recent conflicts is that they are highly public, visible, and thus hard to ignore. In the past—including the Cold War era—much of this turmoil unfolded out of sight of the First Tier public; the emergence of global television networks nowadays ensures greater awareness of those episodes of inhumanity that television chooses to publicize.

In the post–Cold War world, the specter of groups within a state attacking one another with the kind of savagery that only deeply held antagonisms can produce first appeared conspicuously in Iraq, in the attacks by Saddam Hussein against the Kurds and Shiites who had risen in rebellion in the wake of the Persian Gulf War. That his campaign against the Kurds was only the continuation of actions dating back to the 1960s was lost on all but a few experts and partisans; what was remembered were the television pictures of helpless, dying refugees on the mountainsides of southern Turkey. A similar fate has befallen separatist Turkish Kurds at the hands of Turkish forces. Other atrocities have followed in Kosovo, Bosnia and Herzegovina, Somalia, Rwanda, and elsewhere.

What are the underlying causes of this tragic series of events? As we explained in Chapter 8, many have a direct lineal tie to the colonial legacy of multinationalism and lack of political preparation of postcolonial leaders. In many cases, another underlying cause is religion or other divisions that reinforce ethnic differentiation between groups. The problem is not, as was the case in earlier eras, any apparent desire for conversion by the sword; the idea that other groups should be forced to change their religion is never present. Rather, as loyalties to an authoritarian state have dissolved, many peoples are left without substitute symbols of authority with which they can identify. In this circumstance, ethnicity and religion—especially where religion has been suppressed, as in the former Second World—become increasingly powerful as sources of identification and difference. Russians rallying around the Russian Orthodox Church is an example.

Thus, Christian Ethiopians battled and starved Muslim Eritreans until Eritrea won its independence from Ethiopia in 1992; across the border in the Sudan, Muslims from the northern part of the country starved and slaughtered Christians and animists from the south. Christian Armenians and Muslim Azerbaijanis battle over enclaves in each other's states with great passion. Religious differences also underlay much of the violence in the Balkans, where other discernible differences between the warring groups had virtually disappeared.

Case in Point

The Rwandan Tragedy

Among Second Tier internal conflicts, the mass slaughter in Rwanda in the early 1990s stands out for the sheer scale of its horror. By August 1994, there were estimates of as many as 1 million killings in Rwanda, and the UN High Commissioner on Refugees estimated a refugee population of 3.4 million out of a national population estimated at 8.2 million in 1992. Over half the prewar population, in other words, was either dead or displaced by the slaughter—which hardly qualifies as a war, since it consisted mostly of massacres of unarmed civilians, largely from the Tutsi ethnic groups, by militias from the Hutu group. While the killing had abated, many continued to die in refugee camps, and prospects for wide-scale retribution remained a concern. In neighboring Burundi, with an almost identical ethnic mix of 85 percent Hutu and 15 percent Tutsi, inter-ethnic violence also flared in the early 1990s, though it pales in comparison with the Rwandan carnage. The renewal of Hutu-directed violence in 1996 resulted in a coup by Tutsi officers vowing to restore order and to end ethnic violence. Most observers viewed the action as yet another round in inter-ethnic violence and hatred.

The Hutu-Tutsi conflict has long historical roots. The area that is now Rwanda and Burundi was originally inhabited by the Hutu, a farming people, along with a smaller number of Twa, who are pygmy hunters and gatherers. About 400 years ago, the region was invaded by the Tutsi, a warlike people known for their herding of cattle, who effectively reduced the Hutu to a position of serfdom. This relationship between the groups continued until 1959, when the Hutu majority first rose in rebellion, killing large numbers of Tutsi and causing more to flee. By this time, intermarriage had largely destroyed

any true basis of difference, such as physical appearance. When independence was granted to the two countries in 1962 after a half-century of Belgian rule, traditional Tutsi dominance was reestablished in the area. Ethnic conflict continued in various forms, however, and the events of 1994 were just the most recent manifestations of the rivalry.

The conditions that produced the Rwandan tragedy are far from unique. Many other Second Tier countries, especially in Africa, are also potential failed states, because of long-standing patterns of inter-ethnic rivalry and hatred. In fact, Brian Atwood, director of the U.S. Agency for International Development, glumly concluded in 1994, "There isn't a country in Africa that could not become a failed state overnight."

Source: Joshua Hammer, "A Generation of Failure," *Newsweek,* August 1, 1994, p. 32.

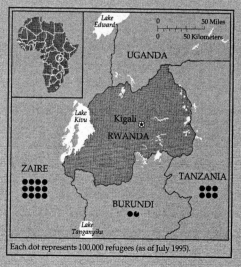

Each dot represents 100,000 refugees (as of July 1995).

Rwanda

With the fall of communism and other authoritarian political systems, religion has become a primary source of identification—and a reinforcement for ethnic division and conflict—in much of the Second Tier. Instead of tributes to Marx and Lenin, Moscow's Red Square now witnesses frequent Russian Orthodox religious processions. This one celebrated Sts. Cyril and Methodius, who traditionally are believed to have converted Russians and other Slavs to Christianity.

National Disintegration

When internal conflicts degenerate into ethnic or other communal violence, there is a strong temptation for one or all groups to settle the problem by disassembling the old state and creating new units aligning more closely with group habitation patterns. The de facto creation of a Kurdistan in northern Iraq is an example, as was the breakup of Yugoslavia and the secession of Eritrea from Ethiopia.

This trend has created a debate about whether secession—the creation of a separate state from part of an existing state—is a "right" of groups within states that supersedes the right of states to maintain their integrity. There is also disagreement about whether secession on the basis of national self-determination is either practical or beneficial. Finally, there is controversy about what role the international community should have in either abetting or discouraging national disintegration.

The question of whether there is a right to secede is a matter of national and international law that can be debated on constitutional and humanitarian grounds. Where a state does not make explicit provision for its members to withdraw from their union, does the right exist? For instance, did the states of the American Confederacy have the right to secede? They thought so; President Abraham Lincoln disagreed. Similarly, did the Baltic states have the right to drop out of the old Soviet Union? The Soviet Union eventually voted its own dissolution, but was there some inherent natural right or legal principle according to which it should have done so?

Traditional notions of international law based in sovereignty imply that there is no such inherent right; otherwise the state would not be given absolute internal authority. The modern notion of national self-determination as a right is associated with Woodrow Wilson, but whether self-determination implies the right to secede is not so certain. The issue becomes particularly acute when a national group within a state is subjected to persecution. There are also practical questions about whether secession should be expected to produce a "better" outcome than continued union. At least three separate objections to secession have been made along these lines.

The first practical objection is economic: by definition, national disintegration produces more and smaller political, and hence economic, units at a time when the global economy suggests the need for fewer and larger economic units. The countries of the First Tier and the more developed Second Tier countries, after all, are joining together in new forms: the European Union, the NAFTA region, the APEC, and ASEAN. Disintegration of Second Tier states runs contrary to this trend and may contribute to a larger gap between rich and poor countries. Moreover, most disintegrating states were economically integrated, so that disintegration requires new structures. Economic stabilization of the Soviet successor states, for instance, is hindered by the need to transform what were intrastate relationships into international ones.

The second objection is demographic: ethnic habitation patterns (where they exist and are a problem) are seldom so separate and distinct that it is possible to redraw the map along ethnic lines. Ordinarily, ethnic populations have intermixed, sometimes on their own (Lebanon) and at other times as a result of conscious state policy (Stalin's Soviet Union, Tito's Yugoslavia). The result is that new minorities may be created when boundaries are redrawn. It is not unknown for yesterday's oppressed minority to become today's oppressor when suddenly put in the majority. This contingency might be prevented by inducing migration, but that is hardly an attractive remedy. Most such migrations in history have been forced and traumatic, as people are uprooted from their homes and communities with little more of their possessions than they can carry. The migrations have also often been accompanied by considerable violence that is a further source of instability, as in Kosovo. The great unknown in the successor states of the Soviet Union is what Russia will do if Russian minorities are mistreated in other successor states. The examples of Bosnia and Lebanon suggest a need for great caution in trying to untangle habitation patterns as a means of separating ethnic groups.

The third objection to national disintegration and secession, raised with particular clarity in 1993 by the American sociologist Amitai Etzioni, is that the current trend toward these phenomena may run counter to the process of democratization that is its partial cause. The crumbling of authoritarian rule has led to demands among formerly oppressed peoples for greater political rights. As the Soviet state crumbled, the cry was for "freedom." In the First Tier, that cry was equated with a demand for political democracy. In Second Tier countries lacking any democratic tradition or culture, however, "freedom" has turned out to mean the right to self-determination—for Serbs to be ruled by Serbs, Armenians by Armenians, and Sri Lankan Tamils by other Tamils. The assertion of this right is often phrased in the form that fellow ethnic group members should be "free" to be ruled by one another. As Etzioni argued, this process in effect reinforces antidemocratic exclusionary nationalism at the expense of a more inclusionary nationalism comporting with democratic theory and practice in the First Tier since the

Case in Point

Nagorno-Karabakh and Nakichevan

The goal of self-determination for national groups divided by ethnicity, religion, and other differences has played an increasing role as the most artificial states of the former Second World crumble in the wake of the end of the Cold War. Bosnia symbolizes that phenomenon in the Balkans; the crises over Nagorno-Karabakh and Nakichevan illustrate the same dynamics in the southern part of the former Soviet Union and, because of their geographic proximity to the Caspian Sea oil and gas fields, how such conflicts may engage the major powers.

The latter problem involves the two adjacent states of Armenia and Azerbaijan, both of which became independent after the Soviet Union disintegrated, with their boundaries remaining as they were when they were Soviet republics. Armenia, a state representing an ancient nation and civilization, has a population within those boundaries of approximately 3.4 million (1992 estimate), of whom about 93 percent are Armenian Christians. Azerbaijan, with a population of about 7.4 million, is predominantly Azeri, and hence Muslim (82 percent), with Armenian and Russian minorities of about 6 percent each.

The problems of Nagorno-Karabakh and Nakichevan are the flip sides of one another. Nagorno-Karabakh is an enclave within Azerbaijan whose predominantly Armenian popula-

tion seeks unification with Armenia by carving out a short corridor linking the enclave to Armenia proper. Fighting over possession of the corridor broke out between Armenian and Azeri forces in 1992, and the Armenian forces have met with some success. Nakichevan, on the other hand, is a part of Azerbaijan physically cut off from the rest of the country by Armenia. Its inhabitants seek linkage to the main part of Azerbaijan by means of a similar (but much longer) corridor, which would have to be created from Armenian territory.

The conflict has been of differing importance to the two states. For the Armenians, it has been

Azeri women mourn a young victim of the war with Armenia.

middle 1950s. Where democracy works, according to the proponents of multiculturalism (the name attached to this approach), it is through the conscious promotion of diversity and toleration of difference, which produces stability and harmony among groups. Reinforcing old prejudices and senses of difference through attempts to create ethnically homogenous communities or states produces a uniformity and spirit of intolerance quite at odds with the emergence of democratic values. In that case, freedom expressed as self-determination is the enemy of freedom as democracy.

Nagorno-Karabakh and Nakichevan *(continued)*

especially important because of their historic mistreatment by Muslims and others and because Nagorno was arbitrarily given to Azerbaijan by Joseph Stalin. As Armenian poet Gevorg Emin puts it, "Barbarism has made us invincible. The barbarism of the Turks, of the Soviets, of the Azeris. When they are all gone, we will be here." The war's toll has not been insignificant for Azerbaijan, however, as Armenian action to create the Nagorno corridor has resulted in a huge outflow of refugees to other parts of Azerbaijan.

The international community has not shown any great interest in solving the conflict. The general attitude has been to let Russia worry about the ancient feud in its old backyard, a prospect that is regarded by the combatants with mixed feelings, since the primary interest of the Russians is presumably in reattaching the area (and especially Azerbaijan's oil reserves) to Russia.

The problem may not remain abstract for the major countries of the First Tier. Negotiations are underway between Azerbaijan and the major energy MNCs to exploit the oil and gas fields of the Caspian Sea. These fields, under Azeri control, are the world's second largest known reserves and are, as such, a potential alternative to reliance on the Persian Gulf—a high geopolitical priority.

The difficult problem is how to get the reserves to First Tier markets. There are three possibilities. One is to run pipelines through Iran to the Persian Gulf, which hardly ends reliance on that area. A second is to run the pipelines through Russia to the Baltic Sea, but that route runs directly across Chechnya. The third route is through Turkey to the Mediterranean Sea, a route transversing Nagorno-Karabakh or other areas of Azerbaijan in which the Armenians are active.

Source of quotation: New York Times (national edition), July 15, 1994, p. A3.

Armenia and Azerbaijan

The Media

As we pointed out earlier, conflicts between ethnic groups have gone on throughout the Second Tier throughout history, but the new role of global television networks has made the First Tier less able to ignore them. Because CNN, ITN, and the various news networks coming on line such as MSNBC are dedicated to around-the-clock coverage and around-the-world broadcasting of news, the extent of their coverage is considerably greater than that of the traditional, nationally based television networks. The result is that television now provides much more extensive visual coverage of international events than was heretofore available.

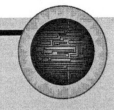

The Impact of Technology
The Media as International Agenda Setters

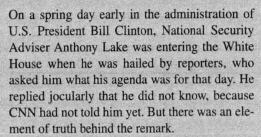

On a spring day early in the administration of U.S. President Bill Clinton, National Security Adviser Anthony Lake was entering the White House when he was hailed by reporters, who asked him what his agenda was for that day. He replied jocularly that he did not know, because CNN had not told him yet. But there was an element of truth behind the remark.

The incident is symptomatic of how people have come to think of the media, and especially global television networks, in the post–Cold War age. Global television coverage seems to be everywhere, reporting, live and in color, events as they unfold around the world. Governments seem confused, even transfixed, by the phenomenon. It took the Chinese days to get the television cameras out of Tiananmen Square during the student protests in 1989. In 1991 the conspirators trying to seize control of the government of the Soviet Union felt the need to call a live, globally televised press conference the day after President Mikhail Gorbachev had been confined to his country house, so as to try to persuade Soviet citizens and the world that what they had done was not really a coup.

Does this explosion of reportage constitute a basic change in how the international agenda is set for foreign policy makers? Are world leaders captive to what CNN and ITN choose to cover—and not to cover? Given that First Tier publics get much of their information about world affairs from television, do the television outlets unduly influence that to which officials must respond?

Conclusive evidence on this crucial matter is lacking. There is, of course, no absence of anecdotal evidence. Without televised depictions of their suffering, would the United States have come to the aid of the Kurds? of the Somalis? of the Rwandans? Would Americans then be concerned about Haitian or Cuban boat people floating in the Caribbean?

People in the media contend that events create the agenda—that they are simply transmitting news, not creating situations to which governments respond. In large measure they are correct, but there is more to the issue than that. Clearly, there are more events in the world that could be covered than are covered. African atrocities, for instance, are not confined to Somalia and Rwanda. That being the case, does the process by which the media choose what to display and what not to become part of the agenda? Almost certainly it does, and it behooves serious students of the process to try to understand more precisely the nature of this relationship.

In the early post–Cold War period, the global, often live television coverage of Second Tier violence created in the First Tier what might be called the "do-something syndrome." When confronted with vivid scenes of tragedy, people naturally react by wanting to alleviate the suffering, to do something. The problem with this response is that the visual images are normally the manifestation of far deeper problems, for which solutions are not readily available. Television coverage may stimulate public demands for action, but when the images are incomplete and the actions inappropriate or ineffectual, as the U.S. intervention in Somalia ultimately became, the reactions in the First Tier can be quite negative, even cynical. The widespread response of the American people to the Somalia experience was "no more Somalias," and a disillusioned First Tier may be more likely in the future to respond in many cases with a "let's-appear-to-be-doing-something syndrome."

Case Study: The Civil War in Congo

In the middle of 1996, a civil war broke out in the country known for a quarter-century of rule by Mobutu Sese Seku as Zaire, and known previously and subsequently as Congo. When it began as an apparent offshoot of the campaign in eastern Zaire to purge Rwandan Hutu militia members suspected of taking part in the 1994 Rwandan genocide, it was lightly regarded as a force for change—largely because it appeared to be the exclusive preserve of ethnic Tutsi, a minority in the country that had emigrated from Rwanda nearly a century ago.

To the amazement of much of the world, the movement grew in strength and size, gradually gaining control of more and more territory, and the Zairian government, especially the army, seemed unwilling or incapable of offering significant resistance. Suddenly the name of Laurent Kabila, an obscure professional revolutionary whose revolutionary roots go back to the 1960s (he is referred to disparagingly by Che Guevara in his *Diaries*) became a household name, and then a national hero. By June 1997, his triumphant revolutionaries had swept into Kinshasa, the national capital, as Mobutu fled into exile, and Kabila declared himself president of the renamed the Democratic Republic of the Congo. A little over a year later, in summer 1998, a movement to overthrow Kabila emerged in the same area of Congo from which Kabila had started. How did it all happen?

Background

The roots of Congolese/Zairian problems go back to the process of decolonization. The process of colonization began in the 1870s, when King Leopold II of Belgium took an interest in the country; after exploration by Henry M. Stanley, the Congo Free State was declared as part of the final partition of the African continent at Berlin in 1884–85. The colony was unique in that it was solely owned by the King of Belgium.

The movement for independence occurred in the 1950s, when similar movements were beginning to sweep Africa. European colonial rulers, exhausted by World War II and concluding that resistance to calls for independence were ultimately futile, were granting

Laurent Kabila, pictured at left, emerged as the rebel leader during the Congolese civil war against Mobutu Sese Seku. After the rebellion succeeded, he named himself president of the newly renamed Democratic Republic of Congo.

wholesale sovereignty to their colonies. Belgian leaders announced the intention to grant freedom to Congo in 1959; on January 27, 1960, Belgian and Congolese leaders announced that independence day would be on June 30 of that same year.

When independence came, the result was almost entirely predictable chaos. During its 75-year reign over Congo, the Belgians had done essentially nothing to prepare the Congolese for self-rule, for reasons discussed in Chapter 8. On independence day, for instance, out of a population of about 30 million, only 12 Congolese had a college degree. Moreover, tribal and regional differences that had preceded the colonial period had never been even mildly resolved. The new country was a powder keg waiting to explode.

The explosion occurred almost immediately, as rivals of Patrice Lumumba, the elected president and a purported Marxist, attacked the capital. Chaos rapidly ensued, and on August 9, the UN Security Council voted to send a peacekeeping force, the United Nations Operation in the Congo (ONUC, after its French spelling).

What must now be viewed as the *first* Congo Civil War raged for nearly four years. The heavy UN involvement at times became partisan (seeking to help prevent the secession of Katanga—now Shaba—Province) and exceeded the original mandate. Its participation in the Congolese civil war is viewed in retrospect as one of the UN's least glorious adventures. The last UN troops left the country on June 30, 1964, but fighting rapidly flared again. From the chaos, General Joseph D. Mobutu, who later changed his name to Mobutu Sese Seku, rose to power in 1965, where he remained until he was deposed in 1997.

Mobutu's rule was disastrous for the country. On paper, Congo (Mobutu changed the name to Zaire in 1971) should be—and may prove to be—one of the richest states in Africa. It is especially rich in natural resources, notably gold in the eastern areas where the Kabila movement began, and diamonds, copper, and cobalt in Shaba Province, and has considerable agricultural potential. Under Mobutu's rule, not only was Congo/Zaire's potential not

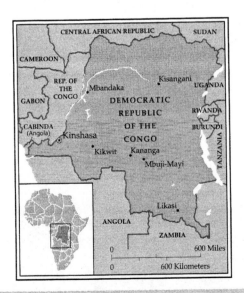

Map 11-4 **Congo/Zaire**

met, but instead the country was systematically impoverished. Due to widespread corruption, including the diversion of unknown amounts estimated in the billions of U.S. dollars into Mobutu's personal Swiss accounts (which the current government seeks to recover), the economic life of the country gradually declined, including important infrastructural elements such as roads, rail lines, and airports.

The Mobutu regime's undoing coincided with and was aided by the end of the Cold War. For all his other failings, Mobutu was an unswerving anticommunist and bulwark of anticommunism on the African continent. Because he was willing to assist in undermining attempts at communist influence—such as supporting Jonas Savimbi's UNITA movement in neighboring Angola—he received considerable support from the West, and notably the United States, which continued its support even though it opposed the quality of his rule.

When the Cold War ended, so did Mobutu's value to the West, which promptly cut him off financially. The result was the utter disintegration of what was left of the Zairian economy. Inflation ran rampant, government workers (including the Army) were unpaid or compensated with worthless currency, and the normal economy simply ceased to exist, reverting to a bartering basis for commerce. According to estimates in the *1996 CIA Factbook,* for instance, per capita GDP stood at about $400, and it took 10,618 zaires (the basic currency unit) to buy a single U.S. dollar. All of this was rightly blamed on Mobutu, whose apparently losing bout with prostate cancer left him with substantially no support in the country. There was growing consensus that his days were numbered.

The Second Congolese Civil War

It is difficult to pinpoint exactly when the revolutionary movement that became associated with Laurent Kabila began its formal campaign to topple Mobutu. It was apparently part of a general attempt to repatriate Rwandan refugees from the 1994 massacre who had fled into what was then Zaire, and it was intermixed with attempts to isolate Hutu refugees from Rwanda who were implicated in the genocide and seeking refuge from prosecution. In its earliest stages, it was unclear whether the "Tutsi militias," as they were generally referred to, had any wider intentions than affecting the refugee problem. Reportage on the movement was noticeably absent in the West; in the United States, for instance, about the only public information came from sporadic coverage in the *New York Times.*

The movement began in the easternmost part of Congo, where the ethnic Tutsi (referred to disparagingly as Rwandese by many Congolese) were concentrated and where most of the Rwandan refugees were located. Gradually, the movement replaced government control and expanded through much of the Kasai region—in the process gaining control of the gold mines, taxes from which were used to finance the revolution as it unfolded.

From this beginning, the Democratic People's Movement—a name with a curiously 1960s Marxist ring—began to extend its sway, picking up additional recruits and supporters (including mercenaries and foreign troops) along the way. There is little current indication that this was so much because of the appeal of Kabila, about whom the average Zairian knew little, or the appeal of his message, about which less was known. Rather, the movement became a simple expression of opposition to Mobutu—anybody had to be an improvement.

As it rapidly spread across the country, first into the mineral-rich southern area of Shaba and then westward toward the capital of Kinshasa, a pattern curiously reminiscent of the overthrow of Cuban dictator Fulgencia Batista by Fidel Castro emerged. There was hardly any fighting along the way—word would simply spread that the revolutionaries were headed toward an area or city, and the army, unpaid in months and in some cases years, either fled or joined the revolution. In most cases, the only fear was of looting by the Zairian Army as they abandoned their posts. When the revolutionary army approached and entered Kinshasa in early June 1997 and the new flag of the Democratic Republic of the Congo replaced Mobutu's Republic of Zaire flag, hardly a shot was fired. Mobutu's regime simply collapsed like a house of cards.

Implications

When Laurent Kabila declared himself president of this newly reconstituted country, much apprehension was mixed with hope about what the future held. There were initial demands for Kabila to open the system and share power with all those who had opposed Mobutu. When he refused to do so without offering detailed explanations and declared a vaguely timed return to democracy, there were worries about whether the tyranny of Mobutu might be replaced by the authoritarian rule of Kabila, a fear reinforced when the new government briefly placed Etienne Tshisekedi, the chief parliamentary opponent of Mobutu, under house arrest.

Allegations also quickly emerged about Kabila's ties to neighboring countries, all of which had reason to exact revenge on Mobutu. There were, for instance, accusations that regular Rwandan army forces participated in the revolution and covered up retributory actions against Hutu refugees (including atrocities documented by Amnesty International and others). Also, the government of Angola, which chafed under Mobutu's support for its UNITA opponents, supposedly contributed arms and other support for the rebels.

It is too soon to sort out all the allegations and to determine the future of Congo. The revolution there may be the harbinger for much of the future in strife-ridden, impoverished Africa, the site of much of the current and possibly future violence in the post–Cold War world.

One thing is already clear, however. In the conduct of the Second Congolese Civil War, the First Tier stayed conspicuously on the sidelines, limiting its participation to sending entreaties to both sides to limit the bloodshed and the privation to innocent civilians. With regard to the rule of Kabila, the First Tier has adopted very much a wait-and-see posture. In 1998, when an anti-Kabila insurgency began (allegedly sponsored by the Rwandan government), the same wait-and-see attitude prevailed as Kabila's forces, augmented by foreign troops (notably Angolan) succeeded in putting down the "rebels." Whether this instability and outside interference is a precedent for the future is an interesting question, one that will be addressed in Chapter 13.

The Changing Contours of Violence

The campaign between the government of Yugoslavia (Serbia and Montenegro) and Kosovar separatists into which NATO intervened with a concerted air campaign in 1999 may be the wave of the future for systemic violence. The heart of the conflict is the Serbian province of Kosovo, an area in the southwest corner of what is left of Yugoslavia that has a predominantly Albanian Muslim population. For strong historic and sentimental reasons

(Kosovo was the site of the decisive battle by which Serbs lost their independence for over 500 years), the Serbs controlling Kosovo refused even to consider the wishes of the Kosovars to regain autonomy, gain independence, or become part of neighboring Albania, with which they share a border. The result was a furtive campaign between the predominantly Serbian government forces and the Kosovo Liberation Army (aided generously from outside) that included numerous atrocities committed against civilian populations and caused NATO's campaign to pressure Serbia to end its systematic ethnic cleansing in Kosovo.

The long-term outcome in Kosovo is uncertain, but the way it is handled may have a good deal to say about the future of violence in the international system and how that system deals with or ignores that pattern. On the one hand, the "war" is typical of post–Cold War internal conflicts: most of the victims are civilians; there is clear evidence of atrocities that fit most definitions of war crimes (and resulted in war crimes indictments against President Slobodan Milosevic and other Serb leaders in May 1999); and there is abundant evidence that something like ethnic cleansing is at work. On the other hand, Kosovo was clearly outside the international spotlight, and it can be argued that no significant interests of major First Tier countries are at stake regardless of the outcome.

What will happen? Will the actions promote the secession of Kosovo? Will the alleged war criminals be brought to justice? Will the NATO bombing provide a precedent for future international reactions against regimes who violate international norms? Or in future, will world public opinion, which has become so used to violence and atrocity on a global scale, simply turn its back and ignore situations like that in Kosovo? It is a situation worth watching.

Review

This chapter examined the nature of security problems in a post–Cold War world environment. In the process, the following points were made:

1. Because of the political and economic similarities among First Tier states, there will not be any military conflicts among them. Violence and instability will occur within the Second Tier, with some security concerns at the intersection of the tiers.

2. Some regional conflicts—long-standing confrontations between Second Tier states—have been muted somewhat since the end of the Cold War. These include the Arab-Israeli conflict and those in the Asian subcontinent. A residual problem is the spread of weapons into the Second Tier, notably NBC weapons and ballistic-missile delivery systems, possession of which is the hallmark of the weapons state.

3. A principal way in which the First Tier seeks to influence regional conflicts, and especially to prevent the rise of weapons states, is through various forms of arms control. Examples include the Limited Test Ban Treaty, the Nuclear Nonproliferation Treaty, and the Missile Technology Control Regime.

4. The most serious conflicts in the Second Tier in the post–Cold War era have been internal wars. Most often occurring in so-called failed states like Somalia, Rwanda, or Haiti, these conflicts are often the result of some combination of governmental failure, ethnic or religious hatreds, and complex processes of national self-determination. They are often extremely bloody and may give rise to numerous atrocities.

5. The First Tier has not devised a comprehensive strategy for dealing with these internal conflicts. Global television coverage makes visual exposure to them inevitable, but the general absence of traditional vital interests in the outcomes makes any comprehensive policy difficult to develop.

Suggested Readings

Bell-Fialkoff, Andrew. "A Brief History of Ethnic Cleansing." *Foreign Affairs* 72, 3 (summer 1993): 110–21.

Cullen, Robert. "Human Rights Quandary." *Foreign Affairs* 72, 5 (winter 1992/93): 79–88.

Deibel, Terry. "Internal Affairs and International Relations in the Post–Cold War World." *Washington Quarterly* 16, 3 (summer 1993): 13–36.

Etzioni, Amatai. "The Evils of Self-Determination." *Foreign Policy*, 89 (winter 1992/93): 21–35.

Kampelman, Max M. "Secession and the Right of Self-Determination: An Urgent Need to Harmonize Principle with Pragmatism." *Washington Quarterly* 16, 3 (summer 1993): 5–12.

Kapstein, Ethan B. "America's Arms-Trade Monopoly." *Foreign Affairs* 73, 3 (May–June 1994): 13–19.

Kegley, Charles W., Jr., and Gregory A. Raymond. *A Multipolar Peace? Great-Power Politics in the Twenty-first Century.* New York: St. Martin's Press, 1994.

Klare, Michael T., and Daniel C. Thomas. *World Security: Challenges for a New Century,* 2d ed. New York: St. Martin's Press, 1994.

Kober, Stanley. "Revolutions Gone Bad." *Foreign Policy*, 79 (summer 1990): 3–24.

Krauthammer, Charles. "The Unipolar Moment." *Foreign Affairs* 70, 1 (winter 1990/91): 23–33.

Mazaar, Michael J. "Nuclear Weapons After the Cold War." *Washington Quarterly* 15, 3 (summer 1992): 185–201.

Millot, Marc Dean. "Facing the Emerging Reality of Regional Nuclear Adversaries." *Washington Quarterly* 17, 3 (summer 1994): 41–71.

Neumann, Stephanie. "Controlling the Arms Trade: Idealistic Dream or Realpolitik?" *Washington Quarterly* 16, 3 (summer 1993): 53–73.

Paschall, Rod. *LIC 2010: Special Operations and Unconventional Warfare in the Next Century.* Washington, DC: Brassey's, 1990.

Quester, George H., and Victor A. Utgoff. "No-First-Use and Nonproliferation: Redefining Extended Deterrence." *Washington Quarterly* 17, 2 (spring 1994): 103–14.

Sullivan, Gordon R. (Gen.), and James M. Dubik (Col.). *War in the Information Age.* Carlisle Barracks, PA: Strategic Studies Institute, June 1994.

Leonard, Sullivan Jr. *Meeting the Challenges of Regional Security.* Carlisle Barracks, PA: Strategic Studies Institute, February 1994.

Prospects for the Future

THE FUTURE OF DIPLOMACY

THE EVOLVING ROLE OF INTERNATIONAL LAW AND ORGANIZATIONS

CONCLUSIONS: THE SHAPE OF THE FUTURE?

PA

...e of ...cy

C H A

This chapter examines the principal nonviolent instrument used by states to communicate and negotiate with one another and to resolve conflicts among them. Topics addressed are the recruitment and functions of diplomats, the development of contemporary diplomatic practices, the contrast between modern and classical diplomacy, signaling and bargaining as techniques of conflict resolution, and the five rules of successful diplomatic bargaining. The chapter concludes with an examination of the role of diplomacy in restoring peace to Bosnia in 1995.

KEY CONCEPTS

diplomacy
ambassadors
modern diplomacy
classical diplomacy
summit diplomacy
Camp David Summit
signaling
ping pong diplomacy

the Astoria affair
bargaining
good offices
mediation
arbitration
ethnic cleansing
Dayton Peace Accords

OUTLINE

Sir Harold Nicolson, a distinguished British diplomat turned scholar, points out that the word diplomacy is used in widely different ways. Some writers use the term interchangeably with foreign policy, while in everyday conversation it is often used to refer to a smooth and conciliatory personal style. For our purposes, we use the term diplomacy to refer to the people, institutions, and processes used by states to conduct their political relations with one another.

As we will explain, diplomacy embraces many tasks, ranging from the mundane issuance of travel visas to intricate negotiations aimed at resolving international conflicts. Stripped of its pomp and ceremony, diplomacy is an indispensable tool in the everyday conduct of international relations. Without its established modes of communication and negotiation, countries would continually have to devise ad hoc procedures for handling issues among them.

While the functions they perform are essential for the smooth handling of international transactions large and small, diplomats themselves are often the object of broad distrust and disdain. The very nature of their work, with its characteristic secrecy, anonymity, and preference for compromise, lends itself to widespread popular belief that diplomats are more interested in preserving cordial relations with their foreign counterparts than taking firm, if contentious, stands on behalf of the ordinary people of their own country. This perception, compounded by the diplomats' lack of dependable political bases in their own countries, makes them uncommonly vulnerable as scapegoats when international dealings turn sour.

Diplomats and Diplomacy

The heart of the diplomatic enterprise is communication. The diplomat's essential calling is to convey his or her state's policies, intentions, and concerns to officials in other states. Through both explicit and symbolic diplomatic means, states communicate to one another such things as a shift in their foreign policy, their unhappiness with the behavior of another state, and their resolve in an international crisis.

The Recruitment of Diplomats

Today's professional diplomats are typically selected from among their countries' most talented elites. In the United States, for example, thousands of young aspirants compete each year for a coveted slot in the State Department's Foreign Service. Successful candidates must first excel on a rigorous written examination and then demonstrate exceptional oral and group skills in a day-long round of oral examinations and group simulations. In a typical year, about 17,000 candidates take the written examination. Of the 2,500 who pass and thus undergo the oral examinations, about 600 are placed on a list of eligible hires, and about 200 of these actually gain entry into the Foreign Service.

Once selected, the most successful diplomats rise through the ranks to reach the pinnacle of a diplomatic career: that of ambassador. An ambassador is a country's senior representative to the foreign country to which he or she is accredited. Each ambassador is in charge of an embassy, which houses and coordinates a broad array of representatives from numerous agencies whose job it is to carry out the country's foreign policy on issues ranging from human rights and environmental protection to trade and national security.

Some countries, including the United States, utilize political appointments to recruit some of their ambassadors. About two-thirds of U.S. ambassadors are career diplomats who have risen through the ranks of the Foreign Service; the other third are political appointees. Of the latter group, some are highly qualified for their positions, having distinguished themselves in some other field of endeavor, such as business, academe, or electoral politics. Others, however, are merely wealthy campaign donors of dubious qualifications for the world of diplomacy. When President Ronald Reagan named Theodore Maino, a St. Louis businessman, to be U.S. ambassador to Botswana, Maino sought to counter doubts about his qualification for the post by arguing that he had a "commitment to public service, having a lifetime association with the Boy Scouts of America."

The idea of a diplomatic career is appealing to many people. To some it suggests a life of adventure in exotic locales, while others are inspired by the prospect of serving their country and, more broadly, advancing global understanding and cooperation. In reality, however, diplomatic life is often difficult and demanding, requiring constant hard work and periodic assignments in hardship areas. The inherent demands of diplomatic work are compounded for some diplomatic corps by shortages in personnel, which force a preoccupation with immediate issues to the detriment of long-range policy planning. Another impediment to effective diplomacy, discussed more fully below, is the difficulty many small and poor countries face in recruiting and supporting an adequate corps of qualified diplomats.

Functions of Diplomacy

As noted earlier, the range of diplomatic tasks is quite broad. The most important functions are (1) representation, (2) reporting, (3) policy management, and (4) negotiation. We will briefly consider each.

Representation. Diplomats posted abroad serve as official representatives of their government. Some forms of representation are substantive, such as serving as the official channel of communication between the government represented and the host government. In other instances, diplomats serve as symbolic representatives of their country at an array of public functions, such as celebrations of national holidays, educational conferences, and media appearances. In these instances diplomats are trying to project a favorable image for their country and foster cordial relations in ways that go beyond formal government-to-government dealings. Because ambassadors in effect personify the state they represent, they are accorded an exceptional degree of deference and courtesy.

Summary

Functions of Diplomats

1. Official representation of their governments
2. Information gathering, analysis, and reporting on local conditions
3. Management of routine foreign relations
4. Conduct of negotiations

Reporting. Diplomats gather, analyze, and report information on local conditions. Although the telecommunications revolution means that officials and ordinary citizens now enjoy unprecedented live access to distant events through CNN and ITN, there is no real substitute for the kind of informed analysis that diplomats posted abroad can provide to their own governments. In all of their dealings, diplomats are alert for new information about political, economic, and social trends that might affect their government's relations with the host country. Successful career diplomats are also talented analysts, skilled at identifying the significance and interrelationship of otherwise isolated facts and figures.

Policy Management. Another key function of diplomats is to manage routine foreign relations. Diplomats posted abroad oversee the day-to-day routines of implementing a wide array of specific foreign policy programs, such as providing assistance to firms at home that are trying to develop business opportunities abroad, overseeing the implementation of treaties and alliances, and administering the distribution of economic assistance. Though seldom glamorous, and often having little impact on the process of making foreign policy, the carrying out of routine policy is one of diplomacy's essential functions.

Negotiation. Diplomats sometimes conduct negotiations. As we will explain on the next page in more detail, the communications and transportation revolutions of the twentieth century now make it possible for governments to maintain much more centralized authority over the conduct of their foreign policy. Through fax and telephone messages, foreign ministries can oversee the most precise aspects of distant talks. Thanks to jet travel, foreign

Case in Point
The U.S. Misreading of Iran

Sometimes the information gathering and analysis function of diplomacy is performed poorly, with harmful effects on policy. An example would be the failure of U.S. officials posted in Iran in the late 1970s to grasp the political significance of the Muslim movement led by Ayatollah Ruhollah Khomeini. Few officials assigned to the U.S. embassy in Tehran spoke the principal Iranian language, Farsi, or had developed contacts among the dissidents that would have alerted them to the movement's explosive potential. Instead, most of their dealings were with the western-educated, English-speaking, pro-U.S. elite that was loyal to the ruling shah.

Better information and analysis would have alerted U.S. officials that the wave of mass discontent fanned by Khomeini could not be stemmed by the Shah's repressive tactics. Continued U.S. support of the doomed Shah meant that the United States would be added to Khomeini's long list of enemies who must be punished once the Shah was toppled. After the Shah fled to the United States for medical treatment, triumphant followers of Khomeini seized the Tehran embassy and held hostage 55 Americans from late 1979 to January 1981, a flagrant violation of diplomatic immunity. The experience embittered both sides and continues to prevent good U.S.-Iran relations.

ministers or even heads of state can quickly converge to take over the negotiations in person. None of this means that the art of negotiation is a less important component of diplomacy today than it was in the eighteenth century. What it does mean is that the identity of the negotiators and the techniques used in negotiation have changed.

The Development of Modern Diplomacy

To a much greater extent than other forms of international conduct, such as trade or warfare, diplomacy is encrusted with an elaborate code of rules, traditions, and protocol that at first glance may strike modern observers as anachronistic. They are the accumulated product of a long history of diplomatic practice. Certainly the extravagant forms of diplomatic address and the immense attention paid to such matters as diplomatic rank and title seem like curious throwbacks, if not downright silly, at the end of the twentieth century. But there is a reason such seemingly antiquated traditions linger. Quite simply, they serve some need. Diplomats keep alive numerous practices that would otherwise be of merely historical interest because they believe that their purposes are better served by observing the tradition than by abandoning it as merely another outdated convention.

Given that contemporary diplomacy is still heavily conditioned by traditions begun long ago, we will survey briefly the development of diplomatic practice. Doing so will not only shed light on the character of contemporary diplomacy, but will also provide insights into the development of the international system. Students of international relations often distinguish between *classical diplomacy* and *modern diplomacy*. What separates the two periods and their respective themes is the influence of Woodrow Wilson, U.S. President from 1913 to 1921. Wilson's idealistic approach to international relations and his sharp attacks on the traditional, balance-of-power diplomacy of Europe helped set in motion a number of far-reaching changes in international diplomacy in the twentieth century. Some of these Wilsonian innovations have proven healthy, while others have been less so. However one evaluates his legacy, there is no doubting that Wilson's presidency marked a watershed in worldwide diplomatic concepts and practices.

Diplomacy in some form dates back to the formation of the earliest human communities. The ancient Greeks, Romans, Chinese, and Egyptians all developed ad hoc procedures for dealing with their neighbors. Treaties were negotiated, official personnel were dispatched, and the policies of rulers were articulated through these early diplomatic channels. Beginning in the sixth century B.C., the Athenians, Spartans, and citizens of other Greek city-states began selecting their ambassadors on the basis of their skill in oration and persuasion. The finest public speakers were sought out and dispatched to articulate their city's policy before the public assemblies of other cities. To the Greeks, diplomacy consisted almost entirely of clever oration; ambassadors were expected to be great speechmakers, not information gatherers or report writers.

Classical Diplomacy. Classical diplomacy began to take more recognizable form amid the chaotic rivalries of the Italian city-states during the fourteenth and fifteenth centuries. Following the lead of the duke of Milan, the various city-states began keeping permanent representatives in each other's capitals. Rather than being merely ad hoc envoys sent out to perform one-time tasks, the diplomats of Renaissance Italy began to acquire the stature of recognized, permanent professionals. But the fact that Renaissance Italy played so crucial a role in defining the essential character of classical diplomacy proved to be very much a double-edged sword. On the one hand, the cultural and intellectual flowering of the time

Contours of the Future?

The Future of Ambassadors

Prior to the advent of electronic communications, ambassadors were accorded broad latitude in representing their states abroad. Given the physical impossibility of communicating detailed directions to ambassadors on a broad array of issues, ambassadorial prerogatives in representation, negotiation, and policy making were often substantial. In the 1990s, however, foreign offices can dispatch instantaneous communications by voice or fax via satellite technology.

As the telecommunications revolution proceeds, with video teleconferencing making possible the "meeting" of a number of world leaders to deal with breaking issues, some believe that the venerable role of ambassador will gradually atrophy into near irrelevance. Others, though, are not so sure. Good ambassadors, they argue, are more than simple executors of instructions from their home governments. At their best, they create a favorable impression of their states through numerous appearances in the host country, and their firsthand contacts with local leaders offer invaluable, nuanced insights that no high-tech revolution can replace.

brought forth a remarkably talented array of representatives who helped to define the essential character of the ambassador. Florence alone produced such diplomatic luminaries as Dante, Petrarch, and Machiavelli. On the other hand, the constant struggle for power among the Italian states and its attendant maneuverings for advantage by forging alliances or hatching secret plots against opposing states gave to classical diplomacy an aura of intrigue, trickery, and amorality that it would never entirely shake.

As Italian diplomatic practices spread throughout Europe, by the seventeenth century France emerged as a leading continental power. Reflecting their political clout, the French contributed heavily to the formation of the institutions and principles of classical diplomacy that would shape international interactions until World War I. Among their other influences, French became the common language of diplomacy, replacing Latin. France's Cardinal Richelieu, a seventeenth-century statesman, stands out as a pioneer of classical diplomatic practice. According to Sir Harold Nicolson, Richelieu advanced the concept that diplomacy revolved around the unsentimental pursuit of the national interest, not the advancement of abstract values. Even though his was an age of monarchs and secret policymaking, he also argued that successful foreign policy ultimately depended on its ability to sustain domestic opinion behind it, an idea that would become central to the challenges of twentieth-century diplomacy.

As we noted in Chapter 3, the European powers towered over the rest of the world from the seventeenth through the nineteenth centuries. It was during this time that the procedures, principles, and styles of diplomatic interaction developed among the leading states of Europe became virtually synonymous with diplomacy itself. Though the European powers engaged in constant rivalries, their diplomats worked to maintain a balance of power amid an ambience of shared cultural values, a shared commitment to

Although the realist-oriented classical diplomacy pioneered by Cardinal Richelieu of France in the seventeenth century has given way to some extent to newer forms influenced by the idealism of U.S. President Woodrow Wilson, the ability to sustain domestic public opinion remains a key ingredient in diplomatic success.

the principle of dynastic succession, and, frequently, personal ties produced by inter-marriages among the ruling elites.

As was established by the Treaty of Westphalia in 1648, states enjoyed sovereign equality with one another. Without agreed-upon rules, however, such mundane matters as which ambassador preceded another in public ceremonies or negotiations provided an endless source of bickering and conflict. Two conferences held early in the nineteenth century finally settled most of these disputes by working out principles for diplomatic protocol. At the Congress of Vienna in 1815 and the Congress of Aix-la-Chapelle in 1818, diplomatic ranks and precedence were standardized in forms that survive today. Four ranks were established, the highest carrying the formal title of *ambassador extraordinary and plenipotentiary,* which designates someone who is fully authorized to represent his or her government and conduct negotiations in its name. As for precedence, some way had to be found to avoid the inevitable friction that would be created by trying to rank diplomats according to the importance of the countries they represent. The solution that evolved was to determine precedence among ambassadors at each capital according to the length of time they have been posted there. Seniority, determined solely by the length of term in a particular capital, provided a simple, noncontroversial way out of the inherent pitfalls of national rivalry.

Before World War I, the limited number of national players, broad agreement on the essential rules of the game, and the secrecy and flexibility available to monarchs unencumbered by democratic politics permitted diplomacy to flourish in the hands of Europe's hereditary elites. The war marked the decline of European supremacy and the rise of non-European powers, especially the United States. More fundamentally, it sparked a broad repudiation of the secret, undemocratic, and often cynical diplomatic scheming that had characterized the classical system. Traditional diplomacy now seemed the playground of an unaccountable, arrogant elite whose bumbling was blamed for the catastrophe that had befallen the people of Europe. The very term "secret diplomacy" became an epithet hurled at Europe's diplomats.

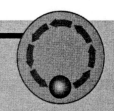

Coming to Terms

Diplomatic Immunity

As any driver in a national capital will attest, the concept of diplomatic immunity often serves as a license for abused privileges, such as avoidance of any penalty for illegal parking. Sometimes diplomatic immunity is invoked to cover more serious criminal offenses, about which a country can do little but expel the offender. However, diplomatic immunity is one of those venerable practices worked out centuries ago to routinize the everyday interactions of states. As Clifton Wilson has written, "The international rules of diplomatic privileges and immunities, which are among the oldest examples of international law, are firmly entrenched in practice, treaties and municipal legislation."

In its origins, diplomatic immunity meant that emissaries of a state were to be regarded as the personal representative of the sovereign, and any disrespect or harm inflicted on them was interpreted as a grave affront to the sovereign. With the passage of time, diplomatic immunity has taken on a wider meaning, effectively placing diplomats above the laws of the states to which they are accredited so that they cannot be harassed or prevented from carrying out their duties.

Source: Clifton E. Wilson, *Diplomatic Privileges and Immunities* (Tucson: University of Arizona Press, 1967), p. vii.

Modern Diplomacy.   Woodrow Wilson, in proclaiming his famous Fourteen Points, propagated a new standard for international dealings. "Open covenants, openly arrived at," was Wilson's memorable plea. Wilson believed that democratic governments are inherently more peace-loving than are monarchies or dictatorships, because a democratic leader must pay attention to the interests and the wishes of the general public, which is presumed to favor peace over war. He acknowledged that not all governments can be expected to become democratic at once, but insisted nonetheless that interactions among governments should be conducted according to the fundamental precepts of democratic governance: openness and accountability to the people.

The distinct forms of modern diplomacy, which have supplemented but not entirely supplanted classical diplomacy, were prompted by the spread of a Wilsonian opposition to diplomacy cloaked in secrecy and intrigue. In addition to Wilson's influence, the gradual spread of democracy, the dramatic proliferation of independent states and of nonstate international actors, and technological advances in communication and transportation have converged to produce diplomacy in its modern form.

Modern diplomacy is distinguished from its classical heritage principally by four characteristics: an expanded, diversified array of diplomats; the declining autonomy of ambassadors; public opinion pressure; and the growing importance of summit diplomacy. Each of these is discussed more fully in the sections that follow.

The Array of Players.   Today's diplomacy is conducted by a vastly expanded and diversified array of participants as compared with the days of classical diplomacy. This

Summary ⸺⸺⸺⸺⸺⸺⸺⸺⸺⸺⸺⸺⸺⸺⸺⸺⸺

Characteristics of Modern Diplomacy

1. Expansion and diversification of the range of diplomatic players
2. Declining autonomy of ambassadors due to the centralization of decision making in national capitals
3. Public opinion pressure for greater openness and political accountability in diplomacy
4. Growing importance of summit diplomacy

change is due principally to two factors: (1) the post–World War II breakup of Europe's colonial empires in Asia, Africa, and the Middle East and the consequent growth in the number of sovereign states; and (2) the modern trend towards global interdependence, which has resulted in the need for formal channels among countries that formerly were largely irrelevant to one another due to vast differences in location, ideology, and economic interests. Modern technologies of mass communication and transportation mean that no spot on the globe is truly "remote" from any other, and growing economic interdependence plus the global reach of electronic media services such as CNN has fueled a need for virtually every state to have some form of diplomatic interaction with every other.

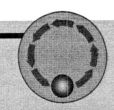

Coming to Terms

Street-Level Diplomacy

As the international dealings of European states became more complex after the Treaty of Westphalia, there arose a need to codify and institutionalize diplomatic procedures. Since ambassadors were considered the personal emissaries of their respective monarchs, great attention was paid to any perceived slight. Illustrative of the endless potential for conflict in the diplomatic encounters of the time was the near incident created when the horse-drawn carriages of the Spanish and French ambassadors converged on a narrow street in the Dutch city of the Hague in 1659. Fearful that yielding would be interpreted as conferring a higher rank upon the other ambassador, and thus upon his monarch and his country, neither ambassador would give way to the other. A potential "crisis" was defused only by the expedient of removing a fence and thus permitting both carriages to pass by simultaneously, as equals.

Silly though the incident sounds, it suggests the need—then and now—for formalized rules of etiquette, rank, and protocol so that everyday diplomatic encounters do not turn into symbol-laden international contests for power and prestige.

Source: Forest L. Grieves, *Conflict and Order* (Boston: Houghton Mifflin, 1977), p. 325.

This swelling of the ranks of diplomatic players has produced some important effects. First, the relative decline of Europe's global influence and the dramatic rise of the United States in the twentieth century meant that English would replace French as the standard language for diplomatic intercourse, just as French had supplanted Latin several centuries earlier.

Second, the attainment of independence by large numbers of new states from nonwestern cultures in Africa, the Middle East, and Asia means that the diplomatic community has lost its old cohesion grounded in the shared values of western civilization. The relatively close-knit world of European elites gave their diplomatic relations a common context of belief and values, rooted in the secular traditions inherited from the ancient Greeks and Romans and the religious traditions of Christianity. Nonwestern countries are not always receptive to these values and insist that their cultural norms be accorded equal legitimacy in international dealings. The rise of cultural diversity does not pose an insurmountable obstacle to effective diplomacy, but it does present an additional source of complexity and greater potential for misunderstandings.

Third and finally, the drastic expansion of sovereign states has meant the addition to the international community of a number of small, poor states that are sometimes hard pressed to recruit and support the full complement of diplomats necessary for global representation. Some are so poor or so lacking in educated elites that they can barely staff even the most important diplomatic postings, such as those at the UN.

Declining Autonomy of Ambassadors. The second characteristic of modern diplomacy is the declining authority of ambassadors due to the centralization of authority in national capitals. Prior to the twentieth-century revolution in communications, diplomats posted overseas depended on the "diplomatic pouch" transported by ship, rail, or horse-mounted messenger to stay in touch with their home foreign ministries. Their instructions were of necessity quite general in nature, sketching the outlines of policy the ambassador was to pursue, but leaving the ambassador with considerable latitude to fill in the details. No longer.

Today's diplomats are never more than a few seconds away from their home governments via electronic communications. This means that not only the broad outlines, but also the smallest details of policy can be centrally directed from national capitals, with detailed and up-to-the-minute instructions flashed instantly to embassies around the world. Ambassadors, therefore, are now much more the executors of policy decisions and play a much less independent role in the shaping and conduct of foreign policy. This trend, coupled with the rise of summit diplomacy that is discussed below, has somewhat reduced the importance of ambassadors as key negotiators and policy makers.

Public Opinion Pressure. The third characteristic of modern diplomacy is the rising importance of public opinion. A product of both the greater availability of information and of the worldwide trend toward some form of political democracy, the new weight of mass opinion in diplomatic dealings means a broad insistence on public disclosure of diplomatic undertakings and a growing demand that the activities of diplomats be subject to the same democratic accountability expected in domestic policy-making.

This factor helps explain in part the unwillingness of the western powers to become more involved in ending the tragic ethnic violence that devastated Bosnia beginning in 1992. In the United States, for example, a number of officials directly involved in Balkan affairs insisted that their government had a moral obligation to use its political and military weight to force Bosnia's Serbs to halt their genocidal campaign against the outgunned Muslims. Within less than a year, two top State Department officials responsible for directing U.S. policy towards Bosnia—George Kenney and Marshall Harris—resigned in protest over what they regarded as undue timidity in their government's policy. Regardless of whether these experts were right in calling for a more forceful U.S. stance, opinion polls routinely showed that the American public was unwilling to commit its fighting men and women to a faraway conflict rooted in centuries of ethnic hatred where no vital U.S. interests were clearly at stake. In the face of those political realities, many U.S. diplomats could only watch with dismay as their exhortations for a more forceful Bosnian policy went largely unheeded.

The United States is not alone in having its diplomacy conducted under the glare of media scrutiny and constrained by the shifting tides of public sentiment. The role of Japan in the Persian Gulf War provides another instructive example. As the unprecedented international coalition came together under UN auspices to expel Iraq from Kuwait, much attention was paid to Japan to see how it would respond. As discussed in Chapter 7, ever since World War II the Japanese had pursued a single-minded quest for economic advancement while generally maintaining a low profile on contentious international political and military issues. By 1990, however, Japan was increasingly being looked to by the rest of the world to take on the responsibilities of international leadership befitting its stature as an economic superpower. To stay on the sidelines while other countries paid the price of maintaining world order would seem to confirm accusations that it was a "free rider" who reaps the benefits of a peaceful and open global system while doing little to uphold it.

Throughout the seven months bounded by Iraq's invasion in August 1990 and its defeat in February 1991, Japan's policy makers—particularly its career diplomats in the Foreign Ministry—attempted to forge the necessary political support and legal authority to dispatch elements of the Self-Defense Forces to perform noncombat support missions in the Persian Gulf area. Members of the legislature, however, were inhibited by public opinion polls that showed overwhelming opposition among voters to any kind of Japanese military role in the crisis. Despite Japan's generous financial contribution to the UN coalition, its conspicuous military absence dealt a severe blow to its international reputation. Once again, the force of domestic opinion overrode the voice of diplomacy.

Summit Diplomacy. The fourth and final characteristic of modern diplomacy is the growing importance of summit diplomacy. Until recent decades, it was unusual for heads of government to meet in person. Slow means of transportation meant that international travel by incumbent national leaders was seldom practical; they could not stay away from home so long. Today, with distances shrunk by jet travel, face-to-face summit meetings between leaders have become commonplace. The trend began earlier in the twentieth century (Woodrow Wilson was the first U.S. President to travel abroad while in office) and has recently grown exponentially. During the Cold War, summit meetings between U.S. and Soviet leaders defined some of that tense period's most memorable moments. Today the annual meetings of the leaders of the seven largest industrial democracies and Russia (G–8) generate much of the same international interest formerly produced by the Soviet-American summits.

Personal diplomacy conducted by national leaders has advantages and disadvantages. On the one hand, by elevating the diplomatic process to the very highest level, summits permit

Case in Point
Soccer Diplomacy

In 1979 Iran underwent a mass-based revolution which rejected modern materialism and reaffirmed the values of fundamentalist Islam. The revolution's leader, Ayatollah Khomeini, identified the United States as the principal enemy of Iran's spiritual renewal. "The great Satan," he called it. Inflamed by Khomeini's rhetoric, Iranian radicals seized the U.S. embassy in November 1979 and held its 55 personnel for the next 444 days. For nearly two decades, relations between the two countries were venomous and dangerous.

However, by the late 1990s, Iran had a new president, Mohammad Khatami. Refreshingly moderate, Mohammad Khatami presented a "message to the American people" in January 1998. In it, he called for a gradual reconciliation between the two countries, beginning with cultural ties. Notably, however, Khatami followed a delicate course to protect himself against a domestic backlash in a country where clerical leaders lead their congregations in repeated chants of "Death to America."

Khatami's protection against a domestic backlash came in the form of a soccer game. In June 1998 at the World Cup games in Paris, Iran was paired against the United States. Some feared the worst—political agitation, professions of hatred on both sides. What happened, in a game that Iran won 2–1, was the best. There were no reported anti-American episodes. In the stands, Iranian fans handed Americans white flowers, symbols of peace. On the playing field, when the game was over, the traditional team pictures were taken. But then both sides agreed to do something that was unprecedented: pose together for a group picture. Back in Iran the exultation of victory seemed pro-Iran, not anti-American. So much for the Great Satan.

Sports do not always facilitate diplomatic communication. As often as not, international sports competitions stir up nationalistic chauvinism and antipathy. But on other memorable occasions, they help diplomats to open and maintain diplomatic communication.

leaders to cut through the thick tangle of bureaucratic politics that often lead to delay, indecision, and stalemate. Another advantage of summit diplomacy is that in bringing powerful decision makers together, it sometimes fosters a personal rapport between them that can facilitate the resolution of outstanding substantive differences between their nations.

Both of these advantages of summitry were evident during the famous Camp David Summit of 1978, where President Jimmy Carter brought together two leaders of profoundly different temperament whose countries had gone to war with each other on four occasions in the previous 30 years: President Anwar Sadat of Egypt and Prime Minister Menachem Begin of Israel. As Carter recounts in his memoirs, only through difficult and often highly emotional direct encounters were the two men able to transcend the enormous obstacles to peace that existed within each country's respective political life. The Camp David accords paved the way for peace between the two archenemies, and stand as perhaps the finest example of what summit diplomacy can achieve.

Amplification

Public Diplomacy

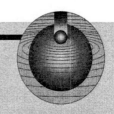

Public diplomacy is the method by which states promote their image, ideology, and message. Typically inexpensive (the National Endowment for Democracy costs less than an F-18 fighter), public diplomacy has turned into highly ideological battles in the United States in recent years. To the likes of Jesse Helms (R-NC), Chairman of the Senate Foreign Relations Committee, public diplomacy smacks of political liberalism. A steady barrage of conservative attacks has shrunk the United States Information Agency (USIA) from 12,600 employees in 1967 to the current figure of 8,500. USIA's personnel stationed overseas have been cut in half. Iran, a Second Tier state, has stronger radio stations than the Voice of America. The failure of U.S. international radio and television is due heavily to its poor quality. Not only have American news and serious programming been lagging behind the competition, but so have U.S. soap operas. The programs of the former Soviet Union, Mexico, Brazil, and a host of other states draw larger audiences than do their American competitors.

On the other hand, summit diplomacy contains built-in pitfalls. Its most obvious disadvantage is that national leaders, perhaps too eager to reach some sort of agreement so that their meeting can be presented as a success, may act hastily and without full consideration of the nuances of complex international issues. Whatever their faults, professional diplomats conducting routine diplomacy typically do so with caution, thoughtfulness, and expertise on the issues at hand. National leaders less in command of the intricacies of the issues may bypass their own experts and enter into agreements that prove ill-advised.

Some historians believe that the notorious Yalta conference illustrates the dangers inherent in summit diplomacy. In February 1945 at the Soviet city of Yalta, the three major Allied leaders of World War II—President Franklin Roosevelt of the United States, Prime Minister Winston Churchill of Great Britain, and Premier Joseph Stalin of the Soviet Union—met to plan the political settlement of Europe once the guns fell silent. Roosevelt was by then old, ill, fatigued, and within two months of his death. Some believe that his personal frailty adversely affected his fateful dealings with his Soviet counterpart. Perhaps eager to placate Stalin and thus hold the wartime coalition together, Roosevelt acquiesced in an agreement that the Soviets would later take as a green light to impose their will on the countries of Eastern Europe.

President Ronald Reagan's 1986 summit meeting with the Soviet Union's Mikhail Gorbachev in Reykjavik, Iceland, similarly illustrates the pitfalls of personal diplomacy at the summit level. Reagan briefly appeared to have agreed to Gorbachev's proposal that both countries eliminate their nuclear arsenals within 10 years, a proposal that would have been detrimental to U.S. interests given the overwhelming Soviet advantage in conventional forces. Only later were Reagan's aides and advisers able to persuade him of the folly of the agreement he very nearly embraced.

The face-to-face contact of summit diplomacy has yielded some dramatic successes. In 1978 in the relaxed setting of his official retreat at Camp David, Maryland, President Jimmy Carter (*center*) was able to mediate the bitter differences between Egyptian President Anwar Sadat and Israeli Prime Minister Menachem Begin, who reached an agreement that led to a peace treaty between their countries the next year.

Conflict Resolution Through Diplomacy

While the ordinary, daily routines of diplomats are essential for the smooth management of international relations and for averting potential conflicts, the inherent nature of the international system, with its absence of an overarching authority and the presence of competing national interests, means that international conflicts are likely to occur. When they do arise, skillful diplomacy becomes even more important. Here we examine two diplomatic techniques that states employ to help resolve international conflicts: *signaling* and *bargaining*.

Two key points need to be emphasized about these techniques. First, they are not mutually exclusive, but rather are often used in combination with one another to suit the circumstances at hand. While signaling is sometimes used alone, it is usually a part of the bargaining process. Second, while we stress the key role of diplomacy in resolving international conflicts, it is not at all the case that policy makers confront an either-or choice between employing these two forms of diplomacy or engaging in armed conflict against an adversary. While most countries would prefer to bargain rather than fight, it is nonetheless true that diplomatic signaling and bargaining are essential policy tools that countries continue to use even while they are fighting. Moreover, to an ever-increasing extent in the contemporary world, diplomacy is used in conjunction with the economic instrument of power as well as the military instrument.

Perhaps the most misunderstood adage in the field of international relations is the famous assertion by Carl von Clausewitz that "war is the continuation of diplomacy by other means." Clausewitz, the nineteenth-century Prussian general whose distinction between the "logic" and "grammar" of war was discussed in Chapter 5, has been mistakenly invoked by those who see war and diplomacy as thoroughly opposite enterprises, so utterly different in their aims that whenever one is present, the other must therefore be absent. But that was not at all his point. Rather, he believed that the grim resort to war should be employed only when other instruments of conflict resolution fail and, more important, that war must then be conducted as a disciplined tool of the state's larger policy objectives. Far from advocating a dichotomy between diplomacy and war, Clausewitz was urging national leaders to avoid allowing the imperatives of military operations to supersede their countries' larger geostrategic policy objectives. Both diplomacy and war should be viewed as instruments for achieving those objectives.

Clausewitz's classic argument is today more important than ever. Given the global proliferation of advanced weaponry, both conventional and the more terrifying weapons of mass destruction (nuclear, biological, and chemical), and the parallel growth in sophistication and political influence of military establishments in many countries, it is more essential than ever before that the leaders of civil governments grasp the kernel of Clausewitz's profound point: a state's policy objectives must always be kept uppermost in mind. When international conflicts do arise, diplomacy is best seen as a continuous policy instrument, augmented, perhaps, but never superseded by war. With these key points in mind, we turn now to examine the two diplomatic techniques states use to attempt to resolve international conflicts.

Signaling

Signaling is the process states use to communicate their intentions and their credibility in conflict situations. Sometimes signaling is done through explicit means, such as formal speeches, published declarations, or official dispatches. At other times, it is carried out through implicit means, such as symbolic actions, the granting or withholding of diplomatic recognition, or the recalling of envoys. Signaling is above all else a process of communication, and like other forms of communication, whether between governments or between individuals, the potential for misunderstanding is ever present. Sometimes one party to a conflict will perceive a "message" by the other side where none was intended. At other times, the method chosen for signaling will be ill-suited to the occasion, with the result that the intended message is either misinterpreted or simply missed altogether. By looking at the various forms of diplomatic signaling, we will see examples of successful and failed communication between states.

Explicit Signaling. Explicit signals ordinarily provide the best opportunity for one party in a conflict to communicate its intentions and credibility with the least chance that its message will be distorted. Official papers, authoritative pronouncements, and formal communiqués represent the most frequently used methods of delivering explicit diplomatic signals. Shortly after Iraq's invasion and annexation of Kuwait in 1990, U.S. President George Bush struck an uncharacteristically Churchillian chord with his unequivocal declaration: "This will not stand." Bush's uncompromising rhetoric was aimed at multiple audiences, including the American public, without whose acquiescence a major military undertaking would be politically untenable, and the international community generally, which shares a broad agreement on the unacceptability of international change through aggression. But Bush's stark declaration was aimed principally at Saddam Hussein and his Baghdad regime. Bush was attempting through forceful words to dissuade Hussein from his dreams of Iraqi military hegemony in the Persian Gulf region and to convince him that Iraqi aggression would be punished by the United States and its allies. Though Bush's words alone proved insufficient to bring about a peaceful resolution of the crisis, they conveyed, clearly and succinctly, the resolve of the U.S.-led coalition to reverse Iraq's actions.

In some instances, however, explicit signaling is conducted in so careless a manner that the signal sent and received is not at all what was intended. Bush's "This will not stand" might not have been necessary in the first place if earlier statements by other U.S. officials had communicated the policy and the resolve of the United States with greater precision. For example, in late July 1990, only days before the invasion of Kuwait, American Ambassador April Glaspie met with Saddam Hussein. In the course of their conversation, Glaspie declared that Americans "don't have much to say about Arab-Arab differences like your border differences with Kuwait. All we hope is that you solve those matters quickly." Glaspie may thus inadvertently have given Saddam a verbal green light to seize a vulnerable neighbor with what he thought would be impunity where the Americans were concerned.

Similarly, early in 1950 U.S. Secretary of State Dean Acheson gave a speech in which he delineated American strategic interests in Asia in the face of perceived communist challenges. Conspicuously missing from Acheson's remarks was any reference to the Korean peninsula. Within a matter of months, tens of thousands of U.S. troops were dispatched to repel an invasion of South Korea by the communist regime of North Korea. While there is no definitive proof that either Glaspie's or Acheson's signals were directly responsible for the subsequent acts of aggression, it seems clear that they were misleading and exacerbated, rather than dampened, tense regional situations.

Implicit Signaling. Implicit signaling occurs through deliberate gestures, such as the recall of envoys, displays of military might, and otherwise unremarkable acts, which subtly convey larger meaning in periods of conflict. Several cases illustrate the uses and the pitfalls of signaling through gestures to help resolve international conflicts.

An interesting example of successful implicit signaling was the unorthodox way the Chinese used to indicate their readiness to reestablish diplomatic relations with the United States. Today it is difficult to convey the bitterness that characterized Sino-American relations from shortly after the communist triumph in mainland China in 1949 until the restoration of diplomatic ties in the early 1970s. For two critical decades, during the most dangerous phases of the Cold War, normal relations were frozen between the two countries— one the world's most populous, the other its most powerful. As China's relations with the Soviet Union, its fellow communist giant, steadily deteriorated, however, Chinese leader Mao Ze-dong decided that old-fashioned power politics would have to take precedence over ideological affinity. By establishing an American connection, China would gain new leverage in its dealings with the Soviets.

As it happened, the new Nixon administration was thinking in similar balance-of-power terms. This was the context for China's famous "ping pong diplomacy." During an international table tennis tournament held in Japan in 1971, Chinese officials invited the American

Case in Point

A Firm Signal

In 1961, at the height of the Cold War, Soviet leader Nikita Khrushchev decided to test the resolve of new American President John F. Kennedy by provoking a crisis over Berlin, a city lodged within Soviet-dominated East Germany and divided between western- and communist-controlled sectors. In a calculated signal of U.S. firmness, Kennedy decided to visit Berlin, where he delivered a dramatic speech proclaiming the inseparability of freedom throughout the world. Kennedy's appearance electrified his immediate audience and, more important, signaled to Khrushchev America's determination to resist a Soviet grab of West Berlin.

Kennedy's central message was not lost despite an amusing linguistic lapse. Seeking to dramatize American solidarity with the fragile enclave of West Berlin, he had intended to proclaim: "I am a Berliner." As he attempted to deliver the phrase in German, however, rather than using the correct "Ich bin Berliner," he instead said, "Ich bin ein Berliner," which means "I am a jelly doughnut." But his physical presence in Berlin and the uncompromising toughness of his message were correctly interpreted by Khrushchev, who backed away from his threats, and the crisis was defused.

In his ringing speech to a quarter-million Berliners on June 26, 1963, U.S. President John F. Kennedy provided an implicit but unmistakable signal of American resistance to Soviet aggression.

team to visit China, ostensibly for a nonpolitical exercise in athletic competition. In most circumstances, such an invitation would cause little notice, especially among foreign policy decision makers. But given the almost complete absence of direct contacts between Chinese and Americans, at both official and private levels, the invitation extended to otherwise obscure American ping pong players created a stir in Washington's highest councils. Beijing's gesture was interpreted, correctly, as signaling a desire for further contacts between the two countries. Later in 1971, National Security Adviser Henry Kissinger made a secret trip to Beijing to prepare for the historic visit of President Richard Nixon to China in 1972. Although China's gesture was an unusual way to convey its desire to reduce its tensions with the United States, it worked.

Another example of diplomatic signaling through gesture illustrates the potential that a message will be seriously garbled between its sender and receiver. Raymond Cohen, in his book *Theatre of Power: The Art of Diplomatic Signaling,* recounts the tangled saga of the *Astoria* affair. In 1938, when U.S.-Japanese relations were in a crisis over Japan's military expansionism in East Asia, Japan's ambassador to the United States died suddenly in Washington, D.C. President Franklin Roosevelt, intending merely a gesture of personal kindness, ordered the U.S. Navy to transport the ambassador's remains back to Japan aboard the cruiser *Astoria.* Japanese leaders, however, read the gesture completely differently. To them, Roosevelt's act carried a political signal of U.S. weakness. Roosevelt, unschooled in the nuances of Japanese culture, was unaware of the exceptional significance the Japanese attach to the rituals of paying tribute to the dead. By honoring a deceased senior Japanese diplomat with a potent symbol of U.S. maritime prowess, Roosevelt inadvertently encouraged Tokyo's military rulers to believe that a political accommodation with Washington was forthcoming, when in fact U.S. policy firmly condemned Japanese aggression.

Bargaining

A second approach to conflict resolution involves bargaining. Countries in dispute with one another confront an inherent dilemma. On the one hand, each desires to prevail over the other. At the same time, there is ordinarily a mutual interest in resolving the conflict if the costs of doing so are not perceived as outweighing the likely gains of continuing the conflict. For bargaining to succeed in resolving conflicts, then, both parties to a dispute need to reach a point where their mutual wish to settle the conflict outweighs either side's wish to pursue unilateral victory over the opponent by keeping the conflict alive.

Scholars of conflict processes sometimes use the term "expected utility" to refer to each side's evaluation of its likely gain or loss in pursuing various alternatives. So long as side A believes that the expected utility of continuing to wage conflict exceeds that of compromising through negotiations, bargaining can occur, but it will be for a purpose other than meaningful conflict resolution. Therefore, one of the critical tasks of a successful bargaining strategy is to alter your opponents' perception of both the costs and benefits that they are likely to encounter if they continue to seek unilateral advantage in a conflict. If they can be persuaded that their original estimate of the utility of engaging in conflict understates the costs and overstates the benefits of doing so, then they are much more likely to engage in meaningful bargaining aimed at resolving the conflict.

As countries in conflict approach the bargaining process, they confront three critical issues that do much to determine the outcome of the negotiations. These are (1) the purpose of the negotiations, (2) the participants in the negotiating process, and (3) the choice of bargaining techniques to be employed.

Reasons for Negotiations.   Countries may enter into diplomatic negotiations for a variety of reasons other than to seek a resolution of the conflict. The most common include scoring propaganda points or buying time in which to enhance one's bargaining position. This description applies, for example, to the negotiations to end the Vietnam War, which dragged on for nearly five years, from 1968 to 1973. Seemingly endless haggling took place over such secondary issues as the location of the talks (Paris was

the eventual site) and even the shape of the negotiating table. North Vietnam's apparent determination to delay the talks at every opportunity reflected their conviction that time was on their side, not the Americans'.

Beginning in 1969, the Nixon administration began the phased withdrawal of its ground forces from Vietnam in order to contain the growing domestic opposition to the war. This policy of "Vietnamization" was intended to gradually hand combat responsibility over to South Vietnamese forces, which were being trained and equipped by the departing Americans. From the North Vietnamese perspective, however, the Americans did not have to be outfought, but only outwaited. They calculated that the growing political clout of the antiwar movement would make it impossible for Nixon to reverse course and reintroduce U.S. forces to shore up a deteriorating military situation in South Vietnam. Further, they reasoned, the very logic of the Vietnamization policy meant that with the simple passage of time the United States would possess less and less ability to punish North Vietnam for either its dilatory negotiating strategy or for violations of the agreements that were eventually reached in early 1973.

For the United States, the Paris peace talks were viewed as a vehicle for attaining a negotiated settlement that would permit American forces to exit the unpopular war while still assuring its South Vietnamese ally a reasonable chance of maintaining its independence from the communist North. For the North Vietnamese, however, the talks were intended principally to avoid the international condemnation that would follow if they refused to negotiate with the Americans. In reality, their "negotiation" consisted principally of running out the clock. Given the entirely opposed purposes with which the two parties approached the negotiations, it is little wonder that they did not lead to a lasting peace for the people of South Vietnam, who were overrun militarily by the North Vietnamese in 1975 and forcibly reunited with the North under communist rule.

Participants in Negotiations. The second decision to be made regarding negotiations, who shall participate in them, involves three distinct issues: (1) the rank of the negotiators, (2) the inclusiveness of the talks, and (3) the possible use of third parties. As to rank of negotiators, most successful negotiations are carried out by professional diplomats who are well schooled in the substantive issue at hand and in the subtleties of bargaining techniques. In exceptional cases, however, negotiation is conducted by the highest leaders of the countries involved. A *summit,* a term that refers to any meeting of two or more heads of government, ordinarily serves to codify actual negotiations already worked out by working-level diplomats. In some instances, though, the heads of government choose to enter into the negotiating process themselves. As we discussed earlier in this chapter, summit diplomacy has resulted in celebrated successes like the 1978 Camp David accord between Begin and Sadat and embarrassing mistakes like Reagan's 1986 nuclear talks with Gorbachev in Reykjavik.

As for the inclusiveness of negotiations, sometimes disputes over whether particular parties may participate in talks are nearly as divisive as the substantive issues that prompted the talks in the first place. In the seemingly endless round of Middle East peace talks, for example, Israel for years had consistently refused to accept the Palestine Liberation Organization (PLO) as a direct participant in peace talks, while most Arab countries have argued that the PLO represents the authentic voice of the stateless Palestinians who live in the Israeli-occupied territories seized in the Six Day War of 1967. Similarly, the Paris peace talks over Vietnam were bogged down for months over U.S. objections to participation by the National Liberation Front, the communist political apparatus within South Vietnam that Washington viewed as a mere instrument of the North, and North Vietnam's parallel objection to a direct negotiating role by the government of South Vietnam, which it viewed as an illegitimate puppet of the United States. (A compromise eventually allowed both to take part.)

The final issue under the heading of who participates in negotiations is the possible use of third parties. As the term suggests, third parties are persons, usually senior career diplomats, whose country is not a party to the dispute but who are invited by the disputing parties to help arrive at a diplomatic resolution. Clearly, the third party must be a person or group that commands the respect and trust of both sides in the dispute.

Third party diplomacy takes several forms, the simplest of which is the provision of so-called good offices. Here the third party works to keep the channels of communication open between the disputing parties, such as by acting as a conduit for messages or providing a place to meet, but does not take a direct role in the substantive negotiations.

Summary

Forms of Third Party Diplomacy

1. Good offices: the third party keeps channels of communication open.
2. Mediation: the third party is actively involved in negotiations.
3. Arbitration: the third party's resolution of conflict is binding.

A more ambitious form of third party diplomacy is mediation. Here the third party not only conveys messages but becomes actively involved in the diplomatic process. Since the mediator's proposed solution is not binding, the success of mediation efforts depends heavily on the wish of each side to work out some sort of compromise. Though mediation efforts fail more often than they succeed, they have led to some dramatic successes. For example, the distinguished UN official Ralph Bunche was awarded the Nobel Peace Prize for his efforts in mediating an end to the first Arab-Israeli war in 1949. President Jimmy Carter's patient mediation between Israel and Egypt made possible the Camp David accords.

Arbitration is the final, and most ambitious, form of third party diplomacy. In this case, the third party actually sets the terms of the settlement to the conflict. The disputing parties agree ahead of time to accept the settlement stipulated by the third party. Although arbitration has often been used to resolve international conflicts, it is ordinarily turned to only in cases where important national interests are not involved.

An example of successful arbitration was the 1988 resolution of the Taba dispute between Israel and Egypt. Taba is a tiny (190 yards wide, 750 yards long) but valuable strip of beachfront on the northern shore of the Gulf of Aqaba, at the edge of the Sinai Peninsula. Under the Camp David framework, in 1982 Israel withdrew from the peninsula,

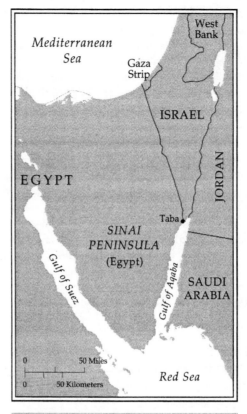

Map 12-1 Taba

©1996 by St. Martin's Press, Inc. From: *Contours of Power,* by Snow/Brown. Reprinted with permission of Bedford/St. Martin's Press, Inc.

which it had taken from Egypt in the 1967 Six Day War. It refused, however, to return Taba, which it claimed was not a part of the Sinai but of Israel proper.

Both Israel and Egypt attached symbolic importance to ownership of Taba. To Egypt, getting it back would fulfill President Anwar Sadat's pledge to recover "every inch" of Egypt's territory taken by Israel in 1967. To Israel, the issue was one of historical legitimacy. Its claim to ownership of Taba rested on a 1906 Turkish map that marks the borders between Egypt and the Ottoman Empire possession then known as Palestine. Moreover, an Israeli entrepreneur had built a $200 million resort, complete with a topless beach, on the site. In 1986 the two countries agreed to turn the dispute over to a five-member arbitration panel consisting of a Swede, a Swiss, a Frenchman, an Israeli, and an Egyptian. In 1988 the panel ruled in Egypt's favor. Though bitter recriminations followed within Israel, the use of arbitration made it possible to resolve a territorial dispute that the two countries were unable to resolve through conventional bilateral diplomacy.

Case Study: Bosnia and the Dayton Accords

The Context

The early years of the post–Cold War era (1991 to 1995) found the international community preoccupied with the horrific carnage in Bosnia. Bringing an end to the wanton slaughter of innocent civilian life as well as that of the armed combatants would require a combination of mediation backed by the threat or actual deployment of armed forces from the sole remaining superpower: the United States. Bosnia was a mix of ethnic tragedy waiting to happen. From the end of World War II until 1991, the highly artificial entity of Yugoslavia, of which Bosnia was a part, was held together by fear of Josip Broz Tito's central government.

Yugoslavia was a melange of different ethnicities, languages, and religions. After World War II, it was given a modicum of order through a distribution of power defined in the Tito Constitution of 1974, in which the country's centuries-long ethnic divisions were codified into political power over the country's regions.

In the west was Croatia, ethnically Slavic and religiously Catholic. Slovenia was in the northwest, also a Slavic and Catholic province. In the center was Bosnia and Herzegovina (hereafter simply Bosnia), of mixed ethnicity but containing a slight Muslim plurality (44 percent), a substantial Serbian, Eastern Orthodox minority (31 percent), and a Croatian, Catholic population (17 percent). The fourth republic was Montenegro, a diminutive Orthodox Christian Slavic republic. The fifth republic was Macedonia, principally Orthodox Christian but multiethnic. Then there was Serbia, the largest republic in the State of Yugoslavia and overwhelmingly composed of Slavic Orthodox Christians. In addition to these six republics there were two autonomous regions. Both were Serb, but one, Kosovo, contained an Albanian Muslim majority, while the other, Vojvodina, had a heavily Hungarian majority.

Yugoslavia was held together, however shakily, until 1991. Tito had died in 1980; now it was Serb dominance that held the wobbly country together. By 1991, however, the entire structure began to collapse, following in quick succession declarations of independence by Croatia, Slovenia, Macedonia, and Bosnia. Only Serbia and Montenegro were left behind under the banner of what had once been a much more robust Yugoslavia.

Of all of Yugoslavia's long-suffering regions, it was Bosnia that was trapped squarely in the cross-hairs of nationalist hatred. Its Muslim plurality marked it for horrific suffering during the Balkan wars of the early 1990s. As John Stoessinger observes, "Bosnia was a truly multiethnic state." (*Why Nations Go to War,* pp. 190–191). It was this polyglot country that would prove to be the vortex of ancient hatreds in the Balkan region. The reason is rooted in the passionate nationalism of people like Slobodan Milosevic, the leader of Serbia and, eventually, the spokesman of Yugoslavia's Serbs. The depth of Milosevic's nationalist passion is indicated by his obsession with the 1389 battle between Serbs and Ottoman Turks known as the Battle of Kosovo. To Milosevic, the distant conflict was the stuff of contemporary hatred because the Serbs lost and thus were forced to live under Muslim Ottoman rule for 500 years. There is no describing the sheer hatred that Milosevic held for the Muslims. Given his strategic plans, that meant hatred for Bosnia's Muslims.

By 1989 the former Yugoslavia was in tatters. All of the generals of the former Yugoslav army were Serbs. They commanded the best-trained forces and had appropriated Yugoslavia's best weapons. In the coming showdown between Serbia and the Muslim-dominated republics, Serbia would hold the upper hand militarily.

Map 12-2   **Yugoslavia**

©1996 by St. Martin's Press, Inc. From: *Contours of Power,* by Snow/Brown. Reprinted with permission of Bedford/St. Martin's Press, Inc.

Croatia and Slovenia each moved for independence in June 1991. This unleashed ethnic passions across the Balkan states that had once been Yugoslavia. Two conflicts were triggered by Croatia's and Slovenia's moves: (1) a brief war between the Slovenes and the Yugoslavian Army, easily won by the Yugoslavs, and (2) a protracted, bloody effort in Croatia in which Milosevic helped the Serbs come to power by introducing one of the most loathsome concepts of warfare of the twentieth century, "ethnic cleansing."

The Descent into Ethnic War

According to the doctrine of ethnic cleansing, people of ethnic homogeneity should work and live homogeneously. Force should be used, if necessary, to move resistant populations out of the way. Clearly, this would mean that minority peoples would live in and work at inferior areas, while the numerically dominant peoples would enjoy the best homes and the best jobs. But it was the ruthless violence that ethnic cleansing required that gave it a particularly contemptible odor.

Ethnic cleansing was first implemented in the breakaway Croatia. While Slobodan Milosevic was the author of the concept, its immediate executor was Ratko Mladic. Illustrative of the sheer brutality of Serbia's concept was the destruction of Croatia's community of Kijevo in August 1991. Serb forces used a relentless artillery assault to literally destroy the village. Croat forces were helpless against the better-armed Serb forces.

The viciousness of the Yugoslav war against Croatia prompted two diplomatic initiatives aimed at restoring the peace. First, the former American Secretary of State Cyrus Vance was tapped to lead a UN mediation effort. In early 1992 Vance brokered a cease-fire agreement in Croatia and the introduction of the first UN peacekeepers. With his cease-fire in place, the UN ground peacekeepers (UNPROFOR) were deployed to Croatia in the winter of 1992. Since the UN peacekeepers were deployed as nominally "neutral" maintainers of the cease-fire, they could not repel the Serbian aggressors to their legitimate territory. Though no one intended it to be the case, the UN forces helped reward the Serbian aggressors by shielding them against Croatian efforts to retake their own territory illegally seized by the Serbs.

Bosnia would prove to be the scene of the Serb dream of a "Greater Serbia" and the consequent use of the gruesome strategy of ethnic cleansing. Bosnia's ethnic Serbs had opposed the creation of an independent Bosnian state in the first place, and when it did occur in March 1992, they immediately rose up in rebellion against the democratically elected government of Alija Izetbegovic, a Muslim. Bosnia's Serbs declared their own independent republic, as did the republic's Croats. Nonetheless, the Izetbegovic regime continued to maintain that it legitimately represented all of Bosnia, and that the two breakaway ethnic "republics" were entitled to no international standing. What followed was three years of war, one whose savagery drew little distinction between armed combatants and innocent civilians.

Bosnia's Serbs quickly gained a decided military advantage, due in large part to the assistance given them by the Serbian-controlled army of Yugoslavia. Their struggle, they insisted, was to reattach Bosnia's Serbs to Milosevic's Serb Yugoslavia and his dream of a "Greater Serbia." By early 1992, Bosnian Serbs controlled two-thirds of Bosnia, thanks in large part to the heavy weapons provided them by Milosevic.

The Major Powers Weigh In

As the war in the Balkans dragged on, outside states asserted their interests, based largely on ethnic-religious ties and historic affinity. Among the Europeans, the Germans took the initiative, announcing their recognition of Croatia and Slovenia without consulting their NATO allies. To the Germans, the Balkans historically fell within their sphere of influence, and the Germans did little to hide their interest in promoting economic ties with Slovenia and Croatia. Similarly, the Russians—by now shorn of their global pretensions—continued to regard themselves as Central Europe's principal protector of Serb interests. Of the remaining major powers, the British and French initially held back, regarding the Bosnian carnage as a local problem to be resolved by normal course of local war.

The United States was the slowest to grasp the necessity for outside diplomatic intervention to end the bloodshed in Bosnia. The Bush administration expected the European states to take the lead and, when they did not, felt no obligation to what it regarded as a European problem. It did, however, take two tepid steps. First, it recognized Serbian Bosnia, Catholic Croatia, and Slovenia as independent states, signaling that the United States harbored no interest—for the time being, at least—in maintaining the territorial integrity and sovereignty of Bosnia. Secondly, seeking shelter behind the United Nations, it joined the UN Security Council in imposing economic sanctions against Serbia and in sending UN peacekeepers to Bosnia to assist in the distribution of humanitarian relief. In order to assure the security of the humanitarian operations, the United States joined the rest of the Security Council in imposing a "no-fly zone" over Bosnia in October 1992, a measure which NATO aircraft began to enforce in April 1993. The United States, however, declined to contribute to the UN peacekeepers in Bosnia, though it did send a token 500-person force to the Republic of Macedonia as part of a UN effort to prevent the conflict from widening. With the United States remaining aloof throughout the Bush administration and in the early years of the domestically focused Clinton administration, diplomatic efforts to resolve the conflicts were left to the UN and the European Union. The first peace plan, which would have rendered Bosnia a highly decentralized federation, was prepared by the European Union mediator Lord David Owen and UN mediator and former U.S. Secretary of State Cyrus Vance. The plan—which was favored by Serbia's Milosevic—was rejected by Bosnian Serb leader Radovan Karadzic.

The United States Moves to End the War

Early in 1994, with the world's television screens drenched nightly with bloody images of the Bosnian Serb ethnic cleansing campaign against non-Serbian soldiers and civilians alike, the Clinton administration stepped up its efforts to halt the Balkan slaughter. Under U.S. prodding, a five-nation "Contact Group" composed of Russia, Britain, France, Germany, and the United States formed with the goal of negotiating a settlement between the warring factions of Bosnia. In the spring of 1994, still hoping to keep Bosnia a single state, the Contact Group presented a cease-fire and political reconciliation plan to each of Bosnia's ethnic factions. Karadzic again rejected a peace plan that did not recognize his Serb's conquest of nearly 60 percent of Bosnia.

By this time, however, three factors were converging that would ultimately drive Karadzic to a peace table in the unlikely location of Dayton, Ohio. First, Serbia's leader Milosevic, by now feeling the economic squeeze of UN economic sanctions, announced in the fall of 1994 that he would no longer provide weapons to the Bosnian Serbs. His dramatic step had the intended effect: the UN lifted some of the economic sanctions that had been in effect since 1992. Secondly, ever more grim images of Karadzic's Bosnian Serb campaign of ethnic cleansing were shown on global television daily, thus further eroding Karadzic's international standing and further degrading the legitimacy of his cause. The most famous of these was the February 1995 shelling of a crowded marketplace in the city of Sarajevo, which caused nearly 70 deaths, all of them innocent non-Serb combatants. Third and finally, the summer of 1995 witnessed a series of military reversals suffered by Karadzic's forces, most at the hands of the Bosnian Croats.

The convergence of these forces led President Clinton to make the United States the leading actor in an all-out diplomatic offensive to end the Bosnian carnage. By the fall of 1995, the foreign ministers of Bosnia, Croatia, and Serbia—which now represented the Bosnian Serbs—were ready for a U.S.-brokered peace arrangement. At a series of meetings

Wright-Patterson Air Force Base in Dayton, Ohio hosted the Bosnian peace talks, one session of which is shown in the accompanying picture. The peace agreement is known as the Dayton Accords because of this location.

held at Wright-Patterson Air Force base in Dayton, Ohio, the experienced American diplomat Richard C. Holbrooke took the lead in brokering a diplomatic resolution to Bosnia's agony. In the end, the three warring Bosnian factions agreed to a settlement which included the following key points: (1) Bosnia's Serbs would receive about one-half of Bosnia, substantially less than their peak military conquests, but substantially greater than their proportion of Bosnia's population. (2) A UN peacekeeping force, including 20,000 U.S. forces, would be interposed between the three factions for as long as needed. (3) Bosnia would remain as a loosely constituted federation, with each of the three factions retaining substantial autonomy. (4) A War Crimes Tribunal would be established to try to punish the most egregious offenders of elemental human rights that occurred during the three-year war.

The last provision elicited the greatest international enthusiasm at the time. Nearly all of those indicted were Bosnian Serbs, including their leader, Karadzic. However, to Bosnia's Serbs, these people are heroes and are therefore sheltered from arrest by Serbian nationalists. To date, little has been done to enforce the War Crimes Tribunal of the Dayton Accords.

Lessons and Conclusions

Among the lessons of Bosnia's agony, five stand out. First, in the post–Cold War era, diplomats can expect to confront long-muted ethnic conflicts that were suppressed under the discipline of the Cold War. Secondly, outside diplomatic intervention will typically be required to bring an end to these ethnic slaughters. Third, diplomacy works best when it is backed by credible military force, as in the case of NATO enforcement of no-fly zones. Fourth, international opinion matters. Bosnia's Serbs committed grisly atrocities against Muslim and Catholic women and children, whose suffering will not soon be forgotten by all who witnessed it on global television. The resulting international outcry generated greater pressure to bring to an end the Bosnian conflict. Finally, for better or worse, diplomatic intervention by the United States is—at this particular moment in history—a necessity for ending the most egregious international conflicts. No other power commands the full armory of diplomatic instruments—including its prestige, economic stature, and coercive capabilities. It follows that the United States will find itself more rather than less involved in the search for peaceful resolutions of the panoply of ethnically fueled domestic and international wars that mark the post–Cold War era.

The Changing Contours of Diplomacy

Diplomats of the twenty-first century will find their work made increasingly difficult by three factors. First, the global communications revolution means that once distant conflicts are now the currency of conversation around the world. In a world where Tibetan monks learn of world events from satellite dish receivers and cities as far-flung as Nairobi, Moscow, and Mexico City have access to ever greater amounts of information from CNN and its European counterparts, diplomats lose their ability to insist that world affairs are the domain of a handful of informed insiders. With increased information comes an ever mounting flow of opinions, though—to be sure—some are better supported and reasoned than others. As we have seen, worldwide outrage at the senseless slaughter in the Bosnian civil war generated mounting demands that the diplomats of the powerful states bring their countries' influence and—if necessary—their armed might to bear to find a peaceful resolution of the conflict. The global flood of information, then, removes the shield of insulation which diplomats once enjoyed, and it generates greater demands on them to end human suffering. Media coverage of global events also subjects diplomats' efforts to ever broadening scrutiny and judgment.

Secondly, the broad trend toward democratization, however wobbly the transition from authoritarianism may be in many instances, brings with it greater demands and constraints for the diplomatic community. In the same sense that diplomats must now deal with a more informed global audience, so too do they find themselves buffeted by the demands and criticisms of mass publics. Not only is it increasingly difficult for diplomatic negotiations to occur in secrecy, it is downright perilous for diplomats to enter into substantive accords whose contents are held secret from the public. Leaks are nearly inevitable, and when they do occur, they generate a sense of outrage and cynicism that no democratic leader wants to face among his or her own people. So the current of democratization, while one of the most hopeful trends of our time, brings with it new pressures and limitations on traditional diplomatic pressure.

Finally, the diplomatic corps—especially that of the First Tier—will increasingly have to work hand-in-glove with their countries' armed forces. In a world in which the number of sovereign states has ballooned from more than 50 after World War II to about 200 today, the agenda of global diplomacy has similarly swollen. At the top of that agenda is the Second Tier ethnic and religious impulses that all too easily lead to civil war, regional wars, and terrorism aimed at the First Tier. For First Tier diplomacy aimed at quelling these destructive impulses to be credible, it is essential that diplomats be able to count on the existence and utilization of their countries' coercive capabilities. "Coercive diplomacy" could be as modest as transferring a small number of weapons to a Second Tier state in order to maintain a regional balance of power, or as massive as the U.S.-led multinational coalition which evicted Iraq from its short-lived conquest of Kuwait at the start of the 1990s.

In sum, the world of diplomacy has forever lost the kind of insularity within which an informed, internationally minded elite could broker agreements, many of which were withheld from public disclosure. The communications revolution, the global trend towards democratization, and the rising importance of "coercive diplomacy" will bring mounting pressures and constraints to the world of diplomacy.

Review

This chapter examined the role of diplomacy in international relations. In the process, the following points were made:

1. The essence of diplomacy is communication. Most states' diplomatic corps are staffed largely by highly trained professionals, although some diplomats are appointed for political reasons.

2. The key functions of diplomacy are (1) representation, (2) the gathering, analyzing, and reporting of information, (3) policy management, and (4) negotiation.

3. Modern diplomacy represents the result of a centuries-long process of development. Much contemporary practice was developed by the European states between the seventeenth and nineteenth centuries. Elaborate protocols prescribe proper conduct among diplomats at official functions.

4. Modern diplomacy is distinguished from its classical heritage by four characteristics: (1) the expansion and diversification of the range of participants, (2) the declining autonomy of ambassadors due to the centralization of decision making in national capitals, (3) the pressure for greater openness and democratic accountability in diplomacy, and (4) the growing popularity of summit diplomacy.

5. Two diplomatic techniques of conflict resolution are signaling and bargaining. Signaling may be either explicit or implicit. With implicit signaling, there is always a risk that the intended message may be missed or misinterpreted. Bargaining sometimes is facilitated by third parties, who may provide good offices or act as mediators or arbitrators.

6. Bosnia's long civil war was ended by a continuous diplomatic effort by states that had long-standing ties to Bosnia, were generally in geographic proximity to it, or calculated that their own national interests would be served by participating in a resolution of the conflict.

Suggested Readings

Bartson, R. P. *Modern Diplomacy.* New York: Longman, 1988.

Cohen, Raymond. *Theatre of Power: The Art of Diplomatic Signaling.* New York: Longman, 1987.

Grieves, Forest L. *Conflict and Order.* Boston: Houghton Mifflin, 1977.

Habeeb, W. M. *Power and Tactics in International Negotiations: How Weak Nations Bargain with Strong Nations.* Baltimore: Johns Hopkins University Press, 1988.

Ikle, Fred C. *How Nations Negotiate.* New York: Harper and Row, 1964.

Kissinger, Henry. *A World Restored.* Boston: Houghton Mifflin, 1973.

Kremenyuk, Victor A. *International Negotiation: Analysis, Approaches, Issues.* San Francisco: Jossey-Bass, 1991.

Lall, Arthur S. *Modern International Negotiation: Principles and Practice.* New York: Columbia University Press, 1966.

Lockhart, Charles. *Bargaining in International Conflict.* New York: Columbia University Press, 1979.

Miller, Robert Hopkins, et al. *Inside an Embassy: The Political Role of Diplomats Abroad.* Washington, DC: CQ Books, 1992.

Nicolson, Harold. *The Evolution of Diplomatic Method.* London: Constable, 1954.

—. *Diplomacy.* New York: Oxford University Press, 1964.

Rapaport, Anatol. *Fights, Games and Debates.* Ann Arbor: University of Michigan Press, 1960.

Sebnenius, James K. *Negotiating the Law of the Sea.* Cambridge, MA: Harvard University Press, 1984.

Strang, William. *The Diplomatic Career.* London: A. Deutsch, 1962.

Wilson, Clifton E. *Diplomatic Privileges and Immunities.* Tucson: University of Arizona Press, 1967.

Wood, John R., and Jean Serrs. *Diplomatic Ceremonial and Protocol.* New York: Columbia University Press, 1970.

The Evolving Role of International Law and Organizations

PREVIEW

This chapter examines international law and organizations, which collectively provide much of the order and structure within which international relations occur. We begin with international law, looking first at the question of whether it qualifies as law, then at what its sources are, and at what role it is likely to perform in the post–Cold War world. We will then turn to international organizations, focusing on the set of institutions that make up the revived United Nations system. The discussion proceeds to an analysis of peacekeeping and peace enforcement, which have played such a prominent part in the revival of the world body, and to the UN role in dealing with internal war in the Second Tier. The chapter concludes with a case study assessing the future of UN activism.

KEY CONCEPTS

international law
law
enforcement
vital national interests
values
World Court (International Court of Justice)
treaties
international custom
general principles of law
judicial decisions and teachings
just war
war crimes

Helsinki Accords
intergovernmental organizations (IGOs)
nongovernmental organizations (NGOs)
United Nations system
functionalism
General Assembly
Security Council
Secretariat
specialized agencies
peacekeeping
peace enforcement (imposition)
humanitarian relief operations

OUTLINE

Every system has a structure with rules that govern the interactions between the parts and thereby help define the system. Within the international system, many of the important rules are included in the body of international law, and much of the systemic structure comes in the form of a web of international organizations.

The early twentieth-century study of international relations was largely the study of international law and organization. Law was a prominent part of the subject because many of the original international relationists came from a legal background and a western tradition that extolled the expansion of the rule of law into the international realm as a way to better order an unruly system. In the period between the world wars, international organization became a focal point for scholars anxious to prevent a repetition of the "Great War"; these idealists emphasized the expansion and perfection of the League of Nations as a means toward this end.

From this dominant position in the study of international relations, law and organization faded after World War II. The original assault on its significance came from the realists, who observed that the structure represented by the League had collapsed as soon as the winds of war began to blow. The realists' emphasis on power rather than law as the motive for national behavior in the international realm further downgraded the role of law. Furthermore, when the quantitative and behaviorist approaches to international relations study became important in the 1950s and 1960s, most of their advocates had backgrounds in social sciences such as sociology and psychology or in the natural sciences or mathematics, and very little background in law. Thus, law became less of a point of reference.

The nature of the Cold War system was another factor in diminishing the apparent importance of international law and organization after World War II. The competing ideologies of communism and anticommunist and the influx of newly independent states with nonwestern values made it difficult to devise rules of international conduct acceptable to all. The paralysis of the peace and security system of the United Nations because of East-West polarization and of UN specialized agencies because of North-South conflicts mean that international organization was also less central to international affairs. Concern for international law and organization was thus consigned to the periphery of international relations as a discipline; the topic was seen as comparatively minor and not clearly focused on the important questions of war and peace, and especially the vital problem of avoiding war between East and West.

Has this trend changed or will it change in a post–Cold War world? As we have noted in passing, there are at least some signs in that direction. For one thing, there is greater agreement among the major states on most political and economic values than there has been since the eighteenth century, and common values are the breeding ground of successful law at any level. It is not hard to imagine a future expanded regime of law regulating, say, most economic relations among the states of the First Tier. Whether such a regime could be extended to encompass the Second Tier is more problematic.

The recent resurgence of interest in the United Nations is also a hopeful sign for advocates of law and organization. One of the major critiques of their approach had been its irrelevance to the most important concerns, those pertaining to war and peace. In fact, the framers of the UN Charter intended that the organization be inoperative in the event of major conflict among the most important states; they realized that cooperation among the major powers was necessary as a precondition for successful operation of the world body in resolving conflict. It remains true today that the UN lacks the capacity to solve conflict among the major powers. But the UN's relevance in resolving Second Tier conflicts may be on the increase. With the end of ideological gridlock in the UN Security Council, the world body has an opportunity to become a central part of the security system—

During the Cold War, ideological conflict paralyzed the United Nations in many respects and served to diminish interest in international law and organization. In a 1960 visit to the UN, for example, Soviet Premier Nikita Khrushchev defied diplomatic decorum by (among other things) challenging Secretary-General Dag Hammarskjöld to quit, calling the Philippines' delegate a "jerk," and taking off his shoe and putting it on his desk, ready to pound it if necessary to emphasize his objections to western proposals.

to the extent its membership wants to expand the UN role and is willing to provide resources for such an expanded role.

The previously moribund area of international law and organization may thus experience something of a renaissance in the new international system. International law and organization may be tools for bolstering peace and prosperity in the First Tier and extending it to the Second Tier. To investigate the change that may occur, we will start with a discussion of international law, its nature and its sources, concluding with some examination of war and international law. We will then examine international organization, principally through surveying the UN system of intergovernmental organizations (IGOs). Because it is so important in any revival of the UN system, we will also discuss the question of UN peace-keeping and peacemaking in the international security system. The chapter will conclude with a case study on the future of United Nations activism in the international order.

The Nature and Sources of International Law

Any examination of the "law of nations" must begin with an explicit recognition of the centrality of sovereignty as the basic underpinning of the system and of law. Sovereignty is the basis for authority within the territorial jurisdiction of the state, and thus the basis for law within the states that are the principal units of the international system. Sovereignty also defines the boundary between domestic and international legal jurisdictions, indicating where each form of law can and cannot penetrate.

Because the concept of state sovereignty means that there can be no legal superior to the state, it has an important impact on the nature of international law. Insofar as this concept is invoked, there can be no police officer in the international system, as there is within states; international law, as distinct from domestic law, may thus be unenforceable. This difference is, of course, intentional: states are unwilling to accept external judgments that may adversely affect their most important interests. They prefer to avoid external judgments rather than to have to defy those that are unacceptable. The exercise of one form of power or another is the preferred method of resolution—especially, of course, among the most powerful states, which dominate the system and make the rules.

It can be concluded that international law is different from law as applied within states—a judgment with which no student of international relations would disagree. Indeed, some have maintained that the difference is so great that international law cannot really be thought of as law. Moreover, to the extent that the concept of sovereignty is invoked, there can be no legislative body authorized to produce international law, as is the case for law within states. Thus, the sources of international law must also be different from those of law within states.

Web Sitings: The United Nations Home Page

The United Nations home page (http://www.un.org) is one of the most useful, best organized sources of information on the Internet. Whether the subject is peacekeeping operations or activities to increase the recourse to international law, it is a resource that you will almost certainly find useful for any number of uses or projects.

Is International Law Law?

Legal scholars and students of international relations have debated this question since the field of international relations began to emerge. We can begin to clarify the issue by looking at a definition of law in general and contrasting it with a definition of international law, both taken from *The American Political Dictionary* (9th ed.):

Law: a rule [or set of rules] of conduct prescribed by or accepted by the governing authority of a state and enforced by courts.

International Law: a body of rules and principles that guides the relations among nations [*states* in our terminology] and between governments and foreign nationals.

How are these definitions similar and divergent? The major similarity would appear to be that both refer to rules defining permissible—and by extension impermissible—behavior within their jurisdictions. Thus, international and domestic legal codes are similar in their basic form: they state, in effect, that some kinds of action are allowable, while others are not. A key area where the definitions differ is in the matter of enforcement. The definition of law per se refers to it as being enforced by courts; the definition of international law, by contrast, makes no reference to enforcement, speaking instead of rules and principles that guide behavior.

Given this distinction, those who argue that international law is law maintain that it is the basic structure and function of law (as prescribing rules of behavior) that gives law its essential character. Critics of this approach argue that unenforceable laws are more analogous to moral and ethical norms or principles than to law; they prefer to think of international law as a branch of ethics (international ethics).

What is most important here is not that there is a difference in enforceability between international law and law in the generic sense, but the question of why there is a difference. The short answer, of course, is sovereignty. But more explanation is needed to understand why states prefer not to have an external regime of law governing their external behavior in the same way as an internal regime.

There are two related reasons for this preference. The first, with which we have dealt previously, stems from the fact that states have vital national interests. To protect and advance such interests, a state will tend to do whatever it can, including going to war or acting in what might be considered an illegal manner within domestic society (such as engaging in espionage). An authority with enforcement powers could interfere with the state's ultimate protection of its own vital interests. To allow independent enforcement of "verdicts" that threaten a state's deeply felt interests would effectively reduce international law to a "suicide pact," in the words of Jeane Kirkpatrick, former U.S. ambassador to the UN.

The other reason states do not want international law with enforcement capability stems from the great diversity of values within the international system. Law that people are willing to have enforced upon them must normally reflect their common values. In a large and diverse world, values in some societies are incompatible with those in others. When this incompatibility cannot be reconciled, there are three basic options: to make no laws pertaining to the disputed areas, to formulate such laws so vaguely as to encompass all views, or to enact laws that are not enforceable. For instance, think of trying to write a meaningful code of law governing the rights of women that would be acceptable today in both western and Islamic fundamentalist societies, a challenge discussed in the Case in Point box "Law, Values, and the Rights of Women."

Clashing values and vital interests do not preclude the existence of some sort of legal regime covering certain limited aspects of international relations; they do preclude a comprehensive regime covering a wide range of international dealings in the same way that domestic law widely regulates behavior within a particular society. The international system's major judicial institution, the World Court (officially the International Court of Justice), illustrates the point. Created in 1945 as part of the United Nations system and as the successor of the Permanent Court of International Justice under the League of Nations, the World Court is intended to promote the rule of law and provide a forum for the peaceful settlement of international disputes. But the Court's jurisdiction is limited. In accepting its authority, states commonly have adopted a restriction or rider, the Connally Amendment (named after the Texas senator who introduced it as an amendment to U.S. acceptance of the court's charter). According to this amendment, the court has jurisdiction in a case only if both parties to an action give it specific jurisdiction for that particular case. This means states appear before the court and grant it the right to decide the merits of a case only when they are willing to. Furthermore, its decisions cannot create precedents. A precedent-setting authority, as is found in American law, is specifically excluded in the constitutional document that created the court. Thus, international legal judgments are enforceable only when the parties to a dispute agree for them to be. Sovereign control over matters of vital interest is thereby protected; expansion of the international regime is not. (Information on the Court, including its charter, can be found through the UN home page on the world wide web.)

Sources of International Law

The conceptual differences between law per se and international law are also reflected in the sources of international law. The definition of law cited earlier says that it is "prescribed by or accepted by the governing body of a state"; for international law, on the other hand, there is no mention of any authority that makes such prescriptions or acceptances. That is, there is no equivalent of a national or other legislative body to create international law.

Hence, international law must spring from different sources than does domestic law. There are several sources generally agreed to be "legitimate"; all lack the characteristic of having been produced by a legislative body, thereby contributing to the disagreement as to whether international law is, properly speaking, law.

Summary ━━━━━━━━━━━━━━━━━━━━

Sources of International Law

1. Treaties and other international agreements
2. International custom
3. General principles of law
4. Judicial decisions and teachings
5. UN declarations and resolutions

Case in Point

Law, Values, and the Rights of Women

The reformulation of international law, like the reform of international relations more generally, is part of the agenda for many feminists, for theoretical and practical reasons. On the theoretical level, feminists often argue that the development of international law has been male-dominated, so that, in the words of one feminist theorist, "international law is not a 'woman'-friendly tradition of thinking" but is a tradition overlaid with considerable "gender encrustations." The reconstruction of concepts advocated by postmodernist feminists includes a broadening of principles of international law to encompass gender-based concerns such as the right freely to choose a spouse.

This theoretical matter is closely related to the more practical concern for enforcing a set of universal rights of women. Efforts to do so are hampered by the historical fact of gender-based discrimination and exclusion of women from power and the absence of common values about women in various cultures and societies today. In many societies, women are still considered second-class citizens with few if any political, social, or economic rights. In Saudi Arabia, for example, women—including foreign women— are not allowed to drive cars. In a few states, women are even regarded as property; and in some places, such as China, it is considered nearly a disgrace to bear female children, who are often abandoned or even killed outright (in fact, there is a "crisis" of sorts in China because unmarried men outnumber unmarried females by a wide margin). Although it is arguable that women in western societies have not gained complete equality with men, their status is in general much higher.

Given this wide disparity of values, it is difficult, even impossible to devise universal rights that would not be culturally offensive to some society. Most westerners think that the principles of the Universal Declaration of Human Rights should apply equally to men and women (the right freely to vote, for instance), but in some cultures clearly they are not applied. In that circumstance, those who favor gender equity have the choice of devising appropriate norms, lobbying for their broad application, and publicizing where they do not exist, or accepting very broad, ambiguous norms that are not offensive to any culture.

Source of quotations: Christine Sylvester, *Feminist Theory and International Relations in a Postmodern Era* (Cambridge, UK: Cambridge University Press, 1994), pp. 128, 129.

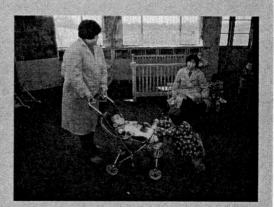

Reformulating international law to include a meaningful set of universal rights of women is difficult given the low status of females in many societies. In China, the site of a major UN-sponsored international women's conference in 1995 at which a code of such rights was adopted, orphanages are crowded with baby girls abandoned by their parents.

The most basic statement of what has been accepted as sources of international law is found in Article 38 of the World Court statute, a document which most countries have signed. The article provides for four sources: treaties and other international agreements, international custom, general principles of law, and judicial decisions (but not specific precedents) and teachings. UN resolutions, especially as they become more numerous and mutually reinforcing in areas such as human rights, may also be added to these standards in the future.

Treaties and other international agreements commit those parties to them to a legal framework of obligations that are as binding on them as domestic law. In some countries, when a treaty obligation clashes with a domestic law or statute, the treaty obligation takes precedence (which is a major reason that treaties must be ratified by the U.S. Senate). It is generally agreed, however, that a treaty between particular countries does not create a legal principle or law regulating other countries—a treaty between Peru and Chile on fishing zones cannot be applied to a similar dispute between Great Britain and Norway.

Treaties are of two basic sorts: bilateral (between two countries) and multilateral (between more than two countries). The more countries that are party to a treaty, the more likely it is to produce general principles of international law applicable universally. The Universal Declaration of Human Rights adopted by the UN in 1948 has been ratified by almost all countries and is thus thought of as essentially universal, although technically those states that have not signed the declaration are not bound by it.

Are treaties law? They certainly provide rules that govern states that are party to them, and can be considered law in that respect. Are they enforceable? In principle they are; the legal principle *pacta sunt servanda* (treaties are to be served as binding) creates an enforceable obligation. Enforcement, however, is indirect; a country that does not fulfill treaty obligations is "punished" by the reluctance of other countries to negotiate with it in the future.

International custom refers to common practices and habits that have taken on an obligatory aspect, in the sense that actions in conformity to the custom are widely expected. For such a practice in relations between states to qualify as law, two criteria are generally applied: (1) recognition of the custom as universal by the international community, and (2) compatibility of the custom with general principles of law to be discussed shortly (the practice in some Islamic countries of cutting off the hands of thieves would fail when placed against more generally accepted standards).

This is clearly a relatively "soft" basis for law. It reflects the Anglo-Saxon basis of much international law; particularly in the British system, custom and practice are important sources for regulating behavior. Finding customary practices that are universal in acceptance is difficult, however, especially in a world of widely varying, even conflicting values from which customs evolve.

Customary behavior becomes "firmer" law when it is codified into general treaties and agreements. Most of the regulations regarding the treatment of diplomatic personnel are of this nature. They all evolve from the original principle of protecting, rather than killing or otherwise harming, negotiators or emissaries from an adversary's camp; a negotiator who risked being killed when in enemy hands would be reluctant to undertake the task. Over time, this principle has been formalized and expanded into detailed conventions governing the treatment of foreign diplomats, as noted in Chapter 12. Violations of these custom-based conventions, such as the seizure of the American embassy in Tehran in 1979, are exceptions that are universally condemned.

General principles of law "recognized by civilized nations" (to quote the World Court statute) refer to the common principles behind bodies of law commonly administered in the courts of most or all states. The basis for making such principles law is the idea that a principle to which a state has agreed to regulate itself domestically should also be a principle by which it is obligated in its relations with other states. This intermestic approach as a means to create international law is, however, not universally accepted.

An example of such a general principle in practice is the rule for determination of boundaries where rivers are the dividing line. In American law, it has been determined that when a river changes course (as mature, meandering rivers occasionally do), the boundary changes as well. The domestic precedent is in litigation between Arkansas and Tennessee over changes in the course of the Mississippi River; the same principle has been applied to the border between Mexico and the United States as affected by changes in the course of the Colorado River.

Judicial decisions and teachings are likewise a general, rather than a specific, source of law because of the ban on precedent contained in the World Court statute. Hence they are considered a subsidiary source. What this source recognizes is that judges are in fact influenced—certainly in a general way—by what their predecessors have done and said, either in judicial decisions or in their writings and teachings. Some advocates would extend this source to include the influence of textbook writings in the field and judicial "reason"—the use by lawyers of similar lines of argument to the point that there is general agreement on certain principles within the international legal community.

Although they are not considered as such in the World Court's statute, UN resolutions are another possible source of international law. International standards regarding such matters as how states may treat their citizens are being set in the form of resolutions in the Security Council. It would stretch international consensus to argue that standards regarding internal atrocities in places like Bosnia and Rwanda can be accorded international legal status. However, such standards could be used to help define or redefine war crimes and the like, just as they do the conduct of war. The creation of a permanent War Crimes Tribunal attached to the World Court (introduced in Chapter 2) will help institutionalize the status of war crimes in the body of international law.

International Law and War

War—its regulation, conduct, and termination—is the most important phenomenon in international relations; and international law is not silent on this topic. International legal debates have long focused on the definition of the "just war"—the question of under what circumstances, if any, states have the right or possibly even the obligation to go to war. Recently the issue has been raised anew in debate over when outside intervention in primarily civil wars is permissible or impermissible, mandatory or not. This important First Tier–Second Tier issue will be further discussed in the next section.

The other area in which international law deals with war is in the rules that govern how war can be fought. Since war is about killing and being killed, imposing limitations on how this may occur may seem strange, especially since such limits are normally couched in "humane" terms. By convention that has evolved over time and been

Contours of the Future?

War Crimes Trials

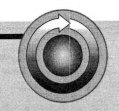

The spate of internal wars marring the contemporary international system has created a debate about defining an international role justifying intervention in these kinds of tragedies that has come to a head over the proposed permanent war crimes tribunal discussed earlier. A major aspect of that debate has to do with international rights and responsibilities for dealing with war crimes and criminals in these situations.

International law places limits on permissible ways to wage war (for instance, banning the use of chemical agents on the battlefield) and the treatment of combatants (conventions on prisoners of war) and noncombatants. Protection of the latter has also been extended under the Convention on Genocide, a treaty initiated within the United Nations that authorizes the convening of a war crimes tribunal under the auspices of the World Court when alleged instances of genocide occur.

In the period from the Nuremberg and Tokyo war crimes trials following World War II to the end of the Cold War, charges of war crimes were rarely made, because they would almost certainly have been impugned as having an ideological base (Khmer Rouge atrocities in Cambodia are a partial exception). The recent reports of horrific acts in internal wars where ideology has played little if any role have brought the subject back to the forefront. In particular, the situations in Bosnia, Rwanda, and more recently Kosovo reactivated international concern and resulted in the establishment of a war crimes tribunal in each case. In Bosnia, accusations of genocide against Muslims and Croats by the Bosnian Serbs resulted in the in-

dictment of a number of Serbian leaders in absentia in 1995; because of the politically volatile nature of the situation, the top leaders remained at large in Serbian Bosnia through 1996.

These proceedings raised several issues. The first was, who should conduct trials? Should it be the international community under UN auspices? or should it be Rwandans or Bosnians themselves? The UN, many analysts believed, had neither the personnel nor the financial resources to conduct timely or comprehensive trials. On the other hand, in the case of Rwanda, for example, trials conducted by the Tutsi-dominated Rwandan Patriotic Front, which controls the country's government, would be subject to the criticism that they represented "victor's law" at best and a vendetta at worst. In the event, the UN decided to assume responsibility for the trials. The Bosnian trials began at the World Court headquarters at the Hague, Netherlands, in 1996.

A second question has to do with enforcement. While the World Court can indict and even try war criminals without their physical presence, bringing them to justice remains a problem. At Nuremberg and Tokyo, the defendants were from defeated countries and were in the physical custody of those conducting the trials. On the other hand, it is not at all clear how any sentences against the top Bosnian Serb leadership can be enforced short of a major change in the ISFOR mission that would allow them to pursue and arrest people in Bosnia. Such an expansion of mission would have unpredictable, and potentially negative, consequences that all parties wished to avoid through 1996.

enshrined in various international agreements, however, certain forms of armaments—such as biological and chemical weapons—are regarded as impermissible, as is the killing or mistreatment of prisoners of war. Reciprocity is the guiding principle: "I will not harm your forces who surrender to me, and in return, you will not harm forces who surrender to you." Violations of the conventions constitute war crimes, as do crimes by military personnel against civilian populations.

In some circumstances, notably internal wars, what constitutes war crimes and who has the responsibility for enforcing sanctions against violators are somewhat ambiguous. The UN Charter provides the leading statements on the subject, but they are ambiguous. On one hand, the charter states that one of the world body's purposes is to promote human rights (Article 1), that doing so is actually an obligation of the organization (Article 55), and that member states are obliged to promote them (Article 56). On the other hand, Article 2 states that there is nothing in the charter to "authorize the United Nations to intervene in matters which are essentially within the domestic jurisdiction of any State."

The principle in Article 2 is under assault. The assertion of an international mandate on human rights—which must underlie any international mandate on war crimes committed in internal wars—is being broadly proclaimed in the light of atrocities against civilian populations in places like Rwanda and Kosovo. Because of the assault on sovereignty contained in these assertions of the human rights mandate, the issue has yet to be resolved.

International Law in the New International System

Clearly, the disorderly way in which international law accumulates is not conducive to the efficient development of a large body of law. This is by design, and it stems from the notion of sovereignty. International law intrudes on the sovereign ability of states to do as they please, and all states recognize this fact. If the members of the international system

Iraqi troops taken prisoner during the Persian Gulf War. International law forbids the killing or mistreatment of prisoners of war by their captors or of civilians by military personnel.

wanted a more efficient and effective way to create international law, they would establish a body with legislative authority. They have not done so as of yet. Is there any reason to expect anything different in the future?

The evolving, tiered international system will surely produce rules of behavior different from those of the Cold War era; some of this change is clearly happening already. Will members of the system decide that formalizing the new rules into something like a legal canon serve them well? That question, in turn, raises two further questions. The first is, will the conditions for forming an international code of law indeed become more prevalent in the future? The second is, are mechanisms to produce such law available? The answers to these two questions really have to do with differences in conditions within the two tiers that compose the system. We will examine the first two questions and then consider how to answer them for each of the tiers.

With respect to the conditions for producing international law, as noted earlier, states behave in accordance with their perceptions of what is in their interest. Where national interests, and especially vital interests, are served by a code of law binding states to observe it, such a code is seen as a tool of potential value. On the other hand, when maximum control by individual states is the object, there will be resistance to institutionalizing legal regimes.

As we have also explained, another requirement for the production of law is a common set of values on which to base it. During the Cold War period, there was sufficient difference between the world views of East and West to preclude law making on many topics. That logjam was broken by the Helsinki Accords of 1975, and then, more completely, by the end of the Cold War. Under the terms of the Helsinki agreement, the states of the West finally accepted the territorial boundaries of Eastern Europe and the Soviet Union resulting from World War II as permanent; in return, the Soviet Union accepted western definitions of human rights and guaranteed it would respect them (a commitment many Eastern Europeans see in retrospect as the beginning of the end of communist dictatorship). The accords also created the Conference (now Organization) on Security and Cooperation in Europe (C/OSCE), which has become a major forum for resolving lingering East-West differences in the wake of the Cold War and is a candidate for the role of overall security regime in Europe, as suggested in Chapter 6.

Common interests and common values translate into general support for a status quo that states are willing to enforce. This is one of the bases for a collective-security system, as noted in Chapter 3. It is also the essential basis for a legal regime.

As for the second question we have raised, whether there are institutions and mechanisms to support such a broadening of law should it be desired, one can safely rule out the prospect that the United Nations or some similar body will be accorded the powers of an international legislative body. How, then, could this law come into being? Since custom, judicial experience, and an expansion of law based on common principles all are slow, cumbersome methods, the only feasible means available are international conventions binding states that are party to them. To what extent might this approach be feasible in the future?

The answer to this question, like the answer to the one about whether general conditions for the expansion of international law will become more favorable, depends on whether one focuses on the First Tier or the Second. We will now examine each tier, focusing in greater detail on the different requirements for the establishment of an international legal regime.

Prospects for the First Tier

By any of the criteria that can be applied, prospects for extending legal regimes to regulate the relations among the countries of the First Tier seem excellent. First of all, the standard of similar values among those who might bind themselves together is clearly met. These values are embodied in the political democracy and technologically advanced capitalist economies that are the defining characteristics of the First Tier. As discussed in Chapter 7, there continue to be differences in culture between the West and Japan, but these are not so fundamental as to preclude agreement on a broad range of matters—for instance, the inviolability of copyrights. Moreover, it is clear that part of the "membership fee" for admission of new states to the First Tier will be acceptance of these common values.

Summary ————————————————————————

Criteria for Development of an International Legal Regime

1. Common values
2. Reinforcing vital interests
3. Support for the status quo
4. Economic interdependence
5. Regime formation mechanisms

Second, the differences in vital interest among First Tier states, particularly in interests that could lead to war, are relatively minor. As has already been noted, the conditions are certainly present for a collective-security regime among them—which is at least one important form of legal regime. Whether there is adequate consensus to extend such a regime beyond the First Tier is problematical.

Third, in the expanding global economy, the First Tier generally supports a status quo of peaceful adjustment of differences because it is quintessentially "good business." There are significant prospects that a global economy, rather than producing winners and losers, can be a positive-sum game benefiting all who play. For it to do so, it may be necessary to develop, through forums like the WTO, legal regimes to help work out the rules.

Fourth, it has been noted that there is a growing economic interdependence among First Tier states. Differences relating to trade barriers and fairness of competition remain, but the central concerns in the future have to do with adjusting to a highly privatized, global economy of stateless corporations. Regulation of such an economy (to the extent that it is desired) is beyond the control of individual states and would require some form of international legal regime.

Finally, there are mechanisms already in place to facilitate agreement among the First Tier states. A G–8 system, somewhat expanded, is a clear candidate to deal not only with a range of economic matters pertinent to internal First Tier concerns but also with a broader range of issues (including such an issue as missile proliferation). The OSCE, although it contains aspirants to the First Tier (the Soviet successor states and Eastern Europe) as well as members, could serve as a forum for producing agreements on security and human rights matters, as could a NATO expanded through the Partnership for Peace.

With so much in common and so little dividing them, there is thus little reason First Tier states cannot evolve lawlike regimes among themselves. In general, however, these conditions do not hold either in the relations among Second Tier states or in the relations between the states of the First and Second Tiers.

Prospects for the Second Tier

Almost none of the circumstances favorable to the development of expanded First Tier legal regimes hold universally within the far more diverse set of states making up the Second Tier. Some of these states, like those of the Pacific Rim, resemble First Tier states and likely will become part of the First Tier. For the remaining majority of states, it is far from likely that a legal regime could develop or gain acceptance.

First, there is no common set of political and economic values. Freedom in the Second Tier often means self-determination that accentuates differences, not inclusionary nationalism and crosscutting democratic tolerance. Economic conditions among Second Tier states are so varied that no common set of aspirations, beyond a vague call for development, is discernible. Cultural incompatibilities abound. The loudest cultural voice is Islamic fundamentalism, but it is by no means a universally accepted credo even in Islamic countries. It is even more difficult to imagine a broad set of international legal standards for the Second Tier that would not be meaninglessly vague.

Second, the vital interests of Second Tier states tend to drive them apart, not bring them together. This is especially true where there are regional conflicts, demanding that the states involved think in terms of national rather than international security. India, for instance, must concern itself with Indian security (notably in relation to China and Pakistan), not some abstract notion of global security that might impinge on Indian vital interests. Economically, the developmental process is a competitive, not a cooperative, enterprise, particularly in the struggle for scarce developmental assistance and in the struggle to attract foreign corporations and investment.

These differences in values and clashing vital interests lead to a third point: there is and for the foreseeable future can be no common vision of a status quo to be enshrined and reinforced in law. Second Tier countries are all, to an extent depending on their locations and their levels of development, at odds with the status quo, which they believe victimizes them, rather than operating to their benefit. This common problem does not, however, translate into a common view of how, for instance, the international economic system should be changed to alleviate their disadvantages.

Related to this is a fourth point: while members of the First Tier enjoy a situation of economic interdependence which they may find in their interests to codify and regulate, quite the opposite is true in the Second Tier. The condition there is one of dependence on the First Tier, a situation that Second Tier states seek to escape. Legal regimes that would reinforce existing relationships are thus undesirable. This does not imply a preference for lawlessness on the part of Second Tier states, only a disagreement about how to bring about change. This clash of economic values helps explain, for instance, the imperfect grafting of the western capitalist system in East Asia that contributed to the financial crisis discussed in Chapter 8.

Fifth, even if the other prerequisites for forming legal regimes were present, there are no suitable structures through which this could be done. During the Cold War, conferences of "nonaligned" states often broke down into parochial bickering, and in most regions there is no effective organization in which Second Tier states might collaborate to develop a legal regime. The universal organization with which they identified themselves in the past was the UN, but for important purposes that body is now dominated by a First Tier in firm control of the Security Council and of the purse strings.

Intertier Prospects

The varying prospects for establishing international legal regimes in the new tiered international system turn out to reflect the general division and dynamic of the post–Cold War order, and the two very divergent realities that exist in these different "worlds." There is an unprecedented opportunity to expand lawlike regimes among the members of the First Tier, while the disarray of the Second Tier suggests the unlikelihood of a parallel development there. What, then, are the prospects for expanding those rules that guide relations between the tiers in more predictable and peaceful ways? Comparing the tiers in terms of the values we have discussed does not lead to an optimistic conclusion.

The wide variation of values within the Second Tier has already been discussed. Some countries of the Second Tier are in the process of adopting First Tier values, but sizable parts of the world—including most of Africa and much of the Islamic Middle East, for instance—instead hold on to values that are more or less at odds with those of the First Tier. The difficulty in the way of adopting universal codes of women's rights, mentioned earlier in this chapter, is a good example of this incompatibility.

The belief system at most obvious odds with that of the First Tier is Islamic fundamentalism—especially in its more militant forms. This conflict is especially important because Islamic fundamentalism is most prominent in that region of the Second Tier where much of the world's petroleum is located, and thus where First Tier vital interests are involved. Access to this petroleum is vitally important to the expanding global economy, but the capitalist principles on which that economy is based are at odds with fundamentalist Islam—which, for instance, considers it a violation of Islamic law to charge interest on loaned money. Furthermore, attitudes toward the legitimate use of violence differ in ways that cause the two tiers to clash. In particular, some Islamic fundamentalist attitudes toward terrorism (at least as categorized by the West) are often relatively tolerant and supportive. For example, the Afghan Taliban, one of the most fundamentalist regimes, granted sanctuary to the terrorist organization of Osama bin Laden. All these differences reinforce the difficulty of devising legal regimes acceptable to all states in the First and Second Tiers.

The two tiers also diverge in the area of vital national interests, and hence in their view of whether their security is served by a legal regime. To reiterate, the countries of the First Tier share a common interest in the spread of democracy and market-based economies—which they believe require and foster peace and stability. This leads to a common preference for the formalization of a legal regime that can develop and support international law and order, and which provides a tranquil setting for extending the general prosperity of the First Tier. Second Tier states, for their part, lack such a common interest. As a group, they are certainly not opposed to a condition of peace and stability, but individually their often conflicting vital interests will make forming an effective legal regime that could enforce the peace favored by the First Tier difficult, if not impossible.

The third factor to be considered, heavily reflecting the first two, is the difference between the tiers in attitude toward the status quo. As has been discussed, the First Tier's prosperity and relative security make it naturally attached to the status quo—and possibly

Case in Point
Law and the Treatment of Terrorists

The spate of terrorist attacks within the United States, along with similar acts in other countries during 1995, 1996, and 1998 has rekindled interest in the capture, prosecution, and suppression of terrorists. This is a hotly contested area, particularly within the counter-terrorist community, which is responsible for preventing and suppressing terrorists.

Although terrorist acts clearly violate the human rights of those against whom they are committed, there is no effective international law in important areas such as definitions of international terrorism—for instance, acts committed on the high seas—or for extradition of suspected terrorists. At the same time, there is no international enforcement regime, making coordination of national efforts more difficult.

Domestically, there are two alternative legal approaches to counterterrorism. One alternative is to treat terrorism as a standard problem of law and order. In this perspective, terrorism is considered criminal activity, and it must be countered within the same legal and judicial limits as other crimes, including adherence to accepted standards of rules of evidence, provisions for search and seizure, and procedures for arrest and trial. Given the highly clandestine nature of terrorism,

these demanding requirements give the advantage to the terrorist. Public frustration at the length of time between the arrest and trial of Oklahoma City bombers Timothy McVeigh and Terry Nichols and Unabomber Theodore Kacyzinski reflects this frustration. States harboring alleged terrorists often insist on such standards before they will allow suspects to be extradited (the Libyan government and the accused bombers of Pan American flight 103, for instance).

The other alternative is to treat terrorism as a military problem. The rationale for this approach is that terrorists have effectively declared war on society and have committed what they say are acts of war. If this position is adopted, the rules of engagement change, and judicial requirements are relaxed, making apprehension easier.

Terrorists prefer to manipulate these alternatives to their advantage: they proclaim themselves at war (thus not to be regarded as common criminals), yet they want to be protected by the the full civilian legal system.

Source: Donald M. Snow, *Distant Thunder: Patterns of Conflict in the Developing World,* 2d ed. (Armonk, NY: ME Sharpe Publishers, 1997), p. 154-57.

to its promotion through a legal regime. Most of the Second Tier, which shares neither the prosperity nor the tranquility of the First Tier, demands development, which means change that will sometimes be reflected in rules about economic and other forms of interaction between the tiers. The entire debate over development, detailed in Chapter 8, suggests the difficulty in finding a commonly satisfactory status quo and hence a system to defend.

The difference between tiers is further reflected in contrasting economic positions. As has been indicated, the states of the First Tier enjoy a high level of economic interdependence that is mutually beneficial, whereas the Second Tier remains in a basic condition of economic dependency, whether one accepts the Marxist trappings of that term or not. From a Second Tier perspective, this dependency is reinforced in parts of international law, such as international commercial law on trade, so that a regime encompassing such law does not seem attractive.

As for the final criterion, the existence of law-making mechanisms, the only comprehensive, international institution encompassing both tiers (aside from the young World Trade Organization) is the UN. The UN not only reflects the diversity and disagreement among Second Tier states but also, as mentioned earlier, is heavily influenced by a First Tier suddenly interested in the world body now that the Cold War is over. Thus, the likelihood that it can serve as a forum for intertier collaboration seems low.

In general, then, the prospects for expanding international law in relations between the tiers are not promising. The diversity of the Second Tier and the gaps in values between the First and Second Tiers militate against any such expansion of international law beyond the First Tier.

International Organizations and the Revived UN

The history and role of international organizations closely parallels those for international law, and hopes for the future of the two are closely intertwined. In fact, law and organizations are often treated as a single subfield of international relations. Both were early approaches to the field, and are, as we have said, an outgrowth of the largely western belief that by extending rules and institutions beyond state boundaries, the world can be made a better, more peaceful place.

International organizations are among the most important nonstate actors, as we discussed in Chapter 2. They come in two basic varieties: intergovernmental organizations (IGOs), whose members are national governments, and nongovernmental organizations (NGOs), whose members are individuals and groups not part of governments. Of these, NGOs are the more numerous, and some of them, such as the International Red Cross, may be quite important. We will limit our discussions to the IGOs, however, because the NGOs are generally less prominent in international relations (an exception being the increasingly important multinational corporations). The crowning jewel of the system of IGOs is the United Nations system, and this will be the center of our attention. We will begin by describing that system, and then will move to assessing its role.

The United Nations System

To many, the term United Nations evokes a picture of the multistory glass building (known as the Glass House) on the East River in New York City, where the organization is headquartered, or televised speeches by world leaders either in the great hall of the General Assembly or in the Security Council. These are certainly important symbols of the world organization, but they reflect only a small part of UN activity. The UN, which came into being at the end of World War II, has two broad missions under its charter: to promote peace and peaceful settlements of differences and to address and help solve social (including human rights) and economic problems. The promotion of peace was the follow-on responsibility from the old League of Nations system, which had been unable to prevent

Amplification

Preamble to the UN Charter

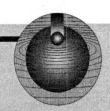

Broad principles of human and international relations are set forth in the text of the Preamble to the UN Charter:

We the people of the United Nations determined to save future generations from the scourge of war, which twice in our lifetime has brought untold sorrow to mankind, and to reaffirm faith in fundamental human rights, in the dignity and worth of the human person, in the equal rights of men and women, and of nations large and small, and to establish conditions under which justice and respect for the obligations arising from treaties and other sources of international law can be maintained, and to promote social progress and better standards of life in larger freedom, and for these ends to practice tolerance and live together in peace with one another as good neighbors, and to unite our strength to maintain international peace and security, and to ensure, by the acceptance of principles and the institution of methods, that armed force shall not be used, save in the common interest, and to employ international machinery for the promotion of the economic and social advancement of all peoples, have resolved to combine our efforts to accomplish these aims.

World War II. The social and economic mission was a new task that reflected values about world peace that emerged from the late interwar and wartime periods.

The theory that underlay the new activity was called *functionalism*. Beginning from the idealist position that national sovereignty was the major cause of international division, and hence of war, the theory's primary apologist, David Mitrany (whose writings during the war provided much of the intellectual framework for the effort), argued for a "functional" approach to replacing national loyalty with loyalty to international organizations. The vehicle for accomplishing this was to be a group of international organizations furnishing the same kinds of services (or functions) as those provided by national governments. Over time, Mitrany's argument went, people would more and more associate the provision of governmental services with international rather than national governments, a shift that would cause a transfer of loyalties to international organizations and render national governments obsolete.

Functionalism is essentially dead, but the structures it inspired have survived as the components of the UN system, as illustrated in Figure 13-1. At the center of the system (and the figure) are the six "principal agencies" of the UN. The three most central are the General Assembly, the Security Council and the Secretariat. At some remove are the World Court (the International Court of Justice), the Economic and Social Council (ECOSOC), and the Trusteeship Council.

At the heart of the UN is the General Assembly, a legislative and debating forum in which all members are represented, each having a single vote. The Assembly is the major forum for debating international issues. It controls the UN budget by determining member

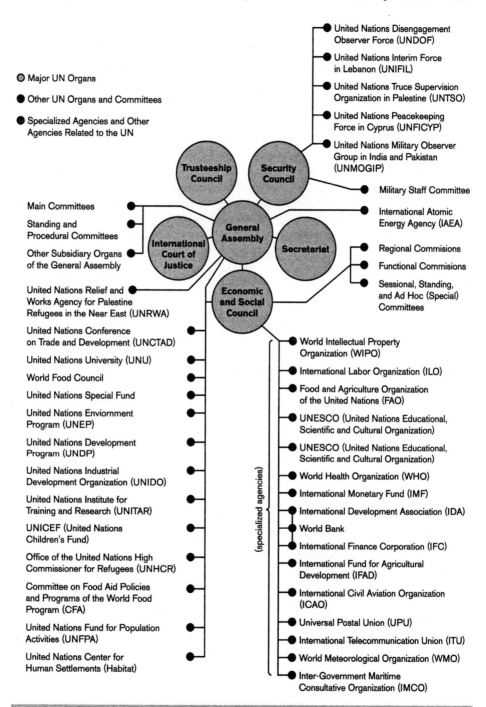

○ Major UN Organs

● Other UN Organs and Committees

● Specialized Agencies and Other
   Agencies Related to the UN

United Nations Disengagement
Observer Force (UNDOF)

United Nations Interim Force
in Lebanon (UNIFIL)

United Nations Truce Supervision
Organization in Palestine (UNTSO)

United Nations Peacekeeping
Force in Cyprus (UNFICYP)

United Nations Military Observer
Group in India and Pakistan
(UNMOGIP)

Military Staff Committee

International Atomic
Energy Agency (IAEA)

Regional Commisions

Functional Commisions

Sessional, Standing,
and Ad Hoc (Special)
Committees

Trusteeship Council

Security Council

General Assembly

International Court of Justice

Secretariat

Economic and Social Council

Main Committees

Standing and
Procedural Committees

Other Subsidiary Organs
of the General Assembly

United Nations Relief and
Works Agency for Palestine
Refugees in the Near East (UNRWA)

United Nations Conference
on Trade and Development (UNCTAD)

United Nations University (UNU)

World Food Council

United Nations Special Fund

United Nations Enviornment
Program (UNEP)

United Nations Development
Program (UNDP)

United Nations Industrial
Development Organization (UNIDO)

United Nations Institute for
Training and Research (UNITAR)

UNICEF (United Nations
Children's Fund)

Office of the United Nations High
Commissioner for Refugees (UNHCR)

Committee on Food Aid Policies
and Programs of the World Food
Program (CFA)

United Nations Fund for Population
Activities (UNFPA)

United Nations Center for
Human Settlements (Habitat)

(specialized agencies)

World Intellectual Property
Organization (WIPO)

International Labor Organization (ILO)

Food and Agriculture Organization
of the United Nations (FAO)

UNESCO (United Nations Educational,
Scientific and Cultural Organization)

UNESCO (United Nations Educational,
Scientific and Cultural Organization)

World Health Organization (WHO)

International Monetary Fund (IMF)

International Development Association (IDA)

World Bank

International Finance Corporation (IFC)

International Fund for Agricultural
Development (IFAD)

International Civil Aviation Organization
(ICAO)

Universal Postal Union (UPU)

International Telecommunication Union (ITU)

World Meteorological Organization (WMO)

Inter-Government Maritime
Consultative Organization (IMCO)

Figure 13-1   **The United Nations System**

Web Sitings: UN Agencies

The United Nations is a complex web of associated organizations, detailed description of which goes beyond present purposes. The UN home page (http://www.un.org) provides thumbnail sketches and references for more detailed information on them.

contributions and expenditures by UN agencies, directs the actions of a number of UN organs, and can make security recommendations to the Security Council.

The second central organ is the Security Council. A kind of executive board of the Assembly, it contains 15 members empowered to decide on security matters as defined in the charter. The five permanent members, each of which has a veto power over any proposed action, are the principal victorious Allies in World War II—the United States, Great Britain, France, China, and Russia (which holds the seat formerly occupied by the Soviet Union). The other 10 members are elected from the Assembly on a rotating base. (A list of the current members at any time can be found at the UN home page.) A major issue currently before the UN is whether to expand the permanent membership, certainly to add Japan and Germany, but possibly to include Second Tier countries as well.

The Secretariat, the third central organ of the system, is the designated bureaucracy of the UN, with approximately 9,000 employees providing services to other agencies. The chief officer—and hence the most visible UN official—is the secretary-general. This position becomes especially important, and occasionally controversial, when the secretary-general becomes involved in peacekeeping missions, either as a participant in defining and directing them or as an advocate of UN involvement. Although the most recent former secretary-general, Egypt's Boutros Boutros-Ghali, maintained that his sole job was to carry out instructions of the Security Council in this regard, he was widely credited with (or accused of) shaping the instructions he implemented, which was part of the reason that the United States announced in 1996 that it would veto his nomination for a second five-year term in office. His successor, Kofi Annan of Ghana, has been less assertive about his role—one reason he was sponsored by the United States.

UN Secretary-General Kofi Annan of Ghana.

The other three principal organs can be treated summarily. The World Court has already been discussed. The Trusteeship Council, which arose from the League of Nations mandate system, is designed to assist non-self-governing states in eventually achieving that status. Currently largely inactive, it has been suggested as a vehicle for restoring legitimate governance in failed states such as Somalia, a suggestion that appears moribund. The Economic and Social Council (ECOSOC), the last principal organ to be mentioned, has responsibility for the added task of promoting social and economic progress, a task it performs mainly through supervision of the specialized agencies of the United Nations.

The specialized agencies represent a novel contribution of the system. In some ways they are implementations of Mitrany's functional dream, although in a number of cases—the Universal Postal Union and the International Labor Organization, for example—they were already in existence when the UN came into being. They cover an impressive array of concerns: financing development and economic stability (World Bank, International Monetary Fund); regulating international interactions (Universal Postal Union, International Telecommunications Union, International Civil Aviation Organization); coordinating scientific and other interchanges (United Nations Economic, Scientific and Cultural Organization, World Intellectual Property Organization, World Meteorological Organization); aiding agriculture (Food and Agricultural Organization, International Fund for Agricultural Development) and world health (World Health Organization). These organizations no longer aspire to supplant national governmental functions, but rather seek to work with and coordinate national efforts. In addition, an impressive array of programs and agencies report directly to the General Assembly, and the various peacekeeping bodies report directly to the Security Council, as the figure indicates.

Prospects for the UN System

Because almost all members of the First and Second Tiers belong to the UN, it provides a unique forum for the interchange of views and opinions; as such, the UN can serve as a kind of honest broker. At the same time, the apparent end of Security Council gridlock raises the prospect of its playing a central role in collective security if a suitable legal regime can be agreed to. First Tier dominance further suggests the possibility that the Security Council could even be used to impose order on a reluctant Second Tier.

The relationship between the tiers, especially but not exclusively in the area of peace and security, will partly depend on how the world body evolves. Previously, it was important mostly to the old Third World, as a tool for publicizing what it viewed as injustices perpetrated by the then First World. The General Assembly was the principal forum for this campaign, because the Third World had more votes (if limited powers) there. Events since 1991 suggest that the First Tier desires a wider role for the UN, principally Security Council action in organizing and enforcing the peace, although the exact dimensions of this role remain uncertain. Much of this debate was crystallized during the celebration of the UN's fiftieth anniversary in 1995, as suggested in the Views from Abroad box "The United Nations at 50."

Three questions with respect to the overall role of the UN stand out in particular. Is the UN role on the world scene to be basically that of a passive servant of member states or that of an activist? How will the UN deal with the diversity of agendas and values of its increasing membership (the size of which may pose a problem in itself)? Can the UN be a vehicle for resolving intertier issues?

Views from Abroad

The United Nations at 50

The summer 1995 observance of the UN's 50 years of existence was a decidedly mixed celebration. The euphoria created by the UN-sponsored expulsion of Iraq from Kuwait had been largely dampened by less successful adventures in places such as Somalia, Rwanda, and Mozambique. Combined with the perpetual financial crisis facing the organization, the UN's future direction is much in question, as reflected in world press coverage.

Madrid's *El Mundo* points to the financial aspect, saying the future will be "very difficult because of financial problems." While advocating a mediating role for the organization, it raises the question "who will pay for it?" Reflecting the UN's traditional role as advocate in Third World problems, the *Katmandu Post* suggests, "The time has come for the world community to make decisions about how to deal with different kinds of conflicts, war, and poverty." The *Philippines Daily Inquirer* of Manila con-

curs, suggesting the need for structural change "to democratize the UN-decision-making process through a fairer representation" of developing countries.

European reaction was more critical. The conservative *Le Figaro* of Paris is highly critical of UN performance, arguing "bloated bureaucracy, the huge costs of its interventions, its failures in Somalia, Rwanda, and Bosnia, and its failure to boost development stress the need for radical reform." Although critical, *Nepszabadsag* of Budapest, Hungary, offers the most balanced assessment: "The slow, hypocritical, and impotent UN is capable of solving problems no other organization could in an efficient, ethical, and quick manner....The UN is both good and bad; it is as complicated and complex as the world in which it operates, but the world would be far more complicated and chaotic without it."

Source: World Press Review, December 1995, p. 5.

The first question can be understood through focusing on former secretary-general Boutros-Ghali. He was clearly an activist who believes the UN as an organization should have a broader role in international relations, a position he more or less directly advocated in a 1992 monograph *An Agenda for Peace* and a *Foreign Affairs* article calling for "empowerment" of the UN. Beyond playing a leading role in shaping the UN's responses to crises, he went so far as to advocate command of UN-delegated national forces by the UN (presumably allowing the secretary-general to have a major role) and creation of a standing UN armed force. Both are sensitive political issues. A number of First Tier states, but most prominently the United States, have resisted these suggestions, and his unwillingness to back away from these controversial positions cost him any chance at a second term.

The desire for a highly active UN, operating more independently of national governments, is thus by no means universal among member states. Previously, the Second Tier was a champion of broadened UN powers as a way to gain leverage against the First Tier. But in a system where that same UN might be regulating the activities of Second Tier states, the enthusiasm for a strong UN role may be more restrained. First Tier states, on the other hand, may find the UN a convenient agency for legitimizing their actions; it is not, however, clear how much sovereign control they are willing to forfeit in the interests of a stronger UN, or how much UN activism First Tier publics will be willing to support.

The second question as to the UN's role concerns not only how it will deal with the montage of diverse agendas and values that members bring to it, but also with the sheer size of the organization. The diversity and size of UN membership may not be a problem as long as the world body is thought of primarily as a debating forum; they become a problem when the UN is seen as an action arm of the international system in the area of peace and security and elsewhere.

The point may be illustrated by an incident in 1993 when a plot tied to radical Islamic fundamentalists was uncovered by U.S. authorities. It involved blowing up several important sites in New York City, including tunnels leading to Manhattan Island and the UN headquarters itself. Further investigation linked the conspiracy to Sudan and, more specifically, to personnel of the Sudanese mission to the UN. The plot was widely and loudly condemned in the West—but almost ignored publicly by UN officials and most Second Tier governments.

If there is a common security goal shared universally within the First Tier, it is the suppression of terrorist acts, especially in the First Tier, a point made forcefully by U.S. President Bill Clinton in a September 1998 speech before the General Assembly. Many Second Tier states concur in this agenda, but not all. Several militant Islamic states condone and even actively support terrorist activity, and some other Second Tier states side with the militants for reasons of Second Tier solidarity. How is a system like the UN—which was itself a victim in this plot but still represents all states—to adopt a commonly acceptable policy that will promote peace and security?

If the process of state disintegration continues, this problem of diversity will only get worse as more new states enter the organization. The breakup of the Soviet Union added 12 new members (Ukraine and Belarus were already members), the disintegration of Yugoslavia added four, and the separation of Czechoslovakia into Slovakia and the Czech Republic added another. These new states reinforce existing value differences, increase the number of voices that must be heard in the deliberative process, and hence make consensus on actions harder to achieve.

The third question about the UN's role is the extent to which it can or should be the "agency of choice" for dealing with First Tier involvement in the internal turmoil within the Second Tier and situations in which Second Tier actions have an impact in the First Tier—such as terrorism. The question has arisen particularly with the end of the Cold War. With superpower rivalry no longer causing paralysis within the Security Council, the UN becomes an institutional candidate for an activist role. With superpower retreat and the dissolution of communism, moreover, has come a rash of internal violence that, in some well-publicized cases, has seemed to demand the attention of outside powers and of an invigorated UN.

Before attempting to define what the UN role can or should be in these situations, we must begin by considering how and where the UN has been active recently in trouble spots around the world and what alternatives have been available to it. That is the topic of the next section. Then, in a case study, we will examine the advantages and disadvantages of employing the UN as the major instrument in the tiered international system's security effort.

Peacekeeping, Peacemaking, and the UN System

The later 1980s and early 1990s produced a wave of violence, mostly confined to the Second Tier, to which the UN was called on to respond by a Security Council no longer divided by the veto. Previously, UN activity in this realm had been confined almost exclusively to the relatively passive job of peacekeeping, or enforcing cease-fires and armistices to which the parties had already agreed. The exception was UN involvement in the former Belgian Congo (later Zaire, now the Democratic Republic of the Congo) from 1960 to 1964, when its forces helped to suppress a secession effort by Katanga (now Shaba) province. This is an adventure most countries involved and the UN itself would rather forget because it was not particularly successful militarily and because it forced the organization to take sides in a civil war, something it is generally reluctant to do.

The newer rash of violence created widespread demand for UN assistance, and the organization responded with an unprecedented outburst of activity. There were 16 active UN missions in mid–1997, of a total of 45 missions in the organization's history. Operations of various sorts were active in most of the world's hot spots: three operations overseeing the Arab-Israeli crisis and another Middle Eastern operation supervising the cease-fire between Iraq and Kuwait, four in the Balkans (Bosnia, two in Croatia, and Macedonia), three in Africa (Angola, Western Sahara, and Liberia), two in the Soviet successor states (Georgia and Tajikistan), and one each in Central America and the Caribbean (Haiti), the Mediterranean (Cyprus), and Asia (India-Pakistan).

The situations are more than geographically diverse; they also cover a wide gamut of different kinds of problems that require different kinds of solutions, including, in some cases, military action. In most of the long-standing operations, the peacekeeping model was adopted by the UN. Peacekeeping was not, however, appropriate to all these circumstances, and so the UN needed to develop a sophisticated understanding of the different roles that could be contemplated and the dangers and pitfalls of various actions.

A Taxonomy of Intervention Forms

Faced with diverse situations apparently requiring diverse responses, the Security Council commissioned Secretary-General Boutros-Ghali to survey the status of peacekeeping operations around the world and make recommendations in late 1991. His response, *An Agenda for Peace,* was produced in 1992 and became—for better or worse—a model for the way the UN and its members have come to categorize various options.

The Boutros-Ghali formulation, including the stage of conflict (active fighting or not) in which various activities presumably take place, is described below:

Some of these categories of response are virtually self-explanatory. *Preventive diplomacy,* in this formulation, refers to diplomatic initiatives undertaken to persuade potential warring partners not to engage in hostilities. *Peacekeeping* refers to actions taken to maintain a peace that has been established; as explained earlier, it is the UN's traditional role of sending forces to interpose themselves between former warring parties and to observe and supervise the cease-fire. (The organization has broadened its definition to include actions to "stop or contain hostilities," a considerable conceptual expansion.) *Peace building* refers to state-building actions taken in an effort to ensure that the causes of conflict do not recur. The largely unsuccessful UN attempts to rebuild Somalia's political system would be an example.

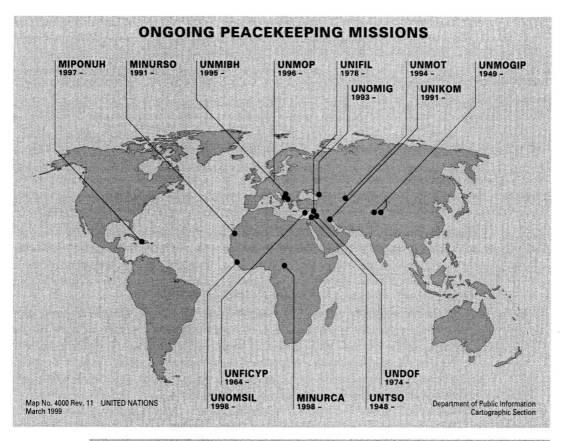

Map 13-1   UN Peace Operations, as of March 1999.
Department of Public Information, cartographic section, Map No. 4000 Rev. 11, United Nations, March 1999.

The designations become murkier, and even misleading, when they deal with actions taken during hostilities. *Peacemaking,* in the secretary-general's formulation, refers and is limited to diplomatic efforts to persuade warring parties to negotiate a cease-fire. The mission of former U.S. Secretary of State Cyrus Vance and British Foreign Minister Lord Owen to former Yugoslavia in 1992–93 would presumably qualify as a peacemaking effort. *Peace enforcement,* on the other hand, refers to actions taken by peacekeeping forces and diplomats to reestablish a cease-fire that has been breached. The U.S. military extends this definition to include military actions (although it euphemistically calls them "peace operations") that might be undertaken to force such a cease-fire in the first place.

This taxonomy is subject to at least four related criticisms. The first is that the wartime definitions fly in the face of normal usage of language. Peacemaking logically includes all kinds of activity that contribute to ending hostilities, not just diplomacy. Peace enforcement is even more misleading: it refers to actions taken to reinstitute a peace that has evaporated, whereas the word "enforcement" implies the existence of peace.

A second problem is that the taxonomy does not include all possible actions. It excludes, for instance, direct military intervention intended to force peace on warring parties by denying them the ability to continue fighting. This is the kind of action the U.S. military misleadingly includes under the term peace enforcement. Peacemaking would be a more accurate word; peace creation or, preferably, peace imposition are alternate terms that are intuitively meaningful.

The exclusion of an active military category of response makes the taxonomy only partially responsive to the real problems the system confronts. It is hard, for instance, to see how any of the options Boutros-Ghali included were applicable to former Yugoslavia from 1992 to 1995 or the Rwandan slaughter of 1994. In both cases, only the use of military forces (peace imposition) had any chance of bringing the fighting to a halt. In Yugoslavia, although peacemaking was attempted and a peacekeeping force was dispatched, that action was clearly inappropriate to and ineffective in the situation (originally meant to enforce a cease-fire between Croatia and Serbia, the force was almost inadvertently thrust into the Bosnian civil war). In Bosnia (and doubtless other places like Kosovo), active, forceful military intrusion may be the only meaningful option, as has been the case with IFOR (renamed the Stabilization Force, or SFOR, in 1997), an active offensive force that was able to create and maintain peace during its duration essentially by intimidating with overwhelming force the formerly warring parties that might challenge it. One can only speculate that the reason Boutros-Ghali excluded it was his assessment that it would be too expensive and controversial a mission for the UN to undertake.

Third, the taxonomy tends not only to downgrade the need for military actions but also to ignore the problems that attend them. In Boutros-Ghali's rendering, the military role remains essentially passive—which is the traditional peacekeeper's role. But not all conflicts can be resolved passively. If the role includes active combat operations, the kinds of forces associated with peacekeeping are woefully inadequate—as the besieged UNPROFOR troops in Bosnia learned at the hands of Bosnian Serbs.

Fourth and finally, the categories of response, with an active military option excluded, suggest a continuity of actions that does not exist in dealing with real military situations. The secretary-general portrays the five actions as though they form a sequence; the actual imposition of force to create peace (what he calls peace enforcement and we shall call peace imposition) is a radically different activity that falls outside any continuum. It is in a wholly different category that is recognized in U.S. policy toward these kinds of operations, as discussed in the Amplification box "U.S. Policy Toward Peace Operations."

Peacekeeping Versus Peace Imposition

To understand the nature of Second Tier conflicts and to frame responses to them, it is vital to recognize that they fall into two basic categories: those amenable to solution through the peacekeeping system of the UN as elaborated by the secretary-general, and those for which such a system of responses is inappropriate. In situations where peace is not the overriding value of all or some of the parties, the only meaningful alternatives are either forceful systemic action or a hands-off approach. When the peacekeeping model is applied to situations where it does not fit, the result can be a Bosnian-style tragedy.

To appreciate the differences involved, we can look at them from two different vantage points. The first is environmental or contextual, referring to the situation that would confront peacekeepers or peacemakers were they to be inserted. The second is the mission requirements, what forces must be physically prepared to do if called upon.

There are two obvious environmental or contextual differences between peacekeeping and peace-imposition situations. First, in peace-imposition situations fighting is going on

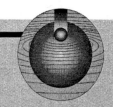

Amplification

U.S. Policy Toward Peace Operations

As noted in Chapter 5, the Clinton administration struggled over the extent to which it should commit U.S. forces to actions under the broad rubric of "peace operations," ultimately adopting a course heavily influenced by the disastrous American intervention in the Vietnam War. The result is a three-stage policy, with increasingly rigorous standards for American involvement as the degree of involvement increases.

The first and least restrictive set of policy guidelines applies to voting to authorize a UN operation with no American participation other than a funding assessment. In essence, the operation in such cases must advance U.S. interests; respond to a real threat to the peace, defined as international aggression, humanitarian disaster, or gross violations of human rights or democracy; have clear objectives; and have available adequate means to succeed. In addition, there must be clear and realistic criteria for concluding the mission, and the possible negative consequences of inaction for American interests must be weighed.

The guidelines are somewhat more restrictive for American military involvement in a peace-keeping operation. In addition to meeting the guidelines for funding a UN operation, three additional requirements are set forth: American participation must be shown to be necessary, there must be public and congressional support, and command and control arrangements must be acceptable. All three of these conditions illustrate the observation that First Tier applications of force are limited primarily by the bounds of public opinion.

Finally, if "significant" American participation in a peace enforcement operation is contemplated, three more criteria are added. First, there must be a commitment of adequate American forces to accomplish the mission. Second, there must be a clear plan to achieve the objective decisively. Third, there must be a commitment on the parts of the administration and Congress to adjust operations as necessary during the course of the operation and a mechanism for doing so.

Source: The Clinton Administration's Policy on Reforming Multilateral Peace Operations. Washington, DC: U.S. Department of State, May 1994.

and the mission is to stop it; peacekeepers, on the other hand, come into situations where fighting has already stopped. Second, in peace-imposition situations, one or more of the parties prefer the continuation of war to peace—presumably expecting to benefit from further combat—whereas peacekeepers enter situations where the parties have agreed on a peaceful settlement of their differences. Thus, peacekeepers are invited guests; peace imposers are unwanted by some or all of the "hosts."

These environmental or contextual factors suggest that the military requirements for peace imposition are more rigorous and difficult than those for peacekeeping. The analogy has been drawn between the peace imposer and a police officer trying to break up a violent domestic quarrel; the effort may be for the greater good (including that of the participants), but the quarrelers do not think so. The role of the peacekeeper is closer to that of a judge

Despite the sign at the Mogadishu airport, in the early 1990s many Somalis did not welcome the entry of UN forces, preferring a continuation of their clan-based warfare to a peace imposed by outsiders. Pakistan, along with Morocco and Ghana, has been one of the Second Tier states that have most often provided troops for UN peace missions.

overseeing observance of a divorce settlement. These differences manifest themselves in three ways as peacekeepers and peacemakers attempt to fulfill their different missions.

The first is in the relative ease or difficulty of maintaining neutrality. Peacekeepers are welcome because they do not take sides. If they cease to be perceived as neutral, they lose their utility; their mere presence, however, is not likely to cause the peace to fail. Peace imposers, whether they like it or not, will be perceived as partisans by whichever side suffers a decline in fortunes by the imposition of peace. Peace imposers in Somalia, for instance, did not enter the country to get into a partisan fight with General Mohammed Farah Aidid, but the dynamics of the situation put them into opposition to him.

A second difference in the challenges posed by the two missions deals with the familiarity or unfamiliarity of the role. Peacekeeping is an established and practiced activity with numerous precedents. Peace imposition, on the other hand, is almost entirely uncharted territory in terms of specific goals, procedures, and measures of success. What, for instance, are the rules of engagement for soldiers in a peace-imposition environment? When (and at whom) may they fire? Who is the enemy? Even among those who initially favor their presence, peace imposers will develop enemies within the target population (they may also make friends by preventing the return of violence). Accidents happen; innocent civilians are killed. The U.S. Marines who were so welcome in Somalia in December 1992 were being booby trapped by the summer of 1993.

Peacekeeping and peace imposing are two missions that also require different kinds of forces. Peacekeepers are typically lightly armed, with exclusively defensive weaponry. Their job is interposition and presence, not combat; they fire only when fired on, and then only with limited firepower. Peace imposers, on the other hand, are combatants entering a combat zone. They must be equipped and configured not only to defend themselves but also to engage in offensive actions designed to accomplish their goal of ending hostilities. The training to develop and maintain this combat readiness is more demanding than that for peacekeepers.

These differences in the context and requirements of the two kinds of missions contribute to a significant difference in the likelihood of success between peacekeeping and peace imposition. If the conditions for peacekeeping exist, peacekeepers can succeed by preventing the recurrence of violence. Peace imposers, on the other hand, must attempt to force peace on those who do not want it. Since most of the candidate situations for peace creation in the contemporary world are internal wars, where outside intervention is problematical at best, prospects for successful intervention are not high. Moreover, even if the peace imposers are able to force a cease-fire, the dynamics of the conflict are likely to result in new hostilities when they leave. Once again, Somalia provides an example.

The IFOR/SFOR and Haitian experiences have suggested the possibility of a hybrid somewhere between peacekeeping and peace imposition, where heavily armed (peace imposition) forces are sent into a putatively peacekeeping environment to enforce a shaky peace for which there may be less than universal support. In this situation, the forces do more than passively peacekeep but less than impose peace. Rather, their interposition is intended to intimidate those who might breach the peace by raising the prospect that a breach would be subject to an overwhelming reaction by the peacekeepers. In both cases, the formidable presence of the occupying forces served to dissuade dissenters from acting while the forces were in place. This model is being applied in Kosovo.

These distinctions between peacekeeping and peace imposition may seem obvious, but the UN's early post–Cold War peace efforts did not take account of them. The most salient example was in Bosnia, where a peacekeeping force was interposed in a peace-imposition situation. It proved utterly ineffectual in solving anything, to its own and the Bosnians' despair. The problem is that many future situations may resemble Bosnia more than they do environments suitable for traditional peacekeeping roles. Understanding that difference is of vital importance to assessing the role of the UN in the future.

An emerging and less controversial form of intrusion by outside forces in Second Tier conflicts is humanitarian relief operations. Often coordinated by the UN, such operations are not new at all. International humanitarian relief has been provided for years in response to natural calamities such as earthquakes and floods. However, major efforts to alleviate the suffering caused by war, especially where large numbers of refugees and both national governments and NGOs are involved, are a new and growing concern. These operations are complex and difficult, especially in the midst of tragedies such as Rwanda. Given the need to coordinate state efforts and those of NGOs and intergovernmental organizations, the UN may prove to be a useful tool to provide coordination among diverse organizations.

Case Study: The Future of UN Activism

The debate about how active the UN should be in dealing with violent conflicts has come to focus on the issue of the size, quality, and commitment of national forces to UN-sponsored actions. It is largely a question of how or to what degree the First Tier, which would have to supply much of the force (at least that devoted to peace imposition), is willing to impose peace on an unstable Second Tier. It also revolves around the advisability of having a standing, permanent UN military force, available constantly for quelling any threats to or breaches of the peace (to paraphrase the language of Chapter VII of the Charter).

The first years of the post–Cold War era offered bright prospects for international activism in this area, with the UN as the centerpiece. However, enthusiasm quickly waned in the wake of overcommitment and reverses, leaving room for somber reflection about the global situation and the UN's role in dealing with unrest. The UN will play such a role in

The Impact of Technology
The Global Refugee Problem and International Responses

By mid-1994 the problem of political refugees, whether outside their countries of origin or in internal exile, had reached epic proportions. Given the nature, extent, and probable persistence of the global refugee problem, what is the international community—and especially the UN—to do? When population flights occur, there is little international concern about where refugees will go or how they will be sustained in the long run; the problem is ameliorating immediate catastrophe, as the Rwandan situation demonstrated.

Modern technology affects these situations in two basic ways. First, global television networks ensure that the suffering of refugees will be widely and dramatically publicized, often more so than the conflict that gave rise to it. The initial slaughter in Rwanda, for instance, was not widely covered because it was too dangerous for journalists to observe; the refugee camps, however, were in relatively safe locations in Congo (then Zaire), and coverage became a daily staple.

The second impact of technology is in responding to disaster. Thanks to increases in airlift and sealift capabilities, it is increasingly possible to mount rapid, massive relief operations into refugee concentrations, and hence in some cases even to reverse the refugee flow. Indeed, it has become a major priority of the American military—which has more of these capabilities than any other national or international agency—to extend its ability to engage in humanitarian relief operations. Although much needs to be done in areas such as coordinating the military logistical aspects of these operations (engineering sanitation, building lodging) with the activities of private humanitarian NGOs, the response to the potentially disastrous Rwandan situation demonstrates the potential for applying military technology to humanitarian ends in conditions that are certain to recur in the post–Cold War world. Among remaining issues for the future is the extent to which the UN will serve as a coordinating agency when these disasters occur.

the future. There is no question about that. What its role will be, however, is a matter of dispute, because there are advantages and disadvantages from the viewpoints of various members to a standing UN force as opposed to intervention on an ad hoc basis by a particular country or group of countries. The alternatives must be weighed as part of any assessment of future UN activism.

Possible Advantages of a UN Force

There are three possible major advantages to a prominent UN role, particularly involving a standing UN force, in organizing and enforcing the future peace. They are the potential deterrent value of a standing force, its readiness, and the greater acceptability that it would engender in countries where it might be used. Each of these advantages, however, is open to questions.

The first apparent advantage of a standing force is its deterrent value. The UN Charter envisaged that a standing force composed of units from the permanent members of the Security Council would be the heart of the collective-security system embodied in Chapter VII of the Charter. The rationale for this idea was to avoid the perceived weakness in the League of Nations Covenant, which allowed only for the hue-and-cry recruitment of forces volunteered by members. The threat of such forces was deemed ineffective, the argument went, because a potential aggressor could often suppose, correctly or incorrectly, that the action it contemplated would not be opposed. The League experience in the 1930s suggested that its own threat was indeed ineffectual; states simply did not respond actively to enforce League recommendations.

A potential aggressor state viewing a standing UN force prepared for and committed to opposing aggression would have to think twice before acting and might more likely be deterred by the prospect. A problem with this view, however, is that most Second Tier conflicts are internal—between groups within a state—so that the dynamics of interstate deterrence may not apply. Outsiders, including the UN, are more reluctant to become involved in such affairs, rendering the threat of intervention less credible. Furthermore, there is little if any evidence that internal movements would be deterred even by a plausible threat of outside intervention—in other words, that an insurgent group in one country would be dissuaded by the threat of outside intervention.

The second supposed advantage of a standing UN force is its availability to be efficiently dispatched to trouble spots. While assembling ad hoc forces volunteered for particular missions can be a ponderous task, a standing force could be ready at once. Moreover, it would already have trained together to create cohesion and effectiveness on the battlefield in diverse missions and contingencies. (As an alternative to a standing UN force, some have suggested "deputizing" NATO forces that have trained together for various combat roles, as in IFOR.) The UN-sponsored mission in the Persian Gulf War was simply fortunate that Iraqi leader Saddam Hussein did not take advantage of his initial success and continue into Saudi Arabia before the UN could get a force on the ground; instead, he allowed it the luxury of several months to group together and organize as his forces remained stationary in Kuwait. A rapidly deployable UN force would have facilitated an improved response in the recent crises in Bosnia, Somalia, and elsewhere.

The drawback here is that a standing force might become too available. In a parallel to the initial American involvement in Vietnam (where a period of preparation for guerrilla warfare had created an apparent capability to intervene in such situations), the availability of a standing UN force could encourage a hair-trigger reaction. What we have called the "do-something syndrome" might come into play, whereas more deliberate counsel could lead to a more reasoned response.

The third apparent advantage of a standing UN force is its acceptability in parts of the world where individual or collective First Tier action is likely to be resented. The UN is, after all, the organization with which much of the Second Tier readily identifies, and the one in which Second Tier countries have traditionally had the most influence. The appearance of "blue berets" is less likely to be viewed as neocolonialist or paternalistic than direct intervention by First World forces.

There are two potential problems here. First, while UN intervention may initially be less objectionable to the Second Tier, it might not be in long-term interventions. Interference is, after all, interference regardless of who is doing it. Second, a UN standing force of any appreciable size and capability would have to be drawn largely from First Tier militaries, which more commonly have the sophistication and flexibility for quick deployment. It would not take long for Second Tier countries to see UN action as a mask for First Tier intrusion.

The Difficulties for a UN Force

In addition to the drawbacks already discussed, there are several other problems or questions involved in empowering the United Nations as the agent of choice to deal with conflicts in the Second Tier, particularly through a standing force. They include the difficulty of determining when to become involved, the necessary dependence of such a force on First Tier troops and resources, and the issue of who is to command and control it.

The first problem is essentially that of who decides when and when not to use UN forces. Assuming there is a standing force, would its deployment be authorized by the Security Council or by the secretary-general? The UN, on its own, has no independent interests, other than possibly broad humanitarian interests (the protection and quality of human life) that could provide a guideline and direction for employing forces. The Security Council, on the other hand, is composed of member states which are generally motivated by their vital interests, particularly in the realm of committing national troops. Those interests will rarely coincide exactly on any given issue. Does this mean that gridlock could return when a permanent member decides a given situation is not in its vital interest and thus vetoes an action that might involve its forces? Or would Security Council members be expected to act out of some other motive than their interests, and run the risk of angering their own populations? In any case, it seems unlikely that the secretary-general would be granted the authority to determine when and where UN forces could be deployed. If the secretary-general were given any such discretion, presumably there would be an escape mechanism for individual First Tier states unwilling to commit forces to particular actions.

This leads to a second problem: the need for First Tier forces, and more particularly First Tier forces from the permanent membership of the Security Council. Such a need arises because the most economically advanced states have the most technologically advanced military forces, and because any large-scale insertion of forces into peace-imposition situations would be beyond the resources of other members. In other words, First Tier states, beyond approving intervention in principle in particular cases, would have to be willing to invest their own troops and resources heavily. The role of the United States is critical here, because the United States has the only global airlift and sealift capacity for rapid, large-scale military or humanitarian deployment, as was so dramatically demonstrated in Rwanda.

A third problem is the issue of command and control: who would have operational control of committed forces? Boutros-Ghali insisted that such forces must come under direct UN control—which is to say under the control of the secretary-general. This is a controversial position in democratic countries, whose troops could be put in harm's way by foreign leaders not directly accountable to domestic restraint. A possible compromise solution would be to invigorate the Military Staff Committee created by Article 46 and 47 of the UN Charter and assign operational authority to it. That provision states that the committee would consist of the chiefs of staff (or their representatives) of the permanent members of the Security Council, who would maintain the veto and ultimately their control.

Ultimately, of course, the question of whether the UN should have a standing force or, more generally, should be activist in dealing with Second Tier instability is a matter for

Views from Abroad

Could Rwanda Have Been Saved?

The slaughter in Rwanda in 1994 was a major embarrassment to the international community, leaving a situation where "the world moves on, face averted," in the words of the *Pioneer* of Lucknow, India. Inevitably, the question of whether the tragedy could have been prevented has arisen, especially on the continent of Africa.

In the African press, the role of the United Nations was especially criticized. When the Hutu rampage against the Tutsi began, the UN actually reduced the number of observers it had in Rwanda to avoid their being caught up in the violence. The organization's "suggestion that an all-African peacekeeping force be assembled" suggested the slaughter was no more than "a racial misdemeanor," according to the *Sun* of Lusaka, Zambia. The *Times* of Zambia, also based in Lusaka, concluded that the UN "displayed poor judgment and inability to read the situation." The *Monitor* of Kampala, Uganda, went so far as to compare the UN's behavior to international inaction in face of the Holocaust: "UN troops walked by while the brutal murder of innocent people was taking place under their very noses."

Regardless of whether anyone might have prevented the tragedy as it unfolded, there was a broader lesson to be learned, according to the government-owned *Sunday Mail* of Harare, Zimbabwe: "It is incumbent upon African leaders at all levels throughout the continent to resist the temptations to exploit tribal and regionalist sentiments in search of a base or political platform. The results can get out of hand, and the countries of Rwanda and Burundi should be a living example of how tragic and ghastly matters can turn out to be."

Source: World Press Review, July 1994, p. 6.

individual members of the international system to determine. Neither the case for nor the case against such activism is thoroughly compelling; either can be plausibly argued. The UN is at heart a tool of its members, who ultimately must decide how they want to use it.

The Changing Contours of Law and Organizations

We have speculated that there is a good chance that international law and organizations may play a more prominent role in the international relations of the current system than they did during the Cold War. The basis of that assessment, of course, has been the reduction in the major friction between the largest members and thus the possibility of greater cooperation in organizing the world. That expansion is by no means inevitable, and it is possible that law and organizations will become less, rather than more, important.

In assessing what will be the case, it is possible to look at a couple of likely lightning rods. If there is an area with great growth potential for expanding international law, it lies in the area of developing rules of behavior for organizing the global economy. Lawlike regimes already are under development among First Tier states in this regard, and the spread of international law will depend on whether Second Tier states seeking to enter the global economy buy into those rules. The friction, even impediment, to this spreading is the fact that the global economy's values are overwhelmingly western, and for nonwestern countries to accept those rules means jettisoning practices and values sometimes long held. As has been argued, the clash of values has been part of the Asian financial crisis, and the extent to which the affected states embrace or resist the imposition of western economic and financial values (through the West's instrument of choice, the IMF) will go a long way to defining the expansibility of lawlike regimes more generally.

The UN is the obvious lightning rod for the growth in importance of traditional international organizations. The heart of the malaise of the UN is its perpetual financial crisis, a product of inadequate dues, the failure of some countries (notably the United States) to pay arrears from unpaid assessments, and, some would argue, the UN's inability to handle its finances. Regardless of the causes, the importance of the UN as an actor in the international system will largely be the result of its financial health. In turn, the willingness—or unwillingness—of the members to provide financial health will be a major indicator of the role the world *wants* the UN to play.

Review

This chapter provided an overview of international law and organization. In the process, it reached the following conclusions:

1. International law is not as developed or comprehensive as domestic law, principally because it lacks an enforcement mechanism. The major reason for this is state sovereignty and the existence of vital interests that states do not wish submitted to a legal regime.

2. For the same reason, the sources of international law (treaties, custom, general principles of law, judicial decisions and teachings) are less precise and less authoritative than domestic law. UN resolutions may become an alternative source of international legal principles.

3. The prospects for an expansion of international law are greatest in the First Tier and in the area of economic relations. The diverse nature of the Second Tier, and especially its lack of shared values on which to base internationally accepted law, make the prospects for legal development less likely there. Essentially the same can be said of legal regimes covering both tiers.

4. A major consequence of the end of the Cold War has been to reactivate interest in the United Nations, as its framers envisaged could happen in the absence of major-power conflict. Renewed UN activism has been especially evident in efforts to settle internal wars in the Second Tier.

5. There remains some conceptual confusion about the different kinds of internal war situations in which the international community may become involved. On the one hand are situations where peace has been restored and needs maintaining (peacekeeping); on the other are ongoing wars, where peace imposition is necessary. The two situations differ in terms of their environment or context and the requirements for intervention, with peace imposition being more difficult.

6. How active the UN will be in this area in the future is problematical, as is the feasibility of a UN standing force; arguments can be made on both sides. The major powers of the First Tier, and especially the United States, will have the leading role in determining the level of involvement.

Suggested Readings

Altschiller, Donald. *The United Nations Role in World Affairs.* New York: H. W. Wilson, 1993.

Blodgett, John Q. "The Future of UN Peacekeeping." *Washington Quarterly* 14, 1 (winter 1991): 30–37.

Boutros-Ghali, Boutros. *An Agenda for Peace: Preventive Diplomacy, Peacemaking, and Peace-Keeping.* New York: United Nations, 1992.

—. "Empowering the United Nations." *Foreign Affairs* 72, 5 (winter 1992/93): 89–102.

Brierly, James L. *The Law of Nations,* 6th ed. Oxford, UK: Oxford University Press, 1963.

Charters, David A., ed. *Peacekeeping and the Challenge of Civil Conflict Resolution.* Fredericton: Center for Conflict Studies, University of New Brunswick, 1994.

Claude, Inis L., Jr. *Swords into Plowshares: The Problems and Progress of International Organizations,* 4th ed. New York: Random House, 1971.

Diehl, Paul. *International Peacekeeping.* Baltimore, MD: Johns Hopkins University Press, 1993.

Durch, William, ed. *The Evolution of UN Peacekeeping: Case Studies and Comparative Analyses.* New York: St. Martin's Press, 1993.

—, ed. *UN Peacekeeping, American Politics, and the Uncivil Wars of the 1990s.* New York: St. Martin's Press, 1996.

Durch, William, and Barry Blechman. *Keeping the Peace: The United Nations in the Emerging World Order.* Washington, DC: Henry L. Stimson Center, 1993.

Metz, Steven. *The Future of the United Nations: Implications for Peace Operations.* Carlisle Barracks, PA: Strategic Studies Institute, October 1993.

Mitrany, David. *Toward a Working Peace System.* London: Royal Institute of International Affairs, 1943.

Natsios, Andrew S. "Food Through Force: Humanitarian Intervention and U.S. Policy." *Washington Quarterly* 17, 1 (winter 1994): 129–44.

Pickering, Thomas R. "The U.N. Contribution to Future International Security." *Naval War College Review* 46, 1 (winter 1993): 94–104.

Snow, Donald M. *Peacekeeping, Peacemaking and Peace Enforcement: The U.S. Role in the New International Order.* Carlisle Barracks, PA: Strategic Studies Institute, February 1993.

Sylvester, Christine. *Feminist Theory and International Relations in a Postmodern Era.* Cambridge, UK: Cambridge University Press, 1994.

Weiss, Thomas G. "Intervention: Whither the United Nations?" *Washington Quarterly* 17, 1 (winter 1994): 109–28.

Conclusions: The Shape of the Future?

PREVIEW

This last chapter will focus on important questions about the future shape of the evolving post–Cold War international system. Three broad concerns will be addressed. The first of these is the question of what state or states will provide primary international leadership, how the roles of different instruments of power will change, and what those new circumstances mean for the security equation in the world. The second concern is how the relationship between the First and Second Tiers will evolve, and particularly how much of a role the First Tier will play in the economic and political development of the Second Tier. The third concern is the future of state sovereignty: to what extent does First Tier involvement in Second Tier internal wars, for instance, constitute a weakening of overall sovereignty? The chapter will conclude with a case study looking at how to address narrowing the gap between likely futures and those that might be preferred.

KEY CONCEPTS

Partnership for Peace (PfP)
ring of market democracies
instruments of power
superpower
internal wars
"clash of civilizations" thesis

humanitarian vital interests
absolute sovereignty
popular sovereignty
economic globalization
policy domain

OUTLINE

The world has changed dramatically since September 12, 1989, when the newly chosen noncommunist prime minister of Poland, Tadeusz Mazowiecki, announced that his government's policy would be the promotion of a fully democratic political system and "a normal market economy." Observers around the globe looked on breathlessly as this first step in the crumbling of the former Second World led to a cascade that left only a handful of nominally communist regimes in power by 1999. Where will it all end?

Two events illustrate this changeover in a clear-cut way. They are the dismantling of the Warsaw Pact by a vote of its members on July 1, 1991, and the peaceful dissolution of the Soviet Union on December 31, 1991. These events altered the global security system of the Cold War by imploding half of the competition. The result, as we have interpreted it here, has been the emergence of a new security system which may eventually bring key players on both Cold War sides under one organizational umbrella. The current, tentative device for incorporation is the vaguely defined association of former Warsaw Pact and Soviet successor states with NATO through the Partnership for Peace (PfP), and more recently the inclusion of former Warsaw Pact members as full members of NATO (Poland, Hungary, and the Czech Republic). The only thing that remains uncertain is the pace and extent of future inclusion of other formerly communist countries, or whether some similar "architecture" such as the Organization for Security and Cooperation in Europe (OSCE) or even the United Nations will provide the common framework.

The end of the Cold War had an impact that goes beyond security concerns. The disappearance of the Second World, the bloc of socialist states—as distinct from the most economically developed states (the First World) and the less developed states of Africa, Asia, and Latin America and the Caribbean (the Third World)—also requires the devising of new ways to distinguish among levels of economic and political development. Our classification device has been a terminology of tiers, distinguishing the wealthy, technologically advanced, market-oriented democracies we call the First Tier from the other countries of the world, the Second Tier, which we have further broken down into four subcategories.

The pace and extent of change in the international system has left scholars, participants, and more casual observers alike with questions the answers to which are beginning to emerge. A major scholarly concern, for instance, is about how fundamental the change is: has there been, as we contend, a genuine revolution, leading to a set of international relationships so different as to constitute a new, distinct system—a new world order—or was the old order merely altered, not fundamentally and radically changed? The latter interpretation recalls the rather cynical view of Marshal Foch that we cited at the beginning of Chapter 1. To Foch, war and suffering are bound to be repeated in endless cycles, with no new order ever emerging. Because of the enormous difference in the world's security system today—the absence of system-threatening military confrontation—we consider the change from the Cold War era substantial enough to constitute a new system.

A related question pertains to the direction the new system is taking. In the initial euphoria over the fall of European communism, it appeared that what President Bill Clinton has called the "ring of market democracies" was inexorably expanding, that the western ideals of political democracy and a market economy would be the global wave of the future, and that a U.S. foreign policy of "engagement and enlargement" of market democracies was the wave of the future. Indeed, in devising a sequential list of subtiers of the Second Tier through which states can "rise" to First Tier status through acceptance of these ideals, we have implicitly embraced this notion.

Optimism has, however, become more tempered since 1989, both because the process of westernization has been bumpier than some hoped and because the new system has witnessed its own complications. The process of change in most of the former Soviet Union and Eastern Europe has proven more difficult than many expected. The Czech Republic, Poland, and Hungary have made some progress toward joining the First Tier, but most of the Soviet successor states and the southern countries of formerly communist Europe have made much less visible progress. China, with the world's most dynamic economy, defiantly flaunts its authoritarian political system and shows a disdain for western notions of human rights. Highly prosperous Singapore, a leading candidate for the First Tier by most measures, demonstrates an antipathy to what many would consider western values by its authoritarian practices in such areas as media censorship and criminal justice—creating international incidents in 1994 and 1995 when an American citizen was caned for acts of vandalism and a Filipino maid was hanged for murder, in both cases on the basis of questionable evidence. Widespread violence in the name of national self-determination has ripped Yugoslavia apart and threatens a number of the Soviet successor states. The smooth transition to a prosperous global economy hit a sizable speed bump in East Asia in 1998.

Demonstrators outside the Singaporean embassy in Manila in March 1995 protest the conviction and death sentence of a Filipina maid in Singapore, Flor Contemplacion. Despite accusations that her employer had actually committed the murders of which Contemplacion was convicted, Singaporean authorities rejected international pleas and hanged her. In words as well as actions, the Singaporean government has frankly expressed its disagreement with Western ideas of democracy and civil liberties.

Such negative occurrences have, to some extent, been balanced by positive events. Despite violent acts of extremists on both sides of the Palestinian-Israeli dispute, there has been dramatic progress toward achieving an enduring peace in the Middle East, more so than at any time since the creation of Israel. The establishment of the North American Free Trade Association and its probable extension into South America (and possibly throughout the Western Hemisphere in the guise of the proposed Free Trade Area of the Americas) holds out the prospect of spreading economic prosperity; the Asia-Pacific Economic Cooperation could yield increased prosperity for the countries of the Pacific Rim if it becomes a free-trade area, as its leaders have repeatedly vowed. Although large nuclear arsenals remain in American and Russian hands, the prospect of their employment in anger has become, as we have noted, increasingly remote.

It has become fashionable among scholars of international relations to talk about the emerging system as more chaotic, less predictable, more unruly, and even more dangerous than the system in place during the Cold War. That was a central message of an influential 1990 article by John Mearsheimer entitled "Why We Will Soon Miss the Cold War." The Cold War era, so this strain of analysis goes, was highly structured and more rationally ordered than is the present era.

We reject this pessimism. The evolving order, indeed, has disorderly aspects. It is unpredictable, but that the old order was more predictable is largely a fantasy. There are certainly things to worry about in the new order, but they are in fact less monumental than those during the Cold War. Most pointedly, the prospect of a nuclear war that could bring civilization to an end no longer looms large on the horizon, and that alone is a great advantage.

In the remaining pages, we will delve tentatively into the future's shape by considering three important questions. The first question relates to the nature of the evolving security system and the topic of global leadership. The second question involves the emerging global economic system, central to which is the issue of whether or how the prosperity of the First Tier can be extended to the Second Tier. The third question is whether the very nature of the international system, as it has existed since 1648, with the sovereign state as its centerpiece, is under siege. The concluding case study will look at a way of thinking about bridging the gap between likely and desirable futures.

International Leadership: Is Anyone in Charge?

It has become commonplace to refer to the United States as the sole remaining superpower in the new international system. Partly, of course, this observation reflects the fact that the United States is the only one of the two Cold War superpowers to survive the turmoil of the past several years intact. At the same time, the lessened importance of major-power military competition and confrontation has broadened the concept of what it means to be a superpower.

Superpower Status

Defining what makes a superpower requires us to return to the idea of instruments of power first introduced in Chapter 2. In traditional geopolitical analysis, three categories of instruments—the military, the economic, and the diplomatic or political—are identified. Within each category are a number of specific actions that can be used to assert a state's interest when that interest comes into conflict with the interest of another state or states.

In the Cold War system, the overarching definition of superpower status was found in military capability, and more precisely the possession of large thermonuclear arsenals. It was by this criterion that the United States and the Soviet Union were the system's superpowers. In fact, it was only by this criterion that the Soviet Union could be considered a superpower, since it lacked significant economic power.

Military power, and especially advanced nuclear weaponry, are less significant as indicators of status in a world of tiers than was the case in the Cold War system. For one thing, the general agreement among the most important states (who are all members of the First Tier) is such that military force as an instrument of power among themselves is essentially meaningless. As we have noted several times, political democracies simply do not threaten or declare war against one another.

The military instrument of power could be relevant in some of the relations between states of the First and Second Tiers—for instance in the event of another threat to the flow

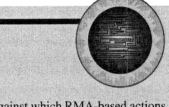

The Impact of Technology

Limits on the Revolution in Military Affairs

The first major hint of the technologies that form the Revolution in Military Affairs (RMA), discussed in Chapter 5, was seen in the Persian Gulf War: smart bombs chasing an Iraqi soldier into a bunker or going down a vent pipe, artillery pounding Iraqi counterparts from outside their range. It is this style of conventional warfare for which most RMA technologies seem most appropriate. But it may be asked whether they could be applied as well in the numerous internal conflicts that Steven Metz and James Kievit describe as "peace enforcement in failed states, new forms of insurgency and terrorism, and 'gray area phenomena,'" where "ungovernability and instability will be the norms with power dispersed among warlords, primal militias, and well-organized politico-criminal organizations."

The answer is that the application to these kinds of situations is uncertain. First, there is likely to be much more institutional enthusiasm for applying RMA to conventional tasks, simply because First Tier military bureaucracies are more comfortable with conventional war. In ad-

dition, groups against which RMA-based actions might be taken will likely develop counterstrategies to frustrate RMA. In Somalia, for instance, the late General Mohammed Farah Aidid made himself largely impervious to American military might simply by hiding among the general population. Resort to guerrilla tactics of dispersal and small-unit activity undetectable by reconnaissance technologies is another possibility. Finally, some of the new technology might actually be used against an RMA-laden force. This technology includes highly lethal yet small and light weapons that can be used against sophisticated targets like jet aircraft and helicopters. The extremely important role of American-produced shoulder-held Stinger antiaircraft rockets used by Afghan rebels against Soviet helicopters during the Soviet invasion and occupation of Afghanistan illustrates this possibility.

Source: Steven Metz and James Kievit, *The Revolution in Military Affairs and Conflict Short of War* (Carlisle Barracks, PA: Strategic Studies Institute, 1994).

of petroleum from the Persian Gulf region, of militarily caused suffering in the Second Tier that First Tier states decide to ameliorate (situations like those in Somalia and Rwanda in the early 1990s and Kosovo in 1999), or of Second Tier assaults on First Tier countries (such as state-sponsored or other terrorist acts). What these situations share, however, is their limited, peripheral impact on the system as a whole. To repeat, Second Tier states do not approximate the states of the First Tier in the amount of force they can bring to bear. Military force is also relevant in the relations between some Second Tier states (regional conflicts) and within some Second Tier states (internal wars).

Within the First Tier, and also in the relations between the tiers, the economic instrument of power has become much more prominent. Within the globalizing economy of the First Tier, economic threats have basically replaced military threats as a means of gaining compliance with state interests. A U.S. threat to attack China to force an end to Chinese violations of intellectual property rights would be hollow; the threat to remove most-favored-nation status may not be. Conversely, the United States believed that moving naval forces into the Straits of Taiwan in 1996 was an appropriate response to Chinese military exercises coinciding with the Taiwanese presidential campaign.

The rise in importance of economic, as opposed to military, threats suggests how the definition of superpower status has changed. In the post–Cold War world, this status is accorded to states that have available to them the full variety or range of effective instruments of power. The United States qualifies as the sole remaining superpower because it is the only state that has both significant economic and significant military power. In contrast, Japan has great economic capacity but little military power, while Russia has military power alone.

This labeling of the United States as sole superpower in the post–Cold War world is not a matter of gloating supernationalism. Rather, it represents a recognition, however cautious and even reluctant, that the United States stands preeminent in the world and has, more than any other single country, the ability to influence events. We do not suggest that it is in a position to dictate world events. What we do assert is that the way the United States acts is a matter of consequence in most situations; the United States has a great leadership role, whether it wants it or not.

Leadership and the Security Equation

As was noted in the case study in Chapter 5 and also in Chapter 7, the degree to which the United States exercises global leadership, especially in the area of peace and security, has varied across time. Before World War II, the United States had the luxury of choosing whether to participate prominently in the international system or withdraw into self-imposed isolation from the political (if not the economic) relations of the world at large. Since World War II, and especially in the emerging international system, that luxury is no longer meaningfully available.

The shape of a post–Cold War security system is not yet clear, because the major powers that will have to organize and enforce that system have yet to reach accord on exactly what kind of status quo they are willing to defend. Despite that general observation, however, the system can be defined to some extent, based in part on a few points made in discussions thus far.

The first and most basic aspect of security in the world of tiers, as has been argued, is the absence of conflicts with military potential in the relations among the most consequential states—all of whom belong to the First Tier. This is important because it relieves these states of the need to maintain the high levels of military readiness for central war (including the associated expenditures) that were deemed necessary during the Cold War. It also means there is essentially no danger of a system-wrenching general war.

This does not mean the emerging order is tranquil. Two major, consequential powers remain outside the First Tier, Russia and China. Despite First Tier assistance, Russia will remain politically and economically unstable for the foreseeable future, as it lurches uncertainly toward the goals of its major reformers, a market economy and political democracy. The possibility of reversion to the past, as exemplified most recently in the collapse of the Russian economy and reshuffling of the Yeltsin government in August 1999, and a xenophobic, authoritarian Russia seeking to recreate something like the Soviet Union could convulse the general tranquility. This prospect, however, seems less than likely for two reasons. First, it would isolate Russia and doom the Russian people to a continuing material poverty that most would reject. Second, Russia has tied itself to the First Tier's security system through participation in such mechanisms as the Organization on Security and Cooperation in Europe, a condition that reversion would likely destroy. Whether Russia

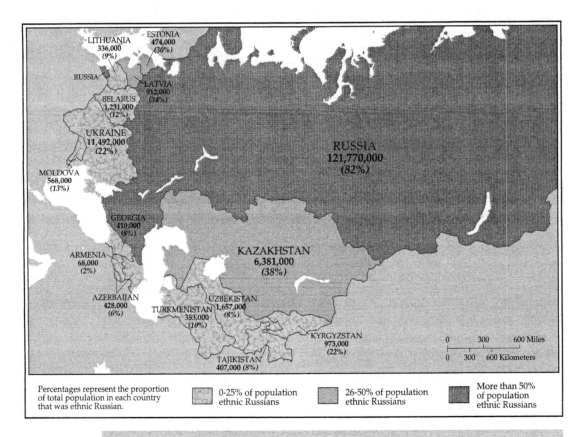

Map 14-1   **Ethnic Russians in the Soviet Union (1989 census).**

©1996 by St. Martin's Press, Inc. From: *Contours of Power,* by Snow/Brown. Reprinted with permission of Bedford/St. Martin's Press, Inc.

will act as a positive force in helping acute systemic stability is discussed in the accompanying Contours of the Future? box.

Although officially committed to communist party rule, the Chinese leadership has enthusiastically abandoned and condemned Marxist economics, retaining only the Leninist facade of authoritarian rule to prevent, in its own rationale, a Soviet-style disintegration of the Chinese state. Democratization, of course, would pave China's entrance into the First Tier; the passage of power to a younger generation offers the greatest hope for the transition. The way China treats Hong Kong now that reunification has occurred will provide a major signal of what the Chinese role will be; the first year of Chinese overlordship suggested at least some basis for tentative optimism.

The more prevalent forms of violence and instability reside in the Second Tier, and especially among and within states in the lower two subtiers (partially developed and developable). As already noted, instability takes the forms of regional conflicts among states—often made more dangerous by NBC weapons capabilities—and especially violence within states, or internal wars. This latter form of conflict is the most frequent and bloody, and it is the form of violence about which there is the most systemic disagreement in terms of regulation and moderation.

After a spate of early actions in trouble spots such as Somalia, the countries of the First Tier have shown considerable reluctance to interfere militarily in internal Second Tier violence. One reason is that the success rate in these situations is negligible; the lesson of "no more Somalias" has become something of a precedent. At the same time, First Tier states usually have no significant interests involved in these situations, and public opinion acts as a significant brake on any large-scale military action. The result is ad hoc policy based on an assessment of individual cases. Beyond an abortive—and by their assessment—misdirected action by France, the First Tier did not respond to the Rwandan slaughter of April 1994 except by dispensing humanitarian assistance after the fact. In Haiti, the United States, under UN auspices, proactively took the lead in reinstalling President Aristide in office and occupied the country until some semblance of order could be restored. After three years of inaction, the NATO-led IFOR/SFOR finally enforced the peace in Bosnia in 1995. In 1999, NATO bombed the Serbs to end their oppression of ethnically Albanian Kosovars and imposed peace with KFOR. Finding a clear pattern was difficult.

Do the evolving rules of the emerging international security system simply write off internal violence in Second Tier countries? Certainly the mechanisms for engagement are available through the Security Council of the United Nations, which has authorized those actions undertaken to date and which is controlled by the major powers. Chapter VII of the UN Charter provides the authority for intervention, despite the breach of sovereignty that may be involved. At a more theoretical, even moral, level, the argument is made that "humanitarian vital interests" dictate intervention to alleviate suffering.

The United States has a key role in determining how the international system will react in such situations in the future. For one thing, the level of American monetary contribution to the UN gives the United States a key voice (in addition to its veto in the Security Council) in decisions. Also, the United States is the only country with global military presence and reach. American logistical assets are necessary to move sizable troop contingents to remote places quickly and to maintain them there, and access to American reconnaissance facilities is basic to good field intelligence. Finally, it is becoming increasingly clear that other First Tier states look to and, indeed, demand American political leadership in crisis situations, where they are reluctant to act when the United States does not lead the way.

Contours of the Future?

Russia as Peacekeeper or Empire Rebuilder?

Among the question marks about the post–Cold War world is the contribution that Russia, as the largest and most powerful of the Soviet successor states, will make to the new order. If one assumes that an aggressive Russian threat against the First Tier states of Western Europe or the formerly communist states of Eastern Europe is not a major concern (certainly an important reason for the Partnership for Peace—and especially the hope for Russian participation in it—was to allay that fear), then three concerns remain about Russia's relations with Eastern Europe and the other Soviet successor states, what Russian officials call the "near abroad."

One concern is what Russia would do in the event of mistreatment of Russian minorities there. In 1993 Russia issued a new military doctrine that warns against "the suppression of the rights, freedoms, and legitimate concerns" of ethnic Russians "in foreign states," which the document says "could be a serious source of conflict." Many in the states with the largest Russian minorities, such as Latvia, Estonia, and Moldova, fear that this rationale could serve as a Russian excuse to reconquer their territory—a policy goal suggested by Russian ultranationalists like Vladimir Zhirinovsky.

The second concern is what the Russians might do in the event of other kinds of instability in the "near abroad." The 1993 military document warns of the consequences of "local wars and armed conflicts" near Russian borders, particularly if foreign forces are involved. Some see such warnings as another ploy to justify reconquest.

The third concern is the most tantalizing: the possibility of Russia acting as a peacekeeper or peace imposer in the successor states. It is a mixed prospect. There is very little enthusiasm in First Tier states for their own involvement, so that the Russians seem the most promising candidates for the role. At the same time, it is not clear either that the Russians would be even-handed interveners (as Abkhazian separatists in Georgia discovered) or that there would not be costs for Russian help (as Georgian President Eduard Shevardnadze learned from the help he received against the Abkhazians; the price was membership in the Russian-dominated Commonwealth of Independent States).

The prospect of Russian forces being employed outside Russian territory in any capacity in the near future has been dampened by their very poor performance in the ongoing attempted secessionist republic of Chechnya (the Chechen Republic). In that situation, untrained Chechen militias continue to hold regular Russian army units at bay, inflicting significant casualties. The attempted secession has not been defeated despite the virtual leveling of the Chechen capital of Grozny during 1995 and 1996; in fact, Chechnya enjoys virtual autonomy within Russia. This poor performance raises the question of whether Russian troops, ineffective inside Russia, would fare any better in the "near abroad."

Source: James F. Holcomb and Michael M. Boll, *Russia's New Doctrine: Two Views* (Carlisle Barracks, PA: Strategic Institute, 1994).

Contours of the Future?

Changing Roles in Bosnia

The Bosnian situation represents, among other things, a prime example of the fluidity of contemporary international relations and the need for flexibility and adaptability necessary to cope with their evolution.

Consider what has happened to the outgrowth of the Dayton Accords. Its primary operational edifice has been the 60,000-troop Implementation Force (IFOR), which was originally scheduled only to be in the country for about a year. That mandate period was clearly inadequate to confront and overcome the multiple ills of the Bosnian society and polity; in 1997, the mandate was quietly extended and the subtle but symbolic change of title to Stabilization Force (SFOR) was accomplished. When U.S. Secretary of Defense William Cohen announced that all troops would be withdrawn by 1998, hardly anyone believed him, and they were not withdrawn.

The mission has expanded as well. Originally, the role of IFOR, particularly as conceptualized by the United States, was little more than that of heavily armed peacekeepers physically keeping the former combatants apart. Of great symbolic value was the role regarding the apprehension of war criminals: there was to be no aggressive campaign to seek out and arrest those accused of war crimes. Because the existence of these individuals provided a constant irritant that was impeding processes of healing within the body politic, that decision was reversed, and in summer 1997 SFOR troops began the aggressive pursuit and apprehension of a number of wanted criminals.

This action clearly expanded qualitatively the potential role of SFOR in the state-building exercise in Bosnia, and many feared that it would create the situation where planned extrication would become impossible. By 1998, it was clear that the SFOR mandate was indefinite and that their continuing presence is necessary for the foreseeable future if the cease-fire is to hold.

In any case, unilateral interventions, except for very limited incursions where a First Tier country has special interests (such as in a former colony), are most unlikely. Instead, burden-sharing organized through some collective entity—the UN or NATO, for instance—is likely to be the form of any action taken.

Power Versus Justice: Relations Between the Tiers

The relationship between the tiers will be governed by more than whether the First Tier decides to develop a collective-security arrangement to stifle Second Tier violence. The question of economic and political development as a way both to extend the general prosperity of the First Tier gradually to larger parts of the Second Tier and to foster peace and stability will also be prominent on the agenda.

Raising the question in this manner invites objections of cultural bias, because it may suggest that the only route to world peace, stability, and happiness is through cloning the economic and social system and values of the West. Critics argue that different cultures and different value systems will have to achieve success in their own way, that First Tier values cannot be grafted onto regions and cultures to which they are alien. Certainly this general line of reasoning applies to the "clash of civilizations" thesis enunciated in 1993 by Samuel P. Huntington and described in the accompanying Coming to Terms box.

Regardless of whether claims of cultural difference have merit, the prospects for elevation to the First Tier are bright in a number of geographic areas. In economic terms, the countries of the Pacific Rim have adopted and mastered most aspects of the First Tier's economic system without apparent cultural trauma; only some relatively minor political and cultural factors (such as the emphasis on stability and social order to the detriment of individual rights in countries such as Singapore and more transparency in financial dealings) stand in the way of full inclusion. The governments of those states have been accorded legitimacy by their peoples in most cases, and their economic relations with the First Tier are already on a nearly equal footing. Meanwhile, in South America, the flowering of political democracy and the rejection of statist economic approaches (including state ownership of important economic sectors) in favor of a free market should foster progress, which could be facilitated either by the extension of NAFTA membership or by implementation of the Free Trade Area of the Americas proposal.

The most basic questions, however, relate to whether, or to what degree, the First Tier will attempt to reach out and assist other Second Tier areas in their quest for inclusion. The question is probably most important with regard to the formerly communist countries of Eastern and Central Europe and the successor states of the Soviet Union, along with China. Most of those countries desperately long for full-scale participation in the First Tier's prosperity. While the association of many of them with NATO through the Partnership for Peace may aid their integration into the First Tier security system, their integration into the economic system remains uneven at present and, in some cases, unlikely in the foreseeable future.

The movement of the formerly communist countries toward the First Tier will be a matter of both how tenaciously their governments and populations pursue the dual criteria of political democracy and a market economy and how enthusiastically the membership of the First Tier accommodates and promotes the process of assimilation. How long, for instance, does democracy have to be in place and operating to meet the political criterion for membership in the European Union, the most obvious vehicle for Eastern European entrance into the First Tier? Certainly, the ability to conduct free elections in which different individuals and parties succeed to office peacefully is an important factor, but how many such elections are enough, and over what period of time? Similarly, the conversion to market economics is a gradual and accumulating phenomenon. At what point in the process do states such as the Czech Republic qualify for membership in the EU? In the dialogue within the EU about the process of union following ratification of the Maastricht Treaty, some of these questions have been muted. They have scarcely been raised at all with regard to the successor states of the Soviet Union.

Prospects for Russia and China are, again, of particular significance. Clearly it is in the broad interest of the First Tier to see both countries become part of the general prosperity. In purely economic terms, Russia and, especially, China represent enormous potential markets that have been a siren's call to Americans as far back as the days of the clipper ships in the nineteenth century. Both countries are also major potential productive centers.

The problems of integration are very different for each. China clearly has the more prosperous and dynamic economy, although market mechanisms are not universally in place. Parts of the country remain highly underdeveloped economically, and the political

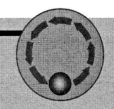

Coming to Terms

The "Clash of Civilizations" Thesis

In a pathbreaking article published originally in the summer 1993 edition of *Foreign Affairs*, Samuel P. Huntington argued that future international conflicts would be based not on political or economic ideology but on cultural differences, the "clash of civilizations." Huntington defines a civilization as "the highest cultural grouping of people and the broadest level of cultural identity people have." He identifies eight divergent civilizations that may be expected to compete: Western, Confucian, Japanese, Islamic, Hindu, Slavic-Orthodox, Latin American, and (possibly) African.

Huntington identifies two sets of reasons for the ascendancy of cultural over political and economic factors. The first set asserts the importance of civilizations, which he describes as "real and basic" and of greater prominence in a shrinking world where cultural contact has eroded other forms of identity. Moreover, he argues cultural identity is more constant than political (national) and economic (class) identity, particularly in a world where economic regionalism is on the rise.

The second set of factors derives from the first and is more directly geopolitical. He argues that the countries with similar cultures are being driven together—the "kin country syndrome." He also notes that the political and military dominance of the West (essentially what we have called the First Tier) is creating an "us versus them" dynamic, "the West versus the rest," which reinforces the cultural identity of non-western countries.

These latter ideas are similar to those we have noted in discussing the issue of First Tier–Second Tier relationships, and Huntington agrees that there is a politico-military tranquillity within the First Tier and an economic tri-polarity involving the United States, Japan, and Germany. He contends that conflict and bloodshed will occur where civilizations collide: "The crescent-shaped Islamic bloc, from the bulge of Africa to central Asia, has a bloody border." This border encompasses the Balkans and the southern border of the former Soviet Union.

Huntington's thesis is not universally accepted; indeed, part of the December 1993 edition of *Foreign Affairs* was devoted to critiques of it. These ranged from arguments questioning the basic concept to the contention that cultural differences are being reduced by the homogenizing effects of economic and political democratization, as has been argued in Chapters 7 and 9. Nonetheless, the thesis remains an important construct that will help form visions of the future.

Source: The Huntington article and rejoinders to it can be found in *The Clash of Civilizations: The Debate* (New York: Foreign Affairs Press, 1993), as well as in the journal itself as cited.

transition has only begun. China's current political stance is most publicly symbolized by the disagreement between the U.S. and Chinese governments over China's treatment of political dissidents. It is clear that China will not fully achieve the "normalcy" expected of First Tier states until political democratization—at least in some Asian variant—takes place. What the United States can or should do to promote such change is highly debatable, as discussed in the Case in Point box "Inducing Change in China."

Including China as well as a number of other Pacific Rim states in the First Tier may require some modification of western definitions of what constitutes political development and stability. A leading proponent of such modification has been the father of modern Singapore, Lee Kuan Yew, who maintains that cultural factors, manifested particularly in attitudes toward order and family, make purely western notions of political democracy inappropriate in an Asian context. While the situation in China hardly approximates even the limited degree of democracy found in Asian countries such as Singapore, some western accommodation with China on this issue may be possible if China makes some progress in political reform.

Case in Point

Inducing Change in China

How, or even whether, to bring pressure on China to democratize—or at least to improve its human rights record—has been a matter of great contention within the U.S. government. The question is not whether democratization of China is desirable but rather whether such a goal is realistic in the short term, given the recalcitrance of the Chinese government in this matter.

Although the Chinese leadership no longer espouses Marxism as an economic philosophy (in fact, it actually discourages other countries from adopting socialism), it continues to support strong authoritarian rule by the Chinese Communist Party, on the grounds that democratization would likely lead to a breakup of the Chinese state into more parts than what occurred in the Soviet Union. Political dissent is not tolerated, and a human rights problem with the United States and other countries has emerged.

What should the U.S. government do? Some argue for the imposition of economic sanctions against China until the human rights record improves (as dissent becomes more permissible and "slave labor" camps are eliminated). At the most extreme are calls for sanctions by revoking China's most-favored-nation (MFN) status, whereby Chinese products enter the United States at the lowest tariff rate. The basis of this argument is that it is hypocritical for the United States to campaign for human rights and ignore Chinese misdeeds; the argument's symbol is the 1989 Tiananmen Square massacre.

The other side of the argument is that U.S. sanctions would be counterproductive. First, the opponents say, they will not work, because they would not be honored by others (notably Japan), so that the United States would unilaterally forfeit the huge Chinese market and the opportunity to have influence over Chinese economic growth. Opponents also note that sanctions would make it politically easier for hard-liners in China to suppress the successors of Deng Xiaoping, such as current president Jiang Zemin. Many argue that given the age of the leadership, change is bound to come before long, and that since little can be done to hasten it, waiting for the inevitable is the proper and prudent strategy.

Up to this point, the opponents of sanctions have basically prevailed. The 1995 review of China's MFN status resulted once again in renewal, although with entreaties to improve the human rights record in the future. In any event, two points stand out: the desirability of moving China toward greater similarity to the states of the First Tier, and the difficulty of doing so.

In Russia (and most of the other Soviet successor states), the structural transition to a market economy has been considerably more difficult than in China. To a very real extent this difficulty has resulted from a lack of strong governmental leadership. There are few government officials who truly understand the workings of the market, there is no infrastructure of laws and procedures for channeling economic transformation, and many Russian people have shown a strong aversion to change. Moreover, those in the private sector who want to invest find the same roadblocks that were present under communist rule (at least partly because the same people inhabit the bureaucracy). The great danger is that economic conditions will continue to deteriorate to the point where the Russian people could make the same kind of Faustian bargain that the Germans made in 1932, when they turned to the Nazi Party in the hope it could relieve their economic woes.

A second aspect of the question about First Tier economic outreach is the extent to which the First Tier seeks to uplift the economic status of countries in the "traditional" developing world, most of which fall in the partially developed and developable subtiers of the Second Tier. This category includes a large number of countries with developmental potential in Asia and Africa, especially the latter. During the Cold War, their fate was geopolitically determined: assistance had an ideological, East-West basis and bias. Now these countries lack the leverage to obtain large-scale assistance, certainly in anything like the amounts demanded by the New International Economic Order that was discussed in Chapter 8.

Are there motives of justice or, perhaps, enlightened self-interest that could lead to a more generous attitude on the part of the First Tier? As telecommunications and transportation continue to develop, parts of the world that were formerly remote and isolated become increasingly more accessible. Given change such as the development of very fast maritime transportation, for instance, it is not difficult to think of multinational corporations building components in Southeast Asia (taking advantage of low wage demands) for assembly in places like Korea or Taiwan. At lower levels of sophistication, European-based firms may foster increased industrialization in some former African colonies.

Economic and security concerns intersect, of course, in First Tier attitudes toward the Second Tier. A reasonably tranquil, stable political environment is required to attract investment, especially from the private sector. What company would be interested in investing in Rwanda, for instance, after the massacres of 1994? At the same time, to attract firms involved in developing sophisticated, complex manufactures it is necessary to have a well-educated, well-motivated workforce with a stake in the system, the requisites of Singer and Wildavsky's "quality economies."

Whether, or to what extent, the bounty of the First Tier will be shared is problematical. It is easy to say that the globalizing economy is a positive-sum game from which all can benefit by expanding the economic horizons. It is far more difficult to devise concrete plans under which such an expansion could occur.

The State Under Siege

A combination of security and economic concerns has given rise to a renewed and reinvigorated debate over the Westphalian basis of the international order—the realist paradigm. Specifically, the outbreak of internal violence and atrocities, sometimes encouraged or perpetrated by governments, has led some to question the inviolability of state sovereignty. At the same time, the globalizing economy, especially as manifested in the stateless corporation, renders the authority of individual states less relevant for some purposes.

Assaulting sovereignty is, and always has been, a favorite pastime of many international relations scholars. Some emphasize that sovereignty, in the sense in which the notion was introduced in Chapter 2, has never been as absolute in practice as it appears in theory. Thus, a more measured description of the extent of sovereignty may be necessary. For other scholars, the assault is a matter of principle: sovereignty, to them, is the last resort of the scoundrels, who hide behind its protection to use and abuse their own citizens. Moreover, to many analysts whose overriding concern is a world in which the instance of war is greatly reduced or eliminated altogether, sovereignty is seen as a concept that allows and even occasionally promotes the recourse to violence.

In security terms, the debate over what to do about internal violence in the Second Tier raises the issue of sovereignty starkly. As the paralysis of the UN Security Council disappeared in the aftermath of the Cold War and the world body adopted a more prominent role in conflict management, the question was joined, largely through the voice of then UN Secretary-General Boutros-Ghali. What obligation does the international community have when members violate the rights of groups and individuals within states? Are there transcendent principles more fundamental and important than state sovereignty?

This debate focuses on the assertion of humanitarian vital interests, the idea that "the rights of individuals and groups" have priority over "the sovereign rights of the state" and that where there are fundamental abuses of individuals or groups, the international community has a right and even an obligation to intercede, even if state sovereignty is violated in the process. This principle was raised with regard to the situation of the Kurds in post–Gulf War Iraq, which is discussed in the Case in Point box "De Facto Kurdistan," and in the cases of Somalia, Bosnia, Kosovo, and Haiti. There will clearly be numerous future cases where the issue can be raised, in parts of the formerly communist bloc, in Africa, and in other parts of the world.

In many ways, this debate has its roots in the philosophical disagreement between those who, like Bodin and Hobbes, argued for absolute sovereignty (the unfettered right of the ruler to govern as he or she determines), and later thinkers, such as Locke and Rousseau, who argued for popular sovereignty (the idea that sovereignty resides in individuals, who may transfer some of their sovereign rights to the state for practical matters). This debate was described in Chapter 2 and need not be repeated. The issue arises today in the realist-idealist dialogue, as well as in feminist critiques. No one argues that absolute sovereignty exists or that it should. But there is disagreement on the extent to which state control has eroded, with the realists generally arguing that sovereignty remains relatively more intact. There is also disagreement over the desirability of this erosion and the extent to which humanitarian interests should be promoted and defended by outsiders, with idealists taking the more activist stand in this regard.

From the perspective of the international system as a whole, the prospect of an erosion of sovereignty raises concern over what principle of organization would replace it. Reorganizing the international system around international organizations, even world government, has often been suggested, but this idea has never attracted much support in a world where nationalism remains a powerful force. States have consistently proven highly resistant to proposals and movements designed to promote their own obsolescence. There is little reason to expect this situation will change.

Case in Point

De Facto Kurdistan

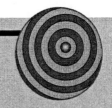

Shortly after his defeat in the Persian Gulf War in 1991, Iraq's Saddam Hussein unleashed his remaining military strength in reprisal against Iraqi Kurds and Shiites who had launched unsuccessful rebellions against his regime. The attacks against the Kurds of northern Iraq were of particular ferocity; helicopter gunships bombarded Kurdish villages with a savagery reminiscent of a similar campaign in 1987 that included the use of chemical weapons. The Kurds, fearing genocide, panicked and fled, many to the bleak mountains of southern Turkey, where CNN broadcast their plight around the world.

What was to be done? Left where they were, most of the refugees would starve or die of disease. Even a massive U.S.-led relief operation was only a temporary solution, and Turkey did not want them to stay. Yet they refused to go back to Iraq, fearing Saddam Hussein's wrath.

The solution adopted by the western allies that had won the war was to move the Kurds back to their homes, but under protection. Declaring Operation Provide Comfort (renamed Operation Northern Watch in 1997), the United States, along with Britain and France, declared the Kurdish zone off limits to Iraqi officials and forces, with the ban to be backed up by allied military force. Iraq, in other words, was not permitted to exercise sovereign authority over what the allies never denied was part of Iraqi territory. Although Kurdish officials denied any intent to create a sovereign

Kurdish state, so-called Kurdistan came to exist in fact if not in name, with a Kurdish authority providing all the basic functions of government.

The situation created two ongoing problems. The first was practical. How long would the exclusion zone (the status of which is reviewed every six months) continue? On one hand, removal of allied protection probably would result in renewed fierce suppression of the Kurds unless the United States was willing to intervene again, probably with ground forces (an unlikely prospect). On the other hand, the longer it lasted, the greater the likelihood of more allied casualties—such as the friendly-fire incident in spring 1994 when two U.S. military helicopters were shot down by American patrolling planes, killing 26 officials. Was the U.S. government irretrievably mired in Kurdistan?

The second problem was precedential. Would the violation of Iraqi sovereignty make it easier to infringe on other countries' sovereignty in the future? No government officials argued that it should, but the fact remained that the United States, Britain, and France acted as if sovereignty—at least for Iraq—was no longer an inviolable principle. This issue was made more complicated by Turkish incursion into Iraqi Kurdistan during the spring of 1995 in pursuit of Kurdish Turks attempting to secede from Turkey. Because of the exclusion zone, Iraq was unable to challenge this violation of its sovereignty either.

At the level of actions, an obligation to intervene globally wherever individual rights are being grossly violated could lead to possible military interventions in a very large number of cases. Although the principle of humanitarian vital interests was not raised during the carnage in Rwanda in 1994, clearly it could have been. Carrying out any universal obligation to protect human rights around the world would clearly go well beyond the very limited resources of the United Nations, especially since such missions normally require a process of peace imposition, which is rigorous, demanding, and expensive. In short, some approach or mechanism is needed to apply this humanitarian obligation and to intervene in sovereign states under certain circumstances.

At least two approaches are possible, and neither is noncontroversial. The first is a commitment of the First Tier in effect to intervene on humanitarian principles when it deems this to be feasible, either unilaterally, multilaterally through the UN, or perhaps through a NATO operation "deputized" by the UN (as was eventually done with IFOR/SFOR in Bosnia and KFOR in Kosovo). Because of its role as the sole remaining superpower, participation by the United States would be critical to such an enterprise. As argued earlier, such acquiescence cannot be presumed, particularly given the generally low level of public support for far-flung military adventures in situations where the geopolitical interests of Americans are not clearly involved.

The other approach to this problem is for states to reach an accord on criteria that would determine when the application of force would and would not be mandated. Such criteria, of course, would need to be restrictive enough to keep intervention obligations at a more manageable level. It has been suggested that a total breakdown in governance in a state (as occurred in Somalia) or a clearly genocidal campaign (such as in Rwanda) might be appropriate situations for intervention.

Of course, questions of consistency arise when one begins to examine real situations. International action in Somalia but delayed in Bosnia, or in Haiti but without ground forces in Kosovo, for instance, is hard to justify in terms of any reasonable principle. Furthermore, many of the situations in which intervention may seem to be called for are extremely intractable, and consequently, the prospects for long-term amelioration as a result of international intervention are dim. Should the prospect of long-term success be a major criterion for activism? In that case, the most difficult situations (like Rwanda) may often be bypassed. Moreover, intervention under any criterion or principle is unlikely to be widely welcomed in Second Tier countries, where these actions are normally implemented.

The demands of economic globalization constitute a less dramatic, if no less pervasive, assault on state sovereignty. Largely driven by advances in high technology, the economic system of the First Tier, extending increasingly into the Second, has leapfrogged state boundaries in ways that leave state jurisdiction more and more irrelevant to regulating economic behavior. As noted particularly in Chapter 9, the result is a global economy much more interdependent than those who first raised the concept in the 1960s could have imagined.

During the 1980s, First Tier policies of economic deregulation and privatization facilitated the movement of ideas, capital, and production across borders. The global recession that gripped most of the First Tier during the early 1990s slowed this trend somewhat and gave rise to a reassertion of economic nationalism. Japan and the United States, for instance, engaged in direct competition over high-definition television (HDTV), and consortia of American and Japanese electronics firms, aided and encouraged by their respective governments, have competed vigorously for supremacy in the vital links in the information revolution. When the American consortium broke through in the competition by successfully digitizing transmission of HDTV images, the accomplishment was heralded as a U.S. triumph.

Nevertheless, an increasingly international economy seems technically and economically inevitable. The movement of ideas and capital is a natural result of continuing improvements in telecommunications, which will allow instantaneous access to all parts of the globe, facilitating penetration of hitherto inaccessible reaches of the Second Tier (if First Tier firms seek such involvement). Breakthroughs in air and sea transportation will make component manufacture and product assembly an increasingly global affair, and international ownership, management, and workforce composition will become increasingly common.

National governments in the First Tier have not come to grips with economic globalization and its consequences. In the privatized, highly prosperous 1990s, governments basked in that prosperity and did not look carefully at its consequences for their own authority. As long as general prosperity and peace among the First Tier continue, the thesis expressed by many business leaders that governments simply do not matter for economic purposes may be adequate. As regional groups such as NAFTA or, more ambitiously, the FTAA, a deepened or widened European Union, or possibly a formalized APEC become increasingly important, common decision structures that dilute individual state control are almost certain to follow.

Case Study: *Envisioning and Shaping the Future*

As one surveys the landscape of the emerging international system, both positive and negative trends become apparent. Where the trends are positive, as in the general nature of relations among the countries of the First Tier, they need to be encouraged. Where the trends are negative, as in the spate of Second Tier violence or the quality of the global environment, then it is appropriate to envision ways in which conditions can be improved.

Changing negative trends into more desirable conditions is the purpose of public policy, whether at the national, subnational, or international levels. The problem of doing so is shown in Figure 14-1. The figure begins with the present: what, for instance, is the current status of efforts to reduce carbon dioxide emissions and thus protect the earth against the threat of global warming? It then moves toward the likely future if there is no increased intermediation: what will the status of carbon dioxide emissions be in five or 10 years if we do no more than we are currently doing to repair the damage? Finally, it portrays the desirable future: what would be the desirable condition after a comparable period of time? The gap between likely and desirable futures represents the policy domain, the area in which choices are made about which problems will be addressed by public policy and the extent to which they will be addressed.

The process of trying to bridge this gap is similar to the decision process introduced in Chapter 1. When confronted with an adverse situation, what do you want to do about it? What will be the responses of opposing parties? What is the likely cost? What uncertainties create risks? What outcomes are likely and possible, and how important or tolerable are those various outcomes? Moreover, what are the diverging interests that various involved parties have in those outcomes?

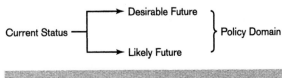

Figure 14-1   **The Policy Domain**

At first blush, a goal such as the prevention of global warming would seem noncontroversial: virtually everyone would want it in principle, and means for achieving it, such as eliminating or reducing carbon dioxide emissions, are well established and scientifically demonstrated remedies. Thus, the policy path between likely and desirable futures would seem simple and straightforward.

But it is not, and the best evidence for that assertion is that the appropriate policies are not universally in place. Why not? For one thing, there are opposing national interests—for instance, automobile manufacturers reluctant to move to cleaner-burning but more expensive engines because of their perception of public resistance. Opponents may also question the scientific data (remember, for instance, that many tobacco companies until very recently vigorously denied claims that cigarettes are carcinogenic, despite mountains of evidence to the contrary). To some governments in the Second Tier, environmental cleanup is held hostage to demands for developmental assistance (as occurred at the Earth Summit in 1992), and there is much international finger pointing as to what states are responsible for certain problems and which must contribute to their solution.

Of all the problems vexing the international system, none is more troubling than the spate of internal violence that is wracking much of the Second Tier. In the absence of First Tier intervention, the situation is likely to get worse. Moreover, the reduction or elimination of internal violence is a value about which hardly anyone would disagree. However, as we have argued in several places in the preceding pages, there is substantial disagreement about the efficacy of outside intervention, and there is an unwillingness to commit the necessary resources even where positive results seem attainable. After an initial flurry of activism, the First Tier has shown only slight interest in the Somalias and Rwandas of this world. Part of the problem is that no one knows how to deal with the underlying conditions, such as violent clan politics in Somalia or the politically induced tribal hatreds in Rwanda, or the irredentist yearnings in Kosovo. At the same time, the publics in First Tier countries may not feel that efforts to solve these problems are sufficiently in their interests—especially when sacrifices may be involved. Many Americans decried the tragedy of starvation in Somalia; when their sons and daughters were dispatched to that land and became victims of its violence, however, support for intervention largely evaporated.

Bridging the gap between likely and desirable futures is never as easy a task as it may seem on the surface. Problems are generally more intractable and difficult than they first appear. To paraphrase former German Chancellor Helmut Schmidt, all the problems for which there are easy solutions have already been solved; what remains are the intractable problems that are not solved, but worked.

Review

This chapter surveyed likely problems for international relations in the future. In the process, the following points were made:

1. Superpower status will be defined differently in the future, with a greater role for the economic instrument of power and less of a role for the military instrument. Only the United States retains a sufficient breadth of power to be thought of as a superpower.

2. Leadership in the area of security will be influenced by the likely pattern of violence in the system, which is (a) an absence of conflict and violence among First Tier states, and (b) a concentration of unrest within the Second Tier, in the forms of regional conflicts, and especially, internal wars.

3. In relations between the tiers, the key issues are how the First Tier will deal with Second Tier violence and to what extent the First Tier will participate in and encourage Second Tier democratization and economic development.

4. The idea of state sovereignty has come under increasing assault, both as a description of reality and as a desired basis for the international system. Related to this assault is the issue of First Tier involvement in internal wars within the Second Tier. The First Tier has yet to develop criteria for when and how it will involve itself in such conflicts, or what mechanisms it will use to make such decisions.

5. A useful way to think of future policy issues is through the prism of likely versus desirable futures. The gap between the two is the domain of policy, where one searches for strategies to narrow the difference.

Suggested Readings

Bloomfield, Lincoln P. "The Premature Burial of Global Law and Order: Looking Beyond the Three Cases from Hell." *Washington Quarterly* 17, 3 (summer 1994): 145–62.

Brzezinski, Zbigniew. "The Cold War and Its Aftermath." *Foreign Affairs* 71, 4 (fall 1992): 31–49.

Cullen, Robert. "Human Rights Quandary." *Foreign Affairs* 72, 5 (winter 1992/93): 79–88.

Foreign Affairs. *Agenda 95*. New York: Foreign Affairs Press, 1994.

Halperin, Morton. "Guaranteeing Democracy." *Foreign Policy* 91 (summer 1993): 105–23.

Helman, Gerald B., and Steven R. Ratner. "Saving Failed States." *Foreign Policy* 89 (winter 1992/93): 3–20.

Huntington, Samuel P. "Clash of Civilizations." *Foreign Affairs* 72, 3 (summer 1993): 22–49.

Layne, Christopher, and Benjamin Schwartz. "American Hegemony—Without an Enemy." *Foreign Policy* 92 (fall 1993): 5–23.

Mandelbaum, Michael. "The Reluctance to Intervene." *Foreign Policy* 95 (summer 1994): 3–18.

Mearsheimer, John J. "Why We Shall Soon Miss the Cold War." *Atlantic Monthly* 266, 2 (August 1990): 35–50.

Metz, Steven, and James Kievit. *The Revolution in Military Affairs and Conflict Short of War.* Carlisle Barracks, PA: Strategic Studies Institute, July 1994.

Neumann, Robert G. "This Next Disorderly Half Century: Some Proposed Remedies." *Washington Quarterly* 16, 1 (winter 1993): 33–50.

Nye, Joseph S., Jr. *Bound to Lead: The Changing Nature of American Power.* New York: Basic Books, 1990.

—. "Peering into the Future." *Foreign Affairs* 73, 4 (July/August 1994): 82–93.

Rosecrance, Richard. "A New Concert of Powers." *Foreign Affairs* 71, 2 (spring 1992): 64–82.

Smith, Tony. "Making the World Safe for Democracy." *Washington Quarterly* 16, 4 (autumn 1993): 197–218.

Snow, Donald M. *The Shape of the Future: World Politics for a New Century,* 3d ed. Armonk, NY: M. E. Sharpe, 1999.

APPENDIX
Countries of the Second Tier

The purpose of this appendix is to explain our classification of individual countries in the various subtiers of the Second Tier. For a discussion of the general principles used in our classification system, see pages 251–262.

Asia and Pacific

Developed (4)

Hong Kong Although not technically a political democracy, Hong Kong is one of the most economically advanced areas in the region, with over 90 percent of the workforce employed in manufacturing, commerce, and service industries. Its future economic status is uncertain because of absorption into China in 1997.

South Korea A fragile, multiparty democracy, South Korea has an economy that verges on First Tier status, with a high per capita income and a large, technologically advanced industrial sector. It is the world's largest shipbuilder, and its electronics industry has become a producer rather than merely a consumer of technology.

Singapore Politically a virtual one-party democracy, Singapore has a very high per capita gross domestic product or GDP ($21,200 in 1996) and an economy structured on a postindustrial, high-technology basis.

Taiwan A two-party political democracy, Taiwan has a high per capita GDP ($14,700 in 1996), a large electronics sector, and a relatively small agricultural sector (4 percent of its gross national product in 1996). Its future depends on possible association with China.

Partially Developed (8)

China Technically still a communist state, China remains under authoritarian rule. The areas designated as Special Economic Zones are among the most economically dynamic in the world; much of China, however, remains at the preindustrial stage of development.

India Like China, India is several countries. A political democracy, it has developed a large middle class (about 100 million) and a sophisticated industrial sector; two-thirds of the workforce, however, are employed in agriculture.

Indonesia A large, diverse partial democracy, Indonesia shows signs of economic growth; the country has large energy resources (oil, coal, and natural gas) and has become a major member of APEC. Its stability has been hurt by the Asian crisis of 1997 and political turmoil.

Malaysia A stable constitutional monarchy with a bicameral legislature, Malaysia has an economy that combines a growing electronics and light manufacturing sector with a continuing high concentration (20 percent of gross domestic product) in agriculture.

Marshall Islands The Marshall Islands are near the border of the developable subtier, with a per capita GDP of about $1,680 in 1996, and have a constitutional government associated with the United States. Tourism is of some significance.

Micronesia A group of islands with a constitutional government associated with the United States, Micronesia is just above the economic line dividing the partially developed from the developable countries, by virtue of a per capita GDP of $1,600 in 1994. The economic structure is preindustrial: fishing and farming are the principal occupations.

North Korea Another country on the border of the developable subtier (per capita GDP of about $900 in 1996), North Korea has a communist government and a centrally controlled but deteriorating economy with an emphasis on heavy industry. It was further weakened by massive crop failures in the middle 1990s.

Thailand A constitutional monarchy since 1946, Thailand has a stable political system. Its major nonagricultural economic sector is tourism, but it seems likely to benefit from regional growth as it recovers from the Asian crisis.

Developable (19)

Afghanistan Prospects for development are particularly grim for Afghanistan, a very poor country with a per capita GDP of $800 in 1996 and an economy and political system that continue to be ravaged by an Islamic fundamentalist civil war.

Bangladesh A combination of adverse climate and topography (notably a proneness to flooding) and overpopulation makes Bangladesh one of the world's poorest countries, with a gross domestic product of about $1,280 per capita in 1996 (largely derived from agriculture). Politically, it is a democracy.

Bhutan Politically linked to India and located almost entirely in the Himalayas, Bhutan is one of the world's poorest countries, with few prospects for short- or medium-term development.

Burma (Myanmar) Given the combination of a repressive military regime and a concentration of economic activity in agriculture and forestry (teak), the developmental prospects for Burma remain clouded.

Cambodia Almost three decades of civil war have left Cambodia's economy largely nonfunctioning. The prospects for progress depend mostly on the success of the government chosen in a UN-supervised election in 1993, and especially its ability to recover from the communist Khmer Rouge insurgency.

Fiji Fiji is politically in transition, with a fragile democracy having been restored after a military coup in 1987. Economically, the country relies largely on agriculture, especially the production of sugar cane; the coup slowed tourism, which had been a major source of income.

Kiribati A republic that gained its independence from Britain in 1979, Kiribati has an economy that relies mostly on fishing and copra. It has very little industry.

Laos Laos remains a communist state burdened by a government-controlled economy in which rice production is the major activity. Any hopes for improvement are tied to deregulation and the development of a private sector.

Maldives A republic ruled by a single clan for several centuries, the Maldives has a preindustrial economy, with emphases on fishing (60 percent of exports) and tourism.

Mongolia A country that has only begun the political transition to democracy, Mongolia has an economy that remains largely preindustrial, with emphases on agriculture (especially livestock) and natural resource extraction.

Nepal A multiparty parliamentary democracy, Nepal has an agriculturally based economy (90 percent of the population works in agriculture, which produces 60 percent of the gross domestic product).

Pakistan A fragile democracy whose military has frequently interfered with governance, Pakistan continues to have a largely agricultural economy, over 50 percent of the workforce. A large (mostly Afghan) refugee population is a problem, as is Islamic fundamentalism.

Papua New Guinea A multiparty parliamentary democracy, Papua New Guinea has an economy that remains preindustrial: 80 percent of the population is engaged in agriculture, and 60 percent of export earnings come from mining.

Philippines A fragile democracy, the Philippines stands on the upper rungs of the developable subtier. Although 45 percent of the population remains in agriculture, there are developing industries in textiles, pharmaceuticals, and chemicals.

Solomon Islands A multiparty democracy with a unicameral parliament, the Solomon Islands is a preindustrial country with about 90 percent of the population engaged in subsistence agriculture.

Sri Lanka A two-party parliamentary democracy, Sri Lanka has an economy dominated by agriculture (which employs about half the workforce). Its high rate of unemployment and the Tamil ethnic uprising remain barriers to economic development.

Tonga A hereditary constitutional monarchy, Tonga is a preindustrial state. The largest elements of the economy are agriculture (70 percent of the labor force) and tourism.

Vietnam Still nominally a communist state, Vietnam has made significant progress in deregulation, privatization, and the attraction of foreign capital. It is a candidate to rise to the partially developed subtier.

Western Samoa A constitutional monarchy, Western Samoa has a periodically active legislature and executive branch. The country's economy is heavily dependent on agriculture, which employs well over half the labor force and produces 90 percent of export earnings; tourism is the next largest industry.

Resource Rich (1)

Brunei Officially a constitutional sultanate, Brunei is a wealthy state, with a gross domestic product of $15,800 per capita in 1996. Its major economic activities are sales of petroleum (about half of gross domestic product) and of other natural resources, such as trees.

Middle East

Developed (2)

Cyprus A nominal republic, Cyprus is effectively two ethnic polities, one Greek and the other Turkish, that have been divided by a UN peacekeeping force since a civil war in 1963. The economy is well developed: 86 percent of the workforce is employed in service or industrial sectors.

Israel A stable, multiparty democracy, Israel has a highly diversified, sophisticated economy with large service and technological sectors. Gross domestic product per capita is also high, at $16,400 in 1996. The major negative factor is the continuing Jewish-Palestinian conflict.

Partially Developed (6)

Egypt Egypt's reasonably stable democracy has been challenged by Islamic fundamentalists, and its economic development has been blunted by public ownership of most industry. Agriculture accounts for 20 percent of its gross domestic product.

Lebanon Historically, Lebanon was the financial center of the Islamic Middle East, but its economy and political system were undermined by its long civil war, which ended in 1990. Some economic recovery, spurred by a strong banking community, has recently occurred.

Malta A parliamentary democracy, Malta enjoys an economic standing that makes it arguably close to the developed subtier. It had a gross domestic product per capita of $12,600 in 1996 and a diversified economy.

Oman One of the world's few remaining absolute monarchies, Oman has a high gross domestic product per capita, $9,800 in 1996, mostly from oil production. It differs from other resource-rich countries in the region by virtue of its growing industrial sector.

Syria A militarily controlled republic, Syria has an economy that suffers from government domination. Most of the country's export earnings come from oil and mineral sales, putting it near the developable subtier.

Turkey A democracy under siege by Kurdish secessionists and other rebels, Turkey has a variety of industries but a fairly large agricultural sector (about half the workforce).

Developable (2)

Jordan A constitutional monarchy with a bicameral legislature, Jordan has a gross domestic product per capita of $5,000, an export profile of mostly natural resources, and a sizable trade imbalance.

Yemen Since unification of North and South Yemen in 1990, the political system has been moving toward democracy. The economy has developmental potential mostly because of projected oil revenues, which can be exploited now that political turmoil has decreased.

Resource Rich (7)

Bahrain A traditional monarchy, Bahrain has no legislature and bans political parties. Its economy is almost totally dependent on its petroleum industry (which provides 80 percent of export earnings). Its only other notable industry is the export of bauxite.

Iran A theocratically controlled republic, Iran has an economy that is almost totally reliant (90 percent of its exports) on petroleum. The rest of its economy was diversifying before the fall of the Shah in 1979 but remains basically preindustrial.

Iraq The economy of Iraq, an authoritarian republic, has been shattered by international sanctions since the country's defeat in the Persian Gulf War. Petroleum formerly accounted for 95 percent of export earnings, but now that has been reduced to 10 percent.

Kuwait A constitutional monarchy that does not allow political parties, Kuwait controls 10 percent of the world's known crude oil reserves. Oil production is virtually its only economic activity.

Qatar A traditional monarchy with a unicameral advisory council, Qatar has a high gross national product per capita ($21,300 in 1996), almost exclusively derived from oil production. The rest of the economy is preindustrial.

Saudi Arabia A monarchy that has never held elections, Saudi Arabia is heavily oil dependent. Unlike many other states in the region, it has made an effort to diversify its economy (22 percent of the workforce, for instance, is employed in service industries).

United Arab Emirates A federation that has neither elections nor political parties, the United Arab Emirates is almost totally dependent on oil-based revenue for its high standard of living.

Latin America

Developed (5)

Argentina Generally considered a fragile democracy, Argentina has an economy that is growing rapidly, due largely to deregulation. Almost 90 percent of the workforce is employed in industry or services, although agriculture continues to provide the bulk of exports.

Brazil By far the largest state in the region, Brazil qualifies as a fragile democracy. It has the resource base (mineral wealth, arable land) for considerable economic growth and industrial diversity.

Chile A stabilizing democracy since its transition from military rule, Chile has a rapidly growing economy. The service and industrial areas employed 72 percent of the workforce in 1996. APEC and Mercosur membership should be an additional boost to economic growth.

Mexico A democracy traditionally dominated by one party and struggling with the transition to full democracy, Mexico is an oil exporter. A high percentage of its workforce (about 67 percent in 1996) is in the service and commercial sectors.

Venezuela A traditionally stable democracy, Venezuela has historically been heavily dependent on oil exports. Its economy has recently been diversifying, particularly into areas such as telecommunications.

Partially Developed (19)

Antigua and Barbuda A parliamentary democracy, Antigua and Barbuda is a member of the British Commonwealth. Its economy is mostly service oriented, with tourism the major base.

Bahamas A stable parliamentary democracy, the Bahamas is a member of the British Commonwealth. Its primary economic activities include tourism (50 percent of gross domestic product) and offshore banking.

Barbados A bicameral, stable parliamentary democracy, Barbados has an economy that historically relied on sugar cane production but is beginning to diversify into areas such as tourism and light industry.

Belize A multiparty parliamentary democracy, Belize has a traditionally agricultural economy (providing 75 percent of export earnings in 1996) that is diversifying slowly into areas such as textiles and tourism.

Bolivia Although one of the poorer Latin American states, Bolivia has a fragile democracy and, if problems such as illicit coca production can be overcome, has the natural resources (such as tin) for moderate growth. It could arguably be placed in the developable subtier.

Colombia A fragile democracy beset by an ongoing narco-insurgency by drug lords, Colombia has reasonable potential for economic growth in areas such as the mining of precious metals and gemstones.

Costa Rica The most stable and longstanding democracy in Latin America, Costa Rica has an economy that remains heavily reliant on agricultural production for export earnings and needs diversification.

Dominica A stable, multiparty parliamentary democracy, Dominica has an economy that relies on agriculture and, to a lesser extent, on industries such as the production of soap and coconut oil and on tourism.

Ecuador A fragile, multiparty democracy, Ecuador has great promise for economic development, based in petroleum wealth and a growing industrial sector that was responsible for 40 percent of gross domestic product in 1996.

Grenada A fragile democracy with a bicameral legislature, Grenada falls toward the lower end of the partially developed subtier. Its economy relies heavily on agriculture and secondarily on tourism.

Guatemala A politically unstable democracy with a history of military interference in political affairs, Guatemala remains largely dependent on agriculture but has an untapped petroleum potential.

Jamaica A stable two-party democracy, Jamaica has a modern telecommunications system, but its economic activity centers on tourism and the production of sugar.

Panama A highly unstable multiparty democracy, Panama is still recovering from the American invasion of 1989. The service and industrial sectors employ about three-quarters of the workforce; illicit drug trafficking is a major problem.

Paraguay A fragile multiparty democracy, Paraguay shows modest growth prospects. Its economy remains agriculturally based, with some light industry.

St. Kitts–Nevis A relatively stable multiparty democracy, St. Kitts–Nevis had a per capita gross domestic product of $5,700 in 1996. Its main economic activities are tourism and sugar production.

St. Lucia A democratic, multiparty state, St. Lucia had a per capita GDP of $4,400 in 1996. Its main economic activities are tourism and banana production.

St. Vincent Like St. Lucia, St. Vincent is a multiparty democracy with primary economic activity concentrated in tourism and banana production.

Suriname A fragile democracy that experienced a military coup in 1990, Suriname has an economy that is basically preindustrial (and relies on the export of bauxite and bananas). It had a per capita GDP of $3,150 in 1996.

Uruguay A multiparty democracy, Uruguay historically has been economically dependent on the export of beef and beef products, but a good telecommunications network and fair infrastructure could fuel future growth and development.

Developable (8)

Cuba Cuba is one of the world's last avowedly communist dictatorships. The Cuban economy has largely disintegrated due to economic sanctions and the loss of economic assistance formerly available from the Soviet Union. Some private enterprise has been instituted.

Dominican Republic A tentative, fragile democracy, the Dominican Republic has an economy that relies on agriculture (notably sugar and tobacco exports), the extraction of mineral resources, and a modest tourist trade.

El Salvador El Salvador has been a fragile democracy since the end of its civil war in 1992. Prospects for economic development depend on the creation of a stable political system and land reform; currently agriculture is the major economic activity and coffee the major commercial crop.

Guyana A fairly stable multiparty democracy, Guyana is one of the region's poorest countries. Its economy is based on agriculture and some light industry.

Haiti Despite the reinstallation of its elected president by the United States in 1994, Haiti is at best a fragile democracy, which has changed or suspended its constitution five times since 1983. It has a largely nonexistent economy, and most of the population lives in abject poverty.

Honduras A fairly stable multiparty democracy, Honduras remains poor, with most economic activity concentrated in agriculture and light industry.

Nicaragua An emerging democratic system recovering from the economic effects of leftist (Sandinista) rule, Nicaragua remains very poor. Because of a deficient telecommunications network and infrastructure, it has little short-term prospect of development.

Peru A very fragile democracy, Peru has been destabilized by the Sendero Luminoso (Shining Path) insurgency. Government austerity measures and success in suppressing the insurgents are currently fueling economic development; Peru had the world's highest economic growth rate in 1994.

Resource Rich (1)

Trinidad and Tobago A stable multiparty democracy, Trinidad and Tobago has an economy heavily reliant on petroleum and petroleum-based products (making up 82 percent of exports in 1996), with a secondary emphasis on tourism.

Former Soviet Union and Eastern Europe

Developed (1)

Slovenia The wealthiest former republic of Yugoslavia, Slovenia has an emerging democracy and an economy that derived over 80 percent of its export earnings from manufactured goods in 1991, before the Yugoslavian war began. Its per capita GDP in 1996 was $12,300.

Partially Developed (8)

Croatia A fragile parliamentary democracy whose development was retarded by the Yugoslavian war, Croatia had the second wealthiest economy in Yugoslavia before the war. Its development could be rapid in the future.

Czech Republic A tentative democracy that survived the breakaway of Slovakia, the Czech Republic has a reasonably developed industrial base, but it must further develop a market-based system and service sector.

Hungary Hungary is a fragile democracy and the Eastern Europe country that has most opened itself to market reforms and foreign investment. It is likely to emerge as a regional leader.

Kazakhstan A nominally democratic state (most of its rulers are former communists), Kazakhstan has economic potential in oil production, but it is burdened by the inability to get oil to market except via pipelines that cross the borders of other successor states. Muslim-Russian ethnic tension is also a problem.

Poland The first Soviet bloc country to elect a noncommunist government, Poland remains a fragile democracy that is experiencing difficulties in making the transition from a state-controlled to a market economy.

Russia At best a fragile democracy that is threatened by economic instability and ethnic tensions, Russia is committed to a market economy but still lacks the infrastructure and financial and legal framework within which to develop a stable market.

Slovakia A fragile democracy that has survived the break with the Czech Republic, Slovakia is somewhat poorer than its former partner and thus probably faces a longer developmental process.

Ukraine An evolving political system that is not yet wholly democratic, Ukraine was the second most important economic unit in the Soviet Union. It has a very strong agricultural base and diversified industry, both of which are in the process of conversion to a market-based economy.

Developable (18)

Albania Although it was one of the poorest and least economically developed of communist states, Albania shows some indications of an ability to develop: a tentative democratic government, exploitable resources, and agricultural self- sufficiency.

Armenia Beset by the ongoing war with Azerbaijan, Armenia has hardly begun the post-Soviet transition. No elections have been held, and there are few signs of economic development or privatization.

Azerbaijan Locked in a war with Armenia that has created a massive influx of refugees, Azerbaijan remains undemocratic and economically underdeveloped, despite the presence of large petroleum reserves that could propel it into the resource-rich subtier when they are exploited.

Belarus Effective political control in Belarus remains in the hands of the Communist Party. Although the economy has both agricultural and heavy industrial strength, the process of transition to a market economy has hardly begun.

Bosnia and Herzegovina Until a Yugoslavian peace occurs, assessing Bosnia is difficult. Politically, its legal government is almost entirely Muslim, and most of its economic activity was suspended by the fighting. Its economy's development remains retarded by the war's aftermath and occupation.

Bulgaria An emerging democracy whose development has been impeded by a strong communist influence (33 percent of the National Assembly seats in 1993 were held by communists), Bulgaria has not truly begun the process of conversion to a market economy. Politically, anticommunists gained control in 1997.

Estonia A tentative democracy, Estonia has an economy that remains largely underdeveloped. Only 30 percent of the workforce is employed in industry, and most exports are limited to natural resources and agriculture.

Georgia A tentative democracy beset by ethnic separatists, Georgia has an economy that continues to be heavily invested in agriculture (fruits and teas), with some residual Black Sea tourist trade.

Kyrgyzstan A tentative democracy at best, Kyrgyzstan remains preindustrial. Its economy relies on agriculture, including livestock.

Latvia A fragile democracy undertaking the transition to a market economy, Latvia has a reasonably diversified industrial base but is conspicuously dependent on Russia for energy (it produces only 10 percent of its electricity).

Lithuania A fragile democracy committed to privatization of the economy, Lithuania has reasonably efficient manufacturing and agricultural sectors, but it is vulnerable because of its need to import almost all natural resources.

Macedonia The poorest successor state of Yugoslavia, Macedonia is an emerging democracy whose economic development is unlikely unless it can resolve disputes over its borders and thus resume relations with its neighboring states.

Moldova Moldova has not made a meaningful transition toward democracy. Its economy has been hampered by ongoing disputes with Russia, Romania, and Ukraine.

Romania A tentative democracy at best, Romania has a reasonably large but aging heavy industrial economic base, which will require considerable modernization and a more predictable energy supply to become competitive.

Tajikistan A country that has not started the democratic transition and has been destabilized by a civil war, Tajikistan has the lowest standard of living of the members of the Commonwealth of Independent States, with an agriculturally based economy.

Turkmenistan A republic effectively ruled by former communists, Turkmenistan employs only 10 percent of the population in manufacturing. Oil reserves that produced 11 percent of Soviet energy represent the main developmental hope.

Uzbekistan A nominal republic controlled by former communists, Uzbekistan has an economy that remains preindustrial, with emphases on agriculture and on oil production and gold mining, which are the major hope for development.

Yugoslavia (Serbia and Montenegro) Deeply torn by wars, Yugoslavia has little chance for political or economic development until peace is achieved. It will require considerable rebuilding from the effects of NATO bombing during the Kosovo conflict of 1999.

Resource Rich (0)

Africa

Developed (1)

South Africa With the transition to multiracial democracy accomplished, South Africa's future will depend on the nature of the political system now that President Nelson Mandela has retired and on its ability to spread the benefits of the economy to underprivileged regions and groups.

Partially Developed (10)

Angola Emerging from a 20-year civil war, Angola has a political system that is not yet democratic. The prospects for economic development are enhanced by large deposits of gold, diamonds, and oil and a large amount of arable land.

Botswana A stable parliamentary republic, Botswana has an economy that remains largely agrarian, but its prospects for economic development are aided by an abundance of mineral wealth, including diamonds and coal.

Cameroon A fairly unstable democracy, Cameroon has an economy that is heavily dependent on petroleum. Therefore, its developmental prospects are heavily tied to oil prices.

Congo Republic A fragile multiparty democracy, the Congo Republic has an economic status and developmental prospects that are closely tied to the investment of oil revenues in diversifying the economy, which appears to be occurring.

Djibouti A nominal republic, Djibouti is a unique case, serving as a free-trade zone and transit point for various states. Its economy is built almost exclusively on the provision of services.

Ivory Coast A country on the boundary of the developable states, Ivory Coast has a relatively stable political system. Its economy is almost entirely dependent on agriculture, principally the production of coffee, cocoa beans, and palm oil.

Mauritius A democracy, Mauritius has maintained its constitution since independence in 1968. Its economy is based on the production of sugar cane, the textile industry, and tourism.

Morocco A constitutional monarchy that allows political parties, Morocco has an economy that depends heavily on the production of food and suffers from a cripplingly high foreign debt.

Nigeria A politically unstable country that has vacillated between democracy and military rule, Nigeria is Africa's most populous state and its leading oil producer. Its future success depends on political stability and productive investment of oil revenues.

Zimbabwe Zimbabwe is a reasonably stable democracy. The basis of its economy is its rich legacy of mineral wealth, notably gold and copper, as well as agriculture.

Developable (37)

Benin Formerly called Dahomey, Benin has been a multiparty democracy since 1989 but remains one of the world's poorest countries. It has few natural resources or other prospects of development.

Burkina Faso A basically one-party state, Burkina Faso has a dense population, few natural resources, infertile soil, and a harsh climate. Its economy also suffers from too much government control.

Burundi Involved in sporadic tribal internal wars, Burundi has an unstable government, and its economy is almost totally dependent on the export of coffee (making up 90 percent of its foreign earnings).

Cape Verde An island state located strategically off the African coast, Cape Verde has a multiparty political system. Its economy combines subsistence agriculture with a sizable service sector (employing 29 percent of the workforce in 1996).

Central African Republic Still in transition from a one-man empire to a multiparty democracy, the Central African Republic has an economy that relies mostly on subsistence agriculture, with a small diamond-mining industry.

Chad An unstable republic scarred by civil war, Chad has an economy almost entirely reliant on subsistence agriculture, with cotton being the major crop. It possesses few natural resources on which to build economic development.

Comoros An island state, Comoros has a highly fragmented government (there are 20 parties in the Federal Assembly). Its economy is mostly subsistence agriculture, which employs 80 percent of the workforce. Comoros is burdened by a high population growth rate and a scarcity of natural resources.

Congo (Democratic Republic of the Congo) A longtime one-man dictatorship now trying to broaden its popular base, Congo (formerly Zaire) has an economy that is a shambles. Mineral reserves and conditions conducive to agriculture are the main hopes for future development.

Equatorial Guinea A republic in transition to multiparty democracy, Equatorial Guinea has an economy concentrated in agriculture, forestry, and fishing, with mineral resources providing some basis for further development.

Eritrea Having gained independence from Ethiopia in 1991 after a long, bitter civil war, Eritrea is extremely poor and politically in transition.

Ethiopia A political system in transition from authoritarian rule, Ethiopia is a desperately poor country. Its economy is mostly subsistence agriculture, with coffee the major cash crop.

The Gambia A multiparty democracy, the Gambia has an economy that consists mainly of agriculture and raising livestock. It had a per capita GDP of about $1,100 in 1996.

Ghana A constitutional democracy, Ghana has an economy based in agriculture (it exports cocoa), gold mining, and forestry. It has made some commitment to privatization in its government-dominated economy.

Guinea A political system in transition from authoritarian rule, Guinea remains poor, with 80 percent of its workforce engaged in agriculture. Its main export is bauxite, of which it contains one-quarter of the world's reserves.

Guinea-Bissau A highly centralized multiparty republic, Guinea-Bissau has an economy among the world's poorest, with 90 percent of the workforce engaged in agriculture.

Kenya A republic in transition, Kenya remains quite poor, with most of the population engaged in agriculture and most exports being agricultural products such as coffee and tea.

Lesotho A constitutional monarchy, Lesotho has an economy based in subsistence agriculture (employing 86 percent of the workforce in 1996), with many workers traveling to South Africa for employment.

Liberia A country beset by internal war that has all but destroyed the economy, Liberia has abundant mineral and other resources for exploitation should civil order return.

Madagascar A multiparty republic, Madagascar has an economy that is one of the world's poorest. Over 90 percent of the workforce is engaged in subsistence agriculture.

Malawi A longtime one-party republic in transition, Malawi has an economy that is among the world's weakest, with most of the workforce and production in agriculture.

Mali A multiparty republic, Mali is another of the world's poorest countries. Eighty percent of its workforce is engaged in agriculture and fishing, and its little arable land is subject to desertification.

Mauritania Mauritania is a reasonably stable political democracy. Its economy is heavily dependent on the extraction of iron ore, a commodity whose value fluctuates widely in international markets.

Mozambique A country recovering from a tribally based civil war, Mozambique is another of the world's poorest countries. It has failed to exploit its considerable agricultural, hydroelectric, and transportation resources, all necessary for economic development.

Namibia An emerging political democracy, Namibia has an economy heavily dependent on mineral extraction (which makes up 25 percent of gross domestic product), while half the population is employed in mostly subsistence agriculture.

Niger Niger is a country in transition toward a representative political system. The economy is tied heavily to agriculture, with some mining (mostly of uranium).

Rwanda Even before its tragic civil war, Rwanda had a highly unstable political system. Its economy was dependent on agriculture and mining and is now virtually nonexistent.

São Tomé and Príncipe A reasonably stable political democracy, São Tomé and Príncipe has an economy that suffers from overdependence on cocoa production, a market that has declined.

Senegal A republic under multiparty rule, Senegal has a reasonably diverse economy, with activity in agriculture, fishing, mining, and tourism, providing some hope for further development.

Seychelles The island republic Seychelles is a reasonably stable political democracy. Its economy is largely dependent on tourism, giving it a large service sector. Its government is encouraging the development of a larger agricultural sector.

Sierra Leone With an already unstable political system, Sierra Leone is enduring a criminal insurgency. Its economy is heavily dependent on agriculture but has been disrupted by insurgent violence. Until the insurgency is overcome, its prospects are bleak.

Somalia Beset by a clan-based civil war, Somalia has been left in near anarchy since 1991 and has one of the world's poorest economies.

Sudan A military dictatorship fighting a bloody civil war, Sudan has an economic system that is based largely on agriculture. The country suffers from one of the world's most crushing debt-service burdens.

Swaziland A traditional monarchy, Swaziland is making the transition to a more representative form of government. Its economy is almost totally dependent on agriculture and food processing, with few prospects for diversification.

Tanzania A multiparty republic, Tanzania has an economy highly dependent on agriculture. Increased exploitation of minerals (especially gold) offers some hope for development.

Togo A republic making a transition from one-party rule to a multiparty system, Togo remains one of the poorer countries of Africa. Almost four-fifths of the population is engaged in subsistence agriculture, and the country exports mainly agricultural goods, along with some phosphate.

Uganda A one-party political system, Uganda has been destabilized by political strife. Its economy has some promise based in fertile soil, dependable rainfall, and minerals (notably copper and cobalt).

Zambia A reasonably stable republic, Zambia has suffered an economic decline for more than a decade due to drops in the price of copper, its primary export.

Resource Rich (4)

Algeria Since nullifying 1994 elections that had been won by a fundamentalist Islamic movement, Algeria's secular government has virtually been at war with fundamentalist insurgents. The economy is highly dependent on the production of oil.

Gabon Gabon, which has an emerging multiparty presidential regime, is one of Africa's wealthiest countries. Its economy is dependent on oil production, with some residual activity in the export of timber and manganese.

Libya Libya remains an authoritarian military republic. The high quality (low sulphur content) of its petroleum makes it one of the primary oil exporters in the world, despite western economic sanctions against it.

Tunisia A fairly stable democratic country, Tunisia is under some pressure from Islamic fundamentalists. Its economy depends mainly on petroleum, with light manufactures, tourism, and phosphate production adding to its economic base.

Source: Most of the basic information used in classification came from *The World Almanac and Book of Facts, 1999* (Mahwah, NJ: World Almanac Books, 1998).

GLOSSARY
Key Concepts

This glossary identifies and defines the key concepts listed at the beginning of each chapter. At the end of each definition, the number of the first chapter in which the term is identified as a key concept is given in parentheses.

absolute sovereignty the idea that a state's authority over internal affairs is complete and inviolable (14)

ambassador a country's senior representative to the foreign country to which he or she is accredited (12)

Amnesty International a nongovernmental organization that monitors human rights violations worldwide (10)

anarchy the absence of government (1)

ancien régime literally, "the old regime"; a term used to refer to the political and social system of Europe prior to the French Revolution (3)

apoliticism lack of political interest or loyalty (3)

arbitration a method of resolving international conflicts in which the opposing parties agree to accept as binding a solution determined by a third party (12)

arms control action to prevent the acquisition of a military capability by countries that do not possess it, or to curb such capabilities (11)

arms freeze an international agreement to limit stockpiles of a particular category of weapons to the level existing at some specified time (11)

arms reduction an international agreement to reduce existing stockpiles of a particular category of weapons (11)

Asia-Pacific Economic Cooperation (APEC) an economic association of 18 states in East Asia and the Western Hemisphere (9)

Association of Southeast Asian Nations (ASEAN) an economic and political association of nine Southeast Asian states (8)

Astoria affair a 1938 diplomatic incident involving President Franklin Roosevelt's offer to return the body of the Japanese ambassador to the United States to Japan on the American naval vessel *Astoria*. The offer was misinterpreted by Japan as a signal of U.S. willingness to accept Japanese expansionism in East Asia. (12)

asymmetry of objectives a situation in which one or both sides in a conflict are fighting a total war, but an intervening outsider has limited purposes and is willing to use only limited means (5). See also limited purposes of war and limited means in war.

• **balance of power** the relative distribution of power among the members of the international system (2)

Bangkok Declaration a statement signed by 40 Asian governments in 1993 asserting that standards for human rights are not universal but determined by regional, cultural, and other factors (10)

bargaining diplomatic negotiation by states to try to settle their disputes peacefully (12)

better state of the peace a pattern of relationships following a war that represents an improvement over prewar conditions for all or some members of the international system (5)

• **bipolar system** a balance-of-power configuration in which two states are so clearly more powerful than any others that they become the organizational axes of the international system (2)

Bretton Woods system the set of agreements and institutions devised at a conference in Bretton Woods, New Hampshire, to restructure the international economic system after World War II; includes the International Monetary Fund, the World Bank, and the General Agreement on Tariffs and Trade (9)

Camp David Summit the 1978 meeting between President Jimmy Carter of the United States, President Anwar Sadat of Egypt, and Prime Minister Menachem Begin of Israel. Held at the presidential retreat at Camp David, Maryland, it produced the Camp David accords, which led to the 1979 Israeli-Egyptian peace treaty (12)

civil (internal) war violent conflict between groups within a state for the purpose of retaining or gaining political control of the state (5)

"clash of civilizations" thesis the idea put forward by Samuel P. Huntington that future international conflict will stem from cultural differences among the world's major civilizations (14)

classical diplomacy the sets of diplomatic rules, traditions, and ranks of personnel begun in seventeenth-century Italy and formalized at the Congresses of Vienna and Aix-la-Chapelle (12)

classical liberalism the body of political belief advocating individual rights, equality, limited government, and free enterprise (7)

cognitive dissonance psychological conflict between existing beliefs and new information (4)

Cold Warriors policymakers and analysts whose view of international relations was shaped by the Cold War, often to the extent that they can view reality only in that context (6)

collective defense a situation in which a number of states with similar interests band together to defend one another in the event of an attack against one or all of them (3)

collective security a situation in which all or the overwhelming majority of the major powers agree that peace is their principal value and that they will enforce that peace on those who would breach it (3)

colonialism the establishment of European political control outside Europe, especially in much of Asia and Africa during the nineteenth century (3)

Commonwealth of Independent States a loose confederation, dominated by Russia, of 12 (of the 15 total) successor states to the Soviet Union (6)

Concert of Europe an informal series of international conferences, created at the Congress of Vienna in 1815, that sought to regulate the war and peace system in Europe during the nineteenth century (3)

context the setting in which change from one international system to another occurs (3)

Convention on the Prevention and Punishment of the Crime of Genocide a document ratified by the UN General Assembly in 1948 declaring that acts of genocide are international crimes (10)

critical events the important occurrences that cause basic change in the operation of the international system (3)

Cuban missile crisis the 1962 confrontation between the United States and the Soviet Union over emplacement of Soviet nuclear missile launchers in Cuba (6)

cultural factors customary beliefs, social forms, and the like which sometimes lead to misperceptions which in turn hamper the ability of policymakers to develop appropriate and national policies to deal with other peoples (4)

custom a source of international law derived from common practices and habits that have taken on an obligatory aspect (13)

Dayton Peace Accords the agreements reached in December 1995 ending the war in Bosnia (12)

debt service the amount of money that a country must pay to public and private foreign lenders in interest on previous loans (8)

democratization the process of the establishment of political democracy in places where it did not previously exist (3)

Deputies Committee a working group within the U.S. National Security Council, made up of relatively senior officials (4)

deregulation the removal of governmental restrictions on economic activity (9)

developmental assistance the provision of economic and human resources to Second Tier countries (8)

diplomacy the people, institutions, and processes used by states to conduct their political relations with one another (12)

disarmament an international agreement to eliminate a particular category of armaments (11)

distribution of power the way in which power is shared among the major states in a given international system (3)

do-something syndrome the tendency when faced with shocking situations to try to rectify them (11)

domestic change agents political, economic, and social factors within states that cause change within the international system (3)

Earth Summit the name given to the international environmental meeting held in 1992 in Rio de Janeiro (10)

economic competitiveness the extent to which a country's goods and services compete successfully in international markets (9)

economic globalization the merging of national economies into a single worldwide economy (14)

economic internationalization growth in interdependence, caused largely by interpenetration of multinational corporations by firms from other countries (9)

economic intertwining the intermingling of private economic concerns across national boundaries (as in the 1970s and 1980s with the rise of multinational corporations), producing a more global economy in which political boundaries become less important or relevant (9)

enforcement the ability to carry out legal judgments (13)

equality of power a condition in which all major members of the international system have relatively equal power and see that condition as desirable; it is one of the requirements for collective security (3)

era of stagnation the Soviet term for the period between the early 1970s and middle 1980s when growth ceased to occur in the Soviet economy (6)

escalation the widening or intensification of a conflict, such as a conventional war into a nuclear war (6)

ethnic cleansing the practice of using force to remove ethnic minorities from a territory or state (12)

European Coal and Steel Community the limited form of common market in coal and steel production agreed to in 1951 by Italy, France, West Germany, Belgium, the Netherlands, and Luxembourg (7)

European Commission the executive and administrative organ of the European Union (7)

European Union (EU) the association of European countries created by the Treaty of Rome in 1957 and previously known as the European Economic Community and the European Community; its current membership is 15 states (7)

failed state a state that over time has consistently shown an inability to engage in effective self-governance (2)

false analogy an attempt to reach a decision by comparing a situation to a past event that is inappropriate for the purpose (4)

feminism an approach to studying international relations which emphasizes the roles of women or the supposed differences that gender makes in understanding and describing international phenomena (5)

first industrial revolution the transition of an economy from a preindustrial state (characterized by subsistence agriculture, extraction, and cottage industry) to the beginnings of industrialization (characterized by heavy industry and the manufacture of basic consumer goods) (8)

First Tier the roughly 25 states of the world that are stable democracies and have wealthy, technologically advanced, market-based economies (1)

First World the Cold War–era designation of the First Tier (8)

flexibility of alliance a condition in which every major member of the international system is willing and able to align with any other member in the event of a threat to or breach of the peace; it is one of the requirements for collective security (3)

foreign policy the individual interactions between governments of states (1)

Four Modernizations Deng Xiaoping's campaign to reform China through scientific and technological advancement, greater industrialization, improved agricultural productivity, and military modernization (7)

Four Tigers the four Asian areas with the most rapidly developing economies: Hong Kong, South Korea, Singapore, and Taiwan (8)

Fourth World the Cold War–era designation of the poorest countries of the developing world (8)

frustration-aggression hypothesis the idea that whenever aggression occurs, frustration must have been present (5)

functionalism a theory, proposed by David Mitrany, to transfer popular loyalty from states to international organizations by giving the organizations the power to furnish the same kinds of services as those provided by national governments (13)

game theory an approach to analyzing the relationship between two competing parties in a particular situation by assigning various values to the different possible outcomes (5)

General Agreement on Tariffs and Trade (GATT) the organization under the Bretton Woods system to promote free trade and to monitor compliance with trade agreements; superceded by the World Trade Organization (WTO) (9)

General Assembly the legislative and debating forum of the United Nations; all members have a single and equal vote (13)

general principles of law one of the sources of international law, based in common principles within bodies of law administered in the courts of most or all states (13)

glasnost a Russian word meaning openness or criticism; one element of Mikhail Gorbachev's reform program (6)

global economy the description of the evolution of an essentially single economy encompassing countries of the First Tier (9)

global television the television networks of CNN and ITN, which collect and broadcast news programs worldwide (2)

global warming the gradual increase in global temperatures as a result of the greenhouse effect (10)

good offices a method of diplomacy in which a third party keeps channels of communication open between disputing parties without taking a direct role in the negotiations (12)

Greater East Asian Co-Prosperity Sphere the name given by Japan to its empire before and during World War II (7)

greenhouse effect the trapping of solar radiation and other heat sources inside the earth's atmosphere (10)

Group of Seven; Group of Eight (G-7, G-8) the association of the seven largest industrial democracies (the United States, Canada, Japan, Great Britain, France, Germany, and Italy), whose leaders meet at least annually to discuss economic matters; when Russia is included, the group is referred to as G-8 (7)

Group of 77 (G-77) the association of developing states, originally numbering 77, whose purpose is promoting developmental assistance (8)

groupthink the tendency for people to be subtly influenced into going along with the prevailing beliefs and behaviors of the people around them, at the expense of individuality (4)

hard currency a currency universally acceptable for payments in international trade (9)

Helsinki Accords a 1975 agreement that guaranteed human rights in signatory states, including Eastern and Western Europe, the Soviet Union, and North America; it also established as permanent the territorial boundaries of Eastern Europe and the Soviet Union resulting from World War II (13)

high-technology revolution the processes and products associated with the revolution in knowledge generation (computing) and knowledge dissemination (telecommunications) (6)

hue and cry the method of recruiting collective-security forces that was used by the League of Nations, which consisted of passing resolutions and calling for volunteers to enforce those resolutions (3)

humanitarian relief operations international efforts to alleviate suffering caused by war or natural disaster (13)

humanitarian vital interests the idea that rights of individuals and groups take precedence over the sovereign rights of states (14)

*   **idealism** an approach to studying international relations which emphasizes the use of research to improve the international system (1)

    ideology an integrated set of political, social, and economic beliefs (4)

    industrial policy a systematic policy of governmental intervention in the economy to promote certain priorities (9)

    industrial revolutions the basic reorientations in the production system on which an economy was based (8)

    infrastructure the basic developmental building blocks of a country, including human attributes such as education and physical attributes such as transportation facilities and sources of power generation (8)

*   **instruments of power** the means a state has available to gain compliance from other states; they include the political/diplomatic, economic, and military instruments (2)

    insurgency an effort by a political group to overthrow and replace a government by employing unconventional military strategies and tactics (5)

    interdependence the mutual dependence of national economies on one another (9)

*   **intergovernmental organizations (IGOs)** international organizations whose members are states; a form of supranational actor (2)

*   **intermestic policy** issues and events that are simultaneously international and domestic (1)

    internal war war within states, normally for control of the political system; also called civil war (11)

    international change agents changes in the relations among major members of the international system that create changes in how the system operates (3)

    international custom common practices and habits that have become widely expected or even obligatory on a worldwide level (13)

    international law a body of rules and principles that guides the relations among states and between governments and foreign nationals (13)

    International Monetary Fund (IMF) the institution created under the Bretton Woods system to stabilize currencies and to promote trade (9)

    international political economy an approach to studying international relations that emphasizes the strong and reciprocal relationship between international politics and economics (9)

*   **international relations** the relations among states (1)

    international security the safety or stability of the international system as a whole (11)

    internationalism active participation in international relations, or a position supporting such participation (5)

*   **irredentism** a situation in which a national group is divided by a state boundary or boundaries and a movement arises to unite the group (2)

    isolationism the desire or practice of remaining aloof from world affairs, historically a prominent strand in American foreign policy (7)

judicial decisions and teachings a source of international law based on the influence of writings and teachings by jurists on one another (13)

just war circumstances in which states are said to have the right or obligation to go to war (13)

law a rule (or set of rules) of conduct prescribed by or accepted by the governing authority of a state and enforced by courts (13)

legitimacy the extent to which a population submits to the rule of law and regards the political system as correct or proper (8)

lethality index a measure of the efficiency of killing and destroying in war (5)

limited means in war the mobilization of less than all societal capabilities in the conduct of war (3)

limited purposes of war a desired political outcome of war that does not require the overthrow of the adversary's government (3)

Limited Test Ban Treaty an arms control agreement signed in 1963 that prohibits the testing of nuclear weapons in the atmosphere (11)

Maastricht Treaty the 1991 agreement further integrating the European Union, which calls for a single European currency and central bank, as well as single EU foreign and domestic policies (7)

Marshall Plan the American program proposed by Secretary of State George C. Marshall in 1948 to provide economic assistance in the reconstruction of Europe (7)

mediation a method of third-party intervention in disputes that includes nonbinding suggestions (12)

Mercosur an economic association of South American countries founded in 1995 to promote free trade among its members

Missile Technology Control Regime the informal agreement begun by the Group of 7 countries to halt the spread of ballistic missiles to the Second Tier (11)

modern diplomacy the results of the alteration of diplomatic practice in response to Woodrow Wilson's call for more openness in diplomacy (12)

Montreal Treaty an agreement negotiated in 1987 that commits signatories to phase out their use of chlorofluorocarbons by the year 2000 (10)

mood theory the idea that American foreign policy historically tends to swing between isolationism and internationalism on the basis of shifts in national mood (7)

multinational corporations (MNCs) private corporations doing business in a number of countries (2)

multinationalism a situation in which more than one national group inhabits a single state (2)

multipolar system a balance-of-power configuration in which more than two states have significant power (2)

N+1 problem the formulation where N represents the number of states possessing nuclear weapons and +1 represents the problems posed by the addition of one more nuclear state (11)

nation an anthropological and psychological term referring to a group of people who feel a common identity and loyalty (2)

national interest the identifiable collective interests held by a state (4)

national security the safety of the state; the traditional basic concern of a state-centric international system (11)

national self-determination the asserted right of national groups to form their own political communities (3)

nationalism the feeling of belonging to a nation or state (2)

nation-state a term sometimes used synonymously with state or country (1)

NBC weapons nuclear, biological, and chemical weapons, collectively referred to as weapons of mass destruction (11)

necessary peace the stabilization in military competition between the United States and the Soviet Union because of the mutual fear of nuclear war (3)

neoisolationism the idea that with the Cold War over, the United States should minimize the extent of its involvement in international relations (5)

New International Economic Order the demand for a large-scale transfer of funds from the First Tier to the Second for developmental purposes (8)

nomenklatura the class of managers of the state-owned production system in the Soviet Union, which owed its position and loyalty to the Communist Party (6)

nongovernmental organizations (NGOs) international organizations with no governmental affiliation, whose memberships consist of individuals or groups from more than one state (2)

nonstate actors entities other than states which are active in international relations, including supranational and subnational actors (2)

North American Free Trade Agreement (NAFTA) the 1993 agreement between the United States, Canada, and Mexico to eliminate all restrictions on trade among them over a 15-year period (9)

North Atlantic Treaty Organization (NATO) the military alliance between the United States, Canada, and European states, currently with 19 members (6)

northern states of Eastern Europe the more prosperous formerly communist states of the region, including East Germany, Slovenia, Croatia, Poland, the Czech Republic, Hungary, and Slovakia (6)

nuclear allergy a repugnance people feel toward nuclear weapons, making it difficult to think dispassionately about them (5)

Nuclear Nonproliferation Treaty the international agreement negotiated in 1968 to halt the spread of nuclear weapons to states that do not possess them and to work toward nuclear disarmament (11)

Operation Restore Hope the code name for the American military operation in Somalia in the early 1990s (4)

Organization of African Unity the association of African states which deals with continental problems, headquartered in Addis Ababa, Ethiopia (4)

Partnership for Peace (PfP) the informal arrangement for loosely associating Soviet successor states and formerly communist states of Eastern Europe with NATO (6)

peace enforcement (imposition) actions taken to establish peace among warring parties or to reestablish a breached peace (13)

peacekeeping actions, normally sanctioned by the United Nations, to maintain a peace that has been established (13)

peace of Westphalia the agreements ending the Thirty Years War in 1648, generally regarded as the beginning of the modern state system (3)

perestroika a Russian term meaning restructuring, the second prong of Mikhail Gorbachev's economic reform program (6)

personality idiosyncrasies the characteristic habits, mannerisms, and ways of thinking that are particular to an individual (4)

ping pong diplomacy the term used to describe the method that China used to signal its interest in establishing diplomatic relations with the United States in 1971; it invited an American table tennis team to visit China (12)

policy domain the area in which policy choices are made about what public problems will be addressed and the extent to which they will be addressed, leaving a gap between likely and preferred futures on issue areas (14)

politics the ways in which conflicts of interest over scarce resources are resolved (2)

popular sovereignty the idea that sovereignty resides in individual citizens of a state, who may transfer some of their rights to the state for practical purposes (14)

population explosion an evocative phrase describing the current high rate of global population growth (10)

Potemkin village a false front, or facade; named after the eighteenth-century Russian prince who supposedly had a number of such facades of villages erected to deceive Tsarina Catherine the Great into believing that Russia was more prosperous than it in fact was (6)

power the ability to get someone to do what that individual would not otherwise do (2)

prisoner's dilemma the theoretical game construct involving prisoners in a cell often used to explain arms races (5)

privatization the movement to turn formerly governmental activities over to the private sector (8)

proliferation the acquisition of a military capability by countries that did not previously possess it (11)

realism the approach to studying international relations which emphasizes the role of power and state sovereignty in an anarchic international system (1)

realist paradigm the worldview of the international system beginning with sovereignty and emphasizing power politics (1)

re-Asianization the proposal by some Japanese commentators to organize the workforce and resources of Asia around Japanese strategic objectives (7)

regional conflict a situation of rivalry among neighboring states, usually with a historical basis, that has erupted into violence or may do so in the future (11)

relative deprivation the extent to which people perceive themselves to be disadvantaged in relation to others, and the extent to which they view this situation as unjust (8)

ring of market democracies the term used by U.S. President Bill Clinton to describe First Tier states, all of which share a commitment to market-based economies and political democracy (14)

scarcity the condition in which all claimants to a valued thing cannot simultaneously have as much of it as they want or need (2)

secession the separation of territory from an existing state to create a new state (11)

second industrial revolution the transition of an economy to an emphasis on the production of sophisticated consumer goods and the provision of services (8)

Second Tier countries that lack a stable democracy, a market economy, or industrial development; essentially, the former Second and Third Worlds (1)

Second Tier subtiers the four categories into which Second Tier countries can be divided on the basis of their economic and political development, including developed, partially developed, developable, and resource rich (8)

Second World the Cold War–era designation of the communist (socialist) countries (8)

Secretariat the designated bureaucracy of the United Nations, with the secretary-general as its chief officer (13)

Security Council the executive board of the UN General Assembly, which deals with security matters (13)

selective activism involvement by First Tier states in some but not all Second Tier conflicts, usually to protect vital interests, prevent massive human tragedy, or provide mutual advantage (6)

self-determination the process by which national and other groups attempt to express and actualize their desires to create independent political entities (3)

signaling the process states use to communicate their intentions and their capabilities in conflict situations; signaling can be either explicit or implicit (12)

social contract in the philosophy of Thomas Hobbes and John Locke, an implicit agreement among human beings about how individuals will live together in groups (5)

soft power the term proposed by Joseph S. Nye, Jr. to describe intangible elements of a state's power such as cultural and ideological appeal (7)

southern states of Eastern Europe the less prosperous formerly communist states of the region, including Bulgaria, Romania, Albania, Serbia/Yugoslavia, Bosnia, and Macedonia (6)

sovereignty complete and supreme authority (2)

Special Economic Zones (SEZs) four areas of southeast China designated in 1979 as laboratories for capitalist-style economic reform (7)

specialized agencies the group of semiautonomous organs of the United Nations dealing with specific international policy areas, such as health and agriculture (13)

state the legal and political term referring to internationally recognized control and jurisdiction by a government over a piece of territory and its inhabitants (2)

state actors states in their role as the primary participants in international relations (1)

stateless corporations corporations so internationally mixed in ownership, management, workforce, and production that they cannot be meaningfully identified with any single country (2)

state of nature the metaphor used by some political philosophers, including John Locke and Thomas Hobbes, to describe the situation of human beings before entering society (5)

submerged Lockean consensus the term used by Louis Hartz to characterize the near unanimity of popular support for classic liberal values in the United States and the notable absence of intellectual self-awareness about it (7)

subnational actors individuals and groups within states who participate in international relations (1)

summit diplomacy face-to-face diplomatic meetings between heads of state (12)

supranational actors the governmental or nongovernmental organizations bridging more than one country (1)

superpower the Cold War–era term applied to the United States and the Soviet Union because of their overwhelming military advantage over all other states; in the post–Cold War era, it is often applied to the United States because of its possession of the full range of effective instruments of power (3)

sustainable development economic development of Second Tier countries in ways that protect the environment (10)

system a number of distinct, independent units that have orderly and predictable interactions and exist within a broader, dynamic environment (1)

terrorism the commission of criminal acts against a target population to frighten that population into acceptance of the terrorists' political demands (5)

third industrial revolution the transition of an economy from the second phase of industrialization (characterized by sophisticated consumer goods and services) to the third phase (characterized by information, technology, and new products and processes) (2)

Third World the Cold War–era designation of the developing countries of Latin America and the Carribbean, Asia, and Africa (8)

total means in war the mobilization of all societal capabilities in the conduct of war (3)

total purposes of war a desired political outcome of war that requires the overthrow of the adversary's government (3)

transnational issues the problems which transcend state boundaries in ways over which states have little control and which cannot be solved by individual state actions alone (1)

treaties the legally binding agreements between states that are a source of international law (13)

Truman Doctrine the policy basis for providing aid to Greece and Turkey, later extended for assistance to other states battling communism (7)

unipolar system a balance-of-power configuration in which one state or empire so dominates the international system that no other political entity rivals it (2)

United Nations system the United Nations and the agencies (IGOs) associated with it (6)

Universal Declaration of Human Rights the document ratified in 1948 by the UN General Assembly asserting political and quality-of-life rights for all people (10)

values the established ideals and ways of life shared by a group (13)

vital national interests conditions considered so important to a state that it will not voluntarily compromise them (2)

war and peace system the ways the international system organizes to control systemic violence (3)

war crimes violations of conventions regulating the conduct of war, including actions against civilians (13)

Warsaw Pact the military alliance between the Soviet Union and six communist countries in Eastern Europe signed in 1956 and dissolved in 1991; also called the Warsaw Treaty Organization (6)

weapons states small, aggressive states armed with weapons of mass destruction and possessing the means to deliver them (11)

Western European Union (WEU) an association of nine Western European states to deal with European security matters (6)

World Bank the institution set up under the Bretton Woods system, designed to make loans for European reconstruction after World War II and, later, for Third World development; formally, the International Bank for Reconstruction and Development (9)

World Court (International Court of Justice) the judicial body within the United Nations system, located in the Hague, Netherlands,which tries cases under international law (13)

World Trade Organization an international organization to promote free trade, approved in 1993 as part of the Uruguay round of GATT; it is the successor of GATT (9)

Yoshida Doctrine Japan's single-minded post–World War II drive for domestic economic development (7)

SELECTED BIBLIOGRAPHY

This selected bibliography contains books and articles for expanded or future reference. It does not pretend to cover all details of either the theoretical or the substantive literature in the field. Rather, it attempts to provide a selection for the student seeking a broader exposure to the field or, for example, conducting research on a paper for this course. Its length and inclusiveness were determined by the dual criteria of including as many important works as possible but not making the list so formidable as to discourage students from trying to use it. The bibliography contains several kinds of entries. Some (generally those with older copyright dates) are important, even landmark books in the theoretical literature of international relations. Other entries are articles and books describing the contemporary world, including many of the works written during the transition from the Cold War to the contemporary world. Still others deal with specific contemporary concerns, such as feminism or interdependence. Hopefully, the entries as a whole provide a helpful sampler from which to begin your study.

Abshire, David. "Strategic Challenge: Force Structures, Deterrence." *Washington Quarterly* 15, 2 (spring 1992): 33–42.

Aganbegyan, Abel. *The Economic Challenge of Perestroika.* Bloomington: Indiana University Press, 1988.

_____. The Economics of Perestroika. *International Affairs* (London) 64, 2, (spring 1988): 177–185.

Akaha, Tsuneo, and Frank Langdon, eds. *Japan in the Posthegemonic World.* Boulder, CO: Lynne Reinner, 1993.

Akhromeyev, Sergei. "The Doctrine of Avoiding War and Defending Peace." *World Marxist Review* 30, 12 (December 1987): 37–47.

Allison, Graham T., Jr. *Essence of Decision: Explaining the Cuban Missile Crisis.* Boston: Little, Brown, 1971.

_____. "Testing Gorbachev." *Foreign Affairs* 67, 1 (fall 1988): 18–32.

Allison, Graham T., Jr., and Robert Blackwill. "America's Stake in the Soviet Future." *Foreign Affairs* 70, 3 (summer 1991): 77–97.

Allison, Graham T., Jr., and Gregory F. Treverton, eds. *Rethinking America's Security: Beyond Cold War to New World Order.* New York: W. W. Norton, 1992.

Alperowitz, Gar. *Atomic Diplomacy: Hiroshima and Potsdam.* New York: Penguin, 1985.

Alperowitz, Gar, and Kai Bird. "The Centrality of the Bomb." *Foreign Policy* 94 (spring 1994): 3–20.

Ambrose, Stephen. *Rise to Globalism,* 4th ed. New York: Penguin, 1985.

Altschiller, Donald. *The United Nations Role in World Affairs.* New York: H. H. Wilson, 1993.

Apter, David. *Rethinking Development: Modernization, Dependence and Postmodern Politics.* Beverly Hills, CA: Sage, 1987.

Arbatov, Alexei. *Lethal Frontiers: A Soviet View of Nuclear Strategy, Weapons, and Negotiations.* New York: Praeger, 1988.

Ardrey, Robert. *The Territorial Imperative: A Personal Inquiry into the Animal Origins of Property and Nations.* New York: Dell, 1968.

Arno, Andrew, and Winral Dissayanake. *The News Media in National and International Conflict.* Boulder, CO: Westview Press, 1984.

Aron, Leon. "The Soviet Union on the Brink: An Introductory Essay." *World Affairs* 152, 1 (summer 1989): 3–7.

Asmus, Ronald D., Richard L. Kugler, and F. Stephen Larrabee. "Building a New NATO." *Foreign Affairs* 82, 4 (September/October 1993): 28–40.

Attali, Jacques. "The Case of Western Civilization. The Limits of the Market and Democracy." *Foreign Policy* 107 (summer 1997): 54–64.

———. "Lines on the Horizon: A New Order in the Making." *New Perspectives Quarterly* 7, 2 (spring 1990): 4–11.

Bandow, Doug. "Avoiding War." *Foreign Policy* 89 (winter 1992/93): 156–74.

Bani-Sadr, Abolhassan. "Azerbaijan: The Muslims Revolt Against Moscow." *New Perspectives Quarterly* 7, 2 (spring 1990): 29-30.

Barnaby, Frank, and Marlies ter Borg, eds. *Emerging Technologies and Military Doctrine: A Political Assessment.* London: Macmillan, 1986.

Barnet, Richard J. "The Disorders of Peace." *New Yorker,* January 20, 1992: 62–74.

———. "Reflections (the Age of Globalization)." *New Yorker,* June 16, 1990: 46–60.

Bartson, R. P. *Modern Diplomacy.* New York: Longmans, 1988.

Battle, John. "In Search of Gorbachev's Revolution from Below." *International Perspectives* 18, 3 (May/June 1990): 7–10.

Beard, Charles A. *The Idea of National Interest.* Chicago: University of Chicago Press, 1962.

Becker, Abraham S. *Gorbachev's Program for Economic Modernization and Reform: Some Important Political-Military Implications.* Santa Monica, CA: RAND Library Collection P-7384, September 1987.

Bell, Daniel. "The World and the United States in 2013." *Daedalus* 116, 3 (summer 1987): 1–31.

Bell-Fialkoff, Andrew. "A Brief History of Ethnic Cleansing." *Foreign Affairs* 72, 3, (summer 1993): 110–21.

Benjamin, Gerald, ed. *The Communications Revolution in Politics. Proceedings of the Academy of Political Science* 34, no. 4. New York: Academy of Political Science, 1982.

Bergsten, Fred. "APEC and World Trade." *Foreign Affairs* 73, 3 (May/June 1994): 20–26.

———. "The World Economy After the Cold War." *Foreign Affairs* 69, 3 (summer 1990): 96–112.

Bertram, Christoph. "The German Question." *Foreign Affairs* 69, 2 (spring 1990): 45–62.

Betts, Richard. "The New Threat of Mass Destruction." *Foreign Affairs* 77, 1 (January/February 1998): 26–41.

Bhagwati, Jagdish, ed. *The New International Economic Order: The North-South Debate.* Cambridge, MA: MIT Press, 1977.

———. *The World Trading System at Risk.* Princeton, NJ: Princeton University Press, 1991.

Bialer, Seweryn. "Gorbachev's Program of Change: Sources, Significance, Prospects." *Political Science Quarterly* 103, 3 (fall, 1988): 403–60.

———. "New Thinking and Soviet Foreign Policy." *Survival* 30, 4 (July/August 1988): 291–309.

———. "The Passing of the Soviet Order?" *Survival* 32, 2 (March/April 1990): 107–20.

Bialer, Seweryn, and Michael Mandelbaum, eds. *Gorbachev's Russia and American Foreign Policy.* Boulder, CO: Westview Press, 1988.

Birdsall, Nancy. "Life Is Unfair: Inequality in the World." *Foreign Policy* 111 (summer 1998): 76–94.

Bissell, Richard E. "Who Killed the Third World?" *Washington Quarterly* 13, 3 (fall 1990): 23–32.

Blaker, Michael. *Japanese International Negotiating Style.* New York: Columbia University Press, 1977.

Blechman, Barry. "The Intervention Dilemma." *Washington Quarterly* 18, 3 (fall 1995): 63–74.

Blodgett, John Q. "The Future of UN Peacekeeping." *Washington Quarterly* 14, 1 (winter 1991): 30–37.

Bloomfield, Lincoln. "The Premature Burial of Global Law and Order: Looking Beyond the Three Cases from Hell." *Washington Quarterly* 17, 3 (summer 1994): 145–62.

Bodin, Jean. *Six Books on the Commonwealth.* Oxford, UK: Basil Blackwell, 1955.

Boniface, Pascal. "The Proliferation of States." *Washington Quarterly* 21, 3 (summer 1998): 111–27.

Borden, William Liscum. *There Will Be No Time: The Revolution in Strategy.* New York: Macmillan, 1946.

Boutros-Ghali, Boutros. *An Agenda for Peace: Preventive Diplomacy, Peacemaking, and Peace-Keeping.* New York: United Nations, 1992.

_____. "Empowering the United Nations." *Foreign Affairs* 72, 5 (winter 1992/93): 89–102.

Bowers, Stephen R. "East Europe: Why the Cheering Stopped." *Journal of Social, Political, and Economic Studies* 15, 1 (spring 1990): 25–42.

Brandon, Harry. "In the Driver's Seat: EC or Germany?" *Brookings Review* 8, 2 (spring 1990): 28–31.

Brandt, Willy. "Will a United Europe Tip Left?" *New Perspectives Quarterly* 7, 2 (spring 1990): 16–18.

Breckenridge, Scott D. *The CIA and the U.S. Intelligence System.* Boulder, CO: Westview Press, 1986.

Brement, Marshall. "Reflections on Soviet New Thinking on Security Questions." *Naval War College Review* 42, 4 (autumn 1989): 5–21.

Brenner, Michael J. "Finding America's Place." *Foreign Policy* 79 (summer 1990): 25–43.

Brierly, James L. *The Law of Nations,* 6th ed. Oxford, UK: Oxford University Press, 1963.

Brock, David. "The Theory and Practice of Japan-Bashing." *National Interest* 17 (fall 1989): 29–40.

Brodie, Bernard, ed. *The Absolute Weapon: Atomic Power and World Order.* New York: Harcourt, Brace, 1946.

_____. *Strategy in the Missile Age.* Princeton, NJ: Princeton University Press, 1959.

_____. *War and Politics.* New York: Macmillan, 1973.

Brown, Harold. "Competitiveness, Technology, and U.S.-Japanese Relations." *Washington Quarterly* 13, 3 (summer 1990): 85–96.

_____. *Thinking About National Security: Defense and Foreign Policy in a Dangerous World.* Boulder, CO: Westview Press, 1983.

_____. "The United States and Japan: High Tech Is Foreign Policy." *SAIS Review* 9, 2 (summer/fall 1989): 1–18.

Brown, Lester. *World Without Borders.* New York: Random House, 1972.

Brown, Seyom. *The Faces of Power.* New York: Columbia University Press, 1968.

Brzezinski, Zbigniew. "Beyond Chaos." *National Interest* 19 (spring 1990): 3–12.

_____. "The Cold War and Its Aftermath." *Foreign Affairs* 71, 4 (fall 1992): 31–49.

_____. "Europe and Amerippon: Pillars of the New World Order." *New Perspectives Quarterly* 7, 2 (spring 1990): 18–20.

_____. "A Geostrategy for Eurasia." *Foreign Affairs* 76, 5 (September/October 1997): 50–64.

_____. "The Premature Partnership." *Foreign Affairs* 73, 2 (March/April 1994): 67–82.

Bueno de Mesquita, Bruce. *The War Trap.* New Haven, CT: Yale University Press, 1981.

Bundy, McGeorge, William J. Crowe, Jr., and Sidney Drell. "Reducing Nuclear Danger." *Foreign Affairs* 72, 2 (spring 1993): 140–55.

Burk, James, ed. *The Military in New Times: Adapting Armed Forces to a Turbulent World.* Boulder, CO: Westview Press, 1994.

Burton, Daniel F., Jr. "Competitiveness: Here to Stay." *Washington Quarterly* 17, 4 (autumn 1994): 99–110.

_____. "High-Tech Competitiveness." *Foreign Policy* 92 (fall 1993): 117–32.

Burton, Daniel F., Jr., Victor Gotbaum, and Felix Rohatyn, eds. *Vision for the 1990s: U.S. Strategy and the Global Economy.* Cambridge, MA: Ballinger Books, 1989.

Butson, Thomas G. *Gorbachev: A Bibliography.* New York: Stein and Day, 1986.

Buzan, Barry. *People, States, and Fear: An Agenda for International Security Studies in the Post Cold War Era.* Boulder, CO: Lynne Reinner, 1991.

Caldwell, Dan. *The Dynamics of Domestic Politics and Arms Control.* Columbia, SC: University of South Carolina Press, 1991.

Caldwell, Lynton K. *International Environmental Policy.* Durham, NC: Duke University Press, 1990.

Carlsson, Ingvar. "The U.N. at 50: A Time for Reform." *Foreign Policy* 100 (fall 1995): 3–18.

Carothers, Thomas. "Democracy and Human Rights: Policy Allies or Enemies?" *Washington Quarterly* 17, 3 (summer 1994): 109–17.

_____. "Think Again: Democracy." *Foreign Policy* 107 (summer 1997): 11–18.

Carr, E. H. *The Twenty-Years Crisis, 1919–1939.* London: Macmillan, 1939.

Carroll, John E. *International Environmental Diplomacy.* New York: Cambridge University Press, 1988.

Carus, Seth. *Ballistic Missiles in the Third World.* New York: Praeger, 1990.

Chaffee, Steven H., ed. *Political Communication: Issues and Strategies for Research.* Beverly Hills, CA: Sage, 1975.

Chalmers, Malcolm. "Beyond the Alliance System: The Case for a European Security Organization." *World Policy Journal* 7, 2 (spring 1990): 215–50.

Charters, David A., ed. *Peacekeeping and the Challenge of Civil Conflict Resolution.* Fredericton: Center for Conflict Studies, University of New Brunswick, 1994.

Chufrin, Gennady, and Harold Saunders. "The Politics of Conflict Prevention in Russia and the Near Abroad." *Washington Quarterly* 20, 4 (autumn 1997): 35–54.

Clark, Jeffrey. "Debacle in Somalia." *Foreign Affairs* 72, 1 (winter 1992/93): 109–23.

Clark, Ronald W. *The Greatest Power on Earth: The International Race for Nuclear Supremacy from Earliest Theory to Three Mile Island.* New York: Harper and Row, 1980.

Claude, Inis L., Jr. *The Changing United Nations.* New York: Random House, 1967.

_____. *States and the Global System: Politics, Law, and Organization.* New York: St. Martin's Press, 1988.

_____. *Swords into Plowshares: The Problems and Progress of International Organization,* 4th ed. New York: Random House, 1971.

Clausewitz, Carl von. *On War.* Princeton, NJ: Princeton University Press, 1976.

Cline, William R. *The Economics of Global Warming.* Washington, DC: Institute of International Economics, 1992.

Cohen, Raymond. *Theatre of Power: The Art of Diplomatic Signalling.* New York: Longmans, 1987.

Cohen, Roberta, and Francis M. Deng. "Exodus Within Borders." *Foreign Affairs* 77, 4 (July/August 1998): 12–17.

Cooper, Richard N. "Toward a Real Global Warming Treaty." *Foreign Affairs* 77, 2 (March/April 1998): 66–79.

Corterier, Peter. "Quo Vadis NATO?" *Survival* 32, 2 (March/April 1990): 141–56.

Coser, Lewis. *The Functions of Social Conflict.* London: Routledge and Kegan Paul, 1956.

Crocker, Chester. "The Lessons of Somalia." *Foreign Affairs* 74, 3 (May/June 1995): 2–8.

Crozier, Brian. "Was It Wrong to Be Right?" *Encounter* 75, 1 (July/August 1990): 6–8.

Cullen, Robert. "Human Rights Quandary." *Foreign Affairs* 72, 5 (winter 1992/93): 79–88.

Curtis, Gerald L., ed. *Japan's Foreign Policy After the Cold War.* Armonk, NY: M. F. Sharpe, 1993.

David, Steven R. "Saving America from the Coming Civil Wars." *Foreign Affairs* 78, 1 (January/February 1999): 103–116.

Davison, W. Phillips. *Communications and Conflict Resolution: The Role of the Information Media in the Advancement of International Understanding.* New York: Praeger, 1974.

Deibel, Terry. "Internal Affairs and International Relations in the Post Cold War World." *Washington Quarterly* 16, 3 (summer 1993): 13–36.

De Michelis, Gianni. "From Eurosclerosis to Europhoria." *New Perspectives Quarterly* 7, 2 (spring 1990): 12–14.

Dessouki, Ali E. Hilial. "Globalization and the Two Spheres of Security." *Washington Quarterly* 16, 4 (autumn 1993): 109–17.

Deudney, Daniel, and G. John Ikenberry. "After the Long War." *Foreign Policy* 94 (spring 1994): 21–36.

Deutch, John. "Terrorism." *Foreign Policy* 108 (fall 1997): 10–22.

Deutch, John N. "The New Nuclear Threat." *Foreign Affairs* 71, 4 (fall 1992): 120–34.

Diamond, Larry, and Marc F. Plattner, eds. *The Global Resurgence of Democracy.* Baltimore, MD: Johns Hopkins University Press, 1993.

Diehl, Paul. *International Peacekeeping.* Baltimore, MD: Johns Hopkins University Press, 1993.

Doder, Dasko. "Yugoslavia: New War, Old Hatreds." *Foreign Policy* 91 (summer 1993): 3–23.

Donnelly, Jack. *Universal Human Rights in Theory and Practice.* Ithaca, NY: Cornell University Press, 1989.

Dougherty, James E., and Robert L. Pfaltzgraff Jr. *Contending Theories of International Relations: A Comprehensive Survey,* 3d ed. New York: Harper and Row, 1990.

Drucker, Peter. "The Global Economy and the Nation-State." *Foreign Affairs* 76, 5 (September/October 1997): 159–171.

Durch, William, ed. *The Evolution of UN Peacekeeping: Case Studies and Comparative Analyses.* New York: St. Martin's Press, 1993.

_____. *UN Peacekeeping, American Policy, and the Uncivil Wars of the 1990s.* New York: St. Martin's Press, 1996.

Durch, William, and Barry M. Blechman. *Keeping the Peace: The United Nations in the Emerging World Order.* Washington, DC: Henry L. Stimson Center, 1993.

Eban, Abba. "The U.N. Idea Revisited." *Foreign Affairs* 74, 5 (September/October 1995): 39–55.

Emmerson, Donald K. "Americanizing Asia?" *Foreign Affairs* 77, 3 (May/June 1998): 46–56.

Etzioni, Amatai. "The Evils of Self-Determination." *Foreign Policy* 89 (winter 1992/93): 21–35.

Evangelista, Matthew. *Innovations and the Arms Race: How the United States and the Soviet Union Develop New Military Technologies.* Ithaca, NY: Cornell University Press, 1988.

Falin, Valentin. "The Collapse of Europe: Moscow's View." *New Perspectives Quarterly* 7, 2 (spring 1990): 22–26.

Falk, Richard. *Legal Order in a Violent World.* Princeton, NJ: Princeton University Press, 1968.

Feinberg, Richard E., and Delia M. Boylan. "Modular Multilateralism: North-South Economic Relations in the 1990s." *Washington Quarterly* 15, 1 (winter 1992): 187–99.

Feld, Werner J., and Robert S. Jordan, with Leon Hurwitz. *International Organization: A Comparative Approach,* 2d ed. New York: Praeger, 1988.

Feldstein, Martin. "Reforming the IMF." *Foreign Affairs* 77, 2 (March/April 1998): 20–33.

Ferguson, Charles H. "America's High-Tech Decline." *Foreign Policy* 74 (spring 1989): 123–44.

Festinger, Leon. *A Theory of Cognitive Dissonance.* Stanford, CA: Stanford University Press, 1957.

Finkelstein, Joseph, ed. *Windows on a New World: The Third Industrial Revolution.* Westport, CT: Greenwood Press, 1989.

Florini, Ann. "The End of Secrecy." *Foreign Policy* 111 (summer 1998): 50–63.

Foreign Affairs. *Agenda* 95. New York: Foreign Affairs Press, 1994.

Forester, Tom. *High-Tech Society: The Story of the Information Technology Revolution.* Oxford, UK: Basil Blackwell, 1987.

Frank, Andre Gunder. "Revolution in Eastern Europe: Implications for Democratic Social Movements (and Socialists?)." *Third World Quarterly* 12, 2 (April 1990): 36–52.

Freeman, Lawrence. "International Security: Changing Targets." *Foreign Policy* 110 (spring 1998): 48–63.

Fromkin, David. *The Independence of Nations.* New York: Praeger Special Studies, 1981.

Fukuyama, Francis. "The End of History?" *National Interest* 16 (summer 1989): 3–18.

_____. *The End of History and the Last Man.* New York: Free Press, 1992.

Gaddis, John Lewis. "Coping with Victory." *Atlantic Monthly* 265, 5 (May 1990): 21–38.

_____. *The United States and the End of the Cold War: Implications, Reconsiderations, Provocations.* New York: Oxford University Press, 1992.

Gaddy, Clifford, and Barry W. Ickles. "Russia's Virtual Economy." *Foreign Affairs* 77, 5 (September/October 1998): 53–67.

Garthoff, Raymond L. "The Warsaw Pact Today and Tomorrow?" *Brookings Review* 8, 2 (summer 1990): 35–40.

Gati, Charles. "From Sarajevo to Sarajevo." *Foreign Affairs* 71, 4 (fall 1992): 64–78.

Gentry, John. "Military Force in an Age of National Cowardice." *Washington Quarterly* 21, 4 (Autumn 1998): 179–92.

George, Alexander. *Forceful Persuasion: Coercive Diplomacy as an Alternative to War.* Washington, DC: United States Institute for Peace, 1992.

_____. *Presidential Decisionmaking in Foreign Policy: The Effective Use of Information and Advice.* Boulder, CO: Westview Press, 1980.

George, Alexander, and Juliette George. *Woodrow Wilson and Colonel House: A Personality Study.* New York: Dover Press, 1964.

Geremek, Bronislaw. "Which Way to Europe?" *National Review* 42, 15 (August 6, 1990): 30–32.

Gilpin, Robert. *The Political Economy of International Relations.* Princeton, NJ: Princeton University Press, 1987.

Goldman, Marshall. *Gorbachev's Challenge: Economic Reforms in the Age of High Technology.* New York: W. W. Norton, 1987.

_____. "Gorbachev the Economist." *Foreign Affairs* 69, 2 (spring 1990): 28–44.

Goldstein, Melvyn. "The Dalai Lama's Dilemma." *Foreign Affairs* 77, 1 (January/February 1998): 83–97.

Gorbachev, Mikhail S. *The Coming Century of Peace.* New York: Richardson and Steirman, 1986.

_____. "The International Community and Change: A Common European Home." *Vital Speeches of the Day* 55, 23 (September 15, 1989): 706–11.

_____. *Perestroika: New Thinking for Our Country and the World.* New York: Harper and Row, 1987.

_____. "Our Ideal Is a Humane Democratic Socialism." *Vital Speeches of the Day* 56, 11 (March 15, 1990): 322–27.

Gottlieb, Gidon. *Nation Against State: New Approaches to Ethnic Conflicts and the Decline of Sovereignty.* New York: Council on Foreign Relations Press, 1993.

Grant, Rebecca, and Kathleen Newland, eds. *Gender and International Relations.* Bloomington: Indiana University Press, 1991.

Grieves, Forrest L. *Conflict and Order.* Boston: Houghton Mifflin, 1977.

Grotius, Hugo. *The Rights of War and Peace: Including the Law of Nature and Nations.* New York: M. W. Dunne, 1981.

Gunlicks, Arthur B, and John D. Treadway, eds. *The Soviet Union Under Gorbachev: Assessing the First Year.* New York: Praeger, 1987.

Gurr, Ted Robert, and Barbara Harff. *Ethnic Conflict in World Politics.* Boulder, CO: Westview Press, 1994.

_____. *Minorities at Risk: A Global View of Ethno-political Conflicts.* Washington, DC: United States Institute for Peace Press, 1993.

_____. "Peoples Against States: Ethnopolitical Conflict and the Changing World System." *International Studies Quarterly* 38, 3 (September 1994): 347–78.

_____. Why Men Rebel. Princeton, NJ: Princeton University Press.

Haas, Ernst B. *Why We Shall Still Need the United Nations: The Collective Management of International Conflict.* Berkeley, CA: Institute for International Studies, University of California, 1986.

_____. "Military Force: A User's Guide." *Foreign Policy* 96 (fall 1994): 21–36.

Haass, Richard N. *Intervention: The Use of American Military Force in the Post Cold War World.* Washington, D.C.: Carnegie Endowment for International Peace, 1994.

Habeeb, W. M. *Power and Tactics in International Negotiations: How Weak Nations Bargain with Strong Nations.* Baltimore, MD: Johns Hopkins University Press, 1988.

Hale, David D. "The IMF, More Than Ever." *Foreign Affairs* 77, 6 (November/December 1998): 7–13.

Halperin, Morton. "Guaranteeing Democracy." *Foreign Policy* 91 (summer 1992): 105–23.

Harris, Owen. "The Collapse of the West." *Foreign Affairs* 72, 4 (September/October 1993): 41–53.

Hartley, Anthony. "And the Wall Fell Down: Mr. Gorbachev and the New Europe." *Encounter* 74, 1 (January/February 1990): 3–7.

Hartz, Louis. *The Liberal Tradition in America.* New York: Harvest Books, 1955.

Hass, Peter M., Robert O. Keohane, and Marc A. Levy, eds. *Institutions for the Earth.* Cambridge, MA: MIT Press, 1993.

Heisbourg, Francois. "The Future of the Atlantic Alliance." *Washington Quarterly* 15, 2 (spring 1992): 127–40.

Helman, Gerald B., and Steven R. Ratner. "Saving Failed States." *Foreign Policy* 89 (winter 1992/93): 3–20.

Hersh, Seymour. *The Samson Option: Israel's Nuclear Arsenal and American Foreign Policy.* New York: W. W. Norton, 1991.

Herspring, Dale R. "The Soviet Military and Change." *Survival* 31, 4 (July/August 1989): 321–38.

Hewett, Ed A. "Is Soviet Socialism Reformable?" *SAIS Review* 10, 2 (summer/fall 1990): 75–87.

_____. *Reforming the Soviet Economy: Equality vs. Efficiency.* Washington, DC: Brookings Institution, 1988.

Heyns, Terry L. *American and Soviet Relations Since Détente.* Washington, DC: National Defense University Press, 1987.

Heywood, Robert W. *The European Community: Idea and Reality.* San Francisco: EM Text, 1990.

Hirsh, Michael. "The Great Technology Giveaway?" *Foreign Affairs* 77, 5 (September/October 1998): 2–10.

Hitchcock, David. "Internal Problems in East Asia." *Washington Quarterly* 21, 2 (spring 1998): 12–35.

Hobbes, Thomas. *Leviathan.* Oxford, UK: Clarendon Press, 1989.

Hoffmann, Stanley. "What Shall We Do in the World?" *Atlantic Monthly* 264, 4 (October 1989): 84–96.

Holloway, David. "Gorbachev's New Thinking." *Foreign Affairs* 68, 1 (winter 1988/89): 66–81.

Holstein, William J. "The Stateless Corporation." *Business Week,* May 14, 1990: 98–105.

Hormats, Robert D. "The Economic Consequences of the Peace 1989." *Survival* 31, 6 (November/December 1989): 484–99.

_____. "The International Economic Challenge." *Foreign Policy* 71 (summer 1988): 98–116.

Howard, Michael E. *The Causes of War.* Cambridge, MA: Harvard University, Press, 1983.

_____. "The Gorbachev Challenge and the Defence of the West." *Survival* 30, 6 (November/December 1988): 483–92.

Howe, Jonathan T. "The United States and United Nations in Somalia: The Limits of Intervention." *Washington Quarterly* 18, 3 (summer 1995): 49–62.

Hughes, Neil C. "Smashing the Iron Rice Bowl." *Foreign Affairs* 77, 4 (July/August 1998): 67–77.

Huntington, Samuel P. "Clash of Civilizations." *Foreign Affairs* 72, 3 (summer 1993): 22–49.

_____. "Coping with the Lippman Gap." *Foreign Affairs* 66, 3 (winter 1987/88): 453–77.

_____. "The Erosion of American National Interests." *Foreign Affairs* 76, 5 (September/October 1997): 28–49.

_____. "No Exit: The Errors of Endism." *National Interest* 17 (fall 1989): 3–11.

_____. *The Third Wave: Democratization in the Late Twentieth Century.* Norman: University of Oklahoma Press, 1991.

Huntington, Samuel P., et al. *The Clash of Civilizations: The Debate.* New York: Foreign Affairs Press, 1993.

Husbands, J. L. "A Buyers Market for Arms." *Bulletin of the Atomic Scientists* 46, 4 (May 1990): 14–19.

Hyland, William C. "America's New Course." *Foreign Affairs* 69, 2 (spring 1990): 1–12.

_____. "Setting Global Priorities." *Foreign Policy* 73 (winter 1988/89): 22–40.

Ihlevan, Moon. "Letter from Seoul: A Nation on the Edge." *Washington Quarterly* 21, 2 (spring 1998): 99–104.

Ikle, Fred C. *How Nations Negotiate.* New York: Harper and Row, 1964.

Inman, B. R., and Daniel F. Burton Jr. "Technology and Competitiveness: The New Policy Frontier." *Foreign Affairs* 69, 2 (spring 1990): 116–34.

Inoguchi, Takashi. *Japan's International Relations.* London: Pinter Publishers, 1991.

Isaak, Robert A. *International Political Economy: Managing World Economic Change.* Englewood Cliffs, NJ: Prentice-Hall, 1991.

Israelyan, Victor. "Russia at the Crossroads: Don't Tease a Wounded Bear." *Washington Quarterly* 21, 1 (Winter 1998): 47–65.

Jacoby, Henry D. Ronald Prinn, and Richard Schmalensee, "Kyoto's Unfinished Business." *Foreign Affairs* 77, 4 (July/August 1998): 54–66.

Jacobson, Harold K. *Networks of Interdependence: International Organizations and the Global System.* New York: Alfred A. Knopf, 1984.

Jaffe, Josef. "How America Does It." *Foreign Affairs* 76, 5 (September/October 1997): 13–27.

Janis, Irving. *Groupthink: Psychological Studies of Policy Decisions and Fiascoes,* 2d ed. Boston: Houghton Mifflin, 1982.

_____. *Victims of Groupthink.* Boston: Houghton Mifflin, 1972.

Jatar-Hausmann, Ana Julia. "What Cuba Can Teach Russia." *Foreign Policy* 113 (Winter 1998-99): 87–102.

Jervis, Robert. *The Illogic of American Nuclear Strategy.* Ithaca, NY: Cornell University Press, 1984.

_____. *Perception and Misperception in World Politics.* Princeton, NJ: Princeton University Press, 1976.

_____. *The Meaning of the Nuclear Revolution: Statecraft and the Prospects of Armageddon.* Ithaca, NY: Cornell University Press, 1989.

Job, Cvijeto. "Yugoslavia's Ethnic Furies." *Foreign Policy* 92 (fall 1993): 52–74.

Johnson, Chalmers. "Their Behavior, Our Policy." *National Interest* 17 (fall 1989): 17–27.

Kagan, Robert, "The Benevolent Empire." *Foreign Policy* 111 (summer 1998): 24–35.

Kampelman, Max M. "Secession and the Right of Self-Determination: An Urgent Need to Harmonize Principle with Pragmatism." *Washington Quarterly* 16, 3 (summer 1993): 5–12.

Kaplan, Morton A. *System and Process in International Politics.* New York: John Wiley, 1957.

Kaplan, Morton A., and Nicholas Katzenbach. *The Political Foundations of International Law.* New York: John Wiley, 1961.

Kapstein, Ethan B. "America's Arms-Trade Monopoly." *Foreign Affairs* 73, 3 (May/June 1994): 13–19.

Kapur, Devesh. "The IMF: A Cure or a Curse?" *Foreign Policy* 111 (summer 1998): 114–131.

Karaganov, Sergei A. "The Year of Europe: A Soviet View." *Survival* 32, 3 (March/April 1990): 121–28.

Kaufman, William W. "Some Small Changes for Defense." *Brookings Review* 8, 3 (summer 1990): 26–29, 32–33.

Keatley, Ann G., ed. *Technological Frontiers and Foreign Relations.* Washington, DC: National Academy Press, 1985.

Kegley, Charles W., Jr., and Gregory A. Raymond. *A Multipolar Peace? Great Power Politics in the Twenty-First Century.* New York: St. Martin's Press, 1994.

Kegley, Charles W., Jr., and Eugene R. Wittkopf. *World Politics: Trend and Transformation,* 6th ed. New York: St. Martin's Press, 1998.

Kelman, Herbert C., ed. *International Behavior: A Social-Psychological Analysis.* New York: Holt, Rinehart and Winston, 1965.

Kennan, George F. *American Diplomacy, 1900–1950.* New York: New American Library, 1951.

———. *Memoirs.* Boston: Little, Brown, 1976.

———. "The Sources of Soviet Conduct." *Foreign Affairs* 25, 4 (July 1947): 566–82.

Kennedy, Paul. *The Rise and Fall of the Great Powers: Economic Change and Military Change from 1500 to 2000.* New York: Random House, 1987.

Kennedy, Paul, and Bruce Russett. "Reforming the United Nations." *Foreign Affairs* 74, 5 (September/October 1995): 56–71.

Keohane, Robert. "International Institutions: Can Interdependence Work?" *Foreign Policy* 110 (spring 1998): 82–96.

Keohane, Robert O., and Joseph S. Nye Jr. *Power and Interdependence,* 2d ed. Glenview, IL: Scott Foresman/Little, Brown, 1989.

———. "Power and Interdependence in the Information Age." *Foreign Affairs* 77, 5 (September/October 1998): 81–94.

Kissinger, Henry A. "Reflections on Containment." *Foreign Affairs* 73, 3 (May/June 1994): 113–30.

———. *A World Restored.* Boston: Houghton Mifflin, 1973.

———. *Years of Upheaval.* Boston: Little, Brown, 1982.

Klare, Michael T., and Daniel C. Thomas, eds. *World Security: Challenges for a New Century,* 2d ed. New York: St. Martin's Press, 1994.

Klineberg, Otto. *The Human Dimension in International Relations.* New York: Holt, Rinehart, and Winston, 1966.

Knorr, Klaus. *The Power of Nations.* New York: Basic Books, 1975.

Knorr, Klaus, and James N. Rosenau, eds. *Contending Approaches to International Politics.* Princeton, NJ: Princeton University Press, 1969.

Kober, Stanley. "Revolutions Gone Bad." *Foreign Policy* 91 (summer 1993): 63–84.

Koppel, Bruce. "Fixing the Other Asia." *Foreign Affairs* 77, 1 (January/February 1998): 98–110.

Korey, William. *The Promises We Keep: Human Rights, the Helsinki Process and American Foreign Policy.* New York: St. Martin's Press, 1993.

Kobrin, Stephen. "Electronic Cash and the End of National Markets." *Foreign Policy* 107 (summer 1997): 65–77.

———. "The MAI and the Clash of Globalizations." *Foreign Policy* 112 (Fall 1998): 97–109.

Kogut, Bruce. "International Business: The New Bottom Line." *Foreign Policy* 110 (spring 1998): 152–165.

Krasner, Stephen D. *Structural Conflict: The Third World Against Global Liberalism.* Berkeley, CA: University of California Press, 1985.

Krauthammer, Charles. "The Unipolar Moment." *Foreign Affairs* 70, 1 (winter 1990/91): 23–33.

Kremenyuk, Victor A. *International Negotiation: Analysis, Approaches, Issues.* San Francisco: Jossey-Bass, 1991.

Kristoff, Nicholas D., and Sheryl Wudunn. *China Wakes: The Struggle for the Soul of a Rising Power.* New York: Random House, 1994.

Krugman, Paul. "America the Boastful." *Foreign Affairs* 77, 3 (May/June 1998): 32–45.

———. "Competitiveness: A Dangerous Obsession." *Foreign Affairs* 73, 2 (March/April 1994): 28–44.

———. "Is Capitalism Too Productive?" *Foreign Affairs* 76, 5 (September/October 1997): 79–94.

Lall, Arthur S. *Modern International Negotiation: Principles and Practice.* New York: Columbia University Press, 1966.

Lampton, David. "China." *Foreign Policy* 110 (spring 1998): 13–27.

LaPalombara, Joseph. "International Firms and National Governments: Some Dilemmas." *Washington Quarterly* 17, 2 (spring 1994): 89–99.

Laqueur, Walter. *The Long Road to Freedom: Russia and Glasnost.* New York: Charles Scribner's Sons, 1989.

_____. "The New Face of Terrorism." *Washington Quarterly* 21, 4 (autumn 1998): 169–78.

_____. *A World of Spies: The Uses and Limits of Intelligence.* New York: Basic Books, 1985.

Lardy, Nicholas R. "China and the Asian Contagion." *Foreign Affairs* 77, 4 (July/August 1998): 78–89.

Layne, Christopher, and Benjamin Schwartz. "American Hegemony Without an Enemy." *Foreign Policy* 92 (fall 1993): 5–23.

Lefever, Ernest. "Reining in the U.N." *Foreign Affairs* 72, 3 (summer 1993): 17–21.

Legvold, Robert. "The Revolution in Soviet Foreign Policy." *Foreign Affairs* 68, 1 (winter 1988/89): 82–98.

Levite, Ariel. *Intelligence and Strategic Surprise.* New York: Columbia University Press, 1987.

Lewin, Moshe. *The Gorbachev Phenomenon: A Historical Perspective.* Berkeley, CA: University of California Press, 1988.

Light, Margot. *The Soviet Theory of International Relations.* Brighton, UK: Wheatsheaf Books, 1988.

Lim, Linda Y. C. "Whose 'Model' Failed? Implications of the Asian Financial Crisis." *Washington Quarterly* 21, 3 (summer 1998): 25–36.

Lincoln, Edward "Japan's Financial Mess." *Foreign Affairs* 77, 3 (May/June 1998): 57–66.

Linter, Valerio. *The European Community: Economic and Political Aspects.* New York: McGraw-Hill, 1991.

Locke, John. *Two Treatises on Government.* New York: Cambridge University Press, 1988.

Lockhart, Charles. *Bargaining in International Conflict.* New York: Columbia University Press, 1979.

Lodge, Juliet. *The European Community and the Challenge of the Future.* London: Pinter Publishers, 1989.

Lorenz, Konrad. *On Aggression.* New York: Harcourt, Brace and World, 1966.

Luck, Edward C. "Making Peace." *Foreign Policy* 89 (winter 1992/93): 137–55.

Luck, Edward C., and Toby Trister-Gati. "Whose Collective Security?" *Washington Quarterly* 15, 2 (spring 1992): 43–56.

Luttwak, Edward. "From Geopolitics to Geo-Economics: Logic of Conflict, Grammar of Commerce." *National Interest* 20 (summer 1990): 17–24.

_____. "The Shape of Things to Come." *Commentary* 81, 6 (June 1990): 17–25.

_____. "Toward Post Heroic Warfare." *Foreign Affairs* 74, 3 (May/June 1995): 109–122.

_____. "Why We Need an Incoherent Foreign Policy." *Washington Quarterly* 21, 1 (Winter 1998): 21–31.

Lynch, Allen. "Does Gorbachev Matter Anymore?" *Foreign Affairs* 69, 3 (summer 1990): 19–29.

Lyon, David. *The Information Society: Issues and Illusions.* Cambridge, UK: Polity Press, 1988.

Machiavelli, Niccolo. *The Prince.* Irving, TX: University of Dallas Press, 1984.

Mahnken, Thomas G. "America's Next War." *Washington Quarterly* 16, 3 (summer 1993): 171–88.

Malmgren, Harald B. "Technological Challenges to National Economic Policies of the West." *Washington Quarterly* 10, 2 (spring 1987): 21–33.

_____. *Reconstructing the European Security Order.* New York: Council on Foreign Relations, 1990.

_____. "The Reluctance to Intervene." *Foreign Policy* 95 (summer 1994): 3–18.

Mandelbaum, Michael. "Preserving the New Peace." *Foreign Affairs* 74, 3 (May/June 1995): 9–14.

Manning, Robert. "The Nuclear Age: The Next Chapter." *Foreign Policy* 109 (winter 1997/98): 70–84.

Mansfield, Edward, and Jack Snyder. "Democratization and War." *Foreign Affairs* 74, 3 (May/June 1995): 79–98.

Manwaring, Max G., ed. *Uncomfortable Wars: Toward a New Paradigm of Low-Intensity Conflict.* Boulder, CO: Westview Press, 1991.

Mao Ze-dong, *Selected Works,* 4 vols. Beijing: People's Publishing House, 1965.

Markuson, Ann, Peter Hall, and Amy Glasmeier. *High-Tech America: The What, How, Where and Why of the Sunrise Industries.* Boston: Allen and Unwin, 1986.

Markuson, Ann, Peter Hall, Scott Campbell, and Sabina Dietrick. *The Rise of the Gunbelt: The Military Remapping of America.* New York: Oxford University Press, 1991.

Marx, Karl. *Capital: A Critique of Political Economy.* New York: Vintage Books, 1977.

Matthews, Jessica Tuchman, ed. *Preserving the Global Environment.* New York: W. W. Norton, 1991.

Maynes, Charles William. "America Without the Cold War." *Foreign Policy* 78 (spring 1990): 3–25.

_____. "The Perils of (and for) an Imperial America." *Foreign Policy* 111 (summer 1998): 36–49.

_____. "Squandering Triumph." *Foreign Affairs* 78, 1 (January/February 1999): 15–23.

Mazarr, Michael J. "Nuclear Weapons after the Cold War." *Washington Quarterly* 15, 3 (summer 1992): 185–201.

_____. "The Pessimism Syndrome." *Washington Quarterly* 21, 3 (summer 1998): 93–108.

McGeorge, Harvey J. "Bugs, Gas, and Missiles." *Defense and Foreign Affairs* 17, 5–6 (May/June 1990): 14–19.

McGowan, William G. "Telecommunications and Global Competitiveness." *Vital Speeches of the Day* 56, 7 (January 15, 1990): 199–201.

Mead, Walter Russell. "The World Economic Order: Perils after Bretton Woods." *Dissent* (summer 1990): 383–93.

Mearsheimer, John J. "Why We Shall Soon Miss the Cold War." *Atlantic Monthly* 266, 2 (August 1990): 35–50.

Medvedev, Zhores A. *Gorbachev.* New York: W. W. Norton, 1986.

Megargee, Edwin I., and Jack E. Hokanson. *The Dynamics of Aggression: Individual, Group and International Analyses.* New York: Harper and Row, 1970.

Merritt, Richard, L., ed. *Communications in International Politics.* Urbana, IL: University of Illinois Press, 1972.

Metz, Steven. *The Future of the United Nations: Implications for Peace Operations.* Carlisle Barracks, PA: Strategic Studies Institute, October 1993.

Metz, Steven, and James Keivit. *The Revolution in Military Affairs and Conflicts Short of War.* Carlisle Barracks, PA: Strategic Studies Institute, July 1994.

Meyer, Stephen M. "The Sources and Prospects of Gorbachev's New Political Thinking on Security." *International Security* 13, 2 (fall 1988): 124–64.

Miller, Abraham H., ed. *Terrorism, the Media and the Law.* Dobbs Ferry, NY: Transnational Publishers, 1982.

Miller, Robert Hopkins, et al. *Inside an Embassy: The Political Role of Diplomats Abroad.* Washington, DC: CQ Books, 1992.

Millis, Walter. *Arms and Men: A Study in American Military History.* Princeton, NJ: Princeton University Press, 1956.

Millot, Marc Dean. "Facing the Emerging Reality of Regional Nuclear Adversaries." *Washington Quarterly* 17, 3 (summer 1994): 41–71.

Milner, Helen. "International Political Economy: Beyond Hegemonic Stability." *Foreign Policy* 110 (Spring 1998): 112–23.

Mitrany, David. *Toward a Working Peace System.* London: Royal Institute of International Affairs, 1943.

Moisy, Claude. "Myths of the Global Information Village." *Foreign Policy* 107 (summer 1997): 78–87.

Moore, Rebecca. "Globalization and the Future of U.S./ Human Rights Policy." *Washington Quarterly* 21, 4 (Autumn 1998): 193–212.

Moran, Theodore H. *Multinational Corporations: The Political Economy of Foreign Direct Investment.* Lexington, MA: Lexington Books, 1988.

Morgenthau, Hans J. *Politics Among Nations,* 6th ed., rev. Kenneth W. Thompson. New York: Alfred A. Knopf, 1985.

Moynihan, Daniel Patrick. *Pandaemonium: Ethnicity in World Politics.* New York: Oxford University Press, 1993.

Mueller, John. *Quiet Cataclysm: Reflections on the Recent Transformation of World Politics.* New York: HarperCollins, 1995.

_____. *Retreat from Doomsday: The Obsolescence of Major War.* New York: Basic Books, 1989.

Muravchik, Joshua. "Gorbachev's Intellectual Odyssey." *New Republic* 920, 3 (March 5, 1990): 20–25.

Nagorski, Andrew. "The Intellectual Roots of Eastern Europe's Upheaval." *SAIS Review* 10, 2 (summer/fall 1990): 89–100.

Natsios, Andrew S. "Food Through Force: Humanitarian Intervention and U.S. Policy." *Washington Quarterly* 17, 1 (winter 1994): 129–44.

Nau, Henry. *The Myth of America's Decline: Leading the World Economy into the 1990s.* Oxford, UK: Oxford University Press, 1990.

Naylor, Thomas H. *The Gorbachev Strategy: Opening the Closed Society.* Lexington, MA: Lexington Books, 1988.

Neuchterlein, Donald. *America Recommitted: United States National Interests in a Reconstructed World.* Lexington: University of Kentucky Press, 1991.

Neumann, Robert G. "This Next Disorderly Half Century: Some Proposed Remedies." *Washington Quarterly* 16, 1 (winter 1993): 33–50.

Neumann, Stephanie G. "Controlling the Arms Trade: Idealistic Dream or Realpolitik?" *Washington Quarterly* 16, 3 (summer 1993): 53–73.

Nicholson, Harold. *Diplomacy.* New York: Oxford University Press, 1964.

Nolan, Janne, and Albert D. Wheelon. "Third World Ballistic Missiles." *Scientific American* 263, 3 (August 1990): 34–40.

Novak, Michael. "Democracy: The Collapse of the Alternatives." *Freedom at Issue* 114 (May/June 1990): 18–20.

Nye, Joseph S., Jr. *Bound to Lead: The Changing Nature of American Power.* New York: Basic Books, 1990.

_____. "Peering into the Future." *Foreign Affairs* 73, 4 (July/August 1994): 82–93.

_____. "What New World Order?" *Foreign Affairs* 71, 2 (summer 1992): 83–96.

_____. "The Case for Deep Engagement." *Foreign Affairs* 74, 4 (July/August 1995): 90–102.

Oberdorfer, Don. *The Turn: From the Cold War to a New Era.* New York: Poseidon, 1991.

Ohmae, Kenichi. "Beyond Fiction to Fact: The Borderless Economy." *New Perspectives Quarterly* 7, 2 (spring 1990): 20–21.

_____. "The Rise of the Region State." *Foreign Affairs* 72, 2 (spring 1993): 78–87.

Olcutt, Martha. "The Caspian's False Hope." *Foreign Policy* 111 (summer 1998): 95–113.

Olson, Mancur. *The Rise and Decline of Nations.* New Haven, CT: Yale University Press, 1982.

Organski, A. J. F., and Jacek Kugler. *The War Ledger.* Chicago: University of Chicago Press, 1980.

Palmer, R. R., and Joel Cotton. *A History of the Modern World Since 1815,* 6th ed. New York: Alfred A. Knopf, 1984.

Paschall, Rod. *LIC 2010: Special Operations and Unconventional Warfare in the Next Century.* Washington, DC: Brassey's, 1990.

Pei, Minxin. "Is China Democratizing?" *Foreign Affairs* 77, 1 (January/February 1998): 68–82.

Peng, Ernest H. "Who's Benefitting Whom? A Trade Agenda for High-Technology Industries." *Washington Quarterly* 16, 4 (autumn 1993): 17–34.

Perkowich, George. "Nuclear Proliferation." *Foreign Policy* 112 (fall 1998): 12–23.

Peterson, Donald K. "Globalization and Telecommunications Leadership: The Future Ain't What It Used to Be." *Vital Speeches of the Day* 56, 17 (June 15, 1990): 527–30.

Pfaff, William. "Invitation to War." *Foreign Affairs* 72, 3 (summer 1993): 107–109.

_____. *The Wrath of Nations: Civilization and the Furies of Nationalism.* New York: Simon and Schuster, 1993.

Pfaltzgraff, Robert, Uri Ra'anan, and Walter Milberg, eds. *Intelligence Policy and National Security.* Hamden, CT: Archon Books, 1981.

Pickering, Thomas R. "The U.N. Contribution to Future International Security." Naval War College Review 46, 1 (winter 1993): 94–104.

Pierre, Andrew J., ed. *A High Technology Gap? Europe, America and Japan.* New York: New York University Press, 1987.

Pipes, Richard. "Is Russia Still an Enemy?" *Foreign Affairs* 76, 5 (September/October 1997): 65–78.

_____. "Why the Soviet Union Thinks It Can Fight and Win a Nuclear War." *Commentary* 64, 1 (July 1977): 21–34.

Porter, Bruce D., and Carlo R. Saivetz. "The Once and Future Empire: Russia and the Near Abroad." *Washington Quarterly* 17, 3 (summer 1994): 75–90.

Porter, Gareth, and Janet Brown. *Global Environmental Politics.* Boulder, CO: Lynne Reinner, 1991.

Pyle, Kenneth B. *The Japanese Question.* Washington, DC: AEI Press, 1992.

Quester, George H., and Victor Utgoff. "No-First-Use and Nonproliferation: Redefining Extended Deterrence." *Washington Quarterly* 17, 2 (spring 1994): 103–14.

Ramo, Joshua. "The Shanghai Bubble." *Foreign Policy* 111 (summer 1998): 64–75.

Rapaport, Anatol. *Fights, Games, and Debates.* Ann Arbor, MI: University of Michigan Press, 1960.

Reich, Robert B. "The Quiet Path to Economic Preeminence." *Scientific American* 261, 4 (October 1989): 41–47.

Repetto, Robert, and Jonathan Lash. "Planetary Roulette: Gambling with the Climate." *Foreign Policy* 108 (fall 1997): 84–98.

Richardson, Lewis. *The Statistics of Deadly Quarrels.* Pittsburgh, PA: Boxwood Press, 1960.

Riker, William H. *The Theory of Political Coalitions.* New Haven, CT: Yale University Press, 1962.

Rikhye, Indar Jit. *The Future of Peacekeeping.* New York: International Peacekeeping Academy, 1989.

Roberts, Brad. "Arms Control and the End of the Cold War." *Washington Quarterly* 15, 4 (autumn 1992): 39–56.

Rodrik, Dana. "Sense and Nonsense in the Globalization Debate." *Foreign Policy* 107 (summer 1997): 19–37.

Rogov, Sergei. "International Security and the Collapse of the Soviet Union." *Washington Quarterly* 15, 2 (fall 1992): 16–28.

Rosecrance, Richard. *Action and Reaction in World Politics.* Boston: Little, Brown, 1963.

_____. "A New Concert of Powers." *Foreign Affairs* 71, 2 (spring 1992): 64–82.

_____. *The Rise of the Trading State: Commerce and Conquest in the Modern World.* New York: Basic Books, 1985.

Rosenau, James N. *Turbulence in World Politics: A Theory of Change and Continuity.* Princeton, NJ: Princeton University Press, 1990.

Rothgeb, John M., Jr. *Defining Power: Influence and Force in the Contemprary International System.* New York: St. Martin's Press, 1993.

Rothkopf, David. "In Praise of Cultural Imperialism." *Foreign Policy* 107 (summer 1997): 38–53.

Rousseau, Jean-Jacques. *The Collected Works of Jean-Jacques Rousseau.* Hanover, NH: University Press of New England, 1990.

Russett, Bruce M. *Controlling the Sword: The Democratic Governance of National Security.* Cambridge, MA: Harvard University Press, 1990.

Sachs, Jeffrey. "International Economics: Unlocking the Mysteries of Globalization." *Foreign Policy* 110 (spring 1998): 97–111.

Sadowski, Yahya. "Ethnic Conflict." *Foreign Policy* 111 (summer 1998): 12–23.

Sanger, Clyde. *Ordering the Oceans: Making of the Law of the Sea Treaty.* Toronto: University of Toronto Press, 1987.

Schelling, Thomas C. *Arms and Influence.* New Haven, CT: Yale University Press, 1966.

Schlesinger, Jacob. "Shadow Shoguns: The Origins and Crisis of Japan, Inc." *Washington Quarterly* 21, 2 (spring 1998): 135–48.

Schlesinger, James. "The Impact of Nuclear Weapons on History." *Washington Quarterly* 16, 4 (autumn 1993): 5–16.

———. "Quest for a Post Cold War Foreign Policy." *Foreign Affairs* 71, 1 (winter 1992/93): 17–28.

Schurmann, Franz. "After Desert Storm: Interest, Ideology, and History in American Foreign Policy." In *Past as Prelude: History in the Making of a New World Order,* ed. Meredith Woo-Cumings and Michael Loriaux. Boulder, CO: Westview Press, 1993.

Schwartz, Herman M. *States Versus Markets: History, Geography, and the Development of International Political Economy.* New York: St. Martin's Press, 1994.

Schwarz, Adam. "Indonesia After Suharto." *Foreign Affairs* 76, 4 (July/August 1997): 119–135.

Sebenius, James K. *Negotiating the Law of the Sea.* Cambridge, MA: Harvard University Press, 1984.

Shevardnadze, Eduard. *The Future Belongs to Freedom.* New York: Free Press, 1991.

Shmelev, Nikolai, and Ed A. Hewett. "A Pragmatist's View on the Soviet Economy: A Conversation Between Nikolai Shmelev and Ed A. Hewett." *Brookings Review* 8, 1 (winter 1989/90): 27–32.

Shulman, Marshall D. "The Superpowers: Dance of the Dinosaurs." *Foreign Affairs* 66, 3 (winter 1987/88): 494–515.

Shute, Stephen, and Susan Hurley, eds. *On Human Rights: The Oxford Amnesty Lectures.* New York: Basic Books, 1993.

Singer, J. David. *The Correlates of War.* New York: Free Press, 1979.

Singer, Max. "The Decline and Fall of the Soviet Empire." *National Review* 42, 13 (July 9, 1990): 26–28.

Singer, Max, and the Estate of Aaron Wildavsky. *The Real World Order: Zones of Peace, Zones of Turmoil.* Revised edition. Chatham, NJ: Chatham House, 1996.

Singh, Jaswant. "Against Nuclear Apartheid." *Foreign Affairs* 77, 5 (September/October 1998): 41–52.

Slaughter, Anne-Marie. "The Real New World Order." *Foreign Affairs* 76, 5 (September/October 1997): 183–97.

Smith, Tony. "Making the World Safe for Democracy." *Washington Quarterly* 16, 4 (autumn 1993): 197–218.

Smith, W. Y. "U.S. National Security After the Cold War." *Washington Quarterly* 15, 4 (autumn 1992): 21–34.

Snow, Donald M. *Distant Thunder: Patterns of Conflict in the Developing World,* 2d ed. Armonk, NY: M.E. Sharpe, 1997.

———. *The Necessary Peace: Nuclear Weapons and Superpower Relations.* Lexington, MA: Lexington Books, 1987.

———. *Peacekeeping, Peacemaking, and Peace Enforcement: The U.S. Role in the New International Order.* Carlisle Barracks, PA: Strategic Studies Institute, 1993.

———. *The Shape of the Future: World Politics in a New Century,* 3d ed. Armonk, NY: M. E. Sharpe, 1999.

———. "Soviet Reform and the High Technology Imperative." *Parameters* 20, 1 (March 1990): 76–87.

———. *UnCivil Wars: International Security and the New Internal Conflicts.* Boulder, CO: Lynne Rienner Publishers, 1996.

Snow, Donald M., and Dennis M. Drew. *From Lexington to Desert Storm: War and the American Experience.* Armonk, NY: M. F. Sharpe, 1994.

Snyder, Richard C., et al. *Foreign Policy Decision-Making: An Approach to the Study of International Politics.* New York: Free Press, 1962.

Solarz, Stephen, and Michael O'Hanlon. "Humanitarian Intervention: When Force Is Justified." *Washington Quarterly* 20, 4 (autumn 1997): 3–14.

Sorenson, Theodore C. "Rethinking National Security." *Foreign Affairs* 69, 3 (summer 1990): 1–18.

Soros, Geoge. "Capitalism's Last Chance?" *Foreign Policy* 113 (winter 1998/99). 55–65.

Spero, Joan Edelman. *The Politics of International Economic Relations,* 4th ed. New York: St. Martin's Press, 1990.

Sprinszak, Ethel. "The Great Superterrorism Scare." *Foreign Policy* 112 (fall 1998): 110–24.

Stanfield, Rochelle L. "Under Europe's Umbrella." *National Journal* 22, 14 (April 7, 1990): 826–31.

Stedman, Stephen John. "The New Interventionists." *Foreign Affairs* 72, 1 (winter 1992/93): 1–16.

Steel, Ronald. "The Rise of the European Superstate." *New Republic* 937, 3 (July 2, 1990): 23–25.

Steinbrunner, John. "Biological Weapons: A Plague Upon All Houses." *Foreign Policy* 109 (winter 1997): 85–95.

Steinfield, Edward. "The Asian Financial Crisis: Beijing's Year of Reckoning." *Washington Quarterly* 21, 3 (summer 1998): 37–52.

Stevenson, Jonathan. "Hope Restored in Somalia?" *Foreign Policy* 91 (summer 1993): 138–54.

Stiglitz, Joseph, and Kyn Squire. "International Development: Is It Possible?" *Foreign Policy* 110 (spring 1998): 138–51.

Strang, William. *The Diplomatic Career.* London: A. Deutsch, 1962.

Sullivan, Gordon R., and James M. Dubik. *War in the Information Age.* Carlisle Barracks, PA: Strategic Studies Institute, June 1994.

Sullivan, John D. "Democracy and Global Economic Growth." *Washington Quarterly* 15, 2 (spring 1992): 175–86.

Sullivan, Leonard, Jr. *Meeting the Challenges of Regional Security.* Carlisle Barracks, PA: Strategic Studies Institute, February 1994.

Summers, Harry G. *On Strategy: A Critical View of the Vietnam War.* Novato, CA: Presidio Press, 1982.

Sylvester, Christine. *Feminist Theory and International Relations in a Postmodern Era.* Cambridge, UK: Cambridge University Press, 1994.

Szabo, Stephen. "The German Answer." *SAIS Review* 10, 2 (summer/fall 1990): 41–56.

Talbott, Strobe. "Globalization and Democracy: A Practitioner's Perspective." *Foreign Policy* 108 (fall 1997): 69–83.

Tanenhaus, Sam. "What the Anti-Communists Knew." *Commentary* 90, 1 (July 1990): 32–36.

Tarr, David. *Nuclear Deterrence and International Security: Alternative Security Regimes.* New York: Longmans, 1991.

Thompson, William R. *On Global War: Historical-Structural Approaches to World Politics.* Columbia: University of South Carolina Press, 1988.

Thucydides. *The History of the Peloponnesian Wars.* New York: Penguin Books, 1954.

Thurow, Lester C. *Head to Head: Coming Economic Battles Among Japan, Europe, and America.* New York: William Morrow, 1992.

Tickner, J. Ann. *Gender in International Relations: Feminist Perspectives on Achieving Global Security.* New York: Columbia University Press, 1992.

Treverton, Gregory. *Covert Action: The Limits of Intervention in the Postwar World.* New York: Basic Books, 1987.

Trofimenko, Henry. "Ending the Cold War, Not History." *Washington Quarterly* 13, 2 (spring 1990): 21–35.

Truman, Harry S. *Memoirs: Years of Decision.* New York: Doubleday, 1955.

Tsepkalo, Valery V. "The Remaking of Eurasia." *Foreign Affairs* 77, 2 (March/April 1998): 107–27.

Tucker, David. "Responding to Terrorism." *Washington Quarterly* 21, 1 (winter 1998): 70–84.

Urwin, Derek W. *The Community of Europe: A History of European Integration Since 1945.* New York: Longmans, 1991.

Van Evera, Stephen. "The Case Against Intervention." *Atlantic Monthly* 266, 1 (July 1990): 72–80.

van Kemenade, William. "China, Hong Kong, Taiwan: Dynamics of a New Empire." *Washington Quarterly* 21, 2 (spring 1998): 105–20.

Vasquez, John. *The War Puzzle*. Cambridge, UK: Cambridge University Press, 1993.

Vernon, Raymond, ed. *The Promise of Privatization: A Challenge for American Foreign Policy*. New York: Council on Foreign Relations, 1988.

Viotti, Paul, and Mark Kauppi. *International Relations: Theory, Realism, Pluralism, Globalism*. New York: Macmillan, 1987.

Walker, Stephen, ed. *Role Theory and Foreign Policy Analysis*. Durham, NC: Duke University Press, 1987.

Waltz, Kenneth. *Man, the State, and War: A Theoretical Analysis*. New York: Columbia University Press, 1959.

_____. *Theory of International Politics*. Reading, MA: Addison-Wesley, 1979.

Wang, Fei-Ling. "To Incorporate China: A New Policy for a New Era." *Washington Quarterly* 21, 1 (winter 1998): 67–81.

Weber. Steven. "The End of the Business Cycle?" *Foreign Affairs* 76, 4 (July/August 1997): 65–82.

Weiss, Thomas G. "Intervention: Whither the United Nations?" *Washington Quarterly* 17, 1 (winter 1994): 109–28.

_____. "New Challenges for UN Military Operations: Implementing an Agenda for Peace." *Washington Quarterly* 16, 1 (winter 1993): 51–66.

Whence the Threat to Peace, 3d ed. Moscow: Military Publishing House, 1984.

Wilson, Clifton E. *Diplomatic Privileges and Immunities*. Tucson: University of Arizona Press, 1967.

Wolfers, Arnold. *Discord and Collaboration*. Baltimore, MD: Johns Hopkins University Press, 1962.

Wood, John R., and Jean Serrs. *Diplomatic Ceremony and Protocol*. New York: Columbia University Press, 1970.

Wright, Karen. "The Road to the Global Village." *Scientific American* 262, 3 (March 1990): 84–94.

Wright, Quincy. *A Study of War,* 2d ed. Chicago: University of Chicago Press, 1983.

Wriston, Walter B. "Technology and Sovereignty." *Foreign Affairs* 67, 2 (winter 1988/89): 63–75.

Yavlinsky, Grigory. "Russia's Phony Capitalism." *Foreign Affairs* 77, 3 (May/June 1998): 67–79.

Young, John A. *Global Competition: The New Reality*. Washington, DC: President's Commission on Industrial Competitiveness, 1985.

Young, Oran B. *International Cooperation: Building Regimes for Natural Resources and the Environment*. Ithaca. NY: Cornell University Press, 1989.

Young, Oran B., and Gall Osherenko. *Polar Politics: Creating International Environmental Regimes*. Ithaca, NY: Cornell University Press, 1993.

Zakaria, Fareed. "A Conversation with Lee Kuan Yew." *Foreign Affairs* 73, 2 (March/April 1994): 109–26.

Ziemke, Caroline F. "Rethinking the Mistakes of the Past: History's Message to the Clinton Defense Department." *Washington Quarterly* 16, 2 (spring 1993): 47–60.

Zuckerman, Mortimer. "A Second American Century." *Foreign Affairs* 77, 3 (May/June 1998): 18–31.

PHOTO CREDITS

515

market-share fluctuation and, 298
political implications of, 320-322
role of state in, 292
technology and, 312-315
tripolarity of, 300, 304
International events, in 18th-century, 73-78
Internationalism, of United States, 164-166
International law, 419-453, 423-424
comparison with state law, 422
definition of, 423
enforcement of, 423
in First Tier, 431-432
general principles of law and, 427
international customs and, 426-427
in international system, 429-435
judicial decisions and teachings, 427
in Second Tier, 432-433
sources of, 424-427
terrorism and, 434
treaties and, 426
UN resolutions and, 427
values and, 423-424
war and, 427-429
and war crimes, 428
women's rights and, 425
International leadership, 457-463
security and, 459-463
International Monetary Fund (IMF), 280, 294, 302
as supranational actor, 54
International organizations (IO)
as supranational actors, 15
United Nations and, 435-441
International political economy (IPE), 290-291, 305
International Red Cross, as nongovernmental organization, 55
International relations
collapse of, 10
definition of, 6-9
personal effects of, 5
players in, 9, 14
scope of, 9
tiers and, 17-26
International security. See also Security
and collective security, 356
definition of, 355
International system, 29-64
change agents in, 71-72
Cold War system, 94-104
components of, 68-73
context of, 68-69
critical events in, 72-73
distribution of power in, 69
evolution of, 66-68
international law in, 429-435
interwar system, 87-94
nation in, 32-33
nation-state in, 33-34
post-Cold War system, 104-109
state in, 31-32
19th-century system, 78-87
transitions in, 68
war and peace system in, 69-71
International Telecommunications Union, 42
International Trade Organization (ITO), 294, 295
Interwar system, 87-94
change agents in, 91-92
context of, 88-89

critical events in, 92-94
distribution of power in, 89-90
summary of, 89
war and peace system in, 91
IO. See International organizations
IPE. See International political economy
Iran
diplomacy and, 401
in Persian Gulf conflict, 362
in 1980s, 115
U.S. diplomacy with, 393
Iranian hostages, 8p
Iraq
cognitive dissonance and, 122
invasion of Kuwait, 108
diplomacy and, 400
Kurds in, 469
irredentism and, 37-38
in Persian Gulf conflict, 362
war with, objectives of, 141
as weapons state, 365
Iron Curtain, 97
Irredentism, 37-38
Islamic fundamentalism, and international law, 433
Isolationism
of Japan, 233, 238
of United States, 216
Israel, diplomacy in, 410
Italy
diplomacy in, 394-395
in interwar system, 93
ITN. See Independent Television Network
ITO. See International Trade Organization

J

Janis, Irving, 117
Japan, 231-242
in 18th-century, 74
in 19th-century, 80
atomic bomb over, 145-146
during Cold War, 96
deregulation in, 317
Diet of, 238-239
diplomacy in, 400
environmental issues in, 350-351
ethnocentrism of, 233, 234
expansion of, 235m, 235-236
future of, 239-242
as international leader, 236-239
in interwar system, 89, 92-93
isolationism of, 233, 238
moralism of, 237
and Pearl Harbor, 93
and Persian Gulf War, 238
place in world order, 241-242
plutonium in, 232
re-Asianization of, 240
relationship with neighbors, 237
relationship with United States, 240-241
relationship with West, 233
security strategy of, 241
self-concept of, 231-233
vulnerability of, 232-233
wartime guilt of, 237
Jefferson, Thomas, 164, 329
Jervis, Robert, 181
Johnson, Lyndon, 296
Johnston, Joseph E., 145

Judicial decisions and teachings, 427
Just war, 427

K

Kabila, Laurent, 383, 383p, 385, 386
Kacyzinski, Theodore, 434
Kai-shek, Chiang, 89
Karadzic, Radovan, 414
Kar, Alphonse, 4
Kaul, Sumer, 205
Keegan, John, 138, 139
Keeping Faith (Carter), 327
Kennan, George, 97, 184, 185
Kennedy, John F., 117, 220, 406
Kenney, George, 397
Keohane, Robert, 290
KGB. See Committee on State Security
Khatami, Mohammad, 401
Khmer Rouge, 363
Khomeini, Ayatollah, 115, 116p, 393, 401
Khruschev, Nikita, 67p, 179, 181, 406, 421p
Kievet, James, 458
Kimble, Melinda, 275
Kim Il-Sung, 375
Kim Jung II, 375
Kin country syndrome, 465
Kirkpatrick, Jeane, 423
Kissinger, Henry, 121, 406
KLO. See Kosovo Liberation Army
Korean War, groupthink and, 118-119
Korea, unification of, 19
Kosovo, 386-387
false analogy and, 121
multinationalism and, 35
Kosovo Liberation Army (KLO), 35
Krauthammer, Charles, 365
Kurdistan, 38m, 469
Kurds, and irredentism, 37-38
Kuwait, invasion of, 108
Kyoto Summit, 351

L

Lake, Anthony, 382
Language, and nation, 32
Latin America
environmental problems in, 348
regional organizations in, 360
Latin American Nuclear-Free Zone Treaty, 180
Law, 419-453. See also International law
definition of, 423
enforcement of, 423
general principles of, 427
and sovereignty, 422
of state, comparison with international law, 422
Law of Nations (Vattel), 40
Law of the Sea treaty, 343
Law on State Enterprise, 186
Lawyers' Committee for Human Rights, 43
League of Nations, 91
Lebanese civil war, 360
Lenin, Vladimir Ilyich, 152
King Leopold II, 383
Lessons of the the Past: The Use and Misuse of History in American Foreign Policy (May), 120
Lethality index, 144
Leviathan (Hobbes), 40

Liberalism, classical, 215
The Liberal Tradition in America (Hartz), 215
Liberia, insurgencies in, 161
Limited means, of war, 140, 140t
Limited purposes, 70, 138-139
Limited Test Ban Treaty, 180
Limited Test Ban Treaty (LTBT), 372
Lincoln, Abraham, 216
Lindbergh, Charles, 218p
Locke, John, 39p, 40, 77, 151, 215, 327, 329
Long telegram, 185
Lorenz, Konrad, 153
King Louis XVI, 78
LTBT. See Limited Test Ban Treaty
Luttwak, Edward N., 139, 293

M

Maastricht Treaty, 229, 301
Machiavelli, Niccolo, 10, 11p
Macrocosmic theories of war, 155-156
Maino, Theodore, 392
Malaysia, 123-124
    environmental problems in, 348
    forest protection in, 344
Manhattan Project, 145
Marginalization, of Second Tier, 281-282
Market-share fluctuations, in international
    economy, 298
Marshall, George, 220, 223
Marshall Plan, 219, 223
Marxism, theories of war of, 151-152
Marx, Karl, 151, 152p
May, Ernest, 120
Mazaar, Michael J., 149
Mazowiecki, Tadeusz, 455
McArthur, Douglas, 118p, 118-119
McDowell, Irvin, 145
MCTR. See Missile Technology Control Regime
McVeigh, Timothy, 434
Mearsheimer, John, 457
Measures-countermeasures arms spiral, 367
Media. See also Telecommunications
    and human rights, 327
    and internal conflicts, 381-383
Mediation, 409
Melting pot, 34
Memoirs (Truman), 220
Metz, Steven, 458
Mexico City, United Nations International
    Conference on Population in, 341
Mexico, in Tier system, 18
Michnik, Adam, 205
Microcosmic theories of war, 152-155
Middle class, in 19th-century system, 85
Middle East
    conflicts in, 360-362
    environmental problems in, 348
Military forces
    during Cold War, 102
    and nongovernmental organizations, 56
Military instruments of power, 48, 50t, 458-459
Military power
    of First Tier, 23-24
    of Second Tier, 25
Military unification, of Europe, 227-228
Mill, John Stuart, 215
Milosevic, Slobodan, 121, 387, 413, 414
Minimax principle, 157
Missile Technology Control Regime (MTCR),
    302, 373

Mitrany, David, 436
Mitterand, FranÁois, 229
Miyazawa, Kiichi, 351
Mladic, Ratko, 413
MNCs. See Multinational corporations
Mobutu, Joseph. See Sese Seko, Mobutu
Modern diplomacy. See Diplomacy, modern
Modernity, and population explosion, 338
Mohammed, Ali Mahdi, 126
Monnet, Jean, 224
Montreal Treaty of 1987, 342
Mood theory, of United States, 217-218
Moralism
    of Japan, 237
    of United States, 217
Moynihan, Daniel Patrick, 10
MTCR. See Missile Technology Control
    Regime
Multilateral foreign aid, 278
Multilateral treaties, 426
Multinational corporations (MNCs), 9, 55-57,
    292, 309-310
    control of, 321
    in Second Tier, 280
Multinationalism, 34-37, 376
    colonialism and, 267
    and Kosovo, 35
    and Soviet Union, 36-37
Multipolar system, 69
    balance of power in, 52-53, 53f
Munro, Ross, 246
Muslims, conflicts involving, 362
Mutual Security Treaty, 241

N

NAFTA. See North American Free Trade
    Association
Nagasaki, atomic bombing of, 145-146
Nagorno-Karabakh, 380-381
Nagy, Imre, 103
Nakichevan, 380-381
Nakosone, Yasuhiro, 239
Napoleonic Wars, 12, 139
Nassar, Gamal Abdel, 103
Nation, 32-33
    characteristics of, 32-33
    definition of, 32
National, definition of, 7
National disintegration, 378-380
National interest matrix, 113-114, 114t
Nationalism, 33-34
    compound, 33
    economic, 321
    post-Cold War, 108-109
Nationality, 32
National security
    and collective defense, 356
    definition of, 355
National Security Council, Deputies
    Committee of, in Somalia, 130
National security state, 99-102
    decline of, 199-201
"The National Security Strategy of the United
    States," 170
Nation-state, 33-34
    definition of, 7, 32
    exclusionary method of, 33-34
    inclusionary method of, 33-34
NATO. See North Atlantic Treaty Organization
Natural rights, 329

Natural state, warfare and, 151
NBC weapons
    and arms escalation, 367
    in Second Tier, 357
Necessary peace, 98
    and end of Cold War, 177-184
Necessary Peace (Snow), 181
Negotiations. See also Bargaining
    diplomacy and, 393-394
Neoisolationism, of United States, 164-166
Netanyahu, Benjamin, 361
New International Economic Order
    (NIEO), 277
New world order, 9
NGOs. See Nongovernmental organizations
Nichols, Terry, 434
Nicolson, Harold, 391
NIEO. See New International Economic Order
Nineteenth-century system, 78-87
    change agents in, 83-86, 86f
    context of, 79-80
    critical events in, 86-87
    distribution of power in, 80
    Europe in, 81m, 84m
    summary of, 79
    war and peace system in, 81-83
Nixon, Richard, 67p, 96, 221p, 294, 296,
    339, 406
Nomenklatura, 185, 186
Nongovernmental organizations (NGOs),
    55, 435
    and humanitarian aid, 56
    human rights and, 327-328
    and military forces, 56
Noninterference, 16
Non-Proliferation Treaty, 180
Nonstate actors, 15, 54-58
North American Free Trade Association
    (NAFTA), and international economy, 301
North Atlantic Treaty Organization (NATO),
    193, 206-208, 219
    in Bosnia, 58-63
    and European unification, 227
    founding of, 97
    membership in, 207t
    web sites for, 208
Northern states of Eastern Europe, 203
North Korea, 19
    weapons in, 373
Notestein, Frank, 336
Nouveau riche, 85
N + 1 problem, 369
Nuclear allergy, 146-147, 184
Nuclear balance, 179-181
Nuclear Nonproliferation Treaty (NPT), 372-
    373, 374
Nuclear power, 96-97
Nuclear stalemate, and end of Cold War, 177-184
Nuclear Suppliers Group, 373
Nuclear testing, 374
Nuclear threshold, 147
Nuclear weapons
    and deadliness of war, 143
    support for, 147
Nuechterlein, Donald, 113
Nye, Joseph, 50, 238, 290

O

Oceans, environmental problems in, 343-344
On Aggression (Lorenz), 153